Adjustment
of
Property
Losses

Adjustment
of
Property
Losses

Fourth Edition

PAUL I. THOMAS
Former Vice President and General Adjuster
Kemper Insurance Companies
Professional Engineer and
Consultant on Property Losses

PRENTISS B. REED, SR.
Late President
National Association of
Independent Insurance Adjusters

GREGG DIVISION / McGRAW-HILL BOOK COMPANY

New York   St. Louis   Dallas   San Francisco   Auckland
Bogotá   Düsseldorf   Johannesburg   London   Madrid
Mexico   Montreal   New Delhi   Panama   Paris
São Paulo   Singapore   Sydney   Tokyo   Toronto

Sponsor: *Edward E. Byers*
Senior Editing Supervisor: *Linda Stern*
Editor: *Marion B. Castellucci*
Production Supervisor: *Gary Whitcraft*
Design Supervisor: *Edwin Fisher*
Book Design: *Graphic Concern, Inc.*
Cover Designer: *Richard Scott*

Library of Congress Cataloging in Publication Data

Thomas, Paul I
    Adjustment of property losses.

    First ed. published in 1929 under title: Adjustment
of fire losses, in the 1st–3d ed. Reed's name appeared
first on t. p.
    Includes index.
    Bibliography: p.
    1. Insurance, Fire—Adjustment of claims. 2. In-
surance—Adjustment of claims. I. Reed, Prentiss B.,
joint author. II. Reed, Prentiss B   Adjustment of
fire losses. III. Title.
HG9721.R4 1977   368.1'1'014   77-821
ISBN 0-07-064215-X

HG
9721
.R4
1977

ADJUSTMENT OF PROPERTY LOSSES, Fourth Edition

2 3 4 5 6 7 8 9 0   DODO   7 8 6 5 4 3 2 1 0 9 8 7

Preface

Publication of the fourth edition of *Adjustment of Property Losses* marks its forty-ninth year as the principal text and reference on the subject in the property insurance field. The first edition, entitled *Adjustment of Fire Losses*, was published in 1929, when a strong distinction was drawn between fire and casualty lines of insurance, especially in the handling of losses and claims. Prentiss B. Reed, a highly regarded and respected independent adjuster, was the author. Numerous innovations and changes in the insurance industry prompted subsequent revisions and updatings of the text.

This fourth edition is, in many respects, a new book. It has been reorganized to move from general to specific and more complex topics. Sections have been revised, consolidated, or dropped completely. Seven new chapters have been added to keep up with industry developments and to bring within the covers all major lines of property insurance.

The text covers the numerous elements that make up the many-sided talents of a good claim representative. It provides guidance and information to enable the claim representative to perform his or her duties in an effective and professional manner. Emphasis is placed on the procedures for investigating the insured and the insurable interests, the property at risk, the insurance coverage, and the cause of loss, all of which may have a bearing on the insurer's liability. The reader is guided in collecting and recording information, choosing the best method for determining value and loss, and negotiating an adjustment that is equitable for all interests.

Stress is placed on the role of the claim representative during the investigation of both small and large losses, especially those in which arson or fraud is suspected. The *implied* and the *actual* authority of the claim representative are discussed, and the unique relationship of the claim representative to the insured is strongly accented. The reader is cautioned about the hazards involved in inadvertent or thoughtless words or actions. In addition, the duties and obligations of the insured after a loss are fully covered.

Many policy forms and endorsements are quoted and discussed to point out the importance of careful reviewing and understanding of coverage prior to accepting or denying coverage or liability on behalf of the insurer. Situations that give rise to a right of action of the insurer against third parties are cited and explained.

As in previous editions, thorough treatment is given to the adjustment of losses involving household furniture, machinery and fixtures, merchandise, business interruption, rental value, extra expense, and additional living expense. New chapters deal with boiler and machinery losses, condominium losses, automobile physical-damage losses, and flood, mudslide, and FAIR Plan losses. Step-by-step procedures are presented for adjusting these and other losses, both when the property is in sight and when part or all of the property is totally destroyed and books of account become the basis of adjustment.

New chapters on important topics include "Unfair Claim-Handling Practices," "Arson Investigation and Detection," and "Negotiations." Application of the insurance and contribution by the insurer are treated in detail, including discussion of excess, deductible, exclusionary, coinsurance, and other limiting clauses. The Guiding Principles for Overlapping Insurance Coverages is reproduced in its entirety. Outline guides for reporting to insurers on various types of property losses are presented to aid in the preparation of preliminary, interim, and final reports.

Many exhibits of forms and documents are shown in the Appendix. They include proof of loss forms; a certificate of satisfaction; a hold-harmless agreement; notice of loss forms for different lines of insurance; a nonwaiver agreement; a subrogation receipt; a loan receipt; a trust agreement; and sample letters demanding examination under oath, requiring appraisal, and rejecting proof of loss.

End-of-chapter questions and problems are used to check the reader's comprehension. In addition to testing mastery of ideas and procedures, they deal with language which gives rise to conflicting interpretations.

The term *claim representative* is generally used in place of *adjuster,* since more and more insurers are using the newer term. The language used in the text attempts to recognize that women are being employed in increasing numbers as field claim representatives, performing the same duties of investigation, evaluation, negotiation, and reporting as their male counterparts.

This edition is a text for both student and instructor; it is a reference for all property claim personnel, whether they are field claim representatives or administrators and supervisors in the insurer's office; it serves as a tool and guide for underwriters concerned with how property claims are adjusted and why they account for a major portion of the premium dollar; and it serves as a text and reference for attorneys, brokers, agents, public adjusters, and others who from time to time represent insureds in the adjustment of losses.

Adjustment of Property Losses is used by the Insurance Institute of America in their program for adjusters as well as by the claim departments and the claim training departments of many insurers. It is used by insurers in insurance buyers courses. Larger independent adjusting firms employ the text to instruct beginning adjusters. Because of the broad coverage the book gives the subject, it is an ideal supplement for colleges and other educational institutions offering courses of study in principles of insurance or general insurance. For those providing courses in insurance claim adjusting, it serves as a principal text.

As the scope of property insurance claim handling continues to expand under multiple-line and multi-peril contracts, it becomes less possible for one individual to be knowledgeable and proficient in all areas. By the same token, no one person could author a text such as this without the counsel and assistance of those who are well informed in specific areas and lines of property claim handling.

The author received generous counsel and advice from independent adjusters, salvors, claim executives, educators, and industry associations. Some undertook to go through the third edition page by page, line by line, to make suggestions and comments. Others reviewed new and revised chapters. Space does not permit mentioning all who gave their time to help shape this fourth edition. The following persons, however, made extremely valuable contributions:

R. G. Anderson, General Adjuster, General Adjustment Bureau, Inc. (GAB), Kansas City, Mo.
W. G. Bates, Secretary, Underwriters Adjustment Bureau, Ltd., Montreal.
Edward F. Brennan, Executive Claim Officer, Commercial Union Assurance Companies, Boston.
Harold Daynard, Daynard & Van Thunen, New York.
Richard H. Greene, Chartered Property Casualty Underwriter and Secretary (and staff), Maryland Casualty Company, Baltimore.

George E. Guinane, Chartered Property Casualty Underwriter and Assistant Vice President, Education and Special Services, State Farm Fire and Casualty Company, Bloomington, Ill.

Max J. Gwertzman, Gwertzman, Nagelberg & Pfeffer, Counselors at Law, New York.

Harry H. Hanson, Property Claims Officer, Kemper Insurance Companies, Long Grove, Ill.

Jon S. Hanson, Executive Secretary, National Association of Insurance Commissioners (NAIC), Milwaukee, Wis.

Wallace R. Hanson, Educational Director, Property Loss Research Bureau (PLRB), Chicago.

Bruce W. Herrick, Director, Industry Communications, Insurance Services Office (ISO), New York.

Frederick H. Hodosh, Chartered Property Casualty Underwriter and Director of Legal and Claims Education, Insurance Institute of America (IIA), Malverne, Pa.

Sylvia T. Jurkovich, Director of Communications, Underwriters Adjusting Company (UAC), Chicago.

W. L. Kennell, Claim Manager, National Flood Insurance Association (NFIA), Arlington, Va.

William H. Kotlowski, Information Director, Defense Research Institute (DRI), Milwaukee, Wis.

H. F. Larzelere, Mid-Atlantic Claim Division, Kemper Insurance Companies, Summit, N.J.

E. L. Lecomte, General Manager, Massachusetts and Rhode Island FAIR Plans, Boston.

John E. Lecomte, Lecomte, Shea & Dangora, Boston.

Robert L. Lusk, Consultant to Property Loss Research Bureau, Chicago.

Dr. A. H. Malo, Staff Psychologist, Kemper Insurance Companies, Long Grove, Ill.

William J. Murray, Assistant Manager, Commercial Multiple Line Division, Insurance Services Office, New York.

Howard P. Osborn, Property Claims, Training and Development, Maryland Casualty Company, Baltimore.

Randall W. Parrish, Boiler and Machinery, Insurance Services Office, New York.

Harold R. S. Perdriau, former Boiler and Machinery Officer, Kemper Insurance Companies, member emeritus, American Institute of Chemical Engineers, co-author of *Primer of Boiler and Machinery Insurance*, Northwestern University and College of Engineering, Boston.

Robert J. Reault, Director, Claim Department (and staff), Aetna Life & Casualty, Hartford, Conn.

Joseph B. Rottman, Regional Manager, Property Claim Services, American Insurance Association (AIA), Rahway, N.J.

Parker W. Schaefer, Secretary (and staff), "The Hartford," Hartford, Conn.

Bruce H. Smith, Executive Vice President, National Association of Independent Insurance Adjusters, Chicago.

John H. Snyder, Vice President, M. F. Bank & Company, Inc., Atlanta.

Dale Stentz, Vice President, General Adjustment Bureau, Inc., New York.

Dale Turvey, Assistant Deputy Commissioner, State Insurance Department, Springfield, Ill.

Marvin E. Verbeck, Vice President and Claim Manager, Kemper Insurance Companies, Long Grove, Ill., and members of his staff, R. L. Harnack, Claim Training, and M. F. Von Leer, Technical Claim.

Ivan M. Willson, Assistant Vice President, Property, Crawford & Company, Atlanta.

John Wrend, Vice President and Secretary-Manager, Property Loss Research Bureau, Chicago.

Special credit and appreciation go to my wife Marie for her role as secretary, typist, proofreader, and consultant over the past two years. Her moral support has been inestimable.

Hendersonville, N.C.   Paul I. Thomas
1977

Contents

FLOODS, MUDSLIDES, AND FAIR PLANS 370

BUSINESS INTERRUPTION, EXTRA EXPENSE, AND ADDITIONAL LIVING EXPENSE 387

RENTS, RENTAL VALUE, AND LEASEHOLD 440

APPLICATION OF INSURANCE, CONTRIBUTION, AND APPORTIONMENT 448

REPORTS TO INSURERS 499

APPENDIX   513

BIBLIOGRAPHY   557

INDEX   561

1

Nature and Significance of Property Loss Adjusting

Until about the middle of this century, individual insurance policies were issued to cover such property as *buildings, building and contents, household furniture, merchandise, furniture and fixtures, machinery,* and *equipment.* These policies were designated property, or fire, insurance policies as distinguished from the traditional casualty contracts, such as auto, liability, workmen's compensation, accident and health, surety bonds, and crime coverages.

The property insurance forms were required to be attached to a *standard fire policy* prescribed by or acceptable to the state in which the policy was written.[1]

With the advent of *multiple-line* and *multi-peril* concepts, the traditional property and casualty coverages are now incorporated, to a large extent, under various personal lines and commercial "package" policies.

TYPES OF PROPERTY LOSSES

This text will deal with the adjustment of losses in the three general classes of property or interest covered: (1) buildings and structures, (2) personal property, and (3) rights of possession or use.

Buildings and structures includes all insurable property identified as a structure and associated with real property.

Personal property, from the claim representative's viewpoint, falls into three groups: (1) personal property in use, such as furniture, fixtures, machinery, equipment, household goods, and other articles that are used and are not for sale in the ordinary channels of trade; (2) personal property for sale, such as raw materials or merchandise, i.e., articles for sale by a producer, manufacturer, or merchant; and (3) automobiles, tractors, bulldozers, road-working equipment, and other motorized equipment.

Rights of possession or use includes those rights described in policies covering *rents* or *rental value;* loss of future earnings of a business as a result of damage or destruction of real or personal property and covered under *business interruption, earnings,* or *loss of income insurance;* loss of a favorable lease canceled under its provisions as a result of damage to or destruction of a building and covered under *leasehold interest insurance;* increased cost of living over the normal cost due to damage to or destruction of the insured's place of residence or its contents and covered under *additional living expense.*

WHAT IS PROPERTY LOSS ADJUSTING?

Claims for losses presented to insurers under policies covering property are generally first-party claims. In other words, the claim is made by the policyholder who is a named insured or by someone with an insurable interest under the policy. The exception is to be

[1]See p. 25.

found when claims are presented under a bailee policy or a trust-and-commissions clause covering property of others than the named insured.

On receiving notice of loss, the insurer inquires into the circumstances of the occurrence and investigates the propriety of the claim. If it is found there is liability, negotiations are commenced to harmonize opposing viewpoints and issues in contention and to establish the amount of loss and the proportion of that loss for which the insurer is liable under the terms of the policy. When these negotiations result in an agreement, the insured and the insurer are said to have made an *adjustment*. While the amount of loss is ordinarily determined by negotiation, in case of disagreement it may be established by *appraisal* as provided for in the policy or by arbitration under arbitration agreements signed by the insurer and the insured.

In the law of insurance the adjustment of a loss is the ascertainment of its amount and the ratable distribution of it among those liable to pay it; the settling and ascertaining the amount of the indemnity which the assured, after all allowance and deductions made, is entitled to receive under the policy, and fixing the proportion which each underwriter is liable to pay. Marsh. Ins. 4th Ed. 400; 2 Phil. Ins., 1814, 1815; *New York v. Insurance Co.*, 39 N.Y. 45, 100 Am. Dec. 400; *Whipple v. Insurance Co.*, 11 R.I. 139.[2]

Property Loss Adjusting Versus Liability Settlements

Claims made under liability insurance policies are generally third-party claims made against the insured for personal injury or damage to property. The person or persons prosecuting the claim are strangers to the contract. Most third-party claims because of their very nature are *settled* by compromise rather than *adjusted*, and negotiations are frequently legalistic. The distinction in adjusting first-party claims is that while basic legal obligations are observed, they are rarely asserted as such. Through experience, the

adjuster, the insured and the producer realize that their interests are parallel and that best results will be obtained generally by tolerance, trust, and cooperation.

PARTIES AND THEIR REPRESENTATIVES

In the adjustment of a loss the insured conducts negotiations, either in person or through a representative, and performs the duties required under the policy. In larger cities the insured is often represented by an *agent*, a *broker*, or a *public adjuster*. On occasion the insured is represented by an *attorney* or by an *insurance adviser*. The insurer's claim representative in the adjustment will generally be a *staff* or an *independent* adjuster. Many insurers permit agents to adjust losses within varying limits of authority.

Staff Adjusters/Claim Representatives

Staff adjusters, or staff claim representatives, are salaried employees of an insurer. They may be residents working from their homes, or they may work out of a branch office or the insurer's home office.

Since the mid-1960s most insurance companies have merged their property and casualty claim-handling facilities and personnel, developing multiple-line claim representatives. While this has enabled insurers to process the great volume of small to moderate-size uncomplicated losses, there remains a recognized need for specialization according to major lines of insurance, such as liability, compensation, accident and health, and property where claims are both complicated and in excess of a few thousand dollars.

Independent Adjusters

Independent adjusters adjust losses and provide other claim services for insurers and in many instances for self-insurers. Their work is done on a fee-and-expense basis. A few are under contract with certain of their clients to service all claims in a specific territory for either a retainer, a percentage of earned

[2]*Black's Law Dictionary.*

premium in the area, or another mutually agreed-upon method of remuneration.

Independents operate either as individuals or as members or employees of an organization. Some have a single office; others have many offices in one or several states, such as Crawford and Company, Gay and Taylor, Inc., James C. Greene Company, Southeastern Adjustment Company, and Brown Brothers on the West Coast. Most of the larger independents now provide multiple-line claim service.

The largest of the independent adjusting firms is the General Adjustment Bureau, Inc. (GAB) with over 600 branch offices. A number of these are in other countries. GAB employs 3,300 adjusters, with an overall personnel of 5,000. Formerly owned by a large group of insurance companies, GAB is a subsidiary of UAL, owner of United Airlines. In addition to adjusting, GAB offers numerous claim-related services including catastrophe operations; appraisals for value or loss; safety engineering; fraud, arson, and subrogation investigations; also technical, accounting, and engineering experts.

Another large independent adjusting firm is Underwriters Adjusting Company (UAC) with over 425 offices and an overall personnel of 3,500. UAC is a subsidiary of the Continental Corporation. Its services include all lines of claim adjusting, catastrophe operations, drive-in claim service, subrogation investigations, and Dial-A-Claim for emergency auto claim handling.

In Canada, the Underwriters Adjustment Bureau Ltd. (UAB) is owned by a group of insurance companies operating in Canada, both stock and mutual. UAB has 85 branch offices across Canada, with 280 adjusters and multiple-line services.

National Association of Independent Insurance Adjusters (NAIIA)

The NAIIA, with headquarters in Chicago, was founded in 1937. It has a membership of 500 independent adjusters or firms. Its standards for membership are on a professional level and it maintains quality control in order to foster and maintain its standards.

Services provided members include two quarterlies—*Adjuster's Reference Guide* and *The Independent Adjuster*. Committees consist of Advisory Council; Catastrophe; Educational; Electronic Data Processing; Forms, Procedures, and Standards; and Legislative. NAIIA is the originator of the Adjuster's Educational Program administered by the Insurance Institute of America (IIA), to which it budgeted large sums for development of the program. Members continue to serve on the advisory committee, approving texts and designing examination questions and answers. The NAIIA still gives financial support.

Agents as Adjusters

The *agent-adjuster* for the insurer generally is limited to small, uncomplicated losses ranging from $50 to $500, although some agents have higher limits. Some insurers also give agents loss-draft authority. Other agents simply agree with the insured on the amount of loss and send the papers to the insurer for processing and payment.

Fast-Track Claim Handling

Fast-track claim handling consists of one of several procedures designed by insurers to quickly process the large volume of small claims. Usually these fall under residential policies and include such losses as glass breakage, cigarette burns to furniture and carpeting, minor windstorm, hail, fire, theft, mysterious disappearance claims, and small medical payments under Section II of the Homeowners policies. These claims do not usually require special investigation or correspondence or the service of a field claim representative.

A common procedure is for the producer, agent, or broker to send a completed *Notice of Loss* form (see Appendix H) to the insurer with a bill or estimate. The insurer's claim department then checks coverage, and, if the amount claimed seems reasonable, the loss is paid. Many insurers take telephone-recorded statements, with the insured's consent, depending on the circumstances and amount of loss. The recording itself is placed in the file, usually untranscribed.

Public Adjusters

Public adjusters are retained by insureds to represent them in adjusting losses with insurers. The public adjuster performs many duties required of the insured, such as protecting the property against further damage, separating damaged from undamaged property, preparing inventories, providing estimates of loss, presenting the claim to the insurer, and negotiating the final adjustment with or without the insured being present. Public adjusters are reimbursed for their services on a percentage of the adjusted loss or on an agreed-fee basis. They usually work under a written contract with the insured.[3] On complicated and large losses they are able to perform valuable service to both insureds and insurers.

The National Association of Public Insurance Adjusters (NAPIA) was founded in 1951. It has 225 member firms with headquarters in Baltimore, Maryland.

LICENSE REQUIREMENTS FOR ADJUSTERS

Of the 50 states and the District of Columbia, 38 have licensing laws of one kind or another for adjusters (see Appendix A).

Staff adjusters must be licensed in 12 states, independent adjusters in 34 states, and public adjusters in 26 states. Licensing is not required in any state to handle catastrophe losses although many states require registration, temporary permits, or special authority. It is recommended that both claim representatives of insurers and public adjusters review the specific licensing legislation of the state or states in which they do business.

THE ADJUSTER'S AUTHORITY

The insurer's claim representative is the *agent* of the insurer for the purpose of adjusting a loss. The claim representative is ordinarily empowered to negotiate agreements regarding value and loss on behalf of the insurer. The stipulations of the policy contract largely determine what facts should be established and what agreements may be made with the insured.

Agreements between adjuster and insured covering matters within the scope of the adjuster's authority, or reasonably believed so by the insured, are binding on the insurer.

An insurer has the power to delegate to employees or independent contractors the manner of investigation and adjustment of losses. Once the adjuster is appointed, the insured has a right to assume that that claim representative has the power to negotiate on the amount of loss and to adjust it. If there are any limitations on the authority of the claim representative, the insured is not bound *unless actual notice has been given of such limitation of authority.*

When an adjuster is delegated by an insurer to adjust a loss, that person possesses extremely great powers insofar as that particular function is concerned. One of the courts in comparing the authority of an adjuster with that of officers of the insurer, said: "An insurance adjuster, while acting in the line of settling and adjusting claims against his principal has the power and authority of the president, vice president, or secretary of such principal. The reasoning is in line with respectable authority." See Flaherty v. Continental Ins. Co., 20 App. Div. 275; 46 N.Y.S. 934; Roberts v. Insurance Company, 94 Mo. App. 142, 72 S.W. 144.[4]

It becomes obvious, in view of the foregoing, that claim representatives should conduct themselves with utmost caution while investigating and adjusting claims to avoid waiving any rights of the insurer. This admonition is especially important when there are questions of coverage or liability.

WORK OF THE INSURER'S CLAIM REPRESENTATIVE

The work of the insurer's claim representative may be divided into four general functions: *investigating, evaluating, negotiating,* and *reporting.* The relative importance of

---

[3]See Work of Insured's Representative, p. 7.

[4]Max J. Gwertzman, *Proceedings,* Property Loss Managers' Conference, New York, 1965.

these functions will vary according to the circumstances in each assignment.

Most property losses are small and uncomplicated, and there is no question about policy coverage. These losses may be handled by telephone or by correspondence. If a field claim representative is sent out, he or she visits the insured, looks at the damaged property, if it is still in existence, discusses the circumstances with the insured, and usually makes an adjustment then and there.

If the property for which claim is made is *totally* destroyed, and more evidence of its existence or value is desired, the claim representative may delay concluding an adjustment pending receipt of such evidence from the insured. In other instances, where the article is damaged and can be repaired, the insured may be asked to have such repairs made and submit a bill. These small losses constitute as much as 75 percent of all property losses.

In larger, more serious losses and in those involving questions of coverage or the liability of the insurer, the function of the claim representative as an *investigator* becomes highly important. If a particular claimant is difficult to deal with or has an inflated idea of the amount of loss, the adjuster's ability as a *negotiator* may be more important than any other qualification. (See Chapter 12, "Negotiations.")

Procedures for careful investigating can soon be learned; and if adequate facts have been obtained, there will usually be no insurmountable problems when it comes to negotiating. Likewise, accepted formats can be followed for reporting. But, when presented with an estimate to repair real or personal property; a schedule of destroyed household goods; an inventory of stock; or a list of destroyed machinery, equipment and fixtures, or improvements and betterments, the claim representative should personally know how to go about evaluating. If the claim representative is not qualified, he or she must know where to obtain reliable and competent experts to do the evaluating.

The insurer can and often does exercise some control over the claim representative's investigation by instructing and counseling either in the beginning or during its progress. But the insurer's control over the determination of value and loss is pretty much limited to designating who will appraise the damage for the claim representative if an expert is needed. Yet that decision also is generally left to the claim representative.

In contrast to liability claim handling, where the insurer usually has complete control over the monetary settlement, in property loss adjusting the determination of value and damage is left in the hands of the claim representative, barring individual insurer limitations on his or her authority. Furthermore, since the claim representative deals directly with the policyholder in negotiating, the company can be committed to any amount agreed upon in the absence of fraud, collusion, or mutual error. This also is at variance with liability claim handling, where the claim representative is dealing with a claimant who is not a party to the contract, and with whom damages are rather freely discussed without committing the insurer. Multiple-line claim representatives must be careful to recognize the distinction between property and liability adjusting when discussing value and loss.

Checklist of Procedure

If the claim representative takes the necessary steps in a particular situation, the work will be completed without essential details being overlooked and information will be acquired that makes possible the answering of any pertinent questions the insurer may ask about the loss.

While different kinds of policies require different approaches to adjusting losses, claim representatives generally take the following steps. The order of procedure should suit the situation. Work done in one step often contributes to what should be done in another.

1. Meet the insured or the person who will act for the insured in the adjustment, get the story, discuss the loss, and make any necessary examination of records.
2. Examine the policy or policies or, if they cannot easily be produced, the

insurer's, agent's, or broker's record of them; list each policy and get a copy of the form or make an abstract of it.

3. Inspect the scene of the loss and examine any of the property still in evidence.

4. Examine available records or reports covering the occurrence of the loss, those of fire department, police, weather bureau, coast guard, or private protective service, watchman's clock records, logbooks, or driver's reports, also any special reports available that may bear on time, place, or cause of loss.

5. Examine records or documents, deeds, mortgages, contracts of sale, leases, warehouse receipts, bills of lading, or other written evidence of title, interest, possession, or liability of the insured or of others.

6. Consider whether any insurance held by others should bear the loss or any part of it, also to what extent the representatives of any such insurance should participate in efforts to have the property protected or salvaged, or should participate in the adjustment.

7. If you believe that the insurance should not cover the loss, withdraw from contact with the insured and report to the insurer, or have a nonwaiver agreement executed before proceeding further.

8. Estimate the situation and the probable results of adjustments made according to the different methods that might be used to determine value and loss.

9. Choose the method of adjustment to be used.

10. Make any necessary preparation for conducting the adjustment according to the method chosen.

11. Negotiate an agreement with the insured regarding value and loss, or if efforts to agree fail, submit the disagreement to appraisal.

12. Check any claim for possible errors and omissions, also for improper inclusion of property, expense, or loss not covered.

13. Apply contract conditions and determine the sum for which any policy, binder, or contract is liable.

14. Gather any necessary information regarding mortgagee or other payee interest, or any claim for payment made by a third party.

15. If, because of a question of liability, the sound value and the amount of loss were fixed under a nonwaiver agreement, make a preliminary report to the insurer and ask for instructions.

16. If no question of liability has arisen, have a proof of loss executed for each policy or contract, and forward it to the insurer with the final report and supporting papers.

17. If any salvage has been sold for account of the insurer and proceeds come to hand after the final report has been forwarded, check the account of sales, expenses, and salvor's commission. Forward to each insurer the salvor's check for the proportions of the net proceeds that the insurer is entitled to receive.

18. Determine what rights, if any, the insurer may have against any party.[5]

Planning the Claim Representative's Work Load

An established claim representative will generally handle several hundred losses every year. Ordinarily, he or she is notified of losses in the order of their occurrence and generally takes up their adjustment in the same order. Sometimes, however, several losses occur at almost the same time. In periods of abnormally cold weather, fire losses are far more numerous than usual. Severe windstorms, hailstorms, and freeze may produce losses by the thousands. Following any sudden increase in the average daily or weekly number of losses, the pressure of work will dislocate orderly attention to it. In almost all adjustment offices, periods of relative quiet alternate with others of tension and confusion. Sometimes losses will be far apart geographically, while at other times they will be confined to a relatively small area. At times, the claim representative's duties are comparatively easy; at

---

[5]What the claim representative should do when it is found that there may be a right of recovery from a third party is discussed at length in Chap. 9, "Subrogation Possibilities."

others, one must travel hard and keep late hours. Like any other person whose work is professional in its nature, the adjuster experiences great irregularity in the demands made.

The claim representative will have days when engagements can be kept and papers cleared according to schedule, but at other times conflicting demands at widely separated points will require much overtime, if the output is not to fall far behind.

The claim representative must follow some consistent general plan in selecting work to be given priority. Any plan should, as far as possible, allow losses to be taken up in the order of their occurrence. This order, however, must necessarily be subordinated to traveling conditions and also to the need of giving prompt attention to losses involving property that may be saved from further damage or restored by appropriate action, postponing losses in which the property or the claimant will not suffer by delayed adjustment. Conservation of time, energy, and expense must also be considered.

Except when working under catastrophe conditions, the claim representative is ordinarily expected to reach the scene of any loss within 24 hours after it is assigned. In areas of sparse population and at long distances, however, the claim representative leaves the office with enough assignments to keep busy on the road for several days. When several losses are to be adjusted in the same community, they should be taken up, as far as possible, in the order that will do most to prevent further damage, but the claim representative must adapt that order to the exigencies of claimants and local agents in order to avoid the ill feelings that arise from delay.

When the claim representative is under such pressure of assignments that it is physically impossible to get to a loss with reasonable promptness, depending on the urgency indicated, it is well to contact the insured by telephone, inquire about the circumstances of the loss, give necessary instructions, and make a definite appointment to visit the insured. *Much of the criticism of adjusters by insureds stems from apparent or actual neglect.* Very seldom will the insured complain if the adjuster telephones or even writes explaining why there will be a delay of a day or two, or several days.

WORK OF THE INSURED'S REPRESENTATIVE

Function of the Insured's Representative

Agents, brokers, accountants, lawyers, and public adjusters are ordinarily expected to (1) guide the insured in the actions required by the insurance contract, or requested or demanded by the insurer's claim representative, (2) aid in obtaining the information necessary to prepare and support a proper claim, (3) negotiate an acceptable adjustment, and (4) suggest any rearrangement or improvement of coverage.

Very rarely does the insured authorize the representative to make an adjustment without previously receiving the insured's specific approval of the claim or of acceptance of any offer of settlement.

Qualifications

The representative, in order to function efficiently on all kinds of losses, should have the following qualifications.

1. A comprehensive knowledge of the insurance contract.
2. Knowledge of classes of property and the rights of possession or interest that are ordinarily the subject matter of insurance contracts.
3. Knowledge of conditions prevailing in the locality where the loss occurred, or the means of gaining such knowledge.
4. Knowledge of costs, depreciation factors, and values, and connections through which can be gained any necessary special knowledge.
5. Knowledge of the statutes and court decisions affecting adjusting work in the locality.
6. Personnel and office equipment to
   a. Prepare inventories, showing costs or values of articles of personal property.
   b. Check inventories for accuracy as to quantities or prices.
   c. Prepare statements, according to the

books or accounting records, of the cost or value of property, or of business-interruption losses.

7. The ability to correlate with any other information possessed the advice received from builders, architects, engineers, repairmen, cleaners, accountants, salvors, or other experts.

What the Insured's Representative Should Do

The procedure of the person who adjusts for the insured is similar to the procedure of the insurer's adjuster. He or she may find it necessary or advisable to take any of the following steps.

1. Get the insured's story. Become familiar with the insured's policies; explain the coverage, limitations, and conditions to the insured; and give pertinent advice.
2. Determine what property or other subject matter in which the insured has an insurable interest has been lost, destroyed, or damaged.
   a. When? Where? How?
   b. By what peril?
3. Give written notice of loss to each insurer.
4. See that the insured complies with policy requirements as to the handling of the property after the loss.
5. Facilitate the inspection of the property by the insurer's claim representative and make agreements as to its handling and preparation of claim.
6. Prepare inventory, estimate, or statement of value and loss, or any account necessary to present claim, and deliver copies to the insurer's claim representative.
7. Try to agree upon value and loss with the insurer's adjuster.
8. Arrange for appeals from any adverse position taken by the claim representative.
9. In case of hopeless disagreement as to value or loss, make arrangements for appraisal.
10. When value and loss have been determined, apply any limitation clauses

and if two or more insurers are interested, apportion the loss.
11. See that proof of loss is executed and filed with each insurer.
12. Suggest to the insured any rearrangement of insurance that will provide better coverage.
13. Follow up on collection of claim.
14. If the insured has any right of recovery against a third party, advise as to rights and be prepared to cooperate with any lawyer retained to enforce them.

DETERMINATION OF VALUE AND LOSS

Generally the first evidence examined after a loss is the property itself or the place it occupied, unless the property has disappeared—as when it has been stolen. By comparing its condition after the loss with its known or assumed condition at the time of the loss, an opinion can often be formed as to its value before the loss, the nature and extent of the damage, and the amount of loss. Records bearing on the property may show quantities, cost, age, history, or condition and thus establish the loss with greater certainty or furnish a stronger base for an opinion of the amount. Statements of persons familiar with the property may be taken. Such statements may cover matters of fact, such as size, weight, quantity, quality, brand, serial and model numbers, use, or condition.

Burden of Proof of Value and Loss

The burden of proving value and loss rests upon the insured who is required to furnish evidence in support of the amount claimed. If there is a mixed loss, that is, a loss part of which is covered by the policy and part of which is not covered, the burden of proving the amount covered by the policy also rests upon the insured.

Policies generally contain requirements that the insured produce specified kinds of evidence bearing on value and loss and also aid the insurer in its efforts to determine value and loss by exhibiting all that remains of the property for examination by the insurer's representative. Most policies, statutory or otherwise, covering property, also require the insured to submit to examination under oath.

Value and loss are usually matters of opinion; only occasionally are they matters of fact or certainty. In most cases, value and loss are established by agreement, in a few by appraisal or arbitration. Fundamentally there are four ways that insureds and adjusters approach problems of value and loss in expectation of reaching an agreement: (1) survey and estimate, (2) acceptance of cost or quantity shown by record, (3) actual repair or replacement, (4) selling of the salvage.

Adjustment Methods Available to Determine Value and Loss

In every covered loss the insured and the insurer's claim representative will seek some practical method for determining value or loss that promises to bring about a fair and equitable adjustment. The choice of the method to be used should be determined by the kind of property, the type of loss, the information to be had about the property, the resources, ability, and attitude of the insured, and the expert advice and services available to the claim representative.

Some of the circumstances under which each method is commonly used are set forth below.

1. *Adjuster and insured go over the property together and try to come to an agreement.* Most small and moderate-sized losses are adjusted by the insured and the claim representative looking at the damage, discussing it, and agreeing on what it amounts to in dollars and cents. The loss may be nothing more than a grease fire on top of the stove that ignited the window curtains, blistered the window trim, and smoked the painted kitchen walls. Under the contents coverage of the Homeowners policy a claim may be made for cleaning dishes and kitchenware, and under the dwelling coverage claim may be made for washing down the walls, sanding the woodwork, and painting the kitchen. The claim representative and the insured inspect the damage

together and agree on the amount of the loss.

In rural areas and in smaller towns and villages many property owners, as well as adjusters who work in the territory, are familiar with simple building construction and are capable of estimating small repair jobs using local material and labor costs. Credit for any betterment as a result of the repairs will be discussed and agreed upon.

Larger mercantile and manufacturing losses also may be adjusted by this method. The insured with the help of employees or the services of a public adjuster may inventory the damaged and destroyed contents and make a claim on each article inventoried. The claim representative and the insured, or the insured's representative, then go over the property, examine each article or lot, and checking the figures on the inventory, try to effect an agreement.

In many cases the claim representative will be handed an inventory prepared by or for the insured with no claim figures. Agreed loss figures are entered as the property is being examined and discussed jointly. In still other cases the insured and the claim representative will together make up the inventory, agreeing as they go along on the quantity, value, and damage to be entered for each article. If the loss is one that must be adjusted from the books of account, the insured and the adjuster will often go through the books together.

2. *Adjuster and insured make or have made for themselves independent estimates which they compare and discuss in an effort to reconcile any differences.* When property of considerable value is involved and the loss is substantial, the insured and the claim representative will ordinarily have separate estimates made by experts and will then try to agree on value and loss by comparing the estimates and discussing differences.

When unusual and expensive buildings are destroyed or damaged, the insured and the claim representative usually have estimates made by contractors or builders and, after comparing them and discussing them, come to an agreement. In many cases there will be no great difference in the amounts of the estimates, but in some cases there will be. The degree of difficulty experienced in making an adjustment is generally in direct proportion to the amount by which the estimates differ. The claim representative, therefore, spends considerable time in analyzing and discussing differences. If the estimate prepared for the insured exceeds the probable cost of rebuilding or making necessary repairs, the claim representative tries to isolate the items in the estimate believed to be excessive and to demonstrate that the extent of work stated in the item, or the cost of doing it, is greater than necessary. If the estimate is properly itemized and shows the quantities and unit costs of the work contemplated, the claim representative should be able to point out any item calling for more work than is necessary, and by making actual measurements show the quantity of material needed and compute the cost of putting it in place. Excessive prices can be demonstrated by comparing them with prevailing local prices for materials and labor.

The claim representative often finds it impossible to bring about an adjustment by dealing with the insured alone. In many cases the insured is unfamiliar with methods of making repairs or the cost of materials or labor and can only rely on figures given by a builder. If the property involved is of complicated or expensive construction, the claim representative may be uninformed on the cost of materials required for repairs or on the amount of work that various classes of mechanics can be expected to perform in a given length of time. He or she must frequently deal with the insured's builder and in many cases will find it wise to have his or her own builder discuss estimates with the insured's builder. If the estimates differ greatly, it is the common practice to have the two builders meet and try to reconcile them.

If the loss involves unusual articles, expensive furniture, or complicated machinery or merchandise, experts will often be employed and will perform the same kind of service as the builders who are employed on building losses.

Likewise, if a loss must be determined from the showing of complicated books and records, the insured and the claim representative may both enlist the aid of accountants.

3. *Adjuster and insured may each select an expert and instruct the two experts to examine the property or the evidence bearing on it, if it has been lost or destroyed, and to try to produce an agreed estimate or determination.* On building losses, if competent and reliable builders are used, this method will most often produce a satisfactory adjustment. It is regularly used in a number of cities.

On personal-property losses this method is generally productive of equitable adjustments when capable experts are employed. It is most serviceable when the property involved is of such a nature that technical knowledge is needed to estimate its value and to determine the damage it has sustained. In such cases considerable time is saved that would otherwise be expended in acquainting both the insured and the claim representative with details that both would then have to discuss in order to settle differences of opinion.

This method works well when the loss must be determined from books and records, if competent accountants are selected to produce the figures.

4. *Adjuster and insured may prepare or have prepared agreed specifications for repair or replacement and submit these to be bid upon.* On losses involving damaged buildings this method will generally produce highly satisfactory results, particularly when, after general specifications have been agreed upon by the insured and the claim representative, a competent builder or an architect prepares detailed specifications.

On large or complex machinery and fixture losses this method is often used.

5. *Adjuster and insured delegate the determination of amount of loss to a single expert.* This method is used infrequently and only when the single expert is recognized as such and is completely satisfactory to both the insured and the insurer. Examples might be a subcontractor, such as an electrician, a painter, or a glazier. In cases involving personal property it might be a jeweler, a reweaver of rugs and fabrics, or a well-recognized restorer of objects of art. Neither the insured nor the claim representative should give such experts a free hand without reserving the privilege of double-checking the results.

6. *Adjuster and insured arrange for the repair or replacement of the property, frequently on a cost-plus basis under proper check, and an accounting of the cost, then agree upon betterment as a result of the repairs or replacement.* Use of this method is rather common on small losses where there is little question that the repairs or replacement will be done to the satisfaction of the insured. It is highly satisfactory where reweaving or reupholstering of furniture or replacing floor coverings, drapes, and similar household furnishings is required. The use of outside firms to do work of this kind should be generally limited to those of well-known competence and integrity. In larger cities there are firms that specialize in insurance repair work. The claim representative should, whenever possible, have the insured make the arrangements with whoever is to do the work with the understanding that satisfaction must be guaranteed before payment.

    This method is an excellent one where the insured business employs its own maintenance and repair force. With such concerns this method should be used as often as possible.

7. *Adjuster and insured accept as a basis for determining the loss the record of cost of construction or purchase.* If the cost record is relatively recent and upon examination is satisfactory in every respect to the claim representative, it may be used as a basis for establishing loss. Any increase or decrease in cost from the date of purchase or construction should be taken into account as well as any betterment. Where this method is contemplated in cases involving destruction of a building, it generally requires the careful checking of original plans and specifications to ascertain their propriety and to eliminate items that are not covered by the policy, such as footings and grading.

8. *In case of disagreement adjuster and insured submit their disagreements to appraisal, reference, or arbitration.* This method is used only occasionally and then more often on building losses. Personal property, rent, leasehold, and business-interruption losses are seldom adjusted by this method.

9. *Adjuster and insured agree on the value of any personal property. The insurer pays on the basis of the agreed value and takes the property for sale as salvage.* This method is in conformity with the policy provision giving the insurer the option of taking all or any part of the articles on which claim is made and paying the insured the agreed or appraised value. The method is usually confined to losses on stocks of merchandise.

10. *Adjuster and insured agree upon the value of personal property and have the salvage sold with the proceeds being paid the insured.* This method is a modification of method 9 by which the insurer pays the insured the agreed value and retains the salvage proceeds. Method 10 is preferred when there is inadequate insurance to cover the loss or when the insured is a coinsurer.

11. *The adjuster exercises the insurer's option to repair or replace the property.* This method is used more often on small losses involving minor building repairs; repairing or replacing household items, such as furniture, cameras, jewelry, carpeting, and appliances. In many cities there are firms that specialize in such repairs and replacements, and insurers and insureds alike find this method expeditious and equitable. In some areas of the country, insurers subsidize or actually own construction

companies, and repair or replacements are made by them.

The procedure works well when the firms making repairs or replacements are well established and of unquestioned integrity. The claim representative may authorize the work to be done or insist that the order come directly from the insured. When the repair or replacement is completed, a *Certificate of Satisfaction* is signed by the insured authorizing the insurer to pay the repair firm directly (see Appendix B).

The Certificate of Satisfaction may be a separate document or may be incorporated into the proof of loss form of individual insurers (see Appendix C). If a separate document is used, a proof of loss is generally prepared for the insured's signature.

However, unless this method is controlled, it tends to create new problems. The insured may be dissatisfied with the repairs after they have been completed, or with the replacement that has been made, and may refuse to accept one or the other. This places the insurer in the position of a defendant in a controversy over specific performance. Furthermore, the general holding of the courts has been that, when an insurer elects to repair or replace, it enters into a new contract with the insured under which its *liability* is unlimited regardless of the policy coverage and amount.

Another caveat is making certain, especially on larger losses, that all interests, mortgagee, public adjuster if one is under contract, and other loss payees agree that the loss is to be paid directly to the firm making the repairs or replacement.

There are occasional situations when either a threat to exercise the option or actually exercising it can be advantageous. These would include losses involving suspected but unprovable fires of incendiary origin; cases involving two or more persons separately insured, each attempting to collect the same loss;[6] or extremely avaricious insureds

who cannot be brought to reason by any other means. If the option is exercised, the claim representative should require a guarantee and a bond from the contractor before any structural or mechanical work is started, or equivalent documents from a supplier or reconditioner of personal property.

PREPARATION FOR ADJUSTMENT

No special preparation is necessary in handling the majority of small or moderate-size losses. The claim representative's general knowledge of property and insurance contracts is sufficient to warrant efforts to agree on an amount of loss when first meeting the insured. If the first meeting is unsuccessful, a second visit may be needed, and in the interim proper preparation should be made.

In complicated losses and those involving large amounts of money, preparation is essential, so that the claim representative will not lack information and evidence and thus be at a great disadvantage in discussions with the insured and unable to make intelligent decisions.

The objective of adjustment negotiations[7] is a final agreement upon the maximum amount of money the insured is entitled to receive under the terms and conditions of the insurance covering the loss. This amount should likewise coincide with the maximum liability of the insurer. Preparation for negotiations includes seeking information and evidence and planning how to use it most effectively. Documents and exhibits should be arranged in orderly fashion so as to be found readily. Such information and evidence should be studied for its probable effect when used in negotiating. Is it such that it is likely to be acceptable to the insured as proof; will it justify an inference; will it impress the insured in a way that will make negotiating easier? How should the material be presented or used? Who should present it, the claim representative or the expert, if one is employed? The time, place, and manner of use or presentation should be planned.

Losses that are likely to involve nonconcurrent or overlapping policies, those pre-

---

[6]See Improvements and Betterments, p. 202.

[7]See Chap. 12, "Negotiations."

senting questions of cancellation and substitution, or those that entail property that is wholly or partly not covered call for careful and thorough preparation for adjustment.

CONCLUDING AN ADJUSTMENT

Claims may be prepared in great detail before there is any discussion of value and loss, or they may be prepared afterward based upon agreements made during adjustment negotiations. Regardless of when the claim was prepared, it should be checked by the claim representative before the amount is computed for which the insurer is liable. Any contribution or limiting clauses are applied, and if more than one insurer is to contribute to the loss, an apportionment should be made. *Proof of loss* is prepared for the insured's signature, either by the claim representative or the insured's representative.

Loss Payees

Proofs of loss submitted to or prepared by the claim representative for presentation to the insurer should include the name of the payee in any mortgage or loss payee clause attached to the policy. The subject of mortgagees and other loss payees is covered in detail in Chapter 5.

Reports to Insurers

When an adjustment has been concluded, the claim representative should prepare without delay the papers necessary to support the amount agreed upon and present them promptly to the insurer's loss department or to the person whose duty it is to check the details and make payment. Generally the final papers will include a *statement of loss* written or typed on the proof of loss by the claim representative or typed on a separate sheet which is attached to the proof of loss, together with estimates, inventories, and schedules or other original papers on which the adjustment was based.

When more than one insurer is interested, it is customary to send the original supporting papers to the insurer that carries the largest amount of insurance. On large or complicated losses, all interested companies frequently receive copies of the supporting papers, together with a proof of loss for their proportion. In some cases, where a great number of insurers underwrite a large industrial or commercial line, each for a small percentage of the total insurance, a single Master Proof of Loss is executed by the insured. This is sent to the insurer carrying the largest amount of insurance; all other insurers receive a copy of the claim representative's report and a copy of the details of the adjustment and apportionment. Reports to insurers are covered in Chapter 28.

Dispatching Papers

The claim representative should systematize the work so that ordinarily he or she will complete the necessary papers immediately after making an adjustment and deliver them by mail or otherwise with the greatest possible dispatch. While occasionally the completion of papers connnected with a loss must be subordinated to other pressing matters, delay should be avoided. The insurer's representative in charge of losses must receive and examine the papers before the claim is paid. The public and the producers expect prompt payment when a loss has been adjusted, and delay tends to cause irritation. If the delay is due to the adjuster's failure to complete and deliver the necessary papers, criticism can be expected. As often happens, the insured may begin to make repairs or replacements immediately after the adjustment and may be dependent upon the insurance money to pay bills. Any delay in receiving it may prove embarrassing and will generally lead to complaints to the agent or broker who in turn will complain to the insurer. If the delay is chargeable to the claim representative, he or she may be blamed, not only by the agent or broker but also by the insurer, as it may have disturbed business relations that the insurer has built up, possibly by years of effort and expense.

CONTROVERSIES BETWEEN INSURERS

In the adjustment of losses in which two or more insurers are interested, controversies at times arise because opinions differ regarding how much each insurer should pay. Situations generally responsible for such controversies are those involving overlapping coverages, apportionments, or respective liabilities.

Nonconcurrencies

Nonconcurrent policies present questions of contribution and apportionment, primary and excess insurance, exclusions, and limitations. With the broadening of the fields of fire, inland marine, and casualty insurance, the extensions of coverage that have come in recent years, and the multiple-line underwriting, there have developed many loss situations in which the coverage of the different kinds of insurance overlaps.

The Agreement of Guiding Principles, which became effective November 1, 1963, establishes rules for apportioning losses when there is overlapping coverage; that is, when more than one policy of insurance covers the same peril but the interest, the property, or the location is not the same. Application of these rules eliminates most disagreements involving apportionments among insurers (see Chapter 27).

Cancellations

Controversies over efforts to cancel and substitute policies often follow the act of an insurer that orders its agent to cancel a policy. As the agent generally wishes to keep the insured covered, he writes a policy of another insurer as soon as he receives the order to cancel and mails the new policy to the insured, asking that he return the first policy as canceled. If a loss occurs before the first policy has been surrendered, a controversy over which insurer shall pay the loss almost always follows.

Arbitration Between Insurers

In most of the controversies between or among insurers over questions of liability, contribution and apportionment, or cancellation and substitution, the insured is annoyed and the payment he needs is withheld because of circumstances which do not affect his interest. There is a strong feeling on the part of insurers that such controversies should not be allowed to involve the insured. There is also a feeling that insurers can do much better by settling their disputes with one another than by taking them to the courts.

These feelings are responsible for the present well-established practice of submitting to arbitration controversies between or among insurers when there is sufficient insurance, the loss has been agreed upon, and the insured is innocent of any wrongdoing.[8]

Property Arbitration Programs

The Property Loss Research Bureau and the Property Claim Services of the American Insurance Association each have a formalized arbitration program for arbitrating differences of opinion respecting application of the Guiding Principles and differences of opinion in first-party property losses and claims arising *outside* the scope of the Guiding Principles. These programs have been in operation for many years to settle disputes between the respective *member companies* of the PLRB and AIA, and companies which are not members of the PLRB or of the AIA but who wish to avail themselves of the respective arbitration programs.

To settle disputes involving application of the Guiding Principles, and also for resolving differences of opinion in the first-party property losses and claims between AIA and PLRB *member companies*, a joint arbitration program was developed in 1975, a program benefiting both organizations and the industry as a whole. The rules and regulations of the joint arbitration program are reproduced in Appendix D. The rules and regulations of the AIA and PLRB arbitration programs for their respective member companies are similar to those of the joint program in many respects and are available through the AIA or PLRB.

A third type of arbitration program is known as the *Fire and Allied Lines Subrogation Arbitration Agreement*. This is for *com-*

---

[8]See also Nationwide Intercompany Arbitration Agreement in Chap. 23.

pulsory arbitration for signatories to the agreement and applies exclusively to the arbitration of *liability* and *damage issues* in losses under $5,000. It has no authorization to arbitrate coverage questions or the application of the Guiding Principles. Geographic jurisdiction is national and served by numerous local appointed arbitration committees. There are presently in excess of 230 stock and mutual insurance company signatories to this program. The first two of the five articles of agreement (see below) state the questions and disputes within the authority of the arbitrators. The full agreement, with rules and regulations, is available through any signatory Company.

Article First. Signatory companies are bound to forego litigation and in place thereof submit to arbitration any questions or disputes which may arise as hereinafter set forth:
(a) Any fire subrogation claim not in excess of $5,000.
(b) Any extended coverage subrogation claim not in excess of $5,000.
(c) Any additional extended coverage subrogation claim not in excess of $5,000.
(d) Any inland marine subrogation claim not in excess of $5,000.
(e) Any first party property subrogation claim not in excess of $5,000, that is not within the compulsory provisions of other industry inter-company arbitration agreements.
This Article shall not apply to:
(a) Any subrogation claim for the enforcement of which a lawsuit was instituted prior to, and is pending at, the time this agreement is signed.
(b) Any subrogation claim as to which a company asserts a defense of lack of coverage on grounds other than
  (1) delayed notice or,
  (2) non-cooperation.
(c) Subrogation claims arising out of policies written under Retrospective Rating Plans, Comprehensive Insurance Rating Plans, or War Risk Rating Plans unless prior written consent is obtained from the Home Offices of the companies in interest.
Article Second. Any controversy, including policy coverage and interpretations, between or among signatory companies involving any claim or other matter relating thereto and not included in Article First hereof or which involves amounts in excess of those stated therein may also be submitted to arbitration under this Agreement with the prior consent of the parties.

PAYMENT AND DISCHARGE

When the amount for which the insurer is liable under the contract has been determined and all requirements in case of loss have been complied with, the loss is payable.

Ordinarily, the insured is the person entitled to receive payment and competent to give a receipt that will discharge the insurer from liability. Losses under many policies, however, are by stipulation payable to some third party, such as a mortgagee, and there are situations in which third parties not named in the policy but possessed of an interest in the property may be able to intervene by legal process and require payment in whole or in part to themselves. In some cases the insured will assign to another person his or her right to collect. While the policy provides that no assignment of the policy itself shall be valid except with the written consent of the company, the provision does not operate as a prohibition against the assignment of a *claim*. If the insured had a valid claim and did assign it, the insurer must recognize the assignee.

QUESTIONS AND PROBLEMS

1. You have been assigned to a building loss in which a serious fire caused extensive damage. You have made a telephone call to meet the insured at the loss, but before leaving the office you decide to write down a number of points you will want to cover in the investigation and evaluation of the loss and in concluding the adjustment. Make a list of at least ten of the points you plan to cover.
2. Discuss briefly the claim representative's authority, *actual* or *implied*, when handling the adjustment of a property loss.
3. Compare the insurer's control over a claim representative assigned to a property

insurance loss with one assigned to a legal liability claim as to (a) investigating, (b) evaluating, (c) negotiating.

4. a. Representatives of insureds on losses include brokers, agents, and public adjusters. To effectively represent insureds they should have certain qualifications. Name four.

b. The general procedure for what the insured's representative should do covers fourteen activities listed in the text. State ten such activities.

5. Visualize a fire loss in a dwelling which causes serious damage to the building and its contents. The loss to contents poses no problem and is worked out between the insured and the claim representative. There are several methods to choose from in deciding how best to adjust the building loss. Considering various possible situations, discuss *three* procedures applicable to this type of loss.

6. a. What is a Certificate of Satisfaction?

b. Describe a typical situation where one would be used.

c. Unless controlled, a Certificate of Satisfaction can cause new problems. Explain.

7. The American Insurance Association (AIA) and the Property Loss Research Bureau (PLRB) each have its own arbitration program for arbitrating controversies between their respective member companies. There are two other important intercompany arbitration programs for arbitrating certain differences of opinion between insurers. Explain briefly the purpose of each program.

2

Unfair Claim-Handling Practices

Most reputable insurers take the view that *prompt, courteous,* and *fair* claim-handling practices are essential to build and retain the goodwill and respect of policyholders, the producers, and the insuring public. This philosophy is also recognized as a viable competitive sales tool for developing new business. Underpayment of claims, insupportable denials of liability and coverage, neglect of or discourtesy toward insureds by claim personnel can be disastrous to an insurer. Likewise, overpayment of claims through carelessness, incompetence, or simply the avoidance of distasteful confrontations with insureds and producers can be equally harmful. The experienced claim representative is keenly aware of the fine line between these two extremes.

Much attention has been given to the technical training and education of claim personnel, because property and casualty insurance is a highly technical business. Training qualified claim people requires continuing study programs. Most insurers maintain an educational department where claim personnel are required to attend claim studies. There are also numerous state and national adjuster and insurance company groups or associations that devote considerable time to workshops and lectures on claim handling. In addition, many schools and institutes offer study courses leading to certificates of accomplishment for claim personnel. The subjects covered by the various educational facilities go far beyond the numerous contracts of insurance; they include such matters as basic and tort law, accounting, salvaging of stocks, building construction and estimating, auto body repairs, methods for investigating causes of loss, and the evaluating of personal property.

Responsible and reputable insurers have long known that the courteous and fair handling of claims is a worthy business tenet. But in today's *consumer-oriented society* it became obvious that for too long too much emphasis was being given to technical training with little or no emphasis placed on indoctrinating claim personnel with this very philosophy. The result has been an oversupply of claim representatives who, when communicating with insureds, show great skill in technical know-how but who exhibit a low profile when it comes to human relations.

This misplaced emphasis is less a criticism of the individuals than of the system under which they operate. The business of insurance claim work is legalistic and technical, mainly because of its legal, contractual nature. Because the majority of insurers are multiple-line in all departments, their claim administrators and field claim representatives need to be qualified to handle claims under many kinds of insurance policies, including auto, inland marine, fire and allied lines, and even workmen's compensation. One assignment may involve negotiating with a *third-party claimant*; the next, with a *first-party policyholder*. The former is a stranger to the policy contract, while the latter is the insurer's own customer. Consequently, the attitude of the claim representative to the one is not necessarily the same as it is to the other. Yet the voice of either as consumers, complaining of unfair treatment to a state insurance department, is equally effective in attracting attention.

UNFAIR CLAIM SETTLEMENT PRACTICES SECTION OF NAIC MODEL ACT

In 1947 the National Association of Insurance Commissioners (NAIC) drafted a model Unfair Trade Practices Act related to the business of insurance. The drafting was stimulated by the Federal Trade Commission Act, some of the language of which was used in the NAIC Model Act.

The NAIC model act did enumerate specific acts, peculiar to the business of insurance, as unfair trade practices and contained an omnibus clause for undefined acts, but required in cases of undefined practices that the commissioner petition the court for a cease and desist order rather than issue the order himself, after hearing.[1]

In 1971 the model act was reviewed and rewritten by the NAIC. This action was aroused by pressures, primarily from two sources. (1) Four Congressional bills were introduced which would give the Federal Trade Commission power to regulate the insurance business, a privilege heretofore enjoyed by the states. (2) A rising consumer movement was more and more demanding protection for the insuring public, a demand generated in part by an unprecedented increase in claim-related complaints.

This dramatic increase in claim-related complaints to state insurance departments by consumers was the principal stimulus for including in the revised NAIC act a section

[1]William H. Huff, Iowa Insurance Commissioner, in a speech, "Unfair Claim Settlement Practices," at Loss Managers' Conference of the Property Loss Research Bureau, Arlington Heights, Ill., 1973.

known as "Unfair Claim Settlement Practices." This section listed the following 14 claim-handling practices designated as unfair, subject to the following condition:

Committing or performing with such frequency as to indicate a general business practice any of the following:

(a) misrepresenting pertinent facts or insurance policy provisions relating to coverages at issue;

(b) failing to acknowledge and act reasonably promptly upon communications with respect to claims arising under insurance policies;

(c) failing to adopt and implement reasonable standards for the prompt investigation of claims arising under insurance policies;

(d) refusing to pay claims without conducting a reasonable investigation based upon all available information;

(e) failing to affirm or deny coverage of claims within a reasonable time after proof of loss statements have been completed;

(f) not attempting in good faith to effectuate prompt, fair and equitable settlement of claims in which liability has become reasonably clear;

(g) compelling insureds to institute litigation to recover amounts due under an insurance policy by offering substantially less than the amounts ultimately recovered in actions brought by such insureds;

(h) attempting to settle a claim for less than the amount to which a reasonable man would have believed he was entitled by reference to written or printed advertising material accompanying or made part of an application;

(i) attempting to settle claims on the basis of an application which was altered without notice to, or knowledge or consent of, the insured;

(j) making claim payments to insureds or beneficiaries not accompanied by statement setting forth the coverage under which the payments are being made;

(k) making known to insureds or claimants a policy of appealing from arbitration awards in favor of insureds or claimants for the purpose of compelling them to accept settlements or compromises less than the amount awarded in arbitration;

(l) delaying the investigation or payment of claims by requiring an insured, claimant, or the physician of either to submit a preliminary claim report and then requiring the subsequent submission of formal proof of loss forms, both of which submissions contain substantially the same information;

(m) failing to promptly settle claims, where liability has become reasonably clear, under one portion of the insurance policy coverage in order to influence settlements under other portions of the insurance policy coverage;

(n) failing to promptly provide a reasonable explanation of the basis in the insurance policy in relation to the facts or applicable law for denial of a claim or for the offer of a compromise settlement.

The condition to which each subsection is subject is an important one, i.e., "committing or performing with such frequency as to indicate a general business practice." Obviously it means more than once and perhaps more than twice. *Frequency* will be a determining factor. Whether this is a decision that will rest with the commissioner or the courts will have to await the test of time.

UNIFORM COMPLAINT-HANDLING PROCEDURE

The NAIC has established a complaint database system through its Uniform Complaint Handling Procedures Task Force of the Unfair Trade Practices Subcommittee. The system, not a part of the NAIC Model Act, is designed to cover (1) unfair sales and advertising practices, (2) unfair underwriting practices, and (3) unfair claims practices.

This comprehensive system is set up for state insurance departments to report complaints by company and by line to the NAIC central office. The complaints are compiled, consolidated, and returned to the state departments. Reports take into account premium volume and relate it to the number of complaints which will hopefully be classified

as *justified* and *unjustified*. The system could allow a commissioner to obtain the *nationwide* complaint figures of a particular company to help establish frequency which would indicate a possible general business practice.

The complaint data-base system was developed between October, 1973, and April, 1974. The state of Illinois served as a pilot for part of 1974 and all of 1975. The computer figures for 1975 are shown in Table 2-1. The total number of complaints received by line of coverage was 12,545. This does not include approximately 5,000 inquiries received by the Insurance Department. "The system, while new and not entirely perfected, does present statistics that show general trends which can be a useful tool for the public, the industry, and the Department."[2]

The number of complaints in each line of coverage is not particularly significant unless it is related to total premium and claim volume. For example, one would expect more complaints on automobile than on fire and allied lines since there are many more automobile claims.

What does appear significant is that the highest number of complaints in all lines of coverage fall under three reasons:

1. Unsatisfactory settlement offer.
2. Denial of claim.
3. Delays in handling claims.

These three reasons together account for the following percentages under each line of coverage:

All Auto 83%
All Fire and Allied Lines 81%
Accident and Health Life 65%
Workmen's Compensation and
    Liability 80%

The data-base system also provides for the *disposition* of complaints. They are tied in to *reasons* but not to *line of coverage*, so that it is not possible to determine disposition by line, something that could be useful. While no attempt is made here to analyze the statistics

---

[2]Dale Turvey, Assistant Deputy Director, Illinois Department of Insurance, in a letter to the author.

TABLE 2-1

Complainant		Complaint Against	
Insured	9,400	Insurer	11,745
Third Party	3,045	Service Organization	800
Other	100	Total	12,545
Total	12,545		

Reason for Complaint	All Auto	Fire and Allied Lines	Accident and Health, Life	Workmen's Comp. and Liability
Premium and rating	311	79	664	33
Refusal to insure	10	2	59	0
Cancellation, nonrenewal	406	89	229	13
Delays (underwriting)	8	2	50	0
Misleading advertising	1	1	8	0
Agent handling	29	14	149	1
Misrepresentation	5	2	198	0
Delays (marketing and sales)	0	0	13	0
Unsatisfactory settlement offer	1,414	267	873	33
Post-claim underwriting	3	0	8	0
Denial of claim	1,853	302	1,425	116
Coordinating benefits	0	0	12	0
Delays (handling claims)	1,380	286	1,279	57
Unsatisfactory repairs	59	3	0	0
Premium notice (billing problem)	4	1	39	0
Cash value	0	0	93	0
Delays (policyholder service)	21	4	254	1
Other	90	6	185	1
Total	5,594	1,058	5,538	255

Miscellaneous-lines complaints including inland marine, 100. Grand total, 12,545.

without more detailed information, it should be noted that of the *Unsatisfactory settlement offer* complaints for all lines of coverage, 58 percent were classified under "Disposition" as *no policy in force, contract provision, no jurisdiction, question of fact* or *Company position upheld*. Of the *Denial of claim* complaints, 77 percent were so classified; but of the *Delays in handling claims* complaints, only 28 percent were so classified.

A conclusion that might be drawn from these statistics is that well over 50 percent of the complaints of "Unsatisfactory settlement offers" and "Denial of claims" had small justification in being reported to the Insurance Department. Lacking more specific data, it might be generalized that there was far less justification for "Delays in handling claims."

OBJECTIVES OF NAIC UNQUESTIONED BY INSURERS

Insurers in general find no reason to question the objectives of the NAIC in promulgating the Unfair Claim Settlement Practices section of the Model Act. "Compliance with these provisions should require no changes in most companies' procedures. In fact, they might be a blessing in disguise. They may have a beneficial effect on a few companies whose standards were not as high as they should have been, and they may have a similar effect on individual claim personnel who, at times, may try to take the easy way out."[3]

[3] Ralph W. Arnold, Vice President, American Family Mutual, "Living with Unfair Claim Practices Acts," *Best's Review*, June, 1975.

POWERS OF COMMISSIONERS TO REGULATE COMPLIANCE

The powers granted insurance commissioners in the model act are substantial and in some respects not unlike the powers in Congressional inquiries. Commissioners have the power to examine and investigate, hold hearings, administer oaths, examine and cross-examine, receive oral and documentary evidence, subpoena witnesses, and compel attendance. Upon failure to comply with a subpoena or to testify in a matter on which a person may be lawfully interrogated, the commissioner may obtain a court order; after determining the person charged is guilty, the commissioner shall issue a cease and desist order and *at his or her discretion*, assess monetary penalties. A person seeking to be excused on grounds that evidence or testimony required may tend to self-incrimination shall nevertheless be directed to give testimony or produce evidence and must comply but thereafter shall not be prosecuted on any matter concerning which he or she may testify except perjury in such testimony; and such testimony shall be admissible in any *criminal* action.

STATE LEGISLATION BASED ON NAIC MODEL ACT

The 1947 NAIC Unfair Trade Practices Act was enacted in virtually every state. The 1971 revised Model Act containing the Unfair Claim Settlement Practices section has been enacted either in toto or adopted with modifications in many of the states, and will eventually be enacted by all states, as was the 1947 Act.

These state statutes or legislative regulatory measures are not alike in all states. Some are more rigid in their requirements, especially with regard to automobile insurers. A few states have used the legislation to expand their consumer-protection programs. The lack of uniformity of legislation in the states places a hardship on insurers doing business in many or all states as they seek to comply with the different requirements. An insurer in compliance in one state may not, under similar practices, be in compliance in a neighboring state.

Certain insurance policies contain verbalism over which there is still confusion and differences of opinion from one jurisdiction to another. The more recent policies, especially the easy-to-read type such as Homeowners-76, Standard and Special Businessowners, and the newer auto policies use words and phrases the interpretation of which may keep the courts busy for a long time. Denying part or all of a claim, *in good faith*, where one of these policies is involved could give rise to a charge of misrepresenting policy conditions or failure to affirm or deny coverage within a reasonable time.

In the NAIC Model Act itself there are words that do not lend themselves easily to the same meaning for all persons. The meaning of such words as a "reasonable man," "reasonable," or "reasonably" (used in eight subsections), "substantially," "prompt," "pertinent," "fair," and "equitable" is dependent on specific circumstances to which each is related or on other qualifying words.

PRECAUTIONS FOR COMPLIANCE BY INSURERS

In handling claims, every representative of insurers, including but not limited to claim personnel employed by the insurer, independent adjusters, agents, experts, accountants, and attorneys, should take the following precautions:

1. Possess a copy of the state legislation adopting or enacting the NAIC Model Act.
2. Obtain the commissioner's *interpretation* of the legislative requirements.
3. Obtain the insurer's *interpretation*.
4. Devise explicitly worded form letters to be sent to insureds and claimants where required under any state legislation.
5. See that claim files contain adequate supporting data for *any* action taken.
6. Maintain a record of written complaints.

Complaints received by other than an insurer's employees should be forwarded to the insurer promptly. Such persons include agents, brokers, and all experts used by insurers in connection with claim matters. In addition, insurers should adopt and implement reasonable standards for prompt investigation of claims.

FAIR CLAIM-HANDLING PRACTICES

As a result of the NAIC Unfair Claim Settlement Practices section of the Model Act, the claim training and educational departments of most insurers are placing more and more emphasis on what might be termed *fair claim-handling practices*.

In this regard, it would seem that the NAIC 14 unfair practices, as they pertain to property claims in particular, could serve as an excellent springboard. Putting these so-called unfair practices in a positive framework, ten *fair claim-handling practices* can be formulated as follows:

1. State pertinent facts and interpret policy provisions honestly.
2. Respond promptly to *notice of loss, correspondence,* and *telephone calls* from insureds.
3. Establish good procedures and standards for making prompt investigations of claims.
4. Make thorough and complete investigations.
5. Affirm or deny coverage to insureds as soon as the facts are known.
6. Make prompt and fair settlements when liability is clear.
7. Make reasonable settlement offers so as not to force the insured to litigate to obtain a greater amount.
8. Be sure the insured understands the coverage on which payment is made.
9. Make every effort to agree on the loss without forcing the insured to go to appraisal or arbitration.
10. Explain pertinent policy provisions when a part or all of a claim is declined.

For additional discussion of the relationship of insured and insurer in the handling and adjusting of claims, refer to Chapter 12, "Negotiations."

QUESTIONS AND PROBLEMS

1. What two important pressures or developments prompted the NAIC to revise the NAIC 1947 Model Unfair Trade Practices Act in 1971?
2. The revised NAIC Model Act included a section known as "Unfair Claim Settlement Practices." This section listed 14 claim-handling practices that were designated as unfair. State, in your own words, 6 of the 14 and give an example of each.
3. In order to be adjudged unfair, each of the 14 unfair claim settlement practices is subject to what important condition?
4. The NAIC established a complaint database system under which each state would put complaints received into their computer. The annual results would be sent to NAIC central office where they would be compiled, consolidated, and returned to the state departments. What are the three broad unfair trade practices in the insurance industry that the system is designed to cover?
5. In general, the objectives of the NAIC in including the section which lists the 14 unfair claim settlement practices are not questioned by insurers. Explain why this is so.
6. While insurers concur that the 14 practices listed by the NAIC are unfair, and would see no reason for not complying, the modifications enacted by some states have created problems. Explain briefly.
7. The powers of insurance commissioners to regulate compliance with the NAIC Model Act are substantial and in many respects similar to those in Congressional inquiries. There are at least ten such powers. State five.
8. State at least three precautions that should be taken by every person who represents an insurer *in any capacity* in the handling of claims so that compliance is assured with both the NAIC Model Act and state statutes growing out of that act.

Insurance Policies Covering Property

An insurance policy is a legal contract, and it conforms to the general laws that govern the making of all contracts. The law requires that (1) there be an offer and its acceptance, (2) the purpose be legal, (3) the parties be competent, and (4) there be a consideration. In the adjustment of losses the legal elements must be in existence *at the time* of loss.

THE INSURANCE CONTRACT

The insurance contract has been variously designated by the courts as (1) *a contract of indemnity*, (2) *a unilateral contract*, (3) *a conditional contract*, (4) *an aleatory contract*, (5) *a contract of adhesion*, and (6) *a personal contract*.

It is important that the meaning of these designations is understood by claim representatives, particularly in light of the discussion in this chapter concerning the interpretation of insurance contracts by courts.

1. *Indemnity* means compensation or reimbursement for loss. Applied to an insurance policy, *a contract of indemnity*, simply stated, is a conditional agreement that, for a consideration (premium), one party will indemnify the other for loss or damage to property, or bodily injury, or for legal liability to third parties. The term *contract of indemnity* no longer enjoys the popular usage in claim circles that it did years ago when it was employed rather ideologically to convey the impression that the intent was *to make the insured whole*. That concept is, of course, not true in many cases.

2. A *unilateral contract* is one in which one party makes an express engagement or undertakes a performance without receiving in return any express engagement or promise of performance by the other. Bilateral (or reciprocal) contracts are those by which the parties expressly enter into mutual engagements, such as sale or hire. Civ. Code La. art. 1765; Poth. Obl. 1,1,1,2; *Kling Bros. Engineering Works v. Whiting Corporation*, 320 Ill. App. 630, 51 N.E.2d 1004, 1007.

   A contract is also said to be *unilateral* when there is a promise on one side only, the consideration on the other side being executed. *McMahan v. McMahon*, 122 S.C. 336, 115 S.E. 293, 294, 26 A.L.R. 1295.[1]

3. A *conditional contract* is an executory contract the performance of which depends on a condition. It is not simply an executory contract, since the latter may be an absolute agreement to do or not to do something, but it is a contract whose very existence and performance depend upon a contingency. *Railroad Co. v. Jones*, 2 Cold. (Tenn.) 584; *French v. Osmer*, 67 Vt. 427, 32 A. 254.[2]

4. An *aleatory contract* is a mutual agreement of which the effects, with respect both to the advantages and the losses,

[1]*Black's Law Dictionary.*
[2]Ibid.

whether to all the parties or to some of them, depend on an uncertain event. *Losecco v. Gregory*, 108 La. 648, 32 So. 985.

These are contracts in which a promise by one party is conditioned on a fortuitous event, *Southern Surety Co. v. MacMillan Co.*, C.C.A. Okl., 58 F.2d 541, 549.[3]

5. The insurance policy as a *contract of adhesion* is one in which there is unequal bargaining strength between the parties. As a result, ambiguities should be interpreted against the party of greater bargaining strength, the insurer, and the party which drew the contract. "... insurers who seek to impose upon words of common speech an esoteric significance intelligible only to their craft, must bear the burden of any resulting confusion. *State Farm Mutual Automobile Insurance Co. v. Oliver*, 406 F. 2d 408 (CA-6-1969)."[4]

6. A *personal contract* is a contract relating to personal property, or one which so far involves the element of personal knowledge or skill or personal confidence that it can be performed only by the person with whom made, and therefore is not binding on the executor. See *Janin v. Browne*, 59 Cal. 44; *Lucas v. J. H. Gross Motor Car Co.*, 27 Ohio App. 183, 167, N.E. 362, 363.[5]

Insurance Services Office

Insurance Services Office (ISO) is a national organization established by the property and liability insurance industry to provide a full range of insurance services, with maximum flexibility and economy, to insurers and other persons and organizations vitally affected by rapid economic and social change.

ISO was formed January 1, 1971, through the consolidation of several national insurance industry service organizations: the Fire Insurance Research and Actuarial Association, the Insurance Rating Board, the Multi-Line Insurance Rating Bureau, and the National Insurance Actuarial and Statistical Association. Also included in the consolidation was the Insurance Data Processing Center, a joint computer facility of two of the predecessor organizations. By January 1, 1972, most of the former state and regional fire rating organizations in the United States also had become a part of ISO.

ISO is licensed in all 50 states and in the U.S. territories and has assumed in those jurisdictions all of the operations of its predecessor organizations. It is licensed as a fire rating organization in most of the jurisdictions and operates as an advisory organization to state fire organizations in the other jurisdictions. It also acts as an advisory organization for other property-liability lines of insurance in those states in which statutory bureaus are operative.

ISO renders a wide range of advisory, actuarial, rating, statistical, research, and other types of services. Many of these previously had been provided by the predecessor organizations. Others have been or will be initiated by ISO.

Among the numerous services which ISO is organized to provide is to develop standard forms of policies and coverages and to act as an agency for filing forms, rules, and rates with state insurance departments. The lines of insurance that come within the purview of ISO are:

1. Boiler and Machinery.
2. Commercial Automobile.
3. Commercial Fire and Allied Lines.
4. Commercial Multiple Line.
5. Crime.
6. Dwelling Fire and Allied Lines.
7. General Liability.
8. Glass.
9. Homeowners.
10. Inland Marine.
11. Nuclear Energy Liability and Property.
12. Private Passenger Automobile.
13. Workmen's Compensation and Employer's Liability.

Kinds of Insurance Contracts

Three kinds of insurance contracts are recognized: *policies, written binders,* and *oral*

[3]Ibid.
[4]Ibid.
[5]Ibid.

binders or *agreements to insure*. The insurance contract is created by agreement between the insured and the insurer, covering the following: (1) the parties, (2) perils insured against, (3) property and location to be covered, (4) amount of insurance, (5) rate of premium to be charged, and (6) time and date of commencement and of expiration. Generally it has been held that the first three items must be agreed upon or there will be no contract.

A *written binder* is a brief preliminary memorandum containing the essentials of the contract, as noted above, which are to be set forth in the completed policy. It is accepted practice that the insurance contract created by the signing or initialing of a binder is the same as that to be embodied in the policy when it is issued.

An *oral agreement* to issue a policy or an endorsement is a binding contract, whether it involves a policy to cover a new risk, renewal of a policy that is expiring, or the issuing of an endorsement to change the amount or add a location to an existing policy. If the agent who made the oral agreement represents only one company, there is no question that the insurer is a party to the contract. If the agent represents several companies and a fire loss occurs before action can be taken on an oral agreement for a new policy, in fairness to all companies, each generally participates in the loss in the same proportion that its fire premium in the agency bears to the agency's total fire premium.

STANDARD FIRE POLICIES

The business of property and liability insurance, exclusive of ocean marine and life insurance, had been traditionally separated into two broad fields under the classifications of (1) *fire and allied lines* and (2) *casualty lines*. The original fire policies limited the peril covered to fire. In the 1943 revision of the New York Standard Fire Insurance Policy[6] the perils of *lightning* and *removal* were added.

The so-called casualty lines of insurance are numerous, but broadly it may be said they include those not classified as fire and allied lines, marine, or life. Specifically, the major lines of casualty are *automobile, workmen's compensation, accident and health, liability, boiler and machinery, crime and surety bonds,* and *glass insurance*.

The Extended Coverage Endorsement expanded the fire policy to include the perils of *windstorm, hail, explosion, riot and civil commotion, aircraft, motor vehicles, smoke damage,* and, in some forms, *sprinkler leakage*. Later, the Additional Extended Coverage Endorsement included the perils of *water damage from plumbing and heating systems, rupture or bursting of steam or hot-water systems, vandalism and malicious mischief, damage by vehicles, glass breakage, falling objects, freezing of plumbing and heating systems,* and *collapse*. To identify policies that included these numerous perils, they became known as fire and allied lines policies.

The fire policy is unique in that it is the only insurance policy that has been standardized to the extent that each state prescribes the exact wording to be used. The first major step to standardize the fire policy was taken by the New York legislature in 1887. That policy was widely accepted by many other states, either verbatim or with moderate changes. Certain provisions and stipulations in the policy later proved to be inequitable, and a number were nullified by court decisions. In 1918 and again in 1943, the policy was revised on recommendation of the National Association of Insurance Commissioners (NAIC). The amending committees in each instance included lawyers and representatives from insurers and producers.

The 1943 New York Standard Fire Policy has been established by law in 32 states and adopted with minor changes in 15 others. Three states—Massachusetts, Minnesota, and Texas—have statutory fire policies which, while similar in most respects to the 1943 New York form, contain differences that could be significant in the adjustment of property losses in those states. These vari-

[6]See Appendix E.

ances will be commented upon in the appropriate sequence when the essential provisions and stipulations of the standard fire policy are discussed later.

It is to the standard fire policy that insurers look most often for available defenses against exaggerated or fraudulent claims.

Forms and Endorsements

The standard fire policy is not a complete policy of insurance until a form or forms are attached to it, together with any endorsements, all designed for the particular risk and the needs of the insured. Forms are intended to clarify the terms of the policy. They do so by describing the interests insured, property or subject covered, perils covered, locations where the insurance is applicable, extensions and exclusions, property and perils excluded, and limitations of liability.

Companies that write fire and allied lines, either under a single policy or under a multiple-line policy, until recently were *required* to attach the statutory standard fire policy prescribed or approved by the state in which the policy was issued. More and more, exceptions are being made, provided the policy being issued contains the same or equivalent provisions of the state statutory fire policy.

STANDARDIZATION OF OTHER PROPERTY POLICIES

Recognizing certain advantages in standardizing insurance policies, companies have voluntarily developed, by intercompany agreement and through bureaus, standard policies for property as well as liability coverages. While the language used in inland marine, automobile, plate glass, boiler and machinery, and other policies promulgated by the various bureaus is not identical (except provisions required by state law), for all practical purposes they are standardized. Companies making independent filings are not bound by the "bureau forms," and consequently their policies may have minor or major differences. The rapid development of multiple-line policies and their collateral competitive aspects have resulted in the appearance of numerous nonstandard and independent policies for various classifications of risks.

MULTIPLE-LINE POLICIES

As a result of the development of a *multiple-line concept* within the insurance industry, fire and allied lines and casualty lines may be merged or combined into a single insurance policy. This transition was made possible by individual state legislative changes, or departmental rulings, which permitted any insurer to write all types of insurance except *life*. All such state licensing changes were completed by the year 1955. The first product to emerge was the Homeowners Program in 1958. Since then the program has undergone many changes.

Following rapidly in the wake of the Homeowners, a number of commercial and industrial multiple-line policies were developed, the trend gaining prominence with the physical merging of fire and casualty divisions of the insurers. The real significance of a multiple-line policy is that it insures against many perils which formerly had to be written under individual policies by fire and casualty insurers. Not all multiple-line policies include liability coverage, but most do include theft, burglary, or other crime coverages.

The following are a few of the important multiple-line coverages available to homeowners, commercial and manufacturing businesses, and institutions.

Special Multi-Peril Policy (SMP) is a program originally intended to provide both broad and all risk of physical loss coverage for businesses that mainly provide services rather than for those engaged in manufacturing or merchandising. Such businesses include motels and hotels, apartments, condominiums, public institutions, offices, builder's risk, commercial properties, colleges, and schools. The program later expanded to include mercantile risks, processors, and manufacturers. The great variety of coverages available extends to practically all of the traditional inland marine, fire and allied lines, and liability. There are special package policies available for every conceivable type of business. Boiler and machinery coverage is optional and includes both direct loss and liability resulting from accidents.

Commercial Property Floater, subject to the standard fire policy, provides all risk property coverage for retail and wholesale mercantile risks. Actually it makes available to merchants the same block protection provided by inland marine insurers for such risks as camera dealers, jewelers, fur dealers, road equipment dealers, and musical instrument dealers. The policy covers anywhere in the United States and Canada and has many exclusions characteristic of inland marine forms.

Public and Institutional Program (PIP) provides broad property coverage for libraries, churches, hospitals, government buildings, and other public institutions. The policy may be written all risk or named perils. Annual inspections and a sworn statement of values are required. Legal liability coverage is not included.

Manufacturers Output Policy (MOP) provides all risk coverage to manufacturers on personal property *away* from the premises. Originally designed for automobile manufacturers, it is presently available to over 300 categories of manufacturers. Personal property may be subject to reports of values. Real property coverage is available by endorsement as is Loss of Income, Additional Expense, and Accounts Receivable. There is no legal liability coverage.

Office Contents Form is a form attached to the standard fire policy affording all risk of physical loss coverage for offices other than those in connection with mercantile or manufacturing risks but not a physician's or a dentist's office. It includes, with limitations, extra expense, valuable papers, money and stamps, and personal effects of officers, partners, and others.

Highly Protected Risk (HPR) policy is designed for large mercantile and manufacturing businesses with a high degree of fire protection usually in the form of sprinklers, fire department, watchman, fire-resistive construction, and/or other features acceptable to the underwriters. This is a named peril policy and includes buildings and con-

tents. This policy is subject to state statutory policy provisions and stipulations. This is also known as *Superior Risk Form.*

Businessowners Program MLB-700 and 701 (Ed. 11-1-75) represents a new format for eligible small- to medium-sized businesses. The program, filed by ISO in 1975, presents both a *Standard* and a *Special* policy. The former is a named peril policy; the latter is an all risks of physical loss policy.

The format includes a booklet-type policy with a table of contents, more legible type, more direct and clearer language, more orderly sequence and continuity of policy provisions, with major headings and marginal captions printed in large type in blue ink for ready identification.

Policies are written for one year, there is no coinsurance, and replacement cost applies to all direct property damage including buildings, stock, contents, and improvements and betterments. The insurer expects the insured to carry insurance equal to full replacement value. The limit of liability on buildings is automatically increased every three months by an agreed percentage. The limit on personal property has a conditional 25 percent automatic increase to provide for seasonal variations.

Comprehensive Business Liability is covered under both Standard and Special policies. Coverage includes Loss of Income as well as Extra Expense.

A number of optional coverages include Exterior Signs for a specific limit of liability; Boiler Pressure Vessels and Air Conditioning Equipment; and Exterior Grade Floor Glass. The Perils and Exclusions Provisions in the policy do not apply, except the War Risk, Governmental Action, and Nuclear Exclusions. Burglary and Robbery is an option under the Standard Policy with limitations.

The provisions and stipulations of the 165-line standard fire policy are included, with some rewording, so that in jurisdictions that so permit the policy will not have to be attached to a standard fire policy.

Difference in Conditions (DIC) is an *all risk of physical loss* form covering property and loss of income but excluding loss caused by, or resulting from, those perils insured against under fire and extended coverage policies, vandalism and malicious mischief endorsements, sprinkler leakage, earthquake, landslide, earth movement, flood, and a long list of perils against which insurance is available under other policies and whether or not insured carries such insurance. It is not an errors and omissions policy but rather one offering protection against the unforeseen, uninsured fortuitous loss. The DIC contains provisions and stipulations of, or equivalent of, the standard fire policy. Reports of values and audit are required. Earthquake and flood coverages are available by endorsement.[7]

Homeowners Policies are probably the best-known multiple-line policies. All of the forms cover the dwelling, appurtenant structures, unscheduled personal property, additional living expense, and liability. There are six forms available under the HO 1-6 series.

Basic Form, HO-1, covers the fire and extended coverage perils, vandalism and malicious mischief, breakage of glass and theft.

Broad Form,[8] HO-2, adds to the perils in the basic form.

Special Form, HO-3, covers all risks of physical loss on the dwelling, appurtenant private structures, and additional living expense. Unscheduled personal property is covered for the same perils as the broad form.

Contents Broad Form, HO-4, covers unscheduled personal property, insured's interest in building additions and alterations, and additional living expense against the same perils provided in the broad form. Sometimes referred to as Tenant's or Renter's form.

Comprehensive Form, HO-5, is the same as the special form but extends all risks of physical loss to unscheduled personal property.

Condominium Unit-Owners Form, HO-6, is similar to the HO-4, Tenant's Broad Form, and includes Unit-Owners Additions and Alterations coverage with a limit of $1,000. It also includes Personal Liability,

Medical Payments to Others, and Damage to Property of Others. Several endorsements are available for broadening coverage.

Homeowners-76 Policy Program (sometimes called the Simplified Homeowners), filed in 1975 by Insurance Services Office (ISO) represented a new format and arrangement which combined ease of reading, somewhat less technical wording, more legible type with major headings and marginal captions printed in blue ink for ease of identification. Provisions and stipulations of the 165-line Standard Fire Policy are included, but they have been reworded and formulated so as to be read in conjunction with other policy provisions of a similar nature, rather than standing alone almost as a separate contract.

This simplified Homeowners-76 Program offers the same six types of policies as its predecessor, namely: HO-1 Basic, HO-2 Broad Form, HO-3 Special Form, HO-4 Contents Broad Form, HO-5 Comprehensive Form, and HO-6 Condominium Unit-Owners Form.

NON-MULTIPLE-LINE POLICIES

There are many policies available which cover buildings and contents, individually or together under one form, but which are not multiple-line policies since they include no liability or other traditional casualty lines. These forms must, of course, be attached to the statutory standard fire insurance policy in the state they are issued.

Dwelling Building(s) and Contents Form (Ed. 9-74), DF Series

This program is basically a fire and allied lines contract covering dwellings and contents. It takes the place of Form 49. Insurance attaches only to those items specifically described and for which a specific amount is shown. Occupancy is limited to four families. Many of the changes are editorial.

DF-1, Basic Form, insures against the perils of *fire, lightning, removal,* and *inherent explosion.* For an additional premium the perils of *windstorm and hail, explosion, riot*

---

[7]See p. 124.
[8]For a discussion of the 18 perils, see Chap. 8, "Verifying Cause of Loss."

and civil commotion, aircraft or vehicles, and *smoke* can be included. For another premium *vandalism and malicious mischief* can be added.

DF-2, Broad Form, insures against 18 perils of fire, extended coverage and additional extended coverage plus replacement cost coverage and additional living expense.

DF-3, Special Form, insures against all risks of physical loss to the dwelling and appurtenant structures; also as respects rental value and additional living expense. Household and personal property are covered against 17 named perils, including freezing and collapse.

DF-4, Household Personal Property Form, a tenant-type form, covers against the same perils available under the DF-1 form.

Removal (to a new location) endorsement is available. Also, Automatic Increase (on buildings) and Earthquake endorsements are available.

Theft or burglary is not covered under any of the forms although *damage* by burglars is covered under DF-2 and DF-3.

These forms attach to standard fire policies.

General Property Form, FGP-1 (Ed. 12-74)

This is a commercial form designed to replace Form 18 and insures basically against the perils of fire, lightning, and removal. Windstorm or hail, smoke, explosion, riot or civil commotion, and aircraft or vehicles may be insured against for an additional premium. Vandalism or malicious mischief may also be insured against for another premium.

The insurance applies only to items specifically described and for which an amount of insurance is shown. Coverage A is buildings or structures; B is business personal property owned by the insured; C is personal property of others in the care, custody, and control of the insured.

Building and Contents Form 18 (Ed. 1972), which has been in existence for many years, is an example of the so-called fire and allied lines policy. It is an appropriate form for small- to medium-size mercantile and manufacturing businesses. The form covers buildings, additions and extensions attached thereto, furniture, fixtures, machinery and equipment, stock and other personal property, and improvements and betterments. The perils insured against are fire and lightning, removal, windstorm and hail, smoke, explosion, riot, aircraft and vehicles.

Form 420-8, North Carolina (Ed. 2-72), is similar to Building and Contents Form 18 but can be used to write fire only or fire and extended coverage.

PROVISIONS AND STIPULATIONS OF STANDARD FIRE POLICIES

Because property insurance policies that include the peril of fire must either include the provisions and stipulations of the standard (statutory) fire insurance policy or their equivalent, a knowledge and understanding of them is essential in the adjustment of property losses. In the following general discussion the 165-line New York Standard Fire Insurance Policy will be used as it is the one common to most jurisdictions. Important variances in other state policies will be commented upon. Also, equivalent wording built into some of the multiple-line policies and intended to take the place of statutory wording will be pointed out. To what extent this rewording of the provisions and stipulations will face interpretation by persons within the industry, or in the courts, must stand the test of time. The purpose and objectives of the drafters are commendable.

Insuring Agreement

The *insuring agreement* states the agreement of the insurer to protect the insured against certain kinds of loss, for a specified period, in consideration of a premium and the insured's compliance with the provisions and stipulations in the policy. The agreement may be found on the Declaration Page of the policy, or, as in some of the multiple-line policies, equivalent wording may be found throughout the policy in conjunction with other provisions of a related nature and purpose. For the standard fire policy insuring agreement see Appendix E.

Inception and expiration dates, under newer forms, begin and end at 12:01 A.M. (standard time), which is uniform with the automobile and other casualty policies. *The insured* is the insured named in the declarations. Forms attached to the standard fire policy, however, may insure others who are not named in the policy. The Homeowners, for example, under Coverage C, Unscheduled Personal Property, covers, at the *option* of the named insured, property owned by others while on the portion of the premises occupied exclusively by the insured. It also covers unscheduled personal property, subject to limitations, while elsewhere than on the described premises, anywhere in the world:

2. At the option of the Named Insured,
   a. owned by a guest while in a residence occupied by an Insured; or
   b. owned by a residence employee while actually engaged in the service of an Insured and while such property is in the physical custody of such residence employee or in a residence occupied by an Insured.

Under Definitions in the Homeowners-76 Program (Ed. 7-1-75):

3. "Insured" means you and the following residents of your household:
   a. your relatives
   b. any other person under the age of 21 who is in the care of any person named above.

Under Coverage C, Personal Property, subject to limits, at the *request* of the insured, coverage is granted on personal property owned by others while the property is on the part of the residence premises occupied by any insured. Also at the *request* of the insured, personal property owned by a guest or a residence employee is covered while the property is in any residence occupied by any insured.

Persons who are covered, other than the named insured, are not identical in all policies.

Legal representatives is a term ordinarily meaning executors and administrators. It is sufficiently broad to include, under certain circumstances, heirs at law, next of kin, legatees, and devisees; in fact, anyone who is legally authorized to act for the insured.

Actual Cash Value

Actual cash value of the property at the time of loss is an indistinct phrase which literally translated means "what it is worth in cash." In seeking a definition many factors must be considered. Personal property in use may have a different value than the same property held for sale. Goods in the hands of a manufacture may have the same or a different value than the same goods in the hands of a retailer. Generally speaking, in most cases, the actual cash value of property is its cost to replace new, less depreciation both physical and economic. Because of the importance of this subject it is discussed in the chapters dealing with specific kinds of property.

Repair or Replace

As stated in the standard fire policy, "The cost to repair or replace the property with material of like kind and quality" is one of the upper limits for which the insurer is liable under the standard fire policy. There are three other limits, namely, the *actual cash value*, the *amount of insurance*, and the *interest* of the insured. The insurer's liability is limited to the least of these. Thus, if the cost to repair or replace the property, as fixed by agreement, appraisal, or actual reconstruction, is less than the other three limits the amount of loss is so determined.[9]

Ordinances or Laws

"Generally ordinances or laws regulating construction or repair will not serve to increase the amount for which the insurer is liable." For example, many building laws or local ordinances provide that buildings of substandard construction prior to enactment of the law or ordinance, if structurally damaged in excess of a specified percentage by

[9]See Valued Policy Law States in Chap. 14.

fire, must be demolished and rebuilt to conform with the building code or ordinance. The standard fire policy limits the loss to the cost of repairing the damage done by fire and specifically excludes the increased cost of construction or demolition of undamaged portions by reason of the local law or ordinance.

It is not uncommon, following moderate damage to a building, for an insured to be faced with completely rewiring the premises to comply with the building code. Similarly, chimneys and fireplaces, though slightly damaged, must be torn out and rebuilt completely to meet the building code. The cost of repairs in excess of the direct damage to the property covered by the policy is excluded.

Some of the requirements under building ordinances in built-up areas and business areas of cities are quite severe. They may specify installation of sprinklers, building of fire walls, fire-resistive construction in place of combustible, or actual changes in building lines. Special endorsements to the policy are available to cover this type of consequential loss.

Loss From Interruption of Business

"Loss resulting from the interruption of business or manufacture" is a consequential loss and is specifically excluded. Loss of anticipated sales, rents, profits, or other earnings is provided for under business-interruption, rental, or other time-element forms which may be attached to and override the conditions in the standard fire policy.

Loss Not to Exceed Insured's Interest

"Nor in any event for more than the interest of the insured" is a limitation in the insuring clause, and the insurer will not be liable for more than such interest.[10]

Direct Loss

"Direct loss caused by a peril insured against" is language in the standard fire policy and other property policies that raises two

[10]See Chap. 4, "Insurable Interests."

questions concerning which there has been no absolute agreement: (1) What constitutes a fire? (2) What is a direct loss?

Friendly Fire Versus Hostile Fire. A *friendly fire* may be said to be one which has been deliberately kindled or lighted for a definite purpose. As long as it remains within the confines intended, it is friendly. A fire in a fireplace, a furnace, a stove, a trashburner or incinerator, an oil lamp—these are friendly so long as they remain within the place intended. Fires become *hostile* when they escape their confines, such as flames licking outside the furnace door or outside the fireplace opening. Burning soot in a chimney is a hostile fire, as also is the roast or steak in an oven actually in flames or burning fat or oil in a cooking utensil on top of the stove.

A trend is developing for the courts to consider the *intensity* of heat from a friendly fire which may be sufficient to place it in the role of a hostile agency rather than a friendly one.

Historically, the courts have drawn a fine line of distinction between a friendly fire and a hostile fire in spite of the absence of any such differentiation in the standard fire policy. However, it is universally recognized that the policy contemplates indemnity only for damage done by a hostile agency.

To have a fire there must be combustion accompanied by a flame or glow. The presence of smoke and/or heat alone is not sufficient to constitute a fire. Spontaneous combustion is a rapid oxidation, but until it is rapid enough to produce flame or glow there is no fire. A pressing iron left too long on fabric may scorch the material. This is rapid oxidation of the fabric, but without glow or flame present there has been no fire either of a friendly or a hostile nature.

Friendly fires, a misnomer, frequently cause damage. A chair left too close to a fireplace may have the arm blistered if the heat is great enough. The damage to the chair is not covered as long as the fire, deliberately kindled, remains inside the fireplace; it is a friendly fire. Claims of a similar nature are encountered in connection with stoves, heaters, and mislaid cigarettes or cigars.

Claims also are made for damage caused by smoky fireplaces, oil lamps, and stoves.

It is reasonable to assert that the mere discoloring or scorching, without ignition, of a table top, tablecloth, rug, or upholstered chair or sofa by the heat of a mislaid cigar or cigarette is not a loss by hostile fire. But it is hard to justify an assertion that there has been no damage by hostile fire if the cigar or cigarette has actually burned a hole in the tablecloth, rug, or upholstery, or has charred the table top.

A hot cooking utensil placed on a Formica counter may scorch or discolor the counter top, or a roast in an oven may char from excessive heat, but the loss in either case was not caused by hostile fire. Synthetic fabrics such as drapes hung over an inadvertently lighted floor lamp may char and shrivel, but in the absence of glow or flame there has been no fire.

Occasionally articles of value, such as jewelry, are unintentionally thrown into fireplaces, stoves, furnaces, or incinerators. Damage or destruction of such articles under these conditions is not covered under the standard fire policy and the courts have consistently so held.

It should be noted that forms covering against all risk of physical loss, or specifically against the peril of smoke damage, afford coverage for loss caused by friendly fires under appropriate circumstances.

Direct Loss—Proximate Cause. The insurance contract covers direct loss caused by any peril insured against, that is, immediate or proximate as distinguished from remote or consequential loss. It is not essential that the proximate cause of loss be a peril insured against, as any ensuing loss caused by such peril is covered. For example, under the standard fire policy the peril of explosion is not insured against but fire ensuing upon an explosion is covered.

The standard fire policies in most states, including those that use the New York form, insure against all *direct* loss by fire and lightning *(and other perils insured against)*. A few states, notably Massachusetts, Minnesota, and California, insure against *all loss or*

damage, omitting the word *direct*. The omission would appear to be unimportant because to recover for a loss under an insurance policy, the peril insured against must be the proximate or *direct* cause of loss.

Consequential losses are insured against only by special stipulation. Two examples follow:

A dealer in fresh meats preserves his stock in electrically operated refrigerators. The building he occupies receives current from a power station some distance away. The transmission lines are carried from the station to the building on poles and pass a structure that burns. Falling walls break the power lines, and new ones are not installed until after the temperature in the refrigerators has risen and the meat has spoiled. The dealer's policy covering the meat will cover the loss only if it contains a consequential damage clause specifically assuming such loss.

In the foregoing situation, if a fire damaged the electrical wiring on the insured's premises and the refrigerating apparatus could not operate, the loss to the spoiled meat would be covered even though no fire, smoke, or water reached the contents of the refrigerators.

A few court decisions indicate *a trend away* from the long-established thinking that damage to power wiring must occur on the insured's premises for the insured to collect under his policy for food spoilage resulting from lack of refrigeration. In each of three of these cases, windstorm damaged the electric power lines some distance away and cut off current to the insured's premises culminating in food spoilage in the cold-storage facilities. The courts applied the test of proximate cause and held that such spoilage was within the contemplation of the provision covering direct loss by windstorm.[11]

A manufacturer of men's clothing cuts the cloth and sends the parts to three different

---

[11]*Lipshultz v. General Insurance Company of America*, Sup. Ct. Minn., 1959, 96 N.W.2d 880. *Fred Meyer, Inc. v. Central Mutual Insurance Company et al.*, U.S. Dist. Ct. Oregon, 1964, 235 F. Supp. 540. *Federal Ins. Co., et al. v. Bock et al.*, Ct. of Civ. Appeals, Texas, Corpus Christi, 1964, 382 S.W.2d 305, 12 F & CC 220.

garment contractors to be made up, the coats to one, the vests to another, and the pants to a third. The coats and vests are made up and returned. The pants are destroyed on the contractor's premises. Unless the manufacturer can buy identical cloth and have the pants replaced, a heavy loss on the coats and vests will result. The loss on coats and vests, due to lack of pants to match, will be covered only if the policies specially provide for it.

When fire in a structure consumes, softens, scorches, cracks, melts, smokes, or evaporates solid or liquid property, or explodes or causes the escape of gaseous property, it does direct damage. The results of fire covered by the fire-insurance policy, however, may include things other than combustion, such as the fall of a building; or injuries to property by water used in fighting the fire, or released by it, by the acts of firefighters, or by efforts of persons to remove personal property to a place of safety. The results of fire may also include rain damage to the interior or the contents of a building, if the owner, acting with reasonable diligence, has not had time to close the roof or windows against the weather. But if the owner, instead of acting with reasonable diligence, should refuse to take any steps to protect the property, and some weeks later further loss should occur as the result of rain, the further loss would be looked upon as damage resulting from the failure of the insured to protect the property as provided for in the policy. A similar situation might be the result of other weather conditions, such as extreme cold.

One of the most important cases on the question of proximate cause in connection with fire losses is that of *Lynn Gas and Electric Co. v. Meriden Fire Ins. Co.*, 158 Mass. 570.

In this case, fire caused a short circuit of electric current in generating machinery. This resulted in great damage to other machinery located in a portion of the (same) building which was untouched in any way by the fire itself. The damage was actually caused as a direct result of the short circuiting of the generating equipment. The general rule enunciated in this case is that when it is said that the cause to be sought is the direct and proximate cause, it is not meant that the cause or agency which is nearest in time or place to the result is necessarily to be chosen. The active efficient cause which sets in motion a chain of events, which brings about a result without the intervention of any force started and working actively from an independent cause, is the direct and proximate cause. In applying this rule to the facts in the case, the court held that the fire actually brought about a destruction of generating equipment. Directly as a result of the destruction of the generating equipment, other machinery was damaged which in no way was touched by fire. However, the fire was held to be the direct, efficient, operating cause and was held to make the underwriter responsible for all of the resulting damage.

To illustrate how far the rule of proximate cause can go in fire losses, we have the interesting case of *Vincent Jiannetti v. National Fire Ins. Co. of Hartford*, 277 Mass. 434. The facts in that case showed that a fire occurred in an adjoining store.

There was no fire in the insured's store, but smoke from the fire entered the store. Firemen removed the skylight in the insured's store for the purpose of permitting the smoke to leave. They then replaced the skylight, but in a negligent manner. Thereafter, rain entered through the defectively replaced skylight and damaged the insured's stock of goods. All of this damage, the court held, proximately flowed from the original fire and the rain did not constitute a separate, independent cause.

It must be remembered, in fire insurance cases, that even though negligence on the part of the insured may bring about the origin of the fire, the insurer is still liable and the insured can still recover. (*Insurance Co. v. Tweed*, 7 Wall 44; *Peters v. Warren Insurance Co.*, 14 Peters 99 [U.S.]; *General Insurance Co. v. Sherwood*, 14 Howard 351 [U.S.]). In order for a fire to be responsible for a given loss, it must be the direct cause and not the remote cause. However, it is often difficult to separate the proximate or direct cause from the remote cause. If there are successive causes, each sufficient, acting independently, to produce an effect such as to cause a loss, the one last operating on the event is the proximate one. But, where there is no order of succession in time and there are two or more concurrent causes of loss, the predominating efficient one must be regarded as proximate, regardless of the position of the event at the time. The cause which sets the other in motion and clothes it with the power to harm at the time of the disaster must rank as predominant. (*Howard Fire Insurance Co. v. Norwich and New York Transportation Co.*, 12 Wall 194, 79 U.S. 194; *Princess Garment Co. v. Fireman's Fund Insurance Co.*, 115 Fed. 2d 380, *Certiorari denied*, 335 U.S. 871.)

In the case of *Tracy v. Palmetto Fire Insurance Co.*, 222 N.W. 447 (Iowa) and again in the case of *Tonkin v. California Insurance Co. of San Francisco*, 294 N.Y. 326, a fire of little consequence caused a driver of a car to lose control and to wreck the car by reason of a collision. Each of the cars carried insurance coverage for fire, but no coverage for collision. It was held in both cases that the fire was the proximate cause, the predominating cause, and was the cause upon which liability rested. The court in effect held that the small fire frightened and distracted the driver so that he lost control of the vehicle and caused the collision and that had it not been for the fire, the collision would not have taken place.

Although we usually expect to pay under a fire insurance policy for damages ascribed to fire only, we should be aware of the fact that damages following from many other causes may be covered under the fire insurance policy by reason of this doctrine of proximate cause.[12]

Removal

"Removal from premises endangered by the perils insured against" constitutes in itself an additional peril covered, subject, of course, to the policy provisions. Any and all damage which occurs *during the removal* is covered whether it be the result of marring, breakage, submersion, or any other cause, including the cost of removal. The removal must be necessary, and the property is covered pro rata for five days at each location for the perils insured against under the policy.

Additional coverages in Homeowners-76 Program (Ed. 7-1-75) provide as follows:

Property Removed. Covered property while being removed from a premises endangered by a Peril Insured Against and for not more than 30 days while removed is covered for direct loss from any cause. This coverage does not change the limit of liability applying to the property being removed.

Assignment

Assignment of the policy is not valid without the written consent of the insurer. After a loss, however, the *proceeds* of any claim may be assigned by the insured without consent of the insurer. It is not uncommon, when property is sold, for the agent, acting on behalf of the company, to assign the policy to the new owner by endorsement. Frequently the purchaser of property is under the impression that the seller's insurance automatically follows the property and it is therefore covered when in fact it is not. A policy covering property which is sold, and which has not been assigned to the new owner in writing, is not void; the named insured simply has no insurable interest.

Conditions and Provisions

Standard fire policies of the various states number each line of the statutory conditions and provisions. The Minnesota policy contains 155 lines, Massachussetts 154, California 157, Texas 146, and Maine 167. The New York policy has 165 lines.

These conditions and provisions set forth the obligations and rights of the insured and the insurer. They deal with concealment and fraud; property and perils excluded; increase of hazard; the adding of other perils, subjects, and provisions; waiver of provisions; and cancellation of the policy by either party. The rest of the conditions, which constitute about 60 percent of the total, concern the duties and rights of the parties following a loss.

Concealment, Misrepresentation, and Fraud. Concealment, misrepresentation, and fraud have always been held to vitiate an

---

[12]Max J. Gwertzman, "A Legal Analysis of the Standard Fire Insurance Policy," in *The Insurance Advocate*, Roberts Publishing Co., New York, 1963.

insurance contract. The standard fire policy stipulates:

> This entire policy shall be void if, whether before or after a loss, the insured has wilfully concealed or misrepresented any material fact or circumstance concerning this insurance or the subject thereof, or in case of any fraud or false swearing by the insured relating thereto.

If this condition were absent from the policy, it would be read into the policy by the courts, for fraud vitiates all contracts as a legal principle. It is placed in the policy as a reminder to the insured. It provides a major defense against false claims arising out of fortuitous losses as well as against false claims of nonaccidental origin. The concealment or misrepresentation must be intentional and the fact must be material.

Insurance may be obtained by concealing a material fact or by misrepresenting the hazard, location, desirability, ownership, interest, or value of the property. In a few instances, owners of outlying property will apply for insurance on it after it has been damaged by a peril, in the hope that the actual date and time of the occurrence cannot be determined. Persons seeking to insure property which (because of indefinite interest, lack of interest, deterioration or other depreciation, excessive hazard, insufficient protection, or dangerous location) would not be accepted for coverage if the insurer learned of the actual conditions may misrepresent such property and thus induce the insurer to cover it. Sometimes values are misrepresented to avoid payment of adequate premiums. The test of misrepresentation is whether the insurer, if it were truthfully informed by the insured regarding all material facts or circumstances, would have refused to write the risk, or would have written it with important restrictions, for a smaller amount, or at a substantially higher rate of premium. If insurance has been obtained by misrepresentation as to the property or the insured's interest in it, the claim representative should ordinarily find indications of the situation when inspecting the property and making inquiry into title, interest, and encumbrances.

If a resort hotel has been represented and insured as a dwelling, the appearance of the ruins after a fire will generally give some idea of the true occupancy and lead to inquiries that will uncover the misrepresentation. Likewise, property described as being under fire protection may be found to be vacant and abandoned, or a stock of merchandise represented as new and valuable, and covered for a large amount, may be found to be an unsalable collection of odds and ends. The most frequently encountered forms of misrepresentation appear in the presentation of claims. Exaggerated schedules, inventories, and estimates of loss and value are submitted; property saved is undervalued; incorrect bills, invoices, and book records are exhibited; dishonest testimony is given under oath; and proofs of loss with false information are signed and sworn to.

An insured's broker, public adjuster, or other agent, acting within the scope of his or her authority, may void the policy by willful concealment or misrepresentation even though the insured is innocent.[13]

If the misrepresentation is material, the insurer need not establish that it suffered a loss or would have suffered a precuniary loss as a result of the misrepresentation. "If the plaintiffs willfully overstated the value of the goods in the inventories or in the proof of loss or if they included items not damaged or lost as a result of the fire, then the defendant is not liable irrespective of whether the misrepresentations caused damage to the defendant or would cause damage if it was required to pay the loss."[14]

A Nebraska amendment to the standard fire policy provision reads:

> Anything in the policy to the contrary notwithstanding, it is understood and agreed that no oral or written misrepresentation or warranty made in negotiation for this policy by the insured, or in his behalf, shall be deemed material or defeat or avoid the policy unless such misrepresentation or warranty deceived the Company to its injury. The breach of a warranty or condition of this policy shall not avoid the

---

[13]*Bockser v. Dorchester Mut. Fire Ins. Co.*, 99 N.E.2d 640.
[14]*Hendricksen et ux. v. Home Ins. Co.*, Oreg. Supreme Court, Dept. One, No. 7631, May 20, 1964.

policy nor avail the Company to avoid liability unless such breach shall exist at the time of loss and contribute to the loss.

The claim representative must be careful, in an analysis of the situation where concealment or misrepresentation is suspected, to distinguish between a matter of honest though unrealistic opinion and a willful misrepresentation or concealment.

Title 18, United States Code, Section 1341, referred to as the Mail Fraud Statute, forbids using or causing the use of the U.S. mails in a scheme to defraud or to obtain money or property by means of false or fraudulent pretenses, representations, or promises. In such cases the U.S. Postal Service has jurisdiction, and venue lies in the federal judicial district in which the mailing was made, as well as in the federal judicial district in which the delivery was effected. The applicability of this statute should be kept in mind in the investigation of a suspected fraudulent claim.

Property Excluded. The New York Standard Fire Policy does

> not cover accounts, bills, currency, deeds, evidence of debt, money or securities; nor, unless specifically named hereon in writing, bullion or manuscripts.

Many of the multiple-line forms attached to the standard fire policy include coverage for these items or provide endorsements to cover them.

All property insurance policies stipulate what property is not covered under certain conditions and what property is not covered under any conditions.

Perils Not Included. The standard fire policy specifically excludes loss caused by

(a) enemy attack by armed forces, including action taken by military, naval or air forces in resisting an actual or an immediately impending enemy attack;
(b) invasion;
(c) insurrection;
(d) rebellion;
(e) revolution;
(f) civil war;
(g) usurped power.

The purpose of this provision is to exclude damage caused by hostile or warlike actions in time of peace or war, including defensive actions against actual or impending attack. The difficulty of adequately defining *war* is evidenced by the numerous terms listed which are related to warlike activities. Forms attached to the standard fire policy frequently expand this provision under the War Risk Exclusion.

Loss is not covered if caused by

(h) order of any civil authority except acts of destruction at the time of and for the purpose of preventing the spread of fire, provided that such fire did not originate from any of the perils excluded by this policy.

This exception within the exclusion is applicable in cases where, by order of civil authority, property is destroyed to prevent the spread of fire, such as dynamiting or tearing down structures. The cause of the fire, the spread of which is being prevented, cannot be from an excluded peril. In any case involving loss caused by order of civil authority, some public official has generally issued the order. Ordinarily, it will be a matter of record, and the claim representative can get a copy of the order. If, however, the order was oral, the person who gave it should be questioned unless it is a matter of common knowledge such as might be the case if a general order was given over the radio or television.

The standard fire policy excludes loss caused by

> neglect of the insured to use all reasonable means to save and preserve the property at and after a loss, or when the property is endangered by fire in neighboring premises.

It is the obligation of the insured to protect the property at the time of loss and after the loss. The insured's obligation for protecting the property from further damage is restated in the standard fire policy under Requirements in Case Loss Occurs. The opportunity for protecting the property must exist, and a reasonable effort to protect it must be made; otherwise, the loss occasioned by the insured's failure to comply is not covered (see Chapter 6).

Loss by theft is excluded under the standard fire policy although it has been held that if the fire is the proximate cause of the theft, recovery will still be permitted.[15]

Conditions Suspending or Restricting Insurance.[16] Under the standard fire policy the insurer is not liable for loss

(a) while the hazard is increased by any means within the control or knowledge of the insured; or

(b) while the described building, whether intended for occupancy by owner or tenant, is vacant or unoccupied beyond a period of sixty consecutive days; or

(c) as a result of explosion or riot, unless fire ensue, and in that event for loss by fire only.

Increase of hazard generally involves a physical change in the risk. The underwriters accept a risk with known characteristics of construction, occupancy, exposure, and protection. The rate and premium charged the insured are based upon these characteristics. It is assumed there will be no change during the policy period which will materially increase the hazards, thereby increasing the loss potential. If the occupancy of the risk is described as a dwelling, the insurer does not anticipate that it will be converted into a restaurant, a dry-cleaning shop, or an automobile repair shop, all of which are more hazardous and for all of which higher premiums are charged.

While the insured is covered for losses due to his or her own negligence, such as careless disposal of smoking materials, if a collapsed roof is permitted to go unrepaired there may well be a basis for suspending the insurance because the hazard is increased.

The increase of hazard must be within the control *or* knowledge of the insured. It must be a material increase as opposed to moderate, slight, or insignificant. A change of occupancy from a one-family dwelling to a two-family dwelling, or even using one room for a beauty parlor, may not be a material increase in hazard, depending on the facts. A material increase in hazard caused by a tenant of the insured's property will not suspend the insurance unless the circumstances were within the control *or* knowledge of the insured.

The rights of the mortgagee are not affected by an increase of hazard unless the mortgagee had knowledge of it and failed to notify the insurer.

Two clauses are commonly used to provide for continuance of protection during increase of hazard: (1) *the work and materials clause* which permits the insured to do such work and use such materials as are necessary to his business, and (2) *the no control clause*, which, however worded, provides that the insurance shall not be suspended or invalidated by any increase of hazard in parts of the premises over which the insured has no control.

In some jurisdictions, the courts treat the provision regarding increase of hazard as applying only to cases in which the increase was responsible for or contributed to the loss.

Vacancy or *unoccupancy* beyond the period of 60 consecutive days permitted constitutes a specific type of increase in hazard which underwriters seek to avoid. A *vacant building* is one devoid of furnishings and human habitation. An *unoccupied building* has furnishings but is temporarily or permanently without a tenant.

The provision must be construed reasonably, giving full consideration to the type of building, the circumstances of the temporary vacancy, and the customary occupation or lack of occupation incidental to its use. The

---

[15]*Hall v. Great American Insurance Co.*, 217 Iowa 1005, 252 N.W. 763. *Queen Insurance Co. v. Patterson Drug Co.*, 73 Fla. 665, 74 So. 807, LRA 1917D, 1091. *Watson v. American Colony Insurance Co.*, 183 S.E. 692. Gwertzman, op. cit.

[16]The provisions concerning uninsurable and excepted property, the exclusion of loss by theft, and suspension of insurance are waived under most homeowner policies.

courts distinguish between temporary absence and unoccupancy. Where the occupant is temporarily away for reasons of health, pleasure, or business, and such absence is not for an unreasonable length of time, the premises would not be considered unoccupied.[17]

A number of forms attached to policies, such as the Building and Contents, Dwelling Property, and Public and Institutional Property forms, grant coverage during vacancy or unoccupancy. Others place further restrictions on vacancy or unoccupancy as respects certain perils. For example, under the peril of "freezing of plumbing, heating and air conditioning systems and appliances," the Homeowners Policy excludes such loss during vacancy or unoccupancy unless the insured uses due diligence to maintain heat or unless the systems and appliances have been drained and the water supply shut off. Also, in the same policy, loss by "breakage of glass" or "vandalism and malicious mischief" is excluded if the dwelling has been *vacant* beyond a period of 30 consecutive days immediately preceding the loss.

When increase of hazard is removed, or vacancy and unoccupancy cease, the coverage automatically resumes and the policy is in full force and effect as before.

Explosion and riot are hazards not insured against *under the standard fire policy*, and loss is restricted to any damage by fire which may ensue.

Waiver Provisions. In drafting the standard fire policy, the following clause was inserted in an attempt to require the waiver of any provision to be in writing:

No permission affecting this insurance shall exist or waiver of any provision be valid, unless granted herein or expressed in writing added hereto. No provision, stipulation or forfeiture shall be held to be waived by any requirement or proceeding on the part of this Company relating to appraisal or to any examination provided for herein.

Most property insurance policies contain wording of similar intent.

Inland Marine policies state: ". . . nor shall the terms of this policy be waived or changed, except by endorsement issued to form a part of this policy."

Businessowners policies state: "The terms of this insurance shall not be waived, changed or modified except by endorsement issued to form a part of this policy."

Homeowners-76 policies state: "A waiver or change of any provision of this policy must be in writing to be valid."

The courts have given prominence to the doctrine of *waiver* and the kindred doctrine of *estoppel* when deciding insurance cases. While the doctrines have come from general law, they have been applied nowhere else with the severity found in the decisions dealing with insurance policies, and in many cases the effectiveness of this provision has been ignored.[18]

Cancellation. The standard fire policy provides for cancellation at any time at the request of the insured, in which case the company shall, upon demand and surrender of the policy, refund the excess of paid premium above the customary short rates for the unexpired term. The company may cancel the policy at any time by giving the insured *five* days of written notice with or without tender of the excess of paid premium above the pro rata premium for the expired time.[19] Notice of cancellation shall state that this excess premium, if not tendered, will be refunded on demand.

Cancellation provisions with respect to the insurer's reasons for canceling, time of notice to the insured, and the basis for the return of premium have been amended in a number of states. Property insurance policies follow state provisions or stipulate conformity to statutes of the states wherein policies are issued. Personal lines policies, Homeowners and Automobile in particular, state in considerable detail the provisions for cancellation.[20]

[18]See p. 80.
[19]See p. 95.
[20]The mortgagee must be given ten days' notice of cancellation. See p. 63.

[17]*Hemenway v. American Casualty Co. of Reading, Pa.*, U.S. Dist. Ct. La. 11F & C 1108, 1963.

A *proper* cancellation prior to a loss relieves the company of all liability. Difficulties arise, however, when the validity of the cancellation by the company is questioned or there is a cancellation by the insured and substitution of a policy with another company shortly before loss occurs. Full investigation of all of the circumstances is essential to determine on what policy or policies the loss will fall and the amount for which each is liable. [21]

Requirements in Case Loss Occurs. One of the most important provisions in the standard fire policy relates to the duties and obligations of the insured in event of loss. If the claim representative is not thoroughly familiar with them, he or she may unwittingly waive one or more of the requirements, and the company will be estopped from enforcing them. Because of the importance of this provision to adjusting procedure and technique, it is discussed in detail in Chapter 6.

Appraisal. The standard fire policy provides for *appraisal* in case the insured and the company fail to agree on the actual cash value or loss. Each selects an appraiser, and the appraisers select an umpire to whom they submit only their differences. An award in writing of any two when filed with the company will determine the amount of actual cash value and loss. [22]

Other Provisions and Stipulations. The provisions in the standard fire policy which deal with a *company's options, abandonment, when loss payable,* and *suit,* since they are closely related to *requirements in case loss occurs,* are discussed fully in Chapter 6. *Subrogation,* because of its special importance in the adjustment of losses, is examined in Chapter 9.

OUTLINE FOR EXAMINING PROPERTY POLICIES

It is not within the scope or intent of this text to annotate the multitude of forms and endorsements in policies covering property. However, a few comments on the typical format will be helpful to the claim representative becoming oriented to the general pattern of most forms in both single-line and multiple-line policies. Once the pattern is recognized it can be followed in examining most policy forms.

Policy forms generally lend themselves to a fairly logical outline. A popular memory aid may be found in questions *who, what, when, where, against what,* and for *how much.* In other words:

1. *Who* is insured?
2. *What* is covered?
3. *When* is it covered?
4. *Where* is the property covered?
5. *What perils* (losses) are insured against?
6. *How much* is it insured for?

It should be remembered that property is *covered,* people or groups are *insured,* and they are insured against risk of loss or *perils.* A reasonable outline for examining an insurance policy, though headings may occur in a different order, is as follows:

1. Interests insured.
2. Property (subject) covered, property excluded.
3. Policy period.
4. Location where property is covered, locations excluded.
5. Perils (losses) insured against, perils excluded.
6. Extensions as to (a) property covered, (b) locations covered, and (c) perils and kinds of losses.
7. Limitations of liability as to (a) property covered, (b) perils and kinds of losses, (c) contribution to the loss, and (d) deductibles.
8. Special clauses, such as (a) subrogation, (b) cancellation, (c) reinstatement, (d) liberalization, (e) waiver of conditions, (f) loss payable, and so on.

Interests Insured

The insured whose name appears in the policy may be an individual, a partnership, or

[21]Chap. 7 outlines the various loss problems involving cancellation and investigating procedures.
[22]See Chap. 6.

a corporation. [23] Most policies, in particular commercial policies, do not define *insured*. Multiple-line policies under Section 2 define both the *insured* and the *named insured*.

The Homeowners Policies (Ed. 9-70) under General Conditions, Definitions, state:

a. "Insured" means
    (1) the Named Insured stated in the Declarations of this policy
    (2) if residents of the Named Insured's household, his spouse, the relatives of either, and any other person under the age of twenty-one in the care of any insured.

The Homeowners-76 Policy Program (Ed. 7-1-75), under Definitions, states:[24]

3. "Insured" means *you* and the following residents of your household:
    a. your relatives;
    b. any other person under the age of 21 who is in the care of any person named above.

Property (Subject) Covered

A policy may cover specific kinds of property, i.e., buildings, contents, buildings and contents, furniture and fixtures, machinery and equipment, or all real and personal property. It may cover specifically described items or articles, as under a personal-articles floater. Subjects of insurance not usually identified as property may be covered inasmuch as they are subject to loss arising out of the damage or destruction of property. These include such subjects as rents, profits, accounts receivable, earnings of a business, tuition fees, and additional living expenses.

Policies describe the property covered with or without qualifications; or they may describe it in general terms and then qualify, limit, or exclude coverage elsewhere in the policy as respects its location or perils insured against. For this reason it is important to read a policy *in its entirety* before concluding that the loss for which claim is being made is covered, limited, or excluded.

Policy Period

Traditionally, fire and allied lines policies have become effective at *12 noon, standard time*, whereas casualty lines policies become effective at *12:01 A.M. standard time*. Some states, notably California and Oregon, require policies to be effective 12:01 A.M. As newer policy programs evolve, the 12:01 A.M. inception time is used. The SMP (Ed. 7-74) and Businessowners policies (Ed. 11-1-75) state:

To the extent that coverage in this policy replaces coverage in other policies terminating at 12:01 AM (Standard Time) on the inception date of this policy, this policy shall be effective at 12:01 AM (Standard Time) instead of at Noon Standard Time.

Under the Homeowners-76 Policy Program (Ed. 7-1-75), the inception and the expiration time is 12:01 A.M. in lieu of "12 noon" as used in the earlier Homeowners Programs. An ISO bulletin states, "This will not require changing the programed inception and expiration *dates* for a renewal. There will be a 12 hour duplication of coverage period for the initial renewal under the new program."

Locations Where Property Is Covered

A policy may cover property at a described location, for example, a building or personal property in a building at a particular street address. Such insurance is referred to as *specific* as to location. The same policy may extend part or all of the insurance to cover similar property within a specified distance of the described building or premises, or at locations away from the premises.

A policy written for a single amount of insurance and covering several buildings, stocks of merchandise, machinery and equipment, loss of earnings, etc., at more than one place is *blanket* insurance as to

---

[23]See Chap. 4.
[24]Note that in these policies "you" refers to the named insured shown in the Declarations, and the spouse if a resident of the same household.

location. As an illustration, a Public and Institutional Property (PIP) form or a special institutional form under a Special Multiperil Policy (SMP) may cover all the public buildings and their contents of a municipality or a county for a single amount of insurance. The description of the locations of the properties may be in the policy or may refer to locations shown on the latest statement of values filed by the insured with the Rating Bureau.

Whether the insurance is specific as to location, is blanket, or is floating, it is important to read the policy for any extensions covering other locations, exclusions of property at specified locations, or limitations of liability at certain locations.

Perils (Losses) Insured Against

The standard fire policy insures against the perils of fire, lightning, and removal. Forms attached to the standard policy enumerate other perils or may specify that the policy covers all risks of physical loss. The former is known as a *specified peril* or a *named peril* policy; the latter, as an *all risk of physical loss* policy.

A named peril policy may characterize, define, and limit a peril, as in the HO-2 (Ed. 9-70) and HO-2 (Ed. 7-1-75) equivalent:

8. *Sudden and accidental damage from smoke, other than smoke from agricultural smudging or industrial operations.*

Or, it may simply state the peril with no clarification or definition. For example, again HO-2 (Ed. 9-70) and HO-2 (Ed. 7-1-75):

1. *Fire or Lightning* or
4. *Explosion* or
6. *Aircraft, including self-propelled missiles and spacecraft.*

Under the Special Multi-Peril (SMP) policy, MLB-104 (Ed. 2-71), the perils of *fire* and *lightning* are not defined or qualified. But the peril of *explosion* not only has a lengthy description of what it includes and excludes, but also lists seven occurrences

which *are not explosions within the intent or meaning of the provisions of explosion.* Form 18 has similar wording with regard to the peril of explosion, as does the Standard Businessowners Policy. The MLB-101, an all risk of physical loss form, has much broader coverage for the peril of explosion, as does the Special Businessowners Policy.

An all risks of physical loss policy insures against all perils except those specifically excluded. It therefore is presumed to cover a loss caused by a *friendly fire* or an electrical breakdown, provided there is no exclusion for these losses.

In the adjustment of losses, more problems arise about whether or not the loss was caused by a covered peril than about whether or not the property involved is covered. The definitions, exclusions, and provisions applicable to the perils covered may be slightly or substantially different from one form to another, and for certain perils the provisions are quite lengthy. Consequently, it should never be assumed that a named peril in one form has identical provisions to those of a similar named peril in another form.

Under an all risks of physical loss policy the perils and losses not covered are usually described under headings such as Exclusions or Special Exclusions. Under a named peril policy the perils and losses not covered may be described under similar headings and also under provisions applicable to the individual perils.

Extensions and Exclusions

Policies may contain provisions either incorporated into the form or by endorsements attached which expand or extend the contracts to cover additional perils, property, locations, interests, or subjects of insurance. The individual provisions of these extensions may contain limitations on the amount applicable; they may exclude or limit the extension to certain perils or to certain kinds and location of property.

Exclusions are placed in the policy to relieve the insurer from exposure to types of losses which are considered undesirable, uninsurable, or are not contemplated in the rate structure. Such losses are usually identified with catastrophes such as earthquake, landslide, and flood; inherent defects or deterioration in property through normal wear and tear (such as settlement of a building or breakdown of electrical apparatus); moral hazards such as mysterious disappearance or theft from an unlocked car; losses associated with warlike activities; losses resulting from nuclear reaction or radiation; and certain losses which are covered under specific types of insurance.

These exclusions may be specifically stated under the description of property or perils covered, while others may be set forth under the heading of Exclusions or Property Not Covered.

An exclusion in one particular form may be specifically covered under a broader form, or coverage may be available by endorsement for an additional premium.

The provisions under extensions of coverage and exclusions relating to property and perils must be examined carefully before one concludes that a particular loss is covered under the policy.

Limitations of Liability

There are several ways in which an insurer limits the amount for which the policy is liable in a given loss situation. These limitations are in addition to limitations concerning insurable interest, the full amount of the insurance, the cost to replace, or the actual cash value, mentioned previously in connection with the standard fire policy.

An insurer may limit the amount of insurance on specified property to a stipulated percentage of the whole amount of insurance covering that property at the principal location. For example, under the Homeowners Policy the amount of insurance covering unscheduled personal property *away from premises* is limited to 10 percent of the amount specified for that property *on premises*, but not less than $1,000. Also, under the Homeowners Policy the insured may apply 5 percent of the limit of liability of Coverage A—Dwelling, to cover trees, shrubs, plants, and lawns against loss by certain enu-

merated perils with a further limit on any one tree, shrub, or plant, including removal of debris thereof.

Limitations are frequently expressed in terms of dollar amounts such as might apply to money, accounts, and manuscripts under the Homeowners Policy and the Valuable Papers and Records Policy, and to extra expense under some of the SMP programs.

Limitations of liability are specified under the conditions of pro rata distribution, coinsurance, full reporting, and similar clauses which require the insured to carry an amount of insurance equal to a stipulated percentage of the value, or to furnish accurate reports of values as the case may be. An insurer also limits liability under the policy by means of "excess" and "other insurance" clauses pertaining to contribution where other policies cover the same interest or property and insure against the same peril.

The use of deductibles is a form of limitation of liability inasmuch as they provide for a deduction of a stipulated amount or percentage from specified kinds of loss.

Special Clauses

There are several fairly well-standardized clauses which are common in many of the policies and forms. These include the loss clause, liberalization clause, alterations and repairs clause, removal of debris clause, electrical apparatus clause, subrogation clause, work and materials clause, breach of warranty clause, and no control clause.

Loss Clause. A loss clause now found in most property policies provides: "Any loss hereunder shall not reduce the amount of this policy." In other words the full amount of insurance continues during and after a loss. Formerly the insurance was reduced by the amount of any loss, and it was necessary for the insured to pay an additional premium to reinstate the policy to its original amount. The loss clause keeps the amount of insurance in force so that should another loss occur before the property is repaired, the whole amount of insurance applies to the second loss.

Liberalization Clause. The liberalization clause provides:

> If during the period that insurance is in force under this policy, or within 45 days prior to the inception date thereof, on behalf of this Company there be adopted, or filed with and approved or accepted by the insurance supervisory authorities, all in conformity with law, any changes in the form attached to this policy by which this form of insurance could be extended or broadened without increased premium charge by endorsement or substitution of form, then such extended or broadened insurance shall inure to the benefit of the Insured hereunder as though such endorsement or substitution of form had been made.

This clause, or one of similar wording and intent, is found in most property insurance policies.

The two key provisions in this clause are that the changes pertain to *the form attached to the policy* and that the extensions or broadening of the form must be *without increased premium charge.*

Alterations and Repairs Clause. An alterations and repairs clause permits the insured to alter, repair, and erect additions to the buildings covered. The policy extends to cover the additions and also to cover contents in the additions insofar as they are covered under the policy. A typical alterations and repairs clause is found in the General Property Form FGP-1 (Ed. 12-74).

8. PERMITS AND USE: Except as otherwise provided, permission is granted:
   A. to make additions, alterations and repairs. This policy insofar as it covers building(s) or structure(s), is extended to cover additions, alterations and repairs, when not otherwise coverd by insurance, including temporary structures constructed on site, materials, equipment and supplies therefor on or within 100 feet of the described premises: and this policy, insofar as it covers contents, is extended to cover in such additions.

This provision does not waive or modify any of the conditions of the Automatic Sprinkler Clause, if any, attached to this policy.

Permission is given under the General Conditions of the Homeowners Policies for the "named insured to make alterations, additions and repairs, and to complete structures in the course of construction."

Special Multi-Peril policies, under Permits and Use, grant permission "to make alterations and repairs." A similar provision is found in the Difference in Conditions policies. Under the Highly Protected Risk and Superior Risk forms, permission is granted "to erect buildings and structures and to make alterations, additions and repairs." Similar provisions are in most property insurance policies.

Removal of Debris Clause. The removal of debris clauses vary in their language. The Homeowners Policies (Ed. 9-70) simply state:

> This policy covers expenses incurred in the removal of all debris of the property covered hereunder occasioned by loss thereto for which coverage is afforded.

The Businessowners Policies provide for removal of debris of the property covered as an unlimited additional amount of insurance. The simplified Homeowners Policy filed in 1976 is broader in that it extends the policy limit.

> **DEBRIS REMOVAL.** We will pay the reasonable expense incurred by you in the removal of debris of covered property provided coverage is afforded for the peril causing the loss. Debris removal expense is included in the limit of liability applying to the damaged property. When the amount payable for the property loss plus the expense for the debris removal exceeds the limit of liability for the damaged property, an additional 5% of that limit of liability will be available to cover debris removal expense.

Special Multi-Peril policies (SMP) cover removal of debris of the property covered, but the limit of liability of each item covered remains the same. Under the SMP Special Building Form, "the cost of removal of debris shall not be considered in the determination of actual cash value when applying the Coinsurance Clause." This appears to be an unnecessary provision.

A question that frequently arises is whether the policy covers removal of debris (such as trees and parts of buildings from neighboring properties) which is blown onto the insured's premises during a tornado or hurricane, for example. Under the above wording, the policy is liable only for the debris of the *property* covered. Also, it should be noted that where trees on the insured's premises are not covered for the peril of windstorm, the cost of removal, if they are blown over, is not covered.

One of the most comprehensive clauses is the debris removal endorsement in the Building and Contents Form 18 (Ed. 11-72) (This coverage applies only to items of insurance covering direct property loss):

> This insurance covers expense incurred in the removal of debris of the property covered hereunder, which may be occasioned by loss caused by any of the perils insured against in this policy.
>
> The total liability under this policy for both loss to property and debris removal expense shall not exceed the amount of insurance applying under this policy to the property covered.
>
> This Company shall not be liable for a greater proportion of such debris removal expense than the amount of insurance under this policy bears to the whole amount of insurance covering the property against the peril causing the loss, whether or not such other insurance covers such expense.
>
> If this policy covers on two or more items, this clause shall apply to each item separately.
>
> Debris removal expense shall not be considered in the determination of actual cash value in the application of the Coinsurance Clause, if any, made a part of this policy.

The debris must be from the property covered and the loss must be from a peril in-sured against. The loss to the property plus the cost of the debris removal cannot exceed the amount of insurance. While the cost of the removal of debris "shall not be considered in the determination of *actual cash value* in the application of the coinsurance clause," *it is part of the loss and as such is subject to coinsurance.* In other words, in determining the insurance required in compliance with the coinsurance clause, the cost of debris removal will not be considered. However, when applying the coinsurance clause, the cost of debris removal is to be included in the loss.

Electrical Apparatus Clause. The electrical apparatus clause states as follows:

> This Company shall not be liable for any loss resulting from any electrical injury or disturbance to electrical appliances, devices, fixtures or wiring caused by electrical currents artificially generated unless fire ensues and, if fire does ensue, this Company shall be liable only for its proportion of loss caused by such ensuing fire.

The burning out of motors, transformers, wiring, and components of appliances by electrical currents is due to heat and not fire. Losses caused by artificially generated electricity are properly termed electrical injury. While the standard fire policy excludes losses of this kind, any subsequent damage by fire which may ensue is covered.[25]

Homeowners, Broad Form HO-2 (Ed. 1-72), as a named peril policy covers:

> Sudden and accidental injury from electrical currents artificially generated to electrical appliances, devices, fixtures and wiring, except tubes, transistors and similar electronic components.

Homeowners, Broad Form (Ed. 7-1-75), covers:

> Sudden and accidental damage from artificially generated electrical current. This peril does not include loss to a tube, transistor or similar electronic components.

[25] See Chap. 8.

The two perils appear to be somewhat different inasmuch as the former limits coverage to electrical appliances, devices, fixtures, and wiring. The latter covers damage to all property under the form. This might include scorched carpeting and furniture as a result of a hot electrical extension cord which shorted out with no ensuing fire.

Homeowners all risks of physical loss policies include sudden and accidental damage from artificially generated electrical current by virtue of not excluding such damage.

Special Multi-Peril, all risks of physical loss policies, and the Special Businessowners policy, also all risk, both exclude damage resulting from electrical injury from artificially generated current unless fire ensues, and then only for the loss caused by such ensuing fire.

Subrogation Clause. Appearing in many forms, this subrogation clause stipulates that the insurance shall not be invalidated should the insured waive in writing prior to a loss any or all right of recovery against any party for loss occurring to the described property.

This is a voluntary waiver by the insurer of its subrogation rights provided the insured has waived his or her rights *in writing* and *prior* to a loss. The insured may not waive such after the occurrence of a loss; otherwise, the claim is forfeited. The provision has a practical application in cases where an insured waives subrogation rights under a lease agreement, a sidetrack agreement with a railroad, a construction contract with a builder, or other types of written agreements. Where these waiver agreements exist the insurer cannot subrogate against the party with whom the waiver has been executed.

Work and Materials Clause. The work and materials clause permits "such use of the premises as is usual or incidental to the occupancy as described herein." The effect is to modify the provisions of the standard fire policy relating to increase of hazard. The insured may keep materials on the premises or perform operations which, though appearing to be especially hazardous, are usual and incidental to the particular occupancy.

Breach of Warranty Clause. The breach of warranty clause, designated in some forms as the Divisible Contract Clause, provides:

> If this policy covers two or more buildings or the contents of two or more buildings, the breach of any condition or warranty of the policy in any one or more of the buildings insured or containing the property insured shall not prejudice the right to recover for loss occurring in any building insured or containing the property insured, where at the time of loss a breach of condition or warranty does not exist.

If an insured breached a condition or warranty involving, for example, an increase of hazard or a change of occupancy in one of the buildings covered, and if a fire then occurred which extended to some other building, the insured would not be barred from collecting for the damage to the other building and its contents. The breach would apply only to the building in which it took place.

No Control Clause. A no control clause, or control of property clause, simply states:

> This insurance shall not be prejudiced by any act or neglect of any person, other than an insured, when such act or neglect is not within the control of any insured.

This clause, common to most property insurance policies under different wordings, is found, for example, in the General Conditions of the Homeowners, Special Multi-Peril policies, Businessowners policies, Dwelling Building(s) and Contents forms (DF series, Ed. 9-7-74, N.Y.), Highly Protected Risk and Superior Risk forms, and Public and Institutional Property forms.

INTERPRETATION OF INSURANCE POLICIES

While much of the language in insurance policies is clear and understandable to the average person, many of the words and phrases are *not* clear even to the courts. Insurance company personnel themselves, those who draft the forms and administer claims made under them, disagree on the precise meaning of the legalistic and technical jargon used in many of the conditions and provisions, limitations, and exclusions in their policies. For example, within the industry and among the courts there is not always agreement on the meaning of words such as *actual cash value, fixtures, equipment, domestic appliances, building structures, occurrence, all risks of physical loss, contamination, mysterious disappearance, appurtenant private structures,* and *collapse.*

Background to the Problem. The burdensome language of contemporary insurance contracts can be attributed in part to legislatively imposed requirements and in part to the common law. The good intent of each molding force is not in question. The nature of the insurance product and legal nuances easily give rise to complex policy wording. It is generally recognized that policy language must be harmonized to satisfy technical, economic and legal requirements of insurance companies, regulators and the courts. Those standard forms mandated by statutes or administrative orders are typically reflections of or reactions to judicial decision. In effect, the courts have been the chief architects of a great bulk of the verbose and highly technical policy language.[26]

For a number of years insurance companies, endeavoring to meet the problem, began drafting radically different policies, such as the *Family Auto Policy* and the *Homeowners Policies.* While these policies were intended to be easier to read, actually they took the direction of broadening rather than simplifying. In fact the early Homeowners Policies inadvertently created more problems of interpretation than they solved by introducing new words and phrases.

The insurance industry was forced to take notice of the question of insurance policy readability in June 1973 when Herbert S. Denenberg, then Pennsylvania Insurance Commissioner, rejected a mail-order auto insurance policy form on the grounds that it was not suf-

ficiently readable. The policy was submitted by Allied Insurance Company, a subsidiary of INA Corp., and Mr. Denenberg's action marked the first time in American insurance regulation that readability was used as a basis for disapproval of a policy filing.

The initial reaction of the insurance industry was predictable—the business was offended by Mr. Denenberg's invasion of its prerogatives—but in a short time a new attitude appeared. Less than two years later, several insurers are marketing more readable policies and others are working on research, development and approval of simplified policies.

The Pennsylvania insurance department has called for all private passenger auto policies written in the state to meet certain readability requirements by February 10, 1976. These requirements include column width, size of margins, type size (at least 10 point, the size used in this article), and substantially improved language as measured by the Flesch Readability Test.

Nationwide Mutual was one of the first insurers to have a simplified auto insurance policy, *Century II,* approved by the Pennsylvania insurance department. It has subsequently been approved in a number of other states. Sentry Insurance also developed a more readable policy, *Plain Talk Car Insurance Policy,* approved in most states in 1975. The Insurance Services Office (ISO) in 1975 filed a new *Homeowners "76"* policy program. The new policy scored twice as high as the original on the Flesch Readability Test.[27]

Simplified, or easy-to-read, policies are emerging in the various lines of insurance. To what extent they will reduce and minimize litigation over interpretation is not presently predictable. The consensus is that they constitute a "giant step" toward improved communications between insureds and insurers.

Traditional Rules of Construction

Historically the courts have looked upon insurance policies as *contracts* and have con-

[26]E. Neil Young, John R. Lewis, and J. Finley Lee, "Insurance Contract Interpretation: Issues and Trends," *The Insurance Law Journal,* February, 1975, No. 625.

[27]Karen Esposito, Editorial Assistant, "Policy Readability: How the Industry Has Reacted," *Best's Review.*

strued them according to the rules of construction that are applied to *all* contracts. At the same time, however, they have generally recognized that the insurance policy is a contract written by the insurer with the insured having no part in the drafting. To protect the so-called *weaker party* to the contract, the courts have considerably broadened the interpretative rules of construction normally applicable to most *noninsurance contracts* where the parties are presumed to have equal bargaining powers.

While there is a diversity of opinion by the courts on similar issues in the various states, there are certain traditional rules of construction generally followed throughout the country. Set forth below is a digest of the *paramount* rules and reasons behind each rule. As a warning against an overly dogmatic approach to this complex problem, attention is called to the fact that, while the courts are generally in substantial agreement in their statements of the rules of construction to be applied, there is much room for differences of opinion in the application of these rules to specific cases. A more important consideration is to be found in the discussion which immediately follows the citing of these rules and which deals with the emergence of a changing judicial perspective, shifting away from the *negotiated contract* concept of an insurance policy to the notion that it is another product placed on the market for the consumer to purchase.

At the outset it must be recognized that an insurance policy is in fact a contract, and is therefore subject to the same rules of interpretation of all contracts.* In this respect, it is fundamental that the purpose of reducing a contract to writing is to preserve the understanding of the parties as to their agreement. Therefore, the written document should reflect with as much certainty as possible, the understanding or agreements of the parties *as they intended it*. This leads to the first rule of construction.

Rule 1: (a) When the contract is clear and precise in its language, there is no need to

---

apply rules of construction in order to determine the *intention* of the parties.

Rule 1: (b) However, when the contract is not clear or is ambiguous, it is necessary to apply rules of construction in order to *ascertain the intention* of the parties. "Appleman, Insurance L & P," vol. 13, Section 7384, "Am. Jur.," vol. 29, Section (Insurance), 247, "C. J. S.," 2d ed., (Insurance vol. 44), Section 291.

Reason: Since the purpose of the written instrument is to reflect the understanding of the parties, if the instrument clearly reflects the understanding of the parties the court cannot change or modify the parties understanding under the guise of interpreting the contract. In the event a contract is ambiguous, obviously it is the prerogative of the court to clarify by interpretation the ambiguity which does in fact exist.

Rule 2: Once the instrument has been reduced to writing, it is presumed that the parties to a contract of insurance fully understand its contents. "Couch on Insurance" 2d ed. vol. 1, Section 15:12, "Appleman, Insurance L & P" vol. 13, Section 7381.

Reason: In the event the contract language is clear, if the parties were permitted to contend that they placed an unreasonable interpretation on it, or did not understand its clear and apparent meaning, then the worth of the written instrument and its practical need would be destroyed.

Rule 3: Once the contract has been reduced to written form, in the absence of fraud or mistake, if the language is clear, resort cannot be made to extrinsic evidence to establish what the parties *thought* they intended or what the parties said or did prior to consummating the contract. In other words, the clearly set forth written instrument speaks for itself. "Couch on Insurance" 2d ed., vol. 1, Section 15:11, "Appleman, Insurance L & P" vol. 13, Sections 7385 and 7387, "C. J. S." 2d ed., vol. 44, Sections 291 and 304.

Reason: This rule of law (Rule 3) is known as the Parol Evidence Rule. The purpose of the rule is to avoid collateral attacks on agreements which have been clearly and precisely stated. It is presumed that the parties knew what they were doing when they reduced their understanding to writing, and that written document

---

*"Appleman, Insurance L & P," vol. 13, Section 7381, "44 C. J. S.," 2d ed., Section 289; "Am. Jur.," vol. 29, Section 245; "Vance on Insurance," 3rd Ed., 1951, p. 808.

best expresses the intent of the parties. Again, if evidence is admitted to change or modify the expressed intent of the parties, there would be no need for the written document, thus the Parol Evidence Rule.

Rule 4: Extrinsic evidence may be introduced to *explain* ambiguities in the policy. "Couch on Insurance" 2d ed., vol. 1, Section 15:56; "Appleman, Insurance L & P" vol. 13, Section 7385, "Am. Jur." Insurance vol. 29, Section 247; "C. J. S." 2d ed., vol. 44, Sections 291 and 294.

Reason: You will recall that under the Parol Evidence Rule evidence is not admissible to change or modify the terms of a written instrument in so far as that instrument clearly reflects the intention of the parties. When the instrument is clear there is no need for such evidence. However, when the instrument is not clear, the evidence is then admissible to *explain* what the parties intended. It should be emphasized that we are not at this point changing or modifying the agreement, but on the contrary, enhancing its effectiveness by clarifying its meaning.

Rule 5: In the event of an ambiguity, then the ambiguity should be resolved by an examination of the policy in its entirety. "Couch on Insurance" 2d ed., vol. 1, Section 15:29; "Appleman, Insurance L & P" vol. 13, Sections 7383 and 7403; "Vance on Insurance" 3d ed., 1951, p. 809, "Am. Jur.," Insurance vol. 29, Section 250.

Reason: In the event of an ambiguity, the intent of the parties is most readily reflected in the whole policy, and therefore it is reasonable to look *first* to the policy to resolve the conflict and ambiguity, then to turn to matters extrinsic to the policy.

Rule 6: In case of ambiguity, the portion of the policy which is unclear in its language should be resolved so as to impose liability on the insurer, or so as to provide coverage for the insured. "C. J. S." 2d ed., vol. 44, Section 297; "Vance on Insurance" 3d ed., Edition 1951, p. 808; "Appleman, Insurance L & P" vol. 13, Section 7403. "Couch on Insurance" 2d ed., vol. 1, Section 15:92.

Reason: A policy of insurance (with particular reference to the property field) is a policy of indemnity and therefore, in construing the pol-

icy, the general intent of the policy is to indemnify, and in case of ambiguity, the general intent should be employed whenever reasonably possible.

Rule 7: No word in insurance policies should be assumed to be superfluous or redundant unless no reasonable meaning consistent with other portions of the policy can be given to it. "Couch on Insurance" 2d ed., vol. 1, Sections 15:43 and 15:44; "Appleman, Insurance L & P" vol. 13, Section 7383.

Reason: Since the policy was written by the parties in order to express their intent, it is assumed that each word selected by the parties was a necessary element in the expression of their agreement.

Rule 8: Specific provisions of insurance policies will prevail over more general provisions. However, specific provisions of insurance policies will override general provisions only where the two cannot stand together. In other words, if there is no conflict between the specific provisions of the policy and the general provisions of the policy, there is no need to employ any rule of construction, for in this case both the general and specific provisions of the policy may be given full force and effect, each without disturbing the meaning of the other. "Am. Jur.," vol. 29, Section 254; "Couch on Insurance" 2d ed., vol. 1, Section 15:70, "C. J. S.," vol. 44, Section 298.

Reason: In determining the meaning of contradictory portions of the policy, it is generally held that the parties express their intention with more certainty in the area where the subject matter is dealt with on a specific basis. Therefore, specific portions of the policy generally override general provisions of the policy when there is a conflict.

Rule 9: Where a policy is on a printed form, portions of the policy which have been completed by typewriter or by handwriting, or by stamp are to be given more weight than printed portions of the policy in governing questions of conflict. "Am. Jur." Insurance vol. 29, Section 255; "C. J. S.," 2d ed., vol. 44, Section 295; "Couch on Insurance," 2d ed., vol. 1, Sections 15:71 and 15:72.

Reason: This rule contemplates the fact that the parties have given more attention to the area where typed or written or stamped information appears, and thus more clearly reflects the intention of the parties.

Rule 10: Where the policy contains portions in large, bold, or italicized print, or portions more prominent than the less conspicuous portions of the policy, that portion of the policy which stands out is given greater weight in construction than the portion of the policy printed in the standard manner. "Am. Jur." Insurance vol. 29, Section 254; "Couch on Insurance" 2d ed., vol. 1, Sections 15:84 and 15:94.

Reason: Again the courts rationalize that the emphasized portion of the policy more readily indicated the intent of the parties because the parties intended that portion more readily expressed their intention.

Rule 11: Policies of insurance are most rigidly construed against the insurer. "Appleman, Insurance L & P" vol. 13, Sections 7401 and 7402: "Vance on Insurance" 3d ed., Edition 1951, p. 808; "Am. Jur.," Insurance vol. 29, Section 258, "C. J. S.," 2d ed., vol. 44, Section 297 (C-1).

Reason: This (Rule 11) is perhaps the most well known of construction and the rationale supporting this rule is predicated on the fact that the insurance company prepared the policies and therefore, as in all contracts, it is construed most rigidly against the party who drafted it, as that party had the best opportunity to express its intent. In this connection, the "standard statutory policy" presents an interesting problem in construction. In the case of the "standard statutory policy," the courts are divided as to whether or not this policy should be construed most rigidly against the insurer. The courts generally are liberal in their construction of a statutory policy ("Couch on Insurance" 2d ed., vol. 1, Section 15:16), but there is considerable authority that the better view would hold that since the insurer did not select the language, no strained interpretations should be made, and the statutory words should be given their plain meaning and no more. "Appleman, Insurance L & P" vol. 13, Section 7404; "C. J. S.," 2d ed., vol. 44, Section 289; "Vance on Insurance" 3d ed., Edition 1951, p. 809.

Rule 12: Usage and custom may be employed to explain the meaning of a particular insurance contract, but before usage and custom are employed, it must be shown that it is well established, notorious, uniform, and reasonable. "Couch on Insurance" 2d ed., vol. 1, Sections 15:24, 15:59, and 15:63; "Appleman, Insurance L & P" vol. 13, Section 7388.

Reason: In case of an ambiguity in an area where specific words have a unique connotation, it is rationalized that the circumstances giving rise to the connotation, i.e. usage and custom, serve as a legitimate means of *explanation*.

Rule 13: A policy of insurance will not be so construed as to make it violative of the law if such a construction can be fairly avoided. In other words, the courts attempt to construe the policy in favor of legality. "Am. Jur.," Insurance vol. 29, Section 249; "Appleman, Insurance L & P" vol. 13, Section 7406.

Reason: It is presumed that the parties intended a lawful result in consummating their contract and therefore the courts will make every effort to give force and effect to a lawful result.

Rule 14: Grammar and punctuation may be considered in interpreting the intentions of the parties, but will not control or change a meaning which is plainly gathered from the words, and arrangement, and the contract. "C. J. S." vol. 44, Section 294; "Couch on Insurance," 2d ed., vol. 1, Section 15:13.

Reason: Once again the court will attempt to carry out the actual intent of the parties without recourse to an overly technical approach to construction. (See Standard of Construction to follow.)

Rule 15: The judicial construction placed upon particular words or phrases made prior to the issuance of the policy employing them will be presumed to be the construction intended to be adopted by the parties. "Appleman, Insurance L & P" vol. 13, Section 7404; "C. J. S.," vol. 44, Section 293.

Reason: There is some diversity of opinion among various courts interpreting the same words and phrases. This merely tends to emphasize the fact that the use of certain words and phrases does create very real problems in policy construction. Once the court has placed a meaning on a particular word or phrase, and this phrase or word is used again in *context*, the meaning placed on the word or phrase, by the court, will be held to be the meaning intended by the party. The fact that the parties were ignorant (unaware) of the court's interpretation of the particular word or phrase will not excuse the parties from being held to have intended to employ the court-determined meaning.

Rule 16: Endorsements and riders are part of the policy and are not to be given greater effect than the body of the policy, *except* to the extent that the endorsement or rider expressly states that it is in substitution for a part of the body of the policy. "C. J. S.," vol. 44, Section 300.

Reason: You will recall that under Rule 7, meaning should be given whenever possible to the entire policy. Therefore, unless a conflict exists, the riders and endorsements should be construed in such a manner as to render meaningful all portions of the riders and endorsements, as well as the body of the policy. In the event a conflict does exist between the rider or endorsement and the body of the policy, it is generally reasoned that the rider or endorsement was affixed to the policy to carry out a specific purpose, and therefore, when that purpose does appear from a reading of the rider or endorsement, greater weight should be given to the rider or endorsement when it is in conflict with the body of the policy.

Standard of Construction. In interpreting all policies of insurance, the courts implied the standard of the "reasonable person." In other words, it is a basic rule of construction that the policy should be interpreted as viewed from the standpoint of "a reasonable person" acting with reference to the circumstances involved in the particular case. This rule can more readily be brought into focus by stating it in the negative. The policy is not construed as it would be interpreted by a person with unique or particular knowledge or skill which would give rise to an insight and understanding not apparent to "an ordinary reasonable person" reading the policy. "C. J. S.," vol. 44, Section 294; "Appleman, Insurance L & P" vol. 13, Sections 7384 and 7402; "Am. Jur." Insurance vol. 29, Section 251; "Vance on Insurance" 3d ed., Edition 1951, p. 809, "Couch on Insurance" 2d ed., vol. 1, Section 15:16.

Caveat—It may, however, be that the "reasonable man" under the circumstances may be held to a unique knowledge because of the circumstances giving rise to the policy. For example, certain marine policies by their very nature imply a knowledge of marine terminology not customarily known to the man in the street.[28]

The Changing Judicial Perspective

The foregoing 16 rules of construction employed by the courts to interpret insurance policies might be viewed as amplification of what are frequently referred to by legal authorities as the Five Basic Rules of Construction. Attorney John W. Morrison,[29] addressing the Loss Managers' Conference of the Property Loss Research Bureau, in Denver in 1975, outlined these five basic rules in a talk entitled "Judicial Approaches: Trend Setting Decisions." In summary they are:

1. *The Literal Reading Rule.* This rule assumes both parties are of equal standing; the contract was a meeting of minds between the parties, and the wording in the contract reflects the intent of the parties.
2. *The Single Interpretation Rule.* This is referred to by lawyers as the rule or doctrine of *contra proferentum.* This doctrine suggests that ambiguities in a contract should be interpreted against the drafter of the contract without considering the intent of the drafter.
3. *Doctrine of Contracts of Adhesion.* This doctrine, similar to the Single Interpretation Rule, is a more severe interpretation from the position of the insurer. It is based on the disparity of bargaining power between the insurer and the insured and suggests that all contract ambiguities should be interpreted against the insurer.
4. *Rule of Reasonable Expectation.* This rule suggests that provisions sought to be enforced by the insurer should not be inconsistent with the reasonable expectations of the insured. In other words, are such provisions at variance with what the insured thought he was getting when he purchased the policy?

[28]From a letter to the author (Paul I. Thomas) by John E. Lecomte, attorney, Lecomte, Shea & Dangora, Boston, Mass. January 28, 1976.
[29]Attorney John W. Morrison, of Clausen, Miller, Gorman, Caffrey & Witous, Chicago.

5. *Rule of the Wayfaring Fool.* This rule states that an insurer must use language that is sufficiently clear that a "wayfaring man, though a fool, might not be deceived."

These five basic rules of construction appeared in *The Insurance Law Journal,* in a very illuminating and important treatise, by E. Neil Young, John R. Lewis, and J. Finley Lee.[30] The following significant conclusion was stated by the authors:

The trend toward expanding policy language in favor of policyholders indicates a shifting judicial perception whereby insurance policies are more frequently being viewed as mass produced, mass marketed consumer products rather than as negotiated agreements. This shift is in consonance with societal demands for increased consideration and protection of the consuming public. With the continuation of the consumerism movement, the trend in insurance litigation is likely to continue. It is unlikely, though, at least for the immediate future—and in the absence of the imposition of additional legislative controls—that an appreciable number of courts will cease to speak of insurance policies as contracts or to discard the doctrinal approaches associated with the law of contracts as tools to assist in resolving disputes regarding the coverage of those policies.

Attorney Morrison, in his talk, added a sixth rule which he designated as the "Rule of Purpose." This is based on his review of a significant number of 1974 decisions from across the country. This rule asks three questions:

1. What *purpose* was the policy provision intended to serve?
2. Has the *purpose* been served?
3. Will the *purpose* be frustrated by permitting the insured to recover?

The prediction of Attorney Morrison was that the Literal Reading Rule, already in disrepute, would be gradually abandoned and the Rule of Purpose would evolve.

Manifestly, this is a perilous position to be in, in light of the substantial consequential and punitive claims that can be made. I would submit to you that our state of uncertainty and our exposure to the adverse effects of claims can be lessened by searching for the PURPOSE of the policy language which may grant or limit a claimant's right of recovery.[31]

Attorney Morrison's addition of the Rule of Purpose is considered an important contribution to the understanding of claim personnel as to how the courts interpret insurance contracts. It is particularly significant in today's *aura of consumerism.* It has also raised a rather stimulating question in some legal minds: Has, perhaps, the Rule of Purpose already been in existence, but masquerading under a different identity, i.e., those rules that examine insurance contracts for *general intent?*

STATUTORY MODIFICATIONS

Many of the states have passed statutes giving interpretations to the language of the insurance contract or modifying it. Most of these statutes relate to insurable interest, valued policy laws, cancellation, mortgagee interests, filing of proof of loss, payment of loss, appraisal, and time for filing suit. Where conflicts exist between insurance policies and statutory provisions, the latter will prevail.[32]

QUESTIONS AND PROBLEMS

1. The insurance contract is a legal contract and conforms to the general laws governing the making of all contracts. There must be an offer and acceptance; the purpose must be legal; the parties must be competent; and there has to be a consideration. The courts, however, have variously designated the insurance contract as a (a) contract of indemnity, (b) unilateral contract, (c) conditional

---

[30]Young, Lewis, and Lee, op. cit.

[31]Morrison, op. cit.
[32]A recommended reference on this subject is *Annotation of the 1943 New York Standard Fire Insurance Policy,* Section of *Insurance Law Journal,* American Bar Association, Chicago, 1967.

contract, (d) aleatory contract, (e) contract of adhesion, and (f) a personal contract. What, in essence, is meant by each of the six kinds of contract designations?

2. Insurance Services Office (ISO) is a national organization established by the property and liability insurance industry and is a consolidation of several insurance industry organizations.

    a. List several of its services.

    b. List at least eight lines of insurance that come within the purview of ISO.

3. A written binder is a brief preliminary memorandum containing the essentials of the insurance contract.

    a. What, generally, are those essentials?

    b. Because binders are not completed contracts in the sense that they do not contain the full policy conditions and provisions, the claim representative is faced with greater than usual responsibilities as an investigator. Explain why this is so.

4. Standard fire insurance policies as well as many property insurance policies insure to the extent of the *actual cash value* not to exceed the cost to *repair or replace* with like kind and quality.

    a. Give a general definition of the term *actual cash value.*

    b. Explain the significance of the terms *actual cash value* and *repair or replace* with respect to being limitations of loss.

5. Give a definition of friendly fire. Comment briefly on the following situations with respect to whether you would consider them to be hostile or friendly fires and covered or not covered under a standard fire policy.

    a. You inadvertently drop your expensive cuff links in the wastebasket and someone empties the wastebasket into the incinerator.

    b. Soot in a chimney ignites and the intense heat discolors the wallpaper on the bedroom wall through which the chimney passes.

    c. An expensive tropical plant is placed on the hearth near the fireplace. Heat from the fire wilts the plant and destroys it.

    d. A large quantity of wastepaper is placed in the fireplace. When ignited, flames lick up and scorch a mahogany mantel.

6. During a fire, the insured and neighbors are able to remove Oriental rugs, valuable paintings, and other articles of value. These are loaded onto a small truck to be transported to the nearest neighbor's home for safekeeping and protection. While being driven across a wooden bridge over a stream, the truck upsets into the stream. Some of the articles are recovered, but the majority are broken or otherwise a total loss.

In adjusting the loss under a standard fire insurance policy how would you handle the property that was damaged or destroyed when the truck upset into the stream?

7. The insurance contract covers direct loss caused by a peril insured against. In other words, the cause of the loss must be immediate or proximate.

    a. Explain what is meant by proximate cause of loss.

    b. Comment on the following situations as to whether the doctrine of proximate cause would apply or not apply.

    (1) A fire in a brick building so weakens the brickwork that one of the walls falls outward crushing the roof of an adjacent dwelling. There was no fire or water damage to the dwelling, only the crushed roof.

    (2) Smoke from a fire a block away soils the curtains and drapes of a dwelling where the windows were open.

    (3) Three weeks after a fire which gutted a brick building, workers demolishing the standing walls cause it to collapse outward damaging an adjacent building.

    (4) Firemen remove a skylight in a building that was filling up with smoke from a fire next door. A few days later during a rainstorm the premises are damaged by water coming in around the skylight. The firemen had not replaced the skylight properly.

8. Under the standard fire insurance policy, a *condition* that will suspend the insurance is *one where the hazard is increased by any means within the control or knowledge of the insured.* Comment on the following with respect to this condition.

    a. A building covered under the policy is

described as occupied as a *garage and automobile body shop.* During the term of the policy the insured converts the occupancy to a doughnut shop. Doughnuts are made on the premises.

b. A lessee of the insured's building occupies space as a real estate and insurance office. A recession in business prompts the lessee to put up a partition to subdivide the space and sublease it, unknown to the insured, to a dry cleaner. Under the long-term lease the lessee is not prohibited from subdividing.

9. The text outlines eight major elements of a property insurance contract which should be examined in analyzing whether a loss falls within the purview of the policy. List these elements or areas in a policy necessary for analysis.

10. The Homeowners policies state, "This policy covers expenses incurred in the removal of all debris of the property covered hereunder occasioned by loss thereto for which coverage is afforded."

The representative finds that during a hurricane a large tree from a neighbor's lot fell across the yard of the insured; silt and debris from neighboring premises were washed or blown onto the insured's property.

a. Does the policy cover the removal of this debris? If so, what part is covered? Explain.

b. If a large oak tree in the insured's yard was blown onto the insured's house, how would you handle the removal of the tree under the terms of the policy?

11. The insured has waived in writing any right of subrogation against the general contractor who is erecting an addition to the insured's plant. An employee of a subcontractor erecting steelwork sets fire to the building while using a welding and cutting torch. What subrogation rights are available to the insurer?

12.a. In your own words, briefly state the principle underlying the Parol Evidence Rule, also known as the Literal Reading Rule.

b. In general how do our courts interpret ambiguities in an insurance policy? Explain.

c. What is meant by the Rule of Reasonable Expectation?

13. Distinguish between the following pairs of terms by definition and example.

a. Vacant and unoccupied.

b. Arbitration and litigation.

c. Named peril and all risk of loss.

Insurable Interests

As a party to a contract of insurance, the insured may be an individual, two or more individuals, a partnership, an association, a corporation, a joint-stock company, or a combination of two or more of these. In some contracts, individuals and partners are designated by trade names. Standard policies insure the insured and his or her legal representatives.

Adjustments are, with rare exceptions, made with the insured, who is obligated by the contract to fulfill certain requirements in case of loss, ordinarily receives payment, and by accepting it discharges the insurer from its liability. If an insured individual dies while an unadjusted loss is pending, or if a loss follows an insured's death, or if such an individual, or any insured individual, partnership, association, or corporation becomes legally disabled to act as a party to a contract, a legal representative or representatives of the insured are entitled to take over, make the adjustment, receive payment, and give a receipt that will discharge the insurer. It is incumbent upon the claim representative to deal with the insured, or a legal representative or representatives, and to satisfy the insurer, when reporting, that he or she has dealt with the right person or persons. While the insured cannot be relieved of the requirements to be fulfilled in case of loss, he or she can properly delegate to another the task of agreeing upon sound value and amount of loss. Except in the larger cities, the claim representative ordinarily deals directly with the insured. Occasionally, however, a local agent will act for the insured. In the larger metropolitan areas, many losses are handled for the insured by agents, brokers, or public adjusters.

The accepted definition of *insurable interest* is any equitable or legal estate, or any right that may be prejudicially affected, or any liability that may be brought into operation by a peril insured against.

Unconditional and sole ownership[1] is the interest most frequently encountered. Other interests are those of part owner, life tenant, remainderman, vendor, vendee, lessor, lessee, bailor, bailee, mortgagor, and mortgagee. No attempt is here made to enumerate all kinds of insurable interests.

Because the amount the insured may collect is limited by his or her interest in the property, it is part of the claim representative's work to determine the nature and extent of the interest and to see that the amount to be paid does not exceed the value of the interest.

INDIVIDUALS

Individuals who are named insureds, such as *John Doe* or *John Doe and wife Mary Doe*, usually act for themselves in loss adjustments. Normally there is no problem of identifying the insured, and the claim representative negotiates with either one or both.

Under Homeowners policies, where there is only one named insured, the claim representative may adjust the loss with the named insured's spouse inasmuch as the definition of *insured* includes the *insured's spouse*, or under HO-76, the insured's relatives as long

[1]See p. 57.

as they are residents of the insured's household.

The same is true on mercantile or manufacturing risks where the insured may be *Frances Doe, d/b/a Doe's Ready to Wear Shop*, or *Robert Doe d/b/a Bob's Auto Repair Shop*.

If the insured has an agent, broker, or public adjuster as a representative in the adjustment, the representative generally satisfies the claim representative as to the authority to act.

Several Individuals Separately Named

If the policy is issued to several named individuals, it is incumbent upon the claim representative to see that all execute the proof of loss, or that one properly authorized executes it on behalf of the others, after securing their agreement to the settlement and their agreement to endorse individually the draft issued in payment.

Several Individuals Not Separately Named

The claim representative will occasionally find policies that have been issued to a group of individuals under such titles as: Heirs of John Smith, Estate of Henry Morgan, Trustees of Main Street Presbyterian Church. In such cases it may be necessary to collect affidavits naming all the individuals the group comprises. In case of doubt, it is well for the claim representative to secure the affidavit of each individual who may be accessible, and in addition the affidavits of two reputable, disinterested citizens, all affidavits naming the individuals who constitute the group and giving their addresses.

LEGAL REPRESENTATIVES OF THE INSURED

The term *legal representatives* ordinarily means executors or administrators. The term, however, is sufficiently broad to include under certain circumstances heirs at law, next of kin, legatees, or devisees.

When an adjustment is made with an executor or administrator, the claim representative should require a certified copy of the letters testamentary or letters of administration to accompany the proof of loss. These letters, which are issued by the surrogate, judge of probate, or other similar official, evidence the appointment and qualification of the person to whom they are issued. Exception can be made in cases of executors or administrators who represent well-known estates, when the endorsement of the company's check or draft by such executors or administrators will be guaranteed by one of the banks in the community. If circumstances are such that claim can properly be made by heirs at law or next of kin, as when an insured dies intestate but leaves no debts, the claim representative should require an affidavit from one of the heirs or kinsmen, also affidavits from at least two reputable citizens of the community, stating the names and addresses of all the heirs or kin, and also the date of the insured's death.

PARTNERSHIPS

The obligations of partnership are such that one partner may bind the other partner, or partners, in any matter of partnership business. Usually one partner dominates the affairs of the firm and, in the event of loss, acts for the copartners, who will be bound by any bona fide adjustment made. If a partnership is insured under a trade name that does not state the names of the individual partners, the names should appear in the claim representative's report. If the partners act under written articles of partnership, their names will appear in the articles. Some partnerships, however, are organized under oral agreement. In such cases, the identity of partners can be established by the affidavit of one of them, though this is rarely necessary.

ASSOCIATIONS AND JOINT-STOCK COMPANIES

The term *association* is used to designate an unincorporated group of individuals who have so organized themselves that they may be bound in matters pertaining to their common business venture by the act of a single designated person or by the act of a small group of their members. An association generally transacts business through a manager, chairman, or attorney, who derives power from the individual members. In some instances, transactions must be approved by a board of directors or supervisors. In dealing with an association, the claim representative should see that the proof of loss is executed by the person or persons authorized to act on behalf of the association.

There is no essential difference between an association and a joint-stock company. Under the common law, a joint-stock company was midway between a partnership and a corporation, lacking the element of a charter granted by the state but presenting a corporate method of doing business and a plan of organization and perpetuation by means of transferable shares. The joint-stock company has capital stock and officers like a corporation, but its members are individually liable for the debts of the company. In some states, statutes have been enacted doing away with all substantial distinctions between joint-stock companies and corporations. Since, in any event, individual shareholders cannot bind the company, the claim representative should see that the proof of loss is executed in the name of the joint-stock company by one of its duly constituted officers.

CORPORATIONS

Because a corporation transacts business through its officers, the claim representative should ordinarily deal with a duly accredited officer. If the officers, however, desire to have the corporation represented by a subordinate employee or other person with technical qualifications, the claim representative should see that the corporation ratifies the adjustment by having one of its officers execute the proof of loss. The minute book of the corporation will show the names of the officers. When the claim representative reports on the adjustment of any important loss sustained by a corporation, the report should give the names of the principal officers.

BAILORS UNDER TRUST AND COMMISSION CLAUSE

As the courts have held that bailors of the property insured in the name of a bailee may adopt the bailee's insurance in event of loss, there are occasions when the claim representative will deal with individual bailors, instead of with the bailee whose name appears in the policy. In such cases, the names of the bailors must appear in the report; and if they do not execute the proof of loss, their names should appear in the proof executed by the bailee. Another practice is for the bailee to present claim on behalf of the bailor; and if several bailors are interested, the several claims are summarized in a single proof under each policy. When payment is made to the bailee on behalf of bailors, it is common practice to secure a hold-harmless agreement from the bailee for the amount of payment.

FOR ACCOUNT OF WHOM IT MAY CONCERN

In some policies the name of the insured is followed by the words, "for account of whom it may concern." In such cases, the claim representative should make careful inquiry into the possible rights of others than the named insured to collect the loss and should, in any case that threatens to produce controversy, take affidavits from all persons claiming a right to proceeds of the insurance. If, at the time of loss, the property involved is found to belong to some person other than the named insured, the claim representative should either secure a written agreement from the owner that the loss shall be adjusted with and payable to the named insured, or the owner should execute the proof. Generally, however, the policy will provide that any loss shall be adjusted with and payable to a designated person, and the situation will present no difficulties.

RECEIVERS AND TRUSTEES IN BANKRUPTCY; GUARDIANS

A receiver in bankruptcy is a custodian of the bankrupt's property of all kinds. A loss remaining unadjusted at the time the insured is declared bankrupt or a loss occurring during the period of receivership may have to be adjusted with the receiver. In either case, the claim representative should have the proof of loss executed by the receiver and should secure a copy of any court order empowering the receiver to adjust, and also a certified copy of the receiver's certificate of appointment. Both of these should be forwarded to the insurer with other final papers.

A trustee in bankruptcy is an officer elected by the creditors, who takes title to the estate of the bankrupt. If a loss is unadjusted at the time that a trustee in bankruptcy takes charge, the loss must be adjusted with the trustee. On completing such an adjustment, the claim representative should secure a certified copy of the trustee's certificate of appointment and should forward this copy to the insurer with other final papers.

If it becomes necessary to adjust a loss with a guardian of an insured, a certificate of the guardian's appointment should accompany final papers, and the reason for the guardian's appointment should be covered in the report to the insurer.

UNCONDITIONAL AND SOLE OWNERSHIP

The interest of unconditional and sole ownership is equal in its extent to the value of the property.

Evidence of ownership of real property is generally documentary, as the owner will hold a deed or can point to a deed or a will on record giving title to the property. Occasionally an owner of real property has inherited it from a person who died intestate and will, therefore, have no documentary evidence of ownership, or perhaps only such evidence as tax receipts.

When dealing with a case of doubtful ownership of real property, the claim representative asks the insured to produce a deed, point to a will, or produce witnesses who can testify to his or her inheritance from an intestate person. In some cases, it may be advisable to have a title search made by a lawyer or an abstract company.

Evidence of ownership of personal property may be an invoice, a bill of sale, a will, or a receipted contract of purchase. Much personal property, however, is acquired by purchase or as a gift without any written evidence of the transaction. Possession and the possessor's assertion of ownership are, at times, the only evidence available.

PART OWNERS

The owner of an undivided half, third, quarter, or other fractional part of property has an insurable interest in the property to the extent of the fraction of its value. Evidence of fractional ownership is similar to evidence of sole ownership, and in doubtful cases the claim representative proceeds as when investigating doubtful cases of sole ownership.

LIFE TENANT AND REMAINDERMAN

Both the life tenant and the remainderman have insurable interests in property. As the relation of life tenant and remainderman is created only by a will, deed, or lease, the evidence concerning the respective interests is always documentary. Formerly, the courts were rather consistent in holding that the life tenant's interest was fixed by his or her life expectancy; if the expectancy were ten years, according to a mortality table, the interest was the expected useful value of the property for ten years. Of late, however, the courts have taken a more liberal view and are inclined to look at the need for the property and what it will cost to put it in shape that will satisfy that need. There is, therefore, no method that can be used in all cases for measuring the interest of a life tenant. Fortunately, most property in which such interests exist is covered by policies insuring both interests. Under such policies, there is no problem of interest to be determined.

VENDOR AND VENDEE

Both vendor and vendee may have separate insurable interests in either real or personal property. Their interests arise because of a contract of sale that has not been completely carried out. The vendor's interest ends when the contract has been fulfilled, and thereupon the vendee becomes the unconditinal owner.

In the case of real property, the contract of sale may be a bond for title, a lease sale contract, or a contract for title.

In the case of personal property the unfulfilled contract will be, legally considered, a contract of conditional sale.

The vendee usually makes a partial payment when the contract is made and is then given possession of the property by the vendor, who retains the legal title until paid in full. The prevalent method of installment buying has been extended to various kinds of machines, fixtures, and appliances, the seller holding title until the purchaser has completed payment, but meanwhile giving the purchaser possession and use of the article.

Practically all vendor-vendee contracts are in writing and may be examined by the claim representative if necessary.

Interest of Vendor

When the vendor has parted with possession and has agreed to deliver title upon receiving a stipulated price, insurable interest in the property is limited to the unpaid part of the consideration due. If property insured solely for the benefit of the vendor is destroyed, the claim representative must determine the amount due the vendor at the date of loss and compare this with the cash value of the property at the time of loss. If this amount is less than the cash value, the vendor is entitled to collect it in full, but if it is greater, the vendor may collect only the cash value. *Recovery in the latter case is limited by the policy condition that insurance is only to the extent of cash value.*

Interest of Vendee

It has been held in many states that a vendee in possession of either real or personal property, under an executory contract of sale and exercising acts of ownership, has an insurable interest in the property equivalent to the cash value, unless the contract provides that the vendor shall reinstate in case of damage by fire or other peril, a provision seldom found.

LESSOR AND LESSEE

The relation of lessor and lessee is created by the act of leasing real estate. If the lessee builds on the property or improves a structure already built, both lessor and lessee may thereafter have insurable interests in the building or the improvements. The insurable interest of the owner, or lessor, is seldom affected by the act of leasing. The insurable interest of the lessee is entirely dependent upon the terms of the lease, as any improvements made to real estate become the absolute property of the lessor, unless the lease specifically provides to the contrary. The lease itself is documentary evidence of the interests of lessor and lessee.

Interest of Lessor

Ordinarily, a lessor is an owner, and his or her interest is that of ownership. In some instances, however, a lessee sublets and by doing so becomes a lessor. The interest, in such a case, will be determined by the terms of the lease. A requirement in a lease that the lessee shall restore the property in case of damage or destruction by fire or other peril does not abrogate the lessor's interest. In theory, the lessor could compel the lessee to make the restoration. In fact, the lessee might be insolvent and could not therefore be made to fulfill the requirement.

Interest of Lessee

A lessee has an insurable interest in improvements and betterments made to the property covered, and if the lease requires that the property be restored in case of destruction or damage, he or she has an insurable interest in the property itself. The courts have generally held that the value of a lessee's interest due to having made improvements and betterments to a building is measured by the cost of the improvements less a proportionate reduction for the expired time of the lease.

OTHER INTERESTS

Builders and contractors have an insurable interest in buildings into which their skill, labor, and materials have gone. Lien holders have an insurable interest in property subject to the lien. Broadly speaking, any person who may suffer a present or future financial loss if the property is destroyed or damaged has an insurable interest in it.

INTERESTS JOINTLY PROTECTED

When two or more insurable interests exist in the same property, the holders often arrange to have them jointly protected by a single policy or set of policies. Joint protection can be accomplished by joining the names of the holders of the interests in the insuring clause of a policy, or by naming one or more as the insured and attaching to the policy a mortgagee or loss payable clause naming the other or others as payee or payees. When all interests are jointly protected, the measure of loss is the value of the property or the damage it has suffered, whichever value is less.

QUESTIONS AND PROBLEMS

1. a. Why is it important for the claim representative to establish insurable interest, or interests, when investigating a claim made under a policy?

b. Name ten different types of entities or individuals who may have an insurable interest under property insurance policies.

2. In your own words, give a definition of *insurable interest*.

3. a. Discuss the insurable interest of the owner of a ladies' ready-to-wear shop in *layaway merchandise*, i.e., merchandise on which the customer has put a deposit and which is to be held until paid for and delivered.

b. Two women each put up $30,000 to buy a building on speculation. Each has an undivided half interest in the property. One of the owners takes out a policy of insurance covering fire and extended coverage for $40,000, the value of the building, in her name only. Shortly thereafter a fire causes damage of $30,000. What is the insurer's liability to the policyholder? Explain your answer. Assume the damage to be $15,000; how would you answer the question?

4. A parent deeds a dwelling to a son and daughter-in-law as a gift. The couple is indigent and neglectful and carry no insurance. The parent, recognizing the hazard of fire possibly due to carelessness, decides to take out insurance. A policy is issued in the name of the parent who wants to be certain that any payment for a loss will be used to restore the property. If a fire damages or destroys the dwelling, what is the liability of the insurer?

5. a. What determines the insurable interest of a mortgagee?

b. In the absence of a lease requirement to replace improvements and betterments made by the lessee, what generally is the measure of the lessee's insurable interest?

Mortgagees and Other Payees

The claim representative encounters four kinds of payees: (1) the payee named or designated in the policy, (2) the person who has an equitable lien on the proceeds of the policy, (3) the assignee of the claim, and (4) the garnishee or judgment creditor. When adjusting losses in which payees are involved, the claim representative is expected to gather and furnish to the insurer whatever information may be necessary to determine to what persons and in what amounts payment should be made. With proper information in hand, the insurer will know what receipts, releases, or other documents should be executed to discharge it from further liability.

If the wrong person should be paid or the insurer should fail to pay a person who is entitled to some part of the proceeds of the policy, the insurer may later be called upon to make a second payment.

PAYEE NAMED OR DESIGNATED IN POLICY

Payees named or designated in policies by their interest, or otherwise, are generally (1) mortgagees of real estate or (2) persons or institutions to whom the insured owner of personal property owes money.

CLAUSES NAMING OR DESIGNATING PAYEES

Clauses naming or designating payees are of two general kinds: (1) *mortgagee* and (2) *loss payable*. Under a mortgagee clause, the

payee is accorded certain rights to independent treatment and payment. Under a simple loss payable clause, the payee is entitled to payment only to the extent that the insurer is liable to the insured, except in those states which by statute or the printed conditions of the standard policy excuse the mortgagee from acts or omissions of the mortgagor, including increase of hazard not known to the mortgagee.

PRINTED CONDITIONS RELATIVE TO MORTGAGEES

The New York Standard Fire Policy, 1943 edition, lines 68 to 85, provides under the heading Mortgagee Interests and Obligations:

> If loss hereunder is made payable, in whole or in part, to a designated mortgagee not named herein as the insured, such interest in this policy may be cancelled by giving to such mortgagee a ten days' written notice of cancellation.
>
> If the insured fails to render proof of loss such mortgagee, upon notice, shall render proof of loss in the form herein specified within sixty (60) days thereafter and shall be subject to the provisions hereof relating to appraisal and time of payment and of bringing suit. If this Company shall claim that no liability existed as to the mortgagor or owner, it shall, to the extent of the payment of loss to the mortgagee, be subrogated to all the mortgagee's rights of recovery, but without impairing mortgagee's

right to sue; or it may pay off the mortgage debt and require an assignment thereof and of the mortgage. Other provisions relating to the interests and obligations of such mortgagee may be added hereto by agreement in writing.

Statutory Rights of Mortgagees

In many states the mortgagee's rights under the policy are set forth in greater detail in a special statute. The claim representative should become familiar with the statutes.

MORTGAGEE CLAUSE

The New York standard mortgagee clause used in connection with first mortgage interests in real estate reads:

Loss, or damage, if any, under this policy, shall be payable to . . . . as . . . .
. . . . . . mortgagee (or trustee) as interest may appear, and this insurance, as to the interest of the mortgagee (or trustee) only therein shall not be invalidated by any act or neglect of the mortgagor or owner of the within described property, nor by any foreclosure or other proceedings or notice of sale relating to the property, nor by any change in the title or ownership of the property, nor by the occupation of the premises for purpose more hazardous than are permitted by this policy; PROVIDED, that in case the mortgagor or owner shall neglect to pay any premium due under this policy, the mortgagee (or trustee) shall on demand pay the same.

PROVIDED, also, that the mortgagee (or trustee) shall notify this Company of any change of ownership or occupancy or increase of hazard which shall come to the knowledge of said mortgagee (or trustee) and unless permitted by this policy, it shall be noted thereon and the mortgagee (or trustee) shall, on demand, pay the premium for such increased hazard for the term of the use thereof; otherwise this policy shall be null and void.

This Company reserves the right to cancel this policy at any time as provided by its terms, but in such case this policy shall continue in force for the benefit only of the mortgagee (or trustee) for ten days after notice to the mortgagee (or trustee) of such cancellation and shall then cease, and this Company shall have the right, on like notice, to cancel this agreement.

Whenever this Company shall pay the mortgagee (or trustee) any sum for loss or damage under this policy and shall claim that, as to the mortgagor or owner, no liability therefor existed, this Company shall, to the extent of such payment, be thereupon legally subrogated to all the rights of the party to whom such payment shall be made, under all securities held as collateral to the mortgage debt, or may at its option pay to the mortgagee (or trustee) the whole principal due or to grow due on the mortgage with interest, and shall thereupon receive a full assignment and transfer of the mortgage and of all such other securities; but no subrogation shall impair the right of the mortgagee (or trustee) to recover the full amount of . . . . claim.

Similar clauses are used in other states.

The full-contribution clause is the same as the New York standard mortgagee clause except for the addition of the following section:

In case of any other insurance upon the within-described property, this Company shall not be liable under this policy for a greater proportion of any loss or damage sustained than the sum hereby insured bears to the whole amount of insurance on said property, issued to or held by any party or parties having an insurable interest therein, whether as owner, mortgagee or otherwise.

Under this clause the loss is apportioned on a pro rata basis to the mortgagee's policy as a matter of contract right.

LOSS PAYABLE CLAUSE

Loss payable clauses generally read substantially as follows:

Loss, if any, under this policy, shall be payable to John or Mary Doe, as interest may appear.

MORTGAGOR AND MORTGAGEE

The mortgagee of real estate usually protects the loan by requiring the mortgagor owner to cover the property with policies containing mortgagee clauses making loss, if any, payable to the mortgagee. In a few states no mortgagee clause is necessary because of the policy conditions and a statute.

The mortgagee clauses create separate contracts with mortgagees. There is, therefore, under any policy containing the same conditions concerning mortgages, a contract with the insured and a separate contract with the mortgagee. In most losses the two contracts will operate alike; in a few, they will operate differently.

PROCEDURE WHEN LOSSES ARE PAYABLE TO MORTGAGEE

When loss occurs under a policy and is payable to a mortgagee, the ordinary procedure of adjustment will be followed if the policy is valid as to the insured, but quite a different one if it is void as to the insured but valid as to the mortgagee. In the first instance, the designation of the mortgagee as payee will require little more of the claim representative than a properly prepared proof of loss. In doing so he or she should note the name of the mortgagee, the amount remaining unpaid on the mortgage, and the date the mortgage is due.

When the policy is valid as to the mortgagee but void as to the insured, the mortgagee may, in rare cases, be well secured by the remaining value of the property and may elect to make no claim whatsoever, knowing that should this be done it would compel an assignment to the insurer of an interest in the mortgage equal to the amount collected. Ordinarily, however, the mortgagee demands payment. Then the claim representative may recommend one of two methods of adjustment: (1) to pay the actual damage and take an assignment or (2) to purchase the mortgage. If the first method is to be used, the amount of loss is determined by agreement or appraisal, the mortgagee taking the place of the insured; if the second, the amount of the mortgage debt is ascertained and becomes the basis of the settlement. The mortgagee's assignment of an interest in the mortgage is subordinate to the

eventual collection of the full debt due. When, however, the full amount of the mortgage debt is to be paid by the insurer and the mortgage is to be purchased, the original note or notes, or other papers recording the debt and any payments thereon, should be examined, and the amount due thus ascertained. Any charges, such as taxes or insurance paid by the mortgagee, should be checked for correctness. Payment and assignment are usually left to the insurer's direction and may be made through an attorney who will arrange for foreclosure, if necessary. The claim representative should not undertake to handle assignments unless specifically directed to do so, as insurers generally prefer to have this done by attorneys.

When loss is made payable to several mortgagees under the same policy, treating with the mortgagees separately may become necessary. Their technical rights in such a case are determined by the order of their priority, the first mortgagee being entitled to satisfaction before the second can collect. When several mortgagees hold separate policies, however, each looks to his or her own policy for the full amount of the loss, though in practice pro rata payments are often accepted in partial losses.

While the mortgagee clause gives the insurer the right to treat independently with the mortgagee when it claims that no liability exists concerning the insured, it may be necessary for the insurer to prove its claim when it initiates litigation to foreclose on a mortgage that it has taken over.

As a rule, the claim representative has no contact with the mortgagee. The loss is adjusted, and the insurer's check or draft is drawn to the joint order of the insured and the mortgagee. In exceptional cases, however, direct contact with the mortgagee is necessary (1) when there is a dispute over the cancellation of the policy before the loss, (2) when the mortgagee objects to the adjustment made by the insured, (3) when the mortgagee refuses to endorse a check or draft payable jointly to the insured and the mortgagee, (4) when the claim representative finds evidence indicating that there is no liability to the insured, (5) when the insured fails to render proof of loss, and (6) when the mortgage debt has been paid off but the policy has not been endorsed to show that losses are no longer payable to the mortgagee.

Dispute Over Cancellation

The mortgagee clause provides, as do lines 68 to 73 of the New York Standard Policy, that ten days' written notice of cancellation must be given to any mortgagee named in the policy as a payee.

Under this requirement the claim representative who encounters a case of disputed cancellation must gather evidence not only concerning cancellation so far as the insured is concerned, but also so far as the mortgagee is concerned.[1]

When Mortgagee Objects to Adjustment

It is the general opinion of claim personnel that, when the claim representative and the insured agree upon the amount of loss and when proof of loss is filed within the time stipulated in the policy, the mortgagee is bound by the adjustment unless there was fraud on the part of the insured or the claim representative, or there was collusion or mutual mistake between them, and as a result, the mortgagee's rights are prejudicially affected.

When Mortgagee Refuses to Accept Joint Payment

In some instances there will be no disagreement about the amount that the insurer should pay, but the mortgagee will refuse to accept a check or draft drawn jointly and will demand independent payment. In such an instance, the claim representative must investigate the situation and obtain evidence that will show how much the mortgagee is entitled to receive and how much the insured is entitled to receive. It is the general rule that a mortgagee is entitled to collect any money to be paid under a policy as payee unless the amount to be paid exceeds the amount of the

mortgage debt, in which case the mortgagee is entitled to the amount of the debt and the insured is entitled to collect the remainder. The amount that the mortgagee may legally claim is, therefore, the lowest of the following: (1) the amount of loss or damage to the property, (2) the amount of the mortgage debt at the date of the loss, (3) the limit of liability under a policy containing an average, coinsurance, or contribution clause.

In some losses, generally those involving mortgages under which payments are in default or mortgages which the mortgagee is anxious to have paid off, acrimonious conflict arises between the insured and the mortgagee, each being anxious to get possession of the money. The insured will want to use it to pay for the repairs necessary to make the property useful. The mortgagee will want to collect against the debt the insured owes. In such losses the claim representative must establish the exact amount of the mortgage debt, and try to get the insured and the mortgagee to agree on a figure. In extreme cases, examination of the mortgage and canceled checks or receipts held by the insured may be necessary.

Liability to Mortgagee Only

When the claim representative finds evidence indicating that the insurer is liable to the mortgagee but not to the insured, he or she must promptly inform the insurer, who may elect to pay the mortgagee the amount of the damage to the property or the limit of liability under the policy and have executed articles of subrogation and assignment,[2] or it may elect to pay the mortgagee the full amount of the mortgage debt and take an assignment of the mortgage.

Liability to Mortgagee Greater Than to Insured

In occasional losses property will be covered by policies, some payable to the mortgagee and others not. In such losses the mortgagee may be able to enforce payment of the full amount of the loss under the mortgagee's

[1]See Cancellation, pp. 95–97.

[2]See Appendix U.

policy or policies. But the existence of other insurance, not payable to the mortgagee, may make the liability to the insured under the policies payable to the mortgagee less than the liability to the mortgagee. The difference will be due to the fact that the liability to the insured under each policy will be its pro rata share of the loss, while the insurers under the policies payable to the mortgagee, if the mortgagee clauses do not contain a contribution provision (or, if they do, are large enough to comply with contribution requirements), may owe the mortgagee the full amount of the loss. But though they may owe the full amount of the loss, they stipulate in the mortgagee clause that if they pay him

> ... any sum for loss or damage ... and shall claim that, as to the mortgagor or owner, no liability therefor exists, this Company shall, to the extent of such payment, be thereupon legally subrogated to all rights of the party to whom such payment shall be made under all securities held as collateral to the mortgage debt....

When Insured Fails to File Proof of Loss

When the insured does not press claim and fails to file proof of loss within the time stipulated in the policy, the claim representative should notify the mortgagee and ask whether he or she will negotiate an adjustment and render proof. Only in rare instances does the claim representative find it necessary to do this.

In some states, statutes require the insurer to make written demand on the insured to render proof of loss if it intends to declare the claim forfeited because proof is not rendered within the stipulated period after date of loss. In most states, the claim representative should serve written notice on the insured to render proof of loss if a mortgagee is named in the policy and the insured is dilatory in presenting claim following a serious loss.

When Mortgage Has Been Paid Off

Occasionally a mortgage is paid off, and the insured fails to take possession of the policy and have it endorsed to show that it is no longer payable to the mortgagee. A loss occurs, and the failure comes to light.

In many cases the insurer will endorse the policy after the loss, or have the claim representative do so, and with the endorsement on record and a report from the claim representative stating that the mortgage has been satisfied, pay the loss to the insured. But the best procedure in such a situation is for the claim representative to get a clearly worded letter or signed statement from the mortgagee setting forth the mortgagee's declaration that the mortgage has been satisfied.

Other Named Payees

Sellers of personal property on the installment payment plan often require the purchaser to take out insurance in his or her own name and include in the policy or policies a clause making loss, if any, payable to the seller.

Banks, finance companies, and others who lend money to producers or traders in similar fashion require the owner or custodian to cover the merchandise by policies making loss, if any, payable to the lender. The clause used in either situation will generally be worded substantially as follows:

> Loss, if any, under this policy shall be payable to John or Mary Doe, as interest may appear.

Under such a clause the payee does not have a separate contract with the insurer. Any right is limited to the collection of any amount payable under the policy to the insured, not in excess of the amount that the insured owes.

Sometimes, as with mortgagees, disputes arise between the insured and the payee, making it necessary to establish the exact amount of the payee's interest.

Likewise, in some instances the debt to the payee has been paid and the loss-payable clause has not been eliminated from the policy. Procedure in such instances should be the same as that outlined in the preceding section dealing with mortgages that have been paid off.

Payees Designated But Not Named

In order to protect the interests of bankers or others who advance money to the buyers of commodities and whose transactions are too numerous to be followed through and covered by specific policies with loss-payable clauses naming the bank or person that advanced the money, a certain form of loss-payable clause is used in policies covering some commodities, notably cotton and wheat. The following is an example:

> Payments or advances, in case of loss or damage to cotton, shall be made to banks or other persons having made advances against such cotton as their interests may appear, or, at the option of this Company, to such banks or other persons and the Insured jointly, provided this Company receives written notice of such interest within ten days after such loss or damage.

When adjusting a loss under policies containing such a clause, the claim representative should determine by investigation what banks or persons have advanced money against the commodity and what amount each has advanced. Investigation generally begins with asking the insured for the information. No final action should be taken until the ten days after loss have gone by.

Generally losses under policies containing this kind of loss-payable clause occur in warehouse or grain elevators that issue warehouse receipts to the owner against units or quantities of property as these are received. The owner sells to the buyer who takes over the warehouse receipt. The buyer then deposits the receipt with the bank as collateral for a loan with which to buy more of the commodity. A loss occurs in the warehouse. The buyer's funds invested may be only 20 percent of the value of the commodity involved. The banks or others who have advanced money with which to finance the business may be interested to the extent of 80 percent.

When dealing with a commodity loss where several banks have made loans to a buyer, the claim representative can often arrange for one bank to take over from the others all warehouse receipts and agree to pay each bank the value of the commodity covered by the receipts taken over. The bank that takes over the receipts from the others then receives the insurer's check or draft payable to the insured and itself, gives the insurer a guaranty or hold-harmless agreement,[3] and surrenders the warehouse or elevator receipts to the insurer.

HOLDER OF EQUITABLE LIEN

Following a loss, a person or an institution not named in the policy may demand payment from the insurer because of an interest in the property or a debt due from the insured. In this case it is important to obtain the facts and report them to the insurer.

While the law regards an insurance policy as a personal contract payable in case of loss only to the insured or the payee named in it, the courts apply the principle of the equitable lien to insurance policies as they do to other kinds of contracts and will, in some situations, decree payment to a third party.

If the owner of property who has promised a creditor to cover it by insurance for the creditor's benefit is found after a loss to hold a policy that does not name the creditor as a payee, the creditor may present this situation in an equity action, and the court will award the insurance payment. The insurer must then pay according to the amount of the lien.

The Supreme Court of the United States, in a decision rendered in 1879, which has been cited by many state courts as a leading authority, said:

> It is undoubtedly the general rule that a mortgagee has no right to the benefit of a policy taken by the mortgagor, unless it is assigned to him. . . . But it is settled by many decisions in this country that if the mortgagor is bound by covenant or otherwise to insure the mortgaged premises for the better security of the mortgagee, the latter will have an equitable lien upon the money due on a policy taken out by the mortgagor to the extent of the mortgagee's interest in the property destroyed.[4]

[3]See Appendix G.
[4]*Wheeler v. Ins. Co.*, S.C.U.S. (1879), 101 U.S. 439.

Equitable liens most often arise in connection with mortgagee creditors. They are, however, encountered in connection with other creditors, as for example, bankers who have lent money to merchants and have required them to promise to carry insurance to protect the loans.

The holder of an equitable lien is entitled to payment not exceeding the value of the interest. In reporting on a possible equitable lien, the claim representative must, therefore, do as he or she should in disputed mortgagee cases, that is, determine the amount claimed by the party holding the lien and try to get the insured to agree to the amount or point out wherein it is wrong. If possible the claim representative should negotiate an agreement under which a check or draft payable jointly to the insured and the lienholder will be accepted and endorsed by both. But, because an insistent lienholder may legally demand independent payment, it is essential that the claim representative put into the hands of the insurer information that will enable it to discharge its obligations to both the insured and the lienholder if independent payment is insisted upon. And because an insurer that has paid a loss is not immune from suit by a third party who may claim that the insurer had notice of a lien but ignored it and paid the loss to the insured, the claim representative should be diligent in following up any indication of third-party interest and in reporting it accurately to the insurer.

ASSIGNEES

If the insured assigns the claim after a loss, the assignee may take control of the adjustment, although he or she may not substitute themselves if the insurer demands that the insured submit to examination under oath. Ordinarily, assignments of all or part of the claim are not made until after adjustment has been completed and the proof has been executed by the insured. In dealing with an assignee whose assignment became effective before adjustment, the claim representative should see that the proof of loss is executed by the insured and that the assignee joins in the execution. The original assignment, or a

certified copy, should accompany the final papers, and the reason for the assignment should be stated in the report.

If the insured assigns a specific sum which is less than the amount due under the adjustment, the claim representative is under no necessity of dealing with the assignee but should transmit the original assignment, or a copy, to the insurer, stating the reasons for the assignment in the report. The insurer is liable to such an assignee.

GARNISHEES OR JUDGMENT CREDITORS

Between the time loss occurs and payment is made, the insured, the agent, or the claim representative may be served with a writ of garnishment or an attachment under which a person who is suing the insured, or who holds a judgment, is seeking to satisfy the claim out of the proceeds of the insurance. The service of such a writ should not be allowed to halt or delay adjustment, but prompt information should be given the insurer, who may elect to employ an attorney to answer or, in some cases, to pay into the court money that may be due the insured.

Sometimes it is possible to negotiate an agreement between the insured and the attorney representing the creditor, under which the writ will be dismissed when the insurer delivers to the attorney a check or draft for the full amount of the loss, payable to the insured, the creditor, and the creditor's attorney jointly.

If two or more writs are issued, it is important that the date and time of the service of each be communicated to the insurer.

ESTATES

Sometimes policies designate the insured as "Estate of . . . ." In other situations the insured has died and the loss proceeds will be payable to the estate. Under these conditions the claim representative obtains from the executor, or the person legally designated to act for the estate, a copy of the certificate from the Surrogate's Court attesting that the person with whom the claim representative is dealing is empowered to act.

QUESTIONS AND PROBLEMS

1. The First Bank holds a mortgage on a dwelling. The policy contains the New York standard mortgagee clause (similar clauses are used in othe states). The insured, a do-it-yourselfer, works out an adjustment of a fire loss with the insurer's claim representative which will enable the insured to do most of the work nights and weekends. The amount of the adjusted loss is quite a bit less than it would be if based on a reliable general contractor's estimate. The mortgagee, hearing of the arrangement prior to proof of loss being executed, files with the insurer a written objection to the amount of the settlement. What are the mortgagee's rights in this situation:

    a. If the amount of the loss as adjusted with the insured is less than the mortgage debt?

    b. If the amount of the loss as adjusted with the insured exceeds the mortgage debt?

    c. If proof of loss had been signed and the insurer had issued a draft in payment including the name of the mortgagee?

2. When the insurer is liable solely to the mortgagee, what options in payment are available to the insurer?

3. A vendor of refrigerated showcases sells such appliances to a butcher shop and requires the vendee to take out insurance with a loss payable clause naming the vendor. Under a loss payable clause there is no separate contract as in a mortgagee clause, and the vendor's interest is limited to the amount owed by the insured at the time of loss.

The appliances in the above situation are three years old at the time of loss. The amount owed is $3,000. The actual cash value of the appliance is $2,800 at the time of loss. What will be the insurer's liability under the policy?

4. A public adjuster, representing an insured, is under written contract stipulating the assignment of any proceeds to the extent of the fee basis in the contract, which is signed by the insured, and a copy is filed with the insurer.

The loss is adjusted and proof of loss is forwarded with closing papers to the insurer. Payment in full is forwarded to the insured. What are the rights of the public adjuster?

5. The owner of a building obtains a mortgage with the Fair Bank. Under the mortgage contract the mortgagor is bound to insure the property to provide better security for the mortgagee. A policy of insurance is taken out but the mortgagee is not named in the policy. A serious loss occurs. What are the rights of the mortgagee?

6. Shortly after occurrence of a loss and prior to payment, the insurer is served with a writ of attachment under which a person holds a judgment and is seeking to satisfy the claim out of the insurance proceeds. In general how should the insurer handle this situation?

Duties of the Insured After Loss

Policies covering property state the specific duties of an insured after a loss. While all policies are not alike in their requirements, they generally provide that the insured will do the following:

1. Notify the insurer promptly or as soon as practicable.
2. Minimize the loss by protecting the property against further damage or trying to recover it.
3. File a *proof of loss* with the insurer within a specified time, along with evidence to support the amount claimed, the insured's interest in the property and the interest of any others, other insurance, if any, and any encumbrances on the property.
4. If requested, furnish special evidence to the insurer.
5. Produce books of account and other records for examination and permit extracts and copies to be made.
6. Submit to examination under oath (except in Massachusetts and Minnesota).

In case of disagreement as to value and loss between the insured and insurer, either may demand an appraisal as provided for in the policy.

In addition, most policies covering property stipulate that the insurer has the option of paying the insured the agreed value and taking the property, or of repairing or replacing it. Generally, policies prohibit the abandonment of property to the insurer.

These duties and requirements of the insured are discussed in the following pages. Claim representatives should be thoroughly familiar with the particular policy provisions regarding the requirements of the insured after loss.

NOTICE TO INSURER

In the ordinary course of business the insured telephones or writes the insurer's local office, agent, or broker, or a public adjuster who in turn gives notice to the insurer (see Notice of Loss form, Appendix H). Failure to notify the insurer will, in some states, bar recovery although the courts have been prone to hold that the provision requiring notice will be waived if the company or agent has learned of the loss and taken steps for its investigation. The courts also tend to hold that if notice is given within a *reasonable* time, the policy requirement has been fully complied with.

Frequently when notice is delayed, the insured will comment on the reason at the time of reporting the occurrence. There are times, however, when notice of loss is given but no mention of the date, and the claim representative is unaware of the delayed notice until investigating the loss. When this happens, an explanation should be requested. If the insurer's interests have been adversely affected, the claim representative should take the matter up with the person to whom such questions are normally reported for instructions.

MINIMIZING THE LOSS

The insured's duty to do everything reasonable to minimize the loss is set forth in *standard fire policies*, to which most forms covering property are attached, in a simple statement that he or she shall "protect the property from further damage." The New York Standard Fire Policy provides in case of loss:

The insured shall . . . protect the property from further damage, forthwith separate the damaged and undamaged personal property, put it in the best possible order . . . .

Newer, easy-to-read policies, such as the ISO's Homeowners 76 Program (HO-Ed. 7-1-75) and the Businessowners Program (MLB-700 Ed. 11-1-75), are not required in many states to have attached the standard fire (statutory) policy. These policies have the insured's duties after a loss built into them. The HO 76 (1975) policies state:

2(b) protect the property from further damage, make reasonable and necessary repairs required to protect the property, and keep an accurate record of repair expenditures.

The Businessowners (1975) policies state:

B(1) protect the building and personal property from further damage, make reasonable temporary repairs required to protect the property, and keep an accurate record of repair expenditures.

Nothing is said with regard to separating the damaged from the undamaged property or putting it in the best possible order—a requirement in the New York Standard Fire Policy.

The *Protection of Property* provision in the MOP and Inland Marine policies states:

In case of loss, it shall be lawful and necessary for the Insured, his or their factors, servants and assigns, to sue, labor, and travel for, in and about the defense, safeguard and recovery of the property insured hereunder, or any part

thereof, without prejudice to this insurance, nor shall the acts of the insured or the Company, in recovering, saving and preserving the property insured in case of loss be considered a waiver or an acceptance of abandonment. The expenses so incurred shall be borne by the Insured and the Company proportionately to the extent of their respective interests.

Methods for Minimizing Loss

The method the insured should take to protect the property from further damage after a loss is dependent on the extent of damage and the nature of the occupancy and contents. Generally, one or more of the measures listed below will be required for protection against the following:

1. The elements and trespassers.
   a. Close breaks or openings in walls and roof.
   b. Board up or replace windows and doors.
   c. Drain plumbing, heating pipes, and fixtures.
   d. Provide watchman service; restore alarms.
2. Moisture and dampness.
   a. Air and ventilate.
   b. Mop floors, scatter sawdust, pump out cellars and pits.
   c. Shut off water when pipes are broken.
   d. Clean and oil metal machinery; dry off furniture and fixtures.
   e. Move contents to better location.
3. Unsafe conditions.
   a. Take down or brace hazardous masonry walls and chimneys.
   b. Remove debris or other contents from weakened floors.
   c. Shore up weak floors and roofs.
   d. Shut off gas and electrical service.
   e. Remove dangerous contents.

In many situations protection against further damage is aided by arranging to have electric lighting or power restored promptly on a temporary or permanent basis.

Specific methods that the insured shall employ to minimize loss are described in later chapters discussing the several kinds of property and risks that ordinarily come before the claim representative, who is expected to enforce the requirement of the policy that the insured minimize loss. Protective measures are usually carried out by the insured, but there are times when the adjuster will find it advantageous to direct or even take over the work.

While the insured is not entitled to collect for further damage that occurs because of failure to protect the property, it is very difficult for the claim representative to exclude any such damage from consideration in the final settlement. He or she should, therefore, endeavor to prevent further damage, so that at least one possibility of controversy will be eliminated from adjustment negotiations.

PROOF OF LOSS

The words *proof of loss* have two meanings: (1) the evidence offered by the insured in support and proof of the amount being claimed, and (2) the statement, signed and sworn to (when swearing to is required) by the insured, setting forth what he or she is required to state according to the policy or according to the blank form furnished by the insurer. (See Appendix C.)

According to the first meaning, the insured makes proof that entitles him or her to collect by tendering to the claim representative the policy covering the property, by exhibiting the remains of the property, by offering testimony or other evidence of loss or damage, by testimony or by fire department or police records indicating when the loss occurred, by testimony, deed, or bill of sale showing interest, and by testimony or documentary or physical evidence bearing on the amount of loss.

According to the second meaning, the insured makes proof when he or she completes, executes, and files with the insurer the blank form used by the insurer and bearing the imprint "proof of loss."

Some policies require the insured to furnish "satisfactory proof of loss," some to furnish "affirmative proof of loss," and others to "file a proof of loss" or "furnish the insurer with a satisfactory proof of loss and interest upon forms to be provided by the insurer."

Time for Filing

Most policies require that proof of loss be filed within a stipulated time following date of loss, usually 30, 60, or 90 days. A few policies provide that unless proof is rendered within the stipulated time, any claim under the policy shall be invalidated.

Many states have statutes affecting the provision in the policy for filing proof of loss. Several require the insurer to furnish the insured with proper blanks upon which to make proof. In some of those states the insurer must notify the insured in writing that proof of loss is required and must furnish the forms. In New York and New Jersey the insured then has 60 days to complete and file the proofs; in others, 90 days.

The courts in some states have held that failure to file proof within the time stipulated in the policy is not a bar to recovery but that the insured may not commence suit until proof has been filed or rendered and the required time, usually 60 days, has passed.

Several states provide that a penalty be assessed the insurer for failure to pay a loss within the time specified by the policy or by statute. Claim representatives should become familiar with the statutes related to filing of proofs of loss in the states in which they handle claims.

Requirements Under New York Standard Fire Policy

The New York Standard Fire Policy and similar policies require that

> ... within sixty days after the loss, unless such time is extended in writing by this Company, the insured shall render to this Company a proof of loss, signed and sworn to by the insured, stating his knowledge and belief as to
> (1) the time and origin of the loss
> (2) the interest of the insured and of all others in the property
> (3) the actual cash value of each item thereof and the amount of loss thereto
> (4) all encumbrances thereon
> (5) all other contracts of insurance, whether valid or not, covering any of said property
> (6) any changes in the title, use, location, possession or exposures of said property since the issuing of this policy

(7) by whom and for what purpose any building herein described and the several parts thereof were occupied at the time of loss, and

(8) whether or not it then stood on leased ground.

As part of the proof the insured "shall furnish a copy of all the descriptions and schedules in all policies."

While the policy requires the insured to render proof of loss to the company, the claim representative will ordinarily suggest that, if the adjustment can be completed without unusual difficulty or delay, a proof will be prepared for the insured's execution when the claim has been adjusted, or it may be suggested that the insured delay making and filing the proof until the adjustment is completed. On the other hand if the claim representative wishes to commit the insured to a definite statement of facts, he or she may ask that proof of loss be filed without delay. In an extreme case, the claim representative may refuse to have any dealings with the insured and await, or call for, the filing of the proof of loss. If the insured is to be examined under oath, or an appraisal is to be held, the filing of the proof of loss may be awaited before commencing examination or appraisal in order to avoid the possibility of a later contention that rendering of the proof of loss has been waived.

Requirements Under Other Standard Fire Policies

Massachusetts' standard fire policy, Requirements in Case Loss Occurs, reads:

> In case of any loss or damage under this policy, a statement in writing, signed and sworn to by the insured, shall be forthwith rendered to the company, setting forth the value of the property described, the interest of the insured therein, all other insurance thereon in detail, the purposes for which and the persons by whom the building described, or containing the property described was used, and the time at which and manner in which the fire originated, so far as known to the insured. The company may also examine the books of account and vouchers of the insured, and make extracts from the same.

There is no provision for immediate notice being given to the insurer and actually no provision for the insured to present claim. He or she is required to submit a written, sworn statement "setting forth the value of the property *described*." Also, there is no provision for the insured to submit to examination under oath.

The Minnesota standard fire policy wording under Requirements in Case of Loss closely follows that of Massachusetts. It provides for immediate notice of loss to the insurer and also has a built-in valued policy provision with respect to buildings: ". . . in case of total loss on buildings the value of said buildings need not be stated." As in the Massachusetts policy, the insured is not required to submit to examination under oath.

Amending Proof of Loss

If a proof of loss is filed claiming a greater loss than is later agreed upon or established by appraisal, it may be amended to conform to the agreed or appraised figure. If only one policy is involved, the amendment may be a simply worded letter, signed by the insured, stating that the sound value and the loss and damage have been agreed on at stated figures. If several policies are involved, a new statement and a reapportionment should be made with a sufficient number of copies to furnish one for each policy. These copies should be dated, signed by the insured, and attached to the original proofs of loss.

Waiver of Proof of Loss

The requirement that the insured render or file a proof of loss may be waived by certain acts on the part of the insurer or its representatives. If the insurer denies liability, either orally[1] or in writing, the insured may proceed to sue at once without filing proof of loss. In some states, the requirement will be waived if the claim representative promises to prepare the proof of loss for the insured. In other states, an attempt to adjust the loss will operate to waive proof of loss, unless the

[1]*Callahan v. London & Lancashire Fire Ins. Co.*, 163 N.Y.S. 322; affirmed, 179 App. Div. 890, 165 N.Y.S.

claim representative puts the insured on notice that proof of loss will be required. The subject is a technical one, and all claim representatives should inform themselves of the customs and court decisions of the territory in which they operate.

Defects, Objections, and Rejection of Proof

The paper offered by an insured as a proof of loss may be technically correct. In that case the insurer may retain it without comment. Failure to object to a technically correct proof does *not* bar the insurer from later contesting the amount claimed or charging fraud. But the courts have generally held that when the insured tenders a technically defective proof the insurer will be held to have waived any defects unless they are promptly pointed out to the insured so that he or she may have a chance to correct them. If they are pointed out promptly and are not corrected, the insured is in the same position as if no proof whatsoever had been filed.

General objections by the insurer have been held to be insufficient; objections must be specific.[2] Specific objections, however, have been held to waive any defects not mentioned.[3] Formerly much attention was devoted to letters[4] rejecting proofs or objecting to proofs that claimed an amount with which the claim representative disagreed. The prevailing practice is toward less formal correspondence, the tendency being to point out any failure to make a required statement, or to pass unanswered a proof of loss claiming more than the claim representative's estimate, unless the claim representative decides to ask for an appraisal or an examination under oath. Ordinarily a proof of loss is nothing more than an ex parte statement of the person signing it and therefore does not establish the amount of the loss.

An objection to a proof of loss on the ground that it does not show in detail how the insured arrives at the figures of sound value and loss or damage will *not* be sustained by the courts. The insured satisfies the requirement of the policy when he or she makes, under oath, the statements that it specifies. If the loss involves personal property, detailed information is to be set out in the inventory that the insured must furnish; if it involves a building, the insurer under a New York Standard Fire Policy may demand verified plans and specifications. It is best to avoid objecting to a proof of loss unless the objection is one that can be sustained, for if the loss becomes the subject of litigation, the court will be inclined to comment unfavorably on any attempt to delay coming to the real issue of the loss by tactics that are not technically correct.

When an insurance case is tried, the insured's proof of loss, if one was made, is ordinarily part of the evidence. The insurer's attorney invariably objects to it if it is offered as evidence to prove the amount of loss, and this objection is usually sustained. The insured's attorney then, as a rule, offers it as evidence that the insured has complied with the policy requirement that a proof of loss be filed. When offered for this purpose, the court allows it to go into the record.

SPECIAL REQUIREMENTS

If required by the insurer, the insured, under the New York Standard Fire Policy, must substantiate a claim by furnishing verified plans and specifications of any building, fixtures, or machinery damaged or destroyed.[5] Also, often as may be required by the insurer, the insured must exhibit all that remains of any property described in the policy.[6]

The insured is bound to comply with special requirements only when notified to do so before the loss becomes payable.

[2]*Victoria Park Co. v. Continental Ins. Co. of New York*, 178 P. 724. *Myers v. Council Bluffs Ins. Co.*, 33 N.W. 453, 72 Iowa 176.
[3]*Paltrovitch v. Phoenix Ins. Co. of Hartford, Conn.*, 37 N.E. 639 143 N.Y. 73. *Peet v. Dakota Fire & Marine Ins. Co.*, 47 N.W. 532, 1 S.D. 462.
[4]See Appendix N.

[5]Not specified in the standard fire policies of Massachusetts, Minnesota, and Texas.
[6]Not specified in the standard fire policies of Massachusetts and Minnesota.

Verified Plans and Specifications

Verified plans and specifications may be required for buildings, machinery, or fixtures. The verification must be made by the insured, and the plans and specifications themselves must be complete. The notice that plans and specifications will be required should ordinarily be given by a letter that states specifically what property is to be covered. The requirement may be enforced regarding any property on which claim is made. Plans and specifications are of the greatest value when the claim involves property that has been totally destroyed. In such a case, the claim representative or the expert working under his or her direction will have little definite information to go on until plans and specifications are prepared. With accurate plans and specifications in hand, the replacement cost of the property can be estimated with reasonable accuracy.

Exhibition of the Remains of Property

The insured, as often as may reasonably be required, must exhibit to any person designated by the insurer all that remains of any property described in the policy. Because of this requirement, the claim representative and any experts employed have access to the property and the right to examine it, a right, however, that must be reasonably used. There are few cases in which it is necessary to make demand for compliance in writing. In such cases, the notice should name the person to whom the property is to be shown and should state the date and hour of the visit. Ordinarily, persons sent to examine property are not asked for credentials, if the insured has been told to expect them. If the insured has not been notified, the persons sent should be furnished with a letter of authority.

Examination Under Oath

As often as may reasonably be required, the insured must submit to examination under oath[7] by any person designated by the insurer

and must subscribe the transcript. In other words, he or she must give testimony under oath and sign the written record of the questions and answers. Formerly many examinations were conducted by claim representatives, but in recent years examinations have more and more been referred to lawyers because of their greater experience in questioning witnesses. When an examination is to be required, the insured should be notified in writing,[8] the notice stating a definite time and place for the examination, and also the name of the person designated to conduct it. It is advisable to state that the time and place named may be changed, if, in the opinion of the insured, they are not reasonable. The scene of the loss is the proper place for the examination.[9]

Prior to the beginning of an examination, the insured should be put under oath by a notary public, commissioner of deeds, or other person empowered by law to administer oaths. The insured's signature to the transcript of the examination should be attested to by the same kind of person, not necessarily the same one.

An examination may be required for the purpose of obtaining information or of committing the insured to known facts. The date on which property was acquired and the price paid for it are often subjects of inquiry. Its use while in possession of the insured and its condition at the time of the loss are sometimes developed by examination. The history of the insured and what he or she has to say about the origin of the fire are, in some cases, worth bringing out. If there are reasons to suspect incendiarism, the examiner may ask what the insured knows about persons who are thought to be in collusion, where they were at the time of the fire, and whether they had possession of keys to the premises. If the loss involves the examination of a set of books, the method of keeping them and the significance of unusual entries may be inquired into. In all such cases, the answers furnish leads that can later be followed, and the findings can be compared

---

[7]Not specified in the standard fire policies of Massachusetts and Minnesota.

[8]See Appendix I.
[9]*Pierce v. Globe & Rutgers Fire Ins. Co.*, 501, 182 Pac. 586.

with other evidence that will corroborate or contradict them. An insured who makes evasive or contradictory statements when not under oath will be compelled, when later put under examination and held to the record of his or her answers, to tell a consistent story or appear ridiculous or be subject to prosecution for perjury or for making false proofs of loss.

An examination may serve the purpose of committing the insured to facts establishing a breach of the policy contract or to statements and figures bearing on the amount of loss. Such testimony by the insured is highly valuable, but it is well to remember that the testimony will not prevent later changes in the story. In such a case, however, the record of the examination may be used to contradict the insured, and question the insured's credibility as a witness when forced to admit that his or her testimony on the two occasions was different.

In many cases, however, an examination is conducted to shake the purpose of an insured who is pressing a fraudulent or exorbitant claim. In these cases the solemnity of the oath, the fear of later contradiction, and the knowledge that each answer will be checked against whatever evidence is available will often work a change in the insured's attitude. The insured will be cautioned that the policy provides for avoidance in case of fraud or false swearing and if false answers are given and contradicted, the claim will be still further endangered. The insured's fear or nervousness will be heightened by questions that indicate that the person asking them knows the facts of the case. Under such circumstances the insured may be driven to admissions that will cause modification or abandonment of the claim.

It is rarely safe to commence an examination until the person who is to conduct it has become thoroughly familiar with all available information and can reasonably expect that the insured will be impressed by certain specific questions. An examination conducted at random may occasionally produce a result favorable to the insurer, *but as a general rule it is a waste of time.*

PRODUCTION OF BOOKS AND RECORDS

As often as may reasonably be required, the insured must produce for examination all books of account, bills, invoices, and other vouchers or certified copies thereof if originals are lost, at such reasonable time and place as may be designated by the insurer or its representative, and must permit extracts and copies thereof to be made. By reason of this requirement, the claim representative is enabled to make a thorough examination of books and records kept by the insured or to have an accountant audit books and report on them. When a written request is made for the production of books, its language should follow that of the policies, and when the books are received they should be listed and identified, and the insured should be required to state definitely whether all books, invoices, and other vouchers connected with the business, or the property involved, have been produced. Extracts and copies are at present most efficiently made by photostatic and photographic processes. Entries that show signs of alterations frequently produce interesting exhibits when photographed through a magnifying lens.

Other Specified Evidence

Some property policies contain an *iron safe clause* or a *record warranty clause* requiring the keeping of books or records in a prescribed manner and their preservation and production in case of loss. A similar stipulation appears in the mercantile-open stock burglary policy, to the effect that the insurer shall not be liable for loss or damage unless records are kept by the insured in such manner that the insurer can accurately determine from them the amount of loss or damage. Burglary policies also generally stipulate that the insurer is not liable for loss unless there are visible marks of felonious entry made by tools, explosives, electricity, or gas or other chemicals. When the claim representative handles a loss under a policy specifying such evidence as a prerequisite to liability, the report must show in detail the evidence that the insured presented for consideration.

APPRAISAL OR REFERENCE

The appraisal provision of the standard fire policy is included to provide a method for settling disagreements about the "actual cash value or the amount of loss" without resort to litigation. The Massachusetts statutory fire policy uses the word "reference," and the provision is applicable where there is "a failure of the parties to agree as to the amount of loss."

Appraisal and reference provisions may *not* be used for determining liability or to settle disputes over interpretation of contracts. These are the concern of the court.

The provision is framed so that, following a disagreement, either the insured or the insurer may demand its use. While disagreement must precede demand, the parties may by mutual agreement institute an appraisal at any time. The standard fire policy sets forth the following language:

Appraisal. In case the insured and this company shall fail to agree as to the actual cash value or the amount of loss, then on the written demand of either, each shall select a competent and disinterested appraiser and notify the other of the appraiser selected within 20 days of such demand. The appraisers shall first select a competent and disinterested umpire; and failing for 15 days to agree upon such umpire, then, on request of the insured or this company, such umpire shall be selected by a judge of a court of record in the state in which the property covered is located. The appraisers shall then appraise the loss, stating separately actual cash value and loss to each item; and, failing to agree, shall submit their differences, only, to the umpire. An award in writing, so itemized, of any two when filed with this company shall determine the amount of actual cash value and loss. Each appraiser shall be paid by the party selecting him and the expenses of appraisal and umpire shall be paid by the parties equally.

Appraisals are usually conducted under written agreement or memorandum[10] naming the appraisers selected, but may be held under oral agreement, as the policy does not provide for a supplementary written contract. When the appraisers are appointed, it becomes their first duty to select an umpire. In several states the laws provide for the selection of an umpire by the court or the insurance commissioner if the appraisers fail to make a selection within a stated time. After the umpire is selected or appointed, the appraisers together estimate and appraise the loss, submitting any differences found to the umpire. In common practice the umpire usually looks over all figures prepared by the appraisers, although examination should be confined to those in which there are differences. The insured is legally entitled to a hearing before the appraisers if requested; if refused, the insured may plead the refusal in objection to the award. An award signed by any two of the three acting as appraisers and umpire fixes the amount of loss. After the award, the insured and the insurer pay the appraiser respectively selected by each, and bear equally the charge of the umpire and the expense of the appraisal.

Demand

Neither the insured nor the insurer may properly demand an appraisal until after an actual disagreement has occurred. Such a disagreement cannot occur before a bona fide effort has been made by both parties to determine the amount of loss. When demand is made by the insurer, it should be in writing, should state that disagreement has occurred, should name and identify the appraiser selected by the insurer, and should call on the insured to select and present an appraiser.[11] Identification by giving the appraiser's name and address is sufficient. A demand should not incorporate any qualifications, such as the elimination of certain property from the purview of the appraisal, or the suggestion that a certain form of memorandum or agreement be signed. A demand may well suggest the signing of an agreement or memorandum as a record but should not insist on

[10]See Appendix J.

[11]See Appendix K.

it. Under policies providing for reference, the demand should nominate three persons from whom the insured is to select one, and should call on the insured to nominate three, so that the insurer may likewise select one.

The courts have regularly held that when the insured demands an appraisal, and the insurer refuses to comply, the insured can sue directly under the policy.

There is conflict concerning whether the insurer can be compelled to appraise on demand of the insured. The New York court has said that, in the absence of a specific provision by the legislature, there is not even a right of specific performance vested in the insured to force the insurer to submit to appraisal proceedings. [12]

The Pennsylvania court in *Robinson v. Lumbermens Mutual Casualty Co. (Penn.)*, 168 A. 321, follows the New York rule. In that case the insurer refused to name an appraiser. The insured named an appraiser and the appraiser named an umpire. The court held that their appraisal award was not competent evidence for the determination of values in an action on the policy. [13]

The Ohio Supreme Court was confronted with a situation in which the insurer refused to name an appraiser, the insured having named one. The insured had applied to an Ohio court to appoint an umpire. The court-appointed umpire and the insured's appraiser made an award. The insurer brought an action to set the award aside on the grounds the insurer had a right to revoke the appraisal provision. The court disagreed, saying that the appraisal provision was a valuable right to the insured and one that should not be denied. [14]

New Jersey follows the Ohio rule in *Drescher v. Excelsior Insurance Co. of New York*, 188 F. Supp. 158, wherein the court recognized the existence of the New York rule but found the Ohio rule preferable.

Notification to Loss Payees and Mortgagees

All parties in interest should be requested to join in the appraisal. If the policy is made payable to a third party, in whole or in part, notice of the demand for appraisal should be served upon such third person; otherwise, the award will not be binding.

The weight of authority is to the effect that a mortgagee, entitled to the proceeds of an insurance policy by virtue of a simple loss payable clause in the policy, is not affected or bound by an adjustment of the claim, whether by arbitration or agreement by the insured and insurer, without prior knowledge and consent. [15]

Under the so-called union mortgage clause, which provides that no act or negligence on the part of the insured shall affect the mortgagee's right to collect, the mortgagee is not bound by an adjustment between the mortgagor and the insurer without the mortgagee's knowledge and consent, and it is not bound by an appraisal unless it had notice and acquiesced in the said appraisal. [16]

Claim Representative's Contact With Appraisers

Theoretically, appraisers are supposed to proceed with the appraisal on their own initiative, first selecting an umpire, or applying to the court for an appointee if selection fails. Actually, the appraisers are seldom free from efforts to influence their judgment by the claimant or his or her representatives whose efforts are directed toward securing the choice of an umpire favorable to the claimant, and an award in keeping with the claim. It is, therefore, important that the claim representative be prepared to consult with the appraiser at any time. There must, however, be no interference with the appraisal, or acts which might be so construed lest the insured plead interference in objection to the award. If the appraisers ask for tes-

---

[12]*Delmar Box Co., Inc. v. Aetna Insurance Company, et al.* (N.Y.), 309 N.Y. 60, 127 N.E.2d 808.
[13]*National Fire Insurance Co. v. Shuman*, 44 Ga. App. 819, 163 S.E. 302, 44 A.L.R.2d 850.
[14]*Saba v. Homeland Insurance Company of America*, 159 Ohio St. 237, 112 N.E.2d 1, 44 A.L.R.2d 841.

[15]*Bergman v. Commercial Assurance Co.*, 92 Ky. 494, 15 L.R.A. 270. *Hathaway v. Orient Insurance Co.*, 134 N.Y. 409. *McDowell v. St. Paul Fire & Marine Insurance Co.*, 207 N.Y. 482.
[16]*Syracuse Savings Bank v. Yorkshire Insurance Co.*, N.Y. 403.

timony, the claim representative should present witnesses and see that their testimony is fairly heard, and likewise see that the insured's witnesses are properly examined by or before the appraisers. The appraisers may ask the parties to examine the witnesses, in which event the claim representative must function in the same way as a trial lawyer. While appraisers are authorized to take testimony, the authority is seldom exercised except in Massachussetts. If the appraisers do not ask for testimony, the claim representative should simply be alert to see that nothing goes wrong in the procedure. In some cases the claim representative may wish to offer testimony. If so, the appraisers and the insured should be notified, and a time and place fixed for the occasion.

Finally the claim representative should see to it that the award is free from errors and is rendered in proper form. If the insurance is written under several items, the award should state separately the appraised sound value and loss on each. An otherwise satisfactory award may be invalidated through neglect to itemize it, and the subsequent refusal of the signers to correct it.

Record of Appraisal

The policy does not require the appraisers to record their proceedings or to sign any writing except the award. For convenience, the memorandum or agreement[17] under which appraisals are conducted provides blank affidavits for the appraisers to execute when they qualify, and blank spaces in which to record the selection of the umpire and the figures of the awards. As awards are sometimes disputed, it is advisable for the insurer's appraiser to keep a record of his or her acts from the time of being notified of selection until the award is made. Such a record should include copies of letters nominating umpires, unless the selection is agreeably made without delay, and a copy of the appraiser's original estimate showing the items agreed upon and those on which there was a difference. A list of differences should be prepared and given to the umpire. Such a record is always useful in case of litigation, errors, or misunderstandings. When an award is to be made, the details on which it is to be based should be checked and a copy retained in preparation for future contingencies.

Award

When an appraisal is held before the filing of a proof of loss, the result of the award can be incorporated in the proof by a statement naming the appraisers and the sound value and loss awarded. But if the proof of loss was filed before the rendering of the award, an amendment (or reapportionment sheets if more than one policy is involved) should be prepared for the proof.

In the absence of fraud, collusion, or mutual mistake, an award is binding. In some states, the use of a professional appraiser by the insurer is held to be fraud.

Charges for Appraisal

The bill of the company's appraiser should be paid by the claim representative, or approved for payment if in order; also the bill of the umpire for one-half that charge and one-half any other proper charges connected with the appraisal.

OPTIONS OF INSURER

Most state standard fire policies give the insurer's options as follows:

> It shall be optional with this Company to take all, or any part, of the property at the agreed value, and also to repair, rebuild or replace the property destroyed or damaged with other of like kind and quality within a reasonable time, or giving notice of its intention so to do within thirty days after receipt of the proof of loss herein required.

The Businessowners Policy (MLB-700 Ed. 11-1-75) states the option in much simpler terms:

> If the Company gives notice within thirty(30) days after it has received a signed, sworn statement of loss, it shall have the option to take all

or any part of the property damaged at an agreed value, or to repair, rebuild or replace it with equivalent property.

The Manufacturers Output Policy (MOP) and the Difference in Conditions policy (DIC) both have wording of similar intent.

The new and simplified Homeowners-76 Policy, under "Our Option," tends to over-simplify the wording and makes no mention of taking the property at an agreed value.

If we give you written notice within 30 days after we receive your signed, sworn statement of loss, we may repair or replace any part of the property damaged with equivalent property.

All of these various options are designed to give the insurer the privilege of taking over damaged personal property at a value agreed to with the insured and paying on that basis, or else repairing or replacing the property, whether it be real or personal property.[18]

ABANDONMENT BY INSURED

Most insurance policies that cover property give the insurer the option of taking over property on which claim is made, but pro-hibit abandonment to the insurer. A stock of merchandise, for example, that has been partially damaged by a peril insured against may be taken over by the insurer at an agreed value. But, the insured may not "walk away from it," so to speak, and tell the insurer to "take it." A shipper or carrier may not aban-don property, leaving it unprotected, and per-mit it to deteriorate on the highway or be subjected to theft.

Inland Marine policies contain a *no aban-donment* provision under "Protection of Property."[19]

The New York Standard Fire Insurance Policy states, "There can be no abandon-ment to this company of any property."

The Businessowners Policy states, "The Company need not accept any property abandoned by an insured."

The Homeowners-76 Policy states, "We need not accept any property abandoned by any insured."

The claim representative must make it clear to the insured that there can be no abandonment of property in whole or in part.

SUIT

The New York Standard Fire Insurance Pol-icy stipulates:

No suit or action on this policy for the recovery of any claim shall be sustainable in any court of law or equity unless all the requirements of this policy shall have been complied with, and unless commenced within twelve months next after inception of the loss.

Most property insurance policies follow this one-year limitation for filing suit, including the Homeowners, Businessowners, Inland Marine, and Special Multi-Peril policies. All, however, comply with the statutes regarding the filing of suit in those states wherein the policies are issued. The time for filing suit has been amended in some states. Nebraska and Kansas, for example, stipulate that suit be filed "within 60 months next after discovery by the insured of the occur-rence which gives rise to the claim." Texas permits *two years* and one day after discovery by the insured of the occurrence. Maine per-mits *24 months* after inception of the loss. Claim representatives should acquaint them-selves with the statutes in the states in which they handle losses. The stipulation can, on occasion, offer a defense against unreason-able and fraudulent claimants.

QUESTIONS AND PROBLEMS

1. Insured, a jute bag wholesale firm in Georgia, sustained a fire loss on July 10. Large quantities of jute bags were wet from the sprinklers though not damaged by the fire. Insured decided to ship the bags to its warehouse in upper New York State where they would be put through dryers and sal-vaged.

[18]Under Adjustment Methods Available to Determine Value and Loss, p. 11, the advantages and disadvantages of exer-cising this option are outlined.
[19]See p. 69.

The bags were shipped in closed railroad cars and were a week in transit. When they arrived at their destination, the insured notified the insurer of the loss and advised where the jute bags could be seen. The insurer's claim representative visited the warehouse and found the bags had been shipped wet and, being a vegetable fiber, had heated en route and become so tender that they were a total loss.

Two policy provisions (**a** and **b**) are involved here. Discuss each with respect to the insured's liability for this loss, or possible basis of adjustment.

a. Notice of loss to the insurer.

b. Insured's requirement to protect the property from further loss.

2. As a claim representative, you are assigned to a fire loss involving a three-story ordinary brick factory occupied for manufacturing plastic toys. The top floor is gutted and the roof is off. It is midwinter. Some windows are out on the second and first floors. Water used to extinguish the fire has accumulated in the boiler room, flooding the oil burning furnace several feet deep. Most of the raw, in process, and finished stock located on the second and first floors has been wet but not affected by the fire. Your insurer is alone on this risk and its policy covers Building and Contents.

Using your imagination, list a number of protective measures that the insured, you, or both should consider undertaking to prevent further damage.

3. The insured satisfies the requirement of the policy as to proof of loss when he or she makes, under oath if stipulated, the statements that the policy specifies. Two separate areas of information are usually required to be answered by the insured. What are they?

4. Comment on the following with regard to filing of proof of loss.

a. Insurer's claim representative, after inspecting the premises, advises the insured that the insurer is not liable for the loss, and tells the insured to file proof of loss.

b. At one time, insurers felt secure in rejecting a proof of loss by letter stating one reason followed by the words, "and for other good and sufficient reasons."

That old dog won't hunt anymore. Explain why.

5. Most property insurance policies provide that the insurer may, at its option, repair, rebuild, or replace the property damaged or destroyed.

Following disagreement over the cost to repair a building damaged by fire in the attic, for which insured has asked $9,000, the insurer elects to exercise its option and engages a contractor to make repairs. The contractor tells the insurer it will cost $7,000. The insurer's contractor turns out to be unreliable and inexperienced in fire repairs. Because he failed to provide a temporary cover for the roof while replacing a few rafters, rainwater enters the unprotected openings over the weekend, floods the interior, and adds damage to building and contents estimated at $30,000. In a heated altercation with the owner over the rain damage the following Monday, the contractor breaks a Ming vase valued at $10,000 over the owner's head, causing painful head injuries. Contractor and insurer are then sued for $200,000 by the owner. The contractor carries no insurance of any kind.

Policy limit on building is $40,000 and on contents $20,000. Discuss this situation with respect to the insurer's liability to the insured.

6. The insured, owner of a retail men's clothing store, occupies space in a one-story-and-basement building. Fire in the basement causes the first floor to collapse, dumping the insured's stock and fixtures into the basement area. The roof subsequently collapses. The insurer is notified and sends a claim representative. There apparently is considerable salvage that can be dug out of the "wreck," but the insured, wholly inexperienced, throws up her hands and says, "It's a total loss."

The claim representative accuses the insured of abandonment which is not permitted under the terms of the policy.

a. Do you agree?

b. What would be a better way for the claim representative to handle this situation to effect a loss adjustment equitable to all interests?

7

Investigation of the Insured, the Property, and the Insurance

The claim representative's work begins with an investigation of the circumstances attending a reported loss and any which might affect the claim. If it is apparent that the policy provides coverage, the claim representative proceeds to determine the amount of loss, and sees that the requirements of the insurance policy are complied with and that any rights of value to the insurer are exercised or preserved.

If it is found that a part or all of the loss is not covered under the insurance, the claim representative avoids acting in any manner that could be construed as a *waiver* of any defense the insurer may have or as an *estoppel* of the insurer's right to use that defense.

The claim representative should begin collecting, as soon as practicable, whatever information is needed to proceed with an adjustment and to report to the insurer. That information should be recorded in an orderly fashion (1) to prevent loss of any part of it due to fault of memory and (2) to make it possible for associates or employees to examine the file and learn where the work on the loss stands whenever the claim representative is not available.

While any loss may have unexpected requirements for special information, the routine data outlined in this chapter in the investigation of the *insured*, the *property*, and the *insurance* should be gathered on all important losses. It should be recorded by

appropriate note or entry on whatever form, blank, or file is normally used or by special memorandum when the information is unusual.

The investigation into the *occurrence and cause of loss* is taken up in Chapter 8, with the exception of a few special types of coverages or kinds of loss treated in separate chapters.

WAIVER AND ESTOPPEL

The claim representative's authority is considerable, and, as pointed out in Chapter 1, agreements with the insured on matters within the scope of the claim representative's authority, or believed so by the insured, are binding on the insurer. In any *written* or *verbal* communication with the insured or by any *act* or *omission* on the part of the insurer or its claim representative, the possibility of a *waiver* or an *estoppel* must be kept foremost in mind.

The courts have given prominence to the doctrine of *waiver* and the kindred doctrine of *estoppel* when deciding insurance cases. While these doctrines have come from the general law, they have been applied nowhere else with the severity found in decisions dealing with insurance policies. The decisions should be studied so that waiver and estoppel may be avoided, as these doctrines play an important part in the claim representative's work with insureds.

Waiver

Waiver is defined as the "voluntary or intentional relinquishment of a known right," *Lehigh Val. R. Co. v. Ins. Co.*, 172 F. 364, 97 C.C.A. 62; *Vermillion v. Prudential Ins. Co. of America*, 230 Mo. App. 993, 93 S.W.2d, 45, 51; "or such conduct as warrants an inference of the relinquishment of such right." *Rand v. Morse*, C.C.A. Mo. 289 F. 339, 344; *Dexter Yarn Co. v. American Fabrics Co.*, 102 Conn. 529, 129 A. 527, 537; *Gibbs v. Bergh*, 51 S.D. 432, 214 N.W. 838, 841. "The renunciation, repudiation, abandonment, or surrender of some claim, right, privilege, or of the opportunity to take advantage of some defect, irregularity, or wrong." *Christenson v. Carleton*, 37 A. 226, 69 Vt. 91; *Shaw v. Spencer*, 100 Mass. 395, 97 Am. Dec. 107, 1 Am. Rep. 115; *Smiley v. Barker*, 28 C.C.A. 9, 83 F. 684; *Boos v. Ewing*, 17 Ohio 523, 49 Am. Dec. 478. "A doctrine resting upon an equitable principle, which courts of law will recognize." *Atlas Life Ins. Co. v. Schrimsher*, 179 Okla. 643, 66 P.2d 914, 948.

Waiver may be implied from some act or neglect on the part of the claim representative, as when, by asking for an estimate or other evidence of the amount of loss or by failing to tell the insured that the facts show the policy is void, the insured is led to believe that a known avoidance of the policy or a forfeiture of right to make claim will be overlooked and the claim will be paid.

Waiver Distinguished From Estoppel

Waiver is distinguished from estoppel in that in waiver the essential element is an actual intent to abandon or surrender a right, while in *estoppel* such intent is immaterial, the necessary condition being the deception to the injury of the other party by the conduct of the one estopped. *Insurance Co. of North America v. Williams*, 42 Ariz. 331, 26 P.2d 117, 119. And *estoppel* may result though the party estopped did not intend to lose any existing rights. *Boyce v. Toke Point Oyster Co.*, 145 Ore. 114, 25 P.2d 930.

Estoppel

Estoppel is an equitable principle to the effect that if one *intentionally* or *unintentionally* creates the impression that a certain fact exists, and an innocent party relies on that impression and is damaged as a result, the guilty party will be estopped from asserting that the fact does not exist. In situations where there is a serious question of liability or coverage, if the claim representative leads the insured to believe the claim will be paid, the company may be estopped later from denying liability or coverage. If the claim representative executes a written agreement covering value and loss, the company is estopped from questioning it unless there was mutual mistake, fraud, or collusion.

Guarding Against Waiver and Estoppel

Because of the consequences, the claim representative should avoid behavior that may imply waiver or create estoppel as carefully as the surgeon tries to avoid infection. The danger of being charged with waiver or estoppel exists in all cases presenting questions of liability. When the facts indicate that the policy is void, that it does not describe the property involved, or that because of the time, place, or cause of loss the contract does not cover it, or that because of failure to comply with contract requirements, or for any other reasons, the insured has lost the right to maintain claim, the claim representative must guard against any act or omission that might warrant the insured in proceeding on the assumption that the insurer has waived its contract conditions or any other defenses and will pay the claim.

When encountering any such situation, the claim representative, as soon as there is knowledge of the facts, should withdraw from contact with the insured and ordinarily have no further dealings. In particular, the claim representative should have no further negotiations looking toward agreement as to value and loss and should report the situation to the insurer and await instructions. Should it be advisable to continue investigating to establish the amount of loss to the property before reporting to the insurer, the claim representative should make a written agreement with the insured that no waiver shall be implied from his or her acts. Such an agreement is frequently made and is known as a *nonwaiver agreement.*[1]

When the facts indicate that the policy is valid and the loss is covered but that the insured must comply with certain requirements in order to prove a loss or perfect a claim, the claim representative must avoid misleading the insured into the belief that the requirements will not be enforced. In some instances it is advisable to put the insured on notice in writing that compliance with the requirement or requirements will be expected.

Comments on Waiver and Estoppel

More good defenses are lost to insurers by acts of claim representatives who commit waivers or estoppels than are lost in any other way. A reading of the decisions of our appellate courts supports this assertion.

The claim representative is not often interested in the matter of express waiver as he is seldom so rash as to state to the insured, unless instructed to do so, that the insurer will waive the benefits or requirements of the contract or the defenses it may have against the claim. He or she is, however, vitally interested so as not to commit an implied waiver or estop the insurer from asserting a right or defense that it may have or from enforcing a pertinent requirement of its contract.

Questions of liability, coverage, and compliance with requirements in case of loss are encountered in many bona fide losses and some fraudulent losses.

As a matter of good human relations, the claim representative should promptly point out anything in the policy that stands between the insured and what is being claimed. If done in a dispassionate manner, this action will not ordinarily arouse antagonism. With the situation clearly understood, the way is open to suggest a withdrawal of the claim or, if there are extenuating circumstances, a fixing of the amount under a nonwaiver or without-prejudice agreement and a

submission of the facts to the insurer. From time to time losses occur that the policy does not cover but that the insurer will, nevertheless, pay on grounds of equity or of business policy. Following such losses it may instruct the claim representative to deny liability but advise the insured that the claim will be paid without admission of liability, or it may have the policy *reformed* by proper endorsement so that it will be legally liable. But while it is the privilege of an insurer to make express waivers when it seems expedient to do so, *a claim representative is not privileged* and must avoid all acts of waiver except those that the insurer permits.

Since the insurer may become a participant in litigation, the claim representative dealing with a loss or claim that presents a question of liability should be doubly careful to avoid acting or speaking in any manner that may give grounds for the imputation of waiver, since an insured seeking to collect under a policy that is void or that does not cover may charge a claim representative with waiver and later substantiate the charge in court to the claim representative's embarrassment and the insurer's cost.

In some instances, an insurer will know, even before it assigns a loss to a claim representative, that the policy is void or that the coverage is suspended. It can, if it wishes to consider the situation, write the insured that, without prejudice to its rights under the policy, it will send a claim representative to investigate and report, but that it will limit the authority of the claim representative to agreeing with the insured on the facts, and that the claim representative will have no power to bind the insurer to a settlement and no authority to waive policy conditions.

A claim representative can, by putting the insured to trouble and expense and misleading the insured, waive a provision of the policy or estop the company from asserting it as a defense.

The courts are sympathetic toward claimants and are ordinarily ready to declare waivers and estoppels on a minimum of evidence. For this reason, the claim representative must be on guard constantly.

[1]See Appendix L.

THE INSURED

Meeting the Insured

In almost all cases the claim representative should arrange to meet the insured, or the person who will speak for the insured, through the agent, broker, or other producer. Introduction by the producer helps the claim representative to gain the insured's confidence and cooperation, which should be sought in all cases except when there is reason to believe that the insured is unreasonable or deceptive.

In many losses the insured is a partnership, a group of persons, an association, or a corporation. In such cases the claim representative may meet only one of the interested partners, members, officials, or officers.

The claim representative meets and deals with the insured for several reasons: (1) to identify the insured, (2) to learn what he or she knows and what information can be produced about the loss or any of the circumstances attending it, (3) to find out what kind of person the insured is, (4) to see that the requirements of the policy in case of loss are carried out, and (5) to make whatever agreements are necessary to a proper adjustment of the loss.

Except in the larger cities, the claim representative ordinarily telephones or calls on the local agent who then goes with him or her to introduce the insured or makes arrangements for the two to meet. In the larger cities, a great number of minor losses are adjusted without meeting the insured, as a broker or a public adjuster will act for the insured.

When the claim representative is dealing with reputable persons on the general run of losses that do not present complicated circumstances, it is seldom necessary to ask the insured for anything more than the information required to fill out a proof of loss and complete a routine report, or to do more than discuss the loss and agree on the amount, and if the policy contains an average or a coinsurance or contribution clause, to agree on the value of the property.

In unusual losses—those that are large or complicated, particularly those attended by circumstances arousing doubt or suspicion concerning their origin—the insured should be questioned at length and may also be asked to produce witnesses and documentary evidence. The identity of the insured or the organization should be established, including the business and insurance history and an account of previous losses. The insured should be asked to state any knowledge, information, or belief as to the time, date, location, and cause of loss. If it is a theft loss or a burglary loss, the insured should be asked whether it was reported to the police. In many instances the insured will be asked to state the nature and extent of any interest in the property, other interests in it, and whether there is any agreement on the part of another to be responsible for the property or to insure it. If the insured is in possession of records bearing on the loss, the claim representative should examine them.

The claim representative by association, discussion, and negotiation forms an opinion of the integrity and ability of the insured. If the property involved in the loss requires special handling to protect it from further damage, to make evident the damage that it has suffered, or to determine the amount of the loss, the claim representative's opinion of the insured will be a guide to the degree of supervision that must be exercised while the property is being handled.

The Insured's Story

The claim representative should get the insured's story, ordinarily at the time of the first meeting. The story is in many instances all the information that the claim representative needs before discussing the amount of loss and trying to reach an agreement. In other instances it is a guide to investigation and often gives indications concerning what will be easy and what will be difficult in the handling of the loss. In losses that are unusual in cause, amount, kind of property, nature or extent of damage, or in losses that are complicated by questions of coverage, liability, apportionment, cancellation, or other circumstances, the insured's story is essential in obtaining the details.

In some cases, the insured tells a story directly and clearly, covering any circumstance pointed out as necessary to complete it or explain its details. In others, he or she will ramble and be difficult to understand, confused, reluctant, nervous, or upset. Sometimes the claim representative encounters an attitude of boredom, irritation, resentment, or hostility when he or she asks the insured for the story or asks questions in order to obtain it or call attention to inconsistencies in it. At all times, patience, tact, and tolerance are essential when interviewing the insured.

The information generally sought from the insured's story concerns the following:

1. When, where, and how the loss occurred.
2. The insured's interest in the property and the nature and extent of any interest held by other persons.
3. The value of and loss to each item of the property.
4. Any encumbrances on the property.
5. Other contracts of insurance, whether valid or not, covering any of the property.
6. Any changes in the title, use, occupancy, location, possession, or exposures of the property since the issuing of the policy.
7. By whom and for what purpose any building described in the policy was occupied at the time of loss.

In unusual losses, the insured's story, if fully developed by discussion and pertinent questions, will inform the claim representative of what facts the insured will allege and try to prove in order to show he or she is entitled to make claim, and what evidence will be offered in support of the amount he or she expects to ask for.

Usually, on first contact with the insured, the claim representative will decide whether the circumstances require obtaining a written statement to make a record of the insured's story. In cases of theft, mysterious disappearance, or questionable statements by the insured relating to how the loss occurred, the value and identification of items, the in-

sured's interest, cancellation, and so forth, it is good practice to get the story in writing early in the investigation.

Statements

Taking written or recorded statements from insureds, witnesses, and claimants is standard procedure in casualty insurance claims because of the need to preserve evidence in the event of litigation. In the adjustment of property losses, where the insured and claimant are one and the same, the occasions when written statements are needed have been relatively few. With the development of package, multiple-line, and multi-peril policies in which traditional casualty and fire lines are merged, more claims involve questions of coverage and liability. The taking of statements, as a consequence, is becoming more frequent. Under property insurance policies the kinds of situations in which statement taking can serve a useful purpose include, but are not limited to, those:

1. Where the cause of loss is of suspicious origin.
2. Where coverage or liability is questionable.
3. Where insurable interest is questioned.
4. Involving possible cancellation of the policy.
5. In which the insurer's rights have been prejudiced.
6. Where the claim is excessive or borders on attempted fraud.
7. Where the claim representative wishes to preserve evidence or place on record the story of the insured or witnesses.
8. That indicate possibilities of subrogation against third parties.

Under insurance policies that contain a requirement that the insured shall submit to examination under oath, the claim representative must guard against having the insured swear to a routine written statement. It has been held that an insured need not submit to an examination under oath more than once. Asking an insured to swear to a routine written statement could bar the insurer from later demanding examination under oath.

Basically, the essential reasons for taking statements are, first, to obtain the story of the person being interviewed and, second, to prevent, if possible, the changing of that story at some later date. There are collateral reasons, such as getting the facts before they are lost to memory or before other interests can take a statement that might not be considered factual.

Regardless of the type of claim, whether first or second party, liability, fire, burglary, etc., no statement can be taken properly nor will it have much value unless the person taking it knows precisely what should be looked for in the way of information; or unless one understands the provisions, conditions, warranties, and other elements of the particular insurance policy involved and has at least a general idea of the occurrence that gave rise to the claim. A claim representative who takes a statement involving a collision loss in a state with contributory negligence laws, and who has no knowledge of the law, is likely to do more harm than good. A person who approaches an agent or an insured to record the story concerning questionable cancellation of a policy before the loss must have some knowledge of what constitutes proper cancellation. In taking the statements of witnesses in those cases that have possibilities of subrogation, the claim representative cannot bring out the information sought unless he or she has some knowledge of the law of torts and law of contracts.

The following ten simple rules will aid in the mechanics of taking signed statements.

1. Write legibly with pen and ink.
2. Number each page, and show place, date, and time at the top of each page.
3. Ask preliminary questions such as name, age, residence, marital status, and occupation to establish identity and to prevent refutation of the statement at a later date.
4. Establish the person's relationship or connection with the occurrence of the loss, the property, or the insured.
5. Take the statement in the first person.
6. Write it exactly as given whether grammatically correct or not. Do not change the person's words.
7. Make no erasures; correct by crossing out and having the person initial it.
8. Do not include irrelevant material.
9. Prompt persons, but do not coach, lead, or put words in their mouths.
10. Have the person sign each page; witness the signature.

Investigating the Insured

In the great majority of losses, there will be nothing connected with the origin of the loss or the claim suggesting improper conduct on the part of the insured. Checking the spelling of the name and making a more or less casual inquiry into the history, occupation, and any previous losses suffered will be all the investigation required. On serious losses it may be necessary to go into the insured's business history and trading or operating methods in order to adjust the loss properly and report it clearly and comprehensively.

It is only when apparent or suspected fraud is encountered that intensive investigation is called for. As indicated previously, intensive investigation begins with identifying insureds and covers their history, status, condition, and prospects.

When partnerships, associations, groups, or corporations are insured, investigation of controlling personalities such as partners, members, officers, officials, and sometimes active employees may be in order (see Chapter 4).

Identification. Generally the agent, broker, or company representative through whom the insurance was placed introduces the claim representative to the insured as the person named in the policy. Identification of a person may require a check of his or her name as given to the claim representative against any other names the person uses or is known by, and against a former name or names if there has been a change of name. Names of parents, or the name of husband or wife, may sometimes be necessary to differentiate one person from another of the same name. Checking names is usually done by interviewing persons and getting their statements and by reading commercial and credit reports. Sometimes the personal factors of sex and age must be considered along with such characteristics as racial origin, color, height, weight, eyes, hair, distinguishing features, scars, deformities, evidences of injuries or impairments, speech, habits, and behavior. Data on personal factors and physical characteristics are obtained through observation, from descriptions given by other persons, from school, hospital, and police records, and from photographs. Fingerprints are accepted as absolute identification.

The claim representative seldom encounters a situation where the identity of the insured is in doubt. *When it is, investigation requires diplomatic handling.*

History. The history of a person begins with the date and place of birth, the occupation and status of the parents, education, religious training, and early employment or occupation. Later places of residence and dates of changes of residence will, if established, connect him or her with various events. Records of businesses engaged in or occupations followed, with locations or addresses, trade or other names used, associates or employers, may be important. An insured's record or reputation for meeting financial or other obligations, together with the record for thrift or extravagance, will be indexes of character. If the insured has been involved in previous losses, their dates, kind of loss, the property involved, the amount of loss sustained, and the insurance collected in each case should be subjects of inquiry. The names of any claim representatives who may have settled such previous losses should be ascertained. Business troubles should be traced: bankruptcy, compromises with creditors, or loss of property due to foreclosure or sale of collateral by a creditor. If the insured has a criminal record, it is advisable to find out for what crimes he or she was convicted, in what courts they were tried, what attorneys defended, and what sentences he or she received. The history of the insured is generally developed by questioning him or her and by checking answers against the statements of persons who know the insured.

Status. The insured's place of residence and place of business or employment will determine his or her movements and, in many cases, habits. Whether single, married, widowed, divorced, and whether there is a family or a group of relatives may affect the insured's conduct. Information as to the status of a person comes from personal observation and discussion, from the statements of others, and from records, such as payrolls, registrations, enrollments, or leases.

Condition. The physical condition of a person, whether well or sick, sound or injured, often accounts for that person's actions. The mental condition, whether the person is sane or insane, alert or dull, happy or unhappy, also affects ability and behavior. So do family life and social contacts. The physical or mental condition of a person is generally noted by others who come into contact with him or her. Morally, a person's condition is evidenced by attitudes toward alcohol, sex, gambling, the money or property of others, and the disposition to live and let live, or to be offensive, oppressive, or extortionate. Financially, the insured's condition will be good if he or she is solvent, enjoys a comfortable income, keeps expenses within bounds, has adequate resources and good credit, and suffers no unusual burdens. It will be bad if the contrary is the case. Financial condition is determined by questioning the insured, by examining records, by questioning informed persons, and by reading trade reports.

Prospects. The prospect that the future may improve or deteriorate conditions may affect the insured's actions; therefore, such prospects at, or immediately before, the time of loss may be worth considering. If threatened with loss of health, income, or property, with family misfortune or other troubles, one may be driven to acts of desperation. Information about the prospects of a person is usually gathered from discussion with them and checked against what others say.

Relation to Producer. It is advisable in any investigation of insureds to find out whether they are new or old customers of the producer, how they came to be customers, and their value to the producer.

THE PROPERTY

The claim representative should examine the property—or if it has been lost or destroyed, the evidence that bears upon it—in order to determine whether it is the property covered in the policy, and also to determine its character and condition, the kind of risk it was, its history, its value to the insured, its prospects, who held title to it, what encumbrances rested on it, and who had possession of it.

The sections of this chapter dealing with the property have to do with circumstances existing prior to the time of loss. What may have happened to the property as a result of the loss is outlined in subsequent sections dealing with the claim[2] and also in the chapters dealing with buildings and personal property.[3]

Identification

Investigation of the property begins with efforts to find out whether it is the property described and covered in the contract of insurance and, if so, whether it was at the location covered or a covered location within the boundaries stated in the contract.

The first step is a check of the property against the policy. Ordinarily, this step identifies the property as that described.

Buildings in cities generally check to street numbers and rarely present any real problem of identification. In outlying and remote areas, ownership and occupancy generally identify them. Occasionally a problem arises because of the proximity of two buildings of the same ownership, either of which fits the description stated in a policy or group of policies covering at the location.

Contents items, such as household furniture, personal effects, fixtures, or machinery and equipment, check to descriptions of the items and generally to the descriptions of identifiable buildings.

Property in the open, in yards, fields, or forests, may be within or without the boundaries stated in the insurance contract. These boundaries must, therefore, be traced and the relation of the property to them determined.

The same work must be done when the property is covered by floating insurance. It must be determined whether the property is within the limits of the floater and whether coverage at the location is excluded.

If the insurance is subject to conditions of average, coinsurance, or distribution, identification and listing of all property covered are essential in order to determine whether sufficient insurance is carried.

If a check of the description and location as stated in any letter, binder, or policy form cannot be made against the property itself, or against remains of it, records such as inventories, contracts, or bills of sale covering the property may have to be scrutinized. If none of these is to be had, the statements of persons familiar with the property may be required to support or disprove the statements of the insured.

Sometimes property is described as being shown on a map or diagram on file in a stated office. If so, a study of the map or diagram may be necessary.

Occasionally, the rate of premium indicates the property intended to be covered. Thus, if two risks are so owned, located, and described as to make it difficult to say which one is covered, the rate may be indicative. If the rate on one differs from that on the other, the higher or lower rate shown in the policy will indicate which is covered.

Ordinarily, it is not difficult to identify the property, but occasionally it is difficult because of ambiguous language in the policy form. In that case the intent of the insured and the insurer must be tested by statements of the insured and the broker on the one hand, and the officer, employee, or agent of the insurer on the other. In some cases it will be advisable to have the statements reduced to writing and signed. They can then be filed with the insurer along with the claim representative's report.

Information acquired from an examination of the property can be preserved in descriptive memorandums or detailed reports, supplemented by photographs, pieces of ma-

[2]See Chap. 11, "Procedure for Checking Claims."
[3]See Chaps. 14, "Buildings and Structures," and 16, "Personal Property in Use."

terials, tags, labels, or other articles carrying identifying names, or impressions or rubbings showing raised or indented letters, numbers, or other characters.

Character and Condition

The character and condition of property are factors that help determine its value, how it will be affected when exposed to the action of one or more of the perils insured against, and how it must be treated if damaged. A brick building is more valuable than a frame building of the same design, a pound of silk than a pound of cotton, a five-carat diamond than a rhinestone of the same size. Frame buildings suffer more from fire than do brick, while cotton fabrics are damaged more by water than are woolens. Truckloads of furs are more often hijacked than truckloads of groceries. Damaged buildings are repaired, damaged baled cotton is dried, picked, and rebaled, while damaged sugar is sent through a refining process.

New property that is sound is more valuable than old property that has suffered from decay, corrosion, or other kinds of wear and tear, or that is damaged. A few kinds of property grow more valuable with age, rare antiques and genuine works of art being examples. Wines and liquors, and some other kinds of personal property that must be aged or seasoned to be at their best, increase in value for a while. But ordinarily the value of property decreases as it grows older and deterioration and obsolescence overtake it.

Some kinds of property will, in one condition, be in greater danger from the same peril than in another. Green hay, for example, if stored in quantity in a barn, at times ignites spontaneously, whereas cured hay does not. Bituminous coal tends to heat and ignite spontaneously if a large quantity of it is piled improperly, but does not do so if properly piled. Newly assembled machinery often develops hot bearings. New buildings tend to settle and in doing so sometimes crack plate-glass windows. Newly installed sprinkler systems tend to develop leaks.

Investigation of the character and condition of any piece, article, or group of property is ordinarily made by an examination of the property itself. Results are recorded as described above, under Identification.[4] Records must be consulted, or the statements of persons taken, if the property has been lost or destroyed.

The Property as a Risk

The features of the property that contributed to the occurrence of the loss, or to the size of the loss, should be noted by the claim representative, also any existing defect or other circumstance that increases the chance of a future loss. They should be presented with appropriate comment by the claim representative in his report. Except in the case of large losses that are investigated by inspection bureaus or special-risk experts, the claim representative is ordinarily the only qualified person who examines the property and possesses the information that the underwriter should have for consideration in future treatment of similar property, or of the same property if it is again offered as a subject of insurance.

In fire losses, construction, occupancy, exposure, and protection are to be noted. When possible, the cause of the fire should be determined, the place of its origin located, and its spread traced. Appropriate comment should be made on any detail of construction, occupancy, or protection that tended to limit or extend the spread of the fire, or lessen or increase the loss.

The claim representative should state whether the risk is of brick, frame, or fireproof construction and whether it is protected or unprotected, also, whether it is within the protection of a public fire station and within 500 feet of a public hydrant. Occupancy and construction should be stated, whether occupancy contributed to the fire, whether construction contributed to the size of loss, and whether there are any physical defects needing correction.

History

The history of property begins with its erection, if it is a building or structure; its manufacture, if a fabricated article; its production,

4See p. 87.

if a commodity; and its assembly, if a group of articles such as the furniture and personal effects in a home, the fixtures in a mercantile establishment or an office, the equipment in a manufacturing plant, or the stock in a store. Investigation into the history of property will, therefore, commence with finding out when and how it was brought into existence, who was responsible for its origin, and what was planned to be done with it. From then on, the character of the property, the use to which it has been put, the effect of its environment and the degree of care and attention it has received will determine the depreciation it will suffer due to deterioration. The mere passage of time will often determine the depreciation due to obsolescence.

The history of property may show that it has been used properly or abused, that owners, occupants, or users have found it desirable or undesirable and, accordingly, have given it care and attention that have tended to preserve it, or have done nothing to keep it from deteriorating. Furthermore, it may show a record of losses indicating dangerous characteristics, poor design, improper operation or handling, inadequate protection, or constant exposure to some besetting hazard or nearby source of danger. A compilation of the history of the property involved in an unusual loss may produce information that will greatly help in weighing its real value and, possibly, the cause of the fire, explosion, or other casualty that occasioned the loss. In some cases, the history of the property when checked against the provisions of the insurance contract will show that the property was not covered when the contract became effective; in others, that it was not covered when the loss occurred.

Ownerships or uses prior to the time the property came into the possession of the insured, and any circumstances indicating past value or lack of it, may, in some cases, be worth studying. If the property has been damaged by previous fires, windstorms, explosions, or sprinkler or water leakages, or has been plagued by thefts or other casualties, their dates and the amounts of loss and insurance collected in each case may be worth finding out and recording. It is always important to know whether the property was rehabilitated after a previous loss, and at times it is worthwhile finding out the cost of doing so.

The date the property was acquired by the insured may be important, as may be also the price paid or the consideration given for it. Terms of payment sometimes indicate the existence of several insurable interests in the same property. The reason for acquiring the property is in some instances worth knowing. Its use since acquisition; its improvement or deterioration; the cost of owning, operating or selling it; the income derived from it; or the loss incurred because of the expense of it may help the claim representative to form an opinion of its real value, and whether the insured had an incentive to preserve it or had found it a burden and wished to be rid of it.

Changes in the property and its surroundings may enhance or lower its value and may increase or decrease the probability that it will be involved in loss.

In ordinary losses nothing is to be gained by any extensive inquiry into the history of the property, but in an occasional loss, history will be all-important. Much of the history of any piece of property can be obtained by questioning the owner. Intensive inquiry leads to the questioning of others and the examination of records.

Subsequently Erected Structures

If a policy covers a group of buildings or their contents, it should be learned whether any building in the group has been erected since the policy became effective, because in the absence of a provision to the contrary, the policy will not cover a structure erected after the policy was issued.

Value

In doubtful or suspicious losses, investigation should be made of the income produced by the property or the benefits the insured derived from its use, and these should be contrasted with the cost of owning and using it. The result of such an investigation will aid in judging what was the real value of the property and whether the insured was interested in preserving it or had decided to realize on the insurance.[5]

Prospects

In doubtful or suspicious losses, the prospects of the property prior to loss should be considered, and in some cases investigated. Any circumstance that threatened the existence, use, or value of the property, whether physical, economic, social, or political, should be brought to light. A building, for example, may be threatened by the caving in of mined areas or the encroachment of an uncontrolled river; or its usefulness may be ended or greatly reduced by a change of street or highway level. A once-prosperous business may drift into bankruptcy owing to the dying off or moving away of the class of customers who patronized it, and a factory may find its product unsalable if a change in import duties allows foreign competitors to flood its market with cheaper articles. Property, once desirable, may tend to become a nuisance owing to neighborhood changes, and property that has been valuable in the past may occupy a site that will be condemned for water supply, power, or flood control. Information on the probable future of any property is generally developed by discussion with persons who are acquainted with it. Records of condemnation proceedings should be examined.

Title

Investigation of title is ordinarily no more searching than asking the insured whether he or she owns the property. The question of title may become important, however, in doubtful or questionable claims, and sometimes in claims when the property was under contract of sale, a change of ownership was to take place at or about the time of loss, and buyer and seller held separate policies or sets of insurance on the property.

In the case of a building, the title can generally be determined by an examination of real estate records. The title to real estate passes only by written instrument, unless the owner dies intestate, when title to real property descends by operation of law to the heirs. The title of an insured who makes claim for the loss of a building can, therefore, be verified by a check of real estate records against any documentary evidence, unless it is asserted that title is by inheritance from an intestate ancestor. In such a case proof of title will be the official records or the testimony of witnesses who can swear to the insured's relationship to the deceased ancestor. In rare situations an owner will hold title by reason of an unrecorded deed. Any such deed should be carefully examined, and the circumstances of its preparation, execution, and delivery investigated. The sale of real property is evidenced not only by deeds but also by such instruments as contracts for title, bonds for title, lease-sale contracts, and contracts of similar purport which may bear other names.

Mere possession of personal property justifies presumption of ownership, as title often passes without the formality of executing a written instrument. Important transfers, however, are generally evidenced by bills or contracts of sale, which are sometimes recorded.

The purchase and sale of merchandise in the regular channels of trade are ordinarily recorded by entries on the books of both purchaser and seller and are evidenced by invoices, except in the case of retail sales to customers, many of which are made without even writing up a sales slip for the purchase.

Commodities in warehouses are often covered by negotiable warehouse receipts, the possession of the receipt evidencing title.[6]

Only a small percentage of personal property is held under documentary evidence of title recorded on public records. The common documentary evidences of purchase have already been discussed. Actual possession and oral statements must, in many cases, be accepted as evidence of ownership where nothing in writing can be found to throw light on the title.

---

[5]Investigation to determine insurable value is discussed in Chaps. 14, 16, and 17, "Mercantile and Manufacturer's Stocks."

[6]See Chap. 21, "Bailee Risks."

Clear title to property is the desirable condition. Clouded title may threaten the possessor with loss and make the proceeds of an insurance policy seem more valuable than the property itself. A clouded title also makes for uncertain adjustment at the peril of having another claimant appear prior to payment of the loss.

Possession

Possession of real property is evidenced by the presence of the person or persons occupying it, by the testimony of the owner or others who are informed on the subject, and by leases, contracts, wills, trust agreements, or other written instruments. Because possession by another than the owner under some circumstances imposes a liability on the possessor for certain kinds of loss or damage, and under others gives rights that affect the owner's interest, investigation of possession is at times important. A lessee, for example, may be under obligation to restore damage from a covered cause or may be in possession under a lease giving an option to purchase the property at a stipulated price. In the first case, investigation will establish the lessee's liability and lead to an examination of all insurance to see whether the lessee is insured; in the second case, investigation may reveal that the owner had agreed to sell the property for much less than the amount of the insurance.

Possession of personal property is evidenced by the location of the article or articles, by testimony of persons who have knowledge of it, and by documentary evidence such as contracts of sale, leases, bills of lading, manifests, processing contracts, warehouse receipts, and a variety of tickets and checks. Book entries, in some cases, evidence possession.

When personal property is in possession of the purchaser under a contract of sale or a lease, the purchaser or lessee is ordinarily free to use it in any manner. In some cases, however, it must be kept at a specified location or used in a specified way. Contracts of sale and leases covering personal property generally stipulate the liability of the person in possession in case the property is lost or damaged.

When personal property is in the possession of a carrier or other bailee, the bailee must handle it in accordance with the terms of the contract set forth in the bill of lading, contract, warehouse receipt, ticket, or other document evidencing possession. In many such documents there is stipulated what charge the bailee shall make for services and also the extent of liability in case of loss. In some cases the bailee holds the property under an oral contract, and the claim representative must establish the terms of the contract by having the parties state their understanding or by questioning them in detail. Often the contract is nothing more than a recognition of the custom prevailing in the trade.

Encumbrances

Mortgages and liens on real property are ordinarily recorded, but those on personal property ordinarily are not. Investigation of encumbrances follows the same general plan as investigation of title, set forth in the preceding section. Excessive encumbrance makes property a burden to the owner. A multiplicity of encumbrances sometimes makes it necessary to seek legal advice on how to pay an adjusted loss. In many mortgage agreements it is stipulated that the mortgagor must carry insurance on the property for the benefit of the mortgagee. Such a stipulation may give the mortgagee a right to participation in any payment made by the insurer.[7]

INSURABLE INTEREST

The interest of the insured in the property is determined according to the way in which the loss to the property will cause a present or future loss, and the amount of that loss. Investigation of interest requires that its nature and extent be determined. In some tangled cases a consideration of the history, condition, and prospects of the interest will be in order.[8]

---

[7]See Chap. 5, "Mortgagees and Other Payees."
[8]Specific discussion of the commonly encountered insurable interests will be found in Chap. 4.

Nature and Extent

The nature and extent of the insured's interest is determined in the same way that title to property is determined. The interests commonly encountered in adjusting losses are those of owners, part owners, mortgagees, bailees, and lessees.

History

In doubtful or questionable losses it may be worthwhile to find out when the insured's interest in the property began, how and why acquired, and what circumstances have made it valuable or a liability. The history of an interest is often so closely interwoven with the history of the property that no separate investigation has to be made.

Condition

At the time of the loss the insured's interest may be undisputed or disputed. Occasionally two persons claim ownership of the same property. The interest may also be valuable or worthless, productive or nonproductive, available for collateral or not available. The value of the interest should be compared with the amount of insurance. The condition of the interest often checks with the condition of the property and does not require separate investigation.

Other Interests

The standard fire policy requires the insured to state in the proof of loss "the interest of the insured and of all others in the property." This requirement imposes on the claim representative the necessity, in uncertain situations, of investigating for other interests. Investigation into other interests begins with questioning the insured and may require a search of property records.

THE INSURANCE

The insurance under which a loss has been reported is examined, and investigation is made in order to determine its validity, what and how it covers, its limitations, to whom it is payable, and how it compares with the property and its value. When there are two or more policies describing the same property but insuring different interests, it may be necessary to determine whether one should bear the entire loss or all should participate in it. Insurance is checked against the insured, the property, the loss, and the claim.

Policies, Binders, and Oral Contracts

Investigation of the insurance begins with requesting the insured to present the policy or policies for examination. If loss has occurred before any policy has been issued, the insured or a representative will generally hold a binder. Binders are usually prepared on receipt of the order to insure, and the insurance begins at the moment the binder is signed or initialed by an authorized representative of the insurer. Presentation of the binder should be requested if there is no policy. In rare cases, claim will be made under an oral contract to insure. In such cases, the claim representative should question both the insured and the agent, or other representatives of the insurer, and afterward ask for separate letters setting out the agreement as each remembers it, or should reduce to writing the statement of each and have the statements signed.

Lost or Destroyed Policies

Occasionally policies are lost or destroyed, destruction generally resulting from fire. In such cases the information on file in the office of the broker, agent, or insurer must be consulted.

Suspected Issuance of Binder or Policy After Loss

Sometimes there is reason to suspect that a binder has been signed or a policy issued after the loss occurred. As many binders are time-stamped, it is possible to determine within a few minutes the time they became effective. It is not, however, so easy to be certain just when an unstamped binder was signed or when a policy was written by an agent. It is next to impossible to disprove the time and date of an unstamped binder.[9]

[9]See p. 25.

If the facts justify suspicion that a policy was issued after the loss, the claim representative should trace as far as possible the course of the daily report from the agent's office to the office of the insurer. If the envelope in which it was mailed can be obtained, the postmark will indicate the approximate time of mailing. If the agent's office is in territory under jurisdiction of a stamping office, the record of when the stamping office received the daily report will throw additional light on the matter. The suspected issuance of a new policy should ordinarily be looked upon more seriously than that of a renewal, but in any case the claim representative should diplomatically, yet thoroughly, cover all sources of information to be found.

Suspected Alteration or Endorsement After Loss

At times a situation similar to that described in the preceding section is created by an alteration of the policy, or by the attachment of an endorsement that, if genuine, would make the insurer liable for a loss that otherwise would not be covered or only partly covered. Suspected alterations or endorsements changing description or location of property, increasing amounts of insurance, eliminating contribution clauses, or adding perils insured against should be investigated by a comparison of the insurer's records with the policy, and in the same general way as outlined in the preceding section.

Policy Differing From Daily Report

There is also the very rare case in which the policy presented in support of the claim will differ radically in amount or form or both from the amount or form on the daily report sent by the agent to the insurer. The amount and premium will be greater, and sometimes the property described will be far more hazardous and undesirable than that shown on the daily report. Any such case calls for investigation *under direction of the insurer.*

Checking Policies

Policies are listed and checked for amount; commencement and expiration dates; insurer issuing; property and location covered;

perils included; payees; and clauses, form numbers, warranties, stipulations, and conditions that may affect the adjustment. The claim representative should always find out who placed the insurance and who wrote each policy. In localities where business is done through brokers, the broker places and the company office or agency writes. In localities where all business is transacted through agents, they both place and write.

Policies Incorrectly Written

Some incorrectly written policies will be encountered. One of the most common mistakes is that of writing a policy in the name of one member of the family when the property belongs to another. Whenever an incorrectly written policy is presented to the claim representative it must be determined whether it was written by the agent or the company and why it was written incorrectly, and the situation must be presented to the insurer. The statements of the insured or the broker on the one side, and the agent or company individual on the other, should be summarized and reported accurately.

History

In the investigation of a doubtful or suspicious claim, the history of the insurance may indicate preparation for willful destruction of the property. It is, therefore, important, when handling such a claim, to find out when the insurance was applied for or solicited and when it was bound or written. Past increases or decreases in the amount should be noted, also any favorable or unfavorable changes in terms. Changes of broker, agent, or insurers may be significant.

Assignment of Policy Before Loss

If an assignment is written upon the policy, it will be discovered by the claim representative when examining the policy. If an assignment is suspected but does not appear on the policy, the claim representative can do no more than require the insured to make a sworn statement that the policy has not been assigned. Discovery of an assignment executed before the loss is usually made at the beginning of negotiations of adjustment, as the assignee is generally anxious to be assured that his or her interest will be preserved and consequently presents the assignment or a copy of it to the insurer or the claim representative.

Other Insurance Held by Insured

A listing of the policies presented by the insured for examination ordinarily brings to light all insurance held by the insured. Such an examination, however, is not conclusive, as it is possible that the insured may have misplaced a policy or overlooked policies that are still awaiting delivery in the offices of agents who issued them. It is also possible that one or more of the policies presented may have been canceled by notice sent to the insured by an agent or insurer. The insured may also be covered by a binder or binders held in an agent's office. If the insured negotiates for insurance through a broker, other policies or binders may be in possession of the broker. The claim representative's investigation, in case other insurance is suspected, should include examination of the policies, a check of the insured's insurance record, interviews with agent who may have issued other policies, and an interview with the broker, if the insured employs a broker. Cases frequently occur in which, after the loss has been adjusted, apportioned, and paid, a policy will be found which should have contributed. It is customary in such cases for the claim representative to prepare a reapportionment and also a proof for the omitted policy. The insurer that issued the omitted policy then reimburses the other insurers that have overpaid and makes a payment to the insured, if the insured contributed as a coinsurer under the original apportionment.

In bailee losses, where the bailee carries insurance covering the property of bailors, or covering the bailee's liability for loss to such property, it becomes necessary for the claim representative representing the insurer of the bailee to find out whether the bailors are carrying their own insurance. Investigation generally begins by instructing the bailee to write each bailor, giving notice of the loss and asking the bailor to fill out, sign, and return an enclosed questionnaire which asks for the particulars of any insurance carried.

Insurance Held by Others

In some instances the claim representative representing the insurer of the owner will find that some other person who has an insurable interest in the property is also insured. In other instances, the claim representative representing the insurer of a person other than the owner finds that the owner is insured. In such a situation the stipulations of the policies and the circumstances attending the loss may indicate that the insurance of the owner should bear the whole loss, or that the insurance of the other person should bear it. Or they may indicate that the loss should be borne partly by the one, partly by the other.

How insurance held by others operates, and what must be covered by the investigation when insurance held by others is encountered, may be illustrated by presenting the situation that arises when cloth is sent to a processing plant for dyeing or finishing and, while there, is damaged or destroyed by fire. If the processor holds insurance covering customers' goods and if the owner of the cloth holds insurance, which insurance should bear the loss? The question can be answered only after both sets of insurance have been examined, and the terms of the contract between the owner of the goods and the processor have been studied. If it is found that the processor had agreed in the contract with the owner to be responsible for any loss by fire while the goods were in the processor's possession, and if the insurance of the processor does not exclude from its protection customers' goods insured by the owners, the processor's insurance should bear the loss.

In such circumstances, claim for the goods can be made under the owner's insurance. But the insurer of the owner will require an assignment to recover from the processor and will, itself, present the claim to the processor or the processor's insurer. Similar situations arise under inland marine policies when an owner insures property shipped by a common carrier that also holds insurance covering its liability as a carrier. In such situations the claim representative should obtain the facts which will show whether the processor, carrier, or other bailee is responsible for the loss.

In *any* loss involving insurance held by others, the claim representative must find out what and how the insurance covers, what contract existed between the holders of the several policies, or what trade custom, statute, or principle of law controlled their relation.

Avoidance of Policy

Concealment or willful misrepresentation of a material fact or circumstance regarding the insurance, the subject thereof, or the interest of the insured, or fraud or false swearing by the insured, whether before or after a loss, will void the insurance.[10]

In some localities policies covering stocks of merchandise contain the *iron safe clause*, which provides that an inventory shall be taken at stipulated times, records of purchases and sales kept, and the books preserved and presented following any loss that occurs while the premises are closed for business. Otherwise the policy shall become void.

The claim representative's investigation of a loss should include an inquiry into any possible avoidance of the policy or suspension of its coverage. If a situation is found in which the facts are such that the insurer is not liable for the loss, the claim representative should not commit the insurer to any course of action until specifically directed to do so. In some cases an honest policyholder will frankly admit the facts that have voided or suspended a policy and will be willing to sign a statement setting them forth. In other cases, the insured will deny them or, if they are obvious, will refuse to be committed in writing. It then becomes necessary for the claim representative to gather evidence that would help to establish the facts should the claim be litigated. In any event, he or she should make a prompt and explicit report to the insurer and await instructions, being careful to avoid doing or saying anything that a court might construe as a *waiver* or an *estoppel*. In many cases, particularly those in which there is possibility of further damage, it is wise to have a nonwaiver agreement or a without-prejudice stipulation executed, after which value and loss may be determined, so that the insured will be free to put the property in order without having to wait until the insurer has decided what action it will take, whether to deny liability, offer a compromise settlement, or waive its defenses and pay in full. While the claim representative should refrain from doing anything that might sustain an allegation of waiver or estoppel, everything necessary should be done to preserve any defenses the insurer may have by collecting the pertinent evidence and making it available for use in possible future litigation.

Cancellation

In a number of cases loss occurs shortly after cancellation of a policy or while efforts are being made to cancel it. The policy prescribes how it may be canceled by the insured and how it may be canceled by the insurer.

The provisions for cancellation by the insured or by the insurer vary in property insurance policies as to the following:

1. Conditions under which cancellation may be made.
2. Effective date of cancellation.
3. Method by which notice is to be given.
4. Basis for refunding the unearned premium.
5. Conformance with statutory requirements.

An effort by either to effect cancellation may be successful or may fail. When such an effort is made by one party to the contract, self-interest or misunderstanding may cause the other to deny its effectiveness.

Methods for Effecting Cancellation. Cancellation may be made by the insurer or by

---

[10]For discussion of policy provisions on these, see Chap. 3, "Insurance Policies Covering Property."

the insured. If the cancellation is by the insured, it is effective on receipt of such notice by the insurer or its agent. Furthermore, to be effective, the policy need not be surrendered by the insured, and the excess of paid premium above the customary short rates for the expired time need not be refunded by the insurer.

If the insurer cancels the policy, the effectiveness will depend on compliance with the cancellation provisions in the particular policy and also on the statutes of the state in which cancellation is undertaken since many states have statutes which affect or modify policy provisions. For example, several states require that the unearned premium accompany notice of cancellation.

Most difficulties arise in proving that notice of cancellation was actually given the insured. While some insurance policies provide that proof of mailing is all that is necessary to prove notice, the standard fire policy has no such provision.

There are at least four methods by which the insurer may undertake to give the insured the written notice required by the policy terms:
(1) by personal service of such written notice upon the insured;
(2) by ordinary letter sent by first-class mail;
(3) by ordinary letter sent by first-class mail, supported by an affidavit as to mailing, and a post office receipt on Form No 3817;
(4) by registered mail addressed to the named insured, with request to the post office that the same be delivered to the addressee only.

The first method is probably the nearest foolproof means but it has the vice of inconvenience and preservation of evidence. It probably requires the affidavit of someone who has witnessed the delivery of the notice to the insured.

The second and third methods are vulnerable because the presumption of delivery of the item mailed is rebuttable, and under the second method, proof of mailing becomes an additional burden for the party maintaining that cancellation notice has been served.

The fourth method is considerably more expensive but continues to enjoy favor in the business because of tradition and experience.

Nearly everyone attaches considerably more significance to the receipt of an item of registered mail than to any other type. While no cases directly in point have been discovered, it seems quite obvious that a handwriting expert might become involved if an insured denied that the signature on the receipt card for an item of registered mail was his signature.[11]

However, even using certified or registered mail has not always been trouble-free. Mail becomes lost; insureds move or go on trips; insureds, unaware of the content of the letter of notification, fail to call at the post office for it; insureds are delayed in picking up the notice or having it picked up by a messenger, or the messenger may lose it. These and similar situations have happened, and the courts have held the insurer liable for losses occurring within five days after the insured has actually received and read the notice of cancellation.

When the claim representative encounters circumstances indicating attempted or actual cancellation, he or she must establish the facts that will prove or disprove that cancellation had been effected prior to the loss. Efforts to cancel may have been commenced too late or may have been otherwise insufficient to complete cancellation before the time of the loss. As a cancellation ends the right of any other insurers participating in the insurance to demand contribution from the canceled policy, another insurer is often the real party interested in the effectiveness of efforts to cancel. On the other hand, cancellation will leave the insured without protection if the canceled policy was the only insurance.

Disputes. Cases of disputed cancellation usually occur when an insurer has ordered cancellation, and loss occurs before the policy is surrendered by the insured. The order to cancel may have been handled by the agent in a way that delays actual cancellation. Efforts to substitute another policy for

[11]Annotation of the 1943 New York Standard Fire Insurance Policy, Section of Insurance Law, American Bar Association, Chicago, 1967.

the one to be canceled are responsible for many of the disputes that arise. The agent may represent several insurers. On receiving from one insurer the order to cancel its policy, the agent will immediately rewrite the insurance and mail the new policy to the insured, asking for the return of the policy ordered canceled. The agent handles the situation in this manner in order to keep the insured covered. If the insured accepts the new policy and returns the one asked for, he or she thereby consents to the cancellation, and the substitution of the new policy for the other is effective. But it sometimes happens that the loss occurs while the insured has both policies or before receiving the second policy. It is under such circumstances that most of the disputes over *cancellation by substitution* originate.

Disputes may also arise over the status of a policy that the insured wishes to cancel. If there is an apparent failure of the insured's attempt to return the policy or give the agent or insurer a definite statement of intention to cancel, and if loss occurs, other insurers insuring the property may dispute the cancellation and demand contribution.

Investigation. The first step ordinarily to be taken when investigating a question of cancellation is a discussion with the agent or other insurer's representative, after which the statements should be summarized and recorded by the claim representative. In some cases the claim representative may find it advisable to have the agent go on record in a letter, a signed statement, or an affidavit. Next, the insured should be questioned, and statements likewise recorded. Occasionally it may be necessary to examine the insured under oath. If notice of cancellation was given by the agent or other insurer's representative, the date and hour of its receipt by the insured should be established. If the notice was given by word of mouth, face to face, or by telephone, the insured may disagree with the agent or insurer's representative about the date and hour of the conversation. If word-of-mouth notice was given in the presence of a witness, the witness should be questioned and statements recorded. If

notice of cancellation is given by registered mail, the claim representative should make an abstract of the notice and record the date and signature on the registry return card. In states where statutes provide special methods of cancellation, the investigation should follow the procedure thus laid down, while in localities where special customs have been established and are acquiesced in by all insurers, the procedure required by custom should be followed.

Reports. The claim representative should report both sides of the controversy plus any recommendation. If a claim representative is acting for all insurers, facts only should be reported.

Arbitration. It has become a general practice for insurers involved in a dispute over efforts to cancel and substitute policies to submit the dispute to arbitration, rather than allow it to become the subject of litigation in which the insured would be burdened with the legal expense of determining which insurer should pay.

Cancellation After Loss. The claim representative investigating a loss may find dangerous physical or moral conditions that must be reported to the insurer immediately so that it may order cancellation of its policy pending a report.

QUESTIONS AND PROBLEMS

1. Why is it very important for the claim representative to keep notes relative to the investigation of the insured, the property, and the insurance on other than small routine losses?
2. Briefly define the terms *waiver* and *estoppel*. What is the essential difference between the two?
3. What is a nonwaiver agreement? What is its main purpose?
4. List at least six situations where it may be desirable to have a nonwaiver agreement executed in order to continue the investigation and determine value and loss.
5. The situations when written or recorded

statements are desirable run parallel in many respects to those when a nonwaiver agreement is desirable. The text lists ten simple rules that will aid in taking a satisfactory written statement. List six, in addition to writing legibly in pen and ink.

6. Investigation of the insured is, in most instances, routine, even on serious and complicated losses. Occasionally the insurer, in possession of a policy written through a distant agent, wants more specific information. The Goody Insurance Company assigns a claim to you under a commercial policy and instructs you to investigate the insured thoroughly because the field agent believes the insured is a poor risk. Outline the areas you would cover in your investigation.

7. **a.** Cancellation by the insured is relatively simple. Explain how it may be done effectively.

b. Cancellation by the insurer is a bit more complicated. Explain how it may be done effectively.

c. Difficulties arise in proving that notice of cancellation was actually given the insured. Give four methods available to the insurer for notifying the insured where the policy provides that proof of mailing is all that is necessary to prove notice.

8. Comment on the relative foolproof value of the four methods of cancellation in question 7.

Verifying Cause of Loss

This chapter is devoted to the investigation and verification of the cause of loss, a function performed very early in the work of the claim representative. If it is found that the loss originated from a peril covered under the policy, that part of the claim handling generally is completed. The claim representative is then free to concentrate attention on matters that lead to concluding an adjustment or settlement.

If the cause of the loss is in doubt or it is found that all or part of the loss was caused by a peril not insured against, the claim representative, in an effort to come to an understanding, discusses with the insured what he or she has found and reports promptly to the insurer for instructions. A Non-Waiver Agreement or Reservation of Rights letter should be instituted when a serious question arises. As in the investigating of any matter affecting the insurer's rights, every effort should be made to avoid actions that might be considered a waiver or an estoppel. However, the claim representative's inspection or interviews of witnesses should not be superficial; nor should the assumptions, opinions, observations, or conclusions of others be accepted without satisfactory verification.

RECORDS, EXPERTS, AND WITNESSES

The extent that it is necessary to check records or to interview and obtain statements of witnesses will be known generally after getting the insured's story and inspecting any of the remaining property.

Burglary and theft claims should be checked against police records. In important fire losses it is advisable to check newspaper accounts and reports of fire departments, fire marshals, and fire patrols, as well as those of police departments. The records of the American District Telegraph, the Automatic Fire Alarm Company, and other private protective services should be checked; also any loss reports made by one of the various underwriting bodies, insurer's engineers, and inspectors should be read. Private records, such as disks in the watchman's clock, should be checked, and any report made by the insured's own organization should be examined.

In all unusual losses where it is essential to obtain facts relating to the cause of loss, the property, the insured's interest, etc., available witnesses should be interviewed and their statements taken down in writing for them to sign.

Where photographs will preserve evidence of damage or lack of damage to buildings or contents, or will identify items claimed and their location, snapshots should be taken. Where warranted, the use of a professional photographer should be considered. Photographs should be marked to identify the subject, the position of the camera, the time and date taken, and the photographer.

Sketches and line drawings are often useful when it is necessary to show the location of property in or on a building, to indicate measurements of a structure, or to illustrate specific areas of damage.

Inspection is aided by flashlights, cameras, sectional ladders, and special clothing, hard hats, boots, and shoes. Measuring tapes, folding rules, and notebooks or pads are necessary for thorough examination work.

Where the amount of damage is extensive, or serious questions of coverage are involved, or, as is occasionally the case, maintaining favorable relations with insureds or producers is desirable, the use of special investigators and experts is necessary to verify whether or not a covered peril caused the loss. The objective in the investigation should not be directed toward supporting an assumption but rather toward determining all the facts in support of a rational conclusion.

FUNDAMENTAL CONSIDERATIONS

An investigation which is concerned basically with the cause of loss poses certain fundamental questions which must be answered.

1. If the peril is known, when did it start to operate?
2. If it was a peril insured against, what set it in motion to cause the loss?
3. Was the loss or damage the direct result of a peril insured against?
4. Was the loss or damage caused by a peril not insured against?
5. Was the loss or damage caused by mixed perils—one insured against, the other not insured against?
6. Was the peril insured against set in motion by the negligence of a third party?

When Did the Event Take Place?

The date and hour when the peril commenced must be determined and, in connection with many claims, the location at which it occurred. *Date and hour place the loss as occurring within or without the term of the policy.* The hour is particularly important if a policy commenced or expired on the day of the loss.

Location and time of loss are particularly important under reporting form contracts that require the reporting of values at new locations in the next succeeding monthly report.

Did a Covered Peril Operate?

Property insurance contracts cover specified perils or all risks of physical loss. The specified perils are not defined in the contract although they are generally limited or qualified in one way or another. The all risks of loss contracts cover *all* perils except those specifically excluded. But, here again, in most such contracts the excluded perils are not defined. For example, the specified perils of *fire, windstorm,* and *explosion* are not defined in a specified peril contract. Likewise, the excluded perils of *contamination, vermin, deterioration,* and *inherent vice* are not defined in the all risks of loss policies. Therefore it is necessary to rely on statutes or court decisions for definitions of the perils covered or excluded.

Frequently claim is made for loss allegedly caused by a specified peril, but investigation discloses that the peril never operated. For example, claim for theft where there was no opportunity for theft and none actually occurred; the property was lost or misplaced. The investigation may reveal complete absence of wind at the time when windstorm damage is claimed, or the investigation may show no lightning at the time and place where loss by lightning is claimed.

When the claim representative finds that the peril for which claim is made did not operate to cause the loss, the investigation generally need go no further. An explanation to the insured, pointing out the facts, usually makes possible closing of the file. If the explanation is rejected, evidence by written statements, photographs, or expert testimony should be obtained promptly.

Was the Damage the Direct Result of the Covered Peril?

The loss must be a direct result of the peril insured against, that is, immediate or proximate as distinguished from remote or consequential.[1]

If the investigation discloses that the peril—fire, sprinkler leakage, explosion,

---

[1]See p. 31, for full discussion of direct loss and proximate cause.

etc.—*did* operate, the claim representative then establishes whether or not the damage claimed was a direct result of the peril. While a covered peril may be the proximate cause of loss, the thing, the person, or the events which set the peril in motion to cause the loss are significant. Fire, for example, may be the proximate cause, but the investigation seeks to ascertain how the fire originated and, particularly, whether or not it started as a result of the negligence of a third party.[2]

Was the Loss Caused by an Uncovered Peril?

An uncovered peril, in a named-peril policy, is one which is either not specified or is excluded; in an all risks of loss policy it is one which specifically is excluded. By inspection of the premises, the property or its remains, one may learn that the peril for which claim is made never operated, and the damage was actually caused by a different peril, one not covered.

For example, it is not uncommon to have a claim made that the roof of a building collapsed as a result of wind, but upon investigation it is found that the real cause was a heavy snow load, defective construction, or rotting of supports. Similarly, claims are made under a specified-peril policy for interior water damage during a windstorm. In the absence of any wind-made opening in the walls or roof, if the water seeped around flashings or under shingles, such loss is the result of an uncovered or excluded peril. Claims also are made for sprinkler-leakage damage, but upon investigation the source of the water often is found to be a leaky or broken domestic water-supply pipe or tank.

Very often the insured and the insurer will disagree on the cause of loss because the circumstances under which it occurred are not determinable or cannot be proved. For example, in a common type of loss involving an electric motor, the insured states that smoke was coming from the unit, and that

the fire department was summoned. On arrival the firefighters shut off the electric power and used an extinguisher on the smoking motor. The claim representative, or an electrical expert, on examining the motor, concludes that no fire occurred and the damage was the result of an excluded peril—an electrical short in the wiring. The insured, on the other hand, is convinced that the motor caught fire. In situations of this kind, the claim representative should submit the facts to the insurer for instructions, and at the same time may wish to make recommendations depending upon how well any of the evidence can be substantiated.

Was the Damage Caused by Mixed Perils?

When a covered peril operates to set in motion an uncovered peril, the entire loss is covered. To illustrate, assume that a fire occurs which sets off a serious explosion in a chemical plant. Though the insurance policy excludes the peril of explosion, all of the damage done by both fire *and* explosion is covered as the fire was the cause of the explosion.

If a strong wind blows over a building which is about to collapse from the weight of a 6-foot snow load on the roof and the policy excludes the peril of collapse, the entire loss is nevertheless covered under the peril of windstorm as it caused the collapse.

In both instances cited, the *covered* peril is said to be the proximate or efficient cause which set the force in motion.

However, if a fire policy does not cover the peril of explosion, and an explosion occurs, followed by fire, only the damage resulting from fire is covered. If a building is flooded by seawater during a hurricane, only the wind damage is covered if damage from the peril of flooding is excluded. In these and similar instances of mixed perils, the investigation should determine as accurately as possible the damage done by each peril. The burden of proof of the amount of loss that is caused by the peril covered rests on the insured.

[2]See Chap. 9, "Subrogation Possibilities."

Was the Covered Peril Set in Motion by the Negligence of a Third Party?

Losses are often caused by the negligence of persons other than the owners of the property lost, destroyed, or damaged. Following payment of such a loss, the insurer acquires a right of action against the person who caused the loss and may sue that individual or entity for damages.[3]

PROCEDURE WITH REGARD TO SPECIFIC PERILS

The prime considerations, when investigating the cause of loss, are *when, where,* and *how.* In most instances the cause will be obvious; it will be the result of a fire, an explosion, a windstorm, hailstorm, or some other apparent peril. The time will be readily established from witnesses or records, and the point of origin usually can be determined. A few preliminary questions on the part of the claim representative, and the investigation of cause will be complete.

In other situations—and there are many—investigation must be made in considerable depth to establish as nearly as possible not only when the loss took place, where it originated, and how it occurred, but also whether the facts as determined will bring the happening within the terms and provisions of the particular policy. For this reason the claim representative should have well in mind all the policy language relating to the particular peril or perils involved. In this way he or she is able to set up guidelines which will give the inquiry direction and purpose.

As the investigation progresses, it is often necessary to examine and study the type and extent of damage to the property in order to be reasonably certain that the peril for which claim has been made did or did not cause the loss. Common examples are found in claims made for cracked plaster and broken windows as result of alleged sonic boom, blasting, or explosions in the neighborhood.

Numerous perils, in addition to fire and lightning, are insured against under multiperil policies. There are many exclusions,

provisions, and limitations with respect to individual perils. The forms used in a number of states have provisions which exclude types of losses that are peculiar to the area. For example, in Florida, where hurricanes are not uncommon, Homeowners forms exclude loss to such property as seawalls, cabanas, or screening and supports enclosing swimming pools and patios. An important part of the investigation of cause of loss is finding out what exclusions are applicable.

There are 18 perils insured against in the Broad Form Homeowners and in the Dwelling Building and Contents policies. Many of these perils are found in Special Multi-Peril, Businessowners, HPR or Superior Risk, and Building and Contents policies, in either their basic or extended coverage forms. In the commercial policies sprinkler leakage is a peril insured against.

The perils of fire and lightning are not defined or qualified in any of the policies. Many perils are qualified in all policies but not identically. Before proceeding with any investigation into the cause of loss or whether a particular peril operated to cause the loss, the claim representative must have in mind or in hand a copy of the policy form.

Investigation of cause of loss under the all risks of loss forms is discussed under a separate section later in this chapter.

Fire

The investigation of a fire loss includes the date, hour, place of origin, probable cause, by whom discovered, when and how alarm was given, what fire-fighting apparatus and water supply were used, the nature and extent of destruction or damage, and the features of the property or the risk that were responsible for the origin of the fire or the extent of damages, or that might cause fires in the future.

In fixing the hour of the fire, the claim representative should compare the statement of the insured to other evidence. In practically all cities records are kept by the fire departments showing the times of fire alarms. While there are no such records in country districts, the people are alert to the happening of fire, and there is usually little difficulty in fixing the time with a fair degree of accuracy. When the exact time is a matter of importance, the statements of neighbors or passersby should be recorded.

Isolated property is occasionally destroyed by brush or forest fires. As such fires are often fought by the owners of threatened property, rangers, or other persons, information concerning the time when the fire reached a given place can sometimes be had from the fire fighters.

Because damage done by a friendly fire is not covered by a specified-peril policy, the claim representative must establish whether the fire was hostile or friendly.[4]

Fires are classified according to the place of origin as *on premises, communicated,* or *extended.* A communicated fire is often described as caused by exposure, the exposure being *internal* if the fire that communicated to the insured property started in another occupancy in the same building, or *external* if it started outside the building. The terms "communicated" and "extended" are properly used also in describing losses caused by smoke, water, or falling debris in premises beyond the range of the fire itself. If a communicated fire originates because of negligence on the part of someone other than the insured, his agents, or his employees, the person or organization responsible for it should be located, and the facts indicating negligence should be established as a preparation for *subrogation* proceedings.

Fires are classified according to their causes as *accidental* or *incendiary.* If a fire is accidental, the cause and place of its origin can, in many instances, be determined. Much will depend on the seriousness of the burning. The more destructive the fire, the less chance there is of pinpointing the cause unless someone witnessed the starting of the fire. Frequently the evidence necessary to establish how the fire originated is destroyed. Fires that originate in proximity to chimneys, stacks, heating devices, electric panel boards or boxes, electric motors and appliances, recent scenes of welding and cutting,

paint spray booths, drying ovens, and other specialized machinery or equipment, and in upholstered furniture are examples of accidental fires the cause of which can usually be determined. At least the place of origin is generally fixed.

Great care should be used to avoid attributing the origin of a fire to a definite cause on *mere speculation.* Far too many fires are reported to have originated from such causes as spontaneous combustion, careless smoking, or defective electrical wiring, appliances, or devices, without any substantiating evidence. A comment or statement about the cause made by the insured, an employee, a neighbor, policeman, or fireman, even though a matter of public record, should not be accepted by the claim representative without corroboration. There are a number of reasons for this. The insurer depends on information of this type for statistical purposes, for future underwriting, and also for considering the desirability of continuing insurance on the particular risk involved. Furthermore, by accepting a statement regarding cause without attempting to confirm it, the claim representative may be diverted from learning the *true* cause which might well involve the negligence of a third party or might reveal a condition which had voided or suspended the insurance *prior* to the fire.

The evidence obtained by the claim representative should be studied and sifted until, by elimination, all other than plausible theories can be abandoned, or until it becomes certain that no definite conclusions can be reached. Should the latter be the case, the claim representative can report the fire only as of unknown or undetermined origin.

Spontaneous Ignition. In some kinds of property subject to spontaneous ignition, destructive fermentation or chemical change precedes the outbreak of fire. When it does, the value of the property will have been destroyed by the fermentation or change *before ignition takes place,* and there will be no loss by fire, because the fire will destroy only the worthless mass. Wool, when wet, may first heat, then disintegrate, then take fire. Its value is destroyed by the heat and the disintegration. In coal piles a hot spot may develop and ignite, causing a true fire to spread throughout the rest of the pile. In hay barns, spontaneous combustion may decompose and fire hay that has been stored while wet, destroying both the remains of the hay and the barn. In losses caused by spontaneous ignition, the question of damage done before the outbreak of fire must be considered and all circumstances carefully investigated.

Incendiary Fires. Incendiary fires fall into two general classes: those set for the purpose of collecting insurance and those set for other reasons. In case of a suspected or demonstrable incendiary fire, it is the claim representative's task to determine whether the insured or an outsider is to be suspected or is guilty. In reports on incendiary fires, *inside incendiarism* indicates that the insured caused or procured the fire, and *outside incendiarism* that an outsider was the incendiary.[5]

Fire Fighting. Ordinarily, investigation of the fighting of fire is not necessary. The premises will speak for themselves, and there will be no need for comment in the report. But in large or unusual losses and in losses involving property privately protected, the claim representative should find out and report how the fire was fought, whether the private protection proved to be adequate, and what was the behavior of the personnel that manned it. If a sprinklered risk is involved, the claim representative should check the heads that opened and report the number.

Many fires produce unexpectedly large losses due to delayed alarms, tardy response of the fire-fighting forces, faulty equipment, poor tactics, or inadequate water supply or pressure. In reporting on such fires, the claim representative should present details clearly and dispassionately.

Nature and Extent of Damage. The claim representative should note what parts of the structure, contents, or other property were burned, scorched, heated, or smoked, what may have collapsed as a result of the fire, what may have been damaged by falling debris, what was marred or broken by fire fighters, what was wet, and what has been left exposed to the weather or other influences that may cause further damage.[6]

Features of Risk or Property Affecting Loss. In large and unusual losses, the claim representative should note the details of construction, occupancy, protection, or exposure that were responsible for the origin of the fire and its spread or confinement, or that increased or reduced the amount of damage ordinarily to be expected. He or she should also note any circumstances that may indicate whether a similar loss is probable in the future.

Lightning

Lightning generally shatters any poorly conducting material that it strikes, for example, brick, stone, tile, and wood. It sometimes fuses metal but rarely damages metal that is grounded. It often sets fire to buildings. It does great damage to electrical equipment by striking power lines or by causing induced disturbances sufficiently powerful to rupture insulation and produce short circuits that overload and burn out the coils of transformers, motors, or generators. In most named peril policies of insurance, clauses are incorporated to exempt the insurer from liability for loss or damage to electrical devices, appliances, and equipment caused by artificially generated electrical current. *Claim representatives should not attempt to handle the investigation of serious damage to important electrical equipment without the aid of a competent electrical engineer.*

Property is damaged by lightning in one of three ways: (1) *a direct hit by a bolt of lightning,* (2) *a ground surge,* or (3) *a near miss.*

The direct hit usually leaves a mark of contact or entry into a building. This may be

---

[5]Chap. 10, "Arson Investigation and Detection," covers this subject.

[6]The subject is discussed in detail in Chaps. 14, 16, and 17.

only the shattering of a few bricks in a chimney, but sometimes there may be violent structural and wiring damage without any discernible pattern of the lightning's path as it traveled through the building; or again there may be ignition of the building with partial or total destruction by fire. In most cases where property has suffered a direct hit by lightning, there is no difficulty in establishing the cause of loss.

Problems are encountered on claims for damage to electrical appliances, fixtures, devices, and wiring which is said to have been caused by lightning with no indication that the property received a direct hit. Also, there is usually no evidence that lightning struck anywhere in the vicinity. The majority of these claims involve television sets, radios, elements in electric hot-water heaters, switches or motors on washing machines and dryers, electric clocks and timers, and similar items. The amounts involved are usually small, and generally the first notice to the insurer is accompanied by a paid bill for repairs. It is not uncommon to find the bill marked by the repair firm, "for lightning damage" or a similar phrase. Thousands of such claims are paid each year by insurers, especially in those territories, such as the Southeast, where the incidence of lightning storms is very high.

Efforts to determine to what extent these losses are the result of *ground surge* lightning, sometimes called *atmospheric lightning*, or whether a portion of them are caused by wear and tear, have not been conclusive. There is reason to believe that many are maintenance problems, but others are probably caused by voltage drops or surges in areas where the power company does not have adequate voltage-regulation facilities.

Whenever electrical appliances, motors, or devices are involved, either the claim representative or his or her electrical expert should examine the equipment on the insured's premises or wherever it has been taken for repairs. If repairs have been made before the claim representative makes an inspection, the person who made repairs should be asked to explain in detail what was found upon examination, what part or parts were repaired or replaced because of lightning damage, and how the lightning caused the damage. If the damaged parts are still available, they should be examined by the expert or, in minor losses, by the claim representative.[7]

Removal

The HO-2 covers the peril of removal, meaning "loss by removal of the property covered hereunder from premises endangered by the perils insured against. The applicable limit applies pro rata for 30 days at each proper place to which such property shall necessarily be removed for preservation from or for repair of damage caused by the perils insured against."

This is, for all practical purposes and subject to any general exclusions, an all risks coverage—but only *during* the removal. The investigation should show that loss for which claim is made occurred during and as a result of the removal of the property covered from the premises endangered. For example, during a widespread brush fire the insured, with the help of neighbors, removes articles of personal property from a home which is threatened with destruction. Certain of the items are damaged by handling, and others are made worthless by submersion when a car in which they were being transported plunges into a lake. As long as the damage in handling and by submersion is the direct result of removal, the loss is covered.

If the claim is made for property that has been removed for preservation and stored in a place other than the described location, the claim representatives should determine: (1) whether it has been stored longer than the number of days specified, (2) whether claim for damage at the storage location is for a covered peril, and (3) what insurance is applicable during the specified period. This would be that proportion of the total insurance on personal property which the value at the temporary storage location bears to the total value of all personal property covered.

[7]See Sudden and Accidental Injury From Electrical Currents, p. 121.

After the period of limitation, under the removal peril, the amount of insurance on "personal property away from the premises" is applicable to the storage location without any limit of time.

Windstorm or Hail

With respect to windstorm and hail, the Broad Form HO-2 (Ed. 9-70) reads as follows:

Excluding loss:
a. caused directly or indirectly by frost or cold weather or ice (other than hail), snow or sleet, all whether driven by wind or not;
b. to the interior of the building, or the property covered therein caused by rain, snow, sand or dust, all whether driven by wind or not, unless the building covered or containing the property covered shall first sustain an actual damage to roof or walls by the direct force of wind or hail and then this Company shall be liable for loss to the interior of the building or the property covered therein as may be caused by rain, snow, sand or dust, entering the building through openings in the roof or walls made by direct action of wind or hail; or
c. to watercraft (except rowboats and canoes on premises) including their trailers, furnishings, equipment and outboard motors while such property is not inside fully enclosed buildings.

The Standard Businessowners Policy follows the above wording but exclusion c reads, regarding property outside of buildings:

(1) awnings of fabric or slat construction, including their supports;
(2) radio or television antennas, including their lead-in wiring, masts or towers.

The Homeowners Special Form 3, an all risk of loss coverage on A and B (Dwelling and certain structures), does not exclude loss to the interior of the building itself as in a and b above. Those exclusions do apply to Coverage C (Personal Property) which is subject to specified perils. The Homeowners 76,

HO-3, has slightly different wording. Exclusion c above is the same in all HO-3 forms.

The Special Multi-Peril (SMP), General Property Form (MLB-100, Ed. 2-71), and the Building and Contents Form 18 (Ed. 3-70) read almost identically. They contain the usual *frost* and *cold weather* or *ice* exclusion; loss to the interior of the building by rain, snow, etc., except when entrance is through openings in roof or wall made by direct force of the wind; and loss by water from the sprinkler equipment unless such equipment is damaged as a direct result of the wind. Both policies contain the following additional exclusions unless liability is assumed in the form or by endorsement:

(a) Windmills, wind pumps or their towers;
(b) Crop silos or their contents;
(c) Metal smokestacks; or
(d) When outside of buildings,
   (1) Grain, hay, straw or other crops,
   (2) Lawns, trees, shrubs or plants,
   (3) Awnings or canopies (fabric or slat) including their supports,
   (4) Signs or radio or television antennas, including their lead-in wiring, masts or towers.

Investigation of windstorm claims should cover the date and hour the damage occurred, the duration of the windstorm, the direction of the wind, and the probable maximum velocity. Such records usually can be obtained from nearby sources such as the U.S. Weather Bureau, local airports, and amateur and professional meteorologists.

There is no uniformity of opinion throughout the country on what constitutes a windstorm. Therefore problems arise, particularly on more serious losses, when there is reason to believe the damage may have been caused by an uninsured peril such as defective design or construction, decay or deterioration of structural members, overloading of floors, weight of snow on roofs, and so forth. While there may have been breezes or light winds in the area at the time of a collapse of a roof or part of a building, there is much justification in such cases for questioning whether an actual windstorm caused the loss. It is well recognized that the burden of proof rests upon the insured to prove a direct loss by windstorm. However, if the insured introduces evidence that the loss could have been caused by windstorm, and the insurer introduces evidence to the contrary, if the jury finds for the insured on the disputed evidence the court will uphold the verdict. It has done so in numerous cases.

In the case of *Clark v. Fidelity & Guaranty Fire Corporation*, 39 N.Y.S. 2nd 377, it was held that a wind which has a velocity of 28 miles per hour falls far short of qualifying under any or all of the definitions of a windstorm.

Many other courts, however, have applied a far different ruling in defining a windstorm. In the case of *Gerhard v. The Travelers Fire Insurance Company*, 18 N.W.2d 336, 246 Wis. 625, the court stated that no definition of windstorm was inserted in the Extended Coverage Endorsement. The court held in the absence of definition or limitation in the policy: "... We think that a windstorm must be taken to be a wind of sufficient violence to be capable of damaging the insured property either by its own unaided action or by projecting some object against it. This is especially true where as here the more violent forms of windstorm are especially named as something different from a mere windstorm. Any other view would work an imposition upon the insured. If defendant wishes to adopt some scale which establishes the velocity of wind necessary for a windstorm, or if it desires to limit its liability beyond the point that we have indicated, it should incorporate its proposed standard in the policy by clear terms and such ambiguities as are left in this policy should be resolved against it."

In this particular case the wind velocity was between 25 and 28 miles per hour. This holding was likewise followed by the Georgia courts in case of *Atlas Assur. Co. Ltd. v. Lies*, 70 Ga. App. 162, 27 S.E.2d 791.

The majority of the courts appear to follow the general ruling that a windstorm is a tumultuous wind, violent in character. The New York courts hold that a wind which is 28 miles or less does not fulfill these characteristics.

Many courts, however, follow the Gerhard case, *supra*, and hold that any wind which is actually capable of doing damage is a windstorm within the terms and conditions of the policy of insurance since the underwriters have not seen fit to insert a definition of windstorm or a limitation of type of wind in the policy contract itself.[8]

Investigation of windstorm losses involving plate glass should determine whether the glass is also covered by plate glass insurance. The Guiding Principles[9] have special rules for apportioning such losses between the building and plate glass insurers.

Frost or cold-weather claims are infrequent.

Ice losses result from falling ice, encrusted on the branches of trees or the upper parts of buildings during an ice storm, and from floating ice on bodies of water. In falling ice losses, the breakage or other damage done by the ice and the statements of witnesses about what happened are, ordinarily, the only evidence the claim representative can obtain. In floating ice losses the property is generally damaged near the ground or the water level. True wind damage is generally high upon a structure. Photographs are useful in floating ice losses.

Snowstorm losses occur when so much snow falls on the roof of a building that its weight displaces or breaks the roof timbers. The condition of the roof and the absence of wind damage in the immediate vicinity of the property are the facts tending to prove that the cause of loss is not wind.

As damage to the interior of a building or to property in it caused by rain, snow, sand, or dust, whether driven by wind or not, is not covered under a specified-peril policy unless there was prior damage to the roof or walls by the wind or hail, investigation must be made in cases involving interior damage to determine whether any such prior damage occurred. The situation most frequently encountered is one in which rain is driven through cracks around windows and doors or penetrates a leaky roof, damaging plaster and

---

[8]Max J. Gwertzman, "A Legal Analysis of the Extended Coverage Endorsement," *The Insurance Advocate*, Roberts Publishing Co., New York.
[9]See p. 466.

decorations. Furthermore, only so much of any interior damage is covered as is caused by rain, snow, sand, or dust entering through openings in roof or walls caused by direct action of wind or hail. Investigation required in cases of interior damage is a careful inspection of the roof and walls of the building for openings made by wind or hail. In losses caused partly by rain entering through such openings and partly by rain that entered around windows or through leaks, the two sorts of damage should be separately listed. In doubtful situations, any persons who were on the premises during the storm should be questioned.

Small losses often result from wind slamming swinging doors or blinds that have been left open and breaking the glass in doors or windows. Blowing through an open house, wind sometimes blows fragile articles off tables or blows breakable articles over or off their supports. Pictures and mirrors hung on walls are examples. Such losses may not be true windstorm losses unless the wind is blowing at storm velocity. Investigation should include an inspection of the broken articles and the door or window through which the wind entered.

Other forms have provisions applicable to windstorm and hail which may be similar or substantially different. The claim representative should have the policy available to check or should carry specimen forms to guide in the investigation.

Wind Versus Water Damage. Losses due to tidal wave, high water, or overflow, whether driven by wind or not, occur on the shores of the ocean and other bodies of water, along the banks of rivers and streams, or in low-lying areas, subject to overflow. The tidal wave, or storm tide, as it is also called, that accompanies hurricanes and other severe storms frequently breaks up and washes away shore structures. It raises the level of the water in bays and estuaries, sometimes enough to overflow the shores and flood structures built on them.

Investigation of such losses requires an inspection of the property or, if it has been washed away by wave action or floated off by overflow, an inspection of the site where it stood. Damage to property that is in evidence should be noted. Water marks left by high water on or in buildings inundated should be observed and the depth of the water in the structure determined by measuring their height. Photographs are useful. If the property has been washed away or floated off, the height attained at the site by the water should be determined if possible. In all losses involving wave wash or inundation, the sequence of events should be a subject of inquiry. Available witnesses should be questioned to determine the course of the storm and whether there was any wind damage to the property prior to the time the water reached it. In many instances, no witnesses are available, as few persons care to be out of doors during a violent storm.

In river country subject to overflow, difficult tasks are set for the claim representative by claimants who state that just before high water reached their property it was blown to pieces by wind.

Where there is mixed damage, part caused by wind and part by flooding, or other water damage not covered by the policy, the claim representative must make a detailed separation. The NFIA Worksheets (Appendix P) or the GAB Special Wavewash Statement (Appendix R) may be used as guides.

Explosion

The peril of explosion is not defined or limited in the broader Homeowners policies HO-2 to HO-6 nor in any of the later HO-76 forms, nor in all risks of physical loss forms except commerical multi-peril forms that include boiler and machinery coverage, in which case loss to steam boilers, steam pipes, steam turbines, or steam engines is not covered against loss caused by any condition or occurrence within those items except direct loss resulting from explosion within the firebox or combustion chamber or within flues, etc.

There are very few cases of explosions in residential properties that create problems concerning the cause. They generally are gas explosions from leaking gas pipes or gas-burning appliances and furnaces, oil-fired furnace-box explosions, and occasional explosions in hot-water heaters or in steam boilers.

Most difficulties involve explosions in commercial and manufacturing risks, either because the exact cause cannot be pinpointed or because there is a lack of agreement between the insured and the insurer that an explosion actually occurred.

Engineers and physicists think of explosion as the rapid and destructive expansion of a gas or gases, sometimes resulting from the failure of containers of compressed gases, or sometimes from ignition or detonation of gases or other substances possessing explosive characteristics.

The courts have been reluctant to accept the opinions of the engineers and the physicists, and in explosion cases have generally allowed the jury to decide whether the evidence presented proved that an explosion had occurred. Consequently, insurers have, in many instances, been held liable for kinds of losses they never intended to cover under contracts insuring against explosion. In an effort to exclude such losses, the provisions applicable to the explosion peril in certain policies have been gradually enlarged upon to except specific occurrences which are not considered explosions under the contract.

The following explosion peril is found in several forms including HO-1, MLB-100, Standard Businessowners Policy, and Building and Contents Form 18.

EXPLOSION, including direct loss resulting from the explosion of accumulated gases or unconsumed fuel within the firebox (or combustion chamber) of any fired vessel or within the flues or passages which conduct the gases of combustion therefrom. [A typical example is the so-called "puff-back" in furnaces.]

This Company shall not be liable for loss by explosion of steam boilers, steam pipes, steam turbines or steam engines, if owned by, leased by or operated under the control of the insured.

The following are not explosions within the intent or meaning of these provisions:

(a) Shock waves caused by aircraft, generally known as "sonic boom,"

(b) Electric arcing,

(c) Rupture or bursting of rotating or moving parts of machinery caused by centrifugal force or mechanical breakdown,

(d) Water hammer,

(e) Rupture or bursting of water pipes,

(f) Rupture or bursting due to expansion or swelling of the contents of any building or structure, caused by or resulting from water,

(g) Rupture, bursting or operation of pressure relief devices.

When investigating explosion losses, the claim representative should determine when and where the explosion occurred, tracing the origin as near as possible to any material, machine, apparatus, equipment, piping, appliance, boiler, or firebox involved. He or she should learn everything possible about the history and function of the unit and whether it was in operation at the time of the explosion. Such inquiry should lead to any witnesses to the explosion, such as passersby or employees who had knowledge of the machinery, equipment, or apparatus involved.

In the case of serious losses the claim representative should bring in experts who specialize in investigating explosion and concussion losses.

The claim representative should proceed on the assumption that a true explosion is the result of the sudden creation or expansion of gas. A variety of gases, fluids, and solids will explode if ignited, heated, or detonated. A mixture of inflammable gas with air or oxygen, or of inflammable dust with air, will, if ignited, explode. Excessive pressure of air or other gas pumped into a tank will explode it.

Ruptures, breakages, and displacements of tanks, containers, pipes, or valves, due to the pressure of fluids, whether static or in motion, are not explosions. The forcing open of the sides or bottoms of bins or structures overloaded with grain, or other masses made up of small particles, no matter how sudden or violent, is not an explosion.

Whether insurance against explosion covers damage due to *implosion*, that is, a bursting inward rather than outward, such as occasionally happens when the contents of a tank or other container are pumped out without admitting air to equalize internal and external pressure, is an unsettled question. *The consensus is that implosion is the antithesis of explosion.*

Explosions, like fires, may be accidental or intentional and should be investigated accordingly.

The inherent explosion hazard is high in gas-producing plants, chemical works, and plants that make explosives, owing to the character of the materials they use. It is dangerous in grain elevators, flour mills, and starch mills because of the inflammable dust they produce; also in some textile plants where operations create quantities of flying lint. In garages, in many manufacturing plants, and in stores, offices, and dwellings there is some degree of inherent explosion hazard due to heating fuels, cleaning fluids, solvents, and other inflammable substances. Occasionally there is a hazard due to operations requiring air or gas to be kept under pressure.

The location of some property exposes it to damage from explosion occurring in other property. Property surrounding gas plants, gas-storage holders, or tanks containing explosive gases or highly inflammable liquids is an example.

Intentional explosions are legally set off by blasters and oil-well operators. Explosion insurance is liable for damage done to other property by such intentionally caused explosion, as there is no doctrine of *friendly* explosion as there is of friendly fire. Intentional explosions are criminally caused by saboteurs, gangsters, and individual bomb throwers. On rare occasions, a policyholder, generally in trying to burn his property in order to collect insurance, willfully destroys it by explosion. Explosives are also used by burglars to blow open safes and vaults. When investigating an explosion loss due to the criminal use of an explosive, the claim representative should bear in mind that burglary insurance covers damage done by persons who break and enter and should discover whether any burglary insurance is carried.

Investigation of explosion losses should include inspection and examination of the remains of the property, or of the site if the property has been obliterated, and the questioning of any persons who have knowledge of the sequence of events leading up to and immediately following the explosion. Evidence to be gathered when any claim is made for excepted losses, explosion, rupture, or bursting of steam boilers, steam pipes, steam turbines, or flywheels should be directed toward determining whether the article of property that exploded, ruptured, or burst was owned, operated, or controlled by the insured and whether it was located within or outside the building or buildings covered by the policy.

When property is covered only by fire insurance and is damaged by both fire and explosion, investigation should seek to determine whether explosion preceded or followed the fire. If explosion occurred first, evidence on the amount of loss caused by the fire must be obtained. The fire insurance policy excludes loss due to explosion and, in case of explosion followed by fire, covers only the ensuing fire loss. The courts have held, without exception, that if fire occurs first and causes explosion, the explosion is an incident of the fire and the explosion loss is part of the fire loss.

When property is covered by separate fire and explosion contracts, investigation should follow the same course.

The covering of both fire and explosion by the use of fire policies with extended coverage endorsements makes it unnecessary to separate fire and explosion damage in most losses involving explosion.

When property is damaged by explosion occurring as the result of negligence on the part of any person who is not a party to the insurance contract, the insurer, on paying the loss, acquires a right of action against such person, as in the case of fire.

A firebox explosion, covered under the extended coverage endorsement of the fire policy, may also be covered under the boiler and machinery policy. The claim representative should always check the possibility that it is covered by examining the insured's policy. Provisions for apportioning such losses between insurers are set forth in the Guiding Principles in Chapter 27.

Blasting Losses. A great number of cases are brought against blasters for damage to adjacent property caused by flying debris or concussion. Investigation of losses due to blasting operations should determine whether the blaster was negligent, used excessive charges, set off blasts too frequently, drilled or blasted too close to other property, or failed to use protective mats to prevent debris from being blown into the air. Any investigation which is made of a blasting loss should include questioning the blaster about possible insurance held by him for the benefit of adjacent property owners. The claim representative should become familiar with the liability of a blaster in the state where any damage caused by blasting occurred.

In dealing with any claim for damage allegedly due to blasting, the first step is always to determine the cause of the damage. The noise of a blast may cause many people in the vicinity to believe that their property has been damaged, and once they begin to look around they are almost sure to discover cracks and foundation failures they have never noticed before. Immediately they file a claim either against the blaster or against the property owner's insurance company. But the matter never stops there, for one claim always leads to another. And before long everyone in the neighborhood is filing a claim. A blasting operation rarely produces a single claim; it produces none at all, or many.[10]

Prompt inspection of the property on which blasting damage is claimed is very important. New and old cracks in materials such as wood and plaster are easily distinguished soon after an explosion. As weeks or months pass, dirt, dust, and spider webs accumulate, making it difficult, in many cases, to be certain whether the cracks are of recent origin or not. Diagrams and sketches of the location, size, and shape of all cracks are important. In many instances photographs are helpful in preserving evidence.

The purpose and the location of the blasting should be determined and the site visited by the claim representative. The party who is doing the blasting (or who did it) should be contacted to obtain the story, examine any records or log, and make inquiry concerning the liability insurer.

Often the adjuster will find that a vibration expert has conducted seismographic tests before or during the blasting operations to determine their results or probable effects. If such tests have been made, the adjuster should make every attempt to secure the information they have revealed. Occasionally, but not often enough, the contractor or his representative makes preblasting surveys to determine the condition of the buildings in the potential area of damage before any blasting occurs. Again, the adjuster will find such information of great value.

If at this point the adjuster is still in doubt about the exact cause of the damage, he should not hesitate to suggest to the company he represents that a vibration expert be retained for consultation. Too many adjusters fail to search out expert advice even when the situation clearly indicates that it is called for.

Vibration is a highly specialized field of study, and vibration experts are scientists or engineers who have made a specialty of the causes and effects of earth movement and air movement. They differ from building contractors, who are qualified to estimate the cost of repairs but generally are not expert in discovering the cause that made those repairs necessary.

If possible, inspection of the damage should be made jointly by adjusters representing the liability carriers and property insurers. The adjusters should always make a point of telling the property owner who the company representatives are, what companies they represent, and what the purpose of the visit is.

If the casualty interests agree that liability exists, they may be willing to take over the adjustment. But if the direct property adjuster is convinced that the blasting did not cause the damage, his company may wish to consult and cooperate in the investigation and defense of the claim with the blaster and his insurance carrier.

In those cases where adjustment is concluded by property insurance carriers, the company may wish to ascertain from counsel

[10]*Blasting Damage: A Guide for Adjusters and Engineers*, by Property Claim Services of American Insurance Association.

whether the blasting took place in an absolute liability state, or whether it is necessary to prove negligence before the blaster can be held liable. Blasting has been held to be an ultrahazardous activity, and some states hold that anyone who carries on an ultrahazardous activity is liable for harm. Other states, on the other hand, hold that negligence must be proved before the blaster can be held liable.

Blasting operations are often carried on under written contracts with indemnifying agreements under which the blaster assumes certain liabilities for damages caused by his operations beyond any liability imposed on him by law, even though he is free from negligence. In some places, the blaster is required to secure a permit or license from a public authority before doing any blasting. And quite often the blaster must agree to pay for any damage caused by his operations before the permit is granted.

Consequently, whenever an adjuster is investigating claims for damage by blasting, he should always find out whether the blaster was operating under any written contract or under the authority of any permit or license. If there is any such arrangement, the adjuster should always be sure to examine all the documents involved, including the blaster's application for a license or permit to determine whether the blaster has agreed to pay for damage caused by him regardless of fault. The adjuster should copy down the text of any such agreement word for word and report it to his company.[11]

Checklist for adjusters:[12]

1. Inspect the property.
2. Itemize the damage.
3. Make an on-the-spot sketch of the damage.
4. Examine the blaster's log.
5. Estimate distance from point of discharge to point of claim.
6. Observe nature of ground.
7. Study seismographic test, if available.
8. Study pre-blasting surveys of nearby buildings, if available.

9. Examine and copy any contract, permit, or license containing agreement by blaster to pay for damage.
10. Consult company regarding expert advice if cause is still not clear.

Riot, Riot Attending a Strike, Civil Commotion

These perils include direct loss from pillage and looting occurring during and at the immediate place of a riot or a riot attending a strike or civil commotion, in addition to destruction or damage to the property covered.

There are two general kinds of riot losses: (1) loss caused by a riot of such proportions as to alarm an entire city or neighborhood and (2) loss caused by a group of persons who operate in a stealthy manner. No special investigation is necessary if a riot is a matter of common knowledge, was handled by the police, and was noted in the newspapers. But when claim is made under riot insurance for damage done by persons who gained access to the premises by stealth and, after damaging or looting them, escaped before the neighbors or the police were aware of what was happening, it is essential that the claim representative try to establish by questioning witnesses whether there were more than two persons in the group that caused the loss. Except in states that have provided otherwise either by court decision or by statute,[13] there is no riot unless at least three persons participate in the lawless act. Sometimes premises are entered in the night, and machinery is smashed or stock is cut to pieces, sprinkled with acid, or fouled with a stench bomb. There will be no evidence indicating whether the damage was done by fewer than three persons or by three or more. In such a case there is no proof of riot.

When loss is the result of breaking and entering or pillage and looting, investigation must determine whether the insured also carries burglary insurance that covers it.

Many of the commercial forms, under provisions applicable to this peril, include

---

[11]Ibid.
[12]Ibid.

[13]A few states have enacted statutes making the joint lawless action of two or more persons a riot. *Walter v. Northern Insurance Company*, 370 Ill. 283, 18 N.E.2d 906.

"direct loss by acts of striking employees of the owner or tenant(s) of the described property while occupied by said striking employees," and unless the policy is specifically endorsed, there is no liability for damage to described property due to change in temperature or humidity or interruption of operations. For example, if strikers shut off the refrigeration in a cold-storage plant, any loss to contents as a result of a change in temperature would not be covered.

The Homeowners Broad Form and the Dwelling Building(s) and Contents policies provide no exclusions to this peril. Both policies include pillage and looting during and at the immediate place of the riot or civil commotion.

Civil commotion is an uprising among a mass of people having for its purpose the defying of civil authority and order. It is generally political in genesis, whereas rioting is more often related to social economics. In some situations the two terms are not easily distinguishable.

The words "riot" and "civil commotion," as used in the contract, in lawsuits will be given their popular or usual meaning by the courts and will be held to imply the wild or irregular action or tumultuous conduct on the part of three or more persons assembled together for the common purpose of doing an unlawful act.[14]

The investigation should include inquiry into whether or not legislation has been enacted making the municipality, county, or state responsible for damage done during riot and civil commotion.

Aircraft, Self-Propelled Missiles, Spacecraft

There are no limiting provisions applicable to the peril of aircraft under the all risks and the broader named peril Homeowners policies. Under other specified peril forms and extended coverage endorsements, aircraft and vehicle perils are usually combined and have specific provisions and limitations.

On occasion, private, military, or commercial planes crash into homes, causing serious damage from impact, as well as by fire if fire ensues. Investigation into the cause of this type is made solely for purposes of subrogation.

Where there is no provision requiring *actual physical contact* of the aircraft with the described property as in most commercial policies, damage caused by sonic boom is covered. Certain forms or endorsements specifically exclude sonic boom; the HRP Form specifically covers *sonic shock wave*. It is therefore important to examine the policy involved to determine coverage.

Sonic Boom. A sonic boom is caused by shock waves which build up around an aircraft flying at supersonic speeds—normally about 762 miles per hour at sea level. The waves form a cone, extending back from the nose of the plane, much like the waves created by a boat speeding over water. The shock waves travel to the ground at the speed of sound and follow the path of the aircraft. The sound waves become audible when they slap against the surface of the earth, just as water washing against the shore can be heard. This same kind of pressure wave is created by a common thunderclap.

Sonic boom is the sound that is heard, whereas the pressure waves are the cause of the damage. The higher the aircraft is flying, the less intense are the pressure waves. Although supersonic flights are not authorized below 35,000 feet, there are occasions when supersonic flights are made at lower altitudes.

As a result of a rather important court decision[15] in 1959, sonic boom is not considered to be an explosion.

Ordinarily, damage from sonic boom is confined to cracked or shattered window glass, bric-a-brac vibrated off shelves, doors slammed open or shut, breaking the door or frame, aggravation of existing plaster cracks, or creation of new cracks in weak or poor plaster. Plaster cracks and structural damage

[14]*State v. Stalcup*, 23 N.C. 30, 35 Am. Dec. 732. *Symonds v. State*, 66 Okl. Cr. 49, 89 P.2d 970, 973.

[15]*Bear Bros., Inc., v. Fidelity & Guaranty Ins. Underwriters, Inc.*, Circuit Ct. of Montgomery County, Ala., No. 24164.

are improbable without extensive glass breakage.

The United States Air Force has conducted numerous simulated bombing runs over various cities, including Oklahoma City, Milwaukee, Chicago, and St. Louis. The tests were publicized in advance by the Air Force with an offer to pay for any resulting damage. Many claims were received but, as in blasting cases, much of the alleged damage was preexisting and the result of settlement, defective construction, and deterioration. People frequently, upon hearing a sonic boom, inspect their property and note preexisting cracks in plaster or other damage which they sincerely believe was the result of the sonic boom.

Insureds should be encouraged to present their claims to the nearest Claims Officer of the United States Air Force, as the Air Force has a preference for dealing directly with the property owner rather than through the insurer. Standard Claim Form 95 should be submitted. If claim is filed by the insurer under a subrogation agreement, the same claim form is used, together with other documents.

Vehicles

Excluded under the HO-2 and residential broad forms is loss to driveways, fences, and walks caused by a vehicle *owned* or *operated* by an occupant of the premises. In the extended coverage endorsement, vehicles are defined as "vehicles running on land or tracks but not aircraft nor movable apparatus covered by this policy."

As with the peril aircraft, the HO-2 does not require actual physical contact by the vehicle. The extended coverage endorsement and HO-1 do require actual physical contact with the property covered. Also, the extended coverage endorsement and its equivalent, in various policies, exclude loss by any vehicle owned or operated by an insured or by any tenant of the described premises, and loss by any vehicle to fences, driveways, walks or lawns, trees, shrubs, or plants. The language varies in the several forms. For that reason the claim representative must keep in mind the particular form to determine whether coverage is available to the insured.

A *vehicle* is "any conveyance used as a means of transporting persons or things on land, in the air, or on water, or a mechanical device running on wheels or tracks." Among the many types of vehicles included in this definition are automobiles, tractors, bulldozers,[16] motorcycles, bicycles, scooters, go-carts, sleds, boats, trains, trolley cars, earth-moving equipment, mobile hoists and derricks, and lift trucks.

Claims are occasionally made for personal property which has been damaged in or on a vehicle or as a result of contact with a vehicle. Under the wording of the HO-2 and similar forms, the following interpretations represent a consolidation of opinions of the Committee on Losses and Adjustments of the PLRB (Property Loss Research Bureau).

There is coverage for the following:

1. Insured's suit torn when he or she is struck by vehicle.
2. Insured's hat crushed when insured is run over by vehicle.
3. Insured's furniture in or on vehicle—struck by a second vehicle.
4. Insured's furniture broken or damaged when thrown from vehicle as result of an accident (such as collision or overturn).
5. Insured's clothing damaged when driver is injured due to vehicle striking object.

There is no coverage for the following:

1. Clothing of insured's child torn when he or she runs into stationary vehicle in driveway.
2. Clothing of passenger torn by catching on projection in or on a stationary vehicle.
3. Insured's fragile article damaged when struck against part of a stationary vehicle.
4. Insured's property, improperly loaded, falling from vehicle—no unusual incident.
5. Insured's property damaged in course of transportation—no unusual incident.
6. Tarpaulin covering contents on top of vehicle or on trailer coming loose and being damaged by excess flapping.
7. Rain or snow damaging contents of vehicle because windows leak or are left open.

[16]*Golding–Keene Co. v. Fidelity–Phenix Co.*, 96 N.H. 64, 69 Atl. 2d 856.

Under the vehicle peril, depending on the particular form, insurers attempt to except damage caused by vehicles owned or driven by tenants, residents, or occupants of the described premises, or *by the insured or his employees.* Where the vehicle is owned by the insured, an occupant, or a tenant of the premises, the language is clear. The HPR Form excludes damage by a vehicle operated by an *employee* of the insured, and here there is no ambiguity.

Problems arise when the damage is done by a vehicle owned or driven by an agent or employee of the insured and the form itself only excludes vehicles "owned or driven by the insured."[17] Is the "agent or employee" synonymous with the "insured"? In *Scranton v. Hartford Fire Ins. Co*, 4 CCH (Auto 2d) 1361, Conn. Supreme Ct. of Errors, 1954, such contention by the insurer was denied.

The course and depth of the investigation into the cause of loss will depend on the circumstances in each case. Where a hit-and-run driver has damaged the insured's building, little more may be necessary than obtaining the story of the insured and statements of any witnesses and getting a copy of the police report if one is available. When any vehicle causes damage to the insured's property, and the vehicle and driver can be identified, the claim representative investigates with the primary object of obtaining evidence for purposes of subrogation.

If the policy requires actual physical contact with the described property as a precedent to recovery, damage by stones flicked up by a passing car and breaking a plate glass window is not covered.

In the absence of a provision requiring actual physical contact with the insured's property, if the vehicle is the proximate cause of loss, the damage is covered. For example, a car strikes a tree in front of the building. As a consequence the tree falls on the insured's building, damaging the structure and its contents. This is a loss by vehicle.

All questions of doubtful coverage should be reported to the insurer along with the facts and a request for instructions.

[17]Standard Businessowners and named peril SMP, FGP-1, Form 18, and other policies.

Smoke

Under the peril of smoke the damage must be *sudden and accidental* as opposed to gradual accumulation over a period of time. The named peril policies generally exclude damage by smoke from agricultural or industrial operations.

Smoke damage is identified by a deposit of soot or smoke film. Smoke marks should be examined and traced to the unit from which the smoke escaped. If the appearance of the property suggests that the damage resulted from a day-by-day buildup of a small volume of smoke, instead of a *sudden and accidental occurrence*, it will be necessary to question the insured rather closely.

Damage resulting from smoke created by friendly fires would be covered under this peril, although damage from the fire itself would not be. Smoke from defectively operating fireplaces, from rubbish and bonfires, from incinerators, and, of course, from faulty cooking and heating units are examples. Unlike the provisions of the extended coverage endorsement, the smoky heating or cooking unit need not be "connected to a chimney by a smoke pipe or vent pipe and while in or on the described premises."

Under the extended coverage endorsement, the source of the smoke is limited to *sudden, unusual, and faulty* operation of any heating or cooking unit excluding fireplaces and industrial apparatus. Under that endorsement, claims are occasionally made for smoke damage caused by squirrels building nests in chimneys, by someone's inadvertently placing something over the top of the chimney, or by bricks falling into the flue and causing a blockage. As a result, the heating or cooking unit emits smoke into the premises. The question arises whether this is a faulty operation of the heating or cooking unit. It is contended by some that the faulty operation is taking place in the chimney, not in the furnace or stove. The majority opinion, however, is that if the smoking is sudden and unusual and emanates from the heating or cooking unit, it is a faulty operation due to lack of proper draft, although the blockage may be up in the chimney or stack.

Full details of the cause of the smoking should be determined by the claim representative. In the more serious cases expert opinion of a heating contractor or an engineer should be obtained. Statements should be obtained from persons who may have witnessed the occurrence, or from maintenance people who had knowledge of the condition and history of the unit involved.

Vandalism and Malicious Mischief

Some of the Homeowners policies add the sentence: "A building in course of construction shall not be deemed vacant." Other Homeowners policies exclude loss, as respects this peril, if the described dwelling has been vacant beyond a period of 30 consecutive days immediately preceding the loss.

The HPR Form incorporates the peril with riot and civil commotion, restricting it to "only willful and malicious damage to or destruction of the described property."

Frequently, in the case of commercial and manufacturing risks, the perils of vandalism and malicious mischief are added to the extended coverage endorsement for an additional premium, but the provisions exclude, among others, the following losses: (1) to glass (other than glass building blocks) constituting a part of the building; (2) by pilferage, theft, burglary, or larceny; and (3) resulting from change in temperature or humidity. There is no liability for loss if the described building(s) had been vacant beyond a period of 30 consecutive days immediately preceding the loss.

Vandalism is the willful destruction or defacement of works of art and things of beauty.

Malicious mischief is the willful and malicious injury to or destruction of the property of others with malicious intent. The two terms are used frequently to mean the same thing, which is unfortunate.

No body of law governing vandalism and malicious mischief losses has, as yet, been developed by litigation. The consensus of opinion is that the act must be *willful, unlawful*, and *malicious*. In most loss situations there is little difficulty in determining whether the first two elements are present. Problems arise, however, in deciding whether those who committed the act had a malicious intent to do harm to a person or a

person's property. Seldom are there witnesses to deeds of malicious mischief which result in claims under the policy. The claim representative must reconstruct the incident from the physical evidence. Many times it is not even possible to tell how many persons were present and what was their age or sex, let alone what their precise intent was.

School buildings, buildings under construction, and vacant or unoccupied buildings are more subject to acts of mischief than others. Also, children and youths are the perpetrators more often than adults. In each situation there is always the question of whether the mischief was malicious. Most losses are small, but serious losses are not uncommon.

The claim representative should obtain evidence bearing on the cause of the loss, if possible, and on the individuals guilty of the crime, and if available, they should be questioned and their statements taken. If the premises were vacant at the time the loss occurred, evidence of when the vacancy began should be sought.

Questionable cases involve damage done by infants. Whether they are capable of malicious intent is especially questionable.

Whether damage done to a building by burglars is covered may depend on the wording of the particular form. Where the form excludes loss by burglary except loss by willful or malicious physical injury to or destruction of a building described, there would seem to be no question that the damage to the building by breaking and entering is willful and malicious. Some forms specifically include damage to the building(s) covered caused by burglars, without stipulating that such damage must be willful and malicious.

There is a divergence in opinion on whether damage done by burglars to *contents* can be considered willful and malicious.

The burden of proving that a loss or damage was caused maliciously is on the insured. *Maliciously* means with a deliberate intention to injure.[18] The scratching, marring, or breakage of furniture in storage is not, in itself, evidence of malicious mischief. If two

---

[18]*May v. Anderson*, 14 Ind. App. 251, 42 N. E. 946.

customers fight in a restaurant and throw dishes at each other with resultant damage to the building or its contents, this does not constitute malicious mischief in the absence of malice toward the owner of the building or restaurant.

Questions of doubtful coverage should be submitted to the insurer together with complete facts which will enable it to form a judgment and give proper instructions.

Theft

The perils of theft, burglary, and mysterious disappearance are examined in detail in Chapter 13.

Falling Objects

Under the HO-2 this peril excludes loss to: (a) the interior of the building(s) or the property covered therein, caused by falling objects unless the building(s) covered or containing the property covered shall first sustain an actual damage to the exterior of the roof or walls by the falling object; (b) outdoor equipment, awnings, fences, including their supports.

Falling objects were defined by the Oklahoma Supreme Court, as reported in *Concordia v. Smith*, 37 CCH. (Auto), 449 (1951). The court said in part:

In the clause "loss caused by falling objects" there clearly appears the idea of objects possessing the attribute of being freed from suspension or support, to drop; to descend by the force of gravity. . . .

We hold that the term "falling objects," as used in the instant insurance policy, means objects impelled by the force of gravity.[19]

The wording of some of the broad Homeowners forms varies; some do not specifically exclude such property as outdoor equipment, awnings, and fences.

Investigation should seek to determine what object fell, what caused it to fall, and whether it was due to a third party's negligence. Do the circumstances indicate it was truly a falling object?

[19]PLRB, *Question and Answer Service*, No. 28.

Weight of Ice, Snow, or Sleet

As with many other named perils, the wording of this one is different in different forms and therefore requires more extensive investigating of the cause of loss under one form than under another. Homeowners Policy HO-2 (Ed. 9-70) reads as follows:

Weight of ice, snow or sleet which results in physical damage to the building covered or to property contained in a building and then only if the weight of ice, snow or sleet results in physical damage to such building, but excluding loss to:

a. outdoor equipment, awnings and fences; and

b. fences, pavements, patios, swimming pools, foundations, retaining walls, bulkheads, piers, wharves or docks when such loss is caused by freezing, thawing or by the pressure or weight of ice or water whether driven by wind or not.

The later Homeowners HO-2(Ed. 7-1-75) is less wordy and less restrictive:

Weight of ice, snow or sleet which causes damage to a building or property contained in the building.

This peril does not include loss to an awning, fence, patio, pavement, swimming pool, foundation, retaining wall, bulkhead, pier, wharf or dock.

The weight of ice, snow, or sleet is an extension of coverage and is not included in such basic forms as Homeowners (HO-1) Dwelling Building(s) and Contents (DF-1) and Standard Businessowners policies. It is available in the Special Multi-Peril policies under the Additional Coverage Endorsement.

The important consideration when investigating the cause of loss under this peril is to have the appropriate coverage in mind, or in hand, to know what property is or is not covered. *It is the weight and not the presence of ice and snow.*

Collapse

This is another peril which is not included in most basic named peril policies but is available by endorsement to some. The broad form named peril policies cover the peril of collapse under wording not unlike the HO-2 (Ed. 9-70), which reads:

> *Collapse of buildings or any part thereof* but excluding loss to outdoor equipment, awnings, fences, pavements, patios, swimming pools, underground pipes, flues, drains, cesspools and septic tanks, foundations, retaining walls, bulkheads, piers, wharves, or docks, all except as the direct result of the collapse of a building.
>
> Collapse does not include settling, cracking, shrinkage, bulging or expansion.

The later HO-2 (Ed. 7-1-75) and the Dwelling Building(s) and Contents—Broad Form cover the peril of collapse with similar wording to that above.

There is no satisfactory definition of the word "collapse" applicable to any and all situations. The later forms indicate conditions in structures which are not considered collapse under the peril, these being settling, cracking, shrinkage, bulging, or expansion. All such conditions have been the basis for claims for collapse at one time or another. Many of the problems encountered in collapse claims involve a question of fact concerning whether a collapse has actually occurred. For example, a basement wall exposed to exterior pressure develops vertical cracks. The cracks begin to open wider after a period, and the wall shows a slight bulge. The cracks get bigger and the bulging continues until eventually the whole wall, or a section, falls into the basement. At that point no one would contend that the wall had not collapsed. There is, however, lack of agreement at what precise point the wall can be said to have collapsed.

Generally, the presence of cracks in masonry basement walls with no evidence of bulging or lateral movement is not looked upon as a collapse. As cracks widen, and the wall begins to bulge, losing part or all of its supporting properties, the probability that a collapse will occur becomes obvious.

When a structural member such as a joist, beam, girder, rafter, or column splits, breaks, cracks, or otherwise loses its property

as a support, and the portion of the structure that it holds up sags, bends, or settles, there is strong probability that there has been a collapse. Not all authorities agree.

The falling of ceiling plaster is usually looked upon as a collapse of a part of the building.

The report to the insurer should include a complete description of the part of the building involved and of the circumstances leading to or contributing to the alleged collapse; pictures; diagrams; and also statements of persons having any material knowledge bearing on the incident.

Sudden and Accidental Tearing Asunder, Cracking, Burning, or Bulging of a Steam or Hot Water Heating System, or Appliances for Heating Water

Not included under this peril is loss caused by or resulting from freezing. The claim representative should make certain, while investigating cause of loss under this peril, that (1) the occurrence was sudden and accidental and not due to normal deterioration, or (2) the occurrence was not caused by a freezing of any part of the systems or appliances enumerated in the peril.

Occasionally when claim is made for loss under this peril, investigation into the cause discloses a leak in a hot water or steam boiler, and the condition appears to be an old maintenance problem. In some instances there is evidence of previous attempts to patch the leak. Another type of claim made is leaking of the boiler in the furnace-box area where an improperly adjusted oil burner flame, over a long period of time, has impinged onto a small surface area and literally burned through the metal. These and similar incidents usually do not meet the requirements of being *sudden* and *accidental*.

Other typical losses which *are* covered under this peril are steam-boiler explosions and burning out of furnaces when the water supply fails and the burner continues to operate. It should be noted that damage to the insured's property also is covered as a result of explosion in a steam-heating boiler located in a building other than the described dwelling.

Accidental Discharge or Overflow of Water or Steam

This peril applies when water or steam overflow

> from within a plumbing, heating, or air conditioning system or from within a domestic appliance, including the cost of tearing out and replacing any part of the building covered necessary to effect repairs to the system or appliance from which the water or steam escapes, but excluding loss:
> a. to the building caused by continuous or repeated seepage or leakage over a period of weeks, months or years;
> b. if the building covered has been vacant beyond a period of 30 consecutive days immediately preceding the loss;
> c. to the system or appliance from which the water or steam escapes; or
> d. caused by or resulting from freezing.[20]

The investigation of claims for damage under this peril should be conducted with special care, using the particular policy provisions applicable as a point of reference. Several important considerations must be kept in mind.

1. There must be a discharge or overflow, and there must be a loss to the property covered as a result. Leaking plumbing pipes from cracked or poor joints under a concrete slab laid on the ground, which results in no loss to the property covered, cannot be the basis for claim to tear out and replace that portion of the building necessary to repair the leaking pipes. Mere discharge or overflow of water from a plumbing, heating, or air-conditioning system or domestic appliance is not covered unless the property covered is first damaged.
2. The discharge or overflow must be *accidental*. For example, if a lawn sprinkler

[20]HO-2 (Ed. 9-70).

is turned on by the insured and it sprays water into an open window and wets rugs and furniture, there has been no *accidental* discharge. There is a distinction between accidental damage and accidental discharge. In the above situation, had a small child unwittingly turned on the faucet to which the sprinkler and hose were attached, the discharge of water from the sprinkler would be considered accidental.

3. The substance causing the loss must be water rather than a chemical, a refrigerant, or such liquids as coffee, tea, or milk which might be discharged or overflow from a domestic appliance. Most insurers agree that sewage, or water containing sewage, comes within the meaning of the term *water* as used in the policy.
4. The discharge or overflow must come from *within* the plumbing, heating, or air-conditioning system or domestic appliance. The water, for example, could not come from "sweating pipes" nor from a tray placed under an air-conditioning unit to catch condensation. If the tray is *inside* the air-conditioning unit, then the overflow from that tray is from *within* the domestic appliance.
5. Considerable discussion continues over the definition of *domestic appliance*. While very few people would contend that washing machines, clothes dryers, window air conditioners, television sets, or electric toasters were not appliances, there is some lack of agreement on whether water softeners or hot-water heaters connected to plumbing systems are appliances.

    The majority of insurers and claim representatives concur that *systems*, including their parts, which heat a building or heat hot water for domestic use, should not be classified as domestic appliances, nor should air-conditioning, plumbing, lighting, and sound or communicating *systems*. There is also agreement in general that there is a distinction between an appliance and a utensil such as a pail or pan.
6. While the peril as stated above includes

the cost of tearing out and replacing any part of the building to effect repairs to the system or appliance from which the water or steam escaped and caused damage, the loss to the system or appliance itself is excluded.

7. There is no coverage for loss as a result of freezing nor for *loss to the building* caused by leakage or seepage that has been going on repeatedly or continuously.

8. Loss is excluded if the building covered has been vacant (not unoccupied) over 30 consecutive days immediately prior to the loss.

Some of the special multi-peril and specified peril forms confine the water-damage peril to *leakage* or discharge which is the direct result of the *breaking or cracking* of any pipes, fittings, parts, or fixtures forming a part of such system or appliance. This wording is quite different from that of the standard water-damage policy, the Broad Form, and the several residential forms. This variation is an excellent illustration of why the claim representative must always be guided in an investigation of cause of loss by the conditions and provisions of the particular forms or endorsements attached to the policy under consideration.

Breakage of Glass

The HO-2 (Ed. 9-70) reads with respect to this peril:

Breakage of glass constituting a part of the building covered hereunder, including glass in storm doors and storm windows, but excluding loss if the building covered had been vacant beyond a period of 30 consecutive days, immediately preceding the loss.

Other residential forms are identical or similar. The Special Multi-Peril (SMP) optional perils endorsement excludes neon tubing attached to the building and has monetary limits per plate and occurrences.

The Businessowners policies contain special provisions.

Breakage of glass is a peril under the Homeowners policies. Therefore any damage to the property described as a result of the breaking of glass, such as particles cutting upholstered furniture or marring tables, is covered in addition to the cost of replacing the glass. There is an exclusion for loss if the described property had been *vacant* beyond a period of 30 days. The special limit of liability does not apply to damage other than to glass.

Problems arise when mirrors are broken, and it is claimed they constituted a part of the building. In the *Question and Answer Service* (No. 38) of the PLRB this question was treated as follows, and the treatment reflects the thinking of a substantial number of claim managers:

In our opinion, the phrase "constituting a part of the building" and the phrase "an integral part of the building" are practically synonymous. We believe that mirrors in a permanently installed medicine cabinet as well as the glass doors in a permanently installed china cabinet constitute a part of the building. This also would apply to mirrors which actually form the panel of a door.

As concerns large mirrors attached to walls, it depends entirely upon the manner of installation and somewhat upon the insured's intent. If a large mirror actually formed the part of a wall or partition and was permanently installed in such manner that it could not be removed without substantial damage to the building, we would consider it a part of the building. On the other hand, the mere fact that a certain mirror might be bolted to the wall does not necessarily make it a building item. Frequently, mirrors are bolted to a wall simply because their weight makes hanging them with picture hooks a bit risky.

Where glass is broken during a windstorm, the question whether the peril is *windstorm* or *glass breakage* arises when a deductible applies to the former but not the latter. It would seem reasonable that the insured have the privilege of electing the peril under which to make claim.

Freezing of Plumbing, Heating, and Air-Conditioning Systems and Domestic Appliances

The residential broad forms cover direct loss to the property covered by freezing, and unless the property covered *suffers direct loss as a result of freezing*, there is no liability under this peril. Frequently, when plumbing and heating pipes freeze, the service returns to normal with no damage after they are thawed out. The cost of thawing out the pipes or system under such circumstances *may not be covered*.

This peril excludes loss from freezing while the building covered is vacant or unoccupied, unless the insured has exercised due diligence in maintaining heat *or* unless the plumbing and heating systems and domestic appliances had been drained and the water supply shut off during the vacancy or unoccupancy.[21]

Most problems develop when it is found that the building was vacant or unoccupied and the loss results from freezing of part or all of the heating system. The claim representative seeks to determine whether the insured exercised due diligence with respect to maintaining heat. For example, the insured and family close their northern house and go South for several weeks during the winter. Before leaving, the insured sets the thermostat at 55° and arranges with the oil company to make periodic visits and keep the oil supply adequate. In spite of these precautions, through error, the oil company does not check the oil. The oil burner soon ceases to operate and the heating system freezes. No one would question that the insured used due diligence in this case. However, if the insured had no contract with the oil company to keep the tank full, though they usually came by during the winter and checked it, and the insured left for the South assuming they would keep the oil tank filled, there might be a question whether due diligence was exercised in the event that the heating system froze when the burner shut off for lack of oil.

In situations where systems freeze during vacancy or unoccupancy, the claim representative should carefully check the sequence of events and conditions preceding the occurrence. The written statement of the insured should be taken and also the statement of each person whom the insured may allege was delegated the responsibility to maintain heat, supply fuel, or drain and shut off the water. If the insured states that an oil-supply firm, a neighbor, or a caretaker was responsible for the failure of the heat supply, that person or firm should be contacted for his story and statement. In the case of the oil-supply firm, any written contract it has with the insured should be examined.

Sometimes the insured will allege that the quantity of oil in the tank was more than ample to maintain heat until he returned. In that event it will be necessary to check oil deliveries and, from records of the oil company, determine the probable number of gallons of oil that would have been consumed during the insured's absence, at the prevailing temperatures.

Sudden and Accidental Injury From Electrical Currents

This peril includes:

Sudden and accidental injury from electrical currents artificially generated to electrical appliances, devices, fixtures, and wiring, except tubes, transistors, and similar electronic components.[22]

Artificially generated current is man-made as distinguished from electric current found in nature, such as lightning. The injury must be *sudden and accidental* and may involve real or personal property classified as electrical appliances, devices, fixtures, and wiring. The exclusion of tubes, transistors, and similar electronic components would take in diodes and rectifiers and items by any other name which perform the same functions.

Basic residential policies *exclude* loss caused by artificially generated electricity to

---

[21]See Vacancy and Unoccupancy, p. 37.

[22]HO-2 (Ed. 9-70).

electrical appliances, devices, fixtures, and wiring but cover any damage from ensuing fire. Broad forms cover it as a named peril. The newer Homeowners HO-2(Ed. 7-75) covers loss from this peril to all property by virtue of not specifying loss to any particular property.

The most common cause of injury is the short circuiting of electric current in wiring of appliances, motors, controls, devices, and fixtures.

Since the *injury* is the *peril*, or at least part of the peril, all damage to the property described that is the direct result of the injury is also covered. For example, a thermostat, which controls heat in a dwelling, short-circuits and fuses the mechanism so that the furnace operates continuously. The excessive heat in the house causes the wallpaper to come loose, and veneered doors and furniture shrink and crack. All the damage is covered. Similarly, if the motor or controls on a deep-freeze unit short out, any loss to the food stored in the unit is covered.

Investigation should include a determination of the cause of the electrical injury to make certain that the repairs contemplated or actually made to the appliance, motor, control, or whatever may be involved are not a matter of maintenance. This can be determined only by inspection of the unit by the claim representative or by a qualified expert in the field. Hot-water heater elements may wear out due to mineral content of the water or from age, motors may break down from wear and tear, certain radio and television components may break down mechanically, and appliances may fail—all as a result of something other than electrical injury or disturbance. Some repair concerns are prone to indicate on their estimates or bills that damage was caused by lightning when in fact it was neither lightning nor an electrical injury from artificially generated electric current.[23]

Sprinkler Leakage

The language of the sprinkler leakage peril varies slightly as used in the several policies and endorsements. In general they cover leakage or discharge of water or *other substance* from within the system, including fall or collapse of a tank. Repairs and replacements to the system are included when damage is caused by breakage of any parts of the system or by freezing. There is generally no liability for loss by water from other than the sprinkler system; while the building is vacant; or *during and resulting from* the making of repairs or alterations involving a wall or support of a floor or wall, or changes in the system after fifteen consecutive days from the beginning of such operations.

The descriptions of what constitutes the term *automatic sprinkler system* are similar. The language of the Sprinkler Leakage Endorsement (Form 172) is:

Sprinkler Leakage: Wherever in this endorsement the term "Sprinkler Leakage" occurs, it shall be held to mean (a) leakage or discharge of water or other substances from within any "Automatic Sprinkler System" or (b) direct loss caused by collapse or fall of tank(s) forming a part of such system.

Automatic Sprinkler System: Wherever in this endorsement the term "Automatic Sprinkler System" occurs, it shall be held to mean sprinkler heads, pipes, valves, fittings, tanks (including component parts and supports thereof), pumps and private fire protection mains, all connected with and constituting a part of an automatic sprinkler system, and non-automatic sprinkler systems, hydrants, stand pipes or hose outlets supplied from an automatic sprinkler system.[24]

The first act of the claim representative in an investigation of a sprinkler leakage claim should be to determine whether the water that did the damage escaped from a sprinkler system or from some other source. Occasionally moisture condenses on the exterior of sprinkler pipes in sufficient volume to drip and damage property directly under the pipes. Unless the damage for which claim is made has been done by water that escaped from a sprinkler system, the sprinkler leakage

---

[23]See also Lightning, p. 104.

[24]Uniform Standard (11-63).

insurance is not liable for the loss. Overflows, collapses, or falls of a tank call only for investigation of their cause.

Sprinkler leakages are usually caused by freezing, by accidental striking of a head, pipe, or other part of the sprinkler system by an employee carrying a ladder or piling stock, by breaking of belts on overhead pulleys, by corrosion, or by failure of joints under pressure. Some losses are due to falling tanks.

Many claims under sprinkler leakage policies are made by tenants whose premises have been wet by water that escaped in other premises, generally on a floor above. Investigation of such claims will sometimes result in finding that the water came from overflowing sinks or toilet bowls.

Indications of negligence in the maintenance of the sprinkler system or the care of the premises should be investigated because of subrogation possibilities. At times, a landlord will fail to maintain heat, and the system will freeze. At times, a tenant will overheat a head, as happens in premises where glass bending, brazing, or other processes requiring the use of heat are carried on.

In connection with sprinkler leakage claims, it is advisable to check with the building superintendent or other informed person to determine how long the water flowed and also to examine any broken pipes, elbows, valves, or other parts that may have been responsible for the leakage.

All Risks of Physical Loss Policies

When the claim representative investigates the cause of loss under all risks of loss policies, the technical approach is slightly different from that used when investigating cause of loss under a named peril policy. In either case the occurrence out of which claim of loss arises must be fortuitous or accidental rather than a certainty. Also, in either case, the burden of proof that loss was caused by a covered peril rests upon the insured. The essential distinction, however, in the claim representative's approach is that under a named peril policy he or she seeks to determine whether or not a specified peril has operated, while under an all risks of loss policy he or she seeks to determine whether or not a specified *exclusion* is applicable.

In a most scholarly discussion, "All Risks of Loss v. All Loss," before the Western Loss Association in Chicago on September 17, 1957, John P. Gorman, attorney, of Clausen, Miller, Gorman, Caffrey & Witous, had this to say:

> What is perhaps the leading case upon this subject is that of *British & Foreign Marine Insurance Company, Limited v. Gaunt*, Law Reports (1921), 2 A.C. 41, decided in the House of Lords, April 1921. In that case, Lord Birkenhead said, pages 46, 47: "In construing these policies it is important to bear in mind that they cover 'all risk.' These words cannot, of course, be held to cover all damage however caused, for such damage as is inevitable from ordinary wear and tear and inevitable depreciation is not within the policies. There is little authority on the point, but the decision of Walton J. in *Schloss Brothers v. Stevens*, on a policy in similar terms, states the law accurately enough. He said that the words "all risks by land and water" as used in the policy then in question "were intended to cover all losses by any accidental cause of any kind occurring during the transit.... There must be a casualty." Damage, in other words, if it is to be covered by policies such as these, must be due to some fortuitous circumstance or casualty."
>
> In the same case, Lord Sumner said, page 57: "There are, of course, limits to 'all risks.' They are risks and risks insured against. Accordingly the expression does not cover inherent vice or mere wear and tear or British capture. It covers a risk, not a certainty, it is something, which happens to the subject-matter from without, not the natural behavior of that subject-matter, being what it is, in the circumstances under which it is carried."

As a supplemental note, Mr. Gorman commented:

> ... It should be noted that the burden of proving exclusion from coverage rests upon the insurer. The courts draw a distinction between the coverage provisions and the exclusion provisions of the policy and, while holding that the

burden of proving coverage rests upon the insured, the burden of proving exclusion from coverage rests with equal force upon the insurer. This is graphically portrayed in the recent Circuit in the case of *Ruffalo's Trucking Service, Inc. v. National Ben Franklin Insurance Company*, 243 F.2d 949, 952, 953, 9 Fire & Cas. Cases 146, 149, wherein the court said: "This distinction between 'coverage' provisions and exculpating or 'exclusionary' clauses has been recognized since then by the New York courts; and the distinction is still the decisive factor in determining which party has the burden of proof on an issue such as the issue here in dispute. See, e.g., *Prashker v. United States Guarantee Co.*, 1 N.Y.2d 584, 136 N.E.2d 871 (1956); *Wagman v. American Fidelity & Cas. Co.*, 304 N.Y. 490, 109 N.E.2d 592 (1952). Thus, although the plaintiff insured may have the burden of proving that the policy covers his loss, the defendant insurance company has the burden of proving any fact falling within an exclusionary clause which, despite the 'coverage' provisions, will bar recovery on the policy. *Prashker v. United States Guarantee Co., supra*, 1 N.Y.2d at 592."

At the 1965 Property Loss Managers Conference in New York, William H. Hope, insurance executive and attorney, in a speech entitled "Risk of Loss—Revisited," said:

I would emphasize that the adjustment of the kind of "All Risk" losses we have been talking about calls for all the resourcefulness an adjuster can muster. I think it may be stated the general trend of the courts, particularly at the trial court level, is to give broader interpretation to the question of what constitutes a fortuitous loss and to narrow the interpretation of the exclusionary language. Despite this trend, it is absolutely necessary for the adjuster to continue to question the element of "fortuity" vis-à-vis "certainty." This applies particularly in those losses involving the elements of weather. Emphasize the requirement that the loss must occur from the operation of an extenal cause of force. Always be on the alert and inquire always into the existence of possible third party liability. Always study thoroughly and seek advice if necessary, on the possible application of exclusionary language to the claim. Much,

much more needs to be done in this area, in my opinion.

DIC (Difference in Conditions Form)

The DIC is an all risks of physical loss form and is designed to cover real property, personal property, improvements and betterments, loss of income, or property in transit. It may cover all of the foregoing property or any one, with specific limits of liability and usually a substantial deductible for any one occurrence. Certain property is excluded.

The usual fire and extended coverage perils used by the underlying insurer are excluded, along with vandalism, malicious mischief, sprinkler leakage—all of these whether or not insurance for such perils is being maintained by the insured.

Flood and earthquake (except by endorsement), earth movement, steam boiler explosion, mechanical breakdown, nuclear radiation, warlike action in peace or war, and a long list of other perils or causes of loss are excluded. Reports of values are usually required.

Investigation into the cause of loss under DIC requires considerable ingenuity on the part of the claim representative. First, the precise cause must be isolated from all others, frequently with the aid of an expert. After the cause is determined, the exclusions of perils and property covered under the DIC should be examined with utmost care.

The cause of the loss, as in all risks of loss situations, must be fortuitous. The fire and extended coverage perils, vandalism and malicious mischief, and sprinkler leakage perils, as set forth in the endorsements used by the underlying or primary insurer, are excluded even though coverage for such perils is not being maintained by the insured. If they are available to the insured by the primary insurer, the company with the DIC does not insure against such perils. The insurer under the DIC may be the insurer with the underlying policy.

Because such coverages are frequently tailor-made under inland marine policies, the claim representative should maintain close contact with the insuring company he represents.

Earthquake

The peril of earthquake is customarily insured against by endorsement attached to other policies. There usually is a special limit of liability for risk other than residential, and also a special deductible. The following, or similar wording, is found in most endorsements:

It is also agreed that each loss by earthquake shall constitute a single claim hereunder; provided, if more than one earthquake shock shall occur within any period of 72 hours during the term of this endorsement, such earthquake shocks shall be deemed to be a single earthquake within the meaning thereof. This Company shall not be liable for any loss or damage caused by any earthquake shock occurring before the effective date at time of this endorsement, nor for any loss or damage occurring after the effective date of the cancellation of this policy.

A few forms, such as Mobile Homeowners, provide earthquake protection. Establishing earthquake as a cause of loss is far less difficult than determining that specific damages to property are the result of an earthquake.

The effect of quakes on buildings varies with the seriousness of the disturbance, the distance from its epicenter, and the type of earth formation through which vibration waves travel. Whether an earthquake actually occurred will, in almost every instance, be a matter of public record as all but minor earthquakes may be detected by seismograph anywhere on earth. Computers are used to determine the location of earthquakes by feeding seismograph data into them. Even minor quakes that result in little or no damage are newsworthy, and the interest and reports of the press help to verify that a real earthquake occurred and not shocks from a sonic boom or local blasting operations.

Earthquakes are sometimes followed by fire or flood with the result that there is mixed damage. Fire damage is an insured peril under property policies; earthquake or flood may or may not be, in which case damage

by quake will have to be separated insofar as is practicable from damage by fire or flood. [25]

QUESTIONS AND PROBLEMS

1. An investigation concerned solely with cause of loss usually focuses attention on six fundamental questions in analyzing whether or not the loss involves a peril covered under the policy and for which the insurer is liable. List or outline the basic questions to be answered.

2. You are sent to thoroughly investigate the cause of a fire that practically destroyed a large home in the suburbs. It is reported in the news that the cause is unknown. Outline the procedure or steps you would take in trying to determine the cause.

3. There are three different ways that lightning can cause damage. Describe each.

4.a. Name three sources you might go to to obtain wind velocities where there is doubt the wind could have caused the damage claimed.

b. Many courts apply a simple rule in defining a windstorm with respect to property insurance claims. What is that rule?

5. The peril of vehicle under Homeowners Broad Form reads: "*Vehicles*, but excluding loss to fences, driveways and walks caused by any vehicle owned or operated by any occupant of the premises."

The insured's mother-in-law came to live with the insured and family. On arrival she drove her car into a 25-foot section of picket fence. How would you handle the claim for the fence?

6. The Homeowners Broad Form states: "This policy insures against direct loss to the property covered by the following perils as defined and limited herein:" Peril 17 provides: "Freezing of plumbing, heating and air conditioning systems and domestic appliances. . . ."

The plumbing pipes freeze in a dwelling. The insured engages a plumber who thaws out the pipes, and the system returns to nor-

---

[25]See Chap. 24, "Floods, Mudslides, and FAIR Plans."

mal operation. There is no leakage, no damage to the property covered. Claim is made for thawing out the pipes. Explain why you do or do not think the policy covers the claim.

7. When the claim representative investigates cause of loss under a named peril policy, the objective is generally to relate the named peril as a direct cause of loss.

    a. What is the objective, when investigating cause of loss under an all risk of physical loss policy?

    b. All risk of loss does not mean "all loss." Explain why it does not.

8. The burden to prove that a loss has been caused by an insured peril rests with the insured. If the insurer cites the cause as an excluded peril, on whom does the burden of proof rest? Give an example.

9. The investigation of the cause of loss under a DIC (Difference in Conditions) Form requires a thorough knowledge of the provisions of the policy and an exacting inquiry into the origin. Explain why this is so.

Subrogation Possibilities

When the insurer makes payment to an insured for loss, the insurer is subrogated, to the extent of the payment, to the insured's right of action against any other person or persons responsible for the loss. The right of subrogation arises out of the nature of the insurance contract, which is one of indemnity. It prevents the insured from collecting twice and places ultimate responsibility for payment on the party primarily liable to the insured.

Because of the subrogation feature of the insurance contract, part of the claim representative's duty is to establish and preserve any right of recovery the insured may have against any party, so that the insurer will have the best possible chance of securing reimbursement *after* it has made payment.

A simple definition of subrogation is the substitution of one creditor for another, the new creditor succeeding to the former's rights.

KINDS OF SUBROGATION

Rights of recovery are of two kinds: (1) those arising out of damage done the insured's property by the wrongful act of another and (2) those arising out of a contractual relation between the insured and a person who is charged with responsibility for the insured's property. In important losses where rights of the first kind are indicated by the facts, the claim representative should promptly notify the insurer, who may wish to have an attorney take over investigation even before adjustment has been made. In losses of the second kind, it is ordinarily advisable to do no

more than agree upon value and loss before reporting to the insurer and asking for instructions. Rights of the first kind properly call for the services of attorneys, because suit against the wrongdoer is often necessary. Rights of the second kind can often be handled by a claim representative because the person responsible for the insured's property will carry insurance protecting liability; and settlement becomes a matter of negotiation between insurers.

VOLUNTEER PAYEE NOT SUBROGATED

An insurer who pays an insured for a loss for which the policy provides no coverage is a mere volunteer payee. There is no right of subrogation. The exception is where a policy violation, breach, or other voidance is waived by the insurer and payment made.

RELEASE OF TORT-FEASOR

The party against whom subrogation is sought may have been released from any liability by the insured prior to the loss in accord with a "subrogation clause"[1] in the policy permitting such release. In that case the insurer has no right of action.

Release of the tort-feasor before a loss, in the absence of a subrogation clause in the policy, or release under any condition subsequent to the occurrence of the loss, will discharge the insurer's liability and entitle

[1]This is a voluntary waiver by the insurer of its subrogation rights, provided the insured has waived any rights, in writing, prior to the loss. See p. 38.

the insurer to recover from the insured any payment made.

The claim representative should promptly warn the insured not to make any settlement with the party unless the party is willing to pay the full loss and the insured is prepared to release the insurer, or unless the terms of the settlement have been approved by the insurer. In many cases a wrongdoer will offer to pay the insured for the part of the loss not covered by the insurance and will try to evade responsibility for the rest of it. The claim representative should explain to the insured that any release of a wrongdoer without the consent of the insurer will justify the insurer in refusing to pay the insured, as the release will deprive the insurer of its right to recover its own loss.

EVALUATING POSSIBILITIES

In the case of a possible right of recovery due to the wrongful injury of the property by a third party, investigation should uncover evidence showing whether something done by the third party or for which the third party was responsible caused the loss of or damage to the insured's property. Investigation should also determine whether the third party is financially able to pay the damages or carries insurance that will do so. In a situation in which a third party was in possession of the property and may be liable for loss or damage to it because of law or contract, investigation should determine (1) whether the loss or damage was due to negligence of the third party, (2) whether by law or contract he or she is liable even if not negligent, and (3) whether he or she is financially able to pay the damages or carries insurance that will do so.

Wrongful damage may occur to a customer's property while it is in the custody of a processor, warehouseman, cleaner, or repair shop. The claim representative's investigation should include statements from the owners or employees as well as a statement from the insured describing the property, its condition prior to injury and afterward, and under what circumstances or agreement it was given to the cleaner or repair concern, or

placed in storage. Original receipts or copies should be obtained and scrutinized for any contractual provisions.

SPECIFIC SITUATIONS

Situations in which a third party may be liable by law or contract are illustrated by losses under owners' policies when personal property is in possession of a common carrier or other bailee. In such losses, the bill of lading or the warehouse receipt, storage receipt, or other contract of bailment should be examined for conditions of liability, and these should be checked against the evidence of the cause of loss. In some losses there will be no documentary evidence of the contract of bailment, which must be established by the statements of the parties and checked against the customs in the trade. Most bailees carry insurance to protect them against losses on goods of others. The claim representative handling a loss for an owner should try to find out what insurance for the benefit of others is carried by the bailee.

Other common types of losses are caused by third parties where subrogation possibilities may exist.

Fires caused by:
1. Painters using blowtorches to burn off old paint.
2. Persons using blowtorches to thaw frozen waterlines.
3. Workers using acetylene or electric welding and cutting equipment.
4. Workers applying highly flammable finishes on wood floors without adequate ventilation. Ignition may occur by friction, careless smoking, etc.
5. Painters using flammable paint remover on floors while smoking, or allowing the fluid to flow into an electric outlet in the floor, resulting in a short circuit.
6. Contractors using salamanders to provide heat for drying plaster or concrete in buildings undergoing construction or alteration.
7. Roofers permitting tar-heating devices to get out of control.
8. Soldering of pipes and connections by plumbing and heating contractors.

9. Improper design or construction of fireplaces by contractors or builders.
10. Careless handling of degreasing equipment in manufacturing plants.
11. Workers repairing and testing oil burners and similar equipment.
12. Delivery of gasoline instead of fuel oil; delivery into the wrong filler pipes; permitting gasoline to overflow on delivery to full tanks; overflowing fuel-oil tanks in basements and other careless handling of gasoline or fuel oil.
13. Provable careless use of smoking materials.

Water damage caused by:
14. Defective water mains under streets.
15. Defective or worn-out plumbing, heating, and air-conditioning systems and appliances.
16. Careless handling of manufacturing processes in which water is used, causing damage to other tenants.
17. Shutting off water by owner without notice to tenants and subsequent turning water on again, where tenants meanwhile have left open faucets or permitted toilets and drains to become blocked.
18. Leaky skylights, windows, or roofs of which the owner had actual or constructive notice.
19. Freeze-up of sprinkler systems or plumbing and heating systems, with water damage caused by subsequent thawing and breaking of pipes and fixtures, all due to owner's failure to provide adequate heat.
20. Carelessness of other tenants or their employees in using sinks and toilets.

Other losses caused by:
21. Aircraft and vehicles of all types including autos, railroad trains, bulldozers, and tractors.
22. Explosions due to processing or blasting; explosions due to careless handling of explosive material, steam boilers, and pressure vessels; and firebox explosions.
23. Overloading of floors by tenants, causing collapse and damage to other tenants.

24. Leaky gas lines or equipment, resulting in fire and/or explosion.
25. Rioting, where municipal authorities can legally be held for damages.

USE OF ATTORNEYS AND EXPERTS

From the foregoing list of cases of possible subrogation arising out of the negligence of third parties, it is apparent that the early use of experts is desirable whenever the expense of such experts is worthwhile. On serious losses, when the subrogation possibilities appear to be strong, it may be advisable to bring an attorney in early and place the investigation under the attorney's guidance and direction. The claim representative and any special investigators or experts will then have their activities organized and coordinated. The selection of an attorney should be done with the approval of the insurer.

There are many attorneys whose firms specialize in the handling of subrogation cases and are well equipped and experienced. Their fees are ordinarily on a contingent basis, and they will often evaluate the possibilities of recovery prior to taking the case. This preliminary counsel is generally done at a relatively modest cost and will depend on the work involved.

There are also special investigators who are called in on subrogation cases. Many of these are also investigators of incendiary fires and other insurance-related matters. In larger towns and cities there are chemists, testing laboratories, electrical firms, engineers, accountants, photographers, and a variety of other firms and individuals whose expertise is employed to gather and preserve evidence.

PRESERVING THE EVIDENCE

Too frequently a subrogation case, with initially good possibilities, is lost to the insurer through early failure to recognize, establish, and preserve physical evidence and to obtain the testimony of witnesses. On serious losses it is important to give early attention to the cause of the loss whether it involves fire, sprinkler leakage, collapse, water damage, freeze-up, or some other peril, in order to learn whether it was due to a third party's negligence. If it appears that subrogation is probable, then the preserving of evidence should begin immediately; if necessary, the persons so engaged may have to work around the clock to prevent time and other people from destroying or rendering the evidence useless.

Normally, it is not wise for a claim representative to remove physical evidence without an attorney's instructions as to what is to be removed, whose permission is to be obtained, and where the evidence is to be placed for safekeeping pending litigation. Occasionally, the presence of building wreckers or of persons engaged in cleaning up, moving contents around, or otherwise threatening destruction or removal of important physical evidence requires that such evidence be promptly preserved. The claim representative may be forced into taking action. Under such circumstances, a public official, the insured, or even a law enforcement official should be asked to cooperate in removing and preserving the evidence.

Whatever procedure is used to remove evidence, it should be done in a manner that will not invite criticism at a later date that it had been altered or tampered with or had been removed or impounded illegally.

SUBROGATION, TRUST AGREEMENT, OR LOAN RECEIPT

Although the right of subrogation does not come into being until claim is paid, it is common practice in most instances for the claim representative to obtain a signed subrogation agreement, trust agreement, or loan receipt at the time the proof of loss is taken.[2] In some cases the adjuster reports the circumstances to the insurer and recommends that, upon payment of the claim, a subrogation agreement be taken.

Under most real-party-in-interest statutes, where the insurer takes a subrogation assignment, it must prosecute the action in its own name. Naturally, this creates a prejudice when a case is before a jury and has caused

disastrous results. Much thought has been given by underwriters to avoid this very realistic situation. In New York State, the Legislature, recognizing the very definite prejudice under which insurers labor in bringing actions in their own name, promulgated Section 1004 of the Civil Practice Law and Rules, which covers the real-party-in-interest provision and has made it possible to bring action in the name of the insured, even though he or she has executed a subrogation assignment.

Other states, however, have not provided similar amendments, and in those states it still remains necessary to enter into the subterfuge of a trust agreement or a loan receipt, in order to enable the insurer to bring the action in the name of the original insured. The rationale underlying the necessity for and the use of loan receipts may be found in the following cases: Sosnow, Kranz & Simcoe v. Storatti Corp., 54 N.Y.S.2d 780, 269 App. Div. 122, aff'd. 295 N.Y. 675; Adler v. Bush Terminal Co., 161 Misc. 508, aff'd. 250 App. Div. 730; Eber Bros. Wine & Liquor Corp. v. Firemen's Ins. Co. of Newark, 30 F. Supp. 412; First National Bank v. Lloyd's of London, 116 Fed. 2d 221; McCann v. Dixie Lake & Realty Co., 162 S.E. 869; Cadillac Auto Co. v. Fisher, 172 A. 393.[3]

NOTIFICATION TO WRONGDOER

If preliminary investigation convinces the claim representative that the wrongdoer should be called to account, the wrongdoer should be promptly notified and invited to participate in the adjustment, so that he or she may have some part in determining the amount for which he or she may later be sued. If the wrongdoer accepts the invitation, the contact may bring about a settlement. But a refusal will generally affect him or her adversely if the case is heard by jury.

REPORTING TO INSURER

When all evidence has been gathered, a summary of it should go to the insurer with a

[2]See Appendix M.

[3]Max J. Gwertzman, "A Legal Analysis of the Standard Fire Insurance Policy," The Insurance Advocate, Roberts Publishing Co., New York, 1963.

report giving the adjuster's opinion of what may reasonably be expected in the way of a recovery. The work should be done with sufficient thoroughness to make possible the recommendation to press claim against the wrongdoer or abandon it, according to the evidence in hand and the financial condition of the wrongdoer.

QUESTIONS AND PROBLEMS

1. Subrogation possibilities, open to insurers, arise from two different rights of recovery. State what these rights are and give an example of each.

2. Comment on these situations with respect to the insurer's right of subrogation:

a. Quick Action Insurance Co. pays a loss and takes subrogation against the wrongdoer. The case is clear-cut, and the insurer has every chance to succeed in the litigation. However, during the trial it is brought out by the defendant's counsel that there was actually no coverage for the loss under the policy.

b. The insured's friend and neighbor, burning rubbish in the yard, leaves the fire unattended and goes in the house for lunch. The rubbish fire extends to dry grass and leaves and travels to the insured's house setting fire to the front porch. The neighbor feels badly and is in tears. Insured says, "Don't worry, I am insured." The insured further consoles the good neighbor with a letter releasing the neighbor of any negligence or financial responsibility in return for $100. The loss is estimated to be $1,000.

3. There are three basic areas of information the claim representative should develop when subrogation against a wrongdoer seems a possibility. What are they?

4. Describe in one or two sentences at least ten loss situations that might give rise to subrogation possibilities by contract or by negligence of a third party.

5. State briefly certain advantages in engaging an attorney in the early stages of investigating a serious loss where subrogation possibilities are strong.

6. **a.** When does the insurer's right of subrogation come into being?

b. A preliminary investigation indicates that a painter, burning off old paint with a blowtorch, set the building afire. Should the painter be put on notice and invited to participate in the loss adjustment? Explain your answer.

7. A subrogation agreement and a trust agreement (or loan receipt) are used under different circumstances. Explain the difference between these documents and their use in subrogation cases. (Exhibits in Appendix M.)

8. You are assigned to investigate a fire loss that occurred in an aluminum casting plant, a tenant in an industrial complex. Your investigation discloses that probably molten metal came in contact with sprayed-on, foam-urethane insulation. The insulation, advertised by the manufacturer as fireproof, ignited; the fire extended to the roof and spread throughout the insured's premises. The insulation was sprayed on by a local contractor three months before the fire occurred.

The owner-landlord of the complex was extending the automatic sprinkler system into an addition to the complex and had shut off the sprinklers the previous day unknown to the insured or the landlord's insurer. The sprinklers did not operate during the fire.

How would you suggest proceeding with subrogation and against whom?

Arson Investigation and Detection

The number of known or suspected arson fires in the United States has increased by a staggering 724 percent since 1964, according to the National Fire Protection Association. The National Commission on Fire Prevention and Control in its report entitled *America Burning* states, "In many large cities, fire chiefs believe that almost half of all fires in their experience have been set." Relating that statement to the fact that each day there are nationally, on average, 139 school and 1,500 home fires, the magnitude of this national disgrace comes clearly into focus.

The crime of arson perpetrated by both organized criminals and private property owners is reaping an annual harvest estimated in excess of a billion dollars a year from insurance companies alone. An apathetic public, including many undermanned and inadequately funded law enforcement agencies, holds the erroneous belief that the cost of fires set by arsonists is absorbed by the insurance companies and, therefore, there is no reason to be overly concerned. Nothing could be further from the truth. Every dollar paid out by insurance companies for incendiary fire claims comes out of the insuring public's pocket in the form of higher premiums. Insurers have no provision in their accounting procedure for deducting arson losses from net profit any more than a supermarket or a department store deducts shoplifting and pilferage from *its* net profit. These losses are built into insurance rates in the first instance and into the cost of the merchandise in the latter instance.

The increased cost of insurance is only a small part of the total dollar cost paid by the public for arson fires. When these fires involve commercial properties, either directly or by exposure, there is unemployment insurance payments and frequently a loss of real estate, income, and sales taxes. Additional costs are reflected in unnecessary fire department services, damage to, and wear and tear on, equipment. To these costs must be added the serious injuries and loss of life of firemen and innocent persons caught or trapped in burning buildings that have been deliberately bombed or torched. The total cost of arson is truly staggering.

The apprehension, indictment, and conviction of those engaged in this stealthy crime will not take place, nor will there be successful civil prosecution, until those charged with the investigatory responsibilities are fully proficient in the knowledge and techniques of arson investigations. The ultimate suppression of incendiary fires rests in no small measure with their detection and proper investigation.

More and more, insurers, fire marshals, fire and police departments, and all concerned law enforcement agencies are looking to the federal government to recognize arson as a national crime as important to the nation as kidnapping, bombings, political murders, and other less costly to the people but given high priority. Also, it is hoped that federal law-enforcement agencies will be permitted to assist the states, municipalities, insurers, and others interested in curbing individuals and organized groups from committing arson.

ARSON DEFINED

Arson may be defined as the willful and malicious burning of property of value whether it is the property of the arsonist or that of another. In most jurisdictions, laws making arson a crime include attempted arson, also aiding, counseling, or procuring the burning of property.

It seems reasonable to include bombing in any definition of arson inasmuch as one or both are used in the willful and malicious destruction of property by sociopolitical individuals and groups. The word *incendiarism* has its derivation in the Latin *incendere* meaning "to set on fire."

ESSENTIAL ELEMENTS OF ARSON

Claim representatives will be better prepared to investigate and gather evidence if the basic elements of arson are understood. To successfully defend an action on an insurance policy, where the insured is suspected of arson, proof of essentially three basic elements is needed:

1. The fire was of *incendiary origin*.
2. The insured had a *motive* to cause the fire.
3. The insured had the *opportunity*, acting directly or through an agent, to cause the fire.

... proof of these elements as part of a defence in a civil action against an insurer requires proof by a "fair preponderance of the evidence" as opposed to proof "beyond a reasonable doubt" in a criminal prosecution.[1]

Arson by legal definition does not require a motive on the part of the arsonist inasmuch

as a mentally retarded or disturbed person, or one afflicted with pyromania, could willfully and maliciously burn property without a rational motive. But arson that is committed by or for any of the interests under an insurance policy almost always entails a motive, usually one of economic advantage. When evidence of a motive is uncovered and proved, the position of the defense is materially strengthened.

BURDEN OF PROOF—CRIMINAL VERSUS CIVIL

The principal distinction between the criminal case of arson and a civil case of arson is not in the nature of the investigation, but in the requirements to sustain a successful presentation in court following that investigation. It is, of course, fundamental law that in a criminal prosecution the prosecution must prove its case "beyond a reasonable doubt," whereas in a civil matter the insurer need prove its defence of arson merely by a fair preponderance of the evidence. *Osvaldo Varane, Inc. v. Liberty Mutual Ins. Co.*, 1972 Adv. Sh. 1336 (1972); *Richardson v. Travelers Fire Ins. Co.*, 288 Mass. 391, 393 (1934). The investigation may develop facts which warrant the conclusion that it is "more probable than not" that the insured is responsible for the arson, in which case, the insurer is justified in denying liability (to the insured). At the same time, these same facts may not warrant the conclusion that the insured-involved arson has been proven beyond a reasonable doubt in which case criminal prosecution is not justified.

In a civil matter, in order to carry the burden of proof, it is not necessary to exclude every possibility that the act complained of happened through some cause other than the act of the plaintiff insured. It is enough to introduce evidence which will remove from the realm of speculation the insured's responsibility and establish that responsibility upon a solid foundation. See *Gates v. Boston & Maine Railroad*, 225 Mass. 297 at 301-302 (1926). See also DeFilippo's case, 284 Mass. 531 at 534. As we have seen, in a civil case the proponent's burden is that of proving his point by a preponderance of the evidence which has been defined as follows: "The weight or preponderance

[1]John E. Lecomte, Attorney, Lecomte, Shea & Dangora, Boston, "The Role of an Attorney in the Investigation and Defence of an Arson Loss," presented at the Massachusetts Property Insurance Underwriting Association arson seminar, Nov. 19, 1974.

of evidence is its power to convince the tribunal which has the determination of the fact, of the actual truth of the proposition to be proved. After the evidence has been weighed, that proposition is proved by a preponderance of the evidence if it is made to appear more likely or probable in the sense that actual belief in its truth, derived from the evidence, exists in the mind or minds of the tribunal notwithstanding any doubts that may still linger there." *Sargent v. Mass. Accident Co.*, 307 Mass. 246, 250 (1940).

The fundamental understanding of the quantum and quality of proof essential in creating "proof beyond a reasonable doubt" will be helpful to the adjuster or fire investigator in appreciating the problems that the public agency has in preparing a case for prosecution. Courts have searched for language which will clearly delineate the boundaries essential to establish "proof beyond a reasonable doubt" and, with particular reference to cases based on circumstantial evidence, the Massachusetts Courts have stated the rule to be as follows: "The Commonwealth's case, therefore, rests solely on circumstantial evidence, the rule for the probative character of which is well settled. It is that the circumstances must be such as to produce a moral certainty of guilt, and to exclude any other reasonable hypotheses; ... the circumstances taken together should be of a conclusive nature and tendency, leading on the whole to a satisfactory conclusion, and producing, in effect, a reasonable and moral certainty, that the accused, and no one else, committed the offense charged." *Commonwealth v. Croft*, 345 Mass. 143, 144 (1962).

This expressionable language is by no means so clearly definitive as to make the application of the rules of "proof beyond a reasonable doubt" equally comprehensible to all people under all circumstances. In the extreme, a case in which the insured is caught with the match and a can of gasoline, the application of the criminal standard of proof is easy. However, in the vast majority of cases, it is essential to rely upon circumstantial evidence in proof of the various elements of the crime or defense of arson, and in these cases the distinction between "proof beyond a reasonable doubt" and "proof by a fair preponderance of the evidence" becomes critically important.

As we have stated, failure to establish evidence with the probative value sufficient to obtain a criminal conviction does not necessarily leave the insurer at the mercy of the arsonist. The attorney's role includes a careful evaluation of the available evidence to determine whether or not the claim of the arsonist can be successfully resisted.[2]

MATTERS FOR CONSIDERATION IN SUSPECTED ARSON

Element 1. Was the Fire of Incendiary Origin?

1. *Eliminate* as many *accidental* causes as possible to narrow the field of probability. Investigate the possibility of the following causes, the ideal being to eliminate *all accidental causes.*
   a. Careless smoking.
   b. Defective electrical wiring, motors, appliances, etc.
   c. Spontaneous combustion in paint materials, hay, etc.
   d. Lightning—either direct hit or ground surge.
   e. Cooking and heating equipment or devices.
   f. Trespassers, burglars, juveniles.
   g. Brush, grass, outside incinerator fires.
   h. Gas leaks in piping or at appliances, furnaces, etc.
   i. Careless use of matches by children or others.
   j. Other miscellaneous causes.
2. Check for all *direct* evidence of possible set fires.
   a. Two or more independent fires may be found burning in a room, in different parts of a building, or in separate buildings.
   b. *Trailers* may be used to spread the fire from room to room, floor to floor, or throughout a large area. Rope, toilet tissue, paper towels, newspapers, rags, bedding and other materials, frequently saturated with a flammable fluid, are common types of trailers used. Prompt action by a fire department or smothering due to lack of ox-

2Ibid.

ygen will sometimes result in parts of such trailers not burning completely and remaining in evidence.

c. Ignition and timing devices are used to permit the arsonist ample time to get out of the premises and perhaps establish an alibi. Some of these are complex and may be mechanical, chemical, or a combination of both. Some have been attached to the telephone mechanism to operate when an outside call comes in. Others are attached to furnaces and operate when the thermostat calls for heat. The slow-burning candle is frequently part of a device. Sometimes oven gas jets are turned on to fill an area with gas fumes which will ultimately be ignited by the pilot light, or when the door bell is operated. In the latter instances the buzzer is arranged to emit a spark.

d. *Chemicals* are occasionally used to set fires, as, for example, phosphorous in water. If the water is allowed to slowly leak from a metal or rubber container with phosphorous in it, the phosphorous will ignite when exposed to the air. This then ignites flammable material conveniently placed within range.

e. Accelerants may be paint thinners, kerosine, gasoline, or other flammables. Frequently the fire setter, usually an amateur, saturates some of the contents of a building or pours the accelerant over the floors and into the plumbing fixture traps and other places.

Deep charring of wood is often an indicator of the possible use of an accelerant. At other times empty or partially empty metal or glass gasoline or kerosine containers in or outside the building arouse suspicion, particularly if such materials are not normal to the use and occupancy of the premises.

f. *Odors* are sometimes an indication that the fire setter may have used chemicals, solvents, liquid accelerants, or bottle gas.

g. Intensely burning fires in the early stages, particularly when accompanied by unusual colored smoke, may indicate the use of chemicals or liquids.

3. Check for *circumstantial* evidence of possible set fires.

a. The *time of the fire*, when considered with all other factors, may support the theory that the origin is nonaccidental. Occurrence of late-at-night and early-morning unexplained fires tends to add some credence to suspicions.

b. *Unusual actions of the insured* on the day of the fire may lead to speculation. An example would be the insured taking his wife and children to dinner the evening their home burned, and for the first time the family pet dog, usually left at home, is taken along.

Another situation is when fire occurs shortly after the owner of a business closes up for the night or the insured leaves home for vacation.

c. Location of the fire on the premises, such as in closets with high values of property claimed, or in storerooms, should lead to further inquiry when the weight of other circumstantial evidence is substantial.

d. When an insured has a frequency record of fires of unexplained origin, the circumstantial evidence grows.

e. Evidence that personal property (stocks, furniture, furs, or jewelry) was removed from the premises prior to the fire adds to suspicion and circumstantial evidence.

f. Contradictory statements and misstatements of the insured regarding cause of fire, place of origin, insured's whereabouts, and other matters are important considerations.

g. Evidence of tampering with thermostatic heat controls, oil or gas lines to furnace, hot-water heater, etc., should be vigorously pursued.

Element 2. Did Insured Have a Motive?

As stated earlier, it is not necessary to show a motive in proving arson, but when the insured is involved, evidence of a motive greatly reinforces circumstantial proof of criminal intent.

Motives of arsonists of all types may be classified under six major headings: economic gain by insured, economic gain by others than the insured, revenge, intimidation, or jealousy, to committing or concealing a crime, sociopolitical reasons, pathological persons.

The first two categories generally encompass the setting of fires for the direct or indirect purpose of collecting money under an insurance policy. The other four categories may, in a few instances, contemplate defrauding an insurer, but the principal motive stems from criminal purposes and emotional or mental disorders. The claim representative, in the course of an investigation, might uncover these latter motives or, being satisfied that the insured is in no way involved, may wish to see that the person who set the fire is brought to justice or otherwise removed from society.

In searching for evidence of motives of an insured who has burned or arranged for the burning of property, the claim representative should check for the following:

1. Fires set for economic gain by insured.
   a. Insured plans to collect the insurance money to pay off bills and debts, such as hospital, doctor, legal, revenue, and gambling.
   b. Insured mortgagor desires to liquidate mortgage.
   c. Insured overinsures a property of recent purchase in an urban core area when property does not qualify for insurance in normal market but is eligible under a FAIR Plan or similar pooling arrangement.
   d. A manufacturer, wholesaler, or retailer wishes to liquidate excessive, obsolete, and hard-to-move stocks.
   e. Insured, a tenant, desires to terminate a long-term burdensome lease with landlord.
   f. Insured desires to relocate a business that has outgrown existing facilities.
   g. Insured wants to avoid impending business failure or bankruptcy.
   h. New highway will bypass insured's place of business threatening severe loss of business.
   i. A declining neighborhood threatens the lowering of realty values, making it difficult to dispose of a piece of property no longer desirable.
   j. Partner desires to dissolve a partnership.
   k. Insurers threaten to cancel insurance on property.
   l. Insured's building is on leased land and must be moved as the land is being sold.
   m. Land would be more valuable without insured's building.
   n. Insured seeks to void an unprofitable contract or franchise.
   o. There is an impending condemnation of insured's building for building violations, widening of street, to make room for highway, etc.

2. Fires set for economic gain by others than insured.
   a. Estate is being liquidated over long period and one or more heirs are impatient for settlement.
   b. Payment is offered arsonist (torch) to set fire.
   c. Mortgagee desires to liquidate the mortgage.
   d. Competitor seeks to eliminate competitor.
   e. Building owner wishes to terminate a low-rental lease and renegotiate a new lease with present tenant or get another tenant.
   f. Building contractor sets fire to obtain the profitable rebuilding contract.
   g. Arsonist seeks to obtain employment as a watchman, guard, fireman, etc.

3. Fires set for revenge, intimidation, or jealousy.
   a. Husband or wife against spouse.
   b. Male or female against lover.
   c. Husband or wife against third party threatening their marriage, happiness, or security.
   d. Hateful revenge.
   e. Strikers in labor-management disputes.
   f. Racketeers intimidating businessmen.

4. Fires set to commit or conceal a crime.
    a. Fires set to do away with a person.
    b. Fires set to cover up evidence of crimes, such as burglary; theft or pilferage in warehouses and stores; murder, rape, etc.
5. Fires set for sociopolitical purposes: Vandals, rioters, subversives, terrorists, and similar groups who bomb and set fires to focus attention on their cause or to force recognition of their demands.
6. Fires set by pathological persons.
    a. Pyromaniac (compulsive fire setter).
    b. Persons who set fires for thrills.
    c. Persons who set fires for sexual relief.
    d. Fires set by mentally retarded, senile, and insane persons.

Element 3. Did Insured Have Opportunity to Cause the Fire or Have an Agent Cause It?

As a rule, one of the most difficult of the three essential elements of arson to prove is that the suspect had an opportunity to set the fire. Evidence is therefore almost always circumstantial. Arson is a crime of stealth, and the arsonist has one thought uppermost in mind: his activity must be carried on without witnesses and without physical evidence of his complicity.

The claim representative, by questioning neighbors, acquaintances, relatives, employees, business associates, and the insured himself seeks to establish the whereabouts of the insured just prior to, at the time of, and immediately after discovery of the fire.

The circumstances giving rise to the inferences of opportunity cannot be viewed in a vacuum, removed from other considerations in the case. The evidence on the issue of motive will frequently be intertwined with the issue of opportunity, and the role of the attorney is to view the facts within the spectrum of the legal principles to be applied. In evaluating and proving an arson case, the attorney's role is not to compartmentalize each element of proof and wipe the slate clean after scrutiny of each element; but, on the contrary, the attorney's obligation is

to assure that his client will get the full benefit of the facts developed.[3]

INVESTIGATIVE PROCEDURE

The experienced claim representative who has knowledge of, and understands the previously discussed special characteristics of, incendiary fires and of those who are responsible for them, investigates with definite objectives in mind. The burden and extent of proof needed is recognized, and the investigation is conducted affirmatively but with care to establish whether or not the origin is *incendiary*; if so, was there an *opportunity* and a *motive*?

The routine pattern to be followed is similar in many respects to that taken in fires of fortuitous or accidental origin insofar as investigating the physical aspects of the property and the insurance (see Chapter 7). Concentration in the investigation, however, will be on the time, place of origin, and circumstances of the fire, and on information concerning the insured's character, reputation, and financial situation.

When the conditions encountered arouse suspicion of incendiarism, the claim representative should endeavor to find out as soon as practicable (1) who was the last person to have access to the property, (2) what persons, if any, were on the property at the time of the fire, (3) if the property was a building or was housed in a building, and if the building was closed, how many keys there were, who ordinarily carried them, and where each key was at the time the fire was discovered, (4) what odors and what kind of smoke were noted during the progress of the fire, (5) whether there were any explosions during the fire, and (6) whether the fire spread with unusual rapidity. Also, a careful inspection of the premises or the debris should be made, noting their appearance and giving special attention to anything indicating the presence of a flammable agent.

Visit the Fire Department

Since the claim representative usually arrives on the scene sometime after the fire has been

[3]Ibid.

extinguished, one of the first actions should be to visit the fire department, talk to the fire chief, and to any of the firemen who attended the fire. If a written report is available, it should be obtained. The *quantity* and *quality* of information the fire department is able to provide will depend on how experienced, well trained, and competent the personnel. Much also will depend on how limited the department is in budget and personnel. Many departments in larger municipalities have at least one trained arson investigator. Under such circumstances it may be well to leave the determination of cause up to such a person.

Talk to the Fire Marshal

When there are local or state fire marshals, they should be consulted if they are working on the case. If not, and the evidence of incendiarism is positive, the fire chief or police chief should be requested to call in the fire marshal.

USE OF ATTORNEYS AND EXPERTS

The consensus is that the average claim representative does not possess either the experience, education, or training to, alone, conduct an investigation of fires of suspected incendiary origin. More important, and even though he or she may be qualified, by conducting or joining actively in the investigation there is always the possibility of both the claim representative and the insurer being sued if incendiarism later cannot be proved.

In view of such a risk, the use of attorneys, professional investigators, chemists, laboratories, engineers, and other independent contractors is highly recommended, with the claim representative cooperating but working in the background.

Where the evidence of arson is especially strong, an attorney should be brought early into the investigation. If a professional investigator is to be employed or if experts are to be used in gathering evidence, they should place themselves under the guidance and direction of counsel. In this way activities can be organized, coordinated, and protected.

PROTECTING THE INVESTIGATION

Vital to a successful defense against fraud is the protection of the investigation to prevent information getting into the hands of the arsonist enabling him or her to compose evidence and alibis.

Losses of suspicious origin do not always have the dimensions that would require both an attorney and an arson investigator. When losses do require both, the attorney working with the arson investigator can take the latter's facts and marshal those facts in his or her own opinion to the insurer. That, then, becomes *attorney-client privilege and is available to no one else unless the privilege is waived.*

The work product concept of the attorney is a concept which should be utilized by the insurer.... Now, not only the work product of an attorney but also the work product of private investigators or staff personnel are generally protected from discovery, provided the investigation was being conducted in anticipation of litigation or for trial.... The suspected arsonist may acquire this investigative material under discovery rules only upon showing he has substantial need of the materials in the preparation of his case and that he is unable, without undue hardship, to obtain the substantial equivalent of the materials by other means.

The key to the protection of investigation from discovery is to establish that the material sought by the suspected arsonist was obtained in preparation of litigation or trial....

At the same time, it is clear that legal opinions, mental impressions and conclusions are not susceptible to discovery. If the matter is substantial and the matter sought to be protected is of importance, it may be desirable to have the information obtained orally by the attorney, from the investigators and be made part of the attorney's file.[4]

PRESERVATION OF EVIDENCE

As a general rule the claim representative should not remove evidence from the premises. This should be done by a qualified

[4]Ibid.

law enforcement or fire department official. Prior to the removal of any evidence of incendiarism, photographs should be taken by a professional rather than an amateur. Photographs may be used later in court to identify a container of flammable liquid, show its location on the premises, show excessive charring, the existence of separate unrelated fires, streamers, or a timing device. The person who took the pictures, developed and printed them, is usually called to testify.

The attorney or the professional investigator is the person best qualified to direct the photographer as to what pictures should be taken and from what angles. The photographs should be part of the attorney's file, not the claim representative's or the insurer's.

Evidence of tampering with gas or oil lines connected to heating or cooking equipment, or with electrical fuses, appliances, or wiring should be examined by qualified experts in those fields. Their reports, supplemented by photographs, drawings, and physical evidence, legally obtained, should be preserved under the direction of the attorney for later use in court if needed. Again, such reports or evidence should not be in the file of the insurer or its claim representative.

Claim representatives, however, should maintain adequate notes during the investigation if it is anticipated by the attorney that they may be called upon to testify. Memory of events should not be depended upon inasmuch as arson cases do not come to trial for months and frequently years after the fire has occurred.

EARLY EVALUATION OF SUSPICIONS

Experienced claim representatives and arson investigators recognize that there is a delicate and thin line separating a fairly obvious case of arson and one that is highly improbable even though fraught with contradictory evidence of possible incendiarism. Too often an inexperienced investigator is inclined to make early and rash judgments and conclude that the fire is of incendiary origin without having obtained adequate informa-

tion. Later, much to everyone's embarrassment and to the insured's resentment, it may be found that the fire was accidental.

The importance of evaluating the validity of suspicions as early as possible cannot be emphasized too strongly. There is a very natural and human inclination to seek evidence which will support one's *first impression* rather than to look for evidence which will eventually lead to a *rational conclusion.*

The person doing the investigating would be well advised to bear in mind the provisions of the NAIC Unfair Claim Settlement Practices Act and any state legislation based on the act.[5]

The point made here is that tact, caution, and discretion should be exercised at every turn to avoid implying or actually making damaging accusations that will have to be retracted and apologized for at a later date. Additionally, if one goes off on tangents and up blind trails, much time and often much money are wasted.

THE ADJUSTER IS NOT A LAW ENFORCEMENT OFFICER

Any inclination on the part of a claim representative to play the role of "private eye" must be suppressed for his or her own protection as well as the safeguarding of the interests of the insurer. The reasons are clearly outlined in the pamphlet *Was It Arson* (p. 10) prepared by R. G. Provencher, National Director, Investigations Division, General Adjustment Bureau, Inc.:

> When at the scene of a fire the adjuster is on private property. He is not a police officer and therefore must conduct himself as a private citizen. Everything in the involved building is private property and if that property is to be removed, such action must be left to the appropriate law enforcement authorities. If the adjuster finds personal property believed to represent evidence, he must obtain assistance from fire marshals or law enforcement officers.

In discussing this same subject in a pamphlet *Role of the Adjuster* prepared by Dan

[5]See p. 18.

Econ of the Property Loss Research Bureau of Chicago, the following admonition is given to claim representatives:

It is important for the adjuster to note that, while a fire marshal or other duly constituted legal authority may make a charge of arson against a person, which later proves to be unfounded, without incurring any liability for such false charge, this same immunity is not extended to the adjuster. It is for that reason the adjuster must avoid the activities which the special arson investigator can indulge in and must keep himself entirely free from all identification with the criminal investigation. The adjuster should not even make an appearance at the office of an investigative official during such investigation. Although it might not have any direct connection with the investigation of a suspect, such activity could result in the institution of a damage suit against the adjuster and his principal.

ANALYSIS OF PROOF OF ARSON REQUIREMENTS IN SELECTED STATES

A state-by-state analysis of the proof needed where arson is a defense has been prepared by the Defense Research Institute. As part of the adjuster's training in the investigation and detection of arson, it is recommended that each case be studied so as to understand the kind of evidence that is likely to establish proof of arson and what kinds have failed.

QUESTIONS AND PROBLEMS

1. Give a brief definition of arson which will be broad enough to include any act of arson.
2. What are the three basic elements which must be proved by a fair preponderance of evidence as part of a defense in a civil action against an insurer?
3. In a criminal case "proof beyond a reasonable doubt" is needed, whereas in a civil matter the insurer need only prove its defense of arson by a "fair preponderance of evidence." In the investigation of a fire of suspected incendiarism there are three different approaches necessary to develop evidence that the fire was "set." One approach is to eliminate all accidental origin, a second is to find direct evidence, and a third is to build up circumstantial evidence. Each is distinctly different. Explain briefly the differences and give at least four examples of each.
4. Motives or reasons for arson may be classified under six major headings. Name four and give a sufficient number of examples to clearly demonstrate the particular motive or reason in the four major classifications you have selected.
5. Evidence of opportunity to cause a fire by the insured, or an agent of the insured, is almost always circumstantial. Why is this so? Tell briefly what steps should be taken by the claim representative in attempting to establish that there was an opportunity.
6. Why is it important to engage legal counsel early in most serious cases of suspected arson? Give three reasons and explain them.
7. As a general rule, a claim representative should avoid removing evidence of arson from the premises. How would you instruct a claim representative to preserve evidence without personally removing it?
8. Explain the importance of early and perhaps periodic evaluations of suspicions of arson.
9. Claim representatives should carefully avoid conducting themselves like law enforcement officers. Explain briefly.

11

Procedure for Checking Claims

A claim should show in detail the insured's estimate or computation of the amount of loss to the property covered by the policy and should contain such other information as may be necessary to make proper application of the insurance or of any clauses or policy provisions affecting the amount for which the insurance may be liable. Investigation of a claim should include the checking of its details, an examination of the evidence that the insured offers in support of it, and in many instances a search for additional evidence.

The great majority of claims are made in good faith for losses that are covered by the insurance. On such claims the claim representative spends most of the time investigating evidence bearing on the amount of loss. In many claims questions of liability of the insurer arise, in some concerning the entire amount of loss, in others concerning part of the loss, in still others concerning the apportionment of the loss. In these claims, evidence bearing on the existence or the extent of liability becomes important. In a few claims, fraud is encountered, and evidence of fraudulent intent becomes highly important.

Claims are presented in the form of estimates, inventories, records, and statements of various kinds. In some claims every detail of value and loss is set forth in writing, while in others cost or value figures will be written up, and the amount claimed stated orally. In many small losses the claim will be stated orally and will be written up by the claim representative after he or she and the insured have agreed upon its details.

QUESTIONS TO CONSIDER

In checking a claim the claim representative should have in mind the following questions:

1. Is the property listed in the claim all or part of the property covered by the policies?
2. If there is more than one item of insurance, is the claim made separately under each item involved, and are the units of property and the items of expense correctly listed under the respective items covering each?
3. Is claim made for total or partial loss on property involved?
4. What evidence, other than his or her own story and the property itself, does the insured offer in support of the claim?
5. Does the property, if in evidence, its remains, or the space it occupied, or the place from which the insured states that it disappeared, confirm or discredit the evidence offered?
6. Does the claim include
   a. Property not described in the item; for example, fixtures claimed under an item covering stock?
   b. Uninsurable property?
   c. Excepted property on which liability

has not been specifically assumed in writing?

d. Property at a location not covered?
e. Property that had not been reported?
f. Property excluded if otherwise insured?

7. Does the claim include any loss or expense not covered because
   a. It was not the direct result of a peril insured against?
   b. It is specifically excluded?
   c. It occurred before the insurance became effective?

8. If the insurance is subject to coinsurance, average, or distribution, is the sound value of the property covered under each item involved stated separately?

9. Are sound value and loss measured by the same yardstick?

10. Are the figures in any estimate, inventory, or statement relative to sound value or loss arithmetically correct?

11. How does the claim compare with the claim representative's ideas of sound value and loss?

12. Does the claim appear to be fraudulent?

Property Listed in Claim

The description and location of the property stated in the insured's estimate, inventory, or statement of claim should be checked against the policy or policies and against the property itself, if it is in evidence. In most losses the check is made almost unconsciously, since the claim representative looking at the claim remembers the property as he or she saw it and has in mind the coverage shown by the policy, if it was examined, or by the policy form or abstract which should be in the file.

Two or More Items of Insurance

When there is more than one item of insurance, the claimant may erroneously claim under one item property covered under another. In some instances, because of inadequate insurance under one item, the claimant will do everything possible to shift some of the property covered under the inadequate

item to another item. For example, items of personal property such as power wiring, fixtures, and equipment may conveniently be included in the building claim.

In some claims involving two or more items of a policy, notably building and contents, covered separately, there will be a list of expenses incurred in protecting the property from further damage, evacuating water, and cleaning up. In such claims the question of how the expenses are to be allocated to the items must be investigated. If rent or business interruption insurance is also involved, the question of allocation must be even more carefully studied.

Total or Partial Loss

Insureds will claim a total or partial loss of property involved according to their ideas of what has happened to it. Generally what has happened is obvious, and the insured's idea will be right concerning condition even if wrong concerning the amount of loss. But there are many claims based on an exaggerated idea of loss or damage, some because of ignorance, some because of uncertainty or bad advice, and others because of the desire to make the largest possible collection under the insurance.

The insured who makes claim for a total loss of a unit of property will assert that it was destroyed or lost. The house may have been burned to the ground, blown away by a tornado, or blasted to pieces by an explosion. Or he or she may have lost a camera overboard while photographing a passing ship from a ferryboat. In such cases the losses are obviously total. But in other cases the desire to turn property into money or to get rid of an old article and get a new one may lead the insured to assert that the loss of a damaged unit is total when, as a matter of fact, it can be repaired and made as good as it was before the loss.

Claims for less than total loss are made on the assumption that the unit can be repaired or reconditioned, in which event the insured will claim the cost of doing so, or perhaps ask an allowance for the damage with the idea that the allowance will compensate for the supposed shortened life, impaired usefulness, or changed appearance of the damaged unit. Such is often the case when floors have been wet and have shown signs of buckling but have not buckled badly enough to justify taking up and relaying. If the cork insulation in walls or ceilings of cold-storage plants is wet, its life will be shortened and its insulating quality impaired. It may be inadvisable, however, to tear it out at the time, and the insured will probably claim a percentage of its value. A rug or carpet may be stained or discolored by water or chemicals used in fighting a fire, and even the best of cleaners may not be able to restore its appearance. The insured may wish to keep the rug and, in addition to the cost of cleaning, will ask an allowance for its changed appearance.

On merchandise, claims for partial loss on articles of stock are often based on the assumption that by reducing the selling price the owner can sell the merchandise. But in many instances the owner will assert that customers will not buy damaged articles and that the loss must be determined by sale of the articles to a salvage buyer.

Partial loss of property covered by an item of insurance may result in reduction of an insurance payment because of the application of a coinsurance or average clause. If the percentage of loss to value under the item is equal to or greater than the percentage used in the clause, payment is not reduced.

Evidence Offered in Support of Claim

In support of a claim the insured will generally offer an estimate, invoice, inventory, books of account, or a record of cost. In some cases the insured offers nothing more than his or her own statements. Whatever is offered is subject to examination and consideration and may suggest special investigation. An estimate, for example, should be examined to see whether it covers only such repairs or replacements as are necessary to restore the property. It is important to know who made it, and their reputation for competence and integrity. An invoice may call for additional evidence proving delivery of the property to the location of the loss. An inventory may be a record of actual count, weight, or measurement or it may be a list prepared from memory or by guesswork. Books of account may be properly or improperly kept. The unsupported statements of some insureds will be truthful and accurate; those of others will require testing and checking.

Check of Evidence Against Property

If the property or any part of it is still to be seen, any statement made by the insured or any documentary evidence offered in support of a claim should be checked against it. Measurement, count, or weight of what remains should be compared with the measurement, count, or weight stated in the claim. The amount of loss claimed should be considered and its propriety judged according to the appearance of the property.

If the property has been destroyed but the space it occupied can be measured, the maximum quantity that could have been stored in the space can be determined and compared with the quantity stated in the claim.

If property has been reported as stolen or has disappeared under circumstances indicating theft, a scrutiny of the place where the owner or custodian says it was last seen may satisfy the claim representative that he or she is dealing with a proper claim or may lead to a contrary conclusion.

Check of the insured's evidence against the property will often lead the claim representative to search for other evidence. After checking the insured's estimate against a damaged building, it may be decided to have an independent estimate made.

Property Not Covered

An item of insurance covers only the property described. A building item, for example, does not cover stock. Policies generally provide that certain kinds of property shall not be covered. The New York Standard Fire Policy lists these as "accounts, bills, currency, deeds, evidence of debts, money or securities." Policies also generally provide that other kinds of property shall be covered only if specifically named in the policy in writing. The same policy lists them as "bullion or manuscripts." Similar provisions appear in almost all policies covering property.

Floater policies often exclude certain kinds of property, also property at certain locations.

Certain forms exclude property otherwise insured, some covering only the excess value over the other insurance on such property.

A check of the details of the claim will detect any property not covered.

Loss or Expense Not Covered

Check should be made of each detail of loss or expense claimed to determine whether it is covered. As usually encountered, loss or expense not covered is due to

1. Perils not insured against under the policy.
2. Excluded perils.
3. Consequential loss.
4. Expense incurred for the insured's benefit, but not for the prevention of loss under the policy.
5. Previous loss.

A common example of the first is the claim under a sprinkler leakage cover for damage done by water from an overflowing sink or toilet or broken service pipe that is not part of the sprinkler system. Another example is collapse damage preceding a fire.

The perils excluded by a policy are listed in the policy.

A common example of consequential loss is the extra cost of replacing old open electric wiring with wiring in conduits required by municipal ordinance.

Expense incurred for the insured's benefit may be overtime paid to mechanics in order to hasten repairs, or the cost of a watchman employed to prevent theft or accidents after a fire.

Claims are sometimes made for old damage that had not been repaired when the loss occurred. The cost of repairing masonry that had been cracked by settling of a building before the occurrence of fire may be included in the claim for the fire loss. Sometimes, when a second fire occurs before the

damage due to the first has been repaired, a second claim will be made for the earlier fire damage.

Claims are also occasionally made for loss due to decomposition, souring, rust, other deterioration, or breakage that occurred before the fire or other casualty.

Contribution, Coinsurance, Average, or Distribution

If the policies contain reduced-rate contribution, coinsurance, average, or pro rata distribution clauses, the claim must be checked for the sound value of the property covered by each item, or the sound value at each location, according to the requirements of the clause. The computation of the amount for which the insurance is liable because of the clause must also be checked (see Chapter 27).

Basis of Value and Loss

If the insurance is subject to a coinsurance or average clause, it is important that value and loss be tested to determine whether both have been measured with the same yardstick. If value and loss are not on the same basis, the purpose of the clauses may be nullified.

In a building loss, for example, the claim may state the value of the building as the amount shown in the last tax assessment, while the loss will be stated at the cost of making repairs to roof, walls, floors, or openings. The tax assessment may value the building at only half what it would cost to build. The amount of the insurance may be 80 percent of the assessed value, and the policies subject to the 80 percent coinsurance clause. Fire, windstorm, or explosion may have destroyed half the building, and the remaining half may be practically as good as before the loss. If the assessment figure is used for value and the repair cost figure for loss, the policy may be called upon to pay a total loss, although only half of the property covered by it has been destroyed. The purpose of contribution, average, and coinsurance is to keep the percentage of the insurance loss on a rough parity with the percentage of the property loss.

When machinery or fixtures are underinsured, the claim may state the value of each machine or fixture at the price for which it would sell in the secondhand market, and state the loss on it at the cost of reconditioning or repairing it. Unless value and loss are put on the same basis, there will be a disproportionately high insurance payment.

When value and loss are based on measurement, weight, or count, the claim representative should find out whether the same care and attention were given to measuring, weighing, or counting undamaged articles included in the value as were given to measuring, weighing, or counting those involved in the loss.

Arithmetic Correctness of Claim

The claim representative must test or exhaustively check for correctness all figures in a claim. When to test and when to check are matters of judgment. Whenever figures are accepted on the basis of a test, the claim representative should so state in the report to the insurer. It is good practice to attach adding-machine tapes to the report attesting to the correctness of the figures submitted.

Comparison of Claim With Claim Representative's Estimate

After any obvious errors in a claim have been found and corrected, the value and loss stated should be compared with whatever data the claim representative has assembled independently in an effort to estimate the loss. All differences must be ascertained and investigated.

In a building loss, the claim, presented in the form of an estimate of cost to repair, may show that the estimator contemplates replacing the entire roof, whereas the claim representative may hold an estimate based on replacing one half and repairing the other half. The question of what should be done to the roof then becomes the subject of investigation.

Genuine or Fraudulent Nature of Claim

The great majority of claims are proper; a few are fraudulent. As investigation progresses, the examination of the evidence offered by the insured and a comparison of it with evidence in hand or developed later will lead to the conclusion that the claim is proper, doubtful, or fraudulent. A fraudulent claim may be presented following a deliberately planned fire or explosion, or the concealment or disposal of property. One, however, may also be made after an accidental loss to collect a materially greater amount than the actual loss. A fraudulent claim may include property valued at much more than its actual worth, or may list, as lost or destroyed, property that never existed. In the first case, the remains of the property will be offered as evidence in support of the claim; in the second, fraudulent testimony, forged or altered invoices or inventories, or falsified books will often be presented. At times, property previously damaged, or damaged elsewhere, is surreptitiously brought into the premises and exhibited in support of a claim. The investigation of a fraudulent claim calls for painstaking work on the part of the claim representative. When suspicion is genuinely aroused, the claim representative should commence at once to check all the evidence he or she can collect. The investigation should include a thorough examination of the scene of the loss, the remains of any property, any records covering it, the history of the insurance, and the history and condition of the insured. In many cases, legal assistance and examinations under oath are advisable.

QUESTIONS AND PROBLEMS

1. Checking a claim usually consists of verifying that the amount is in order for the item claimed, that the property is covered, and that the peril claimed to have caused the damage is one either named in the policy or not excluded.

   a. A claim under HO-2 contains the following items:

   (1) Vacuum cleaner $150
   (2) Man's suit $ 80
   (3) Motorcycle $200

   What questions would you ask once you are satisfied all items are a total loss by fire?

b. A trainee claim representative accompanies you to the loss. He says that the man's suit and the vacuum cleaner should be valued the same as similar items in a secondhand store. How do you answer?

2. An insured lists in the claim $500 worth of frozen foods in an upright freezer and the contents of the medicine cabinet valued at $200. How would you go about checking these items?

3. You are supervising the work of a trainee claim representative and have handed her an inventory and claim on the contents of a retail drug store which sustained smoke damage from a fire next door. You ask her to go to the risk and check the claim but she looks rather puzzled. You then list the various questions that should be considered in checking the items. List at least six such questions.

Negotiations

Every human benefit and enjoyment, every virtue and prudent act, is founded on compromise and barter.

Edmund Burke, *Second Speech on Conciliation With America: The Thirteen Resolutions*, March 22, 1775.

Not all property losses are paid as a result of an *adjustment*, for if there is no disagreement as to insurable interest, coverage, and amount of loss, there is nothing to adjust. Thousands of losses are paid by insurers each year through the simple procedure of communicating with the insured by telephone or mail, getting the necessary information, and, upon receipt of a bill or an invoice for repair or replacement of the property, making the payment and closing the file. It is when the extent of damage, method of restoration, amount claimed, or other issues are in contention that opposing viewpoints have to be brought into proper relationship and harmonized. An agreement must be *negotiated* in order to effect an adjustment. This chapter presents, insofar as it is practical, an organized discussion of negotiating methods and techniques.[1]

THE ADJUSTER AS A SALESPERSON

Tactful and diplomatic conduct toward insureds by claim representatives is essential, or otherwise unnecessary antagonisms may be aroused which, in many cases, cannot be overcome. Feelings and emotions play a large part in adjustment work, so large that unless the claim representative has a marked ability for handling people, it might be better to seek other employment.

Negotiating in a loss adjustment is comparable, in many ways, with the work of a sales representative. Differences of opinion have to be met with an open mind.

[1]Review Chap. 2, "Unfair Claim-Handling Practices."

Selling one's viewpoint as to the amount of loss the insured has sustained and creating an atmosphere of good faith and respect with the insured, the insured's representatives, and everyone else involved in the negotiations are indispensable to a successful outcome. The claim representative's position creates an obligation to deal fairly, and experience should broaden the understanding that nervous and excited actions of persons with whom negotiations are being conducted should not cause irritating reactions but rather indicate ways to be adopted to bring about a condition of confidence and cooperation. To look upon an honest policyholder, who has submitted a claim, as an adversary merely because one does not agree on various issues is a serious error; it is as out of place as a salesperson treating a prospective customer as an opponent. The distinction to be recognized here is, of course, the difference between an honest, though possibly sometimes mistaken, insured and one who is grasping, greedy, or outright dishonest. In all situations the claim representative is well advised to maintain composure and not act impulsively until he or she is certain the direction negotiations should take.

BASIS FOR NEGOTIATION

A simple definition of the word *negotiate* is "to confer with another or others for the purpose of reaching an agreement." The word *negotiations* need not imply a group of people around a conference table trying to reach an agreement. Negotiations on losses are probably more often conducted by *individuals* at the scene of small to moderate-size losses. Usually the parties are the insured and the insurer's claim representative. The foundation for successful negotiations can vary somewhat, depending upon the parties and the issues involved.

If satisfactory results are to be anticipated by all parties in negotiations between insured and insurer as to the amount of loss payable under an insurance policy, four conditions are necessary:

1. The issues must be negotiable.
2. The negotiators must be willing to give as well as to receive.
3. There must be a sincere desire to negotiate.
4. There must be a degree of trust on the part of the negotiating parties.

The Issues Must Be Negotiable

Sometimes in the negotiations, issues will come up which are not subject to negotiation nor compromise. The loss may involve property which is specifically excluded or it may have been caused by a peril which is not insured against. The claim representative is not empowered to change the policy conditions and provisions. If there has been error in issuing the policy or misunderstanding as to coverage requested, any changes or concessions are the prerogative of the insurer. The usual issues which are negotiable are extent or degree of damage, cost to repair or replace the property, and value of all property to determine compliance with coinsurance or other limiting clauses.

The Negotiators Must Be Willing to Give as Well as to Receive

In matters that are negotiable, each party, as a general rule, sets its demand or offer at a level from which there is ample room for bargaining. The claim representative or the insured who meets for the purpose of discussing an adjustment, and does so with a determination *not to give an inch*, has either prepared the case poorly or has no genuine desire to negotiate the differences. There are

exceptions, such as in fraudulent claims or where one or both parties are "pigheaded." Such cases are in the minority, and most of those are not negotiable, with the result that other avenues of settlement are sought.

Where thoughtful preparations are made for negotiating, each side must stand ready and willing to *give and take*. The phrase that "negotiators sit down to the bargaining table" is literally true.

There Must Be a Sincere Desire to Negotiate

Unless all parties and their representatives enter into negotiations with a sincere desire to reach an agreement, the discussions invariably become unnecessarily prolonged and frustrating. For any of the parties, whether insured, adjuster, builders, accountants, or other experts, to attend a negotiation meeting with a fixed determination to prove or substantiate their figures or their opinions can be disastrous. Not infrequently, one individual, unwilling to listen to the opinion of others or to change an original opinion when the weight of evidence indicates otherwise, can undermine the best intentions of the negotiators.

The claim representative and the insured, or the insured's representative, are well advised to counsel any experts or others they will have attending the meeting in order to keep them under control. Lack of confidence and trust will cause one side to be suspicious of the motives of the other side, and the usual outcome is either a stalemate or an unhappy compromise for one or both parties.

There Must Be a Degree of Trust

Samuel Johnson said, "It is difficult to negotiate where neither will trust." Either before or during negotiations the parties will decide to what extent they can trust each other. This may be the result of their actions, statements, attitudes, or general demeanor.

In the great majority of property adjustment negotiations, the parties have honest differences of opinion: the insured wants to be fully compensated, and the insurer's claim representative wants to keep the amount to be paid within reasonable and justifiable limits. Their trust in each other, however, is substantial. That trust, together with a willingness to make concessions on both sides, results in respect for one another and a successful outcome.

On the other side of the ledger, there are numerous cases in which, for many reasons, either one or both parties completely distrust the other. What then passes for negotiations develops into a contest of wills, personalities, and general belligerency. On occasion this condition of affairs can result from an overzealous claim representative who feels a need to impress a superior or an employer. It can also result from inflexibility or inexperience in adjusting property losses and in handling people. It also may be sheer lack of a good personality.

More often, however, highly belligerent conferences are the consequence of deliberately exaggerated or outright fraudulent claims made against the insurer. In situations like this there can be no trust and no negotiating, merely quarrelsome debate. *Negotiating is not winning arguments; it is seeking agreements.*

QUALIFICATIONS OF A NEGOTIATOR

The attributes needed to be a skillful negotiator have more often been acquired through common sense and practical effort than through academic endeavor. Quite a few of our present-day successful negotiators in the field of property loss adjusting have had little formal schooling, but they are students of human nature and of human relations. They have great patience and much empathy, maintain an open mind, and listen well; they are tactful, friendly, fair, but firm. Some represent insureds, some insurers, and some will represent either one. They are attorneys, builders, merchandise experts, salvors, accountants, adjusters, and other specialists.

Although people are not born with a propensity for negotiating, almost anyone by application, study, and experience can learn the art of this important function. Fortu-

nately there are few claim representatives who have great talent for investigation and evaluation but who are completely deficient in negotiating skills. Ignorance of human nature or an unwillingness to observe the fundamentals of human relations, however, will lead to inevitable disaster. The claim representative who cannot gain the respect and confidence of honest claimants assumes the risk of many important negotiations degenerating into unpleasant contests.

Many qualifications could be listed for a successful negotiator and they would probably range from major to minor. There will be varying opinions on not only what they are but how important. The opinions will be influenced to some degree by experience and type of negotiation being considered. Negotiating for labor contracts; in the United Nations with friendly nations, with nations of different ideological backgrounds; condemnation proceedings; realty deals; and property loss adjustments—each may call for common skills and also specialized skills.

The author believes that negotiators in property loss adjustments should have at least the following qualities. (It is assumed they are technically qualified in loss work.)

1. Tact (diplomacy).
2. Ability to be a good listener.
3. Understanding of human relationships.
4. A judicious mien.
5. Patience.
6. Sincerity.

Some will possess most or all of these qualities. Others, possessing some, should strive to achieve *all* of them.

Tact

This is an indispensable tool of the negotiator that involves sensitivity to the appropriate action to be taken or words to be spoken at any given time in dealings with others. The dictionary defines *tact* as "the ability to appreciate the delicacy of a situation and to do or say the kindest or most fitting thing." It should not be overlooked that doing the most fitting thing at a given moment during negotiations may be to listen.

Listening

This is an art which is difficult for most of us to cultivate, but in negotiating it is most necessary. An adjuster who had a nationally recognized talent as a negotiator once remarked that he had negotiated successfully more times by listening than by talking. Too many people seem to feel compelled to give their views on specific subjects which they themselves initiate, which are presented by others, or on related or unrelated topics which arise during a discussion. Too often people are less interested in what the other person is saying than in what they are anxiously waiting to say. The cliché "He was talking when he should have been listening" sums up many dismal failures in negotiations.

A garrulous person often inadvertently gives important information heretofore concealed, or at least not disclosed, which turns out to be advantageous to the other side. A highly regarded senior adjuster in New York City, with legal training, had a reputation in his day for garrulity and for monopolizing the conversation at meetings to the extent that he talked himself into a corner. He was inclined to inadvertently make statements against his own interests which the other side seized upon to its advantage. Attorneys, aware of the dangers of talking too much, are careful to counsel their witnesses to answer the opposing attorney's questions with a "yes" or a "no" as often as possible and to volunteer no information.

A good listener usually invites respect but at the same time may arouse concern as to what he is thinking.

Understanding of Human Relationships

This is an essential ingredient for successful negotiations. It includes understanding human values and human nature. Much of our individual understanding of human nature comes from personal experiences, by trial and error, and by observing action and reaction. Much can be learned from reading. There is a plethora of books on the subject of human behavior, and most writers agree that behavior patterns are influenced by so-called deep-seated *needs* (or wants) of people. Not all agree on the number of those *needs*. Some generalize on as few as four major categories, while others produce long lists. Focusing on the kinds of needs that may have to be recognized and satisfied in the property loss adjustment situation, we suggest the following as a reasonable list. The first two are quite similar to the basic needs in Maslow's hierarchy. The other eight are regarded as appropriate for consideration by a negotiator.

1. Food, clothing, and shelter.
2. Security—job, financial, and social.
3. Affection and attention.
4. Achievement, success, capacity to solve conflicts.
5. Cooperation with others.
6. Acceptance by others.
7. Being needed by others.
8. Opportunity to develop one's personality.
9. Freedom from worry, frustration, fear, and anxiety.
10. Maintenance of one's moral values and ethical standards.

Except possibly for the first two on this list, the degree of importance of each of these needs can be expected to vary from one individual to another. Successful interaction with a claimant will depend on recognizing and being attentive to these differences.

A Judicious Mien

Considering issues, arguments, and presentation of evidence in a judicious manner is an important asset to the negotiator. It is another way of saying that one should exhibit sound judgment at all times.

Patience

This needs no explanation. In its absence, other worthy attributes of the negotiator can be damaged or destroyed, rendering the outcome less than successful.

Sincerity

This could well be at the top of the list of qualifications of a negotiator. Lack of sincerity will not pass unnoticed and can cause the objectives of the negotiator to be suspect.

SELECTING THE PARTY OR PARTIES TO NEGOTIATE

Achieving success in negotiating depends to a large extent on the person or persons selected to do the negotiating. The foregoing discussion of qualifications should be a clue to the person best qualified. In addition to the qualities for a good negotiator, knowledge of the area in which the members of the team, if more than one is present, will be operating is important. If a builder, an electrician, a roofer, salvor, merchandise expert, an accountant, or other specialist is to be present, they should be thoroughly competent in their field. One unqualified person can cast an unfavorable reflection on all members of the negotiating party.

In some situations a member of a negotiating party may be skilled in the technical aspects in his area but lack negotiating ability or, perhaps, a good personality. He should be coached to answer only questions submitted to him as a technician.

The importance of having one individual in control cannot be overemphasized, whether it is a person-to-person negotiation or a group of individuals. Also, no one present should be excess baggage; all should be present to contribute.

OBJECTIVES AND PREPARATION FOR NEGOTIATIONS

A cardinal rule is, "If you haven't done your homework, don't start negotiations." One can have all the qualities of a good negotiator, but if a thorough knowledge of the objectives and the details of the problems involved are lacking, going into negotiations can be disastrous. Investigation and evaluation must be complete.

Not only should the insurer's negotiator know all of the circumstances of the loss, the policy conditions, the extent of damage, and the values involved, but he or she should also have as much information as is available as to the details of the insured's interest, claim, previous loss experience, and any other matters bearing on the subject.

Likewise the insured's negotiator should be equally informed before the start of negotiations. Too often the representative of the insured is inclined to "play it by ear" and, after hearing the insurer's proposal, hope for a compromise. This is often an error and a disservice to the insured.

Fact Versus Assumption

As stated earlier, many elements in losses are strictly matters of opinion. Building estimates for repair or replacement are approximations by definition. Damage to wet, smoked, or stained household goods is a matter of opinion. Details of claims are full of matters of opinion as to degree of damage and cost of restoration. Usually such opinions are based on assumptions subject to adjustment or compromise.

However, there are facts in losses which are not subject to compromise. A dwelling may have so many square feet of floor area. That's a fact. The cost per square foot is a matter of opinion. A stock of merchandise in a department store may have a replacement cost agreed upon at $500,000. That's a fact. Smoke and water damage to the stock is a matter of opinion. Making a distinction between fact and opinion is essential. You can compromise opinion; you cannot compromise facts.

Objectives

A negotiator, whether dealing with an individual or as a member of a group, must have certain objectives well in mind. Compromise may be the outcome of negotiations; it should not be an objective. Neither should objectives be rigid and inflexible, for in negotiations there has to be *give* as well as *take*. As Gerard I. Nierenberg states in *Fundamentals of Negotiating* (recommended reading), "In successful negotiation everyone wins." Entering a meeting with ultimatums in mind, whether it is the insured or the insurer, does not constitute "negotiating." Ultimatums may end negotiations but they do not begin them.

Objectives should center around those areas of difference which are material and not petty or insignificant. However, if during negotiations what appeared to be a material difference dissolves into the trivial or what seemed insignificant suddenly becomes a major issue, objectives can be easily revised.

The process of establishing purposeful objectives prior to negotiating consists of analyzing the relevant material available. Detailed estimates of damage are reviewed, and, if the other party's details are furnished, comparisons should be made to determine differences. If experts have been employed, their reports should be scrutinized and all important points noted.

To gain objectives the adjuster-negotiator's work must, in many cases, parallel that of the trial lawyer, testing evidence, presenting evidence in the most effective fashion, arguing points or appealing to the emotions, and choosing the method that promises the best result. In some respects, the adjuster's work is more difficult than the lawyer's because it must be less partisan and must look beyond the adjustment to the ultimate effects on the business of the principal. The lawyer in court deals with a hostile adversary, but the adjuster deals with many claimants who are long-time customers of the insurer. The adjuster is restrained by many considerations the lawyer may ignore. For instance, when handling an excessive claim made by a desirable policyholder, the adjuster has the lawyer's duty of protecting the interest represented but, in addition, the duty to effect the protection in such a manner as to retain the goodwill and patronage of the claimant.

NEGOTIATING TECHNIQUES

Many techniques used in negotiating are simply applications of our understanding of human needs and human relationships. No one *technique* works in all situations. Some may be looked upon as strategems and used as such; nevertheless, they are essential in making or proving a point.

The following techniques, or tactics, are illustrative of ones more commonly used in property loss adjustments. While many are employed by both sides in person-to-person as well as conference negotiations, they are especially effective in the latter.

1. Humor.
2. Questions.
3. Surprise.
4. Demonstrations.
5. Diversion.
6. Exchange or trade.
7. Concurrence.
8. Silent response.
9. Apparent termination of negotiations.
10. Package proposals—wrap-up.
11. Change of horses.

Humor

The use of humor, preliminary to negotiations, frequently gets the negotiators into a friendly mood, since laughter places people on a common ground. It can also be used to illustrate points during a discussion. Several executives of a large textile mill seriously damaged in a New England hurricane met in the office of a claim representative for a last-ditch attempt to negotiate prior to entering into litigation. The general atmosphere was one of belligerency as they filed into the conference room and closed the door. At this meeting, a company expert was introduced—an old merchandise expert with the widsom of Solomon. As a cub adjuster, the author sat at a desk outside the conference room. The conferees were closeted for half an hour, during which angry voices were heard. Interspersed by the heavy accent of the company expert as he spoke calmly, there came faint chuckles through the glass partition. Then as the expert's voice seemed to dominate the conversation there were bursts of loud laughter. Presently the door opened and all the conferees came out smiling, laughing, and chatting in good humor, on their way to lunch. I learned later that the Solomon-like expert had presented his case and made his points with humorous anecdotes that put everyone at ease. The matter was concluded to everyone's satisfaction several days later.

On another occasion, an avaricious claimant mixed a quantity of obsolete stock in with damaged stock and included it in the inventory of merchandise claimed. The claim representative was not deceived and insisted that the obsolete stock was worthless and should be excluded. The claimant exclaimed, "Why, that's as good as gold." The reply was, "That's better than gold. Gold you will spend, this stuff you will have forever." The claimant could not help laughing, and the obsolete material was deleted from the schedule without further argument.

At a favorable moment in negotiations, a humorous comment or story can do much to relieve tensions and bring the conferees back to a common footing. Great care must be used in the type of humor. It cannot be crude, pointless, or untimely. Humor can be very useful to make and emphasize points as long as the story is relevant to the discussion. *Excessive use of humor, however, should be avoided.*

Questions

Questioning is an obvious method of gathering information during negotiations. It is assumed that the normal pattern of questioning relating to investigation of the insured, the insurance, the property, cause of loss, etc., discussed in the earlier chapters, has been followed. Questions that are generally asked during negotiations pertain to the details of the claim, the purpose being to elicit as much information as possible about the validity of the details, and sometimes motives, other interests, or insurance not heretofore disclosed. On serious and complicated losses there may be reports or estimates of contractors, subcontractors, machinery firms, accountants, and other experts, all of which, if not previously audited, have to be examined and questioned.

The wording and tone of a question can cause the person questioned to be at ease or to have anxiety. It can produce a guarded response or a completely frank one. In one instance there will be very little cooperation; in the other there will probably be full cooperation. For example, the question might be put, "These items of clothing in the claim all show wear. *Why* do you allege there is no depreciation?" In contrast, the question might take this form, "You have had quite a bit of use from these garments for which claim is made. Don't you think the company is entitled to *some betterment?*" While the manner of the person asking the question need not be obsequious or fawning, neither should it be combative.

Sometimes questions are useful to start people thinking and to move them closer to, or even over to, the opposite side. For example, you might hand a person a set of figures saying, "This is the way I have set the loss up. Will you look it over carefully and tell me what you think?" Or again, "Would you like to see my details?"

Frequently a question casually asked gets a person's attention and may open up a fresh viewpoint. To illustrate, during a long, rather argumentive conference-type negotiation, one member, the insured's president, sat quietly throughout. Finally during a lull the insurer's claim representative said, "Mr.—, you've not said a word all this time, but I know you have been listening intently. Would you please tell us all what your views are?" When the executive had concluded his remarks, a whole new approach revealed itself and eventually led to a successful conclusion.

On the other hand, pointless questions or ones concerning trivia are to be avoided as they waste time and identify the questioner as inefficient and sometimes incompetent.

Surprise

A textile expert used the element of surprise in negotiations by making it a practice to know as much about the insured's business as possible before attending a meeting. On first inspecting the premises after a fire, sprinkler leakage, or whatever, he would snip off swatches from the rolls of piece goods, unbeknown to anyone. He identified these swatches with the tags on the rolls. For the next few days he would visit friends in the textile business and learn everything he could about each sample, including where it was made, how many threads to the inch, where it was bleached or dyed, where it could be purchased, and the price per yard. When he attended the meeting to adjust the loss, he astounded everyone, including the insured, with his detailed knowledge. He has been known to obtain a swatch of velvet. At a subsequent meeting he would close his eyes, hold a piece of the velvet behind him and, fingering it, say, "This is French silk velvet. It was made in Lyons, France, and it can be purchased for so much a yard." He had done his homework and surprised everyone with his knowledge of velvets, especially the insured who verified the accuracy of the expert's statements.

It was the practice in one town for building contractors to give an insured two estimates for repairing or replacing damaged buildings. One reason given for this procedure was that certain adjusters felt compelled to use the insured's estimate and arbitrarily reduce it 10 percent or more. The author prepared an estimate to replace a small warehouse owned by a nationally known insured, and attended a meeting with the broker unaware of the two-estimate practice. He was handed the high estimate and anticipated there would be considerable controversy over the loss. He in turn handed the broker his detailed estimate to examine. The broker reached in his desk and pulled out the lower estimate, which was very little higher than the author's. A pleasant surprise.

A claim representative, checking the details of a building estimate on a large industrial building, found the insured's builder had inadvertently measured a large room to be 100 feet long when it was only 50 feet long. The difference in the cost of the flooring and floor construction, plus overhead and profit, was several thousand dollars. Many other things were involved in the final negotiations, and at a propitious moment the adjuster disclosed the discrepancy in the measurements, much to everyone's surprise. It had a salutary effect on the balance of the negotiations.

Demonstrations

Making a convincing physical demonstration in the presence of the opposition will usually resolve a difference of opinion effectively. Presenting, at the proper moment, a sample taken from the building involved of a roof shingle, a piece of wall paper, a swatch of fabric from upholstery, or a cutting from carpeting can dispel any question as to the type and quality of the material. When a statement from a supplier accompanies the demonstration, stipulating the replacement cost, that issue is generally put to rest.

It is not unusual to find that electric motors, machines, appliances, and similar items have been wrongly identified as to model, style, horsepower, capacity, or whatever. Since property of this type is almost never completely destroyed, proper identification at the place of loss satisfies all parties concerned.

Demonstrations to determine whether interior decorations, ceramic tile, brick or stone work, metals, and other materials can or cannot be satisfactorily cleaned are usually convincing. Sending out clothing that has been exposed to water or smoke for cleaning or test cleaning generally directs the negotiating parties toward a mutual agreement. The same procedure applies to carpeting, rugs, drapes, and upholstered furniture.

There are instances where the counting of bottle caps, bottle necks, jar lids, and similar items in the debris of a serious mercantile loss has effectively demonstrated approximate quantities. Likewise, counting metal garment hangers, whether in closets of dwellings, clothing manufacturers, or retailers, has helped establish the quantity of destroyed garments.

Of course an agreement to have the damaged, destroyed, or missing property repaired or replaced is the best demonstration and, when practical, is the most satisfactory procedure.

Diversions

This technique is self-explanatory. It is used most often to divert a person who is either off on a tangent or "spinning his wheels" in a "rhetorical rut" so to speak. The diversion may take the form of deliberately changing the subject or suggesting a "break" in the negotiations. Sometimes when the negotiations are person-to-person, one may mention a prior appointment or suggest postponing the discussion until a later date.

Exchange or Trade

This technique is illustrated by the case of a woman whose beautiful home was damaged, mostly by smoke and water. The negotiations proceeded through the home with adjusters, builders, furniture and antique experts, the woman, and her husband trailing through room by room. When it came to the kitchen, it was noticed that the claim included a new expensive electric range and the replacing of the linoleum. The damage to the linoleum was debatable but the range needed nothing much more than a cleaning. The woman persisted in claiming that the linoleum be replaced. Finally the adjuster said, "We will replace the linoleum for you if you will let us give the range a thorough cleaning." She was delighted and so the matter was settled.

Exchanges are often possible in cases where the underside of rafters in an attic are scorched by fire but not structurally harmed. To remove and replace them might include replacing a ceiling in the attic, the roof decking and shingles. This would be very expensive and cause much inconvenience with little benefit to anyone. By making a substantial monetary allowance, deodorizing and concealing the rafters, the matter is frequently taken care of.

A similar situation arises when the floor joists underneath a tile floor in a bath and shower are scorched, with no structural damage. To remove the joists, bathroom fixtures, and floor would be costly and inconvenient to the occupants. A substantial allowance is often exchanged for scraping, deodorizing, and concealing the few charred joists.

Concurrence

When the other side, in negotiating, makes a valid point or proves a point, concurrence should be made in a timely and gracious manner, never grudgingly. Winning must bring a sense of achievement and success no matter how small the issue.

Silent Response

On occasion during negotiations all of us have had to sit and listen to the other side exaggerate, make false statements, and distort facts to the extent that others are seemingly impressed if not convinced. Sometimes actions of this kind are contrived to throw up a smoke screen or to deliberately confuse, on the theory of Harry Truman: "If you can't convince them, confuse them."

Instead of contesting or debating each issue as it is brought up, keeping silent can be very effective. A New York police official told of a method they frequently adopted when an employee in the garment area was suspected of stealing merchandise from his employer. While the employee was being interrogated by two or three detectives, one detective would sit nearby, stare at the suspect throughout the questioning, but say nothing. Frequently after the others left, not having obtained an admission of guilt, the employee would seek out the silent observer, and confess. The psychology apparently was that the suspect was convinced the silent one knew he was telling a lie and that he was guilty. This compelled him to confess his crime.

When a person is fabricating and exaggerating, nothing is more disconcerting than to have the listener or listeners stare silently and disbelievingly.

Apparent Termination of Negotiations

When all efforts to reach an agreement seem to be of no avail, try this technique: Get up, close your briefcase, and with no comment or a statement like "Ladies and gentlemen, that's all we can do," prepare to leave the meeting. This gesture often brings the other side to the realization that the bluffing is over. If they have been bluffing, they see opportunity going out the door with no assurance that a more advantageous time will present itself.

Package Proposals—Wrap-Up

During some negotiations a realization comes that most of the discussion has been over numerous details, all part of the whole picture. Under these conditions, a solution may present itself in the form of making a package deal—putting all of the parts together in a wrap-up offer. The parts might consist of building repair, contents, and time elements such as rents or loss of earnings. When all are rolled into one offer with no breakdown of each, the result can very often be made acceptable.

Change of Horses

The old saying "Don't change horses in the middle of the stream" may be applicable in specific cases, but its antithesis can work wonders in the middle of negotiations where a personality conflict stands in the way of reaching an agreement. The secret is in recognizing when the personality conflict exists. On occasion, one of the negotiating parties will realize that withdrawal and substitution of someone else is the answer to a stalemate. At other times a third party will have to intercede and either tactfully remove the cause of the personality conflict or have the person "take a back seat" so to speak.

Some people are unconsciously or inadvertently abrasive to others for no readily apparent reason. Something in the physical appearance or demeanor of one person turns another person off. When this becomes apparent or can be foreseen, it is advisable to tactfully and diplomatically make a substitution.

COPING WITH VARIOUS PERSONALITY TRAITS

The majority of negotiations in adjusting property losses are conducted in an atmosphere of considerable trust and good faith with the common objective of reaching a harmonious agreement. There may often be strong positions taken on issues, and not infrequently heated arguments take place between individuals. There may be a certain amount of subterfuge, withholding of pertinent information, bluffing, and the use of other stratagems in an effort to attain objectives. But, generally, there is no rancor and the tone of the parties is comparable to that found in any amicable matching of wits.

However, there are times when strong, undesirable personality traits dominate in negotiations. This can hamper or completely block all efforts of the other side to reach an accord. When confronted with obstacles of this nature, all six of the qualifications of a good negotiator, previously mentioned, must be summoned to cope with the situation. Furthermore, on no other occasion is it more important to be cognizant of the 14 points listed in the "Unfair Claim Settlement Practices" section of the NAIC Model Unfair Trade Practices Act.[2] Particular reference is made to the ten-point "Code of Conduct" for claim representatives based on that section of the NAIC act.[3]

The most common difficult personality traits encountered in negotiations will be found in individuals with the following traits:

1. Reasonable but misinformed.
2. Recalcitrant.
3. Avaricious.
4. Positive.
5. Hostile.
6. Trading-minded.
7. Uncooperative.
8. Emotional.
9. Senile.
10. Fraudulent.

There are no hard-and-fast rules for dealing with persons who exhibit these characteristics, whether they be claimant or claim representative. There are degrees of each, and some individuals are possessed of more than one of the traits. About all that can be done here is to assist the negotiator, particularly one who is relatively new in the field, by offering suggestions based on the experience of others who have been long in the field.

Reasonable but Misinformed Persons

As a general rule, reasonable persons are basically honest and, if misinformed or not knowledgeable on specific matters, are inclined to accept logical explanations and fac-

[2]See p. 18.
[3]See p. 22.

tual demonstrations.[4] The gathering of facts or figures by the claim representative to present reasonable explanations to claimants is often time-consuming and may incur what might be thought of as unnecessary expense. As an illustration, an insured owned a frame summer hotel under construction in the mountains, 150 miles from the city. It was completely destroyed by fire when half completed. The claim representative visited the scene, and his measurements of the remains of the foundation disclosed a building 100 feet wide and 100 feet long. When he returned to the city, he was presented with a claim for a building 100 feet wide but 150 feet long. The insured, a doctor, had not seen the building, having merely let the contract to a local builder. The insured did not believe the claim representative and felt he was being victimized. The adjuster offered to drive the insured to the mountains on a Sunday and have him hold one end of the measuring tape. The offer was accepted and, to the insured's amazement, the claim representative's figures were correct. It turned out that the local builder also named in the policy had exaggerated the length of the building in the belief the insurer would not bother to send someone 150 miles just to measure the foundation. The savings to the insurer was many times the expense.

In difficulties arising out of the insured's lack of knowledge, the claim representative may well spend considerable time showing him or her the truth about the loss and explaining the insured's rights and duties under the insurance policy. Most insureds lack the ability to visualize ways of restoring damaged property to usefulness. Many persons sustain only one loss in a lifetime and therefore have no experience to guide them in handling articles that have been damaged by fire, water, smoke, windstorm, or other perils. Moreover, the people have several misconceptions about an insurance policy, a common one being that nothing should be done to disturb the appearance of the property or to protect it from further damage until the claim representative arrives.

[4]See Demonstrations, p. 154.

Recalcitrant Persons

A stubborn and unruly individual is a challenge to any negotiator. This is not the positive or uncooperative individual so much as one on whom all argument and appeal are alike wasted and who is best characterized as pigheaded. The best procedure with this type of negotiator is to apply sufficient pressure and keep it on until he or she yields. Severity, reasonable delay, studied demands difficult to comply with, perhaps seldom exercised but authorized by the policy, may at length bring the stubborn individual to terms.

On occasion an appeal to a third party, such as an agent or a broker, a relative, the claimant's attorney, partner, or superior officer, will help bring about a favorable result.

Avaricious Persons

Grasping and overreaching persons also need to be brought under pressure to bring them to reason, as in the case of the recalcitrants. Individuals with this personality characteristic not only tend to make a small and insignificant damage larger, but also tend to exaggerate the cost of items, real and personal in nature. In the first instance, the claim representative frequently fortifies a position by bringing in qualified consultants, builders, merchandise or machinery experts, etc., with instructions to prepare estimates of damage which will stand the test of appraisal or litigation. In the second instance, the establishment of proper costs is accomplished through factual sources backed by letters from suppliers, by catalogs, copies of invoices, newspaper ads, and other sources.

Offers to exercise the insurer's option to repair or replace the property or to take all of the damaged property at its agreed value will many times bring about a satisfactory conclusion.

Positive Persons

A different method is to be followed when the claim representative finds the insured to be a person with definite ideas and ready to contend for them. If the insured's ideas are found to be erroneous, the adjuster's task will generally be expedited by selecting one of the several methods discussed under "Negotiating Techniques." On the other hand, the insured may be of the type best handled by turning over all estimates, or other data, letting the insured reach a proper conclusion on his or her own initiative. Other insureds may have a limited capacity to think alone and may require much argument to be convinced.

Often if a positive person is shown to be in error on one or a few items, his or her confidence diminishes. A large wholesale plumbing firm had a one-story frame building, used to store fittings, destroyed by fire. The claim representative visited the loss and found the building destroyed. The only wood remaining was in the concrete floor which had been poured after the building was up and to a depth of about 2 inches above the bottom of vertical 1- by 6-inch boards which formed the sides of the numerous bins for storing pipe fittings. The adjuster's builder dug out several ends of these boards which were charred only on top where they had burned off level with the concrete floor. His purpose was to identify the kind of wood, which was hemlock. At a meeting in the insured's office the general manager was positive the bin lumber was white pine, which was twice the cost of local hemlock. At the right moment the adjuster's builder took the samples from his briefcase and placed them on the general manager's desk. While the manager had been positive, he was honest and readily agreed he was in error. This demonstration paved the way for easier negotiating with the somewhat embarrassed general manager.

An insured, positive that his arithmetic calculations are perfect, will often wilt when a thorough claim representative recalculates and demonstrates significant errors.

Hostile Persons

Claimants are people and as such possess all of the perfections and imperfections of the human race. Hostility to various situations is one of the characteristics found on occasion. This posture may arise from an immediate and instinctive personal dislike of the claim representative. Perhaps it is something the adjuster did or did not do in responding to the notice of loss filed by the insured; it may be the insured's preconceived unfavorable adjuster image, not uncommon in some areas; or the insured may be just naturally a disagreeable, hostile person.

Whatever the cause of the hostility, the claim representative is well advised to seek out the reason. If it is the result of neglect on the part of the producer or claim department, apologies should be made and corrective steps taken to right any wrong. If the claim representative recognizes an instinctive dislike on the part of the insured, every effort should be made to overcome that obstacle; but, if to no avail, and the loss is of sufficient magnitude, or the account is of major importance, introduction of a third party should be considered.

There are times when otherwise meek and inoffensive claimants become extremely hostile. These occasions are most often witnessed in catastrophe losses such as hurricanes, tornadoes, floods, or earthquakes, and the insured along with neighbors learns that certain property is not covered or certain perils (such as wave wash) are excluded. The disposition of an entire community is often aroused to the point of threatening violence to claim representatives. In cases of this kind extreme tact and care are to be exercised until the situation is eased.

Trading-Minded Persons

Certain persons are not content with collecting their full actual loss but seek to get as much as they can by trading tactics. These claimants are quite numerous, for it is human to try to drive a good bargain. Also to be considered is the fact that, in some areas, adjusters have, rightly or wrongly, created the impression in the minds of insureds that when you have a loss, in order to get the actual damage paid, you must inflate the claim because the adjuster will arbitrarily "cut" it.

There is nothing wrong with trading tactics per se on matters of opinion, but when it becomes a game or a contest and involves questions of fact, a disengagement is in order. Pressures have to be put on the trading-minded person. The case is presented in a way as to make the claimant believe he is collecting the last penny on the item, items, or the entire loss. The effort to be expended will vary with the tenacity of the claimant, and negotiations will often take much more time than at first seemed necessary. Trading tactics are usually essential when negotiating with the trading-type claimant.

When the claim representative is quite sure of the position taken as to the amount due the claimant, and trading tactics continue to be taken by the insured, a device often effective is to terminate all negotiations. A few days later a proof of loss is sent to the insured together with a draft or check for the amount the claim representative feels is in order. An enclosing letter simply asks that the proof of loss be signed and returned. The trading-type insured, now with a check in hand, realizes the end of the line has been reached and, particularly on smaller losses, gives up.

Uncooperative Persons

The claimant who will not cooperate with the claim representative has to have pressure applied, much like the stubborn, avaricious, or hostile person. There are certain policy requirements of the insured in case of loss which are enforceable.[5] When pressure is applied through policy provisions, care must be exercised to document such actions in writing, explaining the particular provision to be complied with and the reason. If the matter is of sufficient importance and magnitude, witnesses and experts are desirable.

Emotional Persons

When the claimant is emotionally upset or disturbed, the claim representative should seek the cause without being observably guilty of invasion of privacy. Emotional stress can be caused by a death in the family, an unhappy marriage, job frustration, a financial problem, or any one of a number of other reasons. However, regardless of cause,

emotionally disturbed persons need understanding and patience, and negotiations should not be attempted until the person has calmed down and has been put at ease. Probably the first act of the claim representative is to seek out someone with competence and authority to represent the claimant. That could be a business associate, the spouse, a relative, an attorney, an agent or a broker, or, under some circumstances, a close friend or neighbor.

When the cause of emotional upset is the occurrence of the loss, the claim representative may have to assist in doing many things normally required of the insured such as, on dwelling losses, separating some of the damaged property from the undamaged or even assisting in preparing the claim with the insured's consent on smaller losses.

When the emotional stress results from a family problem, progress in negotiating can be frustratingly slow, and will require the patience of Job. Decisions are difficult to make and indecisiveness is apt to be more the rule. Securing someone to represent the claimant is often the best solution.

A severely emotionally disturbed person is impossible to negotiate with, and negotiating should not be attempted in the absence of a legal representative for the claimant.

Senile Persons

Senility is an infirmity of old age. The predominantly observable symptom is a loss of mental faculties. In other words, the senile person suffers from loss of memory and the inability to think rationally. When it is observed that a person is senile, no negotiations should be entered into without a legal representative of the insured present.

Persons Suspected of Fraud

Fraudulent claims result from one of two actions: (1) the deliberate destruction or disposition of the property by the insured with the intent of collecting insurance,[6] (2) the willful attempt to collect more than one is entitled

---

[5]See Chap. 6, "Duties of the Insured After Loss."

[6]See Chap. 10, "Arson Investigation and Detection."

to. While fraudulent claims may be the result of one or both acts, cases resulting from the latter are the more numerous. To commit the first act, the insured must use some foresight and possess sufficient courage to take the attending risks of burning, blowing up, or otherwise destroying the property, or staging a fake theft. The second is most often committed after the loss has occurred and the opportunity presents itself. The risk is also considerably less for, if detected, an inadvertent or honest mistake may be alleged.

Fraud in making the claim itself is generally in the form of overstating the value of, or damage to, the property. Overstatement may include property never in the insured's possession or property that was removed from the premises before the real or alleged casualty took place. Stocks that are shopworn, obsolete, or difficult to move may be inventoried as new goods. Totally destroyed buildings may be overvalued, or the specifications may be altered or exaggerated in the hope that the claim representative will be unable to obtain sufficient data on construction and condition to prepare an accurate estimate of value and loss.

Claims may also be made for damage to real or personal property that was not caused by one of the perils insured against. Such damages could include burned-out motors and electrical appliances said to have resulted from lightning, whereas the real cause was overloading, short circuiting, or plain wear and tear. Old cracks in masonry walls caused by settling of a building, dry rot, termites, inferior materials or workmanship are sometimes intentionally and fraudulently attributed to fire, windstorm, or some other insured peril.

In handling claims where fraud is suspected, the claim representative must practice extreme tact and caution both in action and in questioning of the claimant (1) to determine whether fraud is *in fact* being attempted, (2) to avoid violating provisions of the NAIC "Unfair Claim Settlement Practices," and (3) to avert possible suit by the insured. At some point and as soon as practicable, an opinion will have to be formed

whether it is wiser to litigate or to negotiate a compromise. In forming the opinion one must bear in mind the uncertainties of all litigation and particularly cases that involve questions of fact. The opinion should be submitted to the person to whom the claim representative normally reports. If the claim representative is empowered to act and the opinion formed is that evidence of fraud is substantial, such evidence should be turned over to an attorney for either development of stronger evidence, suit, or both.

If the evidence obtained is fragile, though still suspect, and the claim representative is empowered to act, a tactful or forceful presentation should be made to the claimant if a compromise is hoped for. The several policy defenses available under the policy should be employed where applicable to bring subtle pressure on the claimant, and the negotiating techniques discussed earlier should be used where appropriate.

QUESTIONS AND PROBLEMS

1. A simple definition of the word *negotiate* is "to confer with another or others for the purpose of reaching an agreement." There are four basic conditions necessary for negotiations to be successful. What are they?

2. The text lists six essential qualities a negotiator should possess for adjusting property losses. What are they?

3. It is important in the understanding of human relationships to recognize that behavior patterns are influenced by deep-seated needs or wants of people. Name at least six such needs besides food, clothing, and shelter.

4. Various negotiating techniques can be used during negotiations to try to convince the opposition and prove points. The text lists eleven. Name at least six. Give an example of three.

5. a. When a negotiator on the other side is apparently a reasonable person but misinformed or mistaken, what generally is the best way to convince him or her, assuming your own position is correct?

b. A young claim representative whom you are supervising tells you he is having trouble with an insured who is very stubborn and unruly. Explain briefly what methods you would suggest to the young negotiator.

6. What is meant by the expression "everybody wins in negotiations"?

7. You have been chief negotiator at meetings that have lasted several days trying to bring about agreement on a serious loss that includes buildings, machinery, stock, and business interruption. Neither side seems willing to completely agree on the amount of loss on any single coverage. They are close on some but far apart on others. It looks like a stalemate. What final negotiating technique or tactic would you be inclined to try prior to engaging in possible litigation or appraisal?

8. State in general terms some of the objectives that a negotiator should bear in mind and how preparations to meet those objectives should be undertaken.

Burglary and Theft

This chapter deals with the investigation and adjustment of claims arising under policies of insurance covering burglary, theft, robbery, and other crimes involving the wrongful taking of someone else's property. These policies fall generally into two categories. One insures individuals under residential theft policies, such as the *broad form personal theft policy* or similar coverage included in the Homeowners policies. The second group insures business firms under one of the numerous *crime coverages*, such as the *Mercantile Open Stock Burglary Policy*; the *Comprehensive Dishonesty, Disappearance, and Destruction Policy*; the *Storekeepers' Burglary and Robbery Policy*; and the several types of *robbery insurance policies*. Certain crime coverages may be included as named perils in multiple-line policies or they may be available by endorsement.

Many inland marine policies cover burglary, robbery, theft, or pilferage on premises or in transit, either as named perils or under all risks of loss forms. The forms for individuals and business firms are too numerous to mention.

Prior to the investigation of any claim under the crime coverages one must carefully examine the policy form and endorsements. The conditions and provisions relating to burglary, theft, etc., can be quite different under different types of policies. Specific limitations for certain kinds of property may also be different. Statutory and policy definitions must be understood by the claim representative.

DEFINITIONS OF TERMS

Common law, statutory, and insurance policy definitions of such terms as *pilferage*, *theft*, *larceny*, *robbery*, and *burglary* have certain variations; with the exception of burglary, however, they are in general agreement. In addition to checking for any policy definition of terms, the claim representative should review the statutory definitions of the particular jurisdiction in which the loss occurs. Definitions in insurance policies take precedence over statutory definitions. The following broad definitions of terms will be found satisfactory for most situations.

Burglary

Burglary is the breaking and entering into the premises of another with the intent to commit a felony, whether or not such felony is actually committed. Some state statutes define the breaking and entering as occurring at *night*. In one state, Louisiana, the mere entry at nighttime to commit a felony, without forcible entry, constitutes a burglary. The intended felony need not be theft but may be arson, murder, rape, or any other crime classified as a felony.

Where *breaking and entering* is a necessary provision to constitute a burglary, there must be visible evidence of physical force at the place of entry. If a thief tries unsuccessfully to pry open a door, leaving clear evidence of the attempt, but finds an open window through which to make entry—there is no burglary.

Commercial or mercantile burglary policies cover only when the premises are not open for business. For example, under a mercantile open stock burglary policy there can be no loss if the premises are open for business twenty-four hours.

Under Storekeepers' Burglary and Robbery Endorsement (MLB-158) of the Special Multi-Peril Policy there would be no liability for theft without evidence of forcible entry. Theft by a person concealed inside the premises and thereafter breaking out would not be considered forcible *entry*, but rather forcible exit. Under Mercantile Open Stock Policies, forcible exit *is* a burglary.

Theft and Larceny

Theft or *larceny* is the fraudulent taking of personal property that belongs to another without that person's consent, with the intent to deprive the owner of its value.

Larceny and theft are often used interchangeably, but the term *theft* has a much wider significance in the penal codes of some of the states. It may apply to any illegal acquisition or wrongful appropriation of property whether by removing or withholding, and may include embezzlement, breach of trust, or conversion.

Pilferage

Pilferage is actually petty thievery. In insurance it is usually defined as the theft of part of a carton or package.

Robbery

Robbery is the felonious taking of personal property in the possession of another, from their person or in their presence, against their will and under constraint of force or fear.

As a rule, the policy definition of robbery is broader than are statutory definitions. Robbery in the Comprehensive Dishonesty, Disappearance, and Destruction Policy includes the taking of covered property "by any other overt felonious act committed in his presence (or that of his messenger or custodian) and of which he was actually cognizant." An insured working in the back room hears the cash register ring and peering out sees a person take money out of the drawer and leave. This is robbery even though the insured has not been threatened and there has been no force or violence.

Mysterious Disappearance

Mysterious disappearance, generally excluded, is the disappearance of property from a known place or location, during a known period of time and under unknown or baffling circumstances for which there is no reasonable or logical explanation.

The term is not defined in any insurance policy and, in spite of much litigation throughout the country, there is no uniform agreement on the elements necessary to constitute mysterious disappearance.

One of the country's outstanding independent adjusters (particularly in the field of inland marine adjusting), who is also an attorney, Harold S. Daynard, has propounded certain principles which bear upon the term *mysterious disappearance* whether it is an insured peril *or an exclusion.* They are compounded from the definitions of terms that in Attorney Daynard's opinion are currently most acceptable.

PRINCIPLE I. Property covered for loss by "mysterious disappearance" is covered when it vanished from a known place under circumstances which defy reasonable explanation, i.e., where the cause cannot be logically determined. Proof of theft is not necessary, though a possibility of theft ordinarily is present to create the element of mystery.

PRINCIPLE II. Proof that property was lost does not qualify it within "mysterious disappearance" coverage even though the precise manner of losing the property, or the precise place of loss is unknown or puzzling. The fact that the property was simply lost is sufficient explanation to eliminate the element of mystery. Similarly, if the facts show some other logical explanation for the loss, "mysterious disappearance" coverage does not apply.

PRINCIPLE III. It follows from principles I and II that if property is lost in a manner or in a place which is known, but the property cannot be recovered or retrieved, then the peril "mysterious disappearance" does not apply. The cause of loss is known and determined and there is no element of mystery present.

PRINCIPLE IV (A). Property covered for "mysterious disappearance" is not covered when owner cannot recall where or when it was last seen, or where it may have been placed by him. In such case, the property has not disappeared, i.e., vanished from a known place or location.

PRINCIPLE IV (B). Property which has been mislaid, left unattended, then discovered missing from a known place, where it is likely to have been stolen, or found and converted to the finder's own use, is covered under theft. It is not a "mysterious disappearance" because the cause of loss is apparent.

PRINCIPLE V. "Theft" is distinguished from "mysterious disappearance" in that it is founded upon specific facts which logically disclose the cause of loss to be the wrongful taking of assured's property by some person known or unknown. Policies which insure theft cover such loss. Policies which insure all risks but exclude "mysterious disappearance" also cover such loss, because the cause has been ascertained to be theft.

PRINCIPLE VI. Property covered under theft or all risk policies which exclude loss by mysterious disappearance is not covered against disappearance where the surrounding circumstances offer no logical explanation as to what happened to it.

PRINCIPLE VII. Property covered under theft or all risk policies which exclude loss by mysterious disappearance is covered for disappearance where the surrounding circumstances show that either theft or some other covered peril is the probable cause of loss.

PRINCIPLE VIII. The standard applied to the interpretation of the term "mysterious disappearance" is: What the normal, average person understands the term to mean after giving due consideration to the type of insurance involved, the type of coverage afforded, and the type of perils excluded.

PRINCIPLE IX. In a suit under an insurance policy, the insured has the burden of proving that the loss falls within the term, location, perils and property covered.

PRINCIPLE X. The burden of proof with respect to a defense based upon a policy exclusion, in a suit on an insurance policy, is upon the insurer. [1]

INSURANCE

The Homeowners HO-2, HO-3, HO-4 (Ed. 9-70), and the HO-76 (Ed. 7-1-75), including the Basic Form HO-1, use the following wording in qualifying the peril of *theft*. This replaces *mysterious disappearance* as a separate peril.

Including loss of property from a known place under circumstances when a probability of theft exists.

In the absence of this wording, the insured would have to prove that a theft occurred. With the wording, all that need be demonstrated is that a probability of theft *existed*. This wording came into being after a number of years of litigation and has done much to clarify the coverage.

Most commercial policies exclude loss of *mere disappearance*, as in Open Stock Burglary and Theft Endorsements, or exclude *loss due to unexplained or mysterious disappearance of property or shortage of property disclosed on taking inventory.* The latter wording appears in both the Standard and the Special Businessowners Policies (Ed. 11-75).

Under crime coverage forms and the numerous endorsements available, specific crime situations, individuals, and property may be covered to fit the business of an insured.

There is no type of claim which better demonstrates the importance of verifying and checking coverage before investigation than one made under the various crime coverages. On all but the most trifling losses, the insured's policy should be examined rather than depending upon a broker's or an agent's information. A record should be made of the type of policy; the policy number; forms, endorsements, and edition dates; the term of

---

[1]Harold S. Daynard, *Trends in Adjusting*, Vol. I, Daynard & Van Thunen Co., Inc., New York, 1967.

the policy; any definitions of burglary, theft, etc.; the declarations on mercantile policies, especially those pertaining to watchman, alarm systems, or other protective features for which there has been a reduction in rate.

The policy should be checked to make certain *what* property is covered; *where* it is covered; whether there are any classes of *property excluded* or any *limitations on specific classes of property*; also whether there is a *deductible*. If the policy lists *scheduled articles*, and they are involved, an exact copy should be made of the description of each article and the amount for which it is scheduled.

Mercantile policies particularly should be examined for *conditions, provisions,* or *declarations*, any of which are in the nature of a warranty relating to such matters as *watchman service, protective devices,* location of property on the premises, and *maintenance of accurate inventories* so that the exact amount of loss can be determined.

Insured

The name of the insured[2] and a brief history should be obtained; also the name of any person for whom claim is being made if the property involved belongs to someone other than the insured—for example, an employee, a guest, a customer, or a bailor. The interest of the person for whom claim is made should be ascertained.

Property Covered

Residential policies in general cover unscheduled personal property owned or used by the named insured, or by members of the insured's family of the same household, and, at the insured's option, similar property of guests and servants all while on the described premises. Wording varies as to property specifically covered or excluded. Commercial policies cover, broadly, property owned by the insured or held by the insured without regard for legal liability.

Premises Involved

The premises on which the crime occurred should be described in full in order to specifically identify it as the premises or as a location at which the policy covers. The policy itself and the declarations indicate the premises to which the insurance applies. The information should include construction, number of stories, occupancy, and type of neighborhood.[3] What part of the premises is occupied by the insured, for what purpose, and whether owned or leased should also be noted.

Under commercial policies, *premises* is defined, generally, as the "interior of that portion of any building which is occupied by the insured in conducting its business." Forcible entry into the front entrance of an office building, but no evidence of forcible entry into the particular office occupied by the insured, would not constitute a burglary. The proprietor of a concession in a department store or a larger discount store may place the day's receipts in a safe located in the office of the owner of the department store or discount house. If the safe is burglarized, the concession proprietor would have no burglary coverage unless the policy was endorsed to protect him or her for burglary *away from the premises.*

Under residential policies, if the loss occurred in a temporary residence or secondary location of the insured, a description and the circumstances under which it qualifies as a temporary residence or secondary location should be recorded. The claim representative should determine whether the portion of the premises in which the loss occurred was occupied exclusively by the insured. If not, the names of other occupants should be obtained and their relationship to the insured noted.

Under mercantile policies, the protective devices should be noted; these would include the type of alarms, ADT connection, and watchman or watchdogs.

Alarm systems and security provisions, made in the declarations, must be operative;

[2]See Chap. 7, "Investigation of the Insured, the Property, and the Insurance."

[3]See Chap. 28, "Reports to Insurers."

otherwise, coverage or liability may be affected. The identity of each watchman or security guard should be established; also their age, period of employment, and whether full or part time. The types of entrance doors and locks securing them should be noted as well as the names of all persons who possess keys. If the loss involves a safe, the report should state where it is located and identify it by make, type, serial number, size, whether burglarproof, and whether anchored. Where theft from showcases or windows is involved, the report should describe them, give their location, and state whether or not they open directly into the interior of the insured's premises. If they do not, the Mercantile Open Stock Burglary Policy (for example) may not afford coverage unless the risk is specifically assumed by endorsement.

Under Three D Policies coverage is granted outside the premises by destruction, disappearance, or wrongful abstraction of money and securities while being conveyed by a messenger or any armored motor vehicle company or while within the living quarters in the home of any messenger. Loss of other property by robbery outside the premises or attempt thereat is covered while such property is being conveyed by a messenger or any armored motor vehicle company or by theft while within the living quarters in the home of any messenger. A messenger is the insured, a partner, or any employee duly authorized by the insured to have care and custody of the property covered outside the premises.

CHECKLIST FOR CLAIM REPRESENTATIVES

The claim representative's investigation under policies that insure against one or more crime coverages should be directed along the following lines of inquiry and action.

I. The insurance.
    A. Examine the original or an exact copy of the policy coverage and list form numbers, edition dates, and endorsements.
    B. Note effective date and expiration date of policy and of endorsements.
    C. Is the property claimed covered, excluded, or limited as to amount? Is it scheduled?
    D. Is there an applicable deductible?
    E. Do the circumstances surrounding the crime place it within the policy (or statutory) definition?
    F. Is there any other insurance to cover in whole or in part?

II. The insured.
    A. Obtain exact name of the insured, and of the person for whom claim is made if not the named insured.
    B. If claimant is not the insured, what is the relationship to insured, i.e., relative, member of the household, employee, business partner or associate, etc.?

III. Property involved.
    A. Describe in full the property stolen, missing, pilfered, etc., as to kind, quality, quantity, serial numbers if any, size, age, present replacement cost, depreciation (physical, obsolescence). What was the original cost? Verify.
    B. Who owned the property? Insured, relative, guest, employee, boarder, roomer, member of the household, bailor, business associate, other?
    C. If not owned, was the property used by the insured?
    D. If property was a gift, determine who gave it to the claimant, when, under what circumstances, etc. If questionable, check back to donor.
    E. Any question that policy covers the property? Any dollar limit?
    F. Was property used in the insured's business?

IV. Location of crime.
    A. Where did the crime occur?
        1. On the street (robbery)? Give details.
        2. Was it from the described premises? If from other premises, are they owned, rented and occupied by the insured? Was the

insured temporarily residing there at time of loss?

3. Are premises or any part used for business? If so, describe in full.

B. Was property taken from a depository? Who put it there? When? Is there a receipt or record? Did depository have insurance? Obtain full details. Who had access to depository?

C. If loss was from a motor vehicle, trailer, or watercraft, was the property attended? If not, was there forcible entry into a closed vehicle or watercraft? Check the particular form as conditions and provisions vary from one policy to another.

D. Did loss occur from a public conveyance, as a bus, train, plane, ferry, etc. Do conveyance owners provide coverage in full or in part?

E. If loss occurred in transit, was the property "in due course of transit"?

V. Circumstances of occurrence.

A. Describe in full the occurrence of the crime as to:

1. Place of crime. On the street, in a public establishment (store, bar, hotel, etc.)?

2. Are premises owned or leased by the insured? Occupied by insured? What part? Who are other occupants?

3. Type of crime? Burglary, theft, robbery?

4. Where on premises did it occur?

B. Who discovered the occurrence?

1. Was notice of loss given to the insurer within reasonable time?

2. If burglary or theft from residence, obtain detailed statement from the insured, members of the family, servants, and all others who may have knowledge of the occurrence and its discovery.

3. If burglary, what is the evidence of forcible entry? At what specific point was entry made?

4. If burglary or theft from mercan-

tile premises, obtain a statement from the insured and all employees having any knowledge of the occurrence and its discovery.

5. If robbery, question the person robbed on all details of the occurrence concerning time, place, method, suspects, etc.

C. If the loss occurred on the premises, were all alarms and other security warranties complied with? Did the alarm operate? Were doors and windows locked? Were showcases, safes, etc., locked? What persons had keys to the premises, safes, showcases, etc.? Has the watchman's clock been checked?

D. If the claim is for safe burglary, is there evidence of entrance to the safe by force through use of tools, explosives, etc.? (Losses from within the safe through manipulation of the combination or other means leaving no visible evidence of force on the exterior of the safe are not covered.)

E. Is the loss a mysterious disappearance?

1. When was the property seen last?

2. Exactly where was the property seen?

3. Who saw it?

4. Describe the circumstances under which the property was last worn or used.

5. Under what circumstances was the property discovered missing? Give details.

6. Did the disappearance take place under circumstances that are baffling or puzzling, and for which there is no logical or reasonable explanation?

7. Extensively question the person who makes the claim on events prior to the discovery that the property was missing, and on events subsequent to the discovery.

8. Has a thorough search been made for the missing property? By the insured? By the claim representative?
9. Have all persons having knowledge of the claimed loss been questioned?
10. Has every effort been made to determine whether the property was *misplaced, mislaid,* or *actually lost?*
11. Was there an opportunity for theft to have occurred?

NOTIFICATION TO POLICE

Has the insured notified the police of the occurrence as required under the policy? The claim representative should obtain a copy of the police report on all claims except the most trivial. On losses in excess of a few hundred dollars he or she should personally contact the police officer assigned to the case to give whatever assistance possible and also to learn what progress is being made in apprehending the criminal and in notifying pawnshops and other places where the stolen articles may be disposed of by the thief.

The claim representative should determine who reported the loss to the police, what was reported stolen, and the values claimed for the property taken. Discrepancies between the report given to the police and the report given to the insurer on the items stolen and their value have occasionally led to the uncovering of fraudulent claims. Police records are not open to the public in all localities. In many cities a written request for a copy of the police report, accompanied by a small fee, will obtain the information.

In most cities of any size, pawnshops are required to report to the police each day on items sold or pawned to them. The larger cities have a "pawnshop detail" who check pawnshops to locate stolen property.

If the insured refuses to notify the police because he or she suspects that a neighbor, a neighbor's child, a guest, or some other person close by has committed the crime, the claim representative may have sufficient grounds for terminating negotiations and declining liability.

NOTIFICATION TO OTHERS

While there is no policy requirement to notify persons other than the police, it is quite common and logical for the insured to notify establishments such as hotels and motels of missing personal property. Railroad, airline, and other transportation systems are frequently notified by insureds that articles have been lost or are suspected of having been stolen. These sources should be checked to learn exactly what was reported missing and the claimed value.

The manufacturers of business machines, outboard motors, and other equipment have a procedure for circularizing dealer, service, and repair facilities of stolen items by model, serial number, and other identifying marks. Recoveries are frequently made by notification to these firms of items stolen.

Prompt notice should be given to banks when checks are stolen, and notice should be given to customers that incoming checks have been stolen. A stop-payment request should be made, and the checks should be reissued, even if letters of indemnity must be furnished to those reissuing.

SUSPECTS

The questioning and apprehension of persons suspected of committing theft, burglary, robbery, etc., are police work and, objectively speaking, should not be undertaken by the claim representative for two reasons: first, the police are more experienced, and second, as in the investigation of any crime, *the possibility of laying the groundwork of a suit against the insurer for libel, whether justified or not, is always present.*

However, through investigation, the claim representative may be able to furnish the authorities with useful leads on individuals considered possible suspects. These clues or leads are usually developed through careful interrogation of the insured and all persons who have knowledge of the occurrence or of the location of the involved property immediately before the event took place.

Burglaries and robberies committed in residences of insureds appear, in many cases, to be deliberately planned by persons who know that the insured possessed articles of value. It also frequently appears that the locations of the items of value are known, for in many cases only the most valuable articles are taken. When the circumstances of a serious burglary, theft, or robbery indicate the perpetrator had some knowledge of the existence and location of the property taken, the investigation should be directed toward ascertaining what persons could have informed the thief or thieves. The insured, members of the family, and any part-time or full-time servants, gardeners, or other domestics should be questioned. Workmen, deliverymen, interior decorators, and all persons presently in the insured's employment, or recently released from employment, should be interrogated and their background and records checked.

The investigation of thefts which are claimed to have taken place during a house party, or when neighbors' children had free access to the premises, requires delicate handling. There is always the chance that the item or items have been mislaid or misplaced or that their disappearance occurred at another time in another place. Insureds are most reluctant to have their friends questioned or their neighbors' children accused. Occasionally the insured will refuse to divulge the names and addresses of friends, neighbors, or children who were on the premises at the time of the claimed theft or mysterious disappearance. Whether such refusal is sufficient to decline liability is a matter for the insurer to decide.

It is generally difficult to find direct evidence of theft and larceny. The evidence is largely circumstantial. The premises may or may not be found ransacked. The prime requirements are that there was an opportunity for theft, that the property was known to be in a specific place or location at a definite time, and that it was later discovered missing.

Consider the following instances of theft: A woman places her handbag or wallet on the counter while shopping in a crowded store. A few minutes later she turns to pick it up but it is gone. An insured reports certain jewelry missing from her dresser. She had placed the items there a few days before. The house was open, and a baby sitter or maid was in attendance or a party was going on the day of the loss. A shopkeeper, showing a customer cameras, stepped away from the counter to answer the phone. When he or she returned, the customer and an expensive camera were missing. Many times the opportunity for theft is not as apparent as in the foregoing instances. For example, a woman leaves her earrings on the stairway to the second floor. The stairway is at the front entrance. It is summer and the front door is left open while she works in the backyard. Later she finds the earrings are missing. The only evidence of an opportunity is that neighbors tell her someone was going from door to door, while she was in the yard, delivering advertising circulars. She found one of these inside her screen door. Circumstantially the opportunity for theft was present.

FRAUDULENT CLAIMS

It is as difficult to prove that a theft or burglary claim is fraudulent as it is to prove arson.[4] There is generally little if any difference in the circumstances of a legitimate theft and those which may be alleged in a claim for a theft which never took place.

The motivations behind fraudulent theft or burglary claims are, in a way, similar to those behind incendiary fires set to collect insurance: greed and financial pressure. In most situations, circumstances will arouse the claim representative's suspicion—for example, there may be untrue or inconsistent statements made by the claimant; an unsatisfactory account of the claimant's whereabouts at the time of the crime, or of the claimant's history, background, or need for ready cash; and possibly an incredible story of how the loss occurred. Most policies provide substantial defenses against fraud. Forms subject to the provisions and conditions of inland marine and multi-peril policies and most of the standard fire policies

[4]See Chap. 10, "Arson Investigation and Detection."

contain specific requirements in case of loss, including submission to examination under oath.

The employment of professional investigators working in conjunction with the authorities and on advice of counsel has proved valuable in serious cases.

Because of the very nature of crime coverages the claim representative must constantly guard against being unduly suspicious. The experienced claim representative learns to recognize the delicate distinction between circumstances which *could* arouse suspicion and those which *definitely do*.

STATEMENTS

The claim representative should obtain written statements from each person whose testimony would be helpful in the following general areas:[5]

1. Details of the occurrence itself; type of crime.
2. Physical condition of the premises (or vehicle) prior to and after occurrence.
3. The whereabouts and movements of all persons who witnessed or have knowledge of the occurrence—prior to, during, and immediately after it. (In losses under residential policies, these persons usually would be the insured, members of the insured's household, and guests. Under business policies these persons may be the insured, the insured's employees, customers, etc.)
4. Description; quantity and ownership of property taken.
5. Value of property taken.
6. Suspects.

The claim representative should have the particular policy involved well in mind before taking any statement. He or she should also know what crimes are covered, the policy definitions, declarations, and all conditions and provisions. In this way it will be known exactly what information to look for in taking the statements.[6]

⁵See Appendix S for form.
⁶See Chap. 7.

SKETCHES AND PHOTOGRAPHS

Simple sketches of the premises showing the locations of doors or windows through which burglars or thieves entered the premises can be very helpful. Such diagrams or line drawings may designate the location of safes, fixtures, showcases, show windows, or dressers and closets from which property was taken.

Photographs showing evidence of forcible entry into a building, safe, depository, or vehicle should be taken on all but trifling claims. Photographs frequently show evidence also of the *lack* of forcible entry when such is required. Where marks of alleged forcible entry appear dubious, old, or doubtful, the claim representative must arrange to have the area photographed immediately to preserve the evidence.

PREVIOUS LOSSES

The investigation should include a statement from the insured listing all previous losses by theft, burglary, robbery, etc. Such a list should show the insurer, the date and kind of loss, and the amount paid. This is important notwithstanding anything in the declarations or Proof of Loss. This kind of insurance carries with it substantial physical and moral exposure. Frequent losses, even though minor, should be called to the attention of the underwriters. Some individuals are prone to be careless in taking care of valuables; other expose their valuables unnecessarily in public. Some business firms because of their physical layout or the nature of their merchandise have a high loss frequency. Some insureds have records of losses of unsatisfactory origin.

SEARCH FOR MISSING ITEMS

It is not uncommon for people to be firmly convinced that personal articles of value have been stolen from their home when, as a matter of fact, they have simply been misplaced. At other times the insured may have no recollection of where the item was placed or seen. Under all risks of loss policies the lost property is covered.

Recognizing that many people are absent-minded, the claim representative should carefully question the insured when the likelihood of a theft seems to be remote. He or she should have the insured mentally retrace his or her steps, going back if possible to the last occasion when the item was used, worn, or seen. Many times after payment of loss the article has been found in a shoe or slipper in a closet, in a place of hiding which was temporarily forgotten, in the pocket of a coat placed in storage or sent to a cleaners, or in other places.

Recoveries from plumbing traps and fixtures are occasionally made when questioning reveals that a ring was last seen just before or at the time of washing the hands, dishes, or clothes in the home.

It is not unusual for insureds to find articles of jewelry, thought to be missing, under beds, sofa cushions, or car seats.

RECOVERIES

Stolen property may be recovered before or after payment by the insurer. If found by the insured, returned by someone who found the property, or recovered by the police from a pawnshop, fence, or the thief, it may be accepted in good condition before any payment is made and that part of the claim may be withdrawn. If it is returned in a damaged condition, the loss to the insured will generally be limited to the cost of restoring it to its original condition—provided its disappearance was the result of theft, burglary, robbery, larceny, pilferage, or some other covered peril, rather than the result of its being lost or mislaid.

After payment has been made by the insurer, recovery of property by the police, by finders, or by the insured raises a problem. Generally the insured cannot be forced to accept the recovered property and return the amount paid by the insurer. If the insured refuses to accept the property, the insurer must dispose of it at the best available price and treat the proceeds as salvage.

Usually, when stolen property is recovered along with a suspect, it must be held as evidence to be presented at the hearing or trial.

In most situations the insured will have to be paid long before the trial comes up. In that event, the insurer takes over and disposes of the property as salvage *after* the trial is over. The net proceeds, in such cases, can be very disappointing.

REWARDS

As a general rule, an insured has the right to pay or offer to pay for the return of personal property which has been lost or stolen and, in the latter case, without compounding a felony. The claim representative should always check with the insurer to find out what the practice or policy is with respect to advertising and offering a reward for the return of lost or stolen property. Many companies consider a reward of 10 percent of the insured value or cash value to be reasonable.

A question that often arises is whether a reward should be offered or paid to police officers who recover or are instrumental in recovering stolen property. Custom differs from one area to another, and much depends on the circumstances. Occasionally where exceptional police work results in partial or full recovery, a donation to an association identified with the police is acceptable.

DAMAGE TO REAL PROPERTY

Damage to the building done during a burglary or attempt thereat is covered under most policies provided the insured owns the building or is liable for such damage. Policies covering mercantile premises against burglary generally cover damage done to personal property as well as real property during a burglary or attempt thereat.

DETERMINATION OF LOSS

The measure of loss under crime coverages is determined as under all policies covering personal property.[7] In most cases the articles or items are gone, and loss under residential policies is usually the replacement cost less depreciation. This measure of loss is applicable whether the property is unscheduled or

[7]See Chaps. 5, 14, 16, and 17.

scheduled, the exception being where the policy schedules articles under such terms as "insured for and valued at" or similar wording. Under policies covering mercantile and other business firms, the measure of loss is the actual cash value. This is the replacement cost new—less depreciation, however caused.

Under residential forms a complete description of the articles claimed should be obtained. In checking claims for such property as cameras, watches, binoculars, guns, pistols, radios, television sets, etc., the identification should include the name of the manufacturer, model, serial number when available, any attachments such as extra lenses for cameras, telescopes for guns, and all physical characteristics that will place the items within their proper price range. The insured should be asked to sketch expensive rings, bracelets, pins, and brooches, and to describe location, kind, and size of any precious stones as well as the type of settings.

In all cases, the date and place of purchase should be requested or, if the item was a gift, the name of the donor. Where original bills or other evidences of purchase are available, copies or transcripts should be made.

BOOKS AND RECORDS

Most commercial policies require the insured to keep books and records of all the property covered in such manner that the insurer can accurately determine therefrom the amount of loss. Such records should be in writing and verifiable, and should be those customarily kept in the insured's line of business. Supplying of details from the memory of an interested party does not meet the books and records requirement.

Thefts or burglaries involving merchandise may necessitate the taking of a physical inventory by the insured or jointly with the insurer following the occurrence of the loss and may also necessitate developing a book inventory. On serious losses an accountant should be engaged to check the insured's claim or determine the loss from the books. Losses disclosed by the insured when taking a routine inventory and losses by normal shrinkage and shoplifting are not covered.

Checking with sources from which insureds allege to have purchased property, while not always practical, should be considered if the claim is questionable.

LOSS OF STOCK AND BONDS

Broad form personal theft policies, Homeowners policies, and similar coverages for individuals have a limitation on securities. Generally, the insured can obtain replacements but must furnish a bond. The loss to the insurer is the premium for the bond up to the limit of liability under the policy.

REPLACEMENTS

The claim representative should consider replacement of jewelry, watches, cameras, etc., through local reliable firms who customarily make replacements for insurers. The insured is frequently satisfied to have the claim adjusted in this manner, and, generally, acceptance of the replacement will more than offset depreciation which would normally be taken. Replacement should always be done with the insurer's consent and according to the insurer's instructions. If the insured does not wish to have the articles replaced, liability is generally limited to the actual cost of replacement.

OTHER INSURANCE

Possibilities of the existence of other insurance which would cover all or part of the loss should be explored.[8] Policies covering vandalism and malicious mischief may be called upon to contribute to the loss to a building caused by burglars breaking and entering.[9]

QUESTIONS AND PROBLEMS

1. a. Most insurance policies that insure against the crime of *burglary* define burglary in the same general terms. With that thought in mind, give a definition of burglary.

   b. The Mercantile Open Stock Burglary

[8]See Chap. 7.
[9]See p. 116.

Policy requires two specific conditions in order for there to be coverage for burglary. What are they?

2. Study each of the following situations and state whether a burglary has been committed under a Mercantile Open Stock Burglary Policy. Give a brief reason for your answer.

a. Investigation of a claim for burglary discloses that the intruder forced open the front door of a public office building one night leaving "jimmy" marks. That person then went through the building apparently trying the doors in the various offices stealing from each one that was not locked. The insured's office was one of those not locked.

b. A thief concealed himself in the rest room of the insured's store. After every one left and locked up, the thief stole money from the petty cash drawer and made exit by breaking a window in the side door to the premises.

c. The circumstances are identical, but the coverage now is under an SMP (MLB-158) Storekeepers' Burglary and Robbery Endorsement.

d. Under a Mercantile Open Stock Burglary Policy, claim is made for a burglary that took place on a Sunday while the insured's employees were taking annual inventory. The thief forced a window in the washroom by breaking the lock. Exit was apparently made the same way. A calculator and a typewriter were stolen.

3. a. Give a definition of theft.
   b. Give a definition of larceny.
   c. What is meant by pilferage?
   d. Define robbery in general terms.

4. A number of commercial policies exclude, under the peril of theft, mere disappearance. Other policies exclude loss by mysterious disappearance of property or shortage of property disclosed in taking inventory.

a. Define "mysterious disappearance."

b. Under most Homeowners policies the peril of theft includes loss of property from a known place under circumstances when a probability of theft exists. A woman shopper returns home to find her wallet is missing. She recalls having it at a department store counter when purchasing perfume but is unable to remember whether she put it back in her purse. She came directly home after buying the perfume. She tells the claim representative it is not unusual for her to put her wallet on a store counter when getting her charge card out and it is possible she left it there. The car is searched and the store contacted. An ad is placed in the local paper but there is no answer to it. The wallet contained a driver's license, identification, and several charge cards, also a large sum of money. Is this a lost item or a theft?

5. a. Under a Homeowners Broad Form, the insured takes the family for a month's vacation in their travel trailer. During their absence the house is rented, furnished, to a neighbor's son and family. When the insured returns, it is found that a $1,000 coin collection is missing, also a small color television set. The neighbor's son and family are also missing. Does the policy cover this obvious theft?

b. While vacationing, this same insured and family were enjoying a swim in a trailer park pool. Their trailer was closed and locked. The door was obviously jimmied open and a quantity of clothing stolen. Is this loss covered under the HO-2 Broad Form? What primary conditions are necessary for coverage?

6. Under HO-1 (Ed. 9–70) a claim is made for theft from the insured's automobile while he and his spouse were having dinner at the Hot-Shot Country Club. The insured stated that it was a rule of the club that members must surrender their keys to the parking attendant. The claim representative, talking to the club manager, learned there was no such rule. Many members parked their own cars. The attendant said the insured's car was not locked although the windows were closed.

a. Discuss coverage for the loss.

b. The HO-2 (Ed. 12–75) provides, "Property is not unattended when the insured has entrusted the keys of the vehicle to a custodian." Would your answer be different than it was for situation a above?

7. With respect to the peril of theft, many

policies exclude "loss caused by theft that occurs away from the residence premises: of unattended property in or on any motor vehicle or trailer—unless there is forcible entry into the vehicle while all its doors, windows and other openings are closed and locked and there are visible marks of forcible entry," or similar wording.

Insured parks her car in a small parking lot. The attendant says, "Take the keys, don't lock the car. We will watch your car." When the insured returns, a suitcase with contents valued at $500 has been stolen from the car. Discuss coverage.

8. Insured parks his car on a side street downtown to do some shopping. He is fully aware of policy provisions, and the windows are closed and the doors locked. A clever thief slips a coat hanger over the window and is able to lift the locking button on the door. Valuables are stolen from inside the car. Discuss coverage.

9. You have been assigned to investigate a claim of burglary in a supermarket. During your discussion with the manager he expresses the opinion that it is an inside job and names an employee whom he suspects. You can call in the local law enforcement agency or question the suspect yourself. Give two reasons why it would be better to bring in the law enforcement agency.

10. Outline some of the advantages of sketches and photographs in more serious burglaries.

11. Claim representative Quick, handling a theft loss under a HO-2, is able to locate the thief and the stolen property, a color television. It is returned to the insured before any payment is made by the insurer. The television picture tube has been broken by the thief.

a. On what basis should Quick seek to adjust the loss with the insured?

b. If the loss was adjusted by Quick, paid by the insurer, and the television was later recovered, what procedure would be followed?

c. The police recover the television and hold it as evidence. The trial of the thief will not come up for six months. What is the usual procedure in adjusting a loss under these conditions?

12. If the insured offers to pay the thief for the return of stolen property, would that action generally be regarded as compounding a felony? Explain your answer.

14

Buildings and Structures

The procedure followed in adjusting building losses is also followed when bridges, bulkheads, docks, fences, piers, platforms, ramps, sheds, stacks, tanks, tipples, trestles, wharves, and other structures, ordinarily real as distinguished from personal property, are involved. Present-day building forms make the insurance cover not only the walls, floors, roof, and other structural parts of the building but also any devices, machinery, or fixtures built into it, as well as, occasionally, specified furnishings and supplies used in its service.

DESCRIPTION AND CLASSIFICATION

Ordinarily a building is described by the number of its stories, the construction of its walls, and the covering of its roof. It is classified according to the purpose for which it is occupied. Wall construction is ordinarily frame, stucco, metal-clad, cement or cinder block, tile, stone, reinforced concrete, or brick. Occasionally adobe and coquina walls are encountered. Roof coverings are generally wood shingles, composition shingles or roofing, tar paper, tar and gravel, metal, tile, or slate. Superior buildings which are constructed of nonflammable materials are often described as *fire-resistive* or, inaccurately, as *fireproof*. Heavily built masonry buildings with thick walls, large-size timber floor supports, and other features that retard the spread of fire are described as *slow-burning*. *Mill construction* is a term used to describe slow-burning buildings that conform to certain prescribed standards. *Brick and joist* and *ordinary brick* are terms used to describe the kinds of brick buildings most often encountered. The most common occupancies are condominium, apartment, bank, barn, church, club, dwelling, manufacturing, garage, hospital, mercantile, office, powerhouse, theater, warehouse, hotel, and motel.

BUILDINGS AND STRUCTURES AS SUBJECTS OF INSURANCE

Buildings are subjects of insurance from the time the first materials to be used in their construction are delivered to the premises until the time the buildings are destroyed, abandoned, or demolished.

The term *building*, as used in reference to the subject matter of insurance, is to be given its ordinary meaning. Any structure with walls and a roof is a building within such ordinary meaning.[1]

A structure is something "built or erected or constructed and the use of which requires more or less permanent location on the ground or attachment to something having a permanent location on the ground."[2] All buildings are structures but not all structures are buildings. A structure may be a fence, a patio slab, a driveway, a retaining wall, a brick and cement outdoor barbecue, or a radio antenna mast on a concrete footing.

Policies that cover *Building*(s) may give a very broad description as *all real property*, followed by a list or description of various kinds of property, real and personal, which is

---

[1]*Ayers v. Palatine Ins. Co.*, 234 N.Y. 334, 137 N.E. 608.
[2]*Holsey Appliance Co. v. Burrow*, 281 P.2d 426 (Okla).

either included or excluded. Other policies give long and detailed descriptions of the coverage, exclusions, and limitations.

Many forms tie the particular occupancy into the description, such as under Homeowners, Businessowners, church, school, and theater policies. Permission is expressed or implied in most forms to make alterations, additions, and repairs and to erect new buildings and structures. The SMP General Property Form (MLB–100, Ed. 2-71) permits the insured to "apply up to 10%, but not exceeding $25,000, of the limit of liability specified for coverage —A—Building(s)" to cover new additions, new buildings, and new structures when constructed on the described premises and intended for similar occupancy. Coverage is limited to a specified period of time. Buildings acquired at any other location within the territorial limits of the policy are similarly covered.

Most policies exclude the cost of excavations and foundations which are below the undersurface of the lowest basement floor or, where there is no basement, which are below the surface of the ground, and also exclude underground flues, pipes, wiring, and drains. Most policies enumerate specific property excluded and provide certain extensions of coverage.

The Homeowners policies permit the insured to exclude from value, in determining whether the amount of insurance equals or exceeds 80 percent of its replacement cost, such items as excavations; underground flues and pipes; wiring and drains; brick, stone, and concrete foundations; piers; and other supports which are below the surface of the ground. *However, loss to any of these items is covered.*

Buildings in the course of construction may be covered under a builder's risk policy either on a specified-peril or an all-risk basis. The policy may be a reporting form or a completed value form. The policy covers temporary structures, materials, equipment, and supplies of all kinds incident to the construction of the building or structure, and also, when not otherwise covered by insurance, builder's machinery, tools and equipment owned by the insured, and similar property of others for which insured is liable.

The interest of the contractor or the owner or both may be covered.

The foregoing comments are made merely to emphasize the importance of reading the description of the subject of insurance in the particular form applicable, to determine what part of the real property is covered, what part of the real property is excluded, what personal property is included under building coverage, where the personal property is covered, and what personal property is excluded.

EFFECT OF PERILS COMMONLY COVERED

Buildings are destroyed or damaged by various perils, commonly insured against as fire, lightning, windstorm, hail, explosion, aircraft, vehicles, smoke, sprinkler leakage, water, flood, tidal wave, wave wash, and earthquake. These perils are discussed in connection with *cause of loss* in Chapter 8.

Fire

Fire may consume a building or create enough heat in consuming its combustible material to destroy the value of its noncombustible material. Fire is seldom checked if it gains real headway in an unprotected frame building, and the building is ordinarily destroyed.

The extent of damage to building materials from the heat that is generated by the combustible parts of the building, but more significantly by the burning of the contents, depends on the temperatures reached and on the length of time the materials are subjected to these temperatures.

Heat causes glass to crack at relatively low temperatures; at about 1600°F glass softens. Plaster tolerates fairly high temperatures before flaking and chalking on the surface, with a change in its chemical composition. Paint softens and blisters in the presence of heat. Most woods shrink slightly as they lose moisture, and boards or timbers of wider dimension frequently check. Wood ignites at approximately 400°F after 20 minutes exposure.

While it is impractical to record either the temperatures that are developed or their duration in fires of accidental origin, it is sometimes possible to estimate the degree of heat by observing the physical condition of glass, metals, and ceramics in the area after the fire. Table 14-1 lists some of the melting or fusing temperatures of materials in buildings.

Table 14-1   Approximate Fusing Temperatures

Material	Degrees F	Degrees C
Tin	449	232
Lead	621	327
Zinc	786	419
Aluminum	1217	658
Copper	1981	1083
Iron (cast)	2250	1232
Sand	2588	1420
Porcelain	2588	1420
Steel (structural)	2606	1430
Chromium	2750	1510

The wooden parts of ordinary brick buildings may be seriously injured by the burning of combustible contents. Under sufficient heat such noncombustible materials as brick, stone, or concrete will crack. Metal parts will soften and, in severe fires, melt. The softening of metal beams or columns is often followed by displacement of parts of the structure that rest on them. Shoring up a floor that has settled and cutting out and replacing bent or twisted metal girders or beams are expensive operations. Heat from the burning of an adjacent building will crack glass in windows or doors.

Water used to extinguish fire injures inside woodwork and, unless drained off or wiped up promptly, may cause wood floors or trim to crack or buckle. Water loosens plaster and wallpaper, discolors paint or decorations, and causes other damage. If a large quantity of water is used to extinguish fire in a building filled with closely packed contents such as sisal, rolls of paper, or bulk cottonseed, which will absorb the water and swell, the swelling of the contents may force outward or even break open the walls of the building. Debris or heavy articles from upper floors may be precipitated by the burning of

supporting columns, girders, or joists and cause serious wreckage in the lower parts of the structure. Falling walls sometimes crush or damage other structures.

If the roof has been opened or the windows broken, a building may suffer further damage after a fire has been extinguished, owing to the freezing and bursting of water pipes, tanks, or plumbing. Rain or snow entering through holes in the roof or through broken windows may do serious injury to plaster, inside woodwork, and finish.

Smoke

Heavy smoke develops when burning materials are shut off from adequate oxygen, preventing complete combustion. Two kinds of smoke can occur during a fire. One is *hot smoke*, the other *cool or cold smoke*.

Hot smoke is found relatively close to the fire and carries the heat of the fire with it. Hot smoke causes the greater damage because it penetrates porous surfaces and because, in contact with cool surfaces, it condenses, leaving heavy stains of tars and resins. Building decorations are readily damaged by such stains and require washing or redecorating or both. Wallpapers touched by hot smoke generally need replacing. Window glass becomes coated and must be washed. Ceramic tile normally has hairline cracks that are almost invisible, and under certain conditions, the hot smoke penetrates through the cracks in the glazed surface and remains in the porous backing. It is impossible to remove and the tile must be replaced, or an allowance should be made for the damage. Enameled and porcelain plumbing fixtures will suffer less than ceramic tile. Test cleaning is the best way to determine whether there has been any permanent injury to tile or porcelain.

Stonework, brick, and cement surfaces are difficult to clean after exposure to hot smoke. Experts should be called in to test-clean such surfaces before an estimate of damage is made. If cleaning or sandblasting is impossible, cement washing, coating, or painting may be satisfactory to all interests.

Smoke that is cold has traveled some distance away from the fire and has cooled and condensed in the air before it reaches the surfaces on which it deposits. It is often in the form of *soot*. Vacuum cleaning, brushing, or washing can many times remove it. Cold smoke does not leave the characteristic pungent smoke odor that results from hot smoke.

Damage During Fire Fighting

A certain amount of damage is caused by firemen in gaining entrance to a building or to the rooms in it. Doors, door jambs, and casings are sometimes broken or chopped, locks are forced, and glass in sash doors is broken. A common practice in good fire fighting is to ventilate the premises. For that reason, firemen break windows or skylights and occasionally chop through a roof to let out smoke and heat. Miscellaneous chopping and cutting may be done by firemen in tracing the course of a fire under floors or in partitions and walls.

In fire-resistive multiple-story buildings, toilet fixtures are sometimes broken or removed so that the accumulation of water on the floor can be squeegeed to the outlet. In buildings that have wood floors, holes may be bored or chopped to drain off water to lower floors.

Lightning

Damage to buildings and structures by lightning occurs in all parts of the continent, but more frequently in the southeastern section of the United States, where the incidence of thunderstorms is higher. Lightning is a high-voltage electrical discharge between the clouds and the earth. The voltage may run into millions, and the amperes into tens of thousands.

Once the discharge takes place, the effect on the subject in its path on earth may be the result of a direct hit by a *lightning bolt*, or the result of an *atmospheric surge* or electricity induced in the area, usually by a bolt of lightning which has struck nearby. The latter is sometimes called a *ground surge*.

Damage caused by a direct hit can be trifling (such as knocking a few bricks from the top of a chimney) or devastating. The knowledge that the objective of lightning is

the ground will aid, perhaps, in understanding the unpredictable and sometimes perplexing path that lightning follows from the point of contact to the place of exit in a building. Where resistance to its path is encountered, instantaneous heat is created, and if the bolt of lightning is a powerful one, the result is explosive. Inspection of a building struck by lightning may reveal a few shattered clapboards, or a corner of a roof or a few bricks knocked off, giving the impression of minor, localized damage. A more thorough survey, however, often discloses a greater injury to the interior than anticipated. Electric receptacles may be scorched or blown out of the wall, cracks may appear in some rooms but not in others, and a joist or rafter may be split. When lightning strikes a structure, it frequently fans out rather than pursuing a direct course, making its path more difficult to trace.

Lightning that strikes behind a concrete-block retaining wall can lay it flat on the ground. Chimneys struck by lightning require careful inspection from top to bottom not only to include all damage caused by lightning, but also to detect and distinguish old cracks and damage caused by age and settlement.

Losses to pole transformers, appliances, motors, and other equipment can be the result of atmospheric or ground surges, and not necessarily direct hits. In most instances examination will show either (1) fusing of a part or parts or (2) explosive effects due to violent interior pressure. Because electrical appliances and apparatus are subject to inherent defects and wear, which bring about shorts and breakdowns, the inspection of damage attributed to atmospheric surges of lightning calls for a high degree of care. Expert advice should be sought when there is serious doubt that lightning is involved.[3]

Windstorm

The degree of damage that a building or structure will suffer from windstorm depends

[3]Paul I. Thomas, *How to Estimate Building Losses and Construction Costs*, Prentice-Hall, Inc., Englewood Cliffs, N.J., 1976, pp. 27–28.

not only on the force or velocity of the wind but also on the quality of materials and workmanship. Inexpensive, lightweight composition shingles will not stand up as well as heavyweight shingles of the same material; neither will stand up if improperly applied. Flimsy, lightweight aluminum storm doors with single-thickness glass will twist and break in relatively moderate winds that do no damage to heavier stock. Buildings with light frame walls, improperly anchored walls, or lightly framed roofs sustain much greater damage in high winds which accompany hurricanes or those on the fringe of a tornado.

A tornado (from the Latin *tornare*, meaning to turn) is one of nature's most violent and destructive windstorms. It cuts a narrow swath as a rule, but levels buildings and structures directly in its path. The cyclonic action produces a vacuumlike effect, causing buildings to explode or collapse as the tornado passes close to them. Wind velocities reach 450 miles per hour.

A hurricane, like a tornado, is cyclonic, but its path is much wider, ranging from 50 to 100 miles or more. The eye or center varies from a few miles wide to 40 or 50 miles. The suction causes extensive damage near the center, and wind velocities range from 100 to 150 miles per hour. It has been fairly well established that very often hurricanes are accompanied by small tornados.

Where wind velocities reach over 100 to 120 miles per hour for any length of time, the roof structures on many buildings start to lift, show windows are sucked out or blown in, and total destruction—even disappearance of small, light buildings—may take place. Wind velocities between 70 and 100 miles per hour usually tear off some or all of asphalt-type shingles, and can cause extensive damage to wood, asbestos, aluminum, slate, and roll roofing. Fences are overturned, depending on their construction and the condition of the wooden posts in the ground. Trees or their heavier limbs, when blown on top of or against buildings, cause varying degrees of damage. Carports or other lightly built structures may be blown over or may collapse. Flying shingles, portions of

roofs, and other debris cause damage to adjacent and nearby buildings. Because windstorms are often preceded, accompanied, or followed by rain, damage caused by rain entering openings made in the roof or walls (including broken windows) by the action of the wind should be included in an estimate of damage. The extent of such damage depends on the amount of water that gets into the premises, and the portions of the building with which it comes into contact. In most cases the damage by water is confined to ceilings, wallboard or plaster, insulation in attics, and decorations in the rooms affected. Occasionally, water on finished floors causes them to "cup," but in most cases they can be resanded and refinished. Wooden doors and windows may absorb water through bare or poorly painted surfaces, causing them to swell so that they will not open or close properly. Veneers may come loose on the lower part of the doors. An important part of a claim representative's job is to separate the damage by windstorm from the damage that may be excluded, such as when the buildings involved also have been flooded by tide water or overflowing rivers, or where water has been driven by wind under flashings and around windows. A satisfactory method is to prepare a two-column estimate.[4] The repairs to be made as a result of windstorm should appear in one column, while repairs by reason of flooding, inundation, overflow, and seepage should appear in the other column. In this way the items are subject to analysis and discussion.[5]

Hail

Damage to buildings by hail depends to a large extent on the size of the hailstones. They can vary from pea size to as large as baseballs. Hail may break windows and puncture or dent roof surfaces. Asphalt materials used on roofs can suffer serious damage in a hailstorm which does little or no damage to tile, wood shingle, and heavy-gauge iron roofing. Large hailstones can

[4]See Chap. 24, "Floods, Mudslides, and FAIR Plans."
[5]Thomas, op. cit., pp. 124–127.

shatter tile roofing and have been known to penetrate roof boards.

Hailstorms of serious proportions dent wood and aluminum siding, aluminum awnings, and canopies. Badly dented aluminum siding or awnings are almost impossible to repair, whereas dented wood siding can frequently be repaired by filling in the dents and repainting.

A hailstorm, even though the stones are not large, can scour paint from the exterior surface of the building on sides exposed to the hail. It can also scour the protective mineral coating from asphalt shingles without denting or puncturing the material.

Broken windows and perforations in the roofing open the way for ensuing damage by rain.

Explosion

In buildings of dwelling occupancy, the most common explosions are in furnace boxes of heating plants, caused by delayed ignition of accumulated fuel gases. The majority of these are low-pressure explosions, and the damage is usually confined to the oil burner, the firebox brick lining, the insulated covering, and the smokestack connecting the boiler to the chimney. Smoke, soot, and fumes may follow such an explosion and be carried to other portions of the premises through open doors and hallways; when drawn into heating ducts they may reach into every part of the building through heat registers. The presence of oil in the smoke or fumes can cause substantial loss to decorations. If fire follows an oil burner explosion, more serious damage by burning of controls and by sooting can be anticipated. Violent explosions have occurred in the fireboxes of furnaces, but they are likely to be more prevalent in large industrial furnaces and also in furnaces that burn gas rather than oil or coal.

Explosions in manufacturing and other industrial plants have many different causes, the most common being ignition of the vapors of flammable liquids. There is also the hazard of dust explosions in plants that process starch, sugar, grains, cork, spices, and numerous other products. Chemical explosions occur in plants experimenting with new products and occasionally in munition plants, fireworks manufacturers, petroleum processors, fertilizer processors, and storage plants. Such explosions can demolish buildings completely or damage them partially, depending on the force and the distance of the explosion from the risk. Masonry or plaster walls often crack. Buildings adjacent or nearby can also be damaged severely, or windows and plate glass may crack or shatter from ground shock or concussion. The damage caused by blasting for roads, foundations, tunnels, and so forth follows a pattern similar to that mentioned above.

Examination of damage done by explosive forces requires great care. The estimating should be confined to explosion damage only, and the wear and tear or other conditions that may be chargeable to maintenance must not be included. An excellent reference on this subject is *Blasting Claims—A Guide for Adjusters*, prepared by the American Insurance Association.[6]

A typical low-pressure explosion, not uncommon during fires, occurs when a heavy concentration of gases of incomplete combustion is ignited. These gases become "pocketed" in blind or concealed spaces, or at one end of a floor with the fire burning in the other end. If the premises are not vented to allow such gases to escape, they can be ignited by heat or flames as the fire approaches the area. Windows, particularly display windows in storefronts, are frequently blown outward by such explosions. Because these explosions are low-pressured, they seldom cause serious structural damage.

Aircraft

Falling aircraft, or aircraft off course, may destroy a small structure or damage the roof or walls of a large one. Objects falling from aircraft or oil or gas spilled from them produce damage in lesser degree.

Vehicles

Damage done by vehicles includes the total destruction of small structures, the smashing of doors and windows, and damage to exterior walls and door frames.

[6]See p. 111.

Sprinkler Leakage and Water

Water from automatic sprinkler systems and fire hoses, or from rain or melted snow entering through windows, doors, or openings in roofs and walls after a fire, hail, or windstorm, causes varying degrees of damage to finished millwork, flooring, plaster walls and ceilings, Sheetrock, Celotex, wallboards, and interior paint and wallpaper.

Electric cable and conduit in walls or floors may suffer damage from wetting. Electric motors that have been wet, even those submerged for a short time, can under most conditions be baked out if handled promptly.

Well-seasoned woods if unfinished absorb water up to about 25 percent by weight, during which time swelling occurs. Plaster softens in the presence of water, and wallboards frequently expand and warp, some of them permanently. The glue on wallpaper softens and the wallpaper may peel off. Water behind paint, particularly enamels and semiglazed surface paints, forms small blisters full of water which ruin the decorations.

The weight of water (64.5 pounds per cubic foot) which has been absorbed by certain types of contents such as paper or fabrics may cause the collapse of wood beams, girders, and sometimes entire floor structures.

In the winter if water freezes during or shortly after a fire it causes further damage by expanding in plaster, water pipes, toilet bowls, traps, and hot-water or steam heating systems.

Flood, Tidal Wave, Wave Wash

Flood, tidal wave, and wave wash do much damage.[7] In many cases the contents of sewers back up and discharge through drains, toilet fixtures, and sinks into basements. In some floods the water level is high enough to fill the first story of a building. In great floods, many light buildings are floated off their foundations, and some heavy buildings are undermined and caused to collapse. Receding flood waters leave inundated buildings filled with mud and filth.

Tidal wave and wave wash generally fill basements and lower stories with water,

often break in windows and doors, sometimes wrench off porches, and if severe, displace buildings from their foundations or even beat them to pieces and wash them away.

Earthquake

Earthquakes crack, strain, tilt, break apart, and at times demolish buildings. They open structures to the weather and by breaking water pipes cause water damage. They also start fires by causing parts of a building to fall and lodge against fireplaces, stoves, or furnaces, or by breaking or cracking chimneys and allowing flames or sparks to reach combustible materials.

Sonic Boom

For a full treatment of sonic boom and its effect on certain structural items, see Chapter 8.

INSURABLE VALUES

Under property insurance policies, buildings are covered to the extent of their *actual cash value* and by extension of coverage in the form, or by endorsement, they may be covered for their new *replacement cost*. Therefore, the insurable value in the first instance is the actual cash value; in the other, it is the replacement cost. Insurable value contemplates only the value of the property covered,[8] i.e., the value of excluded property has been deducted or omitted from consideration.

The amount of insurance carried may be 100 percent of the insurable value, it may be a percentage of the insurable value to comply with a coinsurance or other contribution clause, or it may be substantially less than the insurable value, indicating underinsurance.

Replacement-Cost Value

The replacement cost of a building is the cost of constructing another building of the same design, layout and size with materials

[7]See Chap. 24.

[8]Homeowners forms cover certain underground property, foundations, etc., below the lowest basement floor, but underground property can be disregarded in computing replacement cost.

of like kind and quality. The most reliable method of determining replacement cost is the detailed estimate which itemizes all material and labor costs involved in replacing the building; it includes the contractor's or builder's overhead and profit and takes into consideration all the operations necessary to complete the structure. (See Estimating, this chapter.)

Square-Foot and Cubic-Foot Methods of Estimating. For a quick approximation of the cost of replacing a building, there are two systems in common use: *cost per square foot* and *cost per cubic foot.* Both of these systems are based on the principle that similar buildings of the same size, design, and construction will cost the same per cubic foot of content or per square foot of ground or floor area. Variations in the cost per square foot or cubic foot develop as the size of the building increases or decreases from the "norm" used, and as architectural design, layout, and materials change. In either system the cost per square foot or cubic foot increases as the area or volume decreases. In applying a cost-per-square-foot method, the difference in cost of the building due to variations in ceiling heights is not taken into consideration. In neither system is consideration given in the unit cost to the relationship of the perimeter to the area, which changes as the shape changes. Such changes affect the cost of the exterior wall construction and the cost of the floor and roof construction. The more elaborate manuals supply corrective factors for these variations. The cost of units such as heating, plumbing, chimneys, fireplaces, staircases, cabinetry, ranges, and appliances is not a true function of the square foot area or cubic foot volume of the building, at least not to the same degree as the walls, ceilings, roof, and partitions. Neither system is as accurate as the detailed estimate, even when used by an experienced person, but the cubic-foot method is somewhat more reliable.

Both cost per cubic foot and cost per square foot are acceptable methods of approximating replacement cost as a basis for determining insurable value. The claim representative should not, in case of a total loss, rely on either method unless the obvious inadequacy of insurance in relation to value is great enough to allow for moderate error. In any case, it should not be used without approval of the insurer. An authorized adjustment based on cubic-foot or square-foot valuations should be supported by a statement giving a description of the building, measurements, computations, and the unit cost applied. Neither method should be used on partial losses.

Original-Cost Method. If reliable records are available which show the original cost of a building, they can usually be brought up to date by applying a cost index. The American Appraisal Company, Marshall and Swift Publications Company, and other recognized valuation experts publish cost indexes that can be used with confidence when properly applied. Care must be taken in studying the original cost figures to make certain that items not covered by the particular insurance policy are deleted. Such items as excavations, backfilling, grading, shrubs, and all or part of the foundations and underground piping or wiring are examples of original costs of a building that may not be covered.

Actual Cash Value

Standard or statutory fire insurance policies cover to the extent of the *actual value* or *actual cash value* of the property at the time of loss. These terms, which are interchangeable, have little practical meaning. They are not subject to a *precise definition*, even though they are intended as the very foundation for determining the amount of insurance required and the amount of money payable to indemnify the insured in case of damage or destruction of the property. To say that the term *actual cash value* means actual value expressed in terms of money[9] may provide a broad rule but does not provide a workable formula for determining cash value.

The courts, understandably, have not been consistent or in full agreement on what constitutes the cash value of a building. The

[9]*McAnarney v. The Newark Fire Insurance Co.,* 247 N.Y. 176, 159 N.E. 902 (see also p. 185).

cash value has variously been held to be replacement cost less physical depreciation, or market value; the difference between its cash value immediately before and immediately after the loss, where the building had been condemned prior thereto; its intrinsic value; and a reasonable value.

Insurers, brokers, and agents, in a sincere effort to find a rational formula for determining the proper amount of insurance to be carried on a building, generally use *replacement cost less depreciation*. Recognizing that *depreciation* means a decline in value, no one offers violent objection to this formula. The difficulty arises in distinguishing between physical depreciation (wear and tear) and economic depreciation (obsolescence), and particularly in finding some measure or yardstick for determining obsolescence.

Physical Depreciation. The causes of deterioration in building materials are decay, corrosion, metal fatigue, chemical change, and wear and tear. These causes are productive of results in inverse proportion to the resistance of the materials to deterioration and the effectiveness of protective measures used to retard its action. The resistance that a material ordinarily offers to a given deteriorating cause is primarily determined by the inherent quality of the material. This resistance can be made most effective if the pieces of material used are free from faults or inferiorities, are so placed in the building as to be protected from excessive exposure to the deteriorating influence, and are thereafter cared for. A consideration of specific materials and the causes of their deterioration will illustrate this point.

Wood is the most common material. It is a vegetable product subject to decay due to microorganisms that require darkness and moisture for their existence. The resistance that wood offers to decay will, therefore, be determined by conditions of moisture and sunlight. Moisture is absorbed more freely by porous than by close-grained wood. For this reason, boards or timbers exposed to dampness should be made of close-grained wood. They should be free from incipient decay or inferior streaks in which moisture will accumulate. Sills and floor joists in proximity to the ground are exposed to the moisture emanating from it and tend to decay. Usually they are always in darkness, a condition that makes decay more rapid. In the warmer sections of the country, many buildings are constructed without basements, the sills and first-floor joists being frequently only a few feet above the earth. In the South, pine is the wood most frequently used in building, and pine sills and joists are the rule. Since the heart of the pine tree is closer grained than the outer section, known as the sap, the best floor timbers in Southern buildings are made of heart pine. Timbers that are part sap are inferior, as decay starts quickly in the porous sap unless the timbers are kept dry. To ensure dryness in the space between the ground and the floor timbers, the foundation walls are pierced with openings through which air can circulate. Floor timbers properly selected and protected from prolonged dampness by this method of airing decay slowly. Many buildings in the South are constructed of wood timbers which have been chemically treated to resist termites and other insects.

Another form of deterioration in wood often occurs if boards are exposed to the direct rays of the sun before they have been properly seasoned. In such cases the boards will generally warp and in doing so crack.

The decay of woodwork under the action of moisture is to some degree paralleled by the damage to ironwork and steelwork when attacked by rust. Iron resists the attack if it is free from impurities, but structural steel rusts easily. As rust will start quickly when moisture is present, it is essential that ordinary ironwork or steelwork be protected by a grade of paint that will prevent rain or even the air from coming in contact with the metal. Moisture is always present in the air in varying degrees, according to weather conditions, and, because of this, even interior steelwork or ironwork will tend to rust if not protected or frequently wiped or polished.

The rusting of steelwork or ironwork is only one of the processes of metallic decomposition that must be combated by builders and caretakers of buildings. Metallic parts exposed to the action of corrosive agents, such as acids and alkalies, are gradually eaten away. These agents may be present in liquids that corrode plumbing or tanks, or they may be in gaseous form. The gas given off by burning bituminous coal is the most common of the corrosive gases. This gas, present in the smoke from chimneys and furnaces, is particularly injurious to iron and steel and to galvanized sheets or wires.

The three causes of deterioration so far considered produce their results by working a visible decomposition of the material on which they operate. Shock is another cause of deterioration in metal, but it operates without giving any visible evidence of its effect until a fracture occurs. Shock causes metal fatigue, often termed crystallization. Fatigued metal gives no evidence of its condition until it breaks under a stress that the metal would have resisted before crystallization occurred. Rails, trestle members, bridge parts, and other steelwork subject to repeated stress and shock tend to crystallize and finally fail.

Deterioration of building materials may also result from the wear and tear of the elements, or from the use made of the building. The elements are always exerting a deteriorating influence on exposed material. Sunlight, rain, and changes of temperature deteriorate the materials they reach, while wind works injury by shaking or swaying a building. The chemical action of the sun's rays, particularly in the southern sections of the country, gradually deteriorates paint, while the direct heat of the sun exerts an unfavorable influence on shingles and certain other kinds of roofing by drying out protecting gums or oils. Rain finds its way through cracks and furnishes the moisture necessary to start decay or is absorbed by porous stone or brickwork. If freezing weather follows, the stone or brickwork will suffer, as the freezing of the absorbed moisture will enlarge cracks in the masonry and, at times, cause pieces to break off and fall. Frequent repetition of this kind of injury may badly disfigure the materials. Properly made brick suffers very little from the action of rain and cold, but porous mortar or the softer and more porous stones will in time show serious damage. Rain also rusts metal cornices, gutters, and downspouts, unless they are made of copper or lead. In addition to the damage done by sun, rain, and cold, heavy winds will occasionally sway a poorly braced building until the plaster is cracked, while severe wind stress may permanently strain a building.

Deterioration due to wear and tear of the elements is often accompanied by deterioration due to the use to which a building is put. If heavy loads are constantly trucked over floors, they will become badly worn and require frequent repair or replacement. If the floors are not properly supported or if the building is not braced, vibration from the operation of machinery may dislodge plaster or even piping or other equipment attached to walls and ceilings. If water is frequently used in the building and is splashed on wooden floors or leaks through them, not only will the floors suffer, but plaster or paint on the walls or ceilings below will be injured.

Interior paint, wallpaper, and other decorations lose their freshness and deteriorate in time. The rate of deterioration will be accelerated by smoke or dust and, in unscreened houses, by fly specks.

The claim representative, seeking to become informed on the deterioration of building materials, should study some of the numerous tables that analyze the normal depreciation of a building by showing the expected life of each component part. The claim representative should also take occasion to note the condition of the buildings with which he or she deals and learn to look for the particular kind of depreciation that is ordinarily severe in a given type of structure. For instance, wood shingle roofs on buildings in hot climates suffer severe depreciation.

The claim representative should also learn to look for signs of the care and attention that will retard the progress of deterioration. Thus, exposed woodwork is preserved by regular painting, as are also the surfaces of ironwork and steelwork. Plaster and interior finishing will long remain sound in a building that is weathertight but will deteriorate badly if leaks in the roof go unrepaired.

There are some parts of a building, however, that no amount of care will prevent from deteriorating much more rapidly than the other parts. Plumbing and heating systems are probably the best examples. Ordinarily these corrode and fail and must be renewed before the rest of the building shows appreciable wear.

Book Depreciation. If a building owner maintains account books in which are entered charges for depreciation against separate buildings, the claim representative should become familiar with the owner's method of determining the charges before accepting them as correct. Such charges do not always represent the actual depreciation of the property. Particularly if the charges are based on an arbitrary writing down of value, they may be greater, or less, than the actual depreciation. The accounting method of writing off the value of property over a period of years, known as "amortization," is not to be confused with true depreciation by the claim representative.

Obsolescence. Obsolescence is a decline in value as a result of a process of falling into disuse. In buildings, obsolescence is brought about by changes in architectural design, layout of interiors, materials of construction or finish, and occupancy. Areas and neighborhoods change ethnically, and also because of construction of highways that cut through or bypass, because of changes in zoning laws from residential to business, and because manufacturing firms that employ a high percentage of the people go out of business or move away.

Manifestations of obsolescence in buildings are generally revealed where:

1. Commercial buildings are no longer suitable for their original purpose, such as when theaters shut down entirely or are occupied for garage, light manufacturing, or storage.
2. Buildings have been condemned as unsafe or for demolition.
3. Mansion-type residences have been converted to rooming houses, nursing homes, or multifamily residences, or are owned and occupied by low-income individuals.
4. Old factory buildings are occupied for storage, warehousing, etc.
5. Buildings show evidence of severe physical wear and tear, generally in excess of 30 percent of their replacement cost.

Partial losses in obsolete structures, particularly when policies contain average or coinsurance clauses, are difficult to adjust. Claim will generally be made for the cost of repairs, and value will be stated as the price for which the property could be sold, less the selling value of the land. As a result, a 25 percent physical damage to the building may result in a claim for 100 percent of the insurance. Compromises to some degree are generally in order. Formal appraisals are risky.

In cases where the building has suffered a total loss and obsolescence is a major factor in the cash value, the influence of *market value* is of significant importance in the adjustment. This is of special consequence where it is an established fact that the property has been advertised or offered for sale at a price substantially below replacement cost less physical depreciation. This approach is applicable also to the five classifications of obsolete structures mentioned above.

Attitude of the Courts. While it is true, as previously stated, that the courts have not been consistent or in agreement on what constitutes the cash value of a building, nevertheless we must examine current legal standards of recovery under insurance policies for available methods for determining the proper relation between insurance and value. The courts have uniformly held that an old building may not be valued at its replacement cost, since depreciation for physical wear and tear must be deducted. They are not as uniform in holding that economic depreciation (obsolescence) can be considered. While a number of courts support the view that replacement cost less physical depreciation is the measure of cash value, their rulings are controverted by an increasing number of decisions to the opposite effect. The outstanding case is *McAnarney v. The*

Newark Fire Insurance Company, and because of the prestige of the New York Court of Appeals, as well as the thorough nature of the opinion, the rule set down has been followed by many other states. The facts, briefly, were as follows.

In 1919, during national prohibition, seven large buildings, designed for the manufacture of malt, and the land on which they stood were bought for $8,000. The buildings had not been occupied for any useful purpose after March of that year. Insurance of $42,750 was taken out in January, 1920. Fire occurred in April, 1920, destroying the buildings. Proofs were filed for $60,000 and, in the lower court, the jury rendered a verdict specifying the "depreciated structural value" to be $55,000. This was in direct response to a written question submitted to the jury by the judge. The judge then directed judgment in favor of the plaintiff. The court said to the jury, "Your answer shall not be the market value—shall not be the sum that the buildings would sell for, but what it cost to build them—what it cost to build the structures, less depreciation proven in the case." Evidence was presented that a sign had been ordered erected on the roof by the plaintiff, before the fire, advertising the property for sale at $12,000. The insured also had made an affidavit to the local board of assessors that the property had no value as a brewery and the owners would sell it for $15,000, but that the highest offer they had had was $6,000.

The New York Court of Appeals, in reversing the findings of the lower court and granting a new trial, said in part:

We do not agree ... that, under the standard clause, the sole measure of damage was cost of reproduction less physical depreciation.... Where insured buildings have been destroyed the trier of fact may, and should, call to its aid, in order to effectuate complete indemnity, every fact and circumstance which would logically tend to the formation of a correct estimate of the loss. It may consider original cost of reproduction; the opinions upon value given by qualified witnesses; the declarations against interest which may have been made by the assured; the gainful uses to which the buildings might have been put; as well as any other fact reasonably tending to throw light upon the subject.

In the case at bar the trier of fact, in considering cost of reproduction, was required by the policy to make proper "deductions for depreciation." The word [depreciation] means, by derivation and common usage "a fall in value, reduction of worth" (*N.Y. Life Ins. Co. v. Anderson,* 263 Fed. Rep. 527 at 529). It includes obsolescence (*Nashville, C. & St. L. Ry. Co., v. U.S.,* 269 Fed. Rep. 351 at 355; *San Francisco & P.S.S. Co. v. Scott,* 253 Fed. Rep. 854 at 855). An obsolete thing is a thing no longer in use. In determining the extent to which these buildings had suffered from depreciation the trier of fact should have been permitted to consider that, owing to the passage of the National Prohibition Act, they were no longer useful to serve the purposes for which they were erected. It should have been permitted to consider their adaptability or inadaptability to other commercial purposes.

The McAnarney case did not solve the problem of whether replacement cost less physical depreciation is the measure of actual cash value, or whether market value is the measure. It did set down a long-needed rule that *all* factors having a bearing on cash value must be weighed and considered.

Value of Building to Be Demolished

The owner of a building which is to be demolished ordinarily has in expectation no greater return from the structure than the *profit* from the rent to be collected during the remainder of its life, plus the salvage value of the building material. Its cash value, for the purpose of maintaining insurance or collecting for its destruction, would seem to be limited to the return expected. This theory of expected return has not received judicial favor in most cases.

If a building is sold to wreckers who receive no title to the land, the building becomes personal property, as the sale effects a severance of the building from the realty. If a loss occurs under this condition, the net salvage value of the building after wrecking costs is the measure of the wrecker's loss.

Building Appraisals

Many large commercial and industrial insureds have up-to-date detailed appraisals of their property made by recognized and competent professional appraisers. They show specifications of construction, replacement cost, and depreciation. The majority are very reliable but, because the possibility of human error always exists, the claim representative always should check carefully the details and costs. They should be scrutinized also for any additions, deletions, or alterations made to the property subsequent to the date of the appraisal.

Many times the claim representative will be able to update the figures by using current labor and material prices. Frequently the original appraiser is called in by the insured to bring the figures up to date.

VALUED-POLICY-LAW STATES

The following states have statutes providing for a valued-policy requirement in one form or another.

Arkansas	Nebraska
California (optional)	New Hampshire
Florida	North Dakota
Georgia	Ohio
Kansas	South Carolina
Louisiana	South Dakota
Minnesota	Tennessee
Mississippi	Texas
Missouri	West Virginia
Montana	Wisconsin

Very generally these statutes provide that in the event buildings or structures are wholly destroyed by fire, without criminal fault of the insured, the amount of the policy shall be taken conclusively to be the value of the property when insured and the amount of loss when destroyed.

Valued-policy statutes have been held in conflict with insurable-interest statutes and also with standard-policy statutes inasmuch as the full amount of the policy covering realty is forfeited in case of total loss whether or not insurable interest[10] or cash value is less than the insurance. Valued-policy statutes would also appear to contravene the principle of indemnity, the basis upon which the insurance contract is founded,[11] a principle germane to all important court decisions. In spite of the conflict, a valued-policy statute becomes a part of every policy of insurance on realty, and policy stipulations in conflict with the statute are void.[12]

In Minnesota the valued-policy statute applies to all perils covered. In Kansas the statute is applicable to the perils of "fire, tornado or lightning," while most other statutes read *fire* or *fire and lightning*.

The Louisiana valued-policy statute, unlike those of other states, permits the insurer to replace the property partially or totally destroyed at its own expense and without contribution on the part of the insured. Also, the Louisiana statute provides for adjustment on the basis of replacement cost less depreciation where one of the buildings under a blanket policy is totally destroyed. New Hampshire follows the Louisiana rule.

Where two or more insurers have policies on the same building, either one or a combination of which is in excess of the cash value of the property, the question of whether proration is permissible is unsettled in most states.

It is incumbent upon the claim representative to have for reference, copies of any valued-policy statutes for those states in which he or she adjusts losses. Before committing an insurer, he or she should also report fully in each instance where such statutes appear applicable.

DETERMINING LOSS

The loss to a building that is damaged beyond repair (constructive total loss) is measured according to its insurable value as discussed in the preceding section, subject to policy conditions and provisions. The basis for determining loss will be the replacement cost, the actual cash value, or it will conform to any existing statute pertaining to a valued-policy law in the state in which the loss occurred.

---

[10]*Hunt et al. v. General Ins. Co. of America*, 8 F. & C. 663 (S.C.).

[11]*Harrington v. Agricultural Ins. Co.*, 229 N.W. 792, 68 A.L.R. 1340.

[12]*Ted Ford v. Security State Fire Ins. Co.*, 8 F. & C. 680 (Ark.).

If a building is damaged but not destroyed, the loss sustained by the owner is ordinarily measured by the cost of restoring it to the condition existing before the loss occurred. If necessary repairs are not extensive and do not involve the replacement of entire units, such as roofs, it is not customary to make any deduction from the cost of repairs for depreciation. If, however, repairs are so extensive that a substantial portion of the structure will be renewed, depreciation should be deducted, or allowance taken for betterment; otherwise, the owner, on the completion of the repairs, will be in possession of property more valuable than it was before the loss.[13] Occasionally the question of depreciation is equitably settled by an agreement that the owner will make no claim on damaged parts that were in poor condition before the loss but will be allowed full cost of repair or restoration on the parts that were in good or fair condition.

In some instances damage to a part of the building will be of such a nature as to make complete removal and replacement of a part impractical or inadvisable. In those situations loss will be measured by an amount agreed upon as representing a fair allowance for the shortened life, impaired usefulness, or changed appearance of the part affected. Common examples are smoke-stained ceramic tile; flooring ridged from water and requiring heavy sanding; spalled exterior brick that can be plaster-coated; slightly charred heavy wood beams, girders, and trusses that can be scraped, deodorized, and boxed to the insured's satisfaction; slightly deformed but structurally sound steel girders, trusses, and columns.

Occasionally a partial loss is adjusted by having the repairs made and keeping a record of the total expenditure which, less proper depreciation, is accepted as the amount of the loss. *In such cases the insured should have the work done, and the bills should be checked by the claim representative.*

The company's option to repair is very seldom exercised. Many times on smaller losses

an insured is agreeable or may prefer to adjust the loss for the cost of the material plus a reasonable allowance for his labor.

The adjustment of a partial loss on a building is generally more difficult than the adjustment of a total loss, as there is room for disagreement over both the extent of the repairs and the cost of making them. While extent and cost are usually left to the judgment of builders, there are some claim representatives who on ordinary building losses have the experience and ability necessary to prepare specifications and estimate with accuracy the cost of work.

MAJOR ELEMENTS IN ESTIMATING

Claim representatives who handle property losses should know the principles for estimating simple building losses, most of which average but a few thousand dollars. They should also be competent to check detailed estimates made by a builder for repairing more seriously damaged buildings, or for destroyed buildings. Whether the estimate has been prepared by the insured's representative or by a builder or contractor engaged by the claim representative, it should not be accepted without question until it has been carefully reviewed by the claim representative.

Estimating building losses involves precisely what the word *estimating* means, *approximating*. All estimating is made up of five major elements, whether the subject of the estimate is the cost of making a piece of furniture or a man's suit, or the cost of erecting a building. These elements are (1) specifications, (2) materials, (3) labor, (4) overhead, and (5) profit.

Specifications

Specifications state in detail what work is to be done, how it is to be done, and what kind, size, and quality of material is to be used. The place to prepare specifications for estimating the cost of repairing or restoring damaged buildings covered by insurance is *at the scene of the loss.*

Specifications are set down in an orderly manner as the person recording them in the

[13]See Replacement Cost Coverage, p. 205.

field proceeds from one part of the premises to another. He or she identifies the room, section, or area being considered and lists in detail what must be done to effect repairs or replacement. While noting the work required, he or she measures the areas involved and the sizes of any units, and observes the kind and quality of material when it is in sight and can be examined. All of these factors will ultimately influence the cost, and therefore accuracy in measurement, observation, and note-taking is important. Much lack of agreement can develop later, when adjustment negotiations get under way, about the specifications of an estimate of a building loss. If the insured's contractor and the insurer's contractor visit the damaged building separately and each makes up his own specifications of repair, almost invariably the basis on which their estimates of cost are submitted will be different. One will have more or less plastering than the other, more or less painting, flooring, siding, roofing, or electrical wiring. They may specify different materials: for example, a contractor may specify Douglas fir when the lumber used was actually local hemlock or spruce; another may specify three-coat plaster on wire lath when it actually is two-coat plaster on gypsum lath; in still a third case, white oak flooring may be specified instead of a low-grade red oak.

On serious losses, it is advisable to have the contractors make a joint examination and survey of the building so that they may agree on at least the basic specifications for repair or replacement. The claim representative should be present and also a representative of the insured.

Where there is serious damage to items involving specialty trades—such as electrical wiring, brick masonry, marble work or stonework, plumbing, and heating—the specifications should be established by calling in competent experts to determine the extent of damage and advise what is necessary for restoration. Guessing at matters of this kind, about which the contractor or claim representative may have only limited knowledge and experience, jeopardizes both the insured and the insurer. Frequently

when the specifications are being noted at the loss, certain damaged items may require careful examination to determine whether replacement is necessary or repair will suffice. Typical examples are smoked-stained ceramic tile and plumbing fixtures such as lavatories, toilet bowls, or tanks and bathtubs. Cleaning tests made in the field usually will disclose whether replacement is necessary. Plaster and gypsum board have often survived submersion by flooding or wetting down by water from fire hoses, sprinkler leakage, or leakage through roofs or floors above. Flooring that ridges or buckles will rarely return to normal, but if dried under proper conditions it may only need sanding rather than replacing. Where there is a question, it is best to wait a period of time until the area has dried sufficiently to determine fairly what is necessary to make proper repairs. In many cases, under these circumstances, adjustments are held open or the questionable portion of the repairs is held in abeyance by special agreement, the remainder of the loss being accepted and paid.

Measurements.   Measurements of areas, sizes, and thickness of material, when stipulated in the specifications of repair or replacement, play an important role in the ultimate cost of restorations. Inaccurate field measurements, whether deliberate or inadvertent, will be the basis for estimating the quantity of material. The greater the quantity of material specified the more labor will be estimated to install the material. Overhead and profit, which customarily is in the range of 20 percent of the cost of material and labor, is proportionately affected by inaccurate measurements. Conversely, measurements which indicate smaller quantities than they should will produce a final cost inadequate to do the work. The claim representative should take measurements with care when preparing figures and should check the measurements taken by any builder or contractor who made an estimate.

Materials

Building materials that appear alike to the inexperienced, and not infrequently to the experienced, may have a price spread of several hundred percent. Typical examples are composition floor covering either in a roll or in blocks. There are many grades of materials of the same trade name, such as asphalt or vinyl tile, each of which has a wide price range. Asphalt shingles, wood cedar shingles, Sheetrock, plastic wall tile, paints, hardware, lighting fixtures, painted wood trim, finish flooring, insulation, ceiling tile, and numerous other materials, many of which "look alike," have substantially different price tags. In an estimate a mere statement such as "fifty squares of built-up roofing" or "200 square feet of oak flooring" is as meaningless as stipulating a price for "one ladies' hat" in estimating the cost of a wardrobe. Specifications must be more explicit in describing kind, quality, size, grade, and even make where indicated.

Where large quantities of materials are needed such as barge-loads or carloads of lumber and brick, special prices should be sought from the supplier. Trade and bulk discounts on materials should always be considered.

Labor

Local, current wage scales should be used in preparing the estimate.

Earlier, it was stated that estimating building costs is approximating, and the place where this factor of approximating is most important is in the amount of labor needed. There are many conditions that must be considered in estimating the length of time to perform a particular job or operation. In repairing buildings and structures there is generally a certain amount of demolition or tearing out and carting before new materials can be put in place. There are often unusual physical conditions that may have to be taken into consideration such as working in confined areas, working with tenants underfoot, working under poor lighting conditions, protecting furnishings, and moving furnishings back and forth. In addition there are the ever-present and indeterminate elements inherent in construction such as weather conditions, union regulations, experience and productivity of workmen, organi-

zation and supervision of the men on the job, and building ordinances and inspections.

Under normal working conditions, carpenters, painters, roofers, and other building-trades mechanics install building materials at a fairly uniform rate. Records have been kept over a long period and tables have been devised for the labor requirements for most operations. These are available in many books, periodicals, and government publications.[14]

Overhead

The amount of overhead a builder or contractor must charge varies with his particular method of operation. Overhead is actually all general expense not considered chargeable to any particular work or operation. This includes but is not limited to rent, heat, light, and power for an office and shop; general insurance premiums; office equipment; general telephone, travel, and legal expense; and office and shop payroll. Any expense which is solely chargeable to a specific job, such as builder's risk insurance premiums or supervision, is a direct cost allocated to the job and not to general overhead.

Profit

Profit, when not included in unit costs, or loaded into labor charges, ranges generally in the area of 10 percent of the job cost. Some contractors charge 20 percent for overhead and profit. Others charge 10 percent overhead and add to the total 10 percent for profit which adds up to 21 percent for overhead and profit. A careful analysis of overhead is recommended on losses of any magnitude. Frequently overhead will be found buried in unit costs or in a lump-sum labor item, and also added at the end of the estimate as a separate item.

Most contractors charge 5 percent profit on subcontractors' bids rather than including them in the estimate and charging 10 percent.

[14]Thomas, op. cit., pp. 47–54.

OTHER CONSIDERATIONS

Architects' Fees

Where an architect's services are required by law, or one would be used by the insured under normal conditions, i.e., in the absence of insurance, it is usually a proper charge and is part of the cost of rebuilding. Substantial damage to a school, office building, or palatial residence may reasonably require an architect to draw up plans and specifications and supervise restoration. In some states an architect is mandatory when school losses exceed a specified amount. Moderate or slight damage to the foregoing structures may not need an architect's services. Serious damage to or destruction of an ordinary residence or an older commercial or factory building might well be repaired by a reliable contractor without an architect. The matter calls for realistic judgment. Some policy forms specifically include architect's fees; others exclude them.

Methods of Pricing Estimates

In the larger cities, after catastrophes, and in many smaller cities, the customary method of pricing a building estimate is by the unit-cost system.

In other areas of the country, the material for each operation or unit of construction is priced, and the labor cost for installing or applying the material is figured separately. In still other areas, all the materials are itemized, but the labor cost for the entire job is priced in *one lump sum.*

Unit Costs

Of the three methods mentioned, the first two—unit cost and material plus labor for each operation—are the most reliable and also the most useful in the adjustment of property losses because they are subject to checking. A *unit cost* is the combined cost of the material and labor needed to install a unit of material. For example, if asphalt shingles cost $15 per square (100 square feet) and a roofer, making $8 per hour, can apply a square in 2 hours, the unit cost (omitting nails) would be

1 square of asphalt shingles	$15
2 hours of labor for a roofer at $8	16
Unit cost per square	$31

Though the cost of a square is $31, in some sections of the country the unit would be referred to as costing 31 cents per square foot.

The same principle is applicable to most building materials.

Unit costs are easy to apply inasmuch as, once they are computed, they can be multiplied by the quantities of materials and areas in the estimate. For illustration, an estimate to repair a fire-damaged room would be set up as shown in Table 14-2, excluding overhead, profit, and tearing out.

The advantages of the detailed unit-cost estimate as a device for negotiating the adjustment of building losses are immediately apparent. Such an estimate is comparable to a detailed inventory of stock or household

TABLE 14-2   Estimate to Repair Fire-Damaged Bedroom 12 × 18 × 8 Feet

Item	Quantity	Unit Cost	Cost
Plaster ceiling, two coats on wire lath	24 yd.	$6.00	$144.00
Paint, two coats	696 s.f.	.25	174.00
2-piece 6-inch pine baseboard	60 l.f.	1.10	66.00
New 1 × 3 inch white oak floor	288 b.f.	1.00	288.00
Sand and finish	216 s.f.	.20	43.20
			$715.20

goods. Each item may be discussed if there are differences in the cost. Each item of repair is accounted for. All specifications, sizes, quantities, and qualities of materials can be compared and discussed.

Lump Sum

The lump-sum estimate is one that either shows a single sum of money for the entire job or lists a series of sums for various trades or operations. A series of lump sums, such as might be shown in a recapitulation or summary of an estimate, does not in itself constitute a detailed estimate. It contributes very little as a means of adjusting a building loss, and leads to "horse trading" or settling rather than adjusting. It is impossible to analyze.

Use of Experts and Subcontractors

The claim representative should not hesitate to call in competent experts, when in doubt, to furnish opinions on the extent of damage to specific items or materials, to prepare estimates of the cost of repairing or replacing, or to check the insured's claim for damage. The important thing to keep in mind is that the expert should be qualified and, if possible, a recognized authority in the field. Such questions as whether structural steel has lost its temper, whether concrete floors have lost some of their tensile strength because of fire, and whether brick walls have been materially weakened by fire are questions for experts and not laymen. Problems such as these usually require engineering tests if the answers are to be relied upon.

PROCEDURE

The procedure for adjusting building losses[15] includes (1) getting the insured's story, (2) identifying the property and checking coverage, (3) establishing interests, (4) examining the property and surveying the situation, (5) investigating the cause of loss,[16] (6) taking safety measures, (7) protecting the property from further damage, (8) choosing a method of adjustment,[17] (9) preparing for the adjust-

ment, (10) negotiating the adjustment, (11) obtaining the appraisal, and (12) completing final papers.

OSHA (Occupational Safety and Health Administration)

The following summarization of OSHA rules and regulations relevant to estimating building losses and particularly to building demolition is taken from *How to Estimate Building Losses and Construction Costs*, by Paul I. Thomas.[18]

The U.S. Department of Labor has published safety and health regulations for the Construction Industry pursuant to the Williams-Steiger Occupational Safety and Health Act of 1970.

These rules or regulations, while mostly applicable to heavy construction, are enforceable as respects small contractors and builders of residential properties. Authorized representatives of the U.S. Labor Department have the right of entry to any construction site to investigate compliance with the regulations or may designate the services, personnel, or facilities of any State or Federal agency to inspect.

A complaint of the smaller contractors and builders is that the cost of compliance increases their operating overhead anywhere from 2 to 5 percent with no visible benefits in many instances. Nevertheless OSHA should be taken into consideration in estimating, especially where substantial demolition and removal of debris is involved. Federal Register, Part 2, Vol. 37, No. 243 can be obtained from the Department of Labor. This document outlines the regulations. A brief résumé of *some* of the rules is stated below for illustrative purposes. Note particularly Regulations pertaining to Demolition (Subpart T).

Basically, no contractor or subcontractor shall require any laborer or mechanic to work in surroundings which are *unsanitary, hazardous, or dangerous to his health or safety*. It is the responsibility of the employer to initiate and maintain such programs as necessary to comply.

---

[15]See also p. 5.
[16]See also p. 102.
[17]See also p. 9.

[18]Published by Prentice-Hall, Inc., 1976, and used by permission.

The prime contractor and subcontractor(s) may agree on who shall furnish (for example) toilet facilities, first-aid services, fire protection or drinking water, but such agreement will not relieve either one of his legal responsibility.

Machines or power tools not in compliance with the Regulations must be tagged unsafe, locked, or removed from the premises.

Employer must instruct employees in avoidance of unsafe conditions to avoid exposure to illness or injury. If harmful animals or plants (poison ivy?) are present, the employee is to be instructed regarding the hazards and in any first-aid. The same rules apply where employees are required to handle flammable liquids, gases, or toxic materials.

Employer must insure availability of medical personnel for advice and consultation on matters of occupational health. Provisions shall be made for prompt medical attention in case of serious injury.

If no infirmary, clinic, hospital, or physician is reasonably accessible, a person certified in first-aid shall be available at the work site.

First-aid supplies shall be easily accessible. The first-aid kit must contain approved materials in a waterproof container and contents must be checked by the employer before being sent to the job and *at least weekly*.

Equipment must be furnished to transport any injured person to a physician or hospital, or else communication must be available for ambulance service.

Telephone numbers of physicians, hospitals, or ambulances must be conspicuously posted.

An adequate supply of potable water must be supplied in all places of employment. Containers shall be capable of being tightly closed and supplied with a tap. (No dipping of water from containers.) Container is to be clearly marked. A common drinking cup is prohibited. Where single service cups are supplied, a sanitary container for unused and one for used cups are to be provided.

Toilets are to be provided in accord with the Regulations.

Protection against the effects of noise-exposure shall be provided when sound levels exceed those set forth in a Table of "Permissible Noise Exposures." The protective devices inserted in the ears must be fitted individually by competent persons. Cotton not acceptable.

All construction areas must be lighted to minimum intensities listed in a Table designating "foot-candles" for specific areas.

Hard hats are to be worn by employees working in areas where there is possible danger of head injury from impact, falling objects, or electrical shock or burns (usually supplied by employer). Goggles and face protection are to be provided employees who are engaged in operations where machines or equipment present possible eye or face injury.

Fire fighting equipment shall be furnished, maintained, conspicuously located, and periodically inspected. A fire alarm system (telephone, siren, etc.) shall be established so employees and local fire department can be alerted. Alarm code and reporting instructions shall be conspicuously posted at entrance.

Employers shall not permit the use of unsafe hand tools.

Scaffolding requirements are extensive. They must be equipped with guardrails and also toeboards on all open sides and ends of platforms over 6 feet above ground or floor. If persons are permitted to work or pass under the scaffold a 1/2" mesh screen must be installed between guardrail and toeboard.

Subpart T—Demolition

(1926, 850) Preparatory operations.

(a) Prior to permitting employees to start demolition operations, an engineering survey shall be made, by a competent person, of the structure to determine the condition of the framing, floors, and walls, and possibility of unplanned collapse of any portion of the structure. Any adjacent structure where employees may be exposed shall also be similarly checked. The employer shall have in writing evidence that such a survey has been performed.

(b) When employees are required to work within a structure to be demolished which has been damaged by fire, flood explosion, or other cause, the walls or floor shall be shored or braced.

(c) All electric, gas, water, steam, sewer, and other service lines shall be shut off, capped, or otherwise controlled, outside the building line before demolition work is started. In each case, any utility company which is involved shall be notified in advance.

(f) Where a hazard exists from fragmentation of glass, such hazards shall be removed.

(g) Where a hazard exists to employees falling through wall openings, the opening shall be protected to a height of approximately 42 inches.

(h) When debris is dropped through holes in the floor without the use of chutes, the area onto which the material is dropped shall be completely enclosed with barricades not less than 42 inches high and not less than 6 feet back from the projected edge of the opening above. Signs, warning of the hazard of falling materials, shall be posted at each level. Removal shall not be permitted in this lower area until debris handling ceases above.

(1926, 851) Stairs, passageways, and ladders.

(b) All stairs, passageways, ladders and incidental equipment thereto, which are covered by this section, shall be periodically inspected and maintained in a clean safe condition.

(1926, 852) Chutes.

(a) No material shall be dropped to any point lying outside the exterior walls of the structure unless the area is effectively protected.

(c) A substantial gate shall be installed in each chute at or near the discharge end. A competent employee shall be assigned to control the operation of the gate, and the backing and loading of trucks.

(1926, 854) Removal of walls, masonry sections, and chimneys.

(a) Masonry walls or other sections of masonry, shall not be permitted to fall upon the floors of the building in such masses as to exceed the safe carrying capacities of the floors.

(b) No wall section, which is more than one story in height, shall be permitted to stand alone without lateral bracing, unless such wall was originally designed and constructed to stand without such lateral support, and is in a condition safe enough to be self-supporting. All walls shall be left in a stable condition at the end of each shift.

The word *shall* means mandatory; the penalties can be severe for noncompliance so even small contractors and subcontractors find it expedient to attend and/or have a foreman or superintendent attend training facilities set up by the Department. This can be expensive in time and travel for those long distances from such centers.

THE INSURED'S STORY

In the ordinary building loss, the insured's story requires simply stating the date, hour, and cause of loss, the extent of damage, and the plan and probable cost of repair. The insured, on whom the claim representative will call after a reported loss to a dwelling, may say that on the previous Monday at about 11:00 A.M., a towel left too close to the range in the kitchen caught fire, spread to paper intended for wrapping garbage and to the window curtains, which in burning cracked the glass in the window and smoked up the walls and ceiling so that repainting will be necessary. The local contractor has looked over the damage and will make all repairs for $150.

The owner of a mercantile building may say to the claim representative that the building next door burned, and the heat cracked the glass in the windows on the fire side of the building and scorched the frames. Glass was put in at once, because of the weather. Costs to date, plus what will have to be paid for repainting the window frames, total $238.

The owner of a dwelling may say that last week's storm blew most of the shingles off the west side of the roof. The rain came in and wet the ceilings and walls of the west bedrooms. He or she has an estimate from a builder of $825 to make all repairs.

In the preceding instances, the claim representative needs no more information before going on to the next step in the adjustment.

When damages are extensive, or where their origin is obscure or questionable, the insured should be questioned very carefully as to the cause of the loss, its discovery, and what parts of the structure have been damaged. The questioning should cover the insured's ideas of what repairs or replacements will be necessary, and when, how, and by whom repairs will be estimated or eventually made.

If any temporary or permanent repairs have been made, the claim representative should obtain the insured's story concerning the reason for the repairs and who made them. If any building fixtures or equipment have been removed from the premises as debris, the insured should be asked what the property consisted of, where it was taken, and by whom.

In losses to buildings involving vandalism and malicious mischief, vehicle damage, incendiarism, or burglary, the insured should be requested to give any information that might lead to discovery and apprehension of those responsible.

In total destruction, the insured should be asked for a general description of the building; its size, design, layout, and quality of workmanship; its age, history, and condition; also, what architect designed it, who built it, and whether any plans of it are available.

IDENTIFICATION AND CHECK OF COVERAGE

At the time of first inspection, the claim representative should identify the building as property covered by the insurance and, after doing so, should establish, according to the description and any extensions, exclusions, and limitations, to what extent the building or structure is covered.

In the majority of losses, identification is no problem. The claim representative finds the building by its address or is accompanied to the property by the agent, broker, or some other representative of the insured. The construction and occupancy generally fit the policy description. In a few losses, however, identification is difficult when the policy description of location is vague, as in some rural areas, and also when numerous buildings are covered by blanket insurance, as in industrial complexes, and are identified by number or occupancy.

In most losses the insurance covers all of the building. The ordinary dwelling, garage, barn, store, school, church, or factory is rarely covered in such a manner as to exclude any part of it. But in some instances, one of the walls of a building will be a party wall and will be covered only to the extent of the insured's interest in it, usually one-half. In cases occasionally encountered in congested city areas, a building will cover two lots of land separately owned. If the owners carry separate insurance, the insurance of each will cover only his or her part of the structure. Sometimes two buildings of the same ownership and separately insured are connected by a passageway. Ordinarily the insurance on each building is treated as covering the adjoining half of the passageway.

In leased buildings there are, in many cases, numerous fixtures and substantial improvements made by the lessees and covered by their own insurance.[19]

ESTABLISHING INTERESTS

In owner-occupied buildings, the interests are, ordinarily, only those of the insured and a mortgagee. The existence of a mortgagee interest does not require any special action. The notation in the report that a mortgage for so many dollars is held by a certain person or organization is, in most losses, all that is necessary. The mortgagee's interest extends to the entire building and does not require any segregation.[20]

EXAMINATION AND SURVEY

The claim representative makes an inspection and examination of the building or structure involved to determine the cause of the loss, how extensive the damage is, and what part or parts are not damaged. Since most losses are relatively small, the inspection will require a short time to observe and make note of each item of the structure that has been damaged and to measure areas or quantities, so that then, or later, the necessary materials and labor for making repairs can be computed.

Typical small losses are those involving, for example, replacing a few shingles or a few squares of roofing; painting or washing the walls in a room; glazing a few windows; repairing or replacing an oil burner; patching a few yards of plaster, wallboard, or paneling;

[19]See Improvements and Betterments, p. 202.
[20]See Chap. 5, "Mortgagees and Other Payees."

or any combination of such items. The claim representative should be able to itemize a list of necessary repairs, to take measurements, and to make an intelligent calculation of the probable cost of the work, as though he or she were bidding to do the job. Such examinations should preferably be conducted in the presence of the insured or a representative who is familiar with the damage. The claim representative can then ask questions and get guidance through the premises so that there will be little chance of overlooking anything and the scope of repairs can be agreed upon.

If the damage is extensive and the claim representative does not feel competent to detail the specifications and estimate the cost of rebuilding or feels it is advisable to bring in a qualified contractor to make the estimate, the first inspection, while thorough, will be more general. If the loss is total, there may be little left to examine. A wall or two may be standing, or there may be nothing left but the foundations with perhaps a chimney still standing, as frequently is the case when unprotected dwellings are destroyed by fire.

Measurements of the foundations will establish the ground area covered by the building, and if a chimney or a masonry wall is still standing, the height may be determined by counting the bricks or cement blocks of which it is constructed.

Claim representatives and contractors who are experienced in inspecting and examining constructive total losses to buildings are able to reconstruct much from the remains. The pitch and height of the roof are often revealed by evidences of flashing on a still-standing chimney; the locations of partitions are frequently indicated in the debris; the location and type of bathroom and kitchen plumbing fixtures that have fallen into the basement are readily determined; heating systems are likewise identified; charred remains of wood girders and trusses, and steel columns and girders, are clues to the type of construction; and remains of wood framing or trim, ceramic tile, floor coverings, hardware, light fixtures, plaster, and lath or gypsum board all point to the kind and quality of materials used.

In large and complex losses, when most of the structure remains standing, proper examination will require much time and, in many cases, considerable work. In case of severe damage to large structures where dangerous conditions exist, where access to sections or floors is barred by collapse or large quantities of debris, or where basements are filled with water, it may be necessary to make a preliminary examination followed by several others as wrecking or pumping operations proceed.

No unvarying plan of examination can be offered, but the following outline will cover practically all kinds of losses. In all situations the claim representative should take notes during his or her examination and inspection. Where time or weather conditions make notetaking impractical, a portable tape recorder is recommended.

1. Construction and occupancy.
   a. Number of stories, basement, sub-basement.
   b. Construction—frame, brick, brick veneer on frame, concrete block, metal-clad, fire-resistive, etc.
   c. Interior layout—apartments, loft, offices, fire walls, etc.
   d. Special or unusual architectural features.
   e. Quality of construction—materials, workmanship.
   f. Occupancy—one type or several types.
2. Character and extent of damage.
   a. Peril or perils causing damage—wind, fire, explosion, water, freeze-up, etc.
   b. Sections, stories, parts, or rooms damaged or destroyed.
   c. How damaged or destroyed?
   d. Sections adjacent to damaged or destroyed areas but not damaged.
   e. Roof or exterior walls damaged and open.
   f. Basement flooded or wet.
   g. Elevators and other mechanical equipment operating or out of service.
   h. Heat, light, and power available or not.
   i. Plumbing piping or fixtures damaged.

j. What repairs have been made? Temporary or permanent?

3. Unsafe conditions.
   a. Structural weakness—unsupported walls, weakened or destroyed posts or girders, weak or collapsed floors, hanging cornices, floors overloaded with debris, tank supports weakened.
   b. Is building open to trespassers, children, and others who may be injured?

4. Possibility of further damage.
   a. Openings in roof, walls, outside doors, or windows.
   b. Wet floors or plaster.
   c. Plumbing flowing.
   d. Boilers, tanks, pipes, fixtures, appliances, or sprinkler system exposed to freezing.
   e. Clogged drains.
   f. Heat off.
   g. Dangerous contents.
   h. Any building equipment, such as large motors, wet but otherwise undamaged.

5. Possibility of making an estimate.
   a. Can all damaged portions of the building or structure be examined?
   b. Should temporary or permanent electrical lighting be installed?
   c. Should contents debris be removed first but building debris set aside for inspection?
   d. Should stairways be repaired or reinforced, or ladders made available to estimator?

6. Specifications for repair.
   a. Is the damage such that definite specifications can be prepared, or should work be performed on a time and material basis?
   b. Can damage be repaired, or is replacement necessary?
   c. Are photographs needed to preserve evidence of construction and extent of damage?
   d. Should samples of materials be taken, such as composition flooring, roofing, or woodwork (for example, trim or sheathing), to verify kind and quality for later pricing?
   e. Is there need for specialists (such as mason contractors, structural steel or electrical engineers, foundation and soil engineers) to determine specifications and cost of repair?
   f. Is there need for factory or industry association experts to determine specifications or damage to such things as paint, aluminum siding, and built-up roofs?
   g. Does all damage require repair, or can an allowance for appearance or shortened life be made (such as hail-scarred roofs and siding)?
   h. Are there any *real* contingencies noted for possible unseen damage?

7. Damage not part of claim against insurer.
   a. Caused by peril excluded or not insured against.
   b. Caused by a mixed peril requiring separation.
   c. Due to a structural defect prior to occurrence.
   d. Unrepaired previous loss or damage.

8. Does damage involve property not covered or belonging to others?
   a. Property excluded in policy.
   b. Improvements and betterments.
   c. Property owned and insured by others.
   d. Tenants' fixtures and equipment.

9. Depreciation.
   a. Wear and tear, deterioration by elements or atmospheric conditions.
   b. Obsolescence in design or materials.

SAFETY MEASURES

Buildings that have been damaged by fire, windstorm, explosion, or other peril are sometimes unsafe for occupancy or even entry, and they may menace adjoining property or street traffic. In such instances the municipal authorities generally order the owner to take down or make safe dangerously weakened walls, floors, or other parts of the structure. The claim representative handling a loss of this kind should familiarize himself or herself with the situation, get the advice of a builder or engineer if necessary, and do whatever can be done to see that the owner has the work of wrecking or shoring done properly and economically. Multiple-line policies usually include liability coverage. The claim representative should notify the insurer promptly of conditions which might lead to liability claims. The claim representative must avoid any action that might be construed as an assumption of this obligation by the insurer. But the cost of whatever wrecking or shoring is necessary to the proper repair of the building is part of the insurance loss and is subject to contribution. If by wrecking or shoring, valuable contents can be saved or loss to them reduced, the claim representative should see to it that the owners of the contents or their insurers bear a proper part of the cost.

PROTECTION FROM FURTHER DAMAGE

The claim representative should see that prompt steps are taken to protect the interior of a building from further damage by rain or cold weather if fire or other peril has opened the walls or roof or broken the windows. In cases of emergency, tar paper may be nailed over holes in a roof, and windows may be boarded up. In many cases, however, it will be best to have the work of permanently repairing the roof started at once and to replace window glass or sash without delay, in this way avoiding the additional cost of temporary repairs. If the heating system has been put out of commission and the weather is cold, either the plumbing should be drained or the heating system put in working order without delay. If water is standing on wooden floors, they should be swept and mopped as dry as possible in order to prevent swelling. If premises are fouled with mud or filth left by a receding flood, they should be shoveled out or washed out with hose streams. Wet debris in contact with woodwork should be removed and the building should be aired or dried by artificial heat, according to the weather conditions and available facilities. Removal of the contents may be necessary if there is any danger that they will do further damage to the building because of weight, swelling, or movement. Under proper weather conditions windows should be opened slightly at top and bottom

to permit circulation of air to reduce humidity and dissipate odor.

While the work of protecting the property should be done by the insured, as it is one of the duties imposed by the policy, the claim representative should render every assistance possible. The cost of temporary repairs, or of other protective work in cases of necessity, becomes a proper item in the claim, but like any other item it is subject to contribution. Removal of contents belonging to a tenant should be done by the tenant at his or her expense.

The degree of supervision to give to the work of protection from further damage depends upon the integrity and ability of the insured. Some policyholders can be given a free hand, some must be helped and advised, others must be checked closely.[21]

CHOICE OF METHOD OF ADJUSTMENT

The claim representative can employ one or more of the eleven methods of adjustment outlined in Chapter 1, all of which should be reviewed. The choice should be the ones that promise to produce the most equitable adjustment at least cost, giving proper consideration to the circumstances involved.

As a general rule, for acceptable procedure in ordinary building losses of several hundred dollars and no complications, the claim representative is presumed capable of estimating the cost of repairs and agreeing with the insured, the insured's building contractor, the insured's painter, or whoever is engaged to estimate the damage or do the work. On the more complicated and larger losses, the adjustment is usually concluded on the basis of estimates or bids separately prepared for the insured and for the claim representative by individuals they have selected.

Many building losses are adjusted by the insured obtaining an estimate and the claim representative checking it. When the claim representative understands building construction, is knowledgeable about cur-

---

[21]See p. 69.

rent local costs for labor and material, and is reasonably familiar with the labor requirements for installing and applying material, this method is very satisfactory.

The insurer seldom exercises the option to repair or replace buildings as provided under the policy.[22] "As a practical matter, the repair, rebuild or replacement option is not particularly satisfactory, for the reasons that the exercise of this option converts the insurance contract into a repair, rebuild or replacement contract with all the liabilities such a different contract entails."[23]

There are contrary decisions on whether an insurer may exercise its option in states that have a valued-policy law. Most states have statutes relating to when notice must be given the insured that the insurer has elected to exercise its option. A threat to rebuild is not sufficient election. Where it is difficult or even impossible to estimate the cost of repairing certain unusual types of damage or property, as outlined under method 6, Chapter 1, the claim representative and the insured may agree to have repairs made on a cost-plus basis, subject to audit.

PREPARATION FOR ADJUSTMENT

The purposes and objectives for preparing for the adjustment in advance of negotiating are discussed in Chapter 1, and should be reviewed. On serious losses and also small ones when lack of agreement is anticipated, careful preparation is necessary. The claim representative familiarizes himself or herself with details of the insured's claim, which is usually an estimate made for the insured. The claim representative likewise reviews and checks his or her own estimate or one that has been prepared by the contractor. It is presumed the claim representative has already gone over the physical loss in detail and is familiar with the damage to the property. There are many times when it will be advantageous to take the builder's or the insured's estimate to the property to check the details of either or both to be prepared for discussion of any differences.

As a result of checking or rechecking the various estimates it may be decided to have an electrician, plumber, painter, plasterer, or other subcontractor make an estimate, in order to get another opinion on a controversial item of repair.

Errors to Guard Against

Errors made in estimating fall into three general classifications: (1) errors made in the field when taking notes and measurements, (2) errors made in the specifications for restoration, and (3) errors made in computing the cost of the work. Many errors are very common, and of the estimates made either for new construction or for repairing damaged buildings, only a few do not include one or more of the following errors:

1. Errors made in taking field notes.
   a. Wrong measurements and dimensions.
   b. Inclusion of items that do not exist.
   c. Inclusion of damage from a previous unrepaired loss.
   d. Inclusion of property which is not covered under the policy.
   e. Inclusion of previously existing structural defects.
   f. Inclusion of damage not caused by an insured peril.
   g. Overlooked items of repair or replacement.
2. Errors made in preparing specifications.
   a. Including improvements to the property.
   b. Restoring items that can be repaired.
   c. Including work to comply with local ordinances, or building code requirements.
   d. Not replacing with like kind and quality of material.
   e. Allowances for unseen damage (contingencies).
   f. Overemphasizing details.
   g. Duplications by subcontractors.
   h. Duplications of repairs covered under contents insurance.
3. Errors made in computing the cost of the work.

[22]See p. 77.
[23]Annotation of the 1943 New York Standard Fire Insurance Policy, Section of Insurance Law, American Bar Association, Chicago, 1967.

a. Improper consideration given to the *class* of workmanship involved.
b. Inefficient methods and equipment used by builder.
c. Using improper wage rates.
d. Materials not priced correctly.
e. Inadequate or excessive labor allowances.
f. Inadequate or excessive overhead charged.
g. Inadequate or excessive profit charged.
h. Arithmetic errors in computations.[24]

Checking Estimates Submitted by Insureds

It is common practice for many claim representatives to wait until the insured presents an estimate for repairing or replacing the damaged or destroyed building. The claim representative then takes the estimate to the scene of the loss and proceeds to check the details against the physical damage. Frequently this is done without the insured's presence, in preparation for discussion; at other times it is done in company with the insured or a representative of the insured.

Each item on which claim for damage is made should be checked carefully. Measurements of room or areas should be verified, and quantities of materials, labor required, local cost of materials, and wage rates used should be checked. Discrepancies or differences in opinion, in particular any of the twenty-three errors previously listed, should be noted.

Checking Two Estimates by Comparison

In a great many losses the claim representative will have to compare a detailed estimate prepared by his or her contractor with one submitted by the insured, the total of which is substantially greater. To prepare for adjustment negotiations it will be necessary to determine wherein the two estimates differ.

The most effective way to make an analysis is by direct comparison. A recapitulation is made by building trades, that is, by rough

[24]Thomas, op. cit., pp. 516–532.

carpentry, finished carpentry, masonry, plastering, painting and decorating, roofing, sheet metal working, plumbing, electrical wiring, wrecking and removal of debris, and so forth, depending on the trades involved. When the recapitulations are complete and set alongside one another, the differences will be obvious. Generally, certain ones stand out more than others, and these will require further analysis and checking to determine why they are so far apart. By reviewing these items *in both estimates* in light of the sources of errors previously listed, it is usually possible to account for the differences, which can then be discussed intelligently and factually.

There are many occasions, of course, when compromises of opinion are necessary to bring an adjustment to a conclusion. There are no occasions for compromising on facts.

Meetings of Builders and Other Experts

On serious losses and frequently on smaller losses when builders or other experts do not agree on the cost of repairs or replacement, arrangements are made for them to meet and discuss differences. On these occasions the foregoing procedure is usually followed. The claim representative should be present at these meetings and be completely prepared to enter into negotiations with the insured then or later.

Checking Subcontractors' Estimates

It is very common to have a completely detailed estimate of everything to be done except the work of a subcontractor. Estimates of subcontractors are submitted separately or embodied in the general estimate as a lump-sum amount. They may appear as "electrical repairs," "plastering," "painting," "plumbing and heating," or some other trade classification.

These subcontract estimates may be sizable items, and in a lump-sum form they cannot be checked beyond comparing them with estimates submitted by another subcontractor. This comparison, while looked upon by some as a satisfactory method of checking, is not without pitfalls inasmuch as both could be in error. When two subcontractors show a considerable difference in their estimates, they should be called upon to review the details jointly to reconcile differences.

A far more desirable procedure is to explain to subcontractors before they make up their figures that a complete breakdown is required, showing materials, labor, overhead, and profit. A subcontractor's estimate is no more confidential than one made by a general contractor. The probable reason for lump-sum subestimates is the failure to explain to the electrician, plumber, or whoever may be involved the real purpose of requiring details.

CONSTRUCTIVE TOTAL LOSSES

In cases of severe damage to a building the question frequently arises of whether it is, in fact, a total loss. Where valued-policy statutes are in effect, the answer is very important when the amount of insurance is in excess of the cost of rebuilding. Where valued-policy laws are not in effect, the answer is important if there remains a reasonable portion on which to start rebuilding.

The courts have been quite consistent in applying the following general rule:

> Whether a building is an actual total loss (by fire) depends upon whether a reasonable prudent owner, uninsured, desiring to rebuild, would have used the remnant for restoring the building.[25]

The claim representative should check the decisions in the state in which the loss occurred to prepare for the adjustment.

ADJUSTMENT AFTER REPAIRS

On occasion, damage to a building is repaired by the insured either before the insurer receives notice of the loss or before the

claim representative gets to the risk. If the repairs have been extensive, and in situations where the motive is questioned for making repairs before inspection by the insurer, the claim representative should report to his or her principal for instructions, to avoid waiver or estoppel.

If the claim representative is instructed to check the loss and the claim, the investigation will follow the customary pattern set forth in Chapter 7 concerning property, insured, insurance, and cause of loss. The insured's story concerning each detail of damage and repairs becomes very important in reconstructing exactly what the situation was before repairs were started. Each person who had anything to do with the repairs should be interviewed and the story recorded. Contractors, subcontractors, and frequently the workmen will have to be interviewed to determine what repairs were made and why they were necessary.

In verifying whether the repairs claimed were made necessary by the event or occurrence, persons with knowledge of the incident should be interviewed and statements taken. If it was a fire, the fire chief or firemen who attended should be questioned; if a sprinkler leakage, the building superintendent, maintenance crew, or sprinkler-repair people should be questioned. In multiple occupancies, tenants whose premises have been damaged should be interviewed. If there are other insurers covering the same or other property or other interests, their claim representatives should be contacted for their story.

When the investigation is complete, the claim representative may want to bring in a builder or an expert to check out the specifications and cost of repairs being claimed.

CONDEMNATION AFTER LOSS

Building laws and ordinances of cities, counties, or states frequently provide for the complete demolition of certain structures that are partially damaged by fire or other perils. These laws are usually applicable to buildings built before either the code regulating construction or the laws governing zoning

---

[25] *Glens Falls Ins. Co. v. Peters*, Texas Supreme Ct., Jan. 13, 1965. *Royal Ins. Co. v. McIntyre*, 90 Tex. 170 (1896). *Fire Ass'n. v. Strayhorn*, 211 S.W. 447 (1919).

went into effect. They generally prescribe that if a stipulated percentage of the value of the building is destroyed, the undamaged portion must be demolished.

The standard fire policy contains a provision that an ordinance or law regulating construction or repair will not serve to increase the amount for which the insurer is liable. However, in cases decided under valued-policy statutes, the courts have uniformly held that this provision is overridden by the statute if the loss is total by reason of demolition enforced by law.

It is a general rule that where reconstruction of a building is prohibited by law, recovery may be had for a total loss. However, if the policy excludes "any increased cost of repair or reconstruction by reason of any ordinance or law regulating construction or repairs," another question is presented.[26] There is no uniformity in judicial thinking on this question, and therefore the claim representative should check any court decisions in the state in which he or she adjusts losses.

It is important, in any event, for the claim representative to obtain an exact copy of the ordinance, law, or code under which the order for demolition was given. He or she should obtain the name of the individual issuing the order, a copy of the order, and verification of the authority of the person to issue it. Condemnation orders are not incontestable. Where the ordinance or law provides for demolition if a certain percentage of the value is destroyed, the claim representative should determine what value is contemplated, i.e., market, assessed, cash, replacement, etc. In one instance the ordinance read "if the building is more than 25 percent *structurally* damaged." Although the damage to plaster, paint, floors, and trim far exceeded 25 percent of the cash value of the building, structural damage was found by engineers to be only 10 percent of the value. Condemnation was prevented.

IMPROVEMENTS AND BETTERMENTS

Lessees may install improvements and betterments in order to make a building more suitable for occupancy. They may be covered with insurance. If loss occurs to improvements and betterments, covered as such, the cost of replacing or repairing them is ordinarily estimated as on any other parts of the building.

The question of what constitutes improvements and betterments has puzzled insurance people and the courts for a long time. In *Modern Music Shop v. Concordia Fire Ins. Co.*, 131 Misc. 305, the court said:

> These words [*Improvements and betterments*] imply and mean a substantial or fairly substantial alteration, addition or change to the premises used and occupied by the insured, rising above and beyond and amounting to something more than a simple or minor repair.

As do most definitions of policy terms, this one helps but does not provide a yardstick for determining each case that comes up. For example, what about items in a building that wear out and must be replaced by the lessee under the provisions of a lease? Interior decorating, roofing, a new oil burner, or even the heating boiler itself are items that are often replaced by a tenant under a long-term lease.

There are two schools of thought on whether such items are actual improvements and betterments. One group asserts that they are maintenance items and that no improvement is made to the building by replacing worn-out paint or a leaky roof. Generally, the same group will agree that expensive murals painted on the walls of a showroom or restaurant would constitute an improvement and betterment.

Those holding a contrary opinion believe that if a tenant invests money in materials and labor which become an integral and permanent part of the building, it is not important whether such materials and labor replace a worn-out portion or constitute something new which never before existed.

---

[26]*Fidelity & Guarantee Ins. Corp. et al. v. Mondzelewski*, 10 Ter. 306, 115 A2d 861.

In either case the investment is for an improvement and betterment to the building. It also is contended that if the insurer did not intend to consider the replacement of worn-out portions of the building by the tenant as an improvement or betterment, it would have been quite easy to say so.

The question must be decided in each case by individual insurers. In some sections of the country the cost of paint put on by a tenant is paid for routinely under proper coverage and circumstance. In other sections it is not so treated.

There are three conditions that must be met in any claim for improvements and betterments: (1) the changes must be affixed to and a permanent part of the realty as opposed to personal property, (2) they must have been installed or acquired at the expense of the insured as tenant not owner, and (3) there must be an insurable interest.

Part of Realty

In the absence of a special provision in the lease, the common-law rule is that improvements, when added to the realty, become the property of the owner; that is, the right of reversion to the landlord at expiration of the lease exists by operation of law as though the right of reversion were expressly recorded in the lease.

Today, most forms covering business property stipulate that the improvements and betterments *covered* "are not legally subject to removal by the insured." This takes them out of the classification of personalty.

Installed or Acquired by Insured

If the insured acquires, without expense, the use of improvements made by another party through assuming the lease of that party or executing a new lease, they would not be covered under the policy. If in the transfer of a lease the insured paid for the improvements, they would qualify for coverage.

Most forms covering improvements and betterments specify they must be made to the building described or to the buildings occupied but not owned by the insured. The

Homeowners, Contents Broad Form, under Supplementary Coverages, provides (HO-4, Ed. 9-70, SW):

2. Building Additions and Alterations—Applicable only if the Insured is not owner of the premises. This policy covers under Coverage C, building additions and alterations, defined as fixtures, alterations, installations or additions comprising a part of the described building, only when situated within that portion of the premises used exclusively by the Named Insured, and made or acquired at the expense of the Named Insured for an amount not exceeding 10% of the limit of liability applicable to Coverage C.

Insurable Interest

There is no difficulty in recognizing the interest of the landlord even though the improvements have been made by the tenant and even though the lease is silent as to their ownership.

Occasionally a lease reserves a right to a tenant to remove the improvements at or before expiration of the lease. In that case, it may be doubted that the landlord has an insurable interest, as it has been said that a mere expectancy does not confer an insurable interest.[27]

As ordinarily each party, landlord and tenant, has an insurable interest, each may insure separately for his or her own benefit under the widely recognized rule that was stated by the New York Court of Appeals as follows:

The policies could co-exist, because while relating to the same property they affected different interests therein, and neither the policy of the law nor the contracts of insurance forbid, but on the contrary permit as many several insurances upon the same property as there are separate interests.[28]

[27]See p. 58.
[28]*DeWitt v. Agricultural Ins. Co.*, 157 N.Y. 353, at 360.

Because the improvements are absorbed into the realty and are no longer the property of the tenant whose interest usually is the use-interest while a tenant, the first place to look in ascertaining the tenant's interest in the improvements is the lease. Some leases expressly impose an obligation on the tenant to rebuild or repair in the event of fire. Others may provide simply that at the end of the term the tenant will quit and surrender the premises; or will quit and surrender the premises in good condition, ordinary wear and tear excepted. In such cases the decisions of the courts in the state where the property is located should be consulted to ascertain whether the law imposes any obligation on the tenant equivalent to an express covenant in the lease to rebuild or repair.

Adjustment Procedure

The Building and Contents Form 18 (Ed. 11-72), as do many of the latest forms, stipulates how a loss to improvements and betterments is to be adjusted, depending on whether they are restored (1) by the insured, (2) within a reasonable time, or (3) by others.

IMPROVEMENTS AND BETTERMENTS COVERAGE (Applies Only when the Insured is not the Building Owner and Only when "Improvements and Betterments" is indicated on the first page of this policy as being a part of the Contents Coverage or as a separate item): When insurance under this policy covers Improvements and Betterments, such insurance shall cover the Insured's use interest in Improvements and Betterments to the building described on the first page of this policy.

(1) The term "Improvements and Betterments" wherever used in this policy is defined as fixtures, alterations, installations, or additions comprising a part of the described building(s) and made or acquired at the expense of the Insured, exclusive of rent paid by the Insured, but which are not legally subject to removal by the Insured.

(2) The word "Lease" wherever used in this policy shall mean the lease or rental agreement, whether written or oral, in effect as of the time of loss.

(3) In the event Improvements and Betterments are damaged or destroyed during the term of the policy by the perils insured against, the liability of this company shall be determined as follows:

(a) If repaired or replaced at the expense of Insured within a reasonable time after such loss, the actual cash value of the damaged or destroyed Improvements and Betterments.

(b) If not repaired or replaced within a reasonable time after such loss, that proportion of the original cost at time of installation of the damaged or destroyed Improvements and Betterments which the unexpired term of the lease at the time of loss bears to the period(s) from the date(s) such Improvements and Betterments were made to the expiration date of the lease.

(c) If repaired or replaced at the expense of others for the use of the Insured, there shall be no liability hereunder.

Under (a) if the improvements are repaired or replaced by the insured, at his expense, within a reasonable time after the loss, the insurer is liable for the lesser of (1) the actual cost of repairs, (2) the actual cash value of that portion of the improvements involved.

Under (b) if the improvements are not repaired or replaced within a reasonable time after the loss, the insurer is liable for

$$\frac{\text{Unexpired term of lease}}{\text{Date improvement made to expiration date of lease}} \times \text{Original cost}$$

(The life of the improvements is the period from the date they were made to the expiration date of the lease.)

Under (c) if the improvements are repaired or replaced at the expense of others for use by the insured, the insurer has no liability.

In the event that the lease is canceled after the loss and the improvements cannot be replaced or repaired within a reasonable time, adjustment is in accordance with (b).

When one claim representative is handling claims involving contents and another is handling the building adjustment on the same premises, they should consult with each other and compare notes whenever a claim for tenant's improvements and betterments is indicated.

REPLACEMENT COST COVERAGE

Replacement cost coverage is built into a number of property insurance policies, such as Homeowners, Businessowners, and certain of the Special Multi-Peril policies. It is added by endorsement to some policies. All forms of this coverage are not identical. The provisions under the various policies and endorsements are not all alike; therefore, the claim representative should carefully examine the particular wording applicable to the claim being handled. The replacement cost coverage in the Homeowners (Ed. 1-72)[29] contains the following conditions and limitations that are common to many forms.

Certain kinds of property are not eligible for replacement cost:

1. To qualify for full replacement cost, the insurance, at time of loss, must be equal to or more than a stipulated percentage of the "replacement cost" of the building structure.
2. If the insurance at time of loss is less than required in (1) above, the Company's liability will not exceed the larger of
   a. the actual cash value; or
   b. that proportion of full replacement cost which the amount of insurance applicable bears to the stipulated percentage of the full replacement cost of the building structure.
3. The Company's liability is also limited to the smallest of
   a. the limit of liability of the policy applicable to the damaged or destroyed building structure;
   b. the replacement cost of an identical building structure or part thereof on the same premises and intended for the same occupancy and use; or
   c. the amount actually and necessarily

spent in making repairs or replacements.
4. There is no liability for the full replacement portion of the coverage (amount in excess of actual cash value) if the loss exceeds $1,000 or 5 percent of the insurance, unless actual repair or replacement is completed. Losses under $1,000 or 5 percent of the insurance need not be repaired or replaced in order to qualify for the replacement portion of the loss under either (1) or (2b).
5. The cost of various structural parts of the building is to be disregarded in determining if the amount of insurance equals or exceeds 80 percent of the full replacement cost of the building.
6. The insured may elect to be paid the actual cash value of the repairs or replacement and within 180 days make claim for the portion due under replacement cost coverage.

The provisions in the newer Homeowners 76 Program are similar to the older Edition HO-2(1-72) shown on page 206.

Under some policies, SMP General Property Forms, limited replacement cost coverage is included for losses less than $1,000 provided the insurance carried equals or exceeds a stipulated percentage of the *actual cash value* of the property covered. Full replacement cost coverage is available by endorsement. The SMP Replacement Cost Coverage Endorsement (MLB-126, Ed. 1-71) may be applied to Coverage A—Building(s) and also Coverage B—Personal Property. The HPR and Superior Risk Replacement Cost endorsements may be applied to Item 1, buildings and structures, etc., and to Item 2, all other property. The principal amount of insurance is subdivided, each amount being subject to separate policy provisions.

The Businessowners Policies (MLB-700 and MLB-701, Ed. 12-16-75) provide replacement cost for the property covered with the exception of loss to money and securities. The insurer's limit of liability is the least of the following:

1. The full cost of replacement at the same site.

[29]See p. 206.

2. The cost of repairing the property within a reasonable time.
3. The limit of liability applicable shown in the Declarations.
4. The amount actually and necessarily expended in repairing or replacing the property.

There is no liability for payment on a replacement-cost basis unless and until repair or replacement is made. As under the Homeowners Policy, the insured may opt to adjust on an actual cash value basis and, within 180 days, make claim for the amount due under the replacement cost coverage.

Additional Conditions. HO-2 (Ed. 1-72)

1. **Replacement Cost—Coverages A and B:**
   This *condition* shall be applicable only to a building structure covered hereunder excluding *outdoor radio and television antennas and aerials*, carpeting, awnings, domestic appliances and outdoor equipment, all whether attached to the building structure or not.
   a. If at the time of loss the whole amount of insurance applicable to said building structure for the peril causing the loss is 80% or more of the full replacement cost of such building structure, the coverage of this policy applicable to such building structure is extended to include the full cost of repair or replacement (without deduction for depreciation).
   b. If at the time of loss the whole amount of insurance applicable to said building structure for the peril causing the loss is less than 80% of the full replacement cost of such building structure, this Company's liability for loss under this policy shall not exceed the larger of the following amounts (1) or (2):
      (1) the actual cash value of that part of the building structure damaged or destroyed; or
      (2) that proportion of the full cost of repair or replacement without deduction for depreciation of that part of the building structure damaged or destroyed which the whole amount of insurance applicable to said building structure for the peril causing the

loss bears to 80% of the full replacement cost of such building structure.
   c. This Company's liability for loss under this policy shall not exceed the smallest of the following amounts (1), (2), or (3):
      (1) the limit of liability of this policy applicable to the damaged or destroyed building structure;
      (2) the replacement cost of the building structure or any part thereof identical with such building structure on the same premises and intended for the same occupancy and use; or
      (3) the amount actually and necessarily expended in repairing or replacing said building structure or any part thereof intended for the same occupancy and use.
   d. When the full cost of repair or replacement is more than $1,000 or more than 5% of the whole amount of insurance applicable to said building structure for the peril causing the loss, this Company shall not be liable for any loss under paragraph a. or sub-paragraph (2) of paragraph b. of this condition unless and until actual repair or replacement is completed.
   e. In determining if the whole amount of insurance applicable to said building structure is 80% or more of the full replacement cost of such building structure, the cost of excavations, underground flues and pipes, underground wiring and drains, and brick, stone and concrete foundations, piers and other supports which are below the under surface of the lowest basement floor, or where there is no basement, which are below the surface of the ground inside the foundation walls, shall be disregarded.
   f. The Named Insured may elect to disregard this condition in making claim hereunder, but such election shall not prejudice the Named Insured's right to make further claim within 180 days after loss for any additional liability brought about by this policy condition.

Adjustments should not be made on replacement cost without carefully checking the policy conditions, as there are important differences among policies.

Policies Subject to Coinsurance

When a policy contains a coinsurance or contribution clause, compliance with its provisions as stated in a replacement cost *extension* is most important. If the provisions are not complied with, the insured will be ineligible for replacement cost *on any basis.* Under both the New York Homeowners program and the SMP program, coinsurance under the Extensions of Coverage is applicable to the actual cash value of the building structure rather than to its full replacement cost.

Under replacement cost endorsements, the provisions of any coinsurance or contribution clause are applicable to the *replacement cost* of the property covered. While the endorsements permit the insured to make claim first for the actual cash value loss, and to make further claim later under the endorsement, most forms stipulate that the coinsurance clause, applicable to the replacement cost, shall apply. This frequently places the insured in a position of being unable to collect his full actual cash value loss should he wish to do so before making claim under the replacement cost endorsement, even though the amount of insurance would have complied with the coinsurance clause on an actual cash value basis.

The following example illustrates such a situation:

Amount of insurance	$ 70,000
Replacement cost	$100,000
Actual cash value	$ 80,000
Coinsurance percentage	80%
Cost of repairs	$ 5,000
Depreciation	$ 1,000
Cash value of repairs	$ 4,000

The cash value collectible under the policy, including the replacement cost endorsement, is

$$\frac{\$70,000}{80\% \times \$100,000} \times \$4,000 = \$3,500$$

Property Excluded

Replacement cost coverage under either an extension or an endorsement excludes certain property. Under the Homeowners policies, carpeting, cloth awnings, domestic appliances, and outdoor equipment are specifically excluded whether permanently attached to the building structure or not. The Special Multi-Peril forms exclude, under the extension, floor coverings fastened to the floor or walls, mirrors, air conditioners, domestic appliances, and outdoor equipment whether permanently attached to the building structure or not.

Replacement cost endorsements specifically exclude from coverage numerous items. Not all endorsements exclude the same property; therefore, the claim representative should examine the form before attempting to adjust the loss.

Property not eligible for replacement cost should not be included in determining whether the amount of insurance applicable to the building structure is adequate to comply with the provisions of the extension or the endorsement.

Computation of Liability

In determining the insurer's liability under replacement cost coverages, the claim representative proceeds in an orderly series of steps which generally follow the sequence of the conditions and provisions of the form.

The Homeowners form shown on page 206 is used as an illustration since it contains many of the provisions that are common to most extensions and endorsements.

The whole amount of insurance applicable to the building structure is the amount of insurance on Coverage A, though there is other property covered in addition to the building structure. It is the consensus that the *amount of insurance* cannot be divided in any manner between the building structure and the other property. The effect, therefore, is to give the insured a slight advantage.

In determining to what extent, if any, the insured qualifies for replacement cost, three values must be calculated:

1. The *replacement cost* of the building structure excluding cost of excavations;

underground flues and pipes; underground wiring and drains; and brick, stone, and concrete foundations, piers, and other supports which are below the undersurface of the lowest basement floor or, where there is no basement, which are below the surface of the ground inside the foundation walls.

2. The *full cost of repair* or replacement of that part of the building structure that has been damaged or destroyed.

3. The *actual cash value* of the repair or replacement of that part of the building structure that has been damaged or destroyed.

When Amount of Insurance Is Adequate.

Under (a), if the amount of insurance *applicable to the building structure* is 80 percent or more of its *full replacement cost*, the insured is entitled to the full cost of repair or replacement (without deduction for depreciation).

Insurance on Coverage A—
Building $16,000
Full replacement cost of building
structure $20,000
Full cost of repairs .... $ 500
Depreciated cost of repairs .... $ 400

The amount of insurance equals 80 percent of the full replacement cost of the building structure; therefore, the insured is entitled to the full cost of repair or replacement.

When Amount of Insurance Is Inadequate.

Under (b), if the amount of insurance *applicable to the building structure* is less than 80 percent of its *full replacement cost*, the insured is entitled to the larger of the following:

1. The actual cash value of the loss, or

2. That proportion of the full cost of repair or replacement (without deduction for depreciation) which the amount of insurance applicable to the building structure bears to 80 percent of its full replacement cost.

Insurance on Coverage A—
Building $18,000
Full replacement cost of building
structure $25,000
Full cost of repairs .... $ 500
Depreciated cost of repairs .... $ 400

The amount of insurance is *less* than 80 percent of the full replacement cost of the building structure; therefore, the insured is entitled to the *larger* of the following:

1. The actual cash value of the loss ($400), or

2. The full cost of repair multiplied by the following fraction:

$$\frac{\$18,000}{80\% \times \$25,000} \times \$500 = \$450$$

The insured is entitled to $450, the larger amount.

Further Limitations.

Under both (a) and (b), liability is further limited to:

1. The *amount of insurance* applicable to the damaged or destroyed building structure.

2. The *replacement cost* of the building structure or any part thereof on the same premises intended for the same use.

3. The *amount actually and necessarily expended* in repairing or replacing said building structure or any part thereof.

When Replacement Cost Is Payable.

Under both (a) and (b), if the full cost of repairs or replacement is *more than* $1,000 *or* 5 percent of the insurance applicable to the building structure, the depreciated portion of the loss is not collectible unless and until actual repair or replacement is completed.

This provision permits payment of the full amount due under the policy when the full cost of repair or replacement is *less than* $1,000 *or* 5 percent of the insurance applicable. Otherwise, repairs must be completed before the depreciated portion of the loss is payable. Proofs of loss should clearly indicate the basis for computation of any additional amount owing when repair or replacement has been completed.

Repair or Replacement on Same Premises

Under most replacement cost endorsements and extensions, and excepting losses less than $1,000 or less than 5 percent of the insurance applicable under the Homeowners, the insurer is not liable unless and until the damaged property is actually repaired or replaced by the insured.

However, there appears to be no requirement to repair or replace the building structure or any part thereof identically as it was just before the occurrence of the loss. The cost of repairing or replacing an identical structure or any part thereof is a limit of liability of the insurer, but not a requirement.

BUILDERS' RISK LOSSES

Investigation and adjustment of losses under builders' risk policies follow the same procedure as any other building losses. Coverage should be examined carefully, as most forms are broad and include temporary structures, materials, equipment, and supplies of all kinds incident to construction of the building. When not otherwise covered by insurance, the coverage extends to builders' machinery, tools, and equipment owned by the insured or similar property of others for which the insured is legally liable. Under certain conditions this could include tools and equipment of subcontractors and also workmen by reason of union contracts.

Interests insured should be checked in cases of possible subrogation. Sometimes policies name, as the insured, the owner of the building alone or with the builder or contractor; at other times subcontractors are included as insureds. All contracts and other agreements among insured, tenants, contractor, and subcontractors should be examined whenever questions arise concerning who is insured, what is the insurable interest, and whether subrogation has been waived by the insured in writing or otherwise prior to the loss.

Builders' risk forms may insure against all risks of loss or on a named-peril basis.

The completed value form provides that in the event of loss the liability is limited to that proportion of the loss which the provisional amount of insurance bears to the value of the property *at the date of completion*. The claim representative should determine, from records of the insured, the estimated completed value.

A great many losses to buildings under construction are adjusted with the contractor who is erecting the structure, either using estimates or by permitting the contractor to make repairs on a cost-plus basis subject to audit.

When the insurance covers an extension or addition to an existing structure, the claim representative should check the policy covering the existing structure to determine whether there is contribution under the Alterations and Repairs Clause or another clause covering buildings under construction.

Builders' risk forms, under the Occupancy Clause, provide that the premises shall not be occupied without the consent of the insurer by endorsement on the policy.

ADJUSTMENT NEGOTIATIONS

In taking up adjustment of a building loss, the claim representative endeavors to reach an agreement with the insured on an amount that will reasonably represent the sound value of the building in case of total loss, or the actual or probable cost of making repairs in case of partial loss. If the policies contain a coinsurance or an average clause, both the sound value and the amount of damage must be determined in any partial loss. The negotiations that take place during the adjustment must be in accord with the method that the claim representative chooses as being best adapted to the loss in hand. The methods are described in Chapter 1.

APPRAISALS

If the claim representative cannot negotiate an adjustment of a building loss at a figure approximating the amount he or she thinks is proper, it may be necessary to determine the value and loss by appraisal. Appraisals of building losses, except on obsolete structures, generally result in satisfactory awards.

FINAL PAPERS

The original written estimate presented in support of the insured's claim should be forwarded with proof of loss. If the claim was presented orally, the details should be incorporated into the statement attached to the proof. Any estimate that the claim representative prepares, or has prepared by a builder, should be handled in the same fashion. If the loss has been settled by accepting the record of repairs actually made, an account should be prepared showing the bill, or bills, rendered to the insured. If a loss is settled on the basis of a construction account or cost record, the statement of loss, or the report, should show in detail the data on which settlement is based.

QUESTIONS AND PROBLEMS

1. A 50-year-old neighborhood theater building in a rundown section of town was converted to a warehouse by removing all the seats. No other alterations were made. The claim representative, the insured, and a public adjuster are discussing actual cash value, for which the building is insured, to determine application of an 80 percent coinsurance clause. Agreed cost to repair the damage by windstorm is $20,000, insurance is $50,000, and the insured states he paid $50,000 for the property from a realtor who advertised it six months before the loss. The insurer's builder, who estimated the damage, figured the replacement cost new at $100,000.

Insured contends that the market value is the actual cash value. Public adjuster agrees, but says the new replacement cost less physical depreciation and obsolescence may also be the actual cash value. The claim representative contends that loss and value must be on the same basis; therefore, replacement cost new, less physical depreciation only, is the true measure of actual cash value.

As briefly as you can, discuss each of the three different approaches to actual cash value. If you were the claim supervisor for the insurer, how might you instruct the claim representative to resolve the problem?

2. Among the five fundamentals of estimating, the claim representative has greater control over some phases than others.

   a. Name the five fundamentals of estimating.

   b. Which one especially must the claim representative control in order to control the adjustment? Discuss the reason(s) for your selection.

3. In repairing damaged buildings, there are other factors that influence the hours of labor besides the normal time to perform an operation as would be the case on new construction.

   a. State four such factors peculiar to repair jobs.

   b. State four factors that might affect the price of materials for a given job.

   c. Overhead of a general contractor consists of expenses not considered chargeable to any specific job. Name five such items you might anticipate finding when analyzing a general contractor's overhead percentage.

4. Describe the different situations where you would be inclined to allow for an architect's fee in the adjustment of a building loss. Give an example. Describe different situations where you would not be inclined to include an architect's fee.

5. Builders, contractors, and subcontractors submit estimates of damage in three different ways with respect to material and labor. Describe each briefly and their relative value in adjusting building losses.

6. What is OSHA? Why should claim representatives and insureds be familiar with or have access to OSHA's rules and regulations, especially with regard to "demolition and removal of debris" of a damaged building?

7. Estimating errors fall into three major categories; (1) taking field notes and measurements, (2) preparing specifications, and (3) computing work costs. State five errors in each category, and cite an illustration of each error.

8. A claim representative trainee tells her supervisor that she now has an estimate of building damage from the insured's builder and also one from her contractor. The estimates are far apart on totals. The trainee asks her supervisor how she should proceed

to make a detailed comparison to highlight the major differences so that she can start negotiating with the insured or the insured's builder.

If you were the supervisor, how would you advise the claim representative?

9. A tenant-occupied building that houses a bowling alley is totally destroyed by fire. The tenant had installed wall-to-wall carpeting during the term of the lease, and an argument ensued as to which insurer should pay the carpet loss: Company C insuring the building, Company D insuring the contents, or Company E insuring improvements and betterments.

a. Company C contends that the *Guiding Principles* should apply. State the *Guiding Principles* rule on wall-to-wall carpeting, and give reasons why you believe the rule does or does not apply in this case.

b. Company D claims that Company E should pay. State whether you agree and why. State what further information is needed, if any, to make a decision. Your answer must include the definition of "improvements and betterments" coverage.

c. Assume it is agreed that Company E is to pay the loss. Assume further the following facts:

(1) An adequate amount of insurance is carried.

(2) The building will not be rebuilt.

(3) The lease ran from October, 1967, to October, 1977.

(4) The carpeting was installed October, 1969, at a cost of $5,000.

(5) On the date of loss, October, 1972, the cost to replace the carpeting was $6,000.

What amount should Company E pay? Show your calculations.

10. a. One of the most important provisions in the Homeowners Policy concerns replacement cost coverage. It is essential that the claim representative thoroughly understand the application of this provision of the policy in order to adjust a dwelling loss properly.

(1) What percentage of the replacement cost of the dwelling does an insured have to insure for in order to avoid a possible penalty in the amount payable on a dwelling loss?

(2) (a) Assume an insured has met the percentage requirement in the amount of insurance carried on his dwelling and the cost of repairs exceeds $1,000. Will the insured be able to collect the full cost of repairs prior to completion of the repairs? Why or why not?

(b) What type of settlement could be made prior to completion of repairs?

(3) In computing the amounts of insurance required to meet coinsurance requirements on a commercial risk, and replacement cost coverage requirements on a Homeowners risk, what is the basic difference in formulas used?

b. While adjusting a fire loss to a dwelling under a Homeowners policy, the claim representative determines that the cost to replace the dwelling is $40,000. The limit for Coverage A under the policy is $28,000. The full cost of repairs to the dwelling is $4,800. Depreciation applicable to the repairs is $800. Compute the amount collectible under the policy. Show all computations.

Boiler and
Machinery Losses

Boiler and machinery insurance is a complex type of coverage which affords protection against the risk of *accidental* damage to property arising out of *the operation and use of boilers, pressure vessels, mechanical and electrical machinery or apparatus*, all of which are known in policy language as *insured objects.* [1]

A high percentage of boiler and machinery insurance is written under forms and endorsements drafted and filed by larger insurers who specialize in this line, or under ISO forms and the SMP Endorsement MLB-400. While the basic structure or format of these policies is similar and much of the language is the same, the sequence, arrangement, and descriptive headings are optional with insurers.

Under the Businessowners policies, as an option, there is coverage for "Boiler, Pressure Vessels and Air Conditioning Equipment." Much of the language there also follows that of the fairly standardized policies mentioned above.

ENGINEERING AND INSPECTION SERVICE

All boiler and machinery insurance contracts, whether the SMP Endorsement, ISO Standard Forms, Businessowners Optional

Coverage, or policies drafted by individual insurers, contain the following two important conditions of identical or similar wording.

Inspection. The Company shall be permitted but not obligated to inspect, at all reasonable times, any Object designated and described in a schedule forming a part of the policy. Neither the Company's right to make inspections nor the making thereof nor any report thereon shall constitute an undertaking, on behalf of or for the benefit of the named insured or Others, to determine or warrant that such object is safe or healthful.

Suspension. Upon the discovery of a dangerous condition with respect to any Object, any representative of the Company may immediately suspend the insurance with respect to an Accident to said Object by written notice mailed or delivered to the Insured at the P.O. Address of the Insured as specified in the Declarations or at the location of the Object. Insurance so suspended may be reinstated by the Company but only by an endorsement issued to form a part of this endorsement. The Insured shall be allowed the unearned portion of the premium paid for such suspended insurance, pro rata, for the period of suspension.

A relatively small number of insurers underwrite the major share of boiler and machinery insurance on the so-called larger risks. The reason for this is that they have the capacity and the experience, and they main-

---

[1]Much of the material for this chapter was contributed by Harold R. S. Perdriau, retired Boiler and Machinery Officer, Kemper Insurance Group, and M. E. Verbeck, Vice President and Claim Manager of the same group.

tain a staff of skilled engineers and inspectors whose principal duties are to *prevent* losses.

Engineering and inspection service is an extremely important adjunct to a boiler and machinery insurance policy. Basically this service is concerned with the conservation of human life and physical property. Specifically it is concerned with the prevention of accidents, covered by the policy, which can be reduced or eliminated by the application of engineering knowledge and experience, and the prompt repair and replacement of damage resulting from accidents.

Most of the states and numerous municipalities have laws and regulations requiring periodic inspections of high-pressure power boilers by commissioned or licensed inspectors. Some of these same governmental authorities also require inspections of low-pressure heating boilers and specific types of pressure vessels. Insurance company engineers who have taken and passed national board and certain state examinations are commissioned as deputy inspectors of the states and municipalities in which they work. In most jurisdictions of this kind their inspections and reports are accepted in lieu of the fee inspections performed by government-employed inspectors. As a consequence, the policyholder does not have to pay these periodic fees.

Most boiler and machinery insurance companies also use their field inspectors as claim or loss investigators. This is usually advantageous in that the inspectors know the property and the operating people and are intimately familiar with the insured equipment. As a consequence, they frequently contribute greatly to getting damaged equipment back into service with a minimum of delay. When the time comes for claim settlement, the inspector's viewpoint is that of an informed engineer rather than the deductions of a claim adjuster.

OBJECTIVES OF THIS CHAPTER

An intimate knowledge of the insurance contract is essential in determining the extent of the insurer's liability and the amount of indemnity due the insured. In this chapter

the provisions, exclusions, and conditions that are found in most boiler and machinery policies are analyzed and discussed. Conditions and provisions that are common to most property insurance policies, such as *cancellation*, *subrogation*, and *assignment*, which are discussed in Chapter 3, are not elaborated on here. The trend is toward standardization, and while there is presently no standard policy form which, in itself, may be used as an exhibit, Appendix T is Kemper Insurance Companies' policy jacket. It is therefore important for claim representatives to obtain an exact copy of the policy form and all endorsements applicable to the particular risk under consideration.

BOILER AND MACHINERY POLICIES—PROVISIONS, EXCLUSIONS, AND CONDITIONS

A simple boiler and machinery policy consists of a minimum of three basic forms to make a complete contract: (1) a Policy Jacket, (2) a Declaration and Schedule Form, and (3) a Definitions and Special Provisions Endorsement. The Declaration and Schedule pages may be combined in one or may be two separate forms. The Definitions may be built into the endorsement along with the insuring agreement, conditions, and special provisions, as in the MLB-400 of the Special Multi-Peril Policy.

As previously mentioned, the sequence, arrangement, and descriptive headings may be different in policies, but in most cases similar provisions, exclusions, and conditions will be present because the very nature of the subject of insurance requires underwriters to include them.

THE INSURING AGREEMENT

The insuring agreement provides for payment of loss caused by *direct damage* to the property covered resulting from an *Accident* to a covered *Object while it is in use or connected ready for use* at the described location specified in the schedule.

A. Loss on Insured's Property

1. Actual Cash Value. To pay for loss on the insured's property directly damaged by an Accident (or if the insurer so elects, to repair or replace such damaged property). This includes the Object itself, its contents and all other property of the insured which is not specifically excluded. The loss under this provision is based on actual cash value, which contemplates a reasonable deduction for depreciation and is usually measured on the *life expectancy* of the Object and other involved property. (See Property Valuation on page 216.)

2. Repair or Replacement. Some policies provide for *optional* coverage on repair or replacement, which may be found under this section or as a separate condition, as in the MLB-400. The provision is similar to the repair or replacement coverage in other property insurance policies.[2]

B. Expediting Expenses

This coverage provides for payment of the reasonable extra cost of temporary repairs and for expediting repairs. The latter may include overtime labor, and express or airfreight if necessary to speed up returning damaged property to service. The limit for such expediting is $1,000. Some policies provide for higher limits by endorsement for an additional premium.

C. Property Damage Liability

This covers losses the insured becomes obligated to pay by reason of liability to others for property directly damaged or for loss of use of the damaged property. This coverage is limited to the extent of any indemnity remaining after payment of all loss to the insured's property including expediting expenses.

D. Bodily Injury Liability

Bodily injury liability coverage is optional and not included in most boiler and machinery policies. It duplicates public liability and workmen's compensation insurance.

[2]See.p. 205.

The coverage protects the insured against claims of bodily injury, sickness or disease, including death for which the insured would be legally liable as a result of an Accident to a covered Object. This coverage is excess over any other valid and collectible insurance.

The coverage provides for immediate medical and surgical relief rendered at the time of accident irrespective of the limit per Accident. No coverage is provided to employees covered by a workmen's compensation law, unemployment compensation, or disability benefits law, or any other similar laws.

E. Defense, Settlement, Supplemental Payments

This coverage agrees to defend the insured against claim or suit alleging liability under Property Damage Liability coverage, and also if Bodily Injury Liability coverage is carried and included in the policy.

F. Automatic Coverage

Subject to written notice from insured to insurer within 90 days, coverage is provided on any *similar* Object which is newly installed at any location specified in the policy or which is located at any new location acquired by the insured. If the policy does not cover any Objects *similar* to the one in question, no coverage is provided for the one newly installed.

Losses Payable on Coverages in Sequential Order

A single limit per Accident is specified for each location and is available in full for each direct damage Accident that occurs during the policy term, without charge for reinstatement.

However, it is essential for the claim representative to understand that each coverage agrees to pay *to the extent of any indemnity remaining after payment of all loss as may be required under the preceding coverages* excluding "Automatic Coverage." Therefore, the limit per Accident should be set high enough to provide for all exposures.

A policy with a limit of $250,000 per Accident would pay for an *accumulated* loss of $350,000 as shown in Example 15-1.

EXAMPLE 15-1

Coverage	Loss	Policy Payments
A(1)	$200,000	$200,000
A(2)	25,000	25,000
B	2,500	1,000
C	100,000	24,000
D	22,500	0
	$350,000	$250,000

EXCLUSIONS

The following are exclusions from coverage for a loss from an Accident resulting directly or indirectly from the causes below.

1. The usual hostile and warlike action exclusion.
2. The usual nuclear reaction exclusion.
3. The usual ordinances or laws regulating construction exclusion.
4. a. Exclusion from coverages A and B of fire damage resulting from an Accident whether concomitant with or following the Accident or from water or other means used to extinguish the fire.

   b. Exclusion of loss from an Accident caused *directly* or *indirectly* by fire. Flames and heat from a fire can cause an accident as defined under the boiler and machinery policy. Water used by firemen or from automatic sprinklers during a fire can also result in an Accident to an Object. This exclusion places such losses outside the policy and on any fire insurance policies.

   c. Exclusion of a "combustion" explosion *outside* the Object even though caused by an Accident. Despite precise wording, much controversy has centered about this exclusion. This is especially true when a Boiler or similar Fired Vessel was involved and the

fire and boiler and machinery insurance were issued by individual insurers. The disagreement generally is the result of incorrectly interpreting the definition of Object in the boiler policy.

   d. Exclusion of loss resulting from an Accident which is caused directly or indirectly by a combustion explosion outside the Object.

   e. Exclusion of loss from flood unless an Accident ensues, and then coverage extends only for the damage caused by the ensuing Accident.

   f. Exclusion of loss resulting from delay or interruption of business or manufacturing process. This is classified as an Indirect Damage. Coverage is available for this type of loss by various endorsements such as Actual Loss Sustained, and Valued Daily Indemnity.

   g. Exclusion of loss from lack of power, light, heat, steam, or refrigeration. In contrast to fire policies, the boiler and machinery policy is unique in this exclusion. An Accident to an Object could result in spoilage of goods in process or storage, such as solidification of fluid materials in the course of manufacture, deterioration of foods, etc. Coverage can be added by a Consequential Damage Endorsement or Refrigeration Interruption Endorsement.

   h. Exclusion of any other indirect loss as a result of an Accident, not specifically mentioned.

CONDITIONS

1. Notice of Accident and Adjustment

The insured is required to give notice of Accident as soon as practicable, either to the insurer or any of its authorized agents. The insurer should be given an opportunity to examine the premises before repairs are undertaken or physical evidence removed (except for protection of property from further damage). Insured is required to notify the insurer of any liability claims and forward to the insurer any notice of suit or summons. Proof of loss shall be made by the insured in a manner prescribed by the insurer.

In event of disagreement on amount of loss, provision is made for a formal appraisal as in other property policies (see Chapter 6).

2. Inspection

For a full treatment of inspection, see page 212.

3. Suspension

The subject of suspension is covered fully on page 212.

4. Limit Per Accident

The insurer's liability shall not exceed the "limit per Accident." The term "one Accident" includes all resultant or concomitant Accidents whether to one or more Objects. In other words, if one Accident sets in motion other Accidents in a chain reaction, the entire resulting damage is "one Accident."

5. Property Valuation

This follows basic property policies in stating that the insurer's liability is limited to the actual cash value of repairs or replacement with proper deduction for depreciation however caused.[3]

Repair or replacement cost is discussed under the insuring agreement.[4]

6. Other Insurance—Property

As with other property policies, this condition spells out the liability under the boiler and machinery policy where other insurance exists. Conflicts between fire and boiler policies are usually resolved under the Guiding Principles (Chapter 27).

7. Other Insurance—Liability

As respects the liability coverage for *property of others* and *bodily injury*, the boiler and machinery policy is excess over any other valid and collectible insurance.

8. Cancellation

This condition is similar to the cancellation provisions in other property policies and states how cancellation is effected by insured or insurer.[5]

9. Subrogation

This condition is similar in all respects to those in other property policies.[6]

10. Action Against Company—Property Coverages

No action shall lie against the insurer unless the insured

a. Has complied with all policy terms, and
b. Has filed a claim within 14 months from date of Accident.

11. Action Against Company—Liability Coverages

No action shall lie against the insurer unless

a. Insured has complied with all policy terms.
b. The amount of the insured's obligation has been determined by judgment, trial, or by written agreement of insured, claimant, and insurer.

Any person or organization who has secured such judgment or written agreement shall be entitled to recover under the policy to the extent of insurance accorded by the policy.

12. Assignment

Similar to other property policies.

13. Changes

Similar to other property policies.

14. Premium Gradation

Not relevant to claims.

15. Schedules

Insurance under the policy applies only to losses from an Accident as defined, to an

---

[3]See p. 182, for a discussion of actual cash value of buildings, including the attitude of the courts; see p. 241, for a similar discussion on machinery and fixtures.
[4]See p. 214.

[5]For a discussion of the problems in cancellation, see p. 95.
[6]See Chap. 9, "Subrogation Possibilities."

Object designated and described in a Schedule forming a part of the policy.

16. Malicious Mischief

Subject to exclusion 1 (hostile and warlike action), any Accident, as defined in any schedule, arising out of strike, riot, civil commotion, acts of sabotage, vandalism, or malicious mischief, shall be considered "accidental" within the terms of said definition.

17. Blanket Group Plan

This is a policy arrangement under which certain kinds or classes of Objects may be insured under group descriptions without specifically describing each such Object.

DECLARATIONS

The Declarations Form is made a part of the policy and contains information pertinent to the insurance contract, such as name and address of the insured; policy number and period; premium, limit per Accident, schedules and endorsements, and name of the producer.

SCHEDULES

In some boiler and machinery policies the Schedule and Declarations are combined into one form. In others, there is an individual schedule for each coverage or endorsement. These schedules become part of the policy also. Each is numbered, shows the policy number, inception date of the Schedule, and the name of the insured, and it lists each Object covered, describing and identifying it and stating the location.

Importance of Declarations and Schedules

Because they are an integral part of a boiler and machinery policy, Declarations and Schedules must be checked by the claim representative to be certain that the information is accurate and that the Object is properly described and covered.

DEFINITIONS AND SPECIAL PROVISIONS
ENDORSEMENTS—DIRECT DAMAGE

To complete a boiler and machinery policy, it is necessary to attach one or more schedules or endorsements which define an Accident and the Object(s) covered under the policy. Because of the variety of boilers, turbines, machinery and equipment employed in different types of mercantile and manufacturing occupancies, schedules or endorsements have been designed to give insureds an adequate selection from which to choose the proper insurance program to meet their individual requirements. Some insurers provide endorsements for specific Objects covered; others make available endorsements with various *groups of Objects* from which coverage may be selected.

More and more boiler and machinery policies are becoming standardized as to coverage, definitions, and special provisions. The following discussion is based on what are generally considered standard forms.

Schedules and endorsements contain a Definition of Accident, a Definition of the Object, and Special Provisions applicable to all classes of equipment that are covered under the policy. They are also the basis for any Indirect Damage coverage that may be endorsed on the policy.

DEFINITION OF *ACCIDENT*

Except for optional restricted or limited definitions which are available for boilers and turbines, one comprehensive standard definition applies to *all Objects*. Subject to *exclusions* applicable to each covered Object, this definition states:

> Accident shall mean a sudden and accidental breakdown of the Object, or a part thereof, which manifests itself at the time of its occurrence by physical damage to the Object that necessitates repair or replacement of the Object or part thereof.

The claim representative should apply the test of *what, where, when,* and *how* in order to be certain that the occurrence qualifies as an Accident under this definition.

What	A sudden and accidental breakdown (one unforeseen and unexpected)
Where	of the Object or part thereof
When	which manifests itself at the time of its occurrence (is plainly apparent to sight, distinct and clearly evident at the time of the breakdown)
How	by physical damage to the Object that necessitates repair or replacement of the Object or part thereof. (Destruction, impairment, injury or harm has been done or is sustained of sufficient amount or extent that repair or replacement of the Object or part thereof is necessary to restore it to use.)

This definition of accident is completed by a listing of essential exclusions which relate to the types of Objects covered under the policy. The following exclusions to the definition of Accident are common to most endorsements though there may be others. These exclusions mean that the conditions described are not in themselves *Accidents*.

1. Depletion, deterioration, corrosion, or erosion of material.
2. Wear and tear.
3. Leakage at any valve, fitting, shaft seal, gland packing, joint or connection.
4. The breakdown of any vacuum tube, gas tube or brush.
5. The breakdown of any electronic computer or electronic data processing equipment.
6. The breakdown of any structure or foundation supporting the Object or any part thereof.
7. An explosion of gas or unconsumed fuel within the furnace of any Object or within the passages from the furnace of said Object to the atmosphere.
8. The functioning of any safety device or protective device.

The foregoing exclusions are self-explanatory. Their purpose, in general, is to eliminate from coverage losses that can be anticipated, are not sudden and accidental, and which are caused by ordinary use, lapse of time, or the effects of operating elements, and involve items that have normally a short life expectancy.

In respect to Limited coverage on Boilers, Fired Vessels, and Electric Steam Generators the following applies:

Accident shall mean a sudden and accidental tearing asunder of the Object, or a part thereof, caused by the pressure of water or steam therein, but cracking shall not constitute a sudden and accidental tearing asunder, nor shall accident mean

a. depletion, deterioration, corrosion, or erosion of material;
b. wear and tear;
c. leakage of any valve, fitting, joint or connection;
d. an explosion of gas or unconsumed fuel within the furnace of any Object or within the passages from the furnace of said Object to the atmosphere; nor
e. the functioning of any safety device or protective device.

DEFINITION OF *OBJECT*

Each type of Object that is covered under a boiler and machinery policy is precisely defined both as to *what it includes* and *what it does not include*. It is as important for the claim representative to thoroughly understand the policy definition of an Object as it is to understand the definition of an Accident. These definitions will be readily understood by those who are familiar with the Objects, such as the insurer's loss control representatives or professional engineers. If the claim representative is not familiar with the Object involved, the definition in the policy may have little meaning. If that is the case, a consultant should be brought in without hesitation.

SPECIAL PROVISIONS

The following special provisions where applicable will be found in the endorsement:

1. There is no liability for loss from an Accident to a pressure Object (boiler or vessel) while it is undergoing a pressure test.

2. There is no liability for loss from an Accident to an electrical Object while it is undergoing an insulation breakdown test or is being dried out.
3. There is no liability for an explosion in the furnace of chemical recovery boiler regardless of the cause.
4. As respects mechanical and electrical Objects there is no liability while the Object, or part thereof, is being removed, installed, repaired or dried out.
5. As respects electrical Objects the fire exclusion has been amended to include liability for fire within the confines of the Object itself.
6. If a boiler, fired vessel or electric steam generator uses a heat transfer medium other than water, the name of such heat transfer medium and its vapor are substituted for the words "water" and "steam" wherever they appear in the definitions.

Furnace Explosion Coverage

Under the Definition of Accident (7), *an explosion of gas or unconsumed fuel within the furnace or within the passages from the furnace to the atmosphere is not covered.* Coverage *is* available by endorsement. Because of possible overlapping of this coverage with another property insurance policy, the claim representative should be alert to a possible joint-loss situation.

Ammonia Contamination Limit—Water Damage Limit

Under Systems of Refrigerating and Air Conditioning, Vessels and Piping, coverage provides:

1. A limit of $1,000 for loss caused by ammonia contacting or permeating property under refrigeration or process from any one Accident.
2. A limit of $1,000 for loss on property damaged by water from the system from any one Accident.

The limits are part of the limit per Accident in the policy. They may be increased by endorsement.

Object Limit

This provision is self-explanatory and applies only to damage which is confined to the Object itself.

Coinsurance

This is the only coinsurance provision in the boiler and machinery policy applicable to direct damage. It states that the insurer shall not be liable for a greater proportion of any loss on such an Object than the Object Limit specified bears to the amount determined by applying the coinsurance percentage to the actual cash value of the Object at the time the Accident occurs.

As with the Object Limit, the provision applies only to damage which is confined to the Object itself. If the Object was damaged by an Accident caused by another covered Object, such as the breakdown of a turbine, the provisions (Object Limit and Coinsurance) would not apply.

OTHER ENDORSEMENTS APPLICABLE TO DIRECT DAMAGE

There are many standard and nonstandard endorsements with special provisions modifying the direct damage coverages. The claim representative of the insurer should check the policy carefully for such endorsements.

Some of the more common of these endorsements encountered and which are self-explanatory to an experienced claim representative are:

Loss Payable or Mortgage Interest
Multiple Interest
Deductible Insurance
Explosion Loss Exclusion
Lightning Loss Exclusion
Non-Ownership Explosion

ENDORSEMENTS PROVIDING INDIRECT DAMAGE COVERAGE

All coverages described up to now have involved insurance providing indemnity for loss to *tangible* property caused *directly* by an Accident.

In the majority of Accidents under boiler and machinery policies, loss is seldom confined to real and personal property. Loss of income from goods and services that cannot be produced or sold; spoilage of goods from lack of heat, power or refrigeration; or increased operating expenses incurred by the use of less efficient auxiliary equipment often create financial losses greater than the loss to the Object itself and to the surrounding property.

There are a number of endorsements that can be attached to the boiler and machinery policy to provide coverage for these indirect losses. Some of those more commonly used are briefly discussed below.

Use and Occupancy (Valued Form)

The Valued Form is found most often on smaller business risks where operations are dependent on one or two pieces of equipment. The form is also recognized for ease in measuring loss as it provides for a fixed maximum daily indemnity amount for the risk—for example, $5,000 per day. All reimbursable loss under the endorsement must be *directly related to the business* of the insured, which is specified at the time coverage is written. The categories include production, sales, rent, and income.

Deductibles. The endorsement can be written to become effective at the time of Accident or it can be written with a deductible. There are two types of deductible clauses.

1. Deferred Midnight—liability begins at a specified midnight which follows Notice of Loss being received by the insurer. The Third Midnight is frequently used.
2. Dollar Amount—this is a flat dollar amount deductible. It is not unusual to see deductibles of $25,000 to $100,000 on large risks.

Insuring Agreement. In consideration of the premium and subject to the exclusions and the conditions of the endorsement, the insurer agrees:

1. To pay the amount of the specified daily indemnity for each day of total prevention of business.
2. To pay part of the daily indemnity for each day of partial prevention of business.
3. To pay expenses reasonably incurred by the insured to reduce or minimize the loss, but only to the extent the whole loss under the endorsement is reduced.

Exclusions. There is no liability for payment of any loss or expense

1. Resulting from an Accident to which exclusions 1, 2 and 3 or subparagraphs (a), (b), (c), (d) and (e) of exclusion 4 in the policy jacket apply.
2. For any time for which the business would not or could not have been carried on had there been no Accident (for example: Sundays and legal holidays); and
3. Resulting from insured's failure to use due diligence and dispatch and all reasonable means in order to resume business.

Notice of Accident. Specific instructions are given insured for notifying insurer.

Commencement of Liability. Commencement of liability is dependent upon receipt of *prompt* notice by insurer, and there is no liability to pay for any loss period *prior to 24 hours* before notification.

Definitions.
Day—A period of 24 hours beginning at midnight.
Business:
  Production—Manufacturing on the premises of a finished product ready for packing, shipment, or sale.
  Sales—Gross sales on the premises.
  Rents—Rents that would be collectible from the premises.
  Income—Gross income on the premises.

The following definitions provide the essential key for measuring the amount collectible under the Valued Form Endorsement.

Current Business—One-third of the total business during the three days next preceding the date of loss, or during any three days selected by the insured in any calendar week in the eight calendar weeks preceding the date of loss.

Total Prevention of Business—Prevention of all business on the premises during all of a day.

Reduction of Business—The amount determined by subtracting the amount of total business on the premises for each day following the Accident from the amount of current business.

Partial Prevention of Business—The decrease in business on the premises during part or all of a day, sufficient to make the total business for said day less than current business. The ratio of the *Reduction of Business* to *Current Business* gives the percentage of loss. The percentage of loss multiplied by the daily indemnity would be the loss recoverable under the Valued Form Endorsement.

Measurement of Loss. If there is a total prevention of business, the daily indemnity is paid in full for each such day.

If there is a partial prevention of business, the amount to be paid is determined by applying the following formula:

$$CB - B = RB$$
$$RB \div CB = \% R$$
$$\% R \times DI = \text{Daily Payment}$$

Where:

CB = Current Business
B = Business (Production, Sales, Rents, and Income)
RB = Reduction in Business
$\% R$ = Percentage of Reduction
DI = Daily Indemnity

Reduction of Payment. This condition requires the insured to resume business, in whole or in part, as soon as possible, and to utilize every available means including other machinery, equipment or parts, supplies, reserve stock, etc., which might reduce the loss. The insurer may take measures to reduce or avert loss. All expenses so incurred by the insured are reimbursable as permitted under Section 3 of the Insuring Agreement or by written direction of the insurer. They shall be part of but not in addition to the limit of loss.

Daily indemnity seldom compensates an insured exactly. A business with peaks and lows in sales or production may, depending on when the Accident occurs, recover more or less than the actual loss sustained.

Use and Occupancy (Actual Loss Sustained Form)

This endorsement is the same in most respects as the Valued Form except that recovery by the insured is based on the actual loss sustained instead of on a daily indemnity.

Actual loss sustained is defined, under "Definitions," as

a. Loss of net profits on the Business prevented and

b. That part of the following fixed charges and expenses which the Business did not earn because of an Accident, but which the Business would have earned had the Accident not occurred:

1. Salaries and wages of officers, executives, employees under contract and other essential employees, pensions and directors' fees, but not including the Insured's ordinary payroll expense, and

2. Manufacturing, selling, administrative expenses and any other items contributing to the overhead expenses of the Insured; but due consideration shall be given to the Business before the Accident and probable experience thereafter.

Note: Ordinary Payroll may be covered by Endorsement.

Reports of Values. The insured is required to file an annual Report of Values on which the amount of insurance or limit of loss is based.

Coinsurance. If a Coinsurance Clause is inserted in the endorsement, the insurer's liability is limited to that proportion of the actual loss sustained which the limit of loss bears to the product of

1. The insured's estimated earnings for the 12 months immediately following the loss.
2. The coinsurance percentage if one is specified.
3. The number of days in the rating period if specified for the Object.

Actual Loss Sustained Versus Business Interruption. The Actual Loss Sustained Endorsement is similar in most respects to the Gross Earnings Business Interruption Forms used in fire and allied lines policies. The principal differences will be found in the subjects of insurance and perils (Accidents) insured against. For measuring the amount of loss, the reader is referred to Chapter 25 for a complete discussion of business interruption losses.

Consequential Damage Endorsement

This endorsement restores Policy Jacket Exclusion 4 (g), "loss from lack of power, light, heat, steam or refrigeration resulting from an Accident." Under this coverage the insured must specify

1. Premises (description and location).
2. Limit of liability.
3. Specified property (whether owned by the insured or by others, shall mean only . . .).
4. Coinsurance percentage (100, 80, 50 or 25 percent).
5. Schedules and section numbers of the policy.

Item 3 might be filled in by an overall statement, such as "all products in process or cold storage"; or simply "fruit in storage" depending on the kind of *spoilage* exposure on the premises.

Item 5 requires that Schedules and Definitions in the basic policy be designated.

Insuring Agreement. Subject to premium, exclusions, and conditions of the endorsement, the insurer agrees

1. To pay the insured the amount of loss on specified property of the insured.

2. To pay the amount of loss on specified property of others which the insured may become obligated to pay by reason of the liability of the insured for such loss.
3. To pay the amount of expense which is reasonably incurred by the insured or the insurer to reduce or avert such loss, but only to the extent that the total amount, which otherwise would have been paid under (1) and (2) of this agreement, is thereby reduced.

Limits of Liability. The insurer is liable only for the actual cash value of the specified property of the insured, and *total liability* for any one Accident shall not exceed the amount specified as limit of liability in the endorsement.

Defense of Claims or Suits. This condition is similar to that in the Policy Jacket and in other endorsements where the insured's liability is included in the coverage.

Measurement of Loss. To determine the loss under this endorsement, the claim representative must establish two values:

1. Actual cash value (ACV) of the specified property that spoiled.
2. Actual cash value (ACV) of all specified property covered on the premises at the time of Accident.

If the limit of liability is equal to or greater than the product of the coinsurance percentage multiplied by (2) above, the insured collects the full loss. Otherwise, the application of the coinsurance will establish the insurer's liability.

$$\frac{\text{Limit of liability}}{\text{Coins. \% × Total value}} \times \text{Loss} = \text{Collectible loss}$$

For example:

Limit of liability	$100,000
Total ACV of specified property	$400,000
ACV of damaged specified property	$ 10,000
Coinsurance percentage	50%

$$\frac{\$100,000}{50\% \times \$400,000} \times \$10,000 = \$5,000$$

The insured contributes $5,000 by reason of carrying an insufficient amount of insurance.

Business Interruption Insurance

There are two business interruption forms available under boiler and machinery. One is the Gross Earnings Contribution or Coinsurance Form; the other the Two Item Contribution or Coinsurance Form (see Chapter 25).

CLAIM-HANDLING PROCEDURES

More boiler and machinery losses are handled by the insurer's staff claim representatives and loss control representatives than by independent adjusters. There are several reasons for this:

1. Coverages and terminology in many cases are foreign to the average independent adjuster.
2. The subjects of insurance (Objects) require some mechanical engineering knowledge of their function and inner working parts.
3. Insurers who underwrite any quantity of boiler and machinery coverage employ their own inspectors and engineers who are readily available either to personally adjust a loss or act as consultants to staff claim representatives. Consequently adjustment expense is generally less.

As more boiler and machinery insurance is written covering smaller risks that have only one or two Objects to cover, such as might be the case under Businessowners Policies, the availability of qualified independent adjusters is being considered by insurers.

Investigation Checklist

Claim representatives should review Chapter 7, "Investigation of the Insured, the Property, and the Insurance"; also Chapter 8, "Verifying Cause of Loss." Many of the principles and fundamentals employed in investigating other types of property losses are equally applicable to boiler and machinery claims. The following brief checklist may be found useful to claim representatives.

1. Verification of coverage
   a. Secure the original policy with all schedules, declaration and endorsements; obtain copies or verify through the insurer.
   b. Is a covered Object involved? Get full description. Does the Object meet the policy definition? Have you read and checked all exclusions?
   c. What was the nature of the Accident? Details? Does the Accident accord with the definition? Have you read and checked all exclusions?
   d. Has any municipal, state, or federal agency made an investigation? Is their report available?
   e. When did the Accident occur? Date? Time? Was it within the policy period?
   f. Where did the Accident occur? Describe location. Was it on premises covered by the policy?
2. Questionable coverage or liability
   a. Is there reason to question coverage for the loss or liability of the insurer?
   b. Should written statements be taken? Photographs? Sketches?
   c. Is there reason to preserve evidence?[7]
   d. Should the insurer's engineer, an outside engineer, or other expert be brought in for consultation?
   e. Is the Object involved still under warranty?
   f. Has insured been fully briefed on any questionable coverage? Should insured be notified in writing? Should a nonwaiver be taken?[8]
3. Possibilities of Subrogation
   a. Did the Accident occur through the negligence of a third party such as:
      (1) Workers (not insured's employees) repairing or installing Object, machinery, piping, etc.?

[7]See p. 129.
[8]See Appendix L.

(2) Workers on building—roofer, painter, electrician, plumber, etc.?

(3) Defective installation or repair of equipment by outside firm?

4. Direct Loss. (For a discussion of the investigation and evaluation of real and personal property losses, see Chapters 14, 16, 17 and 19. For determining amount of loss from insured's books and records, see Chapter 20.)

   a. Does policy cover for actual cash value? If so, is depreciation from wear and tear and obsolescence being considered?

   b. If policy covers for repair or replacement, see Chapter 14[9] for handling this coverage.

   c. Has insured started or completed repair or replacement before first inspection by insurer? Have careful records of labor, material, etc., been kept?

   d. Salvage—see Chapter 19.

5. Indirect Loss. Has the policy been endorsed to cover Use and Occupancy, Business Interruption, Consequential Damage, or any other Indirect Loss?

   a. Is everything being done to expedite getting insured back into business— either partially or wholly?

   b. Is there a standby or spare Object available?

   c. Are spare parts on hand for repairs?

   d. Can repairs or replacements be expedited by use of overtime, fast freight, or air express?

   e. Is substitute equipment available?

   f. Does insured have goods on hand to continue operating or filling orders?

   g. Has reasonable use of extra expense been considered to reduce or avert loss?

6. Is there a deductible?

7. Are there limiting clauses or conditions?

   a. Limit of Liability.

   b. Coinsurance or Contribution.

8. Is there a Loss Payable or Mortgagee Clause?

[9]See p. 205.

Liability Claims

Claims made by third parties for either bodily injury or property damage must be investigated with considerable care without committing the insurer. The insured should likewise be cautioned not to make any commitments. Except in all but minor cases, the insurer should be notified immediately of the circumstances and the claim representative should seek instructions.

Other Insurance—Joint Losses

Where other insurance exists which might contribute to the loss with the boiler and machinery insurance, the claim representative should obtain a copy of the *other* insurance policy. Most cases of *other* insurance overlapping boiler and machinery insurance will involve the perils of *explosion, lightning,* and *sprinkler leakage.* A few instances arise when both policies insure against direct loss to refrigeration lines and systems, or direct loss from molten material accidentally discharged from equipment. The chance of losses caused by *fire* overlapping with boiler and machinery insurance has been almost eliminated by two exclusions, 4(a) and 4(b), in the boiler and machinery policy. The exclusions apply to coverages A and B.[10] Also, the boiler and machinery policies endeavor to eliminate overlapping coverage for combustion explosions in furnaces by exclusions 4(c) and 4(d).[11] The coverage is available, however, by endorsement.[12]

Where overlapping coverages do exist they are treated as *joint losses* and apportioned in accord with the Guiding Principles (Chapter 27) by subscribing insurers or by nonsubscribing insurers who, by custom and practice, abide by the Guiding Principles. The rare occasions of nonsubscribers refusing to follow the Guiding Principles are generally resolved either by the terms of the other insurance clauses in each policy or by compromise. Claim representatives must be thoroughly familiar with the coverages as

[10]See p. 214.
[11]See p. 215.
[12]See Furnace Explosion Coverage, p. 219.

well as the exclusions in the policy or policies they represent. Other policies of the insured which are suspected of being contributors to the loss should be examined by the claim representative personally rather than making assumptions or taking for granted the statements of others.

QUESTIONS AND PROBLEMS

1. Discuss briefly the authority for and purpose of engineering and inspection service provided by insurers. Who benefits and how do they benefit?

2. In addition to the inspection provision there is a suspension provision.

    a. Under what circumstances can the insurance be suspended?

    b. Who may suspend the insurance?

    c. How is suspension effected?

    d. How is the suspension reinstated?

3. Boiler and machinery policies insure against risk of loss caused by direct damage to property covered which results from an Accident to a covered Object while connected and ready for use.

    a. Give a comprehensive definition of Accident as it might apply to practically all Objects excluding limited coverage on boilers, fired vessels, and electric steam generators.

    b. There are a number of common exclusions to the definition of Accident that are found on most endorsements. State four such exclusions.

    c. What purpose is served by these exclusions?

4. During a fire in a plant the automatic sprinklers operated. Water from the sprinklers damaged a machine, resulting in an Accident to the Object. Discuss whether or not the damage to the Object is covered and give reasons for your answer.

5. Under a boiler and machinery policy an Accident occurs to an Object, resulting in loss of refrigeration in the warehouse containing frozen foods. The loss to the contents is considerable. Would there be coverage? Explain your answer. Compare this coverage with a property insurance policy covering the peril of fire.

6. A sprinkler head opens as a result of a defect, causing an Accident to a covered Object. Would the boiler and machinery policy provide coverage for the damage to the Object? Explain.

7. A boiler and machinery policy provides for a "limit per Accident" of $100,000. A boiler explodes, setting off an explosion in a second boiler. The loss from both explosions is $150,000. Is this loss the result of two accidents? How much would the boiler and machinery policy be liable for, disregarding deductibles?

8. Strikers rioting in a plant cause an Accident to an Object. Would you consider this to be an Accident under the boiler and machinery policy?

9. Discuss the terms *direct damage* and *indirect damage* as used in boiler and machinery policies.

10. Under the Use and Occupancy Endorsements and other "time element" coverages, commencement of liability is contingent upon arrival of notice of Accident at the insurer's home office. Sometimes notice to an authorized representative, such as the loss control engineer, is acceptable though not in compliance with policy provisions.

If the commencement of liability is stated as determined with respect to "time of accident," there is no liability to pay for any loss period prior to 24 hours before notification. What is the "deferred midnight" deductible? How does it operate?

11. Under a Use and Occupancy Valued Form, the daily indemnity is $1,000. The current business is determined to be $1,500 (actual daily business based on one-third of the three days of business selected by the insured).

At 8 A.M. on a Wednesday the insurer received notice that an Accident took place on Monday at 8 A.M. Commencement of Liability is stated to begin with respect to "time of accident."

Repairs were completed Thursday night and the insured was back in full production Friday morning: Monday, Tuesday, and Wednesday there was total prevention of business. On Thursday the plant did $300 in business.

On these facts what should the boiler and machinery policy pay?

12. Under a Consequential Loss Endorsement the actual cash value of damaged specified property consisting of bananas is $24,000. The limit of liability under the Endorsement for Specified Property is $200,000.

An inventory of all specified property covered is determined to be $375,000. The coinsurance is 80 percent. Compute the insurer's liability.

Personal Property in Use

Personal property is, "in a general sense, everything that is subject to ownership, not coming under domination of real estate. . . . The term is generally applied to property of a personal or movable nature as opposed to property of a local or immovable character such as land or houses, the latter being called real property."[1]

Personal property is considered by underwriters and adjusters to fall into two general categories: (1) *personal property in use* and (2) *stocks of merchandise*.[2] Personal property in use, hereafter referred to as *personal property*, is encountered by the claim representative as specifically described articles or objects, or as specifically described *groups* or *classes* of articles or objects.

Examples of specifically described articles or objects, covered for a specified amount of insurance in a policy, are pieces of jewelry, fur coats, cameras, antiques, art objects, and special types of machines or equipment.

Household furnishings, apparel, equipment and supplies, furniture and fixtures, machinery, and contents of libraries, schools, and churches are also examples of groups of articles covered for a specified amount of insurance.

PERSONAL PROPERTY AS A SUBJECT OF INSURANCE

Personal property is a subject of insurance from the time the raw materials are removed from the earth, while they are being processed and made into finished products,

when they are being stored or transported, when they are being sold or used, and until they are destroyed or made valueless.

Descriptions of personal property vary with the particular form, the occupancy, and the kind of property covered. The description may be quite broad as in the Standard Businessowners Policy which basically *covers replacement cost of the business personal property owned by the insured, usual to the occupancy of the insured*; or as in the HPR and Superior Risk forms which basically cover *personal property of the insured*. Other forms, such as FGP-1 (General Property Form) and Form 18 (Building and Contents Form), are much more detailed in their description.

The description of personal property may be qualified to fit the occupancy, as in a Homeowners policy (ed. 9-70) covering "unscheduled personal property usual or incidental to the occupancy of the premises as a dwelling, owned, or used by an insured." Under the SMP Policy the description of personal property is principally "only business personal property owned by the insured and usual to the occupancy of the insured."

The Office Contents Special Form covers those items "common to office occupancy."

Scheduled property floaters cover specifically described articles or objects for a specified amount of insurance.

PROCEDURE

The procedure for adjusting *all* personal property losses[3] includes (1) getting the in-

---

[1]*Black's Law Dictionary.*
[2]Personal property held for sale or in process of manufacture.

[3]See also Work of the Insurer's Claim Representative, p. 5.

sured's story, (2) identifying the property and checking coverage, (3) establishing interests, (4) examining the property and surveying the situation, (5) investigating the cause of the loss,[4] (6) protecting the property from further damage, (7) separating damaged from undamaged property and putting it in order, (8) saving endangered property or recovering lost property, (9) choosing a method of adjustment,[5] (10) preparing for discussing value and loss, (11) checking the insured's claim, (12) negotiating the adjustment,[6] and (13) preparing final papers. These procedures have been discussed in previous chapters, some of them in considerable detail. They will be examined in this section only insofar as there is a specific application to personal property in use.

I. The property.
   A. Possibility of examination
      1. Is the property on which the insured will make claim in evidence and in such condition that it can be correctly inventoried?
      2. If it is, are all the articles accessible and can their condition be determined by examining them where they are and as they are, or must they be moved, separated, unpacked, or disassembled before examination will be possible?
      3. If the property is not in evidence, are there any physical remains, or is there anything in the appearance of the space or the location where the insured says it was last seen that indicates its existence before the loss?
      4. If it is in evidence but in such condition that it cannot be inventoried, can identity or quantity be approximated by weighing or measuring?
   B. Cause of loss.
      1. What signs are shown by the property indicating that damage was caused by a peril insured against? By a peril not insured against?
      2. Are there indications of previous damage?
      3. Are there indications of intentional damage?
   C. Extent of damage.
      1. What articles are obviously a total loss?
      2. What articles are seriously damaged?
      3. What articles are slightly damaged?
      4. Are any articles undamaged?
   D. Depreciation.
      What indications are there of the age of the property and of its care or lack of care? Of obsolescence?
   E. Probable value and loss
      1. What is the probable value of all property covered by the policies?
      2. What is the probable amount of loss?
II. The premises.
   A. Are there potential liability claims as a result of the occurrence?[7]
   B. What is the condition of the premises? Do they offer safety, space, and facilities for handling the property?
   C. Does their condition indicate cause of loss?
III. The environment.
   A. Is there anything in the environment of the premises and property indicating cause of loss?
   B. Is there anything in the environment that has tended to cause the property to depreciate?
IV. Plans for protecting and handling the property.
   A. Should anything be done to the premises to make them safe to work in while protecting the property?
   B. Should anything be done to the premises to protect the property?
   C. Should the property or any part of it be moved elsewhere for protection?
   D. Should the premises, debris, or site be searched for missing articles?

[4]See Chap. 8, "Verifying Cause of Loss."
[5]See p. 9.
[6]See Chap, 12, "Negotiations."

[7]An important consideration under multiple-line policies covering the insured's legal liability.

E. Should articles moved from the premises be traced?

F. Is any work necessary to make articles that are worth saving accessible?

G. How should the articles be treated to protect them from further damage?

H. How should separation and putting in order be done?

I. Are there articles that, because of ownership or interest, should be separated from the rest?

J. Is there debris that should be held as evidence until inventory is completed and loss agreed upon?

K. Should immediate plans be made to repair the property in place or send it out for repair?

V. Plans for inventory.

A. How should counting, weighing, or measuring of property and describing and pricing of inventory be done?

B. What is the possibility of accurate valuation of the articles and estimate of damage?

C. Should an expert be employed to help with the inventory?

D. Should the inventory be made jointly by the insured and the claim representative or by representatives of either?

E. Should undamaged property be inventoried?

VI. Developing and recording evidence.

A. What records of the acquisition or operation of the property are available?

B. Is there any appraisal of the property?

C. Should witnesses be interviewed and their statements taken?

D. Should photographs be made?

E. Should the style, model, or serial numbers or other identifying marks of any articles be recorded by copying or by making a rubbing?

F. Should measurements or sketches of the premises be made, or should the debris be weighed, counted, or measured for proof or indication of quantities?

RESIDENTIAL PERSONAL PROPERTY

The usual articles found in a residence may be described under policies as "household and personal property" or, as in most Homeowners policies, as "personal property usual or incidental to the occupancy of the premises as a dwelling, owned, or used by the insured." It usually distinguishes itself as personal property of a nonbusiness character even though under some forms certain business property may be covered by reason of not being excluded.[8]

Such property is encountered in dwellings, in apartments, in privately furnished hotel suites, in summer cottages, in transit, in storage, and occasionally elsewhere. Under all forms certain property is excluded or limited as to the peril or the amount of insurance applicable. The forms provide where, when, under what circumstances, and to what extent the property is covered elsewhere than on the described premises.

Effects of Perils Covered

Articles of personal property commonly found in residences can, with few exceptions, be consumed or reduced to junk by fire. Many can also be broken, scratched, torn, or crushed in the confusion of removal when endangered. Small articles are often lost in the debris following a fire. Heat damages plastics easily and also phonograph records, artificial flowers, and similar materials.

Hot smoke during a fire may stain fabrics, books, pictures, and other materials to an extent that they resist satisfactory cleaning. Hot or cold smoke can cause damage of varying degrees to all types of property.

Lightning frequently damages radios, television sets, washing-machine motors, and other appliances connected to the electrical circuits. In other situations artificially generated current causes the injury.

Windstorms, tornados, and hurricanes cause damage to contents of homes. They may be crushed in wind-wrecked structures,

[8]Some business property that does not come within the exclusion under On Premises may be covered on the premises.

blown away, or exposed to rain entering through openings in the walls or roofs.

Water from any source may cause wood furniture, pianos, and organs to warp, or cause the veneer to loosen. Television sets, radios, sewing machines, appliance motors, and other similar articles can be seriously damaged if not cared for promptly. Wearing apparel, rugs, drapes, linens, bedding, etc., when wet, may mildew or rot if not dried, unless the temperature is quite low. Sheet music, books, and foodstuffs are highly susceptible to damage by water.

Faulty operation of oil-burning heating equipment often covers the contents of a home with soot or oily deposit. Occasionally the entire contents have to be removed and cleaned, and in more serious cases some replacements are required or furniture has to be reupholstered.

Explosions in steam or hot-water systems, in gas-fired furnaces, in hot-water heating systems, from dynamite, and from other sources cause damage to personal property ranging from minor to extensive.

Vehicles cause damage to personal property as a result of their running into dwellings; also as a result of striking individuals, damaging their apparel. Personal property in or on a vehicle, if damaged when struck by a second vehicle, is covered under most forms as vehicle damage.

Personal property is damaged occasionally by persons intent on malicious mischief, or by persons attempting or perpetrating a burglary.

Personal property can be crushed, scratched, broken, torn, or otherwise damaged when a building or part of it collapses due to wind, weight of snow, etc.

Window glass, shattered inward by baseballs or stones, frequently cuts upholstery, mars wood furniture, or otherwise injures personal property.

Insurable Value

Personal property, such as household furniture and personal effects, is covered under most policies for its actual cash value. This is the insurable value. Policies covering works of art or other valuable articles for specific amounts of insurance, such as a Fine Arts Floater, may be written so that at the time of loss the amount of insurance is the agreed value.

Actual Cash Value

The courts have been quite consistent in holding that, as respects household goods and other personal property in use, the replacement cost *new* at the time of loss, less reasonable depreciation, is a proper measure of the actual cash value. Evidence of the value of such property in the secondhand market, such as used furniture or clothing stores, is not the test, and it is doubtful that such evidence would be admissible.[9] Where property such as household goods and wearing apparel has no recognized market value, the actual value to the owner must be determined without resort to market value.[10] We find no recognized authority which would hold the insured to a recovery based solely on the proceeds on a secondhand market[11] *of household goods.*

Original Cost. The original cost of an article is not necessarily the replacement cost *at the time of loss*, which is usually the starting basis for determining *actual cash value*. When the present-day replacement cost cannot be determined or is difficult to determine, if the original cost and date of purchase can be learned, a comparative guide to present-day replacement can usually be established. The insured should be asked the following questions, any one or more of which may provide a solution or lead into other areas of investigation:

1. When was it purchased?
2. Where was it purchased (name of store)?
3. How much was paid for it?
4. Was payment made by check or cash?
5. Is the canceled check stub available?
6. Does the insured have the original invoice?
7. Can a duplicate invoice be obtained?

[9]*Lake v. Dye*, 232 N.Y. 209,214.
[10]*Britven v. Occidental Ins. Co.*, 234 Iowa 682.
[11]*Crisp v. Security National Ins. Co.*, Tex. Supreme Ct. 6-26-63, 369 S.W.2d 326.

8. Was the article purchased on time?
9. Is there a sales or financing contract? (Interest, insurance, and carrying charges should not influence actual cash value.)
10. Does the store have a sales record?
11. Was it bought on a charge account?

A claim representative who regularly handles personal property losses should keep informed on the current costs of articles of furniture, furnishings, clothing, household appliances, and similar property that he or she commonly encounters.

Articles Difficult to Value. The value of articles that cannot be replaced, such as antiques or works of art, is what they could be sold for. Their value is therefore a matter of expert opinion. The amount of loss that results from any damage to them is also a matter of expert opinion. The kinds of property that produce most of the problems of value are antiques; statuary; oil paintings; engravings; rare books; specially made furniture; draperies and tapestries; tailor-made suits, coats, and dresses; furs; expensive items of jewelry; coin and stamp collections; and ceramics. Oriental rugs, imported laces, linens, and glass are hard to value. Such articles should be examined by an expert, and preferably the claim representative should participate in the examination. The expert's opinion should be in writing and available for use in any discussion of the adjustment with the insured.

Depreciation. *Depreciation* means loss of value. Depreciation in personal property may be physical (wear and tear) or obsolescence (change in style or function).

Women's clothing, particularly millinery, dresses, shoes, and coats, is subject to frequent changes in style. High styling involves extreme changes, and high-fashion clothes are short-lived, frequently not lasting more than one season. Styles in men's clothing change but less frequently and radically than women's.

Domestic appliances change frequently in both style and function. Television sets, radios, tape recorders, and combinations of these; washing machines; refrigerators; and air conditioners are examples of appliances with built-in obsolescence due mainly to style change and partly to functional change. Many items of personal property are less subject to obsolescence. These include men's shirts, handkerchiefs, undergarments, pajamas, robes, etc.; most cooking utensils, dishes, linens, bedding, draperies, curtains, and rugs; electronic organs, pianos, better grades of cameras, optical equipment, high-grade furniture, guns, fishing tackle, and golf clubs.

Physical depreciation due to wear and tear is usually easier to measure than loss of value due to obsolescence. The former is based on physical condition and probable life expectancy while the latter involves the less tangible factor of economic value. While physical depreciation is not subject to exact calculations, if an article has a life expectancy of two years, at the end of one year it has served half of its life. Therefore depreciation of approximately 50 percent would seem reasonable provided it has had normal wear and tear. A suit of clothes with a life expectancy of five years, if given reasonable care, would depreciate at the rate of 20 percent annually.

Not all persons treat property with the same degree of care, and therefore each situation has to be examined accordingly. Furniture on which children and pets are permitted to jump, walk, or eat food as they wish would be expected to depreciate much more rapidly than the same furniture in the home of a more disciplined family or one without children.

Wood furniture should be examined for deterioration of surface finish indicating lack of care or age, for scratches or other marrings, for cracks, and for loss of handles or drawer pulls. Upholstered furniture, rugs, and carpets show wear by becoming threadbare. The armholes of men's suits should be examined, as age will be indicated by wear and stain; wear on the cuffs of sleeves and around buttonholes also indicates use. Ornate brass bedsteads are out of date, as are marbletop tables, though they are in vogue as antiques. With the passage of time homes have, in the past, tended to accumulate a substantial number of articles that were set aside because they were no longer needed or because something that was more needed took their place. As a consequence attics, basements, and storerooms are often filled with these set-aside articles. Indefinite plans for some future use of them, a dislike of seeing them carried off by the trash collector, and sometimes a sentimental desire to keep them cause the owners to hang on to them. If they are lost or damaged, the insured and the claim representative may frequently have radically different ideas as to their value.

The present trend is to use the term *betterment* in place of *depreciation* as one which is more readily understood by the insured in negotiating an adjustment. It is intended to convey the impression that by replacing an item the insured is better off financially because "new" has been given for "old."

Replacement Value Coverage by Endorsement

Replacement value is available under the Homeowners policies, meaning "the current cost at time of loss without deduction for depreciation to replace the damaged, destroyed or stolen property with articles of like kind and quality." Important provisions are:

In consideration of an additional premium, this Company agrees to substitute the term "replacement value" for "actual cash value" as it applies to the following:

1. Section I—Coverage C—Unscheduled Personal Property
2. Section II—Supplementary Coverage— Damage to Property of Others.

"Replacement value" means the current cost at time of loss without deduction for depreciation to replace the damaged, destroyed or stolen property with articles of like kind and quality.

THIS ENDORSEMENT SHALL NOT APPLY TO:

1. PROPERTY WHICH BY ITS INHERENT NATURE CANNOT BE REPLACED,
2. PROPERTY NOT MAINTAINED IN GOOD OR WORKABLE CONDITION,

3. PROPERTY NOT BEING USED BY THE INSURED OR STORED FOR SUCH USE.

THE COMPANY'S LIABILITY FOR LOSS ON ANY PROPERTY INSURED UNDER THIS ENDORSEMENT SHALL NOT EXCEED THE SMALLEST OF THE FOLLOWING:

1. THE COST OF REPAIR OR RESTORATION,
2. THE REPLACEMENT VALUE AT TIME OF LOSS,
3. 400% OF THE ACTUAL CASH VALUE AT TIME OF LOSS, OR
4. ANY LIMIT, OR SPECIAL LIMITS, OF LIABILITY DESCRIBED IN THE POLICY.

THE COMPANY WILL NOT BE LIABLE FOR ANY LOSS UNDER THIS ENDORSEMENT UNLESS AND UNTIL ACTUAL REPAIR OR REPLACEMENT IS COMPLETED. THE NAMED INSURED MAY ELECT TO DISREGARD THIS ENDORSEMENT IN MAKING CLAIM UNDER THIS POLICY, BUT SUCH ELECTION SHALL NOT PREJUDICE THE NAMED INSURED'S RIGHT TO MAKE FURTHER CLAIM WITHIN 180 DAYS AFTER LOSS FOR ANY ADDITIONAL LIABILITY BROUGHT ABOUT BY THIS ENDORSEMENT.

All other provisions of the policy, including any applicable deductible, not in conflict with this endorsement remain unchanged; however, if this policy provides replacement cost for Coverages A and B, the exclusion in Section I, Additional Condition 1, Replacement Cost— Coverage A and B, relating to outdoor radio and television antennas and aerials, carpeting, awnings, domestic appliances and outdoor equipment is deleted.

Identification and Check of Coverage

Identification of the insured and the property is generally a simple matter in the majority of losses involving residential personal property. The claim representative goes to the address given by the company or agent and asks for the insured or a member of the family, who exhibits the damaged property or describes it in case of theft or burglary.

Questions of identification and coverage of specific property arise occasionally, under a Homeowners Policy, when the articles on which claim is made are owned by employees and the loss occurs elsewhere than on the premises, or when they are the property of roomers or boarders on the premises. Similar questions are posed when the articles lost or damaged are, or appear to be, business property, either on or off the premises. Claims made for lost or damaged property of the insured's sons or daughters while residing elsewhere than on the premises involve inquiry to determine whether they are considered "residents of the insured's household."

In many residences, jewelry, furs, cameras, and other valuable articles or objects are scheduled under a Homeowners Policy or a Personal Effects Floater and are separately described and covered for a specific amount of insurance. When handling losses under these schedules, the claim representative should identify the specifically described and covered articles so that they will not be included inadvertently in the claim under unscheduled property.

Residential personal property is frequently lost, stolen, or damaged while in public warehouses, cleaners, furriers, jewelers, and other establishments for repairs or storage. The question of the legal liability of the bailee must be established, and the existence and coverage of the bailee's insurance must be determined (see Chapter 21). Property damaged or lost while in custody of carriers requires similar investigation.

Questions involving overlapping coverage should be resolved as provided for in the Guiding Principles (see Chapter 27).

Examination and Survey

In the ordinary household-furniture loss in a protected area, examination and survey are as informal as is the identification of the property. In almost all such losses the two steps are combined.

In total destructions of homes by fire, wind, or water, the claim representative looks at the site as the insured tells his or her story, and tries to recognize in the debris the remains of anything that the insured may mention.

In large and complicated losses, when a home of many rooms filled with expensive furniture has been badly burned, examination and survey include a roof-to-basement inspection of the building and, frequently, a tour of all out buildings to which any articles may have been moved for preservation.

In many of the larger losses, the insured's story and the appearance of the property will check, as they do in most small losses. Household furniture, however, produces a number of difficult claims, and in support of some of them the insured's story will put the claim representative on notice to carefully examine the evidence offered by the insured and search for other evidence that will confirm or controvert what the insured says concerning the cause of loss, the existence of articles not in evidence, their value, or the damage.

In some losses the insured's story will describe the destruction of clothing, linen, drapes, rugs or other articles and state a value that will, in the claim representative's opinion, be utterly out of keeping with the appearance of the premises, the neighborhood, or the insured. Hearing such a story, the claim representative will expect the insured to present an inventory that was made from memory and that will give the claim representative a difficult task when he or she tries to verify or disprove it. Pictures, stamp collections, and at times manuscripts will be listed as stolen and there will be no physical evidence and no convincing documentary evidence of either their existence or their value.

Stories are at times told of eyeglasses, fountain pens, dentures, or other small articles lost in the confusion attending a fire or windstorm, or of valuable jewelry that has mysteriously disappeared. Such stories raise questions of existence, value, and cause of loss, questions that can be very difficult. Stories of lost heirlooms, antiques, inherited articles, or wardrobes of deceased members of the family prepare the claim representative for troublesome problems of valuation.

In dwellings not under fire department protection, there are many total household furniture losses, and the claim representative finds nothing tangible to identify except the debris of noncombustible articles. Tornados sometimes demolish a dwelling and blow away the furniture. In such instances identification is made by location and the statements of the insured and witnesses.

Search for Missing Articles

It is rarely necessary to search for missing articles after a fire loss. Sometimes, however, the insured will be quite positive that valuable jewelry was in a room that was completely burned out. When such is the case, the ruins should be carefully searched for the jewelry. Anything that is noncombustible and claimed by the insured as lost in a fire should be in the ruins and should in most cases be found by a careful search. Not infrequently articles like jewelry and watches have been recovered by sifting ashes after a fire.

Following fires that do not destroy the premises, the insured will occasionally note that valuable articles have disappeared from places that were not reached by the fire. Such disappearances are frequently due to theft, which is easy to conceal during the excitement attending a fire, but they are occasionally due to removal by some well-intentioned person who sought to save the article from being destroyed. Articles stolen during a fire are seldom recovered. Articles removed often turn up when the persons who removed them recover from the excitement of the fire.

Tracing Articles Removed From Premises

In serious losses, pieces of furniture, silver, draperies, clothes, and other articles are frequently moved during or immediately after the occurrence and taken to a place of safety. Removed articles should be traced, located, and examined, otherwise they may be later inventoried as destroyed, to the detriment of the insurer or, if damaged, omitted from the inventory to the detriment of the insured.

Making Property Accessible

In seriously damaged dwellings, access to some of the contents may be cut off by burned-out stairways or collapsed roofs or floors. The cost of temporary repairs necessary to make the contents accessible, particularly to save it, should fall on the household insurance. The cost of removing building debris should fall on the building insurance, as the debris must be removed before the building can be repaired. In either case the cost is part of the loss and is subject to the provisions of any contribution or coinsurance clause in the policies.

Protection From Further Damage

Refrigerators that have been put out of operation should be cleared of food that will spoil and foul them. In closely built-up areas where no yard space is available but where laundry and cleaning service can be had, wet bedding should be sent to the laundry or dry cleaner as soon as possible. Wet draperies, linens, and wearing apparel should be treated in the same fashion. Before wet carpets and rugs are sent to the cleaners, they should be swept clean of any broken plaster or other pieces of debris that may have fallen on them.

Books, pictures, sheet music, and sporting and traveling equipment should be wiped off and spread about, in or out of doors, to dry. Wood furniture should be wiped dry. Metal furniture, sewing machines, and mechanical appliances should be wiped dry and oiled to prevent rusting.

Radios, television sets, pianos, clocks, and other articles of like susceptibility to damage by neglect should go to competent repair firms as soon as possible.

If there is enough floor space available in portions of the dwelling, apartment house, or other structure in which the loss occurred that are safe against the weather, much of the work of protecting the property can be done on the premises. If the roof has been burned through, immediate roof repairs, temporary covering with tarpaulins, or temporary repairs with tar paper may be advisable. If the entire roof is gone, it may be advisable to remove the property to another building.

Separation and Putting in Order

If the work of protecting wet household articles from further damage is properly handled, the damaged and undamaged articles will be separated as the work proceeds. If the damaged articles are not worth saving, they should be put where they will not endanger undamaged property because of their damp or dirty condition. Charred articles will soil anything they touch, and mildew starting in wet susceptible articles will, in warm, damp weather, spread to other wet or damp articles of similar nature in the immediate vicinity. Total-loss articles in sight must be kept until they have been inventoried and their value agreed upon. Property that has undergone removal needs sorting and matching up of separated parts, such as replacement of drawers in dressers, setting up of bedsteads, and assembling of sets of books. If part of the contents of a home is saved by removal and the rest burns, the work of putting what is saved in the best possible order eliminates the uncertainty of whether specific articles were burned in the fire or are hidden in the salvage.

If the loss has been caused by removal only, and the house escaped injury or has been made safe and habitable after the fire, the property should be wiped off, moved back, and set up just as it was before the fire. If only part of the house can be made safe, the furnishings of each room should, as far as possible, be kept together when moving them into the available space.

Inventory

If the furniture and other furnishings are in the rooms where they belong, the inventory may be taken by listing in some logical order the contents of each room. Much time will be saved in the adjustment if the inventory is taken in this way. Most inventories of property in sight are checked against the articles when the claim representative examines the property. Therefore, the entries should be in such order that the claim representative,

when checking them, can pass from article to article with the least possible delay or inconvenience.

If the property has been moved to a warehouse or other place of temporary storage, it may be well to list the furniture proper as one group, floor coverings as another, pictures as a third, bedding as a fourth, linen as a fifth, clothing as a sixth, and china and glass as a seventh, and to make such other groupings as may be necessary to facilitate the work.

If much property is to be inventoried, numbered tags should be attached to each article or set. The property should then be listed in numerical order, as this will greatly facilitate the checking of the inventory, or the finding of any article that needs special study or attention.

If the property is a total loss, the inventory may simply enumerate each article, set, and give the actual or replacement cost of each. But if the inventory is to include damaged articles, the amount claimed on each should be shown in a separate column. A suggested inventory sheet is shown in Appendix P.

Preparation for Adjustment

In the great majority of household losses, no special preparation is necessary. The amounts involved are small, the losses are free from complicating circumstances, and the claim representative knows enough about the values and characteristics of the property that has been destroyed or damaged to discuss adjustment at a first meeting with the insured. A typical instance is the loss resulting from the damage to an upholstered chair by glass breakage or by a careless smoker. The chair may require upholstering, the extent of which will depend upon the ability of the upholsterer to match the fabric and do the work in a way that will make the chair look as good after the repair as it did before it was damaged. The claim representative will know from experience with other chairs in the same territory that the cost of the work should be about so many dollars and, after hearing what the insured has to say, will give his or her own estimate of the cost. If the chair is to be completely done over, an amount will be suggested to be deducted from the total cost because of the betterment, unless the chair is a new one and no betterment will be made. Any differences of opinion will be ironed out, and the loss will be settled.

There are, however, many household losses that are attended by circumstances that make them difficult or complicated, and there are a few of doubtful honesty. In order to handle these losses the claim representative will find it necessary to be prepared in considerable detail before making an intelligent decision on the disposition that should be made of any given claim and on how to proceed in order to have the best chance of success.

In occasional losses, the household possessions involved will be difficult to value; in others, difficult to repair or restore. In many losses questions of depreciation on total-loss articles or betterment on repaired articles will be serious. In a few losses, the claim representative will have reason to believe that much of the property for which claim is made, perhaps all of it, never did exist except in the imagination of the claimant.

Household possessions are generally accumulated over a period of time during which things are bought, made in the home, inherited from persons who have passed on, or received as gifts. Ordinarily no record is made of the acquisition of the possessions. Only in a few homes is there any effort made to keep inventories of the contents. In some of the expensively furnished homes, which are a very small percentage of the total number of homes, the owners will have appraisals listing and valuing the contents. It is a rare occasion when the householder whose possessions have been completely destroyed by fire or other peril can list in correct detail the property that has been lost.

Many policyholders resent being called upon by fire or other accident to make any expenditure on their own account, even though they will benefit from it. The renovation of a damaged article may make it decidedly better than it was before. The upholstered chair can again be used as an example. It may have been worn and due for reupholstering within the next year or two. Yet, in many instances, the insured owner of such a chair will insist that the cost of the work, even though all the fabric on the chair is being renewed and the frame is being completely refinished, should be borne by the insurer, arguing that he or she was satisfied with the chair as it was and is no better off with the renovated chair than previously.

The preparation that should be made before taking up the adjustment of any difficult, complicated, or doubtful loss will depend upon the circumstances that are responsible for the particular problem or problems presented by the loss.

Property in Sight

When the property is in sight and can be identified and properly described when inventoried, the problem will be one of value or damage.

Problems of damage call for examinations and estimates or bids from laundries, dry cleaners, rug and carpet cleaners; upholsterers, furniture repairers; radio, television, or other technical service persons; electricians; and perhaps others. Unusual problems make it necessary for the claim representative to find experts capable of restoring damaged paintings; repairing costly violins; reweaving holes in rugs, tapestries, laces, or garments; rehabilitating a damaged piano; or rebinding a rare book.

The problems of value that are generally encountered in connection with the ordinary kinds of replaceable furniture, furnishings, clothing, and other articles arise because of differences of opinion on depreciation and, occasionally, on cost of replacement. The only real preparation for an argument over depreciation is an examination of the property and a notation of where and how it shows signs of wear, tear, or other deterioration, or of the details of it that show whether it is out of date or in style.

Property Out of Sight

Because many things in a home, notably clothing, linens, bedding, draperies, and pictures, can be completely destroyed by fire without leaving any evidence of quality or quantity, the unscrupulous claimant will often present an inventory of out-of-sight articles the stated value of which will be many times greater than the value actually destroyed.

When the claim representative suspects that a claim for out-of-sight articles is exaggerated, perhaps to the degree of listing property that never was in the insured's possession, preparation should include a request that the insured produce for examination any bills, contracts, or canceled checks covering purchases of any of the articles listed. This history of the property should be obtained. The insured should be questioned about when and where it was bought, what was paid for it, and how he or she made the payment, by check or by cash. It may be well to question other members of the household and any neighbors or visitors who are willing to talk. Careful attention should be given to physical conditions. Debris should be examined for remains of the property and the premises examined for markings tending to prove or disprove its existence or destruction. Sometimes none of the buttons, buckles, casters, locks, or other indestructible pieces that should be left in case of destruction by fire can be found. Sometimes the space that the insured claims was used to keep the articles before the loss will be found, on measurement and calculation, too small to hold them. In closet fires, hangers may show that they held nothing when the fire occurred. In some such fires, there will be no scorching or smoke markings of the interior of the closet, indicating that the garments were partly burned somewhere else and then hung in the closet to support a claim. Care must be taken when considering the evidence offered by debris. Pieces of a half-dozen picture frames will justify the inference that six pictures were burned, but they will not indicate whether the pictures were valuable or worthless.

In questionable claims for out-of-sight property, it is advisable to make inquiry into the insured's financial condition and past income and also to compare the claim with other possessions. There should ordinarily

be some consistent relation between what the insured owned immediately before the loss and his or her income or resources at the time it was acquired.

In cases that threaten to produce litigation, notes made by the claim representative and reports made by experts will be useful. Photographs will be particularly useful.

FURNITURE, FIXTURES, EQUIPMENT, AND SUPPLIES

Personal property in use, as discussed in this section, includes furniture, fixtures, equipment, and supplies found in or on the premises of all business properties both commercial and manufacturing, and also on the premises of public and institutional properties, and service organizations.

Furniture includes tables, chairs, desks, file cases, cabinets, and safes.

Furniture, household furnishings, and the like are not fixtures.[12] *Fixtures* may include counters, shelving, bins, showcases, paneling, railings, signs, awnings, and mechanical fixtures, such as soda fountains, bars, stoves, refrigerators, boilers, scales, meat slicers, lighting fixtures, and air-conditioning units. All these and similar chattels are usually considered *trade fixtures* insofar as they are not affixed to the realty or, if they are, removal is possible without material injury to the realty.

Technically and legally a *fixture*, as distinguished from a *trade fixture*, something installed or placed on the premises for the purposes of trade or conducting a business, is "something that is personal in its nature but so annexed to realty as to have become a part of the realty."[13] Saying the same thing another way, if the article, object, or whatever of a personal nature can be removed without material injury to the realty, it will not ordinarily be considered a fixture.[14] The rule most often applied in determining whether

[12] *Commercial Finance Co. v. Brooksville Hotel Co.,* 123 So. 814, 816, 98 Fla. 410, 64 A.L.R. 1219. *Klaus v. Majestic Apartment House Co.,* 95 A 451, 458, 250 Pa. 194.
[13] See 25 Tex. Jur. 2d 392, 393.
[14] *Crabb v. Keystone Pipe and Supply Co.,* 177 S.W. 2d 989; 25 Tex. Jur. 2d 398, 399.

the property in question is a fixture or personal property (a trade fixture) involves answering these questions: (1) Was there actual and real annexation to the realty? (2) Was the article or object suitable or adaptable to the uses or purposes of the realty to which it is affixed? (3) Was the intention of the party making the annexation that it become a permanent part of the realty?

It becomes apparent, in the application of the rule of *annexation, adaptation,* and *intention,* that under one set of conditions a particular item of personal property is a fixture, while under other circumstances the same item is personal property. For example, a refrigerator or stove installed by a tenant in a residence is personal property. Identical objects, installed by the landlord for the use of a tenant, are fixtures. An appliance, to become a fixture, need not be so affixed that its removal would injure the realty.

Property which the law regards as fixtures may be considered as personal property by parties to a deed, lease, or other agreement, and by the same token, that which is considered in law as personal property may be regarded as fixtures.[15]

Equipment here extends to a multitude of articles and objects, usually of a movable nature, needed for the efficient operation and conduct of a business or service organization. While the word is broad enough in scope to take in items of furniture, fixtures, supplies, and machinery, it is more often thought of by insurers as all the personal property in use that is not specifically identified as furniture, fixtures, supplies, and machinery. This may include furnishings such as floor coverings, rugs, carpets, and draperies; trays, boxes, baskets, sign holders, dishes, cutlery, tablecloths, and napkins; typewriters, adding machines, calculators, and other business machines; surgical equipment; cameras, enlargers, and projectors; transits and levels, tools, implements, hammers, saws, and scoops.

Supplies are stationery, pencils, pens, clips, and janitor's supplies.

Effects of Perils Covered

Furniture, fixtures, equipment, and supplies sustain damage from perils covered to the same degree as described for residential personal property.[16]

Furniture, Fixtures, Equipment and Supplies as Subjects of Insurance

Furniture, fixtures, equipment, and supplies are covered under a variety of forms. In some of these the description is very broad. Under SMP General Property Form, "all fixtures, machinery, and equipment constituting a permanent part of and pertaining to the service of the building" are covered under "Building(s)." Under "Personal Property," "furniture, fixtures, equipment and supplies, not otherwise covered under this policy" are included.

Most building forms include coverage on fixtures, machinery, and equipment as in the SMP, and most forms covering personal property or contents include furniture, fixtures, machinery, and equipment. The wording varies.

Most policies that cover improvements and betterments include, in the description, "fixtures" not legally subject to removal by the insured and/or "comprising a part of the described building." These are "building fixtures" as opposed to "trade fixtures."

Actual Cash Value

There has been considerable uniformity in the court decisions where fixture and equipment values are at issue. It is the general rule that replacement cost new at the time of loss less depreciation in its broadest sense is the measure of actual cash value. This would include physical depreciation and obsolescence or inadequacy.

Where an owner has purchased secondhand furniture, fixtures, or equipment, if the policy covers their cash value, careful investigation is necessary to uncover their history. The cost of the items in the secondhand market, and in the condition they were at the time of loss, should be a reasonable basis for valuation.

---

[15]*Smith v. Waggoner,* 6 N.W. 568, 50 Wis. 155. *Hunt v. Bay State Iron Co.,* 97 Mass. 279. *Ford v. Cobb,* 20 N.Y. 344. *Tifft v. Horton,* 53 N.Y. 377, 13 Am. R. 537.

[16]See p. 229.

Depreciation

Heavy articles, such as counters and shelving, depreciate slowly. Depreciation on mechanical equipment and floor coverings is quite rapid. Improvement in mechanical equipment is going on at such a rapid rate that much loss in value is due to obsolescence, even though a machine in use functions properly. Stationery and supplies are usually worth the cost of replacement unless they are out of date or have been carelessly stored or handled.

If the books of a business are investigated in connection with a claim on furniture and fixtures, the claim representative will generally find that an accounting depreciation has been charged against them that is quite at variance with the actual depreciation. Since it is good accounting to depreciate fixtures as rapidly as the income tax authorities will permit, in many businesses the book value of fixtures will be far below their actual value. In a going business, replacements and additions generally prevent the fixtures as a whole from depreciating more than 25 or 30 percent.

Identification and Check of Coverage

Identification of all furniture, fixtures, and equipment involved in a loss should be made with the same care as in any personal property loss. Where possible the manufacturer should be determined, and all model, style, or serial numbers should be recorded. The kind of wood, finish, and design of wood shelving, paneling, bins, and showcases should be identified.

In the great majority of fixtures and equipment losses, the claim representative will encounter property of standard design that can be valued by getting replacement-cost quotations from reputable manufacturers, but in losses involving such property as specially made draperies and decorations, it is necessary in almost all cases to learn from the insured something about its origin and history. The same is also the case in connection with many installations of fixtures and equipment put in by one owner and afterward acquired by another.

Check of coverage is usually made to determine what property is covered and what is excluded.

Under the improvements and betterments coverage of fixtures and equipment items, it is highly important to have the insured state what will be claimed on property covered under the insurance, which might otherwise be covered under the insurance of the building owner. The improvements and betterments claim representative who has this information can compare notes with the claim representative who is handling the building claim and, generally, prevent any double payments on improvement items.

When fixtures and equipment insurance is held by the owner of a building who occupies it, any permanent fixtures covered under the building insurance must be identified so that they will not find their way into the claim under the fixtures and equipment insurance.

Establishing Interests

In bowling alleys, bars, grills, delicatessens, shoe-repair shops, and butcher shops, the claim representative will often find that such things as bowling alleys, balls and pins, bar fixtures, juke boxes, computing scales, meat slicers, shoe-stitching and sanding equipment, and refrigerating equipment have been bought under contracts of conditional sale. Dental engines, dentists' chairs, X-ray equipment, infrared and diathermic apparatus, and other devices in the offices of dentists, doctors, and technicians will also often be found subject to such contracts. Almost always, these contracts make the purchaser liable for loss by fire, and there is generally little for the claim representative to do beyond determining the insured's interest and liability.

Examination and Survey

When going into a store or office to make the first inspection of a reported loss, the claim representative may find that a small fire has scorched a few articles of furniture, all of which can be repaired and made as useful and presentable as before the fire. The articles will not require protection from further damage, and it will not be necessary to rearrange the other furniture or fixtures while they are being repaired. In such a situation, examination and survey are limited to a look at the articles. No formal survey and examination are necessary when damage consists of nothing more than locks broken by firemen or slight wettings of fixtures or equipment caused by dripping of water used to extinguish fire on an upper floor.

In serious losses, however, examination and survey must include all the property covered by the fixtures and equipment insurance and in some instances all other contents of the building and the building itself. Preservation of the fixtures from further damage may require some contribution by the stock insurer to the cost of moving property within the premises so as to make the fixtures accessible. Some fixtures will be found to be total losses and should be inventoried and moved out of the way so that salvage operations or building or other repairs can proceed. Some fixtures should go out to repair shops, and others should be protected in place until repair firms can begin work on them. In some losses, it is important that debris be held undisturbed until it can be carefully examined, inventoried, and, perhaps, photographed.

Protection From Further Damage

The work of protecting movable furniture, fixtures, and other furnishings should follow the general plan outlined for household furniture. Special attention, however, must be given to wet or exposed mechanical fixtures and equipment. It is often advisable to urge the insured to bring in repair firms to inspect such fixtures as soda fountains, motor-driven refrigerators, or air-conditioning systems, and to send wet typewriters or other business machines out for prompt overhauling.

Separation and Putting in Order

Generally, there is not much separating or putting in order required when only fixtures or pieces of furniture are involved. Desk drawers that have been pulled out should, as soon as they are dry, be put back. If draperies have been taken down or rugs rolled up and removed, they should be laid out in orderly fashion. Light equipment, dishes, knives, forks, spoons, and table linen in a restaurant, for example, require real putting in order if they are to be inventoried accurately. Stationery and supplies should be promptly separated, otherwise the dampness in the wet articles will affect the dry. Envelopes with gummed flaps must be given preferred handling. If the flaps stick, the envelopes become so much scrap paper.

Inventory

An inventory of fixtures and equipment in sight is generally best made in some geographical order so that a check of the inventory against the property will be easy. In small stores all the fixtures can be seen from any spot, and order is not so important as in the large establishments where the fixtures, furnishings, and equipment are distributed over several floors and floor divisions.

Inventory descriptions should be concise but accurate so that any entry can be checked with assurance against the article it describes.

New fixtures and equipment can often be priced from purchase invoices or installation contracts. Old articles must generally be priced according to the estimated cost of replacement. In large mercantile establishments, the books will include a fixtures account which will be helpful with newly purchased fixtures but will give little help with the old ones.

In a few mercantile establishments, fixtures and equipment inventories are made at regular intervals. Such inventories are of great help in making an inventory following a loss.

Almost all chain stores are supplied with illustrated catalogues, known as fixture books, which show pictures and prices of the standard articles of equipment used by the chain.

When a store is destroyed and all fixtures and equipment are out of sight, an inventory must be made from the record of purchases shown by the books or from the memory of the insured or the employees, unless the insured can produce an inventory made before the loss. In the absence of such an inventory, it may be necessary to make up floor plans of the fixtures and obtain estimates of the cost of reproducing them from manufacturers.

Preparation for Adjustment

Preparation for adjustment is generally limited to getting in hand estimates of value and loss or cost of repair. When fixtures require intricate wiring and piping connections, special attention should be paid to these and estimators cautioned to compare notes with the building contractor and not include building wiring or plumbing in the fixture estimate. When betterments and improvements are involved, it is advisable to learn what work will be included in the building owner's claim so that double payment may be avoided.

MACHINERY

The term *machinery* is extremely broad and includes machines, engines, apparatus, appliances, and other devices for doing types of work, as well as combinations of these. It may include anything falling within this description from a small electric motor to a highly complicated computer, from a bench grinder to a huge papermaking machine, or from a forklift to earth-moving machines.

Machinery may be attached to the walls, floors, or ceilings of the structure housing it; it may rest on the floor or may be portable or mobile, moving under its own power. While machinery is ordinarily constructed of metal parts, there are many that combine metal, glass, porcelain, leather, rubber, cloth, synthetics, or other materials in their makeup.

Effects of Perils

All machinery is subject to direct fire damage, breakage due to falling timbers or other debris, and deterioration following wetting or exposure unless properly handled. Massive machinery will sometimes go through severe fires with little damage. Enough heat, however, will reduce any machine to scrap

value, particularly if water is played on it while hot, for the sudden contraction often cracks the metal. All metal parts expand under heat, and if expansion and cooling are not uniform, the parts may be badly warped. Parts made of aluminum or brass melt at lower temperatures than do iron or steel parts, and the babbitt metal in bearings melts at a still lower temperature. Stone, porcelain, and glass parts crack under heat. Belts, aprons, rolls, and parts made of leather, fabric, rubber, or cloth burn easily. Explosions break or bend parts of machinery, sometimes by direct force, sometimes by showering machines with missiles. Windstorms damage machinery by wrecking buildings in which it is located. Large traveling cranes, bridges such as those used in coal- and ore-loading operations, are at times twisted or toppled over by wind.

Water used during a fire, or water from leaking sprinkler systems, broken service pipes, or rain or snow entering a building through roof or walls ruptured by fire, wind, or other peril, does direct damage to vulnerable machine parts such as the cloth of a carding machine, and causes rust or pitting on metal parts if they are not wiped off and oiled or otherwise cared for. In low areas the machines in a plant are occasionally covered by water during a flood. The same situation is sometimes found in basements when great quantities of water are used to fight a fire in the upper part of the building.

Machinery is frequently damaged in transit as a result of improper packing or by collision or overturning. Machinery is occasionally dropped during loading or unloading, and also during installation in or on a structure.

Motors, generators, and similar equipment used in conjunction with machinery can be seriously damaged by artificially generated current or by lightning.[17]

Actual Cash Value

Like fixtures, equipment, and supplies, in many states, machinery can be covered for its actual cash value, or its replacement cost

[17]See Electrical Losses, p. 245.

without deduction for depreciation. The insurable value is that value upon which the amount of insurance should be based to comply with the particular policy provisions and conditions.

The courts are quite uniform in holding that the actual cash value of machinery is its replacement cost new, at the time of loss, less a reasonable deduction for depreciation in its broadest sense. Such depreciation would include wear and tear, also obsolescence or inadequacy.

While physical wear and tear on machinery, due to use, is subject to reasonable measurement through examination, or through inquiry in event of total destruction, obsolescence or inadequacy can be best measured by comparison with similar machinery in the market. Unlike residential personal property of individuals, there is a market for used machinery. It is well known that many plants are equipped with machinery purchased in the secondhand market and that others make replacements of worn-out machinery in that market.

An important decision relating to this subject was upheld by the United States Court of Appeals for the Seventh District in the case of *Wisconsin Screw Co. v. Firemen's Fund Ins. Co.*, 297 Fd.2d 697. Considerable loss had been sustained by the plaintiff because of destruction or damage to machinery. The plaintiff contended that the *actual cash value* provision required such value be determined on the basis of replacement cost less depreciation, without reference to other factors.

The defendant's evidence of loss on the machinery destroyed was based on market value, at the time of loss, by reference to the used-machinery market, plus freight and installation charges. The District Court concluded that the recoverable loss and damage on the machinery item was in the sum of $316,982.50, the figure resulting from the use of the market-value basis employed by defendant's witnesses. The Court of Appeals upheld the District Court's decision, quoting from *Pinet v. New Hampshire Fire Insurance Co.*, 100 N.H. 346, 126 A.2d 262, 61 A.L.R.2d 706, where the court observed that the actual cash value clause in an insurance

policy does not in itself establish any rule for determining the amount of loss but simply imposes a limitation upon the amount which may be recovered. The court also stated:

> In this state the court has had no occasion to commit itself to either the fair-market-value test or the test of replacement cost in determining the actual cash value of the insured's property. See *Huckins v. People's Mut. Fire Ins. Co.*, 31 N.H. 238; *Wood v. Manufacturers & Merchants Mut. Insurance Co.*, 89 N.H. 213, 195 A. 667. However, we are impressed with what might be denominated a third rule which has received support in New York, Massachusetts and South Dakota. *McAnarney v. Newark Fire Insurance Co.*, 247 N.Y. 176, 159 N.E. 902, 56 A.L.R. 1149; *Kingsley v. Spofford*, 298 Mass. 469, 11 N.E.2d 487; *Lampe Market Co. v. Alliance Ins. Co.*, 71 S.D. 120, 22 N.W.2d 427. In these jurisdictions neither market value nor replacement cost is an exclusive test. Evidence of both market value and replacement cost with depreciation may be introduced as evidence of actual cash value. These jurisdictions stress the fact that variations in the types of property and the conditions under which they are destroyed prevent the adoption of any single test for all cases. The objective in these cases is to see that the insured should incur neither economic gain nor loss if he is adequately insured and suffers partial fire loss. See Howland, Depreciation and Partial Losses, Proc. A.B.A., Section of Insurance Law, pp. 90, 95 (1952)....
>
> In the last analysis the "actual cash value" of the plaintiff's loss must be expressed in terms of money which is a matter of opinion. The trier of fact in determining that question may receive evidence whether there is a fair market value or replacement cost and in either case what it may be. Both fair market value and replacement cost are permissible standards for determining fire losses but they are standards and not shackles.

Measure of Loss

Machinery loss and damage are ordinarily estimated or agreed according to actual cash value, or replacement cost new if the policy so provides. Partial loss to machinery is determined by the cost of repairs less depreciation for any betterment resulting from the repairs. Frequently when machinery is repaired, it is completely overhauled and all badly worn parts are replaced. These are subject to negotiated depreciation generally based on normal life expectancy.

Depreciation

Wear and tear, rust, corrosion, and metal fatigue are the principal causes of deterioration in machinery. The invention of new and more efficient machines is the cause of obsolescence. In the competitive markets of today, the manufacturer whose machinery is worn or out of date cannot expect to survive, and the average useful life of machinery tends to become shorter. Depreciation of certain kinds of machinery proceeds, therefore, at a rather rapid rate.

On machinery that operates with noise and shock, wear and tear will generally be great. Machinery that handles coal, stone, or ore is an example. Woodworking machinery, grinding machinery, and mixing machinery also tend to wear out rapidly. Machinery that works two or three shifts daily and seven days a week will suffer more rapid physical wear and tear than the same machinery worked one shift five days a week.

Boilers, pipes, tanks, and pumps often suffer from rusting or corrosion because of the water or other liquid they must handle. All metal parts that are subject to stress or shock tend to develop metal fatigue.

Machinery that is kept clean and properly oiled and greased will depreciate less rapidly if regularly operated under normal load than if allowed to stand idle. Rust is more dangerous than friction.

Obsolescence is unpredictable. Sometimes in whole industries the important mechanical units lose value overnight because machinery makers put on the market competing units that cost less or are more economical to operate.

Age is the general guide in estimating depreciation. Many tables have been compiled by students of depreciation who have attempted to determine the average useful life of different kinds of machines and from the average produce an annual rate of depreciation. These tables are of great usefulness, but the claim representative handling machinery losses must keep in mind the fact that depreciation due to wear and tear will vary according to the varying degrees of care that different operators give to their machinery. Some factory managers are good housekeepers, others are not; consequently the machinery in one plant will be depreciated less than in another of the same kind and age. Conditions of use must be considered as well as age.

Depreciation as shown by books of account is not always a true reflection of the actual depreciation of the machinery. The tax authorities have prescribed rates of depreciation that manufacturers may charge against their various kinds of machinery when making up, for tax purposes, a profit and loss account of the year's operation. These rates are, in a sense, arbitrary, as they apply, without variation, to all manufacturers in the same industry. Depreciation computed according to these rates will not reflect the effects of any special care or lack of care for the machinery of a given plant. Book depreciation is generally higher than actual depreciation. In many instances a machine will be written off the books as 100 percent depreciated when it is still in service and perhaps highly efficient.

Pattern and die losses produce troublesome questions of depreciation. In the absence of records that clearly show their use in a plant, it is difficult to separate the active from the obsolete. A "live" pattern or die may be worth the full cost of reproduction, but a "dead" one has only junk value.

Standby machinery is, in some instances, outmoded. If so, its depreciation will be great. Used parts held as possible spares are generally heavily depreciated, often presenting the same depreciation problem as patterns.

Identification and Check of Coverage

Identification of pieces of machinery specifically covered is generally made by checking the model and serial number of the machine. Identification of the machinery covered under a machinery item or a blanket item in a fire policy is made according to location. Identification is ordinarily an easy task.

Check of coverage is usually made to determine whether personal property of owners, officers, or employees is included, or whether property otherwise covered is excluded. When machinery insurance is held by the owner of a building who occupies it, any machinery used for the service of the building must be identified so that it will not find its way into the claim under the machinery insurance. When machinery insurance held by a tenant includes coverage of betterments and improvements, efforts should be made to agree upon what items of repair are to be charged against the tenant's insurance and what against that of the building owner.

Whenever there is separate insurance on building and machinery, the subjects of wiring and piping become important, because electricity, gas, and water are often brought into a building from the outside and carried by wires and pipes that are parts of the building to various points from which they are distributed to the machines that will utilize them by other wires and pipes that are parts of the machinery. Claim representatives speak of "building wiring and piping" and "power wiring and piping." Check of coverage should include any business interruption or extra expense insurance, as either kind may, in many instances, be called upon to bear part of the expense of protecting or handling the property, particularly when overtime is involved.

In some groups of machinery there will be machines owned by the insured and others that are leased. When dealing with such groups, the claim representative should determine whether the leased machines are covered as well as the others. In many instances they are separately insured.

Establishing Interests

A substantial number of machines are purchased from manufacturers on a deferred-payment plan or with funds advanced by a fi-

nance company. Until the purchaser makes the last payment, title to the machine remains in the manufacturer or in the finance company. Often such machines are specifically covered by separate policies written in the name of the purchaser with loss payable to the manufacturer or the finance company. In some instances the manufacturer or finance company will carry blanket or floating insurance covering unpaid balances. Printing presses and typesetting machines, power saws and planers, traveling cranes, and a variety of other machines are, because of the method of their purchase, held by the shop or plant as bailee. In case of loss, the legal or contractual liability of the bailee must be established.

In some industries, notably shoe manufacturing and canning, much of the machinery is leased and always remains the property of the lessor. The leases under which it is operated stipulate who shall be responsible for loss or damage, and a large proportion of such machinery is covered by insurance held by the lessor.

Many vendors and lessors service the machines they sell or lease and in case of damage are prepared to make repairs at reasonable cost.

Machines for temporary use are occasionally brought into manufacturing plants and afterward sent to other plants. As an example, a special machine designed for grinding the heavy rolls of large paper-drying machines is rented from time to time by paper mills as the surfaces of the rolls become pitted and rough. The owner of the machine maintains a crew that operates it, and the mill pays shipping charges and wages and expenses of the crew.

Examination and Survey

In the ordinary machinery loss, the insured or some person familiar with the property shows the claim representative the machine or machinery involved and points out the visible evidence of damage or demonstrates that it will not operate or that its operation is faulty. While doing so, the claim representative is told how the damage was actually or probably caused, and, in many instances, an opinion is expressed on what will be necessary in the way of replacement or repair, how it should be done, and what it will probably cost. The claim representative listens, examines the machine or machinery, and notes the markings that indicate the cause of the damage and whether it is slight or severe. Fire damage will be evidenced by the metal parts that have been melted, fused, warped, or discolored; explosion damage, by parts that have been shattered, broken, bent, or displaced; and water damage, by the presence of water or rust. The degree of damage is generally shown by the requirements for reconditioning them or the necessity of replacing them. After noting the damage, the claim representative will, in many instances, find it advisable to go through the premises and examine any burned, scorched, or smoked parts of the building, or water stains on walls or ceilings. If the loss was due to water from a broken service pipe or a leaking sprinkler system, the claim representative will examine the pipe or the system, and will look over the machinery in the rest of the shop, factory, or plant to get an idea of how well it is kept in repair and to approximate the total value of the property if the insurance is subject to average, coinsurance, or contribution. In the ordinary machinery loss, examination and survey require very little time or effort. The claim representative quickly gets in mind the circumstances that require consideration and is ready to begin adjustment negotiations or is prepared to tell the insured what must be done before an adjustment can be made.

In machinery losses that are outside the ordinary class, examination and survey require thought, time, and effort according to the kind of property involved, how it was damaged, whether the damage is slight or serious, and in some instances, because of the insurance covering it.

The insured's story will be a guide in the approach to the situation and will indicate what circumstances must be investigated and what questions will probably be difficult to handle. In many of these losses, it will be advisable to develop the story at length and in great detail by discussion and questioning. In some instances, the insured should be asked to support or amplify any story by producing for examination records that cover the acquisition, construction, use, or maintenance of the machinery.

When the cause of loss is, or may be, doubtful, the story should include the insured's knowledge or belief regarding the cause. Cause of loss is often doubtful in the situations outlined in the following paragraphs.

Electrical Losses

Examinations of damaged motors, generators, and other pieces of electrical equipment, made for the purpose of finding out whether the damage was the result of electrical injury or disturbance or of fire, are probably the most numerous of the examinations of machinery for the purpose of determining cause of loss. The appearance of the windings of a damaged motor and sometimes of the other parts that are conductors of the operating current will indicate very clearly in many instances the effect of the heat of the current in the conductors or of any fire that may have occurred in the insulation. Excess current can generate a very high degree of heat, high enough to melt any metal. The degree of heat generated by the burning of the fabrics and gums, out of which insulation covering wires is made, is relatively low, not high enough to melt copper. If, in the examination of a damaged motor or generator, the claim representative finds fused or melted wires or other conductors with little or no evidence of actual fire, he or she will know that the damage was probably due to electrical action.

Standard fire policies covering machinery include the peril of lightning but not that of electrical injury. The forms attached to such policies generally contain a stipulation (1) that the insurer shall not be liable for electrical injury to electrical equipment or wiring, or (2) that it shall not be liable for any such injury unless fire ensues and then only for the fire damage, or (3) in connection with power stations and utility risks, that it shall not be liable for such injury unless fire ensues, but if fire does ensue, it shall be liable for both the electrical injury and the fire damage. The scorched or burned insulation of a damaged generator, motor, or other piece of electrical equipment will speak for itself, but questions of whether the damage was the result of lightning or of overload due to some other cause and whether fire ensued must be considered in the light of what the insured has to say about what happened and what anyone saw or heard or afterward found out. In many power plants a record of operations is kept in a logbook which the insured should be asked to produce for examination in support of any story covering any loss involving the equipment.

In many cases the facts on which to base an opinion can be determined only by disassembling the unit and having it examined by an electrical expert.

Hot Bearings and Belts

Damage to bearings that run hot or belts that stick and are worn thin by pulleys are at times accompanied by fire, and claims are presented for the costs of repair or replacement. The insured's story about the length of time that the belt or bearing was in trouble before flame appeared may disclose that its value had been destroyed before it caught fire and, therefore, that the insurer is not liable for the loss.

Processing Losses

Damage to ovens and driers that use the direct heat of gas, oil, or other fuel is at times caused by overheating and ignition of the contents. The insured's story of the operation and the quantity of the contents will be a guide to ascertaining or estimating whether any part of the damage was due to overheating before the fire occurred or whether all of it was a result of the fire.

Boiler Losses

When claim is made for fire damage to a boiler that is found empty after a fire, the insured should be asked to state whether it contained water before and during the fire. The shell and tubes of a boiler are rarely damaged by fire unless the boiler is empty. If there was

a rupture or explosion of the boiler, the insured's statement about the time of the explosion should be taken. Explosion of a steam boiler, unless caused by hostile fire, is a peril excluded by the fire policy. If the boiler is on the insured premises, the explosion peril is also excluded by the extended coverage endorsement.[18]

Glass and Metal Furnace Losses

In glassworks and metal-smelting plants serious damage is at times done by molten cullet or metal when furnaces break and the incandescent mass flows over the floor, setting fire to flammable materials and causing damage by reason of its heat. Unless the insurance contract contains the molten-glass-or-metal clause, the insured's story of the cause of the break must be obtained. In the absence of this clause, the heat damage will not be covered unless the break was the result of fire. Such damage is at times serious, as molten cullet or metal flowing around the base of a steel column may soften it and possibly cause displacement of whatever the column supports.

Collapse Losses

In cases of building collapse due to a peril insured against, the insured's statement of what machines were in the structure and where each was located is a necessary preliminary to planning the work of salvaging them. The same is true when mining machinery is involved and has been buried or cut off by cave-in or by seals built for the purpose of smothering a mine fire.

Sprinkler Leakage

In some losses resulting from the discharge of water from a sprinkler head, the insured will have given notice of loss to the companies carrying the fire insurance and also to those carrying the sprinkler leakage insurance. The story will be that the head opened because of the fire in the forge, furnace, or other fire-using device underneath the sprinkler head. In such a situation, the claim

---

[18]See Chap. 15, "Boiler and Machinery Losses."

representative must examine the device and its surroundings for indications of any outside fire that might have been responsible for the rise in temperature that opened the head. If there was no hostile fire, the cause of loss was sprinkler leakage.

Smokestack Losses

When claim is made under windstorm insurance for the blowing over of a metal smokestack, the stack should be examined with particular attention to the thickness of the metal along any lines of breakage as contrasted with the thickness it had when new. Rust or corrosion due to acids generated by the burning of the fuel used in the furnace or firebox may have destroyed so much of the metal that the toppling or breaking of the stack was the result of its weakened condition and *not* the result of windstorm.

Where windstorm is determined to be the cause of the toppling, inspection and examination of the base of the stack is still important to approximate the extent of depreciation.

Explosion Losses

The rupturing of tanks and other containers and of pipes or valves caused by pressure of liquids; the rupture, bursting, or operation of relief valves; water hammer; electrical arcing; and numerous similar occurrences are frequently the basis of claim under the peril of explosion. Most policies covering commercial and industrial properties exclude these. The reader is referred to the section on Explosion in Chapter 8 for a detailed discussion of the subject.

Fire Losses

Following destruction or damage by fire of a building that houses machinery, an examination of the various machines and pieces of equipment should be made and the evidences of damage noted. While in many instances it is advisable to have an engineer or other expert pass on the question of damage and possibly on that of repair, the claim representative should form an opinion based on what he or she sees. Serious fire damage to machinery is quite evident. When all metal parts are found to be melted, fused, or warped, their subjection to a high degree of heat is indicated, and the machinery will ordinarily be a total loss. When iron or steel parts are found to be covered with scale, they will ordinarily have to be discarded unless they are extremely heavy. Scaling indicates great heat. When bright surfaces of iron or steel are found to have turned yellow or blue, a lesser degree of heat is indicated. In some instances the degree of heat to which a machine has been subjected can be approximated after careful observation of the immediate surroundings and an examination of the small parts of the machine itself, also of the grease cups and the bearings. If the paint on a nearby wall is not blistered, if the needles, teeth, or other small parts of the machine are not out of shape, if the babbitt in the bearings is not melted and the grease is still in the cups, it can be assumed that the degree of heat was not great. Such observation and examination should be made when the insured claims that a machine was damaged by heat, but the machine itself shows no evidence of damage. A frequent claim of this sort is that certain parts of the machine have had the temper drawn. Such a claim calls for an examination of the parts, a determination of what kind of metal they are made of, and what were the processes by which they were produced. Cast iron, machine steel, and wrought iron, for example, do not take tempering. In many instances, the only parts of a machine that have been tempered are the springs. Another claim of this sort is that parts of the machine have been warped and have pulled moving parts out of alignment. Such a claim calls for examination of the machine by an expert who can test it and make gauge measurements if necessary.

Disassembling to Examine

In some pieces of machinery the working parts are enclosed and cannot be examined unless the machine is opened up. Other machines of various types must, in many instances, be dismounted or disassembled after being damaged before any real examination can be made of them.

New machines dropped in loading or unloading, damaged during installation, damaged in transit, or otherwise injured by a covered peril, usually have to be taken down, checked, and tested by a manufacturer's representative to ensure continuance of warranties and guarantees.

Total Loss and Out-of-Sight Machinery

When machinery is in sight, its condition at the time of loss will generally be evident, but if it has been lost or so badly damaged that its condition cannot be determined with certainty, the insured should be questioned in a way that will ascertain whether the machinery was old or new, in good repair or run down. In some losses, whether the machinery is in sight or out of sight, the question of value must be approached by leading the insured to outline the history of the machinery, stating when and how it was purchased or built, how it had been used prior to the date of loss, and whether it had suffered any previous damage or developed any unusual troubles. It may be well to ask the insured to supplement the history by stating whether the machinery, at the time of loss, was useful, valuable, efficient, and in regular operation, or whether it was experimental or idle, or equipment used only in emergencies. In some instances, the story should be even further developed to cover the insured's plans for the future use of the machinery.

Choice of Method of Adjustment

A great many losses to machinery are adjusted on the basis of estimates of the cost of making repairs or replacements, with due consideration to betterment. The estimates may be those of the insured's representative or the claim representative's, and in either case the specifications for repair or replacement should be checked.

Machinery losses are frequently adjusted by having the repair or replacement made by someone mutually agreed upon, and the cost checked by the claim representative.

Frequently, insureds are equipped to repair damaged machines with their own employees and loss is handled in this way to the satisfaction of both insured and insurer.

The use of machinery experts, electrical engineers, and other specialists is common in serious losses, in losses involving expensive or complicated machinery, and in losses where the cause of loss or extent of damage is questioned by the claim representative. In losses that involve business interruption or extra expense insurance, when business can be saved by speedy resumption of operations, immediate repair or replacement of machinery is often necessary.

Recovering Machinery and Making It Accessible

Following severe damage to buildings, piers, platforms, or other structures that house or support machinery, machines or equipment may be dropped into lower floors and basements or into rivers or harbors, or may be covered by debris. Questions then arise of what shall be done to recover them or make them accessible. The cost of recovery or opening the way will, in many cases, be relatively high if the work is pushed as an independent operation and relatively low if done in connection with the removal of the structural debris. The value of the machine out of place or inaccessible, the need for it, and the rate at which it will take on rust or other further damage unless cared for must be given consideration.

Expense incurred by the insured in recovering machinery and making it accessible becomes an item of claim to the extent of the value saved, if there is no business interruption insurance involved, or to the extent that the business-interruption loss is reduced, if such insurance is involved. As a part of any claim under insurance covering the machinery, the expense is subject to contribution or coinsurance. Under business interruption insurance, however, it is not.

Protection From Further Damage

The great majority of machinery losses are of small or moderate size. It often is found on arrival at the premises that the insured has already done what is necessary to protect the property from further damage.

In serious losses, however, following fire, explosion, windstorm, flood, sprinkler leakage, service-pipe break, or other casualty, the claim representative will generally find when he or she arrives that the machinery is subject to further damage. Rust, clogging of the machines by the material in process, or breakage from collapse of weakened parts of the structure will result unless protective steps are taken.

In some losses the building must be made weathertight and the machinery cared for on the premises. In others, the building is so badly damaged that it must first be made safe by pulling down dangerous walls, heavy beams or timbers, or by shoring and bracing, after which the machinery must be removed to a place of safety. In other cases, the condition of the building will have no bearing on the situation, as the condition of the machinery itself will determine whether it should remain in the building and be protected there or should be removed. Temporary covers, sometimes nothing more than tar paper, at other times substantial timber and board structures, must, after some losses, be placed or built over machines and remain there until the building has been put in good shape.

When machinery that was in operation at the time of loss is filled with stock in process, and the stoppage of its operation will result in its becoming clogged with the material, or rusty because of water in the material, the stock should be promptly removed from the machines as a preliminary to cleaning and possibly greasing them. Machines that mold chocolate candy are examples of the kind that may become clogged, as the warm candy that passes through them will harden when it becomes cool. Looms and knitting machines are examples of machines that may be rusted because of the wetting of stock in process. Unless they are promptly stripped of wet thread and cloth or knitted products, rusting will be serious.

Wet belts should be taken off pulleys and cleaned of all dirt. Aprons of cloth that absorb water should be removed from machines and dried.

Wet machines should be wiped as dry as possible and, if safe against rain or the drip of water from upper floors or broken pipes, should, with the exception of motors or generators, be liberally slushed with heavy cylinder oil to prevent formation of rust. If there is danger of further wetting, a heavier grease is necessary. Lubricating grease or compound will, in such situations, give the maximum protection. Spare parts and small tools may be put into wire baskets and dipped into barrels of oil for quick greasing.

Electric motors or generators that have not been submerged and do not need to be sent to a repair shop equipped to bake them should be cleaned of dust, charcoal, or fallen plaster and covered with tarpaulins if there is danger of further wetting.

Greasing should be done with special attention to milled, ground, or polished iron or steel surfaces where smoothness is essential. Ordinary rusting will do no damage to cast-iron frame members of a machine, but great damage will be done by rust if it pits the surface of a roll or plate that has been milled or ground to do precision work.

Wet machines with small and delicate parts should be dismounted as quickly as possible to facilitate the work of checking rust. In many cases the parts should be dropped into kerosene as soon as they are taken out of their mountings, then scoured and afterward kept in a thin lubricating oil until they are assembled into the machine. A wet linotype or knitting machine will be undamaged if promptly taken apart, dried, cleaned, greased, and assembled. Left uncared for until rust has made the small parts stick together, the same machine will require much labor to recondition it, and some of the parts will be found so roughened by pitting that new ones will be required.

On machines that are generally sent out for repair as soon after damage as they can be handled, the work of protection from further damage is often combined with the work of repairing and reconditioning. Electric motors that have been under water are often promptly removed from their bases and sent to a repair shop for cleaning and baking. Voltmeters and other panel instruments are generally handled in the same way.

Separation and Putting in Order

Because of their fixed positions there is no separating to be done with most machines. Spare parts, tool dies, and other such movable articles should be matched up and grouped or lotted so that counting will be easy.

Inventory

An inventory of machinery should be made in such order as to permit checking with a minimum of difficulty. Generally, the only descriptions necessary are the names of the machines—looms, bandsaws, lathes, drill presses, and such. In serious losses, however, engineers will frequently give specific descriptions and machine numbers that will enable an office staff to take prices from manufacturers' catalogs or write the manufacturers for replacement prices with assurance that their letters specify the machines involved and will bring the proper answers.

In many plants, cards are maintained for each piece of machinery, giving the manufacturer's machine number and description, date of purchase, cost, and frequently, also the cost of transportation and installation. When such cards are available, a very accurate machinery inventory can be made. In plants that do not maintain cards, a machinery inventory will sometimes be found and almost always a machinery or equipment account. Such an account is generally of little value except as a guide to dates when equipment was purchased and, therefore, to the dates of invoices that should be looked up. Some machinery accounts give practically no help toward pricing an inventory and no indication of the value of the machinery in the plant. If the original machinery invoices have been discarded, the account will, ordinarily, be of little help.

If the equipment is too badly burned or broken to permit the making of an inventory that will be accurate in count and descriptions, it may be advisable to employ an engi-neer to make a floor plan, locate the machines on it, and then list and price the machinery from whatever evidence can be obtained. When a building of two or more stories is destroyed, the machinery debris may be so badly broken and mingled as to make a physical check impossible without the help of persons who were familiar with the machinery.

An inventory intended to reflect actual cost or replacement cost of machinery in place should be noted to show whether the prices are f.o.b. at points of shipment or include transportation and installation costs.

Preparation for Adjustment

In the ordinary machinery loss, the claim representative seldom finds it necessary to make any special preparation before discussing adjustment. He or she listens to the insured's story, examines the machine, and begins to check the damage. Sometimes it is better to employ a repair firm or an engineer to make an examination and prepare an estimate or report, or in other instances, call on the representative of the manufacturer of the machine for an opinion. One who handles a number of losses on the same kind of machinery will become proficient in estimating the cost of repairs and, on the usual run of losses, will only occasionally need outside help.

In serious and unusual machinery losses, preparation is always necessary. In many losses all that is required is the employment of a competent expert to examine the property and report in detail on value and loss, to be available for conference should the claim representative need more information, or, perhaps, to help in discussions with the insured. In some losses, however, the situation demands the joint efforts of claim representative and expert if effective preparation is to be made.

Preparation may require a review of the insured's story with the request that it be put in writing. It may be advisable to abstract, copy, or photostat any financial, property, or operating records covering the machinery.

Ordinarily, however, a study of the machinery itself is the most important part of the work of preparation. Accurate descriptions of the machines should be written up, all evidence of damage should be recorded in notes, and, when advisable, photographs should be made. Specific identifications of machines, such as manufacturer's name, machine number, power or capacity rating appearing on nameplates or stamped on the frames, can be graphically recorded by tracings, rubbings, or plaster-of-paris impressions.

In two kinds of machinery losses—secondhand machinery and experimental machinery—preparation must include a study of the history of the machinery. Both kinds of machinery can be most troublesome subjects of adjustment because of the difficulty of valuing them.

QUESTIONS AND PROBLEMS

1. Under a Homeowners policy an insured sustained a fire loss which was confined to the basement although heavy smoke came in contact with the contents in the rooms above. Claim has been presented and you are assigned to discuss the details with Mrs. Insured, a widow. Several items in the claim could be potential problems in the adjustment. Explain briefly how you would handle the following articles that were damaged beyond repair.

a. Several suits that belonged to Mrs. Insured's husband who passed away a year ago.

b. Mrs. Insured's 25-year-old wedding gown.

c. Three oil paintings of landscapes, painted recently by Mrs. Insured, who is taking lessons with a local group of retirees, all of whom are amateurs.

d. A box of baby clothes once worn by her son now married and living elsewhere.

e. An old victrola record player.

2. a. In your discussing the claim with Mrs. Insured in problem 1 above, she says that the clothes in the closets and dresser drawers are so badly smoke-stained that they are a total loss. You inspect the clothing in question and are almost satisfied that everything is ruined. Would you send it all

out to cleaning establishments or pay on the basis of a total loss?

b. Mrs. Insured, during negotiations, declares, "There is nothing in the policy about depreciation; the word isn't even used. Why are you telling me I have to depreciate these items?" How do you respond convincingly?

c. Mrs. Insured says, "OK. I understand that, but what is this obsolescence and physical depreciation? What is the difference if it's all depreciation?" How do you explain? Cite examples of each.

3. Improvements and betterments covered under a policy are fairly well characterized in the wording "but which are not legally subject to removal by the Insured."

a. How are trade fixtures of a tenant usually characterized?

b. A fixture, as distinguished from a trade fixture, is characterized differently by the courts. What is that difference?

c. In determining whether the property in question is a fixture or personal property (a trade fixture), a rule frequently applied is the rule of annexation, adaptation, and intention. Explain the rule.

4. a. In establishing the actual cash value of machinery in a large machine shop, would you apply the same rule as you did on establishing the actual cash value of household goods under a Homeowners policy? What essential difference, if any, is there?

b. The insured owns and operates a large food cannery that works 7 days a week on three 8-hour shifts daily. The plant is wrecked by a fire, and the insured and the claim representative are discussing the actual cash value of the machinery and equipment.

The insured presents the claim representative with a schedule of annual depreciation percentages for machinery of all types compiled by a large appraisal company. The claim representative's accountant has determined from the books that most of the machines have been depreciated down to one dollar. Discounting all other factors, would it be equitable to use the book value, the depreciation schedule submitted by the insured, or some other test to estimate the probable physical depreciation to be deducted in establishing actual cash value?

5. In sawmills, canneries, and other risks, some of the equipment and machines is custom-designed and made by the insured. Many times such equipment and machinery cannot be bought on the market, and in some instances the insured protects various features with patents.

Assume a loss occurs involving one of these insured-made machines. On what basis would you establish loss and value?

17

Mercantile and Manufacturer's Stocks

This chapter includes all types of movable property which is held for sale in retail and wholesale establishments; which is in factories; which is held in warehouses, elevators, or storage tanks; which is stacked or piled in the open; which is on cars or trucks; and which is in transit. This chapter also includes raw stock, materials and supplies, and stock in process on the premises of manufacturers, converters, processors, and others.

STOCKS AS A SUBJECT OF INSURANCE

Stocks of merchandise is a subject of insurance under a myriad of property insurance contracts classified as fire, inland marine, multiple-line, multi-peril, boiler and machinery, ocean marine, and the traditional first-party casualty policies. Claims for loss or damage to such property also are recognized and adjusted under various liability coverages where liability is accepted.

Mercantile and manufacturer's stocks are usually included in policies under the heading of Personal Property or Contents and, in addition to stock, cover furniture, fixtures, machinery, equipment, and other personal property. The trend in description in forms is toward the broad cover of *business personal property owned by the insured, and usual to the occupancy of the insured,* as used in the SMP, FGP-1, and Businessowners forms. Under Building(s) and Contents Form 18, stock may be covered as a separate item or included under the contents item. Improvements and betterments are usually covered under contents or personal property when the insured is not the owner of the building occupied; and there are frequently provisions to cover, with limitations, personal property elsewhere than on the described premises.

Stock coverage is also found in the many specific fire insurance forms, in inland marine policies, comprehensive crime, and boiler and machinery policies.

As in the adjustment of losses under other property coverages, the original or copies of the policies, forms, and endorsements should be examined with care before proceeding.

DAMAGEABILITY OF STOCKS

Finished stocks of merchandise, stock in process of manufacture, and raw materials may be destroyed, lost, or damaged by the action of one or more of the perils insured against. The damageability of the different kinds of stock depends on a number of factors which may or may not exist prior to, during, and after the occurrence. Damageability is closely related to salvage and salvaging. This subject is discussed in Chapter 19.

INSURABLE VALUES

All insurance policies covering property state in either broad terms or precise language the basis on which the amount of insurance is to be carried and on which losses are to be paid.

As an example of broad terms, the standard fire policies insure

> ... to the extent of the actual cash value of the property at the time of loss, but not exceeding the amount which it would cost to repair or replace the property with material of like kind and quality within a reasonable time after such loss.

A number of important considerations are necessary in determining the actual cash value in loss situations.[1]

Superior Risk forms are more specific and provide coverage under the following:

> VALUE OF PROPERTY: The value of the following property shall be determined as follows:
> 1. raw stock, supplies and other merchandise not manufactured by the Insured, the replacement cost;
> 2. stock in process, the value of raw stock and labor expended, plus the proper proportion of overhead charges;
> 3. finished stock manufactured by the Insured, the regular cash selling price, less all discounts and charges to which such finished stock would have been subject had no loss occurred;
> 4. a. records, manuscripts and drawings, not exceeding their value blank plus the cost incurred for actually transcribing or copying them, except as provided in b.;
>   b. media for, or programming records pertaining to, electronic and electromechanical data processing or electronically controlled equipment, including the data thereon, not exceeding the cost of such media or programming records blank plus the cost of reproducing the data thereon from duplicates or from originals of the previous generation, but no liability is assumed hereunder for the cost of gathering or assembling information or data for such reproduction.

The Businessowners policies cover the

> Replacement cost of the Business Personal Property owned by the insured, usual to the oc-

cupancy of the insured, at the premises described in the Declarations to which a limit of liability is shown....

Replacement coverage endorsements determine insurable value of stocks when such endorsements are part of or attached to a policy. Some stocks may be valued at cost of manufacture, selling price, or the insured's cost plus a stipulated percentage profit.

Reference to the policy and its endorsements is essential to determine the insurable value to be dealt with in the adjustment of a loss. The intent of the insurance policy is to compensate the insured fully in accord with his policy valuation provisions.

Personal Property in the Hands of a Merchant

A dealer in stocks of merchandise may be a wholesaler, a broker, or a retailer. Ordinarily, merchandise in the hands of a dealer can be replaced reasonably promptly if lost or destroyed. The majority of court decisions in cases bearing on this subject hold that *cash value* means replacement cost rather than the dealer's selling price. It is accepted adjusting practice under cash value policies to value retail and wholesale stocks at the cost of replacement. The courts justify this position by stating that recovery is limited to indemnity and should not include, as a result of the loss, unearned and unrealized profits which would be included in the selling price of the merchandise;[2] "replacement in kind necessarily accomplishes indemnity."[3]

To the invoice price that must be paid in case of replacement there is added the cost to the insured of any freight or other transportation charges necessary to deliver the stock to the place of the loss. All trade and cash discounts are deducted. In some instances the cost of receiving, opening, tagging, marking, and arranging the merchandise for sale is properly added. There are two schools of thought among claim representatives and insurers on this subject. One group holds

---

[2]*Niagara Fire Ins. Co. v. Heflin*, 22 Ky. Law Rep. 1212, 60 S.W. 393.
[3]*McAnarney v. Newark Fire*, 247 N.Y. 176, 159 N.E. 902.

[1]See p. 30.

that the inclusion of these costs does not increase the actual cash value of the property and that these charges are part of the operating cost to do business; they should therefore be claimed under business interruption insurance. The second group believes that the actual cash value of merchandise is the value at the time and place where it is covered by the policy. As a practical matter, little difficulty is experienced in this area inasmuch as most insureds do not include these charges in their values for insurance purposes, and they are aware that, in case of loss, inclusion of such charges may cause them to suffer a penalty by application of a coinsurance, contribution, or full-reporting clause.

In those cases where a dealer cannot replace his stock within a reasonable time and therefore misses the market, replacement cost may provide restitution but not indemnity. Active merchandise that, if lost or destroyed, cannot be replaced within a reasonable time is worth to the owner what it could have been sold for. It should be valued accordingly.

In adjusting practice, commodities such as wheat, corn, soya, and cotton, which are bought and sold on established exchanges, are valued according to exchange prices. If the scene of the loss is at a distance from the exchange, the cost of shipping the commodity to the city in which the exchange is located is deducted.

Merchandise bought abroad, in many instances, is dutiable. Duty constitutes a proper item in the computation of replacement cost. Imported merchandise subject to duty may be stored in a bonded warehouse, payment of the duty being deferred until the merchandise is taken out or the time limit for paying the duty expires. If it is destroyed while in bond, there is no obligation resting on the owner to pay the duty, and the duty is therefore not considered in adjusting the loss. If merchandise is destroyed after the duty has been paid but before being moved out of the warehouse, the duty, under some circumstances, is recoverable from the federal government. Efforts to recover any duty should be made through a customhouse bro-

ker. Whiskey on storage in a bonded warehouse is valued at the in-bond price.

Many retail stores sell articles under a "layaway" plan whereby a customer makes a down payment, or sometimes pays in full, and the item is held for later delivery. Such merchandise is sometimes referred to as will-calls or "goods sold but not delivered."

In larger mercantile establishments the values of layaways may run into thousands of dollars. While there is no uniformity of opinion on whether the insured's cost or the selling price should be the basis of determining the insurable value, in many areas it is accepted adjusting practice to use the selling price both for value and loss. The reason given is that the insured earned the profit as a result of the sale, not the loss. Where the insured cannot replace the article from stock and must obtain it from a manufacturer, distributor, or competitor, the practice would seem to be a proper one. Under reporting policies, producers counsel insureds to include layaways at selling price, and in case of loss, adjustment is made accordingly.

Depreciation. On personal property held for sale, depreciation is usually recognized by the courts and a deduction is required.[4] The courts, however, are not always clear in their use of the term *depreciation*. In its broadest sense it includes both obsolescence and physical wear and tear.

Stocks of merchandise may show physical depreciation because of shop wear; poor storage or handling; deterioration; attacks by insects, rats, or mice; or the influences of climate, weather, or location. Shop wear is shown by soiling, fraying, rusting, tarnishing, fading, denting, or chipping. Poor storage may expose merchandise to moisture and heat conditions that produce mildew and fermentation. Excessive heat and cold are injurious to certain stocks; thawing and refreezing frozen food products causes deterioration; and certain food stocks, such as raw fruits and vegetables and bakery goods, are at their best for only short periods. Dried foods such as figs lose quality rapidly.

[4]*Grubbs v. N.C. Home Ins. Co.*, 108 N.C. 472, 13 S.E. 236.

Flies speck the surface of articles. Weevils invade grain and grain products. Rats and mice cut containers and damage foodstuffs. Moths and beetles attack furs and woolens. Location may expose a stock to such deteriorating influences as excessive smoke or corrosive gases from nearby plants. Sun fades many types of merchandise on display in shopwindows. Obsolescence in merchandise reveals itself in style changes, unseasonable goods, incomplete assortment, poor selection, failure to clear out odds and ends, irregular sizes, overbuying, and poor general or local business conditions. All these factors prevent the clearing of stock, and the insured is compelled to reduce prices. When a merchant marks down the selling price in order to move the stock, its "cost value" is proportionately reduced.[5]

Personal Property in the Hands of a Manufacturer

Since the majority of the court decisions hold that the cash value of merchandise in the hands of a dealer is based on the price of the goods in the dealer's normal, current market, one might conclude that the same measure of value would apply to merchandise in the hands of a manufacturer. Most of the cases, however, hold that cash value is to be measured here by the manufacturer's current selling price,[6] contingent, of course, upon any policy conditions and upon whether any unincurred charges exist, as would be the case with goods in process for which the costs of selling, wrapping, and shipping had not yet been incurred.

Two explanations have been offered for the courts' departure from the replacement-cost rule.

1. Manufacturing costs are more difficult to determine than is the selling price at the time of loss.
2. A manufacturer who has sustained a loss to merchandise may be unable to remanufacture it in time to avoid missing the market.

Finished merchandise in the hands of manufacturers may require considerable time to reproduce, if destroyed, and is often covered by policies containing a stipulation that the merchandise shall be valued at what it could be sold for, less the costs that would have been incurred in selling it had there been no loss. In treating with merchandise so covered, it is the practice to examine the sales record, or the price list of the manufacturer if the business is highly active, and price the merchandise accordingly, deducting sales discounts and outbound freight or commissions, if the manufacturer customarily pays either.

Canned, frozen, or dried meats, fruit, or vegetables in the hands of the processor are valued at selling price, less unincurred costs of selling. The insured is able to obtain what is processed only by contracting for it before the season begins, and if the product is lost it cannot be replaced until the next season except by purchase from a competitor. Some policy forms specify the precise basis for evaluating various kinds of personal property in the hands of a manufacturer. The HPR and Superior Risk forms are noteworthy in this regard.[7]

Most manufacturers, in the absence of policy provisions to the contrary, insure on the basis of the cost to manufacture, and they anticipate recovery, in case of loss, on that basis. When the policy contains a contribution clause or a full-reporting clause, the insured usually presents claim only for the value on which the insurance is based, to avoid a contribution or reporting penalty.

Depreciation. On stock in the hands of a manufacturer, depreciation is usually not as prevalent as on that in the hands of a merchant. There are two general exceptions: (1) decline in value caused by overproduction, particularly of seasonal goods; (2) changes in style, as in wearing apparel, and changes in model, as in the case of such electrical appliances as refrigerators, washers and dryers,

[5]See p. 317.
[6]*Boyd v. Royal Ins. Co.*, 111 N.C. 372, 16 S.E. 389. *Birmingham Fire Co. v. Pulver*, 126 Ill. 329, 18 N.E. 804. *Hoffman v. Aetna Fire Ins. Co.*, 1 Rob. 501 (N.Y. Super. Ct.,)1, affirmed, 32 N.Y. 405.

[7]See p. 254.

television sets, electric and gas kitchen ranges, air conditioners, cameras, and projectors.

PROCEDURE

Procedure in stock losses is similar to that followed in losses on other kinds of personal property. Books and records, however, are examined more often and stock is more frequently taken for sale as salvage.

Procedure includes (1) getting the insured's story, (2) identifying the stock and checking the coverage, (3) establishing the interest of the insured and of all others in the stock, (4) saving endangered stock or recovering lost stock, (5) examining the stock and making a survey and estimate of the situation, (6) choosing a method of adjustment, (7) protecting the stock from further damage, (8) separating the damaged and undamaged stock and putting it in order, (9) preparing for discussion of value and loss, (10) agreeing upon value and loss, or agreeing upon value and taking all or part of the stock, or arranging to have it sold as salvage, and (11) checking the claim.

Procedure in any loss will depend largely upon how much of the stock has been involved and how it has been affected. In some losses, the quantity of lost or destroyed stock will be indicated by circumstantial evidence, such as fire marks on the side of a bin, the walls of a building, or the shell of a tank. In others, while all value will have been destroyed, physical remains will evidence the identity and quantity of the stock. In some losses, however, there will be no trustworthy physical indications of the existence of the stock or of the part of it that is missing. Here getting the insured's story and examining the books and records will be the important steps in the procedure.

The Insured's Story

Most stock losses are relatively small or moderate in size and free from complications. Adjustment procedure will be quite routine. The insured's story is usually short and simple and ties in with what the claim representative observes. The damaged materials are examined, if still in existence, verification of values claimed is made from the books of account or other records and sources, and settlement or adjustment is concluded. If any stock is partially damaged and subject to salvaging, the claim representative agrees that it either will be retained by the insured or taken over by the insurer at an agreed value.

On the more serious or complicated losses the insured will be questioned in greater detail as to the time and probable cause of the loss, and any of the insured's employees or associates may be similarly questioned.[8]

Careful questioning of the insured should disclose what kind, quantity, and quality of property is involved, the extent of damage to it, and the insured's opinion of both value and loss. The claim representative may also wish to question the insured about what was the salability of the stock prior to the loss, what it would cost to replace it, and perhaps how it might be handled in the absence of insurance.

The insured should be questioned about the total insurance covering the stock, and whether or not there are consignees, concessionaires, or others who might have an interest in or insurance on any part of the stock. As early as possible the insured should be asked what books of account and records are kept, where kept, and what system of bookkeeping is maintained.

Cooperation of the Insured. In adjusting stock losses in mercantile and manufacturing risks, close cooperation of the insured is very essential to obtain the best results for everyone concerned. Most businessmen with whom the claim representative negotiates will be found successful managers who have considerable knowledge of their own business, whether it is a corner restaurant, a haberdasher, or a manufacturer of electronic equipment. Few claim representatives handle claims in a large variety of retail stores and manufacturing firms. Fewer still, in the course of adjusting a loss, remain on the premises for a sufficient length of time to

---

[8]See Chap. 7, "Investigation of the Insured, the Property, and the Insurance."

become other than superficially acquainted with the intricacies of the operation of the business.

For these reasons, the claim representative is well advised to solicit the help of the insured, who is usually more familiar with the stock than anyone else. While the claim representative is obtaining the insured's story, an opportunity presents itself to learn something about the insured's method of buying, selling, processing, or manufacturing, as the case may be.

The great majority of merchants and manufacturers maintain pride in their business and find pleasure in explaining their operation to interested and ready listeners. Though a claim representative has handled several or many claims in a particular kind of commercial or industrial risk, not all of each kind are conducted identically; and in each case new methods of purchasing, accounting, storing or processing materials, and selling goods may be learned. The more comprehensive the knowledge the claim representative acquires, the better is the insight into the insured's problems and point of view, and the better the perspective developed on what procedure will bring the adjustment to a satisfactory conclusion.

Identification and Check of Coverage

Stock is identified by comparing it, or the space it occupied before its loss or destruction, with the description and location that are stated in the policy or policies.

Coverage should be checked in accordance with the procedure outlined in Chapter 7, with particular attention to property covered, excluded property, provisions for valuation, and locations excluded.

Establishing Interests

In most stock losses, the insured is the sole and unconditional owner of all merchandise on the premises. Invoices showing purchase will be evidence of ownership.

In many losses, however, the stock covered by the insurance is made up of merchandise, some of which is owned by the insured and the rest by others. Merchandise

owned by others may be the property of consignees, concessionaires, or persons who have sent it to the insured for storage, processing, assembling, or manufacturing. In many instances, the merchant, warehouseman, processor, or manufacturer agrees to assume liability for loss, protecting himself by insuring against the liability, or agrees to maintain insurance on the stock itself for the benefit of the bailor. In other instances, the bailor agrees to carry insurance.

In any event, bailor and bailee have each an insurable interest in the property: the bailor, generally, because of ownership; the bailee, because of charges and because he or she may be liable for it if it is lost or damaged.[9]

In department stores and shops that maintain repair departments, there will almost always be on hand at the time of a loss a number of household articles that belong to customers and that are being altered, renovated, or repaired. Such stores and shops are not thought of as bailee risks, but in their repair departments they are.

Interests in merchandise on the premises belonging to others should be established through examination of written contracts or memorandums, or by oral or written statements of both bailor and bailee.

Examination, Survey, and Estimate of the Situation

In the general run of stock losses, the claim representative gets the insured's story, identifies the stock, checks the coverage, examines the merchandise, surveys the situation, and adjusts the loss, all during a single visit. In the exceptional losses, examination and survey are independent and time-consuming operations.

In losses involving the contents of driers, ovens, or other devices utilizing heat, the residue of the contents should be examined and also the interior of the device, as it may or may not show fire marks.

Claims for damage by smoke are occasionally made by merchants who sell high-priced wearing apparel because an electric

[9]See Chap. 21, "Bailee Risks."

motor operating one of the services in the premises has overheated and given off smoke. In such claims, the survey must include an investigation of what actually happened in the motor, whether or not there was fire as distinguished from electrical overheating if such loss is excluded in the policy.

In all losses involving water damage, a sufficient survey of the premises and, at times, of the surroundings must be made in order to determine the source from which the water came and the channel by which it reached the stock.

On arriving at the scene of a loss, the claim representative should note the general condition of the stock and the premises. In many instances, all the stock will be in sight and the premises weathertight. The character of the merchandise will be such that it will not deteriorate because of a few days' stoppage of business or suffer further damage if left as it is. It is accessible, and accurate inventory can be made of it, the damage to it can be estimated with a fair degree of certainty, or it can be offered for sale to a salvage buyer without first having to be reconditioned or removed to a warehouse or other place of safety.

A retail shoe store, for example, may occupy the first floor of a building as selling space, receiving and unpacking cartons of shoes in the basement. Fire may occur in the basement, break through to the first floor, and do some damage before it is controlled. No stock is burned out of sight, all pairs of shoes can be identified, and the stock is not wet enough to go bad if left alone. By keeping the heat on or airing the store properly, the stock will dry where it is. An inventory can be made and the loss adjusted with no preliminary handling of the shoes.

There are many losses, however, in which the claim representative will find the premises wrecked, part of the stock destroyed, part requiring removal and drying, and part requiring protection where it is, often to be given by closing the premises against the weather. It will be possible to inventory part of the stock. The value of the rest will have to be established by examining the books. In a few losses, the claim representative will find wet merchandise that, if processed without delay, will produce perfect finished materials or articles. An example of this is wet raw furs.

In serious losses, the claim representative should promptly determine what merchandise is in sight and whether there is reason to believe that other merchandise of substantial value is buried under debris, covered by snow, or submerged in a flooded basement or in the water under or adjacent to a fire-damaged pier.

Merchandise in sight should be examined to ascertain whether a substantially correct inventory can be made of it and to gain some idea of the sound value involved and the nature and extent of the damage. In cases of severe damage, particular attention must be given to the probable value remaining in the damaged commodity or articles, whether it is great enough to warrant the expense of efforts to save it. When merchandise in sight is worthless, the cost of removing it must be given consideration if the insurer is liable for the cost of its removal.

When there is reason to believe that merchandise worth recovering has been buried, covered, or submerged, survey of the situation should include inquiry into the possibility of exploratory or recovery work in conjunction with wrecking or debris-removal work, if such work is planned for the benefit of any other interest.

The space occupied by merchandise that, according to the insured's story, is out of sight should be surveyed for size, area, markings, or other physical evidence indicating quantity. Any remains of merchandise should be examined to see whether they substantiate or refute the insured's statement of what or how much was destroyed.

When merchandise in sight has been so badly damaged that it cannot be inventoried, or when merchandise is out of sight, the survey of the situation should include inquiry into what books and records the insured may be able to produce that will show quantities or values.

The work of examination and survey should be done with dispatch. The claim representative should become familiar with conditions that indicate how any stock in sight should be treated in order that its maximum value may be realized by the insured, if kept, or by the insurer, if it is taken and sold as salvage. The claim representative should also be familiar with the circumstances that determine how procedure should be planned in order to obtain, at minimum expense, the best information to be had on value and loss.

The following outline fairly well indicates what may be necessary.

I. The situation in general.
   A. What is involved.
      1. Which of the following situations is found at the premises where loss occurred?
         a. Part of the stock is damaged, the rest undamaged.
         b. All of the stock is damaged.
         c. Part of the stock is a total loss, the rest damaged in whole or in part.
         d. All of the stock is a total loss.
      2. Is all merchandise on which claim will be made in sight?
      3. If not, what is in sight, and what, according to the insured's story, is out of sight?
   B. What is required.
      Which of the following must be determined because of any full-reporting, distribution, contribution, or coinsurance clauses in the insurance?
      1. Amount of loss only.
      2. Insurable value on the premises and amount of loss.
      3. Insurable value in all structures and on yards at one plant.
      4. Insurable value at a number of locations.
II. Merchandise in sight.
   A. Possibility of examination.
      1. Is all merchandise in sight accessible and subject to examination for identity and condition?
      2. Can examination be made where it is and as it is, or must the merchandise be moved, separated, or unpacked before examination?

B. Possibility of inventorying.
   1. Is the condition of the merchandise such that all of it can be counted, weighed, or measured?
   2. If any of it is in packages or containers, are the labels, tags, or other identifying marks legible or have they been washed off, destroyed, or obliterated?
   3. Has the merchandise been so badly mauled, mixed with other merchandise, or scattered as to make the cost of counting, weighing, or measuring prohibitive?
   4. Will any other condition make inventorying impossible or inadvisable?
C. Condition of merchandise and premises.
   1. Is the merchandise in a place of safety and not subject to further damage?
   2. If not, is its probable remaining value great enough to warrant the cost of efforts to save it?
   3. Is it a kind of merchandise that, because of what has happened to it or to the premises containing it, must be used, distributed, or processed without delay in order to preserve its value?
   4. Is it, or are the premises, in such condition that action is necessary to protect it from further damage?
   5. Will the space and equipment available on the premises, and the condition of both, permit whatever handling of the merchandise may be requisite to its examination?
D. Treatment of the merchandise.
   1. Should the merchandise remain on the premises or be moved elsewhere?
   2. Should arrangements be made for sale, use, distribution, processing, or reconditioning without delay?
   3. Should all undamaged merchandise that is part of the sound

value be inventoried in place or checked out as it is shipped or removed?

III. Merchandise out of sight.

A. Does the appearance of the premises tend to support or discredit the insured's story of what merchandise is out of sight?

B. Should any debris be separated, counted, weighed, or measured?

C. What physical evidence other than debris indicates identity or quantity of stock out of sight, or indicates that no stock was destroyed or lost?

D. Should debris be removed before the inventory of stock has been completed?

IV. Books and records.

Has the insured kept and can he or she produce books or records showing the quantity or value of any stock not in sight, or of any stock in sight that cannot be inventoried or that it is inadvisable to inventory?

V. Obtaining and recording evidence.

A. Should any witnesses be interviewed and their statements taken?

B. Should any photographs be made?

C. Should the reading of any labels, tags, or other package marks be recorded?

D. Should any counting, weighing, or measuring be done, or any sketches made?

Choice of Method of Adjustment

The choice of method by which a loss on a stock of merchandise is to be adjusted should be made according to the circumstances attending the particular loss. The loss may involve stock in sight, stock out of sight, or both. Some losses involve complete destruction of part of the stock and general damage to another part, while the rest of the stock has escaped injury.

When all the stock is in sight, and the salvage value is less than the probable cost of saving and selling the merchandise, determination of the sound value will also determine the loss. In such a case, only two steps need be taken: (1) to agree upon the replacement cost of the merchandise and, if applicable, (2) to agree upon the amount to be deducted for depreciation. The difference between replacement cost and depreciation will represent both insurable value and loss. When salvaging can produce a net return, the property must be protected from further damage and inventoried. The claim representative must then decide whether to adjust the loss by agreeing with the insured on its amount or by agreeing on the value and taking the merchandise to be sold as salvage.

Many of the methods of adjustment for all types of property losses, outlined in Chapter 1, are used at one time or another for losses involving stocks of merchandise. The methods below, however, are the most commonly used.

Method 1. Agreement on Value and Loss. If the insured is to retain the merchandise, the claim representative may try to reach an agreement on value and loss with or without the help of an expert. Usually the claim representative and the insured discuss the probable outturn of the damaged goods, giving consideration to trade conditions and other matters bearing on the insured's opportunity to dispose of them. Quite often, however, the claim representative will bring into the discussion salvors who make a business of trading in damaged stocks.

Efforts to agree are generally made after the merchandise has been separated, put in order, and inventoried, and the claim representative is familiar with the inventory. Occasionally, efforts are made to agree upon percentages of loss to the various lots of stock with the understanding that they will thereafter be inventoried.

The percentage of loss to merchandise held for sale is the ratio expressed by the amount that the selling price, before the loss, must be reduced to move it, *over* the price it would have sold for at the time of loss. To determine the *dollar amount* of loss, the percentage of loss is applied to the selling price when the merchandise is insured for selling price; it is applied to the actual cash value when the merchandise is insured for actual cash value.

EXAMPLE 17-1

Before the Loss

Selling price of stock..........................	$30,000	100%
Cost of stock.................................	18,000	60%
Gross profit	$12,000	40%

After the Loss

Selling price of stock ($30,000 less 25%)........	$22,500	100%
Cost of stock ($18,000 less 25%)..............	13,500	60%
Gross profit	$ 9,000	40%

For example, a stock of suits in a men's clothing store suffers smoke damage from an exposure fire. The claim representative and the insured agree that if the stock is marked down 25 percent, it can be sold. The *retail value* of the stock is $30,000; the *cash value* (insured's cost less any depreciation) is $18,000. If the stock is insured at selling price, the loss is 25% × $30,000, or $7,500. If it is insured for actual cash value, the loss is 25% × $18,000 or $4,500. Percentage of loss means *percentage of loss to value insured.* [10]

In the foregoing illustration, the insured operated prior to the loss on a 40 percent gross profit, or margin. Applying the agreed percentage of loss to cost or actual cash value, insured can still maintain a 40 percent gross profit after the loss. See Example 17-1. The insured received the full cost ($18,000) of the stock by sale ($13,500) plus the amount paid by the insurer ($4,500). The gross profit of $9,000 represents a loss of $3,000. This is *an earnings* or *profit loss*, not a property loss.

Manufacturers whose plants operate in a way that permits the refinishing or reconditioning of damaged products, parts, or goods in process can ordinarily do better with it than outsiders. Usually, when a percentage of loss is agreed to on the raw stock or stock in process, the percentage may represent the cost of reconditioning the stock or the dif-

ference between the value just before the loss and immediately after the loss.

Method 2. Taking Stock for Sale as Salvage. [11] When, because of the character of the merchandise, the class of trade, the lack of facilities for handling damaged merchandise, or other valid reasons, the insured cannot sell damaged merchandise to the trade, it is advisable to adjust the loss by having the salvage sold for account of the loss or by taking the merchandise at an agreed value and selling it for account of the insurer. Use of this method of adjustment must be limited to merchandise that, prior to being damaged, was salable and to situations in which it is possible to make a fair agreement on the value of the merchandise to be taken.

If the insured cannot dispose of the merchandise except by selling it to an outsider, a competent salvor or salvage organization should ordinarily be able to get a higher net return from a sale of the merchandise than the insured. [12] Taking stock for salvage should be avoided in losses of doubtful origin and in losses involving out-of-date, inferior, contaminated, ill-assorted, or otherwise undesirable merchandise. Where it is essential to remove damaged stock to protect it from further damage in the foregoing situations, removal should be done under appropriate agreement and if necessary under a nonwaiver agreement.

---

[10]See Chap. 19, "Salvaging and Use of Salvors."

[11]See Chap. 19.
[12]See Chap. 19.

Method 3. Sale, Use, or Reconditioning. In some losses, the amount of damage can be kept at a minimum by arranging for the prompt sale of merchandise that, if left where it is, will deteriorate or spoil. Perishable stocks, fresh meat, fruits, vegetables, dairy products, and many other foodstuffs, when involved in loss, must be sold promptly if any value is to be realized. In the normal operation of a grocery store, meat market, or delicatessen the stock must turn over rapidly even when the premises are in order and all refrigerating equipment is working. If the premises are damaged and the equipment is put out of commission, only prompt action will save the stock. Transfer of retail perishable stocks to other refrigerated premises can seldom be made economically. Quick sale to consumers is almost always the only way that such stocks should be handled. Sale should be made by the insured under whatever check is deemed advisable. Its result will establish the amount of loss.

Immediate use will at times prevent loss of damage of wet merchandise. Gray goods, raw furs, hides, and skins are examples. If wet gray goods can be moved at once to a bleaching and finishing plant and processed without delay, they will often be returned to the owner without loss, or with only slight damage, but if they are left uncared for, very serious loss can be done by mildew. Wet raw furs, hides, or skins, if sent at once to the dressers, tanners, wool scourers, or other processing agents who would normally handle them, will also often be returned without loss. In such situations the insurance loss will be limited to extra costs of handling, if any, plus the amount of any damage due to the wetting that is found upon inspection of the finished merchandise.

Green coffee that has been wet should go at once to the roasters, and wet, unground pepper and spices should go to the pepper and spice grinders, as drying is one of the normal steps in handling.

When it is practical to take an accurate inventory of the remaining damaged and undamaged merchandise, subtracting the value of this merchandise from the inventory obtained from the books will disclose the value of the out-of-sight merchandise.

In many metal-worker losses rusted parts should be sent through pickle baths or polishing processes and afterward inspected, with rejection of the parts that have failed to come through in serviceable condition.

Merchandise that has absorbed the odors of smoke can, in many instances, be restored to good condition by smoke-odor treatment. Odors absorbed from stench bombs are often neutralized in the same way.

Lots of finished stock should, in some instances, be repacked or relabeled.

Use of method 3 must be limited to instances in which the insured is trustworthy and competent and can be relied upon to sell, have processed, or recondition merchandise prudently and account for the results accurately and honestly.

Method 4. Books and Records. Resort to books and records becomes necessary when a loss involves an appreciable quantity of out-of-sight merchandise. Honestly and accurately kept books and records will very closely reflect the value of the merchandise. They will not, however, show removals of stock due to theft. Their showing may be distorted by mistakes of employees in handling merchandise and the memorandums covering it. There is often a lag between the movement of a unit or lot of merchandise and the book entry recording the movement. Books should, therefore, be examined and their showing checked against all other evidence indicating value, and not considered alone.[13]

Method 5. Space, Debris, or Other Physical Evidence. Method 5 should be used when the physical evidence is conclusive. When the property can be counted, weighed, or measured after a loss with the same result as before the loss, no better evidence of its quantity can be had. If the space it occupied can be definitely determined and measured, its cubic content can be determined. A tank cannot hold more than so

[13]See Chap. 20, "Books and Records."

many gallons; a bin of known size, no more than so many bushels. If the property is broken into bits but no part of it is lost, its weight can be established by collecting and weighing the bits. In some losses, evidence of the value of masses of shattered bottles or piles of broken mirrors can be determined by weighing the fragments of glass. Frequently, remaining metal containers, bottle tops or caps, barrel hoops, and similar pieces of evidence can be counted.

Method 6. When Merchandise and Records Are Destroyed. There are occasions when all or most of the insured's merchandise is destroyed as well as records and books of account. While it is the obligation of the insured to establish the loss under these conditions, it often is advisable, in the absence of suspected or attempted fraud, to cooperate with or guide the insured in reconstructing records. In most cases the services of a competent accountant are recommended, particularly if the loss is substantial or complicated.

There are several sources of information usually available to aid in developing, within reasonable accuracy, a book statement of the value on hand immediately before the loss occurred. These may include but are not limited to the following:

1. Duplicate purchase records from suppliers.
2. Bank statements of deposits and withdrawals.
3. Income tax returns.
4. Credit reports.
5. Any statements filed in applying for loans.
6. Duplicate sales records from regular customers or purchasers of large quantities in the case of wholesalers and manufacturers.
7. Written statements from the insured and/or associates on inventories, purchases, and sales.
8. Annual audits or profit and loss statements from a prior year or years that may be in the possession of insured's accountant or others.

9. Information from local or national trade associations with which the insured is affiliated.
10. Comparison of insured's business with firms of like size and kind, situated in a similar environment.[14]

Method 5 should be used with method 6 as a double check insofar as practical, particularly making certain that the space the various types of stock are said to have occupied will reasonably contain the amounts claimed.

Method 7. Part of Stock in Sight, Part Out of Sight. In many cases, part of the merchandise is completely destroyed while the remainder may be undamaged or partly damaged but subject to a physical inventory. It is customary to make a physical inventory of the stock in sight and to subtract its value from a properly prepared book inventory. The difference represents the value of the out-of-sight stock.

Book inventory at time of loss...... $ ....
Less physical inventory of stock
in sight .... $ ....
Value of stock out of sight....... $ ....

Protection From Further Damage[15]

After a stock has been involved in a fire, explosion, windstorm, or other casualty, the merchandise that has not been lost or destroyed may be subject to further damage unless steps are taken to protect it. The methods described in Chapter 16 for protecting personal property in use are also employed to protect merchandise.

If merchandise is submerged in a flooded basement, the water must be evacuated so that the goods can be taken out. If the drains are clogged, they must be opened. If there are no drains or the drainage is inadequate, bailing or pumping will be necessary.

Steps should be taken to close all openings in the exterior walls and roof to protect the

---

[14]For example, *Expenses in Retail Businesses*, The National Cash Register Company, Merchants Service.
[15]See p. 69.

property from the elements, at the same time making certain there is adequate air circulation. In cold weather, heat should be restored, if the service has been interrupted, to prevent damage to stocks that may be injured by freezing. Plumbing and sprinkler systems should be secured against freezing or leaking and causing additional damage to contents.

Stocks which have sufficient remaining value to warrant protection that cannot be provided for in a damaged structure should be promptly moved to another location pending final disposition. Typical stocks include such perishables as fresh vegetables, fruits and meats, frozen foods, dairy products, baked goods, and other items in cold storage.

The handling and protection of specific kinds of stocks of merchandise are discussed in Chapter 19.

In practice, expense incurred by the insured in protecting merchandise from further damage, to the extent that it reduces loss, is accepted as part of the loss and is collectible out of the insurance, subject to contribution or coinsurance provisions.

Separation and Putting in Order

In many stock losses, particularly those of small or moderate size, the insured, acting alone or under the advice of an agent, broker, or public adjuster, separates damaged merchandise from the undamaged without awaiting the arrival of the claim representative. He or she will dry such things as wet garments, sometimes even pressing them, wipe or grease pieces of wet furniture or articles of hardware, and often arrange the property so that it will be easy for the claim representative to count, weigh, or measure it. In other losses, however, nothing is done until after the claim representative arrives and goes over the situation.

When the claim representative finds that no separation has been made, it will generally be advisable to make a joint examination of the stock with the insured and try to agree upon what merchandise is damaged and what undamaged, also how the separation should be made and the merchandise put in order.

There are many times when, for one reason or another, joint examination cannot be made. At such times, the claim representative should advise the insured to go carefully over the stock, and make a physical separation unless the damaged merchandise can remain where it is without danger of deteriorating or spreading damage to the undamaged merchandise. Sometimes tagging, marking, or listing of the damaged articles or lots will make a practical separation. Such a practical separation saves labor and will suffice if the merchandise can be properly examined where it is. If it cannot, physical separation becomes necessary.

Separation is sometimes made by authorizing the insured to deliver or ship all merchandise that is undamaged, recording quantities and setting aside the damaged merchandise as it is reached.

In order to make a proper separation of some stocks, it may be necessary to remove debris that blocks access to the merchandise or chokes the floor space needed to spread it out or to brace weakened parts of a building that are dangerous, so that people may work in it.

Whenever the condition of a stock will permit a definite separation of damaged from undamaged merchandise, separation should be made, although at times, spotty or irregular damage makes definite separation too expensive to warrant the work.

Under the requirement in a standard fire policy that the insured separate damaged and undamaged personal property and put it in the best possible order, the cost of separating and putting in order falls on the insured. In serious losses, however, the work of separation and putting in order is often treated as part of a general salvaging operation in which the damaged merchandise is, itself, separated and put in order for use or sale, sometimes as is, sometimes after being reconditioned. Such an operation is ordinarily conducted by a salvor. In such losses, the expense is treated as part of the cost of salvaging.

Retail stocks should have the articles separated according to their character, the kind of damage they have suffered, and the space available in the store for handling them.

When any kind of stock is handled, the damaged units or articles that are not worth saving should be set aside, counted, and held, pending adjustment.

Inventory

After the damaged merchandise has been separated from the undamaged and put in order, an inventory should be made. The inventory required by the New York Standard Policy is

... a complete inventory of the damaged and undamaged personal property, showing in detail quantities, costs, actual cash value and amount of loss claimed.

In mercantile and manufacturing operations, merchandise is inventoried by count, weight, or measurement, as dozens of garments, tons of coal, gallons of oil, or yards of cloth. The details of an inventory are (1) quantities, (2) descriptions, and (3) prices. Treatment of these details often differs in the different trades and industries, and in different businesses and organizations within a trade or industry, according to the special information regarding stock on hand that may be desirable.

The work of making inventories ranges from the simple task of the small owner, who counts, lists, and prices his merchandise on hand at a given date, to the highly specialized operations of inventorying the stock of a large department store or manufacturing plant.

Specially designed sheets, mechanical aids such as tape recorders, trained inventory-taking crews, and routines developed by experience are used by large organizations to reduce the time and expense needed to count, weight, or measure stock and to describe and list it.

In the great majority of losses involving merchandise, the claim representative must check an inventory made by the insured after the casualty or must help make one. He or she should learn about the methods that are ordinarily used in inventorying the kinds of merchandise which are most often encountered. In the more important losses in areas

covered by the operations of competent salvors, many of the inventories submitted by the claimants are, at the claim representative's direction, checked by a salvor. Many inventories, however, are made jointly by the salvor and the insured.

Quantities are determined by counting, weighing, or measuring. Counting can often be expedited by making a count in a unit of area, a single bin, when all bins are of the same size, or a single section, and multiplying the result by the number of the units, bins, or sections. The count of the small articles in a pound—screws, bolts, or nuts, for example—can be made, and thereafter the articles can be weighed and their number almost exactly determined. In some industries, automatic machines have been developed that count articles, and some machines even sort the articles according to sizes and deliver them in counted lots.

Commodities in bulk that are sold by weight would not often be inventoried if it were necessary to weigh the poundage or tonnage on hand at the inventory date. A large quantity of any commodity, powdered, granulated, or in lumps, would require too much time and expense for power or labor to transfer, by hand or mechanically, into boxes or bags that could be weighed. Weight is, therefore, satisfactorily determined by measuring size and computing volume. When commodities are stored in bins or sections of a structure of known dimensions, their volume and, from it, their weight can be determined. Sometimes such commodities are accumulated in conical or mound-like piles. When they are, the volume is determined by the engineering method of making measurements and the geometrical formula for computing the cubic content of the type of pile.

Linear measurement, ordinarily a slow procedure with tape or rule, is facilitated when the yardage in bolts of cloth is run through a measuring machine or spotted with only a small margin of error by a mechanical device used in many stores.

Descriptions taken from invoices covering the purchases or sales of a particular kind of merchandise will identify it and aid in pricing the inventory. Descriptions of commodities should include type and grade or quality. Cotton, for example, may be of the short-staple or long-staple type and of middling, strict middling, or good middling grade. Descriptions of packaged goods should show the different sizes of the packages when there is more than one size. When the same kind of merchandise is handled in different sizes, shapes, or colors, it is important to include them in descriptions. Models or styles should be included. In many businesses stock numbers are allotted to the various kinds of articles sold. These make effective descriptions. Rejected articles and second-hand articles acquired by repossession, trade-in, or purchase should be so described. Descriptions should show whether articles or lots in a manufacturing plant are raw material, in process, or finished goods.

Prices in a mercantile inventory may be those of acquisition or of replacement. In businesses that use the retail accounting system, the inventory may show selling prices. When priced on a cost basis, there should be a consistent treatment of the cost of freight or other transportation and of trade and cash discounts. Markdowns should be used in making any selling-price inventory.

A manufacturing inventory should ordinarily show prices for raw materials at acquisition or replacement cost and prices for stock in process and finished goods at cost of production or reproduction. If the manufacturer's insurance covers finished stock at market value, less unincurred expense, the inventory prices for finished stock should be those shown on the manufacturer's price list or by the record of recent sales of equivalent quantities; in any case, deduction should be made for unincurred selling costs.

Making an Inventory. When an inventory is to be made, the premises should, first of all, be cleaned up. Following the fire, windstorm, or other casualty that caused the loss, they are generally in a confused state and littered with debris. In cleaning up, care must be taken not to throw away any of the remains of the merchandise, as these must be held, pending adjustment.

The making of the inventory should follow a plan that will make its check and verification easy. The stock should be sorted; the pieces of any unit, such as the two shoes of a pair or the coat, vest, and pants of a suit should be matched up and the merchandise then arranged on the shelves, counters, tables, racks, or in the bins, following, if possible, the order that existed before the loss. If the fixtures have been destroyed, the merchandise may be laid out on the floor.

Stock from each department should be kept separate, and as far as possible, the articles of each style and price within a department should be kept together, except that the damaged should be separated from the undamaged, with further separation of damaged into lots of slight, moderate, and severe damage. Special lots should be made of worthless damaged articles. It is customary to assign a letter to each department to be used as an inventory symbol. Each lot of merchandise should be marked with a numbered tag, which should be conspicuous. If tagging is done before the lots are counted, weighed, or measured, the quantity found can be written on the tag, thus enabling the person or persons who are to write up the inventory to record it promptly. When practicable, a single lot number may cover an entire section or area if the merchandise within it can be readily checked to the inventory entry or entries and vice versa. Lotting and tagging will expedite any future examination by the claim representative or by the expert, if one is called in to give an opinion on values, damage, or salvage possibilities.

Since those who will follow the maker of the inventory cannot know what he or she had in mind, no abbreviations should be used in descriptions except those common to the trade or otherwise readily understandable.

All prices should be for the unit of quantity given unless otherwise shown. If the unit is a dozen, the price by the dozen should be given, unless there is a supplementary notation showing that the price is by the gross or the single unit. An accurate count of the items in each lot must be made.

When, because of confusion, quantities

cannot be determined, the inventory should be explicitly marked *estimated*, and when prices must be averaged, they must be stated as *averaged*. Unless this is done, they will be assumed to be actual.

If there is doubt or suspicion about the cause of loss or the honesty of the claim, it is of great importance that the person making the inventory get accurate descriptions as well as an exact count of items. Style numbers, manufacturer's name and number, or other marks of identification on the merchandise should be included in descriptions so that all items can be traced to the invoices covering their purchase, or directly to the manufacturer, importer, or dealer from whom they were purchased.

Sizes, styles, and colors in garment stocks will usually indicate whether merchandise is current or obsolete. Original invoices will show its age. If the merchant disposes of desirable sizes, leaving only small or large sizes, the chance of selling the leftovers is greatly reduced. Styles in women's wear, millinery, novelties, and specialties change almost overnight. This is also true of certain classes of men's wear, though generally to a lesser extent.

If loss has occurred shortly after an inventory of the stock was taken in the regular course of business, it may be possible to save labor by checking the regular inventory against the stock and noting corrections. The corrected inventory can then be copied.

When part of the stock is out of sight and its value must be determined by deducting from the book value of the stock the sound value of the stock in sight, the inventory should be priced according to the book value of the merchandise. Any merchandise that was listed in the last inventory taken prior to the loss should be inventoried at the prices used in the last inventory, while merchandise purchased since the date of the last inventory should be priced at its actual cost. If this is done, the inventory and the book value of the stock will be on the same basis, and deducting the one from the other will show the book value of the stock out of sight.

When all the stock is in sight, the inventory may be priced at actual or at replacement cost, unless the insurance covers under a reporting form. When such is the case, the inventory should be priced on the same basis as the reports of value, otherwise a strict verification of the last report of value cannot be made.

Spot-Checking or Testing an Inventory. If an inventory appears to be correct, circumstances may justify its acceptance without a complete verification. In such cases it is well to make a general examination of the stock, noting whether the lot numbers follow some regular order and whether the material corresponds to the general description. If values appear to be in order, certain lots should be selected at random and accurately counted, following which the price stated should be traced to the bills of purchase or market reports. If a sufficient number of lots are thus tested, a fair idea can be gained of the general accuracy of the inventory. If material discrepancies are noted in quantities, descriptions, or values, a complete verification or a new inventory should be made. If, however, the lots selected for testing are found to be correct, it is fair to assume that the inventory is reasonably correct and can be accepted. This method is often used when the damage is slight and the claim appears to be in order.

Verifying an Inventory. When an inventory has been furnished by the insured, determining with certainty whether it is correct regarding all quantities, prices, extensions, and additions will sometimes be advisable. If it has been taken in some definite order, it can be checked with certainty; if not, it may be confusing. If it is badly out of order, making a new inventory may be better than trying to check the old one. If the inventory made by the insured seems to be intelligently prepared, a start should be made by comparing the description of a specific item with the item itself and noting the correctness, incorrectness, or insufficiency of the description. The quantity should be checked, and then the price and the extension. Often, items are consolidated to save time and labor, and prices are averaged, frequently at too high a figure. Each lot should be carefully counted, weighed, or measured to see that it corresponds to the count, weight, or measurement stated on the inventory. Prices should be checked with invoices. If there is a discrepancy, it should be noted opposite the lot by an entry of the correct figure. The verification being completed, a list of overs and shorts should be compiled, and a final calculation should be made so that the proper amount may be added to, or deducted from, the inventory, according to the result of the calculation.

Preparation for Discussing Value and Loss

While the claim representative should always be properly prepared to discuss value and loss, in most situations he or she will be dealing with a reputable claimant. The merchandise involved will be new, recently purchased, and in current demand. The amount of loss will not be great or hard to determine. There will be nothing unusual requiring consideration, and the claim representative will not need to make special preparation before a discussion of value and loss.

In many losses, however, the claim representative encounters circumstances which are unusual or unfamiliar. He or she must be prepared to deal with these circumstances. The loss may involve large quantities, high values, many locations, extensive or questionable damage, or unusual or a special kind of merchandise; or the loss may be problematical; or there may be early indications that the claimant will be unreasonable or difficult to deal with.

A large stock loss may require the inventorying of several locations, moving lots of undamaged merchandise, reconditioning damaged merchandise or selling it, whether "as is" or after reconditioning, and examining books and records. In such a loss, much work must be done in order to produce the information that must be in hand before dependable figures of value and loss can be made. Competent help is almost always required: inventory checkers, salvage handlers, value experts, and accountants.

Repeated examinations of the merchandise and close contact with the persons who are inventorying or handling it are necessary to familiarize the claim representative with whatever special problems are presented by the character, condition, or quantity of the merchandize in sight. Adequate study of the records is often necessary as part of the search for information on the value of the merchandise, whether in or out of sight.

Whenever possible, the claim representative should work with experts so that when their opinions are to be discussed with the insured, he or she will have them well in mind.

Preparation, when a stock loss is large and complicated, is generally made by arranging for the proper treatment of sizable lots of merchandise and the development and study of a comprehensive body of information bearing on sound value, salvage value, and amount of loss.

The sale of food and drugs is subject to regulation by local boards of health and also by the U.S. Department of Agriculture. In many instances, one of these civil authorities will condemn food or drugs involved in a loss as unfit for use, or will lay down requirements for their treatment before they can be sold. For example, the Department of Agriculture has, in some instances, refused to permit wet wheat to be dried and sold to millers for grinding into flour, but has approved the use of the wheat as poultry or stock feed. In any loss on which one of the civil authorities decides to act, the claim representative should know the position its representatives intend to take before beginning to discuss value and loss.[16]

When value and loss are problematical, preparation should include obtaining the evidence offered by the stock itself, if any part of it is in sight. The claim representative, together with any expert employed, should examine the merchandise, note its quantity, grade, or quality, if it is a bulk commodity, or the exact description of each lot, if it is a group of packages or articles. Marks or tags should be examined for cost and selling

[16]See Chap. 19.

prices, *with special attention to markdowns or price cuts*. The kind of damage suffered — fire, smoke, water, breakage, or scattering — should be particularly noted and the degree of damage estimated. The replacement cost of the grade or quality of the commodity, or of each kind of package or article, should then be established.

The replacement cost of staple merchandise in the common trades can ordinarily be established by making an examination of the invoices kept on file by the purchaser. In case of doubt, the sellers should be interviewed and asked to quote prices at which they will sell in the quantities involved. After replacement cost has been established and a proper deduction made for depreciation, the remainder will represent cash value. In periods of steady business conditions, there is seldom any difficulty in establishing the replacement cost of staple merchandise. In periods of commercial depression, however, much conflicting information will surface in connection with prices. If the depression is severe enough, jobbers will sometimes offer to sell the merchandise they have on hand at lower prices than those quoted by manufacturers who would produce the goods only on order. It is difficult to determine actual cash value in such periods. In any period, prosperous or depressed, the real value of merchandise that has been purchased in job lots, at bankruptcy sales, or from sellers in financial distress is uncertain. Such merchandise will sometimes be incorporated into the stock of an enterprising merchant who will sell it at a substantial profit, possibly getting for it the same prices as for new goods of like kind that were bought in the open market. On the other hand, the merchandise may prove hard to sell and may have to be disposed of at a substantial loss. Its value is entirely dependent on the ability of its possessor to sell it, and no hard and fast rule can be laid down for fixing that value.

The books of a business will often throw much light on the value of merchandise as well as show the prices at which it was purchased. If the books record the selling prices of the individual articles, they should be compared with the cost prices. There is gen-erally a normal rate of markup at which a business must sell its merchandise. If the books show that the goods are being sold at less than this normal rate, one should try to find the reason for it. Such a condition may indicate a decline in the market. On the other hand, it may indicate the possession of a badly selected stock or one that has been run down to the point where sales can be made only at reduced prices. If the books do not show the selling prices of individual articles, some idea of the condition of the stock, and therefore, of its value can be gained from the rate of turnover. Rapid turnover at a normal markup indicates well-selected merchandise, while slow turnover indicates that the merchandise is hard to sell. *Merchandise that is hard to sell is not worth the cost of replacing. Its value may be only a small part of original or replacement cost.*

When a considerable quantity of merchandise is, or is claimed to be, out of sight, all books and records should be examined before discussing value and loss. If the books are intricate or the entries bearing upon the acquisition and disposition of merchandise voluminous, an accountant should be employed. Any book showing should be checked against whatever physical evidence is to be had on quantity, such as debris, bin, or tank space, or floor area occupied or fire-marked; also, in doubtful situations, the book showing should be checked against the statements of persons who knew the stock and are willing to talk.

When the merchandise is in sight and the amount of loss is problematical, it will be advisable, in some situations, to get a firm bid for the salvage from a reliable buyer as a guide to estimating the amount of loss and as evidence to offer in discussion with the insured if the claim seems to be excessive.

Alcoholic beverages, tobacco, and certain drugs are sold under check of the Bureau of Internal Revenue. When losses on such merchandise involve substantial quantities, the reports made to the Bureau should be checked. Customhouse records covering merchandise in bond should be checked when in-bond merchandise is involved.

When fraud is encountered or suspected,

the business history of the insured should be investigated and all available commercial and credit reports studied. In some instances a merchant whose past record includes bankruptcy or other business embarrassments will have in the premises a stock made up of the odds and ends of various lines of merchandise that have little real value. If the damage to these by fire or other casualty is not so severe as to destroy their identity, their doubtful value will be evident upon examination. If they are destroyed, the history of the insured may indicate the real state of affairs. In suspected claims, everything must be done to establish actual quantities and accurate descriptions of any merchandise in sight, also its status before the casualty, whether it was new or old, unused or secondhand, sound or previously damaged. Generally, it is best to delay examination of the merchandise and the books until after the insured has presented a claim in writing that will commit him or her to the story told about what was on the premises. In serious cases it will be advisable to organize a thoroughgoing investigation by attaching to an expert, who knows the kind of merchandise involved, a field stenographer to whom the expert may dictate a report of what the articles are, what they were worth sound, how they have been damaged, and an idea of the amount of loss. An accountant should also be employed and arrangements made to get as soon as possible transcripts of the expert's dictation. The claim representative should keep in constant contact with both expert and accountant, correlate the information they produce, and furnish each with the leads suggested by the findings or comments of the other. By thus correlating the work of the two, the claim representative will, in the end, produce a history of the stock, evidence of its condition, and perhaps evidence indicating intent to defraud the insurer.

Check of Claim

Stock claims should be checked for nonstock articles, such as tools, equipment, and floor coverings; for merchandise belonging to others, unless it is covered by reason of the trust and commission clause; for merchandise lost or damaged at any location not covered; and for merchandise otherwise insured. Stock claims under fire, windstorm, explosion, and other policies that exclude theft should be checked for loss due to theft.

When claim is based on a value obtained from the books, and from such value there has been deducted the inventory value of merchandise saved, the inventory value must be checked to determine whether it has been computed on the same price basis as the book value. Overpricing of a salvage inventory will reduce the out-of-sight loss, underpricing will increase it. If the book value, for example, has been determined on the basis of the actual cost of merchandise and if the inventory of the saved merchandise has been taken at replacement-cost prices that are less than the original-cost prices, a deduction of the inventory total from the book value will give an excessive figure as out-of-sight loss, and vice versa. In like manner, if the inventory total of the saved merchandise is computed on the same price basis as the book value, but part of the saved merchandise was stolen before the inventory was made, a deduction of the inventory total from the book value will give an out-of-sight loss that includes the theft loss.

Appraisals

Appraisals of stock losses have shown rather irregular results and have already been discussed in connection with the various classes of stocks. In recent years the number of stock losses submitted to appraisal has tended to decrease.

Final Papers

The inventory, with proper notations written upon it, or accompanied by a statement setting out all details of the adjustment, should be forwarded with the proof of loss in cases other than those involving the taking or selling of salvage. When salvage is to be sold, the inventory is given to the salvor to check out the merchandise and to be assured that all articles to be taken are delivered. The salvor in due course is expected to advise of any shortage or overage in the inventory, in order that the adjustment may be made on correct figures. The total of the inventory and any shortage or overage in these cases should be reported, either in the statement of loss or in the letter explaining the adjustment. Any agreement should always show the inventory total corrected by shorts or overs, unless made before the inventory is completed, as in the case of moving a stock for better protection. A copy of the agreement should appear among the final papers. If the loss is settled by appraisal, the original award should always be sent to the insurer.

QUESTIONS AND PROBLEMS

1. The insurance policy and any specific endorsements are essential in establishing the basis for insurable values of the property covered. Considerations must include, also, court decisions as to the cash value of property under different circumstances and in the hands of individuals or entities with different interests, such as a homeowner, a retailer, a wholesaler, or a manufacturer.

Consider the proprietor of a toy store that is burned out on October 30. The insured, Mrs. X, is unable to rebuild and obtain stock to replace that destroyed in the fire in time to get the benefit of pre-Christmas sales. Consequently, all the profit on her anticipated sales is lost. The SMP (MLB-100) insures Mrs. X for the actual cash value.

a. Insured states that, had the loss not occurred, she would have been able to sell the stock and earn a profit on it. Therefore, the actual cash value to her is the selling price. How do you respond?

b. In computing actual cash value, the starting point is invoice cost at the time and place of the loss. One charge is to be added to invoice, one item of account is to be deducted. What are those items?

c. The Liberal Insurance Company, under an actual cash value policy covers the building and contents of a large department store. A fire destroys 100 pianos and other stock on the eighth floor. The insurance company's claim representative obtains the invoice cost of each of the

pianos, adds transportation costs to the store, and deducts trade and cash discounts.

The insured takes the position that the insurance policy insures for ACV, and that the value of the pianos is the value at the time and place where the loss occurred. That place, says the insured, was on the eighth floor of the store and not down in the street in front of the store where the pianos are to be delivered. Do you agree? Is there more than one school of thought? Explain your answer.

2. One of the questions asked in Chapter 4 (Insurable Interests) concerned a retailer's insurable interests in "layaways" or will-call merchandise. The answer, simply stated, was that the insured's interest was the full value of the layaway.

a. State two justifications for adjusting a loss on layaways based on the insured's selling price under an ACV policy.

b. To replace ladies' dresses and similar merchandise that has been damaged or destroyed, an insured must send buyers from Washington, D.C., to the New York City garment center to shop various manufacturers for desired styles, patterns, sizes, etc. This is the insured's normal method for buying such merchandise. Because of the relatively small quantity of damaged stock that is being replaced, the buyer's expenses increase the regular invoice cost about 20 percent. Would you consider the added cost to obtain the stock as part of its actual cash value? Disregard other insurance such as business interruption.

3. **a.** The actual cash value of merchandise in the hands of a manufacturer is not the same as merchandise in the hands of a retailer or wholesaler. Most of the court cases hold that cash value is to be measured—by what formula?

b. Two explanations are offered for the position taken by the courts. What are they?

4. Many adjustments are made on losses that involve partial damage to merchandise, such as by smoke or water, by agreeing on a percentage of loss to value. In a men's cloth-

ing store, the stock is said to have suffered a loss ranging from 10 to 80 percent. How is percentage of loss determined and to what values is it applied to establish the dollar amount of loss? Explain your answer and show an example of how you might determine and apply a percentage of loss to a retail stock of men's suits covered under an ACV policy.

5. a. Discuss the reasons for soliciting the insured's close cooperation in adjusting losses in mercantile and manufacturing risks.

b. State several causes of depreciation in mercantile and manufacturing stocks.

6. Claim representative Quick is handling a large stock of piece goods, all of which has been slightly wet during a sprinkler leakage. Rather than trying to dry and recondition this stock, the insured and Quick discuss a percentage of loss of 40 percent. The stock is covered under an ACV policy. The current net invoice cost of the stock to the insured is $30,000; the sales value is $40,000. Insured is "hung up" over coming to terms, stating that Quick's method of determining percentage of loss based on sales value is not equitable. He says he has been operating on a gross profit of 25 percent, and if the 40 percent loss is applied to cost, he can no longer realize his usual 25 percent gross profit. How does Quick counter the insured's argument with facts and figures? Show all calculations.

7. a. In the foregoing problem, claim representative Quick might have used one of two optional methods to firmly establish the loss to the piece goods. Explain briefly.

b. Assume this to be a fire loss and the piece goods involved (only a small part of the insured's total inventory of piece goods) is completely destroyed. By what method would you recommend Quick to determine loss and value?

c. Assume the entire building was destroyed along with all the insured property and books of account. State six sources of information that may be available to Quick or Quick's accountant to develop a book statement of the value and loss.

Reporting Form Losses

The reporting form of policy, as the name indicates, is one that provides for the insured to report values periodically to establish average values at risk during the policy year. Reporting forms are designed for insureds whose inventory values fluctuate widely. A provisional amount of insurance is established at the inception in an amount sufficient to cover the peak values. Thereafter, reports are filed with the company, usually monthly, and at the end of the policy year an average value is obtained by dividing the total by 12. Premium is paid on this average value, and therefore, ideally, the insured is adequately covered at all times and is charged only for the amount of insurance he uses. The reporting form has aptly been referred to as "metered" insurance.

Reporting forms as discussed in this chapter are those usually attached to fire and multi-peril policies. They are variously called *stock reporting*, *general cover*, *multiple-location*, and *reporting* forms.

MULTIPLE-LOCATION FORMS

The two most common reporting forms in use are Multiple Location Reporting Form A (ML-10) and Multiple Location Reporting Form with Premium Adjustment at Average Rate (ML-1). They are referred to as Form A and Form 1, respectively.

Form A can be written to cover either a single location or multiple locations. Form 1 must be written to cover a primary location and at least one additional location.

Form A is written with a specific premium at each location, while Form 1 is written at an average rate for all locations.

If the insured is delinquent in the first report, under Form A, recovery for loss is limited to 75 percent of the applicable limit of liability for the location involved. In a similar situation under Form 1, recovery is limited to 90 percent of the loss or of the applicable limit, whichever is less.

There are two multiple-location reporting form coverages available under the Special Multi-Peril Program. Form MLB-119 is the Reporting Endorsement to be attached to the SMP General Property Form MLB-100, a named-peril policy, and covers only personal property.

Form MLB-116 is the SMP Special Property Reporting Form which insures against all risk of direct physical loss to Coverage B, personal property.

Both forms (MLB-119 when attached to MLB-100) *exclude coverage* of property which is more specifically covered in whole or in part. In other words there is no requirement for the insured to report specific insurance and if there is insurance more specific than that under the SMP forms, the property is not covered under the SMP forms.

Other than minor differences, forms ML-10 and ML-1 are quite similar from the adjustment standpoint. For the purpose of the following discussion, Form A (ML-10, Ed. 6-70) will be used as it is more commonly encountered than other forms. The claim representative is cautioned not to assume that the conditions and provisions cited under Form A are identical in other forms and should not attempt to investigate or enter into adjustment negotiations until he or she has carefully examined the policy, form, or endorsements involved.

Property Covered

Policy Form ML-10 (Ed. 6-70) is to be used only with Form ML-38 (Ed. 6-70) which specifies the *property covered, schedule of locations,* and *limits of liability.* One or more of four classes of property may be covered by placing an X in the box opposite the one(s) desired. They are:

1. Stock owned by the insured, consisting principally of . . . .
2. Contents except Stock, owned by the insured.
3. Improvements and Betterments (only when the insured is not the owner of the building).
4. Personal Property owned by Others while in the care, custody or control of the insured consisting of . . . .

If two or more classes of property are covered at a location, the insurance is blanket over the items.

Personal property owned by others may be covered for a specific amount only when stock, or contents except stock, owned by the insured, are also covered. If no X is placed in the box for Personal Property owned by Others, the insured may apply 2 percent of the amount of insurance applicable to the location where loss occurs, as an additional amount of insurance, but not in excess of $2,000, on personal property of others similar to that covered by the policy and while in the care, custody, or control of the insured subject to the provisions of the form.

Debris Removal Clause

Removal of debris is covered, but the Company's liability is limited to the same proportion of debris expense as its proportion of the loss to the property covered. Also, the Company's liability for both loss and debris expense shall not exceed 100 percent of the amount for which the Company would be liable if all property covered at the location had been destroyed. In other words, if all the property at the location is entirely destroyed, the insurer will not pay for debris removal. The limit of liability under the policy is the value of the property covered at the location of the loss.

Property in the Open

The policy covers personal property (except improvements and betterments) in the open on the described premises, within 100 feet of the described buildings on the described premises, and in or on railroad cars or other vehicles in the open on the described premises or within 100 feet of the buildings on the described premises.

Limited Coverage on Certain Items

The policy limits coverage on books of account, abstracts, drawings, card index systems, and other records to the *cost of blank material plus the cost of labor incurred by the insured to transcribe or copy such records.*

There is also a limitation of coverage on film, tape, disc, drum, cell and other magnetic recording or storage media for electronic data processing, not to exceed *the cost of such media in unexposed or blank film.*

Property Not Covered

There is *no coverage for aircraft* or the contents thereof, *except aircraft held for sale or in process of manufacture. Vehicles licensed for use on public highways* and *growing crops* are not covered; nor is *property in transit or waterborne, or at exhibitions, expositions, fairs, or trade shows.*

Property is not covered at a location not declared at inception of the policy, unless it was included in the first report of values as required and then subject to the limit of liability for an acquired location.

Amount of Insurance Clause

Since an accurate amount of insurance cannot be established until the insured has submitted all the reports of values for the policy year, a provisional amount is agreed upon. A *deposit* premium is paid on the provisional amount of insurance, and later adjusted on the basis of the average of the values reported.

The Amount of Insurance Clause reads as follows:

AMOUNT OF INSURANCE: The amount of insurance for which this policy is written is provisional and is the amount upon which the provisional premium is based. The actual amount of insurance under this policy at any location shall equal this policy's proportion of the total actual cash value of the property covered at that location, subject to the limit of liability and all other provisions of this policy.

The Premium Adjustment Clause provides that an average of the total monthly values reported less any specific insurance will be computed and the premium calculated. If that premium exceeds the provisional premium, then the insured will pay the excess. If the premium is less than the provisional premium, such excess will be refunded to the insured.

The values reported, less specific insurance, are to be used in the computation even though the average of such values exceeds the specified limit of liability at any location. The underlying reason is that rates are based on 100 percent insurance to value and, since the policy is written without coinsurance, the insurer is exposed to all partial losses up to the applicable limit.

When monthly values are reported in excess of the limit of liability, *there is no obligation on the part of the insurer to increase the limit or limits shown in the policy.* These issues have been tested in and upheld by the courts.[1]

Contributing Insurance

Contributing insurance is insurance written subject to the same terms, conditions and provisions as those contained in this policy.

Specific Insurance

Insurance other than contributing insurance is *specific insurance*.

Excess Clause

The Excess Clause in the Multiple Location Reporting Form A is a true excess clause and reads as follows:

This Company shall not be liable for any loss

under this policy until all specific insurance, as defined in this policy, has been exhausted. This Company shall then be liable for its proportion of loss which is in excess of the sum of "1" and "2" below:
"1" the amount due from such specific insurance (whether collectible or not),
"2" the amount of loss, if any, which is uncollectible from such specific insurance because of the application of any deductible, franchise or similar provision in such specific insurance,
but not exceeding the limits of liability set forth in this policy.

Premium under the reporting form is paid only on values in *excess* of any specific insurance as defined in the Specific Insurance Clause. The amount of specific insurance is deducted from the total values reported monthly. If the amount of specific insurance is equal to or more than the reported values, there is no value remaining upon which the reporting policy insurer may charge premium.

For this reason the Excess Clause requires that, in case of loss, nonreporting form insurance must exhaust its liability as though it alone covered the loss before the reporting policy attaches or becomes insurance. The amount due from the specific or nonreporting insurance, whether collectible or not, must include application of any contribution, coinsurance, or other clauses contained in such policies.[2] If written without coinsurance, the specific insurance will pay its face value.

Occasionally the existence of specific insurance is not disclosed until after a loss. Though no credit has been given in determining monthly values upon which the reporting form premium is based, the provisions of the Excess Clause will be enforced. The specific insurance must first exhaust its liability before the insurance under the reporting form attaches and is applicable.

[1]Bert Cotton, "Metered Fire Insurance," *New York Insurance Law Journal*, April, 1958.

[2]*Gillies et al. v. Michigan Millers Mutual Fire Insurance Company et al.*, Fire & Casualty Cas. 257, 98 Cal. App. 2d 743, 221 P.2d 272.

Limit of Liability Clause

The Limit of Liability Clause in ML-38 provides for inserting the insurer's percentage of the total contributing insurance. The liability of each insurer is limited to the same percentage of any loss. When there is one insurer, the percentage is indicated as 100 percent. When there is more than one insurer with contributing insurance, the sum of the percentages should be 100 percent. If it is less, the existence of other insurance should be inquired into; if there is none, the insured must bear the deficit. This situation arises when two or more insurers have stipulated percentages of the total contributing insurance but at the time of loss one policy has been canceled, has been allowed to lapse, or for other reasons is invalid.

The Limit of Liability Clause also provides for listing the specific locations to be covered with a corresponding limit of liability shown for all contributing insurance. Other locations acquired since the inception of the policy and between reporting dates are automatically covered until the next report is due, provided a stated limit of liability is shown for the item.

If the insured does not report an "acquired location" and includes the values in a report other than the next succeeding monthly report of values, there is no coverage. Even though the insured had no values at the "acquired location" or, because of the nature of the operation, values were zero at the end of each month, that location must be reported in conformity with the provisions of the "any other location item." A location used or occupied by the insured over a period of time but not reported as required will not qualify as an acquired location under the automatic pickup even though the location and values are reported at a subsequent date.

Claims made under the "any other location item" should be carefully investigated by the claim representative to enable him or her to inform the insurer of the date the location was acquired and how it was used by the insured, and to furnish a record of monthly values at the location since its acquisition. Such investigations are frequently made under nonwaiver agreements in order to protect or salvage property and determine value and loss.

If the insured has a location which is not reported at policy inception, there is strong support for the contention that "the policy would appear to preclude coverage at that location for the balance of the policy term even if a value is reported for the premises in a subsequent report filed before any loss occurred."[3]

The "any other location" provision reads as follows:

> At any other location, within the above geographical limits, acquired after the inception of this policy if such acquired location is included in the next succeeding monthly report as required by the Value Reporting provisions in Form ML-10.

Miscellaneous Clauses

Under the *Increase in Limits Clause*, increases in limits of liability at existing locations may be added by written endorsement and payment of additional provisional premium.

The *New Locations Clause* permits adding new locations by written endorsement. However, the limit of liability for the new location must exceed the limit of liability provided for the "acquired location" in the Limit of Liability Clause. Payment of additional provisional premium is required.

Value Reporting Clause

An important provision in ML-10 and also ML-1 is the Value Reporting Clause. It is important to the insured, the insurer, and the claim representative when a loss is to be adjusted. It reads as follows in the ML-10 (Ed. 6-70):

> VALUE REPORTING: Not later than 30 days after the last day of each calendar month, the Insured shall report in writing to this Company, as of the last day of such month:
> 1. the exact locations of all property covered hereunder,

---

[3]Ibid.

2. the total actual cash value of such property at each location, and
3. all specific insurance in force at each of such locations.

If the inception date of this policy is the last day of a calendar month, the first report due shall be as of that date.

At the time of any loss, if the Insured has failed to file with this Company the reports as above required, this policy subject otherwise to all its provisions, shall cover only at the locations reported in the last report filed prior to the loss and, at the location where the loss occurs, shall cover for not more than its proportion of an amount equal to the value reported, less the amount of any specific insurance reported, in such last report. If such delinquent report is the first report herein required to be filed, this policy shall cover only at the locations specifically listed herein and for not exceeding its proportion of 75% of each specified limit of liability.

Form ML-32 (Ed. 6-70) is a form for reporting monthly values to the insurer. A comprehensive Guide for Reporting Values is printed on the back to aid the insured.

How, When, and What to Report. The insured must *report in writing* to the insurer *not later* than 30 days after the last day of each calendar month the following:

1. Exact location of all property covered.
2. Total cash value at each such location.
3. Specific insurance in force at each location on the last day of each calendar month.

Insurer's Liability When Reports Are Delinquent. At the time of loss, if reports have not been filed as required, the policy will cover:

1. *Only* at locations included in the last report.
2. For *not more* than amounts included in the last report filed prior to the loss less the specific insurance reported.

Delinquent Report Is First One Required. If the above delinquent report is the first one

required to be filed, the policy will cover:

1. *Only* at locations specifically named.
2. For *not more* than 75 percent of the applicable limit specified.

It should be noted that delinquency in filing reports, as required, does not void the policy but rather confines coverage to those locations included in the last report filed (or to specified locations if no report has been filed) and sets new limits of liability. The insured may still collect partial losses up to the amount of the last report of value, if it was correct.

Delinquency in filing reports bars any benefits of automatic coverage at acquired locations in view of the provision that the policy covers only at locations specifically named, in the event no reports have been filed, or at locations included in the last report filed.

FULL REPORTING CLAUSE: The liability of this Company shall not exceed that proportion of loss (meaning the loss, as provided in the Excess Clause above, at the location involved), which the last reported value filed prior to the loss, less the amount of any specific insurance reported, at the location where the loss occurs, bears to the total actual cash value, less the amount of specific insurance, if any, at that location on the date for which the report was made.

At any location acquired since filing the last report of values, the liability of this Company shall not exceed that proportion of loss (meaning the loss, as provided in the Excess Clause above, at the acquired location), which the total of the values last reported and filed prior to the loss, less the total of the amounts of any specific insurance reported, at all locations, bears to the total of the actual cash values, less the total of the amounts of specific insurance, if any, at all locations on the date for which the report was made.

The clause may be formularized to apply to three different loss situations, bearing in mind that the controlling report of value is the *last report of value filed prior to the loss*.

EXAMPLE 18-1

There Is No Specific Insurance

$$\frac{\text{Last report of value}}{\text{Actual value}} \times \text{loss*} = \text{insurer's liability}$$

EXAMPLE 18-2

There Is Specific Insurance

$$\frac{\text{Last report of value less specific insurance reported}}{\text{Actual value less specific insurance in force}} \times \text{loss*} = \text{insurer's liability}$$

EXAMPLE 18-3

Loss Occurs at Location Acquired Since Filing of Last Report

$$\frac{\text{Total values (less specific insurance) reported at all locations}}{\text{Total actual values (less specific insurance) at all locations}} \times \text{loss*} = \text{insurer's liability}$$

*Loss is the excess after deducting the liability of the specific insurance.

This is tested against the *actual value* on the date for which the report is made. See Examples 18-1 to 18-3.

Other Clauses

Other clauses in the reporting form either are not material to the claim representative's work or are fairly standard and found in many property policies with which he or she is familiar.

ADJUSTMENT PROCEDURE

In investigating the insurance, insured property, cause of loss, payees, value and loss, and other fundamental considerations, the claim representative follows the same procedure under reporting forms as under other property insurance policies. The conditions and provisions of the reporting form that are unique, however, pertain principally to a determination of the amount the insurer is li-

able for in the event of loss. The following outline will alert the claim representative to these specific matters to be investigated in properly completing the adjustment under Reporting Form A.

I. Property covered.[4]
   A. What property is covered?
   B. When any combination of items 1 to 4 is covered, the amount of insurance is blanket in determining values and loss.
II. Exclusions.
   A. Does the form exclude certain property or property damaged by certain perils?
   B. Is the location excluded because the insured had property there but failed to declare it or to include it it the first report of values?

[4]See p. 275.

III. Amount of Insurance and Location
  A. What limit of liability is provided for the location?
    1. Is location named in the policy?
    2. Is it a new location not named but covered under the "any other location" item in the form? What is the limit for that item?
    3. Was the location actually acquired in the month preceding the Report of Values as provided in the Value Reporting Clause?
    4. Is it a location added or deleted by endorsement?
  B. Has the limit of liability been increased or decreased since inception of the policy?
  C. Is there *specific insurance* on any item or items covered under the reporting form?
  D. What coinsurance or other contribution clause is in the specific insurance?
  E. Is there *contributing insurance* (other reporting form insurance)?
IV. Verifying Reports of Values (see Chapter 20).
  The last Report of Values filed prior to the loss is the report that controls under the Full Reporting Clause. Reports of Values filed after a loss, though not delinquent, will not prevail, in view of the words "filed prior to the loss" in the Full Reporting Clause.
  A. On what date was the last Report of Values due?
  B. Was a report filed as required?
  C. If not, when was the last Report of Values filed and as of what month?
  D. What actual cash value and what specific insurance in force were reported?
  E. Did the report include all property covered?
  F. What was the actual cash value of all property, and what was the actual specific insurance in force as of the reporting date?
V. Value at Time of Loss
  A. What was the actual cash value of all property covered at time of loss?

Note: The only application this has is to determine the limit of liability of specific insurance under coinsurance or other contribution clauses. It has no application to the liability of the reporting form insurer.

Determining the Limit of Liability

The amount the reporting form insurer will be called upon to pay in any loss situation will depend on the particular circumstances disclosed by the investigation, as outlined above. The most common situations encountered and the methods of determining the insurer's liability under Reporting Form A are illustrated in Examples 18-4 to 18-12.

Check of Last Report From Books of Account

If the last report of stock values is reasonably accurate, book or physical inventories for a date prior or subsequent to the loss should check out after adjustments for sales and purchases. In other words, a report of stock values is equivalent to stating an inventory value as of the end of a particular month. If the flow of merchandise and cash *since* the date for which the report was made is traced, a book value so obtained (as of the date of loss) should coincide with a book value obtained in the normal manner.

For example, a loss occurs on May 15, 1976. The last report of values filed with the company shows merchandise of $355,000 as of March 31, 1976. To determine the merchandise value on the date of loss, purchases between January 1 and May 15 are added to the January beginning inventory, and sales during that period are deducted. Similarly, purchases between March 31 and May 15 are added to $355,000, and sales during that period are deducted. The two book values thus computed should coincide.

Backing up to January 1 from the value reported for March 31, by *deducting* purchases and *adding* sales, should bring the March 31 values in line with the year's beginning inventory.

EXAMPLE 18-4   Values Correctly Reported—No Specific Insurance

Coverage
Stock..⎫
Contents except stock...⎬ $500,000 limit
Improvements and betterments...................................... Nil
Property of others.. Nil
Last report of values, July 15—as of June 30, 1976 .... $493,000
Actual value, June 30, 1976... $491,375
Agreed loss...................... $10,500...........................
Limit of liability for the location ...... $500,000.........................
Reporting form insurer pays insured in full .... $ 10,500

EXAMPLE 18-5   Values Correctly Reported—Specific Insurance

Coverage
Stock ....⎫
Contents except stock ....⎬ $400,000 limit
Improvements and betterments ....⎭
Last report of values, April 10—as of March 31, 1976
Stock............................. $300,000
Contents except stock.............. 75,000
Improvements and betterments...... 25,000
Total $400,000
Specific insurance reported $100,000 blanket, coinsurance 100%
Actual values March 31, 1976....................................... ⎫ $400,000
Value date of loss, April 26, 1976.................................. ⎬ $500,000
Agreed loss to all items............... $70,000

Specific insurer pays its limit of liability ... $\dfrac{\$100,000}{100\% \times \$500,000} \times \$70,000 =$ $ 14,000

Reporting form insurer pays excess of loss .... $ 56,000
Insured receives full payment .... $ 70,000

EXAMPLE 18-6   Specific Insurance Reported—None in Force

Use the figures in Example 18-5, with the exception that it was discovered there was no specific insurance in force, though $100,000 was reported.

In this situation the provisions of the Full Reporting Clause limit the liability of the insurer to that proportion of the loss which the last reported value, less the amount of the specific insurance reported, bears to the actual value, less the amount of specific insurance on the date for which the report is made.

The insured reported specific insurance where none was in force and received credit for it from the reporting form insurer. Therefore, under the Full Reporting Clause, the liability of the reporting form insurer is treated as though the specific insurance actually existed.

Last reported value as of March 31, 1976 .... $400,000
Specific insurance reported... 100,000
                                                                         $300,000

Actual value as of report date......... $400,000
Actual specific insurance in force....... Nil
                                       $400,000

Reporting form insurer pays........................... $\dfrac{\$300,000}{400,000} \times 70,000 =$ $ 52,500

Insured contributes 17,500
Total loss... $ 70,000

EXAMPLE 18-7   Specific Insurance in Force—None Reported

The figures in Example 18-5 may be used here also, with the exception that specific insurance which was in force was not reported by the insured.

The provisions of the Full Reporting Clause control, limiting liability to that proportion of the loss (meaning loss after deducting the liability of the specific insurance) which the last reported value, less the amount of the specific insurance reported, bears to the actual value, less the amount of specific insurance on the date for which the report is made.

Last reported value as of March 3, 1976 .... $400,000
Specific insurance reported ....   Nil
                                                                           $400,000

Actual value as of March 3, 1976...... $400,000
Actual specific insurance in force 100,000
                                        $300,000

Specific insurer pays .... $\dfrac{\$100,000}{100\% \times \$500,000} \times \$70,000 =$ $ 14,000

Reporting form insurer pays excess of loss.................................   56,000
   Insured collects... $ 70,000

EXAMPLE 18-8   Values Underreported—No Specific Insurance

Coverage, item 1, stock, $50,000 limit. No coverage on other items.

Last report of values, June 15, as of May 30, 1976 .... $30,000
Actual values as of May 30, 1976...   40,000
Loss date: June 30, 1976
Agreed loss... $ 8,000
Reporting form insurer pays .... $\dfrac{\$30,000}{\$40,000} \times \$8,000 =$ $ 6,000
Insured contributes...   2,000
   Total loss... $ 8,000

EXAMPLE 18-9   Values Underreported—Specific Insurance

Coverage same as in Example 18-8.

Value at time of loss $50,000
Specific insurer pays................................ $\dfrac{\$10,000}{80\% \times \$50,000} \times \$8,000 =$ $ 2,000
   (Excess of loss = $6,000)
Reporting form insurer pays............................... $\dfrac{\$30,000}{\$40,000} \times \$6,000 =$ $ 4,500
Insured contributes   1,500
   Total loss... $ 8,000

EXAMPLE 18-10   Coverage on Two Items—Values for One Reported

Coverage, item 1, stock, ...⎫
Coverage, item 2, contents except stock . . . .⎬ $200,000 limit
⎭

Under these circumstances the values for stock are generally reported, but failure to report values for item 2 results in underreporting.

Though no values have been reported for item 2, any loss to that item is covered, subject, however, to the provisions of the Full Reporting Clause (see Examples 18-8 and 18-9).

EXAMPLE 18-11   Coverage on One Item—Value for Other Items Also Reported

Coverage, item 1, stock, ... $200,000 limit
Coverage, item 2, contents except stock . . . . Nil
Coverage, item 3, improvements and betterments . . . . Nil

Under these circumstances the insured will invariably overreport values by including property for which no coverage is afforded. Any loss to item 2 or 3 would not be covered regardless of the fact that values had been reported.

EXAMPLE 18-12   Delinquent Reports

The claim representative should be aware of two situations under the Value Reporting Clause. The first is when the insured has been filing reports but the reports (or the last report) are delinquent. In that situation the policy covers only at the locations and for not more than the amounts included in the last report of values, less the amount of the specific insurance reported, filed prior to the loss.

The second situation concerns a delinquent *first* report required. Then the policy covers only at the locations specifically named and for not more than 75 percent of the applicable limit of liability specified in the Limit of Liability Clause.

In both situations, a location acquired since the last reporting date, but before a later report became due, would not be covered.

On serious losses, the claimed value at the time of loss, whether based on a book statement or on physical inventory, should be adjusted back to the last report of values. If they do not coincide reasonably, it is apparent that one or the other is wrong.

Check of Reports of Values With Person Who Prepared Them

The compiling of Reports of Values is generally left to an accountant, a clerk, or some individual who is not familiar with the reporting form policy of insurance. They are frequently unaware of the basis on which values are covered, i.e., whether stock is at cost or selling price. It is not unusual to find that they do not know what is covered, if anything, aside from stock. Improvements

and betterments are often left out; new machinery may have been installed or old machinery removed, and stock may have been transferred in or out, all without the knowledge of the person responsible for preparing monthly reports.

The claim representative, in seeking to verify values, should therefore seek out the individual who makes up the reports and should carefully review the work papers.

QUESTIONS AND PROBLEMS

1.a. Under Reporting Form A (ML-10), what is meant by the following terms: *provisional amount* of insurance and *actual amount* of insurance?

b. The Premium Adjustment Clause provides that an average of the total monthly values reported less any specific insurance will be computed and premium calculated. Define specific insurance.

c. If the values reported, less specific insurance, exceed the specified limit of liability at any location, is premium based on those values or on the limit of liability? Explain the reasoning behind your answer.

2.a. The Excess Clause in a reporting form is said to be a true excess clause. Why is it a true excess clause?

b. If the specific insurance policy contains a 100 percent coinsurance clause, and the insured is a coinsurer, is the coinsurance penalty picked up by the full reporting form? (Disregard any other limitations or provisions in the reporting form.)

c. If the specific insurance happens to be written without a coinsurance, contribution, or deductible clause, what is its limit of liability before the reporting form is called upon to pay the excess of loss up to any specified limitations?

3. The Limit of Liability Clause provides, among other things, for the listing of specific locations covered and a corresponding limit of liability shown for all contributing insurance. Also, there is an item for inserting a corresponding limit of liability for any location acquired if included in the next succeeding monthly Report of Values as provided in the Value Reporting Clause.

a. If the insured acquires a location after inception of the policy, but no limit is shown for the "any other location item," is that location automatically covered until it is reported in the next succeeding monthly Report of Values?

b. Insured acquires a new location after inception of the policy, but because there are no values the location is not included in the succeeding monthly Report of Values. Several months after the location is acquired, stock is placed there, and the insured reports the values. In event of a loss, is there coverage under the reporting form? Insured has a $100,000 limit for the "any other location" item in the policy.

c. An insured had a location which was not reported at the inception of the policy, because it was used only occasionally to warehouse excess stock. Several months after the policy is written, a large amount of stock is placed therein. It is reported in the next succeeding monthly Report of Values. Would this location qualify as "an acquired location" and be automatically covered under that item in the Limit of Liability Clause?

4.a. Under the Value Reporting Clause in a reporting policy, the insured must report in writing, not later than 30 days after the last day of each calendar month, three facts with respect to the property covered. What are the three facts?

b. If reports are delinquent, the policy covers only at what locations, and for what amount?

c. If the delinquent report is the first one required, the policy will cover only where, and for what amount or limit?

5.a. The Full Reporting Clause has provisions that apply to specific locations in the policy and which have specified limits of liability. State the provisions briefly, and the purpose of the Full Reporting Clause.

b. The Full Reporting Clause also has provisions applicable to any location acquired since filing the last report of values. Briefly, tell what those provisions are.

6. A department store fire occurs June 10. Last report of values was filed with the insurer on April 3 and was for the month of March. The insured's controller realizes that no report of values was filed for the month of April and immediately sends it to the company by registered mail. Under the Full Reporting Clause state the limit of liability of the reporting policy.

7. You are adjusting a loss under Reporting Form A (ML-10) covering $500,000 blanket on stock, contents except stock, and improvements and betterments. Date of loss is January 15, 1977.

Last report of values January 10, as of December 31, 1976:

Stock............................	$350,000
Contents except stock........	100,000
Improvements and betterments	50,000
Total........................	$500,000

Specific insurance reported, $100,000. Coinsurance, 100%.

Actual values on December 31, 1976.......	$500,000
Value on date of loss, January 15, 1977..........	$600,000
Agreed loss to property covered	$180,000

What amount will the specific insurance pay? What amount will the reporting form pay? Show calculations.

8. In the foregoing problem it was discovered at the time of loss that there was no specific insurance although the report of values as of December 31 showed $100,000 specific insurance subject to 100 percent coinsurance. Calculate the liability of the reporting policy in this situation.

9. The Acme Furniture Company suffers a loss on September 5, 1976. The insured under Reporting Form A (ML-10) had filed reports of values as of July 31 on August 29, 1976, showing a value of the property covered of $100,000. No specific insurance was reported. Limit of liability at the involved location is $150,000.

Claim representative Quick learned during his investigation that the actual value of the property covered was $120,000 on July 31 and there was specific insurance of $30,000 with an 80 percent coinsurance clause. Actual value at the time of loss was $75,000. The agreed loss is $10,000.

Calculate the liability of the specific and the reporting insurance policies. Show all calculations.

10. In problem 9, above, assume there was no specific insurance and none was reported. Calculate the limit of liability under Reporting Form A (ML-10). Show all calculations.

Salvaging and Use of Salvors

The term *salvage* is variously used to mean (1) all property covered by the insurance that escaped destruction in the fire or other casualty that caused the loss, (2) the damaged property that, following a loss, is to be sold in order to determine the amount of the loss, and (3) the amount of money received from the sale of the damaged property. The last meaning is much better expressed if the amount is referred to as "proceeds from the sale of salvage." The term *salvor* is applied to a person or an organization equipped to save, protect, inventory, recondition, and sell damaged property.

Salvaging is the work of saving property from loss, or from further loss, during and after the occurrence of fire, windstorm, sprinkler leakage, collapse, explosion, or other covered peril. In the adjustment of losses it also may include separating and putting in order, inventorying, reconditioning, and, in many cases, selling the salvage.

PROFESSIONAL SALVORS

With the exception of the most trivial loss, claim representatives should avoid taking over and selling salvage or personally conducting salvage operations without the assistance of a professional salvor. Reputable and competent salvors perform numerous important services which include inventorying, separating damaged from undamaged stocks, appraising damage, protecting and arranging for reconditioning, and removing and selling stocks. This is their day-to-day business. The experience and judgment built over the years makes their services invaluable to insurers, especially on serious losses. Their acquaintance with salvage buyers in every locality and their knowledge in how best to negotiate with individual buyers are essential in keeping losses to a minimum when salvage is to be sold. Part of the service of qualified salvors is the documentation of their activities, their inventories, sales, and expenses.

Underwriters Salvage Company of Chicago

The Underwriters Salvage Company of Chicago and the Underwriters Salvage Company of New York, both organized and owned by a large group of stock insurers, operated independently until 1975 when they merged under their present name, the Underwriters Salvage Company of Chicago. They are the largest salvors in the country. They provide a complete line of salvor services through 31 offices in major cities with five "convenience" offices. Fourteen of their offices are equipped to handle auto and heavy equipment salvage. Two retail outlets are located in the Chicago area through which merchantable stocks are sold retail to the public. A warehouse is maintained where stocks can be sorted and dried to retain maximum value.

Independent Salvors

There are a number of highly competent independent salvage companies and salvors. The oldest and largest of these is M. F. Bank & Company, Inc., with headquarters in Minneapolis, Minn. This organization, operating through ten offices, provides a full line of salvor services excluding auto salvage. The firm conducts the largest retail salvage store in the country, occupying a five-story, 150,000-square-foot building with retailing, warehousing, reconditioning, drying, and refrigerating facilities.

Another long-established independent salvor is Geo. M. Ruddy & Co., with offices in the Boston and New York areas, Baltimore, Atlanta, and Montreal. Full salvor services are provided. While this organization does not maintain warehousing or reconditioning facilities, it is able to procure such services whenever necessary. Geo. M. Ruddy & Co. does not sell through a retail outlet.

SERVICES PERFORMED BY SALVORS

The claim representative uses the services of salvors for several purposes, depending on the particular situation in which salvaging is indicated. It is the claim representative's responsibility to determine what is to be done, and the decision in this regard will govern his or her relationship with the salvor.

In general, experienced salvors offer the following services. Claim representatives may make use of any one or any combination of these services as the circumstances require.

1. Counseling in person or by phone.
2. Providing emergency protection and first aid to property.
3. Separating and putting stock in order.[1]
4. Preparing inventories.[2]
5. Checking inventory of claimant.
6. Verifying value and loss.[3]
7. Assessing degree of damage.

8. Removing of part or all of stock for sale.
9. Dealing with local, state, and federal agencies.

Counseling by Salvor

In some loss situations, a claim representative will find after a survey of the premises that he needs guidance and advice from a salvor to decide the best procedure to follow. The problem may involve a part of the stock or all of it; or it may concern a particular type, quantity, or condition of a stock. The claim representative is looking for suggestions, for alternate actions to be taken. The circumstances are outlined to the salvor, i.e., the kind of stock, its condition, quantity, location on the premises, insured's attitude and facilities for handling, and other facts to give the salvor a basis for advice. Simple matters can be handled by telephone, but on the more serious the salvor will want to visit the premises before expressing an opinion.

This may be the only service the salvor gives as from then on the claim representative may be able to conclude the adjustment through negotiation and having the insured retain the damaged stock.

Emergency Protection and First Aid

Following a fire, sprinkler leakage, windstorm or other type of loss, some kinds of stock, such as frozen or refrigerated foods or fresh produce must have quick emergency protection to prevent damage or, if damaged but salvable, additional injury.

It is essential that claim representatives understand what the problems are in this area of emergency protection. Priorities must be promptly recognized and established inasmuch as many dollars can be saved by first aid. For example, if a loss occurs in a grocery store or a supermarket, by attending to the damage to the costly cash registers and produce scales at the checkout counters, the gross loss may be reduced substantially more than if such equipment were ignored and efforts were directed to salvaging the stock. Circumstances as to relative values and damages will determine where priorities lie.

[1]See p. 265.
[2]See p. 266.
[3]See p. 269.

Other examples are to be found where carpeting and rugs are saturated by water; wet sheet steel or tin, piece goods, light hardware, canned goods, auto parts, grains in storage, and pianos. Salvors, by experience, are knowledgeable in handling such stocks; they have facilities for temporary reconditioning, such as drying, or they know where such facilities are available. Whether the quantity involved is small or large, this service may be all the claim representative requires.

Separating and Putting Stock in Order

If the work of separating the damaged from the undamaged stock has not already been done, the salvor will usually do the separation in connection with the temporary protection. This service is important to keep wet, heavily smoked, or otherwise damaged stocks from contaminating undamaged stocks. Separating and putting stocks in order is also a preliminary to inventorying.

Preparing Inventories

One of the most important functions of salvors is that of preparing inventories following a loss. The inventory may take in the entire contents of the premises or only a portion; it may be an inventory of only damaged stock or of both damaged and undamaged.

The inventories made by salvors may be only for count, but generally they are made for count, value, and damage. When a joint inventory can be made with a representative of the insured and the salvor working together, best results are obtained as there is little if any question as to quantities.

Checking Inventory of Claimant

There are many occasions when all that a claim representative needs is to have a qualified expert check the inventory submitted by an insured or a third-party claimant. The salvor provides this service.

Verifying Value and Loss

The broad experience of reputable salvors, their knowledge of replacement values, market values, depreciation, and their ability to check invoices and book records qualify them to assist claim representatives in establishing loss and value. Whether or not a salvaging operation is necessary, salvors make available the above service.

Assessing Degree of Damage

After an inventory has been prepared and checked and an agreement has been reached between the claim representative and the insured as to its sound insurable value just prior to the occurrence of loss, the next step is to determine its value immediately after the occurrence. The difference will be the extent of damaged suffered. This appraisal or assessment of the degree of damage is another service the professional salvor offers. His knowledge of what the liquidation market is on any damaged items should provide the claim representative with a "dollar backstop" to negotiate with the insured. Likewise, the appraisal will indicate approximately how much return might be anticipated in the event it is taken over to be sold as salvage.

Removing Part or All of Stock for Sale

At some point in the negotiations with the insured, a decision will be reached whether to leave the stock with the insured at an agreed percent of damage or to have part or all taken over by the insurer. In the latter circumstances the claim representative calls in a salvor to sell the stock as is, where is, or to remove it from the premises and sell it at some other location. In either event it is ultimately removed from the insured's place of business by buyers or the salvor.

This is the principal service of salvors for which they are uniquely equipped and qualified. The selling of salvage, accounting for the results, distribution of proceeds, and the forms and papers ordinarily used will be discussed later in this chapter.

Dealing With Local, State, and Federal Agencies

Salvors are usually on a friendly working basis with regulatory authorities within the area in which they normally operate as frequent losses bring them together. Claim representatives should be aware of the many state, federal, and municipal agencies that could be involved in a loss. Some of the more frequently encountered are state and federal food and drug or consumer protection administrations, environmental protection organizations, and also OSHA. Consequently, a professional salvor is the best person to negotiate with, cooperate with, or confront these regulatory authorities.[4]

RESPONSIBILITY FOR SELECTING SALVOR

The appointment of a salvor to handle salvage is basically the prerogative of the insurer. Staff claim representatives either know their company's preference or can quickly find out from the branch or home office. Independent adjusters should determine what salvor their principal prefers before appointing one, so that there will be no embarrassment later. On routine, moderate-size losses, insurers, if more than one, are inclined to follow the top line insurer's selection of a salvor. But on the more serious losses particularly, one insurer may insist on the appointment of a salvor whom they deem to have special qualifications or experience.

Selection of Salvors in Catastrophes

In catastrophes, such as hurricanes and floods, the claim representative may be confronted with numerous individuals representing themselves as salvors. Some will be actually salvage buyers who provide no services other than purchasing stocks. The claim representative should be cautious in employing any but salvors of proven qualifications and experience.

There are situations in which a claim representative is handling one or more mercantile or manufacturing risks and finds stocks that need immediate handling. With no well-known salvor available at the time, it may be necessary to have the stocks handled promptly under a limited agreement spelling out what is to be done pending arrival of a salvor known to the claim representative. The foregoing list of salvor services may be used as a guide in specifying the extent of any urgent salvaging.

DAMAGEABILITY OF STOCKS

The salvage value of stocks of merchandise after occurrence of a loss is related to their exposure to the peril or perils, susceptibility to a physical injury, and the subsequent marketability in a damaged condition. The insurable loss that stocks of merchandise can sustain as a result of fire, windstorm, or other peril depends on several factors of which the ones discussed below are usually most significant.

Susceptibility—Inherent Damageability of Material

Merchandise may be destroyed, lost, or damaged by the action of one or more of the various perils commonly covered.

Different materials used in the manufacture of goods exhibit varying degrees of inherent resistance to damage by heat, smoke, water, crushing, or whatever during or immediately following the occurrence of a loss. Stocks of inflammable gases, oils, liquids, and metals—or combinations such as hydrogen, acetylene, gasoline, benzol and naphtha, nitroglycerine, alcohol and turpentine, magnesium and potassium, ammonia nitrate, fireworks, or celluloid—explode or burn when ignited.

Cotton, silk, wool, and stocks of fabrics or garments made from them, as well as stocks or products of paper or wood, burn to ashes.

Stocks of articles made of magnesium will burn. Lead, zinc, and alloy stocks, such as pewter, solder, or type metal, melt at low temperatures and are often lost in the burning of buildings containing them. A stock of brass, copper, iron, or steel articles will fuse into a mass of scrap if the fire is intense. Stocks of lard, butter, tallow, bacon, or hams will burn. The action of heat cracks or melts glass.

Fresh food produce, such as vegetables, meats, fruits, and nuts, is highly susceptible to heat, smoke, water, and contamination. Loss of heat or refrigeration, depending on the kind of produce, causes spoilage to set in.

Some losses are caused by smoke. Delicate fabrics that will not stand cleaning suffer severely from smoke damage. Smoke is injurious in direct proportion to its heat, as its heat determines the amount of distillate that it will deposit when cooling. Smoke is hottest immediately over the fire producing it and tends to cool rapidly as it drifts or is blown away. Distance from point of origin is an index of the temperature of smoke.

Severe smoke damage occurs when hot smoke comes in contact with articles and covers them with a film of gum or oil that the fire has distilled from resinous or greasy substances. Slight damage results when smoke that never was very hot, or that has had a chance to cool, deposits particles that can be wiped, dusted, or blown off.

In some instances smoke impregnates fabrics, foodstuffs, or tobacco with an odor that may or may not persist. Butter, cheese, and ice cream retain smoke odor. Tobacco may or may not retain it.

Merchandise is buried, crushed, or broken by falling walls, timbers, or other building debris when the structure containing it is wrecked by fire, explosion, windstorm, or the impact of an airplane, automobile or other vehicle. Liquids in tanks, vats, or other vessels holding them will be lost if the vessels are ruptured. Similar destruction and damage occur when loaded trucks or freight cars are involved in collisions.

Great damage is done by water. Stocks such as zinc sulphate, sugar, or salt may be dissolved. Liquid stocks in open vats or tanks lose value by being diluted. Other stocks are injured if water causes the articles to become mixed. Chemicals may be washed together by the action of water, with resulting loss. Articles that tend to become sticky suffer great damage when they are wet; stocks of paper envelopes usually become total losses if wet enough for the gummed flaps to adhere. Staining and discoloration due to the mingling of colors, and changes in flavors of foodstuffs, are common results of water damage. Stocks such as cement, flake or powdered glue, and sugar may be solidified by the action of water. Cloth often shrinks after being wet. Many metal stocks will rust unless immediately dried and cleaned.

In many commodities or articles, wetness and dampness produce mildew. Stocks of cottonseed, linseed, hay, or mixed feed will heat after being wet, and the heat will increase if the mass is great enough, until there is spontaneous ignition. Water coming in contact with potassium produces combustion. Stocks of lime develop enough heat when wet to ignite the barrels. Stocks are also washed away or submerged by floods.

Raw Materials

Raw materials are stock intended for conversion into finished goods, and they embrace all supplies expended in completing the final product. Commonly encountered raw materials include sheet, plate, and bar metals; cotton and wool in bulk or yarn; various synthetics; crude rubber; chemicals in powder or liquid state; fibers; logs; food products for processing; and piece goods.

While most of these materials, in one form or another, are found in goods in process and in finished goods, generally the nearer they are to the *raw* state the lower their susceptibility to damage. Much, of course, depends on the particular material. For example, under similar physical conditions attending a loss, baled wool and cotton sustain less damage than yarns of the same material; logs sustain less damage than rough lumber, which in turn is less damageable than finished lumber. Finished lumber, in addition, usually suffers less than most finished wood products. Pig iron is less damaged than rough casting, and rough casting less than finished products. Flour and sugar will sustain moderate damage compared to finished bakery goods and candy products.

Goods in Process

Stock in process of manufacture is quite different from anything found in other kinds of contents losses. Because it is made up of parts or combinations of parts of the manufacturer's product, it is usually valuable only if it can be reconditioned and finished economically by the insured. For this reason, it is the portion of the stock that has the greatest damageability and is often the most difficult to handle, either as damaged goods or by sale as salvage.

Manufacturing plants turning out finished merchandise on a highly efficient production line usually find it economically unfeasible to sort out and repair smoked, wet, or otherwise damaged parts of goods in process and place them back into production. Examples are manufacturers of radios and television sets, garments, shoes, wood or upholstered furniture, millinery, and toys. In serious losses the problem may be made more difficult when parts are scattered, mingled, or lost. The labor cost of collecting, identifying, and matching up is frequently greater than any savings anticipated.

Finished Stocks

The damageability of finished stocks of merchandise has a wide range. The inherent susceptibility of the material itself to physical injury has been previously discussed. Several other factors affecting damageability include (1) exposure—methods of packaging and wrapping, (2) exposure—how and where stored or displayed, (3) market level covered by the policy, (4) quantity and quality of merchandise, and (5) the reaction of the consumer who eventually purchases the salvage.

Exposure

Methods of Packaging and Wrapping. Protection against heat, moisture, smoke, crushing, marring, soilage, and contamination by certain types of packaging and containers used in shipping considerably lessens the damageability of merchandise. Injury tends to be minimized by the use of heavy cartons, often tightly sealed; reinforced or moisture-proof paper; plastic wrappings; and fiber and metal cans or drums. Packaging products for the retail trade is a major industry in itself today. While much of it is designed for "eye appeal" and ease of merchandising, particularly in self-service stores, in some cases it does provide better protection against many of the perils covered under an insurance policy. Examples are boxed items with cellophane wrapping; personal effects in cellophane; numerous small articles in sealed plastic on cards; cameras, small radios, and similar fragile goods enclosed in form-fitting Styrofoam containers; and of course a multitude of products in cans and glass or plastic bottles.

All of the above mentioned would be protected to some degree from smoke, but the stock may not fare too well against heat and moisture damage. Most packaging plastics have a low melting point and some are not sealed. When moisture gets into the partially closed package, mildew and deterioration are accelerated. Each case must be analyzed, the problem pinpointed, and the appropriate action taken.

Methods of Storage and Display. Approved methods for storing stocks of merchandise in factories, warehouses, and retail stores greatly reduce its damageability. Some of these include the use of skids to raise the stock several inches above the floor, perforated steel shelving or slatted wood shelving with the lower shelves several inches above the floor, keeping merchandise away from walls to prevent contact with water flowing down the walls, and maintaining adequate clearance below sprinklers to permit their proper functioning.

Newsprint stored on end will absorb water and "mushroom," reducing its salvage value below that generally obtainable when rolls are laid on their sides. The converse is usually the case with rolls of carpeting and linoleum, which have greater salvage value from water damage when stored on end rather than on their sides. Waste paper in bales, unless separated into piles of a few hundred tons with wide aisles between, presents fire-fighting problems and greater damageability prospects.

Merchandise displayed in showcases suffers relatively less damage from smoke and water, depending on the construction of the cases and how airtight they are. Showcases can be conveniently covered with tarpaulins by firemen and in many instances are covered by the insured at night with a light, waterproof dust cover. Suits, coats, and ladies' ready-to-wear, when displayed in wall cabinets, sustain less injury than when displayed in the open on racks. Plastic garment covers aid in reducing smoke and water damage. Stock taken out of wrappers and displayed in the open, on shelves, in show windows, or on counters is subject to considerable damage from fire, smoke, and water. Under-counter stock sustains less damage than that on top of counters.

Market Level at Which Stock Is Covered by Insurance

The *market level* of the insured's product has a direct bearing on the probable *percentage of loss to value.* A salvage buyer will pay the same amount for a stock whether it is on the premises of a manufacturer, a wholesaler, or a retailer; he offers one price for it. But the percentage of loss to value on a damaged stock of ladies' dresses, for example, on the premises of a garment manufacturer may be quite different from the percentage of loss to value on the same stock on the premises of a retail store, because of the market differential. Example 19-1 will illustrate this situation.

If the retailer were insured at selling price, the loss would be as shown in Example 19-2.

One of the first questions a salvor asks is "At what market level is the stock insured?" He knows that the loss to insurance (or loss to value) will be greatest on the retail level and lowest on the manufacturing level. Consequently, the susceptibility to loss, as far as the insurer is concerned, follows the same pattern.

Quantity of Stock Involved

The quantity of stock involved in a loss often affects its marketability, sometimes to advantage and at other times to disadvantage. A large stock of staples such as men's suits, women's dresses, or shoes, in fair condition, will usually attract a sizable group of salvage buyers with ready outlets. This is especially true if the stock is of well-known brand or brands and has a good range in sizes, styles and patterns. On the other hand, a large stock of canned sprouts, surgical sutures, artificial flowers, or out-of-season merchandise will have a limited demand and therefore bring a lower return.

Quality of Stock Involved

As to quality, stocks in medium grade bring better returns in salvaging. High-style or expensive shoe and clothing stocks usually have the greatest damageability because their loss to value, in terms of net salvage proceeds, is greatest.

Salvaged merchandise eventually finds its way to the consumer market. If a stock is

---

EXAMPLE 19-1

Manufacturer		*Retail Store*	
Cost	$10,000	Cost	$12,000
Salvage value	4,000	Salvage value	4,000
Loss to insurer	$ 6,000	Loss to insurer	$ 8,000
Percentage of loss	60%	Percentage of loss	66⅔%

EXAMPLE 19-2

Cost	$12,000
Mark up 66⅔%	8,000
Selling price	$20,000
Salvage	4,000
Loss to insurer	$16,000
Percentage of loss	80%

displayed as "damaged" or "salvage," or is retailed by a known salvor, the persons normally buying that type of merchandise do not expect to pay proportionately more for expensive merchandise than for lower-grade or lower-quality merchandise. Such merchandise as the better-grade women's pocketbooks, costume jewelry, millinery, furs, evening and wedding dresses, men's neckwear, cosmetics, umbrellas, and gloves also fall into this category.

Consumer Reaction

There is a psychological reaction of the buying public toward certain classes of salvage merchandise. Examples are infants' wear, particularly from a layette department, because of a reluctance to expose infants to anything which is less than sterile. Merchandise worn next to the body, such as brassieres, lingerie, and hose, are also in this class.

RELATIVE DAMAGEABILITY OF MERCHANDISE

In most losses no one of the foregoing conditions or factors will solely determine the damageability of stocks or merchandise. It may be necessary to examine many, perhaps all, such factors in order to make an adequate judgment. If all types of merchandise could be, in theory, exposed to similar loss conditions, the classifications in Table 19-1 are a rough guide to the physical damage-

TABLE 19-1

Slight Damageability	Moderate Damageability	Serious Damageability
Grain in elevators	Jewelry (good)	Costume jewelry
Feeds	Rayon piece goods	Pocketbooks
Heavy hardware	Upholstered furniture	Drugs and sundries
Dry goods	Women's shoes (medium price)	Wood furniture
Cotton piece goods	Children's shoes	Stationery
Woolen piece goods	Dress gloves	Millinery
Men's suits and coats (medium price)	Haberdashery	Miscellaneous novelty stocks
Men's shoes	Corrugated cartons	Produce
Sugar	Men's suits and coats (expensive)	Meats
Crude rubber	Women's better dresses	Objects of art
Glassware and china	Knitwear	Electronic equipment
Hides and furs	Wholesale paper	Precision instruments
Raw furs	Pianos	Ladies' high-style shoes
Liquor	Automotive supplies	Christmas decorations
Grain	Tobacco	Artificial flowers
Work clothes	Lingerie	Trimmings and laces
Linoleum		Fur coats
Carpets and rugs		Wallpaper
Paints		Finished leather goods
Baled cotton		Goods in process
Wool		Infants' wear
Cigarettes		Brassieres
Lumber		
Vegetable oils		
Work shoes		
Burlap		
Silverware		
Housedresses		
Work gloves		
Electrical appliances (large)		
Farm equipment		

ability of the stocks listed. Certain stocks, i.e., liquor in bottles, may have a slight physical damageability but poor salvage value due to restrictive state regulations in the matter of resale.

PROCEDURE WHEN SALVOR IS EMPLOYED TO HELP CLAIM REPRESENTATIVE

The procedure is informal when the claim representative employs a salvor to help make an equitable agreement with the insured on sound value and loss. The employment is ordinarily arranged orally, either by telephone or by direct contact, and the claim representative and the salvor make joint or separate inspections or examinations. The salvor may or may not be asked to participate in discussions with the insured, but after the loss has been closed, he or she will be asked to file a report stating briefly what has been done and also the amounts of value and loss as estimated. In some losses, the salvor will be asked to do no more than verify an inventory. Following such losses the salvor will report on the inventory, stating overs and shorts found.

When a salvor is employed to help, the entire bill is chargeable to the insurer or insurers represented by the claim representative. Ordinarily, the salvor presents a bill when submitting a report. The salvor customarily apportions the expenses and service charge to the various insurers, billing each separately and sending the bills to the claim representative to be approved and forwarded to the insurers with the claim representative's report.

SALE BY INSURED

Many merchants and manufacturers regularly dispose of their leftovers, trade-ins, damaged articles or materials, waste, cuttings, or scrap to persons who are able to use or sell them advantageously. These persons are often interested in buying damaged material from an owner whom they know and are willing, in many instances, to pay more for it than strangers. There are occasions

when the insured, if competent and enterprising, can sell salvage of considerable value for a better price than can a professional salvor.

In many packing-house losses, the insured's salesmen will promptly telephone the butchers, hotels, and restaurants to whom they sell to come in and buy at moderate reductions in current prices the fresh meat and meat products in the refrigerator rooms before the rise in temperature due to interrupted refrigerations causes spoiling; producers or wholesalers of commodities that are not easily damaged, such as sulphur, which, when wet, is damaged only to the extent of the cost of drying, can often distribute their merchandise to their own customers by making moderate allowances for the extra cost of handling.

When the insured is to sell the salvage, ordinarily it is sold on the premises. At times, however, it is advisable to send it away for reconditioning and sell it from the premises where it is reconditioned.

Little difficulty attends the selling of salvage by the insured. Details requiring attention by the claim representative are (1) a definite agreement with the insured about what is to be sold, (2) a decision on whether the claim representative should check the selling and the attendant expenses or should accept the insured's record of sales and cost of selling, and (3) seeing to it that the insured clearly understands that the selling is subject to the terms and conditions of the insurance contract, particularly if the insurance is inadequate and coinsurance or contribution requirements will prevent the insured from collecting the full amount of loss.

When the insured sells salvage, he or she retains the money received and credits the amount less any necessary cost of selling against the loss.

PROCEDURE WHEN MERCHANDISE IS TURNED OVER TO SALVOR

In many instances the claim representative finds that the insured is unable to protect the damaged merchandise and put it in order because of lack of the necessary labor, space, and equipment. In others, the claim representative will have reasons for believing that, if the merchandise is handled by a competent salvor, a greater saving of value will result than if handled by the insured, also that the salvor will produce an accurate inventory in much less time than would be needed if the insured made an inventory and the claim representative had it verified. In such instances, the claim representative, after going over the situation, will propose to the insured that all or some part of the merchandise be turned over without waiting to determine values, damage, interests, or insurance coverage. The insured will agree, the agreement will be put in writing, and the salvor will take possession of the specified merchandise. It will almost always be removed to other premises, since it then can be handled better and will increase in salvage value. When it has been put in order and inventoried, the salvor will deliver copies of the inventory to the insured and the claim representative, and the two will examine the merchandise.

If they agree upon its sound value and the amount of the loss, the salvor will be paid a fee for services, plus expenses, and will return the merchandise to the insured. If insurance equals or exceeds coinsurance or contribution requirements, the entire bill of the salvor will be paid by the insurer or insurers; if not, the cost is subject to coinsurance or contribution as it is part of the loss.

In many instances, however, the claim representative will find, after discussion with the insured and the salvor, that the salvor can sell the merchandise at a figure that will produce a smaller loss to the insurer than would result from settling the amount of loss with the insured. In such a case he or she will negotiate an adjustment under which the insured, if adequately covered, will be paid by the insurer for the sound value of the merchandise and will assign any interest in it to the insurer, after which the salvor will sell it and pay to the insurer the net proceeds resulting from its sale. If inadequately covered, the insured will be paid an amount determined by coinsurance or contribution

provisions and, after the salvage has been sold, will receive from the salvor a part of the proceeds determined by the deficit in the amount of insurance.[5]

In some areas, the procedure is different. The claim representative does not arrange for the insurers to pay the insured the sound value of the merchandise, if adequately covered, or the proportion of the sound value determined by the application of coinsurance or average provisions. Following the procedure employed by cargo surveyors in handling losses under policies of marine insurance, an adjustment is made stipulating that the merchandise shall be sold and the net proceeds paid to the insured, who will then file proof for the difference between the sound value of the merchandise and the amount paid. Under such an adjustment, the operation of coinsurance or average is determined in a single computation.

In other instances, the merchandise is turned over to the salvor to be sold for account of whom it may concern. The salvor sells the merchandise and pays the net proceeds to the insurer, the insured, or others entitled to receive them.

In some other instances, the insured protects, separates, puts in order, and inventories the merchandise. Afterward he or she discusses value and loss with the claim representative, but they may not agree upon the amount of loss. If so the claim representative often works out an agreement with the insured that the insurer shall pay the sound value of the merchandise. The claim representative then calls in a salvor to take it over and sell it, instructing the salvor to pay the net proceeds to the insurer. In the smaller losses, the same result is achieved without calling the salvor to the premises. The claim representative looks over the merchandise with the insured, the two agree upon its sound value, and the claim representative prepares proofs of loss for the value and gives the insured written instructions to ship the merchandise to the warehouse of a salvor.

In rare instances, a loss involving merchandise will be appraised, resulting in the

---

[5]See Apportionment of Proceeds, p. 301.

award of an amount of loss that the claim representative can reduce by taking the merchandise at the appraised value and selling it. In such instances, he or she calls in a salvor to sell it.

When merchandise is taken that has not been previously turned over to a salvor under a written agreement, the claim representative should put in the hands of the salvor a letter addressed to the insured with instructions to deliver the merchandise to the salvor. Such a letter is commonly called a *delivery order*.

Whenever merchandise is to be put into the hands of a salvor, the transaction should be covered by a formal written agreement or by a letter or letters.

BAILEE RISKS

In cotton warehouses, grain elevators, and other bailee risks, a serious damage often produces confusion of goods.[6] Salvage will be mixed and unidentifiable. When such is the case, it is customary to sell the unidentifiable salvage for account of whom it may concern and distribute the net proceeds to the owners or to their insurers if the insurers have paid the losses.

QUESTIONS WHEN MERCHANDISE IS TO BE TAKEN OVER BY SALVOR

If merchandise is to be turned over to a salvor, answers to any of the following questions may be important:

1. Are the premises safe for salvage operations and will they protect the merchandise from further damage until it can be removed?
2. If not, should building, equipment, and time-element interests, if any, share in the cost of making them fit to give protection or should the salvor be directed to have the owner of the premises do what is necessary and charge the cost against the work of salvaging the merchandise?

6See Chap. 21, "Bailee Risks."

3. Will building-wrecking operations or the removal of heavy equipment be necessary to recover the salvage?
4. If so, has the building owner, the machinery owner, or their insurers made the necessary contracts?
5. Will the local board of health, the Department of Agriculture, or other federal or civil authorities having jurisdiction permit the use or sale "as is" of the salvage or will they require special disposition or treatment of it?
6. Should part or all of the merchandise be turned over to the salvor?
7. If in bond, what is necessary to get permit for removal?
8. What will be the fee of the salvor if the insured retains the merchandise, or what will be the commision of the salvor if he is directed to sell the merchandise?
9. If the amount of insurance is inadequate and if the insured must bear part of the loss and, therefore, part of the cost of the salvor, has the situation been explained and has the insured been informed about the salvor's fee or commission?
10. Does the insured ask that the merchandise be removed from the premises by a certain date?
11. Does the insured insist that the merchandise must not be sold in a certain territory or until after removal of marks and brands?
12. Have all charges accrued against the merchandise to the date of turning it over to the salvor been paid by the insured?
13. If the merchandise is turned over to the salvor by a bailee, has the bailee filed with the salvor a list of all property belonging to bailors and a statement of accrued charges?

INSURER MAY TAKE SALVAGE "AS IS"

In exercising its option to take all or any part of the property at its agreed or appraised value, the insurer may do so without permitting the removal of trademarks, brands, or labels identifying merchandise as the product of the manufacturer, unless the policy specifically provides to the contrary.

BRANDS AND LABELS CLAUSE

The company's option to pay the agreed or appraised value of personal property and take the salvage is occasionally modified by a clause permitting the insured to remove identifying marks from salvage or mark the goods taken so that they cannot be handled in trade channels except as damaged articles. The use of such a clause tends to increase the extent of loss because, in the event of salvage operations, its presence will usually result in the salvage being sold at a lower figure than would be obtained if the original marks had not been removed or if the articles had not been marked or branded to show that they were involved in a loss.

While the wording in "Brands and Labels" clauses varies, the general intent is the same. The following is a typical clause used in HPR and Superior Risks Forms.

BRANDS AND LABELS. If brand or labeled merchandise covered by this Policy is damaged and the Insurer elects to take all or any part of such merchandise at the value established by the provisions of this Policy, the Insured may, at his own expense, stamp "salvage" on the merchandise or its containers or may remove or obliterate the brands or labels, if such stamp, removal or obliteration will not physically damage the merchandise, but the Insured shall re-label the merchandise or containers in compliance with the requirements of law.

INSURER MAY SELL SALVAGE IN ANY MARKET

The insurer, on taking salvage, is free to sell it in any legal market. The insured is not entitled, under the policy, to require the insurer to sell in or outside specified territory.

SALVAGING AGREEMENTS

Salvaging agreements should always be put in writing. They should be signed by the insured and the claim representative unless the

property is in charge of a bailee, such as a warehouseman of baled cotton or the operator of a grain elevator, when it will be advisable to accept the signature of the bailee and commence efforts to save the property without delay.

Two forms of agreement are in common use: one for use when merchandise is to be turned over to a salvor for protection; the other when it is to be turned over for sale.

Since in some losses the entire stock is to be turned over while in others only a part is to be turned over, the agreement must clearly specify just what merchandise is to be handled

Cargo surveyors do not use formal agreements. They address to the insured a letter suggesting that, without prejudice, the merchandise be sold for the purpose of determining its damaged value.

Forms of agreement tend to become more simply worded. The claim representative should use a form that is current in his or her territory. Salvage companies will supply them.[7]

Use of Formal Agreements and Letters

The various steps in the handling and selling of salvage are ordinarily covered by the agreements or letters noted in the following outline:

I. When the insured and the claim representative turn merchandise over to a salvor under a protection agreement.
   A. If negotiations result in an adjustment under which the insured is to keep the merchandise and be paid on the basis of an agreed amount of loss.
      1. Letter from the claim representative to the salvor directing the return of the merchandise to the insured.
   B. If negotiations result in an agreement that stock is to be sold by the salvor.
      1. Letter from the insured to the

[7]See Appendix O.

salvor or signature of authorization on protection agreement authorizing the salvor to sell stock.

2. Letter from the claim representative to the salvor directing him to sell stock for account of
   a. The insurers.
   b. The insured.
   c. Whom it may concern.

II. When the insured and the claim representative turn merchandise over to the salvor to be inventoried, put in order, and sold.
   A. Sale agreement.

III. When merchandise is taken by the claim representative who employs a salvor to sell it.
   A. Letter from the claim representative to the salvor instructing him to sell the stock and enclosing
      1. Inventory or invoice of stock to be taken.
      2. Delivery order, signed by the adjuster, directing the insured to deliver the merchandise to the salvor, or
   B. Letter from the claim representative to the insured directing him to ship the merchandise to the salvor, and
   C. Letter to the salvor enclosing copy of letter to the insured, and invoice or inventory of merchandise (letter should direct the salvor to sell).

RELATION OF CLAIM REPRESENTATIVE AND SALVOR

The claim representative is responsible for the outcome of the adjustment, and the salvor is under the representative's authority. Each should ordinarily limit activities to the duties listed in the two subsections following, but must always cooperate with the other if satisfactory results are to be achieved.

Duties of Claim Representative

The duties of the claim representative in connection with the handling and selling of salvage turned over to a salvor include the following:

I. When the insured and the claim representative turn merchandise over to a salvor under a protection agreement, the claim representative should
   A. Decide whether to turn over to the salvor
      1. All the merchandise in the premises, or
      2. Part of the merchandise.
   B. Tell the insured what is advisable to do, ask that a copy of the protection agreement be read and, after that has been done, explain how salvaging operations are carried on under it, and
      1. If insurance is adequate, make it clear to the insured that the salvor's costs and expenses will be borne wholly by the insurers; there will be no need to go into details of the salvor's fee or commission, or
      2. If insurance is inadequate, make it equally clear that the insured will have to bear part of the fee and expenses, as they are part of the loss and subject to the provisions of the coinsurance or average clause; it is obligatory to go into details about the salvor's fee or commission, since otherwise there may be a complaint when the salvor's bill is presented.
   C. Write up the agreement, specifying the merchandise to be handled, join with the insured in executing it, and deliver copies to the insured and the salvor.
   D. Negotiate with any building, equipment, or time-element interests for proper sharing of any expense necessary to make the premises safe or protect from further damage.
   E. Make or provide for proper contacts with such civil authorities as may have special jurisdiction over the

merchandise; boards of health, U.S. Department of Agriculture, Bureau of Internal Revenue, or U. S. Customs Service.

F. Watch handling operations and confer with the salvor on expenses incurred and value recovered.

G. Be available for examining promptly any merchandise which, if properly disposed of, will expedite operations or reduce loss on
   1. Total-loss merchandise that should be dumped.
   2. Merchandise that the insured can use advantageously or sell if it can be released for use or sale without delay.

H. Authorize any special expenditures, getting the insured's agreement if insurance is inadequate.

I. Give the salvor necessary instructions in writing when merchandise that has been turned over under a protection agreement is to be
   1. Returned to the insured, or
   2. Sold for account of
      a. The insurers,
      b. The insured, or
      c. Whom it may concern.

II. When the insured and the claim representative turn merchandise over to a salvor to be inventoried, put in order, and sold, the claim representative should

A. Do everything outlined in sections A to I inclusive, under I, also everything outlined under III and IV.

III. When it has been agreed upon by the insured and the claim representative that merchandise originally turned over to a salvor under a protection agreement is to be sold by him, the claim representative should

A. Give the salvor the benefit of any useful information about the merchandise gained from an examination of the books of the insured.

B. Direct to the salvor any persons interested in buying the merchandise.

C. Inform the salvor of any agreement that may have been made with the insured which restricts the disposition of the merchandise.

D. Inform the salvor of any agreement made with the insured that the merchandise will be removed from his premises prior to a given date.

E. See that any removal of marks or brands from the merchandise is done in strict compliance with any marks-and-brands clause in the insurance contract or with the approval of the insurers.

F. See that the insured pays any accrued charges on merchandise that is to be sold.

IV. When merchandise is taken by the claim representative who then employs a salvor to sell it, he or she should

A. Do whatever is pertinent as covered in items D and E, under I, and A to F, inclusive, under III.

B. Give the salvor
   1. Inventory or invoice of stock taken, and
   2. Delivery order directing the insured to deliver merchandise to salvor.

V. In all situations, I, II, III, and IV, the claim representative should

A. Instruct the salvor that any stock to be sold is to be sold for the account of
   1. The insurers
   2. The insured, or
   3. Whom it may concern.

B. Furnish the salvor with the information necessary to apportion proceeds and draw checks to insurers or others entitled to payment.

C. Examine the salvor's account and apportionment, criticize it or approve it, and forward copies and checks to the respective insurers or other payees, or instruct the salvor on the distribution of checks.

Duties of Salvor

The duties of the salvor will be determined by the purpose for which he is employed in the particular loss. They can be generalized as follows.

I. When the insured and the claim representative turn merchandise over to a salvor under a protection agreement, the salvor should
A. Do any necessary work of protection and remove merchandise.
B. Save, separate, and put in order the merchandise worth saving.
C. Inventory the merchandise, having the insured verify quantities and furnish descriptions and prices, sometimes before the merchandise is removed, sometimes afterward.
D. Give the claim representative any proper criticisms of descriptions and an estimate of the amount that the merchandise should bring if sold as salvage.

If instructed to return the merchandise to the insured
E. Check it out to the insured by the inventory, return it to the premises, and get a receipt.
F. Prepare an account of expenses and fee, make any necessary apportionment, and put bill or bills in the claim representative's hands for approval and payment or for presentation to the insurers and the insured.

If instructed to sell the merchandise (see section IV below).

II. When the insured and the claim representative turn merchandise over to a salvor to be inventoried, put in order, and sold, the salvor should
A. Do any necessary work of protection and remove merchandise, if advisable.
B. Decide whether to separate, put in order, and recondition or to sell *as is, where is.*
C. Inventory the merchandise, having the insured verify quantities and furnish descriptions and prices, sometimes before the merchandise is removed, sometimes afterward.
D. See section IV below.

III. When merchandise is taken by the claim representative who employs a salvor to sell it, the salvor should
A. Inspect the merchandise and decide where and in what condition to sell it.
B. Verify the inventory given him by the claim representative and report any overs or shorts to the claim representative.
C. See section IV below.
IV. In all situations, I, II, or III, the salvor should, if instructed to sell,
A. Notify possible buyers or advertise merchandise.
B. Sell.
C. Prepare account of expenses and commission; apportion, if necessary; and forward to the claim representative, for approval and delivery, copies of account and apportionment together with checks drawn to the order of each insurer or others entitled to payment, or forward the copies and checks as instructed by the claim representative.

Comment

In the preceding sections a strictly technical presentation of the duties of the claim representative and the salvor has been made. In practice the work is done with much less formality and rarely develops snarls.

ACCOUNT FOR WHICH SALVAGE IS SOLD

Salvage is sold for account of (1) the insurers, (2) the insured, or (3) whom it may concern. Selling for account of the insured is termed *account of the loss.*

Selling is done at the joint order of the insured and the claim representative except in those cases where the claim representative takes the merchandise and the salvor is not employed until after it has become the property of the insurers.

Following an adjustment in which the claim representative has agreed that the insurers are to pay the insured the insured value of the merchandise and take it, the salvor is instructed to sell it for account of the insurers as it has become their property.

Following an adjustment in which the value of the merchandise has been agreed upon and the amount of loss is to be determined by selling the merchandise, paying the proceeds to the insured, and having claim made on the difference, the salvor is instructed to sell the merchandise for account of the insured, or account of the loss, as the merchandise is never the property of the insurers.

In situations where it is advisable to sell the merchandise before details on the payment of the proceeds can be worked out, or when the insured as well as the insurers will be entitled to part of the proceeds, the salvor will be instructed to sell the merchandise for account of whom it may concern. In such situations the merchandise is never the property of the insurers.

SELLING METHODS

Salvage is sometimes sold at private sale to a buyer who offers a satisfactory price for it. Generally, however, it is sold to the highest bidder after giving all interested buyers the opportunity of examining it. One method of such selling is to advertise the merchandise, often by circulars, and to ask the buyers who come in and examine it to submit sealed bids for all or any part of it, the bids to be opened at a time and place specified in the advertising. Another method is to advertise and afterward sell at public auction.[8]

PREVENTING MISUNDERSTANDINGS WITH BUYERS

Salvage is offered for sale (1) from the warehouse or other location to which it was removed by the salvor or (2) from the premises where loss occurred. When offered from the warehouse or other premises, it will have been inventoried, the buyer will know what

is to be delivered, and there will be little chance of misunderstanding. When, however, salvage is offered for sale from the premises where loss occurred, there may be no inventory and it may even be impossible to see all the merchandise. Under such circumstances, misunderstanding can easily occur.

When badly damaged merchandise is offered for sale on the premises where loss occurred, particularly when it has been mixed or covered by debris, it may be impossible to make an inventory except at a cost that will not be warranted. In such a situation it must be clearly explained to buyers that what is offered is whatever there is within the premises or within a specified space. There must also be a clear understanding about what shall be done with stock debris, whether the buyer must clean up the premises or will be permitted to take what he wishes and leave the rest.

There must be a clear understanding about when, where, and how payment is to be made. For example, when merchandise is sold on a definite inventory out of a warehouse, payment should be made before the goods leave the premises. When an indefinite amount of merchandise is being sold, the amount to be determined by what the buyer actually finds in the premises, payment should be made on an estimated basis before the merchandise is removed, with an agreement that proper adjustment shall be made if the quantity found runs over or under the estimated amount.

APPORTIONMENT OF PROCEEDS

When merchandise is sold for account of the insurers, each receives from the salvor a check for its proportion, as salvage proceeds are apportioned on the same basis as loss payments.

When merchandise is sold for account of the insured or for account of the loss, no apportionment is necessary. The full amount of the net proceeds is paid to the insured. He or she deducts the amount from the agreed value of merchandise and bases claim on the remainder. If adequately insured, he or she

[8]M. F. Bank & Co., Inc., is well known for its successful retail operation in which most stocks are sold and an accounting is given the company. John Werling & Son also retails many stocks, as does the Underwriters Salvage Co. of Chicago.

collects the full amount of loss; if not, the insurers pay their respective limits of liability, and the insured bears the balance of the loss. Each insurer issues its loss draft, and there is no salvage check for it to handle later.

When merchandise is sold for account of whom it may concern, the proceeds may be paid to the insured, who will account for them in the reduction of loss, or paid to the insurers, who may have already paid the insured the sound value of merchandise or may agree that they will do so. In some losses, however, the insured will also have an interest in the proceeds. Then, an apportionment is made by treating the insured as a coinsurer and paying the proper proportion. See Examples 19-3 to 19-5 for the different situations encountered.

EXAMPLE 19-3   Sale for Account of the Insurers

Loss as adjusted:
Sound value $50,000
Merchandise taken $25,000
Paid by insurers to insured $25,000

Apportionment of Payment	Insures	Pays Insured
Company A	$20,000	$10,000
Company B	20,000	10,000
Company C	10,000	5,000
	$50,000	$25,000

Net proceeds of salvage $12,500

Apportionment of Proceeds	Insures	Receives
Company A	$20,000	$ 5,000
Company B	20,000	5,000
Company C	10,000	2,500
	$50,000	$12,500

EXAMPLE 19-4   Sale for Account of the Insured (Account of the Loss)

Loss as adjusted:
Sound value $50,000
Merchandise damaged $25,000
Net proceeds of salvage paid insured 12,500
Net loss to insurers $12,500

Apportionment of Loss	Insures	Pays Insured
Company A	$20,000	$ 5,000
Company B	20,000	5,000
Company C	10,000	2,500
	$50,000	$12,500

EXAMPLE 19-5   Sale for Account of Whom It May Concern
Under 80% Average
Insurance and Merchandise Damaged as in Examples 19-3 and 19-4

Loss as adjusted:
Sound value $100,000
Merchandise turned over to salvor for sale .... $ 25,000
Under terms of 80% average clause, insurers pay insured:

$$\frac{\$50,000}{80\% \text{ of } \$100,000} \times \$25,000 = \$15,625$$

Apportionment of Payment	Insures	Pays Insured
Company A	$20,000	$ 6,250
Company B	20,000	6,250
Company C	10,000	3,125
	$50,000	$15,625

Net proceeds of salvage $12,500

$$\text{Insurer's proportion} = \frac{\$50,000}{80\% \text{ of } \$100,000} \times \$12,500 = \$7,812.50$$

Apportionment of Proceeds	Insures	Receives
Company A	$20,000	$ 3,125.00
Company B	20,000	3,125.00
Company C	10,000	1,562.50
	$50,000	$ 7,812.50
Insured, a coinsurer	30,000	4,687.50
	$80,000	$12,500.00

QUESTIONS AND PROBLEMS

1. a. It is very important for a claim representative to know what services can be performed by professional salvors. State six such services.

b. Salvors stress the importance of recognizing priorities in salvaging the contents in serious losses that involve such occupancies as food supermarkets, discount stores, department stores, auto parts, and light hardware stores. What do they mean by "recognizing priorities"?

2. Salvage value of stocks of merchandise after a loss is related to their (1) exposure to the peril or perils insured against, (2) susceptibility to physical injury, and (3) subsequent marketability in a damaged condition.

Discuss briefly each of these three factors which influence the salvage value of stocks and tell how, using examples.

3. Define the terms *salvage, salvor,* and *salvaging.*

4. a. A Brands and Labels Clause in a policy tends to reduce salvage value. Explain why.

b. The insurer, through a professional salvor, takes over a large stock of men's suits and pays the insured the value of the stock. Insured then contends that the salvor must remove the stock to a distant city so as not to affect the normal trade of the insured. How would you respond?

5. Two different salvaging agreements are used when part or all of the damaged property covered is to be taken over.

One agreement is for a specific purpose or function of the salvor. The other has two purposes, one or both of which may be agreed to. What is the name and purpose or purposes of each? How and by whom are these agreements executed?

6. Distinguish between the following terms and give an example of each.

    a. *Sale for account of the insurer(s).*

    b. *Sale for account of the insured (account of loss).*

    c. *Sale for account of whom it may concern.*

7. a. Salvage has been sold for the account of the insurers. Show each insurer's loss payment to the insured, and each insurer's share of the net salvage proceeds.

Loss as adjusted:

Sound value	$100,000
Merchandise taken over	$ 50,000
Paid by insurers to insured	$ 50,000

Insurer	Insures	Pays Insured
Company A	$ 40,000	?
Company B	40,000	?
Company C	20,000	?
	$100,000	?

Net proceeds of salvage, $20,000

Apportionment of Salvage Proceeds	Insures	Receives
Company A	$ 40,000	?
Company B	40,000	?
Company C	20,000	?
	$100,000	?

b. Salvage has been sold for the account of the insured (account of the loss). Show each insurer's loss payment to the insured.

Loss as adjusted:

Sound value	$100,000
Merchandise taken over	$ 50,000
Net salvage proceeds paid to insured	$ 20,000

Paid by Insurers to Insured	Insures	Pays Insured
Company A	$ 40,000	?
Company B	40,000	?
Company C	20,000	?
	$100,000	?

8. Salvage has been sold for the account of the loss. Show each insurer's loss payment and apportion the net salvage proceeds among all interested parties. All policies are subject to 80 percent coinsurance.

Loss as adjusted:

Sound value	$150,000
Merchandise taken over	$ 60,000
Net proceeds	$ 24,000

Apportionment of Payment	Insures	Pays Insured
Company A	$45,000	?
Company B	30,000	?
Company C	15,000	?
	$90,000	?

Apportionment of Proceeds	Insures	Receives
Company A	$ 45,000	?
Company B	30,000	?
Company C	15,000	?
	$ 90,000	?
Insured, a coinsurer	$ 30,000	?
	$120,000	?

20

Books and Records

Books and records are the written day-to-day history of a business. They account in detail for all financial and merchandise transactions in such a way that their totals and summaries can be compiled by the owner or the management to show the results of operations and the financial position of the business. Because of their detail, they contain many facts of value, and it is customary, and usually necessary, in merchandise losses to examine them in the course of the adjustment. Through checking, testing, or making computations from them, much information will be brought to light that would remain hidden if examination were limited to the goods themselves.

Books of account contain both quantity and dollar evidence. They show data bearing on the quantities of goods on hand and on their pricing. They are useful in establishing facts necessary to the fixing of both value and loss. The ways in which they are used vary, depending upon the circumstances and extent of each loss. If the goods are in sight and are their own evidence of quantities involved, the books will help to establish the value of the commodity or the articles. If the goods are out of sight, in whole or in part, the books may be the only means of establishing the quantities destroyed and their values.

When books and records are dealt with, one of the most difficult tasks is to appraise their reliability. If they are adequately kept and if the entries are properly managed and controlled, they will be correlated with the movement of the merchandise. But the accounting may be inadequate, poorly maintained, or even falsified. The procedure that should be followed in connection with books and records when dealing with either insight or out-of-sight merchandise losses is explained in this chapter, but it is not possible to list all the steps of audit that may be desirable. The extent to which books of account are relied upon, the methods by which they are checked, and the validity of the conclusions drawn from them are in many respects matters of judgment and cannot be prescribed in detail.

STOCK IN SIGHT

When the merchandise is all in sight, its value cannot be assumed to be conclusively established by the price tags. The books sometimes enable the claim representative to determine that articles have been incorrectly listed or priced or that the merchandise should be subject to depreciation. If the books show the history of the stock, its cost, its age, and the rate of selling, they may establish that the merchandise has become hard to sell or is wholly unsalable, because of style, obsolescence, changing demand, defect, or other cause.

Stock in sight can be inventoried physically and usually presents few problems where identification and count are possible.

A general examination of the books is warranted in many cases, even though all the stock is in sight. The rate of stock turnover is worth knowing, as it reflects the general condition of the business. Likewise the rate of profit, the trend of the business, and the relation of indebtedness to assets should be determined whenever a serious loss has occurred.

STOCK OUT OF SIGHT

The quantity of merchandise burned out of sight may occasionally be determined by making measurements of the space that it occupied. If the length, breadth, and height of the space can be measured, the quantity of the merchandise can be approximated and its value determined. It is, however, seldom possible to make accurate measurements when any considerable loss has occurred, as the premises are generally wrecked and do not show one or more of the points where measurements should begin or end. For this reason, the majority of losses involving considerable quantities of stock out of sight are necessarily adjusted on the evidence furnished by the books and records of the insured.

Determination of the value of the destroyed merchandise from evidence furnished by the books and records is generally made by one of two methods, either of which should be corroborated by the other whenever possible.

1. The *book-statement* method, whereby an approximate computation of the stock value *in total* is determined from the financial accounts of inventories, sales, and purchases.
2. The *unit* or *quantity-analysis* method, whereby an approximate determination of the stock in units is made either *(a)* by reference to perpetual-inventory unit records, if available, or *(b)* by adjusting the insured's last inventory listings for all interim purchases and sales in units to the date of the loss.

The valuation of stock on hand produced by the book-statement method is one in which quantity and prices are not determined separately but value is determined in total (or by major classes). Regardless of the method employed, verification of the books and records by the claim representative, possibly aided by a certified public accountant, must usually be undertaken to substantiate the claim for loss when all or part of the stock is out of sight.

Books and records may be quite simple. In some cases a single warehouse receipt or a single invoice will be adequate proof of the insured's loss. In other cases, a complete set of books, reflecting the results of numerous transactions over a considerable period of time, may have to be examined. Such a set of books may cover business done at a number of different locations or in a number of departments. Any complete set of books, correctly kept, will show in one way or another the costs and quantities of commodities or articles purchased or manufactured and the amount realized from sales. Perpetual-inventory records may not be kept in terms of money, but they do generally show quantities received and quantities delivered. Warehouse and department records sometimes deal in quantities only. After familiarizing one's self with the entries appearing in such records, a person proficient in accounting methods can evolve a statement that will show the cost or quantity of merchandise that should be on hand at a given date. This cost or quantity is, of course, theoretical but, in the absence of better evidence, is accepted in lieu of the physical inventory that the insured is required to furnish. It is often termed the *theoretical inventory*.

A *book statement* (which is a theoretical inventory but in money amounts only) may be quite simple or highly complicated, depending upon how many entries must be summarized in its preparation. If the entire stock on hand consists of a single purchase of merchandise, there may be only a single invoice or a single purchase entry to consider. But if the stock of an active business that has been in existence for several years is destroyed, the book statement must commence with the amount of the last inventory taken before the loss and must summarize all entries of purchases and sales, together with charges and credits affecting them, from the date of that inventory to the date of the loss. To support the book statement, it is necessary for the claim representative or accountant to review the showing of the books and records for one or more prior years.

THEORY OF BOOK STATEMENT

The book statement of stock value is based on the fact that the books of the business show its history and that, from these books, the present condition of the business can be established. Because purchases and sales of merchandise have been recorded as they occurred, the cost of stock on hand can be established without counting, weighing, or measuring it. If the cost of all goods sold is deducted from the total cost of all goods taken into the premises, the remainder will represent the cost of stock on hand. The total cost of all goods taken into the premises is made up of the totals of the last inventory and the subsequent purchases, and also any charges such as freight, trucking, or express necessary to receive the merchandise. Cost of materials may be reduced as a result of cash discounts taken. In the case of a manufacturer, there are also charges for labor and factory overhead which enter into the cost of production.

Accountants sometimes refer to the book statement as a computation of inventory on the gross profit basis. As the record of merchandise sold seldom shows its cost, this cost is theoretically determined by deducting a percentage of gross profit (or known margin of markup) from the amount of the sales. This percentage is obtained by finding the gross profit earned in the past and adjusting it for known changes in conditions affecting the business to arrive at the approximate gross profit earned during the period under consideration. The method is based on the proposition that the relationship between sales and cost of goods sold should be fairly constant from year to year in the same business, unless the books themselves show a reason for variation or unless a varying factor in business conditions is known to exist. Much of the work of the claim representative or of the accountant employed to examine merchandise claims is devoted to a proper determination of the relationship between sales and cost of goods sold.

It is important for the claim representative to understand fully the principles on which the book statement is based. The principles are demonstrated by the oversimplified illustration in Example 20-1.

No loss should be adjusted on the uncorroborated evidence of the books unless the stock and the premises have been so badly burned that a complete physical inventory cannot be taken or approximated. While books are indeed evidence bearing on the possession and cost of merchandise, they are not the conclusive evidence that is offered by the merchandise itself. At best, a statement prepared from the books is only a calculation of what *ought* to be on hand. If the statement is prepared shortly after the taking of an accurate inventory, the result will be more trustworthy than if it is prepared many months later, during which time numerous purchases and sales have operated to change the amount of stock on hand.

To understand the book-statement method, one must remember that it is a substitute for a physical inventory in dollars at the time of the loss. The assumption upon which it is based is the consistent effect of the

EXAMPLE 20-1

Last physical inventory before loss, Jan. 1		$100,000
Purchases, Jan. 1 to date of loss, Mar. 16, including freight-in, and after deducting cash discounts		50,000
		$150,000
Less goods removed by sale to customers from Jan. 1 to Mar. 16:		
Sales, at selling prices, after deducting returns, allowances, and discounts	$75,000	
Less average markup (gross profit) realized on sales, as established by previous history of the business, 20%	15,000	
Goods removed at cost		60,000
Stock on hand at the time of loss		$ 90,000

expenditure of money; for example, in the case of a manufacturing business, it is assumed that a given expenditure will produce, under representative conditions, a given number of units. It follows that the number of units indicated by the value shown in the book statement may be distorted by changes in conditions during the period under consideration as compared with the prior periods from which the rate of gross profit has been determined.

A manufacturing plant that maintained a fairly uniform flow of production throughout the year would ordinarily produce the same number of units at the same cost during any two periods of equal length On the other hand, consider a seasonal business that produces one-third of its annual production during the first half of the year and two-thirds during the remainder of the year. Depending on the cost system in use, the units manufactured during the first half of the year might carry a much larger portion of the fixed or nonvariable expenses, such as depreciation, insurance, rent, and taxes. In this case, to avoid an overstatement of stock on hand, it is necessary to reapportion the nonvariable expenses before preparing the book statement.

In preparing the book statement of loss it is well to bear in mind that, while the basic principles of accounting hold good with respect to all businesses, the details of bookkeeping are subject to many individual peculiarities. Add to this condition the many possible errors of omission or commission due to ignorance, together with the occasional misuse or alteration of entries to accomplish fraud, and it will be seen that the task of preparing the book statement can easily be full of difficulties. Errors of all kinds must be eliminated from the books as early in the examination as possible, and the claim representative or accountant must acquire some understanding of the peculiarities of the set of books he or she is dealing with. Afterward attention can be devoted to testing the authenticity of the records, and with their degree of authenticity established, evaluate them as evidence of the cost of stock on hand at the time of the loss.

VERIFICATION OF BOOK STATEMENT

Verification of the results shown in the book statement resolves itself into proving the reliability of the principal known components: (1) opening and closing inventories, (2) cost of purchases or production, (3) sales, and (4) gross profit percentage.

In the process of testing the reliability of the component accounts, it is necessary also to determine whether treatment of the transactions included within them has been consistent. Any inconsistency of treatment can create error in the final result. For example, in arriving at the gross profit experience of the business, such items as cash discounts or freight on purchases may be deducted from purchases in the period of the book statement computation. The accuracy of the book statement depends to a large degree upon uniformity of treatment of each component.

It is vital to verify the reliability of the factors of opening and closing inventories, cost of purchases or production, amount of sales, and the gross profit percentage for the period under consideration, as these items will become direct factors in substantiating the insured's claim. Likewise, testing the accuracy of the gross profit percentage is mandatory, as the percentage used is a highly important element in the computation.

Verification of each of the four factors will be considered separately, though it is to be remembered that the procedures suggested are merely indicative and not all-inclusive. It must be remembered also that particular industries are subject to operating customs and peculiarities that should be studied thoroughly in conjunction with the books to determine the influence of their unusual factors on the ultimate loss computation.

INVENTORIES

There are two methods of accounting for inventory: the *periodic* inventory and the *perpetual* inventory.

The periodic inventory is an actual physical count of each item of stock. It is usually taken as of the date of the closing of the books. As such it is the *ending inventory* for the period and the *beginning inventory* for the next period.

The inventory may be written up on formal inventory sheets or in notebooks, or it may be recorded on tape. It may be taken by departments of the business, by floor, room, or other meaningful and identifiable area depending upon the size and type of operation. Each item or article on the inventory is priced to arrive at the dollar value.

A perpetual inventory, as the name implies, consists of a continuous recording of items received and items sold. The perpetual inventory system is more suitable for some types of business than for others. It is possible to prepare an income statement more frequently inasmuch as the inventory cards show at all times the goods received, sold, or issued, and the balance. While perpetual inventories are convenient they usually have to be reconciled periodically with physical inventories because of shrinkage in stocks from theft, mysterious disappearance, lost items, or deterioration.[1]

A mercantile inventory consists of stock purchased for resale. A manufacturer's inventory consists of material purchased for conversion into finished stock, goods in process, and finished stock.[2]

PRICING INVENTORIES

Inventories prepared in the usual course of a business may be subject to the application of varying accounting procedures in pricing, not all of which would necessarily result in establishing the actual value of the goods on hand at the time of the inventory. For example, inventories may properly be priced for accounting purposes either at actual cost or at market cost, whichever is lower.

Cost may be determined by the specific identification method or on the basis of first-in, first-out; average cost; last-in, first-out; or any of several other varying yet generally accepted practices. The last-in, first-out method is likely to produce, after a loss, the greatest distortion. A company whose inventory is based on this method may show on its books an amount varying greatly from the actual value of the inventory, and it would ordinarily be necessary to reprice such an inventory on the basis of market value at the same date in order to establish a proper starting point for the book-statement method.

Some retail inventories are priced at a fixed percentage above invoice cost. In some cases the increment may be intended to cover the cost of getting the goods into the premises, i.e., the cost of freight or trucking. A great many department stores and other retail stores compute their book inventories by the gross profit method.[3] Physical inventories when taken at the retail selling price are also reduced to cost by the gross profit method.[4]

In other cases, the increment is arbitrary, sometimes being made to protect the business from too much price cutting by salesmen. Some inventories are priced to allow for deterioration or obsolescence on an item basis. Others at times provide for deterioration, obsolescence, or decline in market by a final deduction of an estimated amount.

If the pricing principles of the various inventories are not the same, they should be made the same, otherwise no accurate computation of gross profit will be possible. Consistency is of prime importance in developing a reliable book statement.

In the case of a mercantile concern, inventory prices can be tested by reference to purchase invoices. As the preparation of a book statement requires that consistent allowance be made for such factors as freight charges, cash discounts, and various costs, it is essential that their influence on the inventory total be clearly established. Likewise, the inclusion of such costs as import duties, insurance expense, and warehouse and handling charges should also be clearly determined. The insured should be asked to explain his customary method of treating the several factors, and his explanation should be checked as closely as possible. If any appreciable quantity of merchandise is left in

[1]Perpetual inventories are also discussed on p. 325.
[2]See also p. 266.

[3]See also p. 328.
[4]This subject is discussed in detail on p. 315.

an identifiable condition, it should be examined for cost marks or price tags, and the costs or selling prices shown should be compared with those in the latest inventory.

MANUFACTURERS' STOCKS

The prices applied to stock in the hands of a manufacturer should always be checked against the book records, as these prices are built up by allocating costs of material, direct labor cost, and manufacturing expenses to the various units of production.[5] Whenever accurate cost-finding records are maintained, this work is considerably easier than when costs must be averaged or estimated. Whatever method is used, tests should always be made to ascertain the accuracy of the allocation of costs to the units produced. For instance, if the direct-labor unit charges are applied to the total production quantities, the result should approximate the actual direct-labor payroll. The total production

[5]See p. 315.

quantities of various classes, when multiplied by the raw-material costs applied to each, should equal approximately the actual cost of raw materials used during the period, as shown by the raw-material purchases adjusted by the increase or decrease in raw-material inventories. Similarly, the amount of overhead expenses included in unit costs of the merchandise produced should be equal to the actual overhead expenses incurred.

If no cost-finding records are maintained, a test check for overall reliability of claimed costs should be made. Example 20-2 illustrates how this may be done.

In instances where adequate cost-finding records are available, consideration of the principles used in the allocation of costs should indicate the figures that need to be verified. For example, if the cost records show the use of a fixed or standard percentage of direct-labor cost as the charge for overhead expenses against units of production, the total of such overhead included in the costs should be compared with the actual overhead incurred. It may be found that a

EXAMPLE 20-2

Assume that a manufacturer produced five articles and the estimated costs used in the inventory are:

Product	Costs
1	$3.50
2	6.19
3	3.81
4	4.50
5	9.10

Reference to the records discloses the following total expenditures for the year's operations:

Raw materials	$ 40,000
Direct labor	60,000
Overhead expenses	90,000
Total	$190,000

Production for the year was 6,000, 4,000, 3,000, 20,000, and 11,000 units, respectively, for the five articles. An application of the unit costs used in the inventory to the quantities produced during the year would reveal a considerable overstatement of the inventory unit prices, as shown below.

Product	Units	Inventory Unit Cost	Total
1	6,000	$3.50	$ 21,000
2	4,000	6.19	24,760
3	3,000	3.81	11,430
4	20,000	4.50	90,000
5	11,000	9.10	100,100
		Total	$247,290
		Total actual cost	190,000
		Difference	$ 57,290

plant has a total actual overhead expense of $300,000, whereas the application of the standard overhead rate of 150 percent to a direct-labor cost of $250,000 resulted in the erroneous inclusion of $375,000 as overhead. This would mean that the unit cost of each item of production was overstated.

IMPORTANCE OF VERIFYING INVENTORIES

Substantiation of the insured's last and next-to-last inventories is exceedingly important. Verification of the clerical accuracy of an inventory is the first step to be taken. This involves testing the extensions and footings, and noting whether the inventory sheets contain any references to the presence of consignment merchandise, customers' merchandise held for repair, merchandise sold but held pending periodic shipping instructions, merchandise at other locations, quantities in transit, or any other data that may be pertinent in later establishing the location or ownership of the goods.

An illustration of why the verification of inventories is vital in establishing the correctness of the book statement is pertinent here. While the correct statement of all inventories is important as a gross-profit-rate factor, the inventory used in the last closing of the books before the date of loss deserves special consideration because of the twofold effect that any inflation of this inventory will have in computing the value of the merchandise destroyed. For example, a concern based its claim for loss on a book statement set out in Example 20-3.

Correction of the overstatement of the inventory reduced the percentage of gross profit to be used in computing the value of stock on hand. It also reduced the total cost of goods taken into the premises. The reduced percentage of gross profit reduced the loss by $6,000, and the reduced amount of the inventory reduced it by an additional $10,000.

PURCHASES

Under the general heading of purchases are included all cost components. In the case of a nonmanufacturing enterprise, these will generally be limited to merchandise, freight, and cartage. When manufacturing is carried on, there will be raw material, freight, cartage, labor, and manufacturing expenses.

The verification necessary to substantiate the various cost elements attaching to the goods on hand will depend to a large extent upon the adequacy and accuracy of the cost system, if there is one; upon the control and accuracy in handling receiving tickets, shipping tickets, debit memorandums, credit memorandums, and related documents; and upon the reliability of the accounting period "cutoffs" or closings.

Purchase entries should be supported by original invoices except in those businesses that do not receive invoices for all purchases. The original invoice and the freight bill ordinarily furnish satisfactory evidence of purchase and receipt of merchandise. If the purchase is subject to a cash discount, the terms are usually stated on the invoice. Country stores often do not receive invoices, as many purchases of local produce are made from farmers who give none.

Invoices for purchases of materials or supplies should be carefully checked, not only with purchase records but also with receiving books, express receipts, freight bills, drayage tickets, or similar records. Errors and attempts at fraud may be revealed by such checking.

The importance of examining freight bills in conjunction with purchase invoices was forcibly emphasized in an investigation of a retail lumberyard loss. The insured purchased most of his lumber in carload lots from distant mills. Five carload shipments were included in the claim, the invoices bearing dates earlier than the date of the loss. The invoice dates indicated that the lumber might easily have been received before the fire. No freight bills, however, could be located, and inquiry at the railroad offices established the fact that these shipments were all in transit at the time of the fire.

Freight and Cash Discounts

If the method followed by the insured in pricing the goods does not provide for an

EXAMPLE 20-3

Computation of gross profit:

Sales, calendar year		$200,000	100%
Inventory, Jan. 1	$ 30,000		
Purchases for year	170,000		
	$200,000		
Less inventory, Dec. 31	50,000		
Cost of sales	$150,000	150,000	75%
Gross profit		$ 50,000	25%

Computation of stock on hand at date of loss:

Inventory, Dec. 31		$ 50,000	
Purchases, to date of loss		100,000	
		$150,000	
Sales	$120,000		
Less gross profit, 25%	30,000		
Cost of sales	$ 90,000	90,000	
Stock on hand at date of loss		$ 60,000	

Upon investigation, it was found that the inventory of Dec. 31 was overstated by $10,000; therefore, the following corrected computations were made:

Computation of gross profit:

Sales, calendar year		$200,000	100%
Inventory, Jan. 1	$ 30,000		
Purchases for year	170,000		
	$200,000		
Less inventory, Dec. 31	40,000		
Cost of sales	$160,000	160,000	80%
Gross profit		$ 40,000	20%

Computation of stock on hand at date of loss:

Inventory, Dec. 31		$ 40,000	
Purchases to date of loss		100,000	
		$140,000	
Sales	$120,000		
Less gross profit, 20%	24,000		
Cost of sales	$ 96,000	96,000	
Stock on hand at date of loss		$ 44,000	

increase over invoice prices to cover freight charges and for deductions to allow for cash discount, an amount equal to the freight charge necessary to replace the stock should be added to the inventory, and the amount that would be saved by taking all cash discounts should be deducted. If the inventory consists of a few large items on which freights and discounts can be traced, the exact amount of the freight charge and of the cash discount can be determined. If, however, it consists of a great number of lots of different kinds of goods on which freight charges and cash discounts are not uniform,

it will be necessary to use average figures. As a rule, the average rate of freight paid and the average rate of cash discount covering a year's purchases will be equitable. These rates can be determined by examining the accounts that cover purchases, freight, and cash discount. Sometimes the average rates should be modified, particularly if just before the date of the inventory there were large purchases on which the freight charges, and the cash discounts are entered in a later period, thus upsetting the yearly average. An illustration of average figures is shown in Example 20-4.

EXAMPLE 20-4

Year	Purchases	Freight		Discount	
		Amount	Rate, Percent	Amount	Rate, Percent
1973	$ 35,272.92	$ 465.03	1.32	$1,769.18	5.02
1974	24,787.50	313.88	1.27	1,256.13	5.07
1975	28,045.67	406.82	1.45	1,344.83	4.80
1976	35,684.57	465.18	1.30	1,596.37	4.47
1977 (6 mo.)	14,318.19	157.87	1.10	728.06	5.09
Totals	$138,108.85	$1,808.78	1.31	$6,694.57	4.85

Trade Discounts

Certain established discounts are customary to purchasers of merchandise in some lines of business. Typical of such trade discounts is the 8 percent off ready-to-wear merchandise invoices. There are also bulk-purchase discounts, and sometimes allowances of additional items over and above the quantity ordered but not priced on the invoice. These discounts do not always appear on the invoice and are disclosed by matching the payment instrument or the purchase account with the invoice. They are not to be confused with cash discounts, which are deductions allowed to induce customers to pay their bills within a specified time.

Purchase Returns and Allowances

Purchase returns and allowances may be recorded in a journal or in a specific account book for that purpose.

Method of Recording Purchases

In checking purchases it is important to determine the insured's method of entering the purchases on the books. Purchases entered when paid, usually in the subsequent month, will distort the purchase account by being a month behind actual purchases. Books kept in this fashion cause no special problems under normal conditions. But if, because of serious damage or destruction of the property, the flow of cash and merchandise stops on the day of the loss, the claim representative may find that the books overstate the true value.

Transfers and Direct Shipments

Stock transfers should be checked carefully where the insured has more than one location or where a transfer is made from one department to another.

Occasionally, insureds place large orders such as carloads of lumber from a mill or supplier, ship them directly to the customer, and enter them in the purchase account. Such merchandise never went into inventory and should properly be handled by separate accounting records.

Merchandise in Transit

It is not uncommon for wholesalers and persons selling bulk quantities of second-hand articles to have the merchandise shipped directly to the purchaser. The goods never became part of the insured's inventory. Also, many firms enter invoices in the purchase account when the purchaser pays the invoice. The merchandise has not yet reached the insured's place of business. Frequently it is en route or held up for one reason or another by the shipper.

Verification is therefore necessary to make certain that all stock entered as received has in fact been delivered to the premises of the insured.

Irregularities in Purchase Accounts

If possible, all large entries in the purchase record should be traced to their origin, as some entries may not represent purchases. In one instance, it was found that a $25,000 loan was credited to the purchase account in order to keep the liability off the balance sheet. The account was debited a year later when the loan was paid. A fire loss occurred that same year, following which a claim was prepared from the books without an adjustment of the purchase account to correct the spurious entries covering the loan. The claim was overstated, not only by the amount of $25,000 falsely charged as a purchase, but by an additional amount due to an inflated gross profit computed on the false purchase reduction in the previous year.

In rare cases, purchase records have been heavily padded in anticipation of a loss by forging invoices and issuing checks to fictitious sellers, the checks being deposited by the maker in a private account kept under an assumed name. A case of this sort was unearthed by comparing the endorsements appearing on the checks with the signatures. Enough similarities were found to warrant investigation.

Some investigations should be pushed to the extreme of interviewing the sellers whose names appear on the invoices. Merchandise may have been returned without a record, or invoices may have been raised. When sellers allow their records to be investigated, the result will be conclusive so far as the buying of the goods is concerned, unless there is collusion, which is rare.

Frequently, if the insured is a member of an affiliated group of companies manufacturing identical products or parts of a particular product, intercompany charges for material may not necessarily be the cost applicable to the inventory for insurance purposes. For example, a furniture manufacturer may be "purchasing" its lumber from a subsidiary at a price determined for federal income tax purposes, much higher than might prevail elsewhere. In fact, transactions with affiliated companies almost always require special scrutiny of the propriety of prices and charges. The absence of "arm's-length" dealings in such cases may be the occasion for fictitious, overstated, or understated transactions designed solely to serve management objectives. Such devices, however innocent otherwise, may seriously distort a loss computation.

SALES

In computing the theoretical amount of stock on hand under the book-statement method, the sales item is the third major factor. Generally, this factor is made up of both cash and credit sales, the original record of the former being in some cases the daily reading of the cash register. Credit sales are usually entered in a sales book, on sales tickets, or on sales invoices. The total cash sales and the total credit sales are later posted to the sales account in the ledger. In many establishments, sales are recorded in a sales book that shows carbon copies of the sales invoices.

Cash and Trade Discounts

Trade and cash discounts granted by the seller are deductions from the list or invoice price in arriving at "net" sales, or the amount of cash actually received.

Returns and Allowances

Goods which are returned, for various reasons, by the purchaser and accepted by the seller are also deducted to net out sales.

Method of Recording Sales

The method used in recording sales should be checked out by the claim representative. Some merchants take merchandise out of the stock record when a credit sale is made or a down payment is made. Others do not remove it from stock until the item is fully paid for. The same variation applies to "layaways" or "will-call" merchandise which may be partially or fully paid for by the customer. In situations of this kind a complete analysis may have to be made of the sales records.

Irregularities in Sales Accounting

When sales records are kept accurately, it is easy to verify the sales account, but when they are not, the problem of determining the total sales may become complex, as there is considerable possibility of manipulation. Examination of individual sales invoices and comparison of them with shipping records will sometimes reveal discrepancies. Occasionally it is found that large quantities of merchandise have been shipped out shortly before the loss, although copies of the sales invoices show negligible amounts. Again, shipments may be made without any sales invoices being prepared, the freight or cartage bill in such cases being the only evidence of the transaction; or customers may be billed for work in process in the plant though no shipments have been made.

During the investigation of a loss in a department store, a large freight bill purporting to cover the shipment of a single pair of shoes was discovered. Actually, 1,461 pairs had been shipped by a dishonest employee who was using understated sales invoices to conceal his thefts from the insured. Another case involved a retail lumber dealer who had sold several cars of lumber shortly before a loss. Delivery was made directly from the mill to the customer, an unusual procedure, as the dealer ordinarily made sales from the yard in small quantities. The sales invoices had been made out, and the claim for loss was prepared according to the book showing. A check of the records revealed that accounts receivable were out of balance with the controlling general-ledger account by the exact amount of the large sale. The insured had charged the customer with the shipment but had made no corresponding credit to the sales account. This indicates the necessity that all ledgers be in balance, or that the cause of any discrepancy be made known.

In another instance it was found that the insured was billing certain customers on cash-sales tickets when, as a matter of fact, the transactions were on credit. No entry was made in connection with a sale at the time the merchandise was delivered, but when the account was collected, the cash-sales account was credited. Unpaid cash-sales tickets were kept as memorandums until paid. Numerous gaps in the serial numbers on the sales tickets brought about inquiries for the missing tickets and uncovered several thousand dollars of otherwise unrecorded sales.

In the search for suppressed sales, it is often necessary to analyze the general ledger accounts, particularly accounts payable or loans payable. Analysis should also be made of cash transactions and reconciliations of bank statements. A case was discovered in which the insured had entered sales to a large customer as a liability under the customer's name, in lieu of a credit to the sales account. In another case, the insured made no record whatever of sales to certain customers. When cash was received from these customers, it was deposited in the bank but not entered in the records. This falsification of the book showing was promptly disclosed when a reconciliation of the cash records and the bank statements was attempted. In still another case, a manufacturer credited sales to a loans payable account, indicating that the proceeds of the sales were loans from himself to the business. In each of these cases, the failure to deduct the suppressed sales would have resulted in a substantial overpayment of loss. In small businesses, such as grocery stores or drugstores, the owner is always tempted to pocket some of the cash receipts without recording them, thus saving sales taxes and income taxes.

The sales record and the sales-return record, following procedures similar to those discussed under the purchase record, should also be checked against the inventory for out-of-period items.

Frequently, computation of accounts-receivable ratios or turnover ratios, and comparison with those of previous periods, will indicate the reasonableness or unreasonableness of the total sales figure. Monthly statements or internal-management reports may be requested for further verification of book figures; frequently, the monthly reports will indicate unusual trends or activity that should be critically examined.

While it is admittedly difficult to detect manipulation of sales, the records will give in most cases some indication of irregularities when they exist. Any such indication must be noted and run down to a point at which the reason for it and the type and extent of falsification will become clear.

GROSS PROFIT

In a merchandising operation, gross profit is the difference between the *cost of goods sold* and its selling price. The cost of goods sold is the purchase cost. Gross profit, gross margin, or margin, as it is variously called, is the income of the business. All operating expenses are paid out of the gross profit, and the remainder is the net profit or net loss, as the case may be.

In determining gross profit, the essential difference between a manufacturing operation and a merchandising operation is that in the manufacturing operation the cost of goods sold is the *cost of goods manufactured*. This consists of (1) *direct materials* consumed in manufacturing, (2) *direct labor* applied to materials, and (3) *manufacturing overhead or expense*.

1. *Direct materials*, frequently referred to as *raw materials*, are those that become part of the finished product.
2. *Direct labor* is employees who work directly upon the material by hand, tools, or machines to convert it into the finished product. Direct labor is distinguished from supervisory employees and other *indirect labor*.
3. *Manufacturing overhead* includes all costs that cannot be identified as material or direct labor. It includes heat and light; power used in manufacturing; depreciation and maintenance of buildings and machinery; and foremen, engineers, and other indirect labor.

No unvarying method can be laid down for reviewing manufacturing overhead. For practical purposes, it is perhaps sufficient to say that there should be included only those items having to do solely with the production of the finished products, and that care should be taken to exclude from consideration those having to do with their sale or with the strictly administrative affairs of the business.

Manufacturing overhead is subject to differences in treatment in different businesses. It is, therefore, generally necessary to familiarize oneself with the insured's accounting methods and to agree on what items are to be included. Consistency of treatment is essential both in the period on which the rate of gross profit is computed and in the period of the book statement. For example, if a manufacturer considers buying expense as part of the cost of merchandise, it is necessary to consider buying expense as part of the cost of goods sold when computing gross profit. Likewise, a clear determination should be made of the insured's policy of accounting for tools, small machine parts, or supplies having relatively short useful lives. If they are carried in the accounts of one period as inventories and in another machinery and equipment, a decided distortion will appear in the ultimate determination of stock on hand.

In order to facilitate early month-end preparation of financial statements, many medium-size and large companies apply manufacturing expenses to production on some predetermined basis such as a fixed percentage of direct-labor cost. Such a method, though useful for accounting purposes, will never achieve exact absorption of the actual manufacturing expense incurred; under many circumstances, it may be necessary, in order to restate these items correctly, to adjust the cost of production and the closing inventory for the over- or underabsorbed burden.

Markup

When a merchant buys an article for resale, he or she marks it up to a price that, it is hoped, the customer will pay for it. The difference between the cost and the price at which it is offered for sale is called the *markup*. In dollars it is equivalent to the gross profit discussed above.

However, *gross profit percentage* is always the ratio of the gross profit in dollars to sales in dollars. Most accountants and merchants refer to the *markup percentage* as the ratio of markup in dollars to the cost of the goods. Because there are a few who relate markup to sales, which produces the same percentage as gross profit percentage, the claim representative should be certain that the insured or accountant is using these terms in the same manner. Example 20-5 illustrates the problem.

Markup percentage in this text refers to cost, not sales, and therefore should not be confused with gross profit percentage.

EXAMPLE 20-5

Cost of article	$ .60
Markup	.40
Selling price	$1.00

Markup on cost: $\dfrac{.40}{.60} = 66\frac{2}{3}\%$

Markup on selling price: $\dfrac{.40}{1.00} = 40\%$

Gross profit percentage: $\dfrac{.40}{1.00} = 40\%$

EXAMPLE 20-6

Original selling price	$10.00	100%
Gross profit on selling price	4.00	40%
Original cost	$ 6.00	60%

(The markdown from the original selling price was $2, or 20%.)

New selling price	$ 8.00	100%
Gross profit on selling price	3.20	40%
	$ 4.80	60%

Markdown

A merchant may mark down articles of merchandise for a number of reasons. The items may have suffered obsolescence or may be shopworn; they may be out of season or damaged; the size, color, or style ranges may be broken, leaving odd lots and remnants; or the merchandise may have otherwise lost its former sales appeal. Merchandise may also be marked down solely for promotional sales. In each situation markdowns are taken to move stock more rapidly, generally in order to replace it with new stock.

Markdown Percentage

The markdown percentage is the ratio of the amount of the markdown to the selling price. For example, when an item is marked down from $10 to $8 it is said to have been marked down 20 percent.

Markdowns play an important role in determining the actual value of stocks of merchandise. When the selling price of an item is reduced in the retail system, a new cost is established. In the above example, if the item selling for $10 cost the seller $6, the margin or gross profit is $4, or 40 percent. When the retailer marks the item down 20 percent to $8, the new cost value is now $4.80. This gives the retailer the same 40 percent gross profit he was operating at before the markdown. (See Example 20-6.)

A merchant operates at a fairly consistent gross profit percentage. The merchandise cannot remain long on the shelves; it must move to make room for new merchandise in order to maintain a normal turnover for his particular type of business. Spring stock must make way for summer goods, for example, and summer goods must make way for fall stocks. Items that will no longer sell at their original markup must be marked down. When a merchant voluntarily reduces the cost of items to move them, it is generally an admission that they are no longer worth the cost of replacement.

Turnover

The term *turnover*, also called *stockturn* or *rate of selling*, means the number of times the average inventory is sold or replaced during the year. This may be determined by dividing the cost of goods sold by the average inventory at cost. If there is a seasonal fluctuation of inventory, turnover is computed by averaging the end-of-month inventories during the year with the beginning inventory. (See Example 20-7.)

EXAMPLE 20-7
Stock Turnover

Cost of goods sold	$140,000
Inventory beginning of year	$60,000
Average monthly inventory	40,000
Average inventory	$50,000

Stock turnover: $\dfrac{\$140,000}{\$50,000} = 2.8$

The rate of selling is useful in approximating inventory values because in many lines of business the turnover of stock falls within a certain range depending on such factors as annual sales volume, whether the business is located in a city or a suburb, and whether it is a cash store or a credit store. For example, retail furniture stocks turn over 2 to 2.5 times annually; jewelry stores have a low turnover range, generally between 1 and 1.5; whereas grocery stores and meat markets have a high rate of turnover.

The rate of turnover is also useful in determining whether a stock of merchandise is slow-moving as compared with similar businesses in the same general area. Such stocks may be subject to depreciation because, as previously stated, hard-to-move goods are not worth their replacement cost.

Checking Turnover by Items

If the books are kept so that the selling prices of specific articles can be compared with the cost prices, the claim representative should not be content with a verification of the cost prices shown on the inventory but should trace through the books a number of sales in order to determine whether the merchandise was being sold at a normal rate of profit. A claimant may present an inventory priced according to what the merchandise cost and may submit original invoices to substantiate the prices. The invoices should be examined and the dates appearing on them noted. If the invoices are dated prior to the current season and cover any appreciable quantity of stock, the claim representative will be warranted in assuming that the stock has not sold well and is not worth the cost of replacement. Under such circumstances, it is important to trace a number of sales, as they may show that the goods were sold at less than normal selling prices, perhaps at less than cost. If the tracing is carried out to the extent of following through all sales of a given kind of goods, and if the dates of the sales are noted, it will establish the time at which the stock commenced to be hard to sell.

In some cases, however, low selling prices may indicate nothing more serious than a decline in the market for the particular kind of merchandise, which will, therefore, have a replacement cost less than its original cost. If a large percentage of sales of standard merchandise were made at less than cost, one may assume that the business is under financial pressure.

When selling prices of individual articles are not shown by the books, the claim representative usually finds in the records a reliable indication of the condition of the stock. If the inventories taken in the regular course of business have been preserved, the claim representative should compare the quantities of various kinds of goods in the inventory taken after the loss with the quantities in the previous inventories. The comparison may show that some lots of stock were on hand for several seasons. If goods of the same kind and in the same quantity appear in one inventory after another, and if there are no invoices to show that new goods of the same kind were bought, there is but one conclusion: the goods did not sell. The same type of data may be uncovered from inventory-control records, if available.

GROSS PROFIT PERCENTAGE

The percentage or ratio of gross profit, the fourth major factor in the book statement, is frequently the one uncertainty. Inventories, purchases, and sales can in many instances be reduced to certainty by carefully checking the records, but the ratio of gross profit that should be used to reduce sales to a basis of cost cannot always be determined with precision. Consequently, when the other factors have been established, this one, in many cases, becomes a subject for intelligent judgment. In properly kept sets of books, the ratio of gross profit for any given period between physical inventory dates can be readily ascertained. But when a loss has occurred some months after the date of the last inventory, and after substantial purchases and sales have changed the quantity of stock on hand, the question arises whether the sales made after the inventory produced the same rate of gross profit as those made before. Unless the accounting system shows the cost as well as the selling price of each article sold, this question cannot be definitely answered.

The operating history of the fiscal year immediately preceding the loss is generally used as a basis for computing the ratio of gross profit, on the theory that the year is a guide to conditions existing at the time of the loss. Since this is not always true, it is highly important that adequate consideration be given to factors operating to change the ratio. Usually the ratio òf gross profit does not fluctuate greatly from year to year. In periods of changing general economic conditions, however, or when internal or external forces bear upon the normal operation of a given industry or individual business, the ratio of gross profit can change materially in a short time.

Neither party to the adjustment should offer to accept the ratio of the previous year or period until after careful consideration of the factors that might operate to increase or decrease the ratio of gross profit made on sales following the last inventory, and thus increase or decrease the final showing of stock on hand. It often happens that the ratio experienced for this fiscal period is so distorted as to be unfit for use as a factor in determining the theoretical amount of stock on hand. Equally often, changed conditions from the end of that period to the date of the loss may make an otherwise indicative ratio of previous periods wholly inapplicable.

Influencing Factors

Variations in the ratio may arise from many causes, only a few of which need be mentioned:

1. Changes in purchase prices, freight, or cash discounts.
2. Changes in selling prices, sales discounts, or distribution methods.
3. Changes in costs through strikes, changes in production efficiency, revised wage rates, or new plant methods.
4. Special sales promotions or price wars.
5. The period of the year represented by the sales, if one season normally shows higher profits than another.
6. Introduction or elimination of certain lines of goods.
7. Changes in normal lines of goods owing to scientific improvements or to expansion of the business.
8. Prosperity or dullness of conditions in the period covered by the sales as contrasted with the period before the last inventory.
9. Methods of pricing inventories which vary from year to year.
10. Changes in "mixture" of goods sold, when at varying rates of gross profit.

The first four of these causes need no explanation. The fifth may be explained by calling attention to the method prevailing in some agricultural sections where staples, sold at a small profit, constitute the bulk of the business during the period of planting and cultivating the crops, and where luxury items bringing higher profits are sold after harvest. The sixth includes the opening up, or closing out, of lines of merchandise on which the profit is greatly above or below the average of the business. The seventh is a situation common to business evolution, as when a manufacturer of radios changes to television, or a producer of machinery offers automatic operating features that develop a new and profitable demand. The eighth involves the rise or fall in prices that accompanies unusual times, good or bad, caused by general or local influences, such as the effect of a national political campaign on a manufacturer of campaign buttons.

The ninth and tenth warrant some discussion. Inventories are not always taken on the same basis from year to year. Instead of inventorying goods at the prices paid for them, some merchants inventory their stock according to what they deem the goods to be worth at the time of inventory or at arbitrary prices influenced by income tax considerations. The original invoice price of each article is thus lost unless there is sufficient detail on the inventory to make it possible to trace the invoice. In the case of such inventories, the ratio of gross profit becomes an uncertain factor and, if improperly calculated or applied, may work injustice either to the insured or to the insurer. If a stock is inventoried on a price basis different from that appearing on the purchase record and if the difference is not accounted for by obsolescence, the ratio of gross profit will be in error. This error becomes a factor in increasing or decreasing the amount shown by the loss calculation according to the increase or decrease in the price basis used in the last inventory.

EXAMPLE 20-8

Inventory, Jan. 1, 1976, 501 units at $25		$12,525
Purchases, 1976		37,500
		$50,025
Inventory, Jan. 1, 1977, 400 units at $20		8,000
Cost of goods sold		$42,025
Sales, 1976	$50,031	
Cost of sales	42,025	
Gross profit	$ 8,006 (16% of sales)	

To illustrate: Assume that a merchant whose stock on January 1, 1977, consisted of 400 units, at an invoice price of $25 a unit, had arbitrarily entered them on his inventory at a figure of $20, although the market value was unchanged. If this should pass unnoticed, the rate of gross profit would be as shown in Example 20-8.

Assuming that the market remains unchanged until the time of the loss and the merchant to continue his practice of marking up 25 percent of invoice price, a book statement using the foregoing gross profit percentage gives a result materially at variance with the true state of affairs. Comparing a statement by count with a statement based on 16 percent gross profit, and using in each

the same figures for purchases and sales, the result is as shown in Example 20-9.

Importance of Consistent Inventory Pricing

The foregoing illustration shows the importance of consistent inventory pricing. The varying effect on gross profit and net income is set forth in the following four rules:

1. When beginning inventory is overstated, the gross profit and net income are reduced.
2. When beginning inventory is understated, the gross profit and net income are increased.

EXAMPLE 20-9

Actual Count

Inventory, Jan. 1, 1977, 400 units at $25		$10,000
Purchases to date of loss, 1,875 units at $25		46,875
Total, 2,275 units		$56,875
Sales, 1,750 units at $31.25	$54,687	
Cost of sales, 1,750 units at $25		43,750
Loss, 525 units at $25		$13,125

Statement Based on Percentage of Gross Profit

Inventory, Jan. 1, 1977		$ 8,000
Purchases to date of loss		46,875
		$54,875
Less computed cost of goods sold:		
Net sales	$54,687	
Less 16% gross profit	8,750	45,937
Computed stock on hand at date of loss		$ 8,938
Actual loss count	$13,125	
Loss based on percentage of gross profit	8,938	
Difference	$ 4,187	

3. When ending inventory is overstated, the gross profit and net income are increased.
4. When ending inventory is understated, the gross profit and net income are decreased.

If the ratio of gross profit used in preparing the statement of stock on hand has been determined from transactions between inventories that were made without allowance for obsolescence or other depreciation, the statement will show the theoretical cost of the stock. If, however, accurate allowances for depreciation have been made in each inventory, the ratio of gross profit will produce a statement showing the theoretical depreciated cost of the stock. But if the values used in one inventory have been reduced to take depreciation into account and those used in the other have not, the ratio of gross profit will produce a statement showing a larger or smaller theoretical amount than should be employed. If only the first inventory is depreciated, a higher gross-profit ratio is shown; if only the second, a lower.

A business sometimes makes an unusually high gross profit in a given year because of a single highly profitable transaction. For example, a wholesale grocery company suffered a loss and presented a claim based on a gross profit of 12.13 percent, which was the operating experience of the year preceding the loss. It was found, however, that for many years the percentage of gross profit had been about 6 percent and that the increase for the year before the loss had been caused almost entirely by transactions in the sugar market. Since no such transactions had been made during the year of the loss, the insured's claim was adjusted on the basis of a 6 percent gross profit, which materially reduced the amount of the loss.

When a business is losing ground and its sales are decreasing, it is usually found that the ratio of gross profit shows a yearly decrease. In such cases, the rate of decrease should be ascertained and the ratio of gross profit adjusted according to the trend.

Any marked change in the character or composition of sales produces a corresponding fluctuation in the gross-profit ratio. An excellent example of the effect of such a change was noted in the case of a concern that did both wholesale and retail business. During one year, the sales were divided as shown in Example 20-10.

During the following year a loss occurred. Sales to the date of the loss were $200,000, and a claim was filed using the average gross profit of 26.3 percent, or $52,600. An analysis of the sales showed that the ratio of wholesale to retail sales had materially changed and that sales in the two classes were equal. The loss was recomputed using the separate ratios of 30 and 15 percent as shown in Example 20-11.

EXAMPLE 20-10

	Retail	Wholesale	Total
Sales	$300,000	$100,000	$400,000
Cost of goods sold	210,000	85,000	295,000
Gross profit	$ 90,000	$ 15,000	$105,000
Percentage of gross profit	30%	15%	26.3%

EXAMPLE 20-11

	Retail	Wholesale	Total
Sales	$100,000	$100,000	$200,000
Gross profit	30,000 (30%)	15,000 (15%)	45,000 (22.5%)
Cost of goods sold	$ 70,000	$ 85,000	$155,000

Thus the greater proportion of low-profit wholesale volume depressed the general gross-profit ratio from 26.3 to 22.5 percent, and the original loss claim was, therefore, overstated by $7,600. A similar result is found when a concern sells a number of products at varying rates of gross profit, and the proportion that each bears to the total sales varies from year to year. In other words, attention must be given to the composition of sales in different fiscal periods and at different times of a single fiscal period, because of its possible effect on the rate of gross profit.

Because of the foregoing situations, which are not uncommon, and in spite of the fact that the experience of prior periods is always of value, it is important to make some sort of *direct* check on the actual gross profit, if possible. This may be done by analyzing the cost of the sales of the period in which the loss occurs. The method may be illustrated as shown in Example 20-12.

The gross profit is 156/648, or 24.1 percent. If this figure agrees substantially with the ratio experienced during the prior year, it is reasonable to assume that no radical change has occurred in the relation of selling prices to material prices, labor costs, or other items, and that the prior year's ratio is being repeated.

The number of sales invoices to be analyzed depends entirely upon the individual case. When sales are individually large and few in number, all sales invoices should be analyzed. When, however, their number runs into the thousands, complete analysis will be impracticable. In this event it is best to analyze *all* the sales for a certain period: two weeks, one month, or two months. Care should be exercised to cover a representative group of sales; otherwise the test will be ineffective. If a concern sells five different products in about equal amounts, testing a group of sales of only two or three of the products is insufficient.

For manufacturers, the cost prices may be obtained from the cost records, if accurately maintained; for nonmanufacturing businesses, from purchase invoices on file.

DETERMINING MERCHANDISE VALUE AND LOSS FROM BOOK STATEMENTS

Forms of book statement, based on applying a gross profit percentage to sales and generally used in computing merchandise value at date of loss, are shown in Exhibits A and B (Examples 20-13 and 20-14) for manufacturing losses and in Exhibits C and D (Examples 20-15 and 20-16) for mercantile losses.

DETERMINING STOCK ON HAND BY QUANTITY ANALYSIS

From comments on the uncertainties of the book statement, based on gross profit, it is evident that radical changes in a business may make the book-statement method inequitable as a basis for establishing the value of stock on hand at the time of loss. For example, the profits of a young and undeveloped business that is growing rapidly during its first year, or during an experimental period,

EXAMPLE 20-12

Sales Invoice No.	Selling Price	Cost	Gross Profit
1	$100	$ 75	$ 25
2	175	110	65
3	228	202	26
4	145	105	40
	$648	$492	$156

may not be representative of conditions during a subsequent period.

In such instances, and particularly if the business is small, the merchandise on hand can sometimes be determined with a greater degree of accuracy by the *unit method*, also known as *quantity analysis*. If the insured maintains a perpetual inventory, a stock book, or a stock-control record, it should be examined. If not, quantities can sometimes be established from the last inventory, the purchase invoices, and the record of sales.

Where the perpetual inventory is controlled by, or balanced with, the general books and is also substantiated by periodic physical inventories, it is a proper basis for loss computation.

A perpetual-inventory record is a running account of stock on hand, classified according to units, in which are recorded quantities purchased and sold. When the unit of value is large, as in the case of machinery or precious stones, the perpetual-inventory method is generally an effective means of stock control. But when an attempt is made to adapt this kind of record to a business having rapid turnover, and there are large numbers of units of small individual value, inaccuracy and unreliability may be anticipated. Although many of the perpetual-inventory

EXAMPLE 20-13   Exhibit A

Computation of Gross Profit and Cost of Goods Sold
The Shade Manufacturing Company
Year Ended December 31, 1976

Gross sales				$853,835.17
Less sales discounts and allowances				12,694.26
Net Sales				$841,140.91
Cost of goods sold:				
Inventory, Jan. 1, 1976			$ 47,950.04	
Purchases:				
Mirrors	$ 7,677.10			
Shades	184,571.48			
Lamps	156,210.24			
Wrought iron	74,848.51	$423,307.33		
Less discounts		12,292.14	411,015.19	
Labor:				
Shades	$ 94,372.06			
Lamps	93,301.27			
Wrought iron	35,407.36			
Manufacturing expenses:				
Depreciation of machinery	4,500.88			
Rent	22,427.16			
Machinery maintenance	3,451.09			
Light, heat, and power	5,562.86			
Insurance	7,273.82			
Freight, express, and cartage	6,965.30			
General expense	1,002.25			
Designing	7,284.26	281,548.31		
		$740,513.54		
Less inventory, Dec. 31, 1976		101,934.48	638,579.06	
Gross profit (24.08% of net sales)			$202,561.85	

records in use are manifestly ill adapted to the business involved, and many more are carelessly or inaccurately kept, a claim is almost invariably made by the insured for the open or unsold items in this record without correction or revision. In these cases, purchases and sales should be carefully checked with the record, at least on a test basis, before it is accepted as correct. As a countercheck, a regular book statement should be made, as it may verify or disprove the showing of the perpetual inventory. A well-kept perpetual inventory or stock record may often be put to valuable use in ascertaining the rate of turnover, which will indicate the salability of the merchandise on hand. For example, the inclusion of a quantity of obsolete machine parts may be revealed by the date of the last

EXAMPLE 20-14   Exhibit B

Computation of Merchandise Value at Date of Loss
The Shade Manufacturing Company
Year Ended March 9, 1977

Inventory, Dec. 31, 1976			$101,934.48
Purchases:			
Mirrors	$ 507.59		
Shades	36,063.38		
Lamps	27,161.08		
Wrought iron	23,422.00	$ 87,154.05	
Less discounts on purchases		1,702.84	85,451.21
Labor:			
Shades		$ 16,138.13	
Lamps		15,955.55	
Wrought iron		6,055.23	38,148.91
Manufacturing expenses:			
Depreciation of machinery		$ 923.58	
Rent		3,927.67	
Machinery maintenance		349.35	
Light, heat, and power		985.96	
Insurance		438.38	
Freight, express, and cartage		1,874.93	
General expense		222.93	
Designing		712.43	9,435.23 $234,969.83
Deduct computed cost of goods sold:			
Sales		$127,798.53	
Less sales discounts and allowances		2,660.05	$125,138.48
Deduct computed gross profit (24.08% of net sales)			
(see Exhibit A)			30,133.35 95,005.13
Total computed merchandise value			$139,964.70
Deduct:			
Inventory at 1516 Montpelier Street not touched by fire			67,497.43
Total computed merchandise value at 422 North Eighth Avenue			$ 72,467.27
Add:			
Computed inventory of shipping supplies			5,150.90
Total computed merchandise value at 442 North Eighth Avenue Mar. 9, 1977			$ 77,618.17
Deduct:			
Agreed value of salvage			9,423.05
Merchandise value destroyed			$ 68,195.12

EXAMPLE 20-15   Exhibit C

Computation of Gross Profit and Cost of Goods Sold
The Jobbers Merchandise Company
Year Ended December 31, 1976

Gross sales			$464,396.93
Less:			
Discounts on sales		$ 9,078.07	
Allowances		147.37	
Out-freight and drayage		4,710.17	13,935.61
Net sales			$450,461.32
Cost of goods sold:			
Inventory, Jan. 1, 1976		$ 29,463.20	
Merchandise purchased	$492,891.60		
Less discounts on purchases	5,815.94	487,075.66	
In-freight and drayage		4,813.80	
		$521,352.66	
Inventory, Dec. 31, 1976		119,031.40	402,321.26
Gross profit (10.69% of net sales)			$ 48,140.06

EXAMPLE 20-16   Exhibit D

Computation of Merchandise Value at Date of Loss
The Jobbers Merchandise Company
Year Ended March 31, 1977

Merchandise inventory, Dec. 31, 1976		$119,031.40	
Merchandise purchased	$48,376.17		
Less discounts on purchases	737.36		
	$47,638.81		
In-freight and drayage	429.37	48,068.18	$167,099.58
Deduct computed cost of goods sold:			
Gross sales		$ 56,511.45	
Less:			
Discounts on sales	$ 1,133.24		
Allowances	71.99		
Out-freight and drayage	694,33	1,899.56	
		$ 54,611.89	
Less computed gross profit			
(10.69% of net sales)			
(See Exhibit C)		5,838.01	48,773.88
			$118,325.70
Deduct:			
Merchandise in transit and out on consignment			$ 7,519.50
Total computed merchandise value on hand, Mar. 13, 1977			$110,806.20
Deduct:			
Agreed value of salvage			32,500.00
Merchandise value destroyed			$ 78,306.20

entries showing acquisition of the parts, and by the absence of any recent credits for withdrawals for assembly purposes.

An accurate perpetual-inventory record may also serve to disclose errors in the general books. It is, therefore, desirable to reconcile the two whenever possible. In one instance, a perpetual-inventory record reflected a value at the time of the loss that was $15,000 in excess of the amount shown by a book statement. As a few minor errors were noted in the perpetual-inventory record, it was at first believed that the record was unreliable. An attempt was then made to reconcile the perpetual-inventory record with the general books, as of the date of the last physical inventory. A large error was disclosed, which had resulted in a considerable understatement of the physical inventory. The correction of this error affected the rate of gross profit and the result of the book statement to such an extent that the value as shown by the perpetual-inventory record at the time of the fire was substantiated.

A perpetual-inventory record of stock is useful for loss purposes only to the extent that it is accurate and reliable. Some indication of the reliability of the record can usually be observed from the frequency of corrections or adjustments in entries. Even the best of well-kept records would normally require correction from time to time. The lack of such entries might be an indication that errors are permitted to accumulate without correction.

It is becoming a rather common practice to rely upon perpetual-inventory records for control of stock, even to the exclusion of annual physical-inventory counts. Under this procedure, the unit records for the stock on hand are posted daily for acquisitions and withdrawals, and the balances are maintained currently. At periodic intervals, test counts are made of the actual quantities of the stock for a section of the perpetual-inventory records, and these counts are compared with the book balances. This is usually done on a rotating basis so that the entire stock is checked at least once a year. At the close of the year, the inventory quantities are listed from the balances shown by the unit records, and no special count is made at that time. A claim representative who encounters such a situation should make a careful examination of the procedure of test counting, especially to see that it accomplishes the purpose intended, that the stock is carefully counted at least once a year, and that the records are adjusted for any differences shown by the counts. If a company has a continuing experience of discrepancies disclosed by actual counts, the claim representative should not place too much reliance upon these records.

In a large number of cases, the perpetual-inventory record is merely a memorandum of doubtful utility, as in the case of a clothing company that recently made claim for a loss of $29,000 on the basis of its perpetual-inventory record. It was found that this record had been kept in a slipshod manner, and when a comparison was made between the book balances and the actual count at the time of the last physical inventory, the discrepancies shown in Example 20-17 were revealed.

Upon examination, errors of the following nature were disclosed:

1. Purchases were entered in duplicate, and often quantities were not as shown on purchase invoices.
2. Sales were not always recorded in the perpetual-inventory record.
3. Cost prices were incorrectly stated.

EXAMPLE 20-17

	Physical Inventory	Stock Record	Difference
Woolens	$19,687.46	$29,570.09	$ 9,882.63
Finished goods, overcoats	2,066.50	5,926.75	3,860.25
Finished goods, suits	4,950.00	6,911.09	1,961.09
Totals	$26,703.96	$42,407.93	$15,703.97

4. Items were always carried at original cost, although some were several years old and were without value.

These errors were sufficient to eliminate this record from further consideration, and a computation by the gross-profit (or book-statement) method reduced the loss from $29,000 to slightly over $9,000.

Occasionally, it is found that no general books worthy of the name have ever been maintained. Such was the case in a recent claim for over $100,000. The insured was engaged in the sale of articles whose unit values were sufficiently large to warrant using the perpetual-inventory method. The insured kept no general books, had no purchase or sales invoices, had lost or misplaced most of the bank statements, and had never filed a federal income tax return. The stock record was what might be termed a rudimentary perpetual-inventory or stock book. In it were listed purchases individually and, when an article was sold, it supposedly was crossed off from the list. Claim was based upon the open items in this book, over 1,000 in number. An analysis of transactions brought out the fact that the insured had apparently paid for purchases of at least $60,000 in excess of the total available cash. No additional funds had been invested in the business, and therefore, either sales were understated or purchases overstated. An inspection of the scene of the loss made it doubtful that 1,000 articles could have been on hand. The insured sold about one-third locally and two-thirds by mail order. A large number of express shipping receipts were accidentally located and, while no single receipt could be identified with the shipment of a particular unit, the number of receipts could be compared with the number of sales month by month. For some months it was found that the shipping receipts were in excess of the recorded sales, and the test as a whole indicated that mail-order sales were understated by at least one-third.

While no purchase invoices were available at the insured's premises, copies were obtained directly from the manufacturers, and by comparison with the so-called stock book, it was discovered that numerous invoices were duplicated. These disclosures sufficed to eliminate the stock book as a basis for loss computation.

RECONSTRUCTING UNIT RECORDS

Many times it is possible, in the absence of perpetual-inventory records, to reconstruct unit records for the goods on hand by analyzing and tabulating the quantities represented in the last physical inventory and in the subsequent purchases and sales to the date of the loss. The procedure is usually the simple one of setting up work sheets in these steps:

1. Segregate the last physical inventory into units of each product.
2. Add thereto the respective quantities purchased or manufactured during the period under review, as determined by an analysis of purchase invoices or production records.
3. Deduct the net quantities of each product sold or shipped, as revealed by an analysis of shipping records or sales invoices.

The result of such a compilation is in reality the construction of a perpetual-inventory record in the form of totals by products on hand at the date of the loss, based upon the recorded transactions of the insured during the period subsequent to the last physical inventory. This method is especially practical in the case of a jobber or manufacturer dealing in a few products. It may also be applied to a small business where complete general records are not available, such as that of a dealer in raw hides or in automobile tires.

As a case in point: While a fire in a paper warehouse was under examination, it was found that scarcely any evidence remained of a large quantity of wrapping paper in rolls which the insured claimed were on hand at the time of the loss. Rolls of wrapping paper are not easily obliterated, and for that reason the purchases and sales of wrapping paper for several years were analyzed in detail. This analysis resulted in definite proof that the amount of wrapping paper on hand had been overstated 500 percent by the insured.

When fraud is suspected and particularly when a loss occurs shortly after the close of the fiscal year, every possible method of checking inventory quantities should be employed. A few illustrations will reveal the extent to which it is sometimes necessary to go. A large jobbing house suffered a loss on the first day of the year. The insured stated that the physical inventory had been taken on the afternoon of Dec. 31. The quantities stated in this inventory seemed inordinately large but, owing to the fact that some of the records had been destroyed, lost, or concealed, a check by complete analysis of purchases and sales was impossible. It was noted, however, that on many branch-store requisitions certain items were marked "Back Order" by the stock clerks, indicating that these items were out of stock at the time. Subsequent purchases and shipments of these were traced, and in many instances it was found that the insured could not possibly have had on hand the amount stated on the inventory. The correspondence files showed that the insured had sent the branch offices weekly bulletins that often listed the current stock shortages. When these shortages were investigated, numerous other discrepancies in inventory quantities were uncovered. In this manner, the purported physical inventory was sufficiently discredited to be eliminated from consideration in determining the amount of loss.

In another case, the insured attempted to defraud the insurance company by arbitrarily raising the quantities of various items on the inventory sheets. The insured made the mistake, however, of using an indelible pencil when increasing them, while the original figures had been made with an ordinary lead pencil.

When the procedure of quantity reconstruction is undertaken, it is important that the claim representative be satisfied that the beginning quantities shown in the last physical inventory are accurate. Purported physical inventory listings should not be accepted without some verification. Testing of computations and totals of the last physical inventory is always important because it may establish that the quantities have been deliberately raised. The submitted inventory should be scanned for clerical correctness,

and its total should be compared with the general-ledger account and the figure appearing on the insured's federal income tax return for the same date.

Another excellent test of the correctness of a submitted physical inventory for a prior date is computing the rates of turnover for several years and comparing them. Turnover rates are computed by dividing the cost of a year's sales by the average inventory. A comparison of the rates of turnover will sometimes show that the last inventory is suspiciously large. For example, the records of an insured for successive years are shown in Example 20-18. Subsequent investigation proved that the 1976 inventory had been padded.

Inventory padding may be continuous for a period of years, and therefore attention may well be directed to prior stock-taking data. Padding has been found in more than one case, not necessarily "in preparation for a loss," but for the purpose of misrepresenting financial condition to bankers, stockholders, or others.

Quantity analysis is highly desirable in all instances where the work involved is within reasonable limits. Whenever physical inventories are suspected of being fraudulent, a quantity analysis in accordance with the foregoing outline offers a workable method by which they may often be proved fictitious. In such a compilation, it may be necessary to consider only a few of the principal products making up the major value of the purported physical inventory.

RETAIL-INVENTORY METHOD

Department stores have almost all adopted the retail-inventory method of merchandise accounting.

Stock control in an establishment of this nature, with its rapid turnover, its numerous selling items, and its many "sales" and other merchandising schemes, is a difficult problem. One of the essentials of the retail-inventory method, as a means of solving this problem, is a high degree of accuracy in record keeping. The value of stock on hand determined by this method, when it is properly

EXAMPLE 20-18

	1974	1975	1976
Cost of goods sold	$611,000	$500,000	$377,000
Average inventory	117,000	164,000	258,000
Rate of turnover	5.22	3.05	1.46

applied, is almost as accurate as that determined by means of a physical inventory with correct unit prices for the units counted, weighed, or measured.

The brief summary in Example 20-19 shows the steps involved in the application of this method.

The following points are to be emphasized: (1) This method is an almost perfect example of the book statement. (2) The decline in salability is automatically accounted for by the markdowns taken.

The method requires that all inventories and purchases be recorded at both the cost and the selling price, that additional markups be considered as being purchases at 100 percent profit on selling price, and that markdowns be treated as sales. At the end of any given period, the resulting percentage relationship between the Cost column and the Selling column is the percentage relationship between the sales made during the period and the cost of these sales.

However, when the retail-inventory method is not correctly applied, the showing of stock on hand will not be substantiated by physical inventory. A large department store recently suffered a loss of considerable amount. Upon investigation it was found that markdowns were habitually considered as deductions from the accumulated selling total instead of being considered as sales. To illustrate the effect of this erroneous procedure, the foregoing example has been recomputed in Example 20-20 according to the method employed by the insured.

The stock on hand (at cost) computed by this method amounts to $1,212.93, as compared with an actual $1,147.02. In the department-store loss mentioned above, the inventories were very large, and the resultant overstatement of the claim was considerable.

LOCATION AND OWNERSHIP

Not all stock on hand determined by an accounting computation is necessarily on the destroyed or damaged premises. Nor is all merchandise on hand necessarily owned by the insured. After an agreement has been reached on the approximate amount of the total value of stock in question, whether by book statement, by perpetual-inventory record, or by unit reconstruction, it is important to verify the *location and ownership* of the merchandise on the date of the fire.

EXAMPLE 20-19

	Cost	Selling	Markup
Inventory, beginning of period	$1,000.00	$1,500.00	$ 500.00
Purchases during period (net)	2,150.00	3,000.00	850.00
Additional markups	—	100.00	100.00
	$3,150.00	$4,600.00	$1,450.00
Percentage of markup 1,450/4,600 = 31.522%			
Sales during period (net)	?	2,675.00	?
Markdowns for sales, etc.	?	250.00	?
	$2,002.98	$2,925.00	$ 922.02
Inventory, end of period	$1,147.02	$1,675.00	$ 527.98

EXAMPLE 20-20

	Cost	Selling	Markup
Inventory, beginning of period	$1,000.00	$1,500.00	$ 500.00
Purchases during period (net)	2,150.00	3,000.00	850.00
Additional markups	—	100.00	100.00
	$3,150.00	$4,600.00	$1,450.00
Less markdowns for sales, etc.	—	250.00	250.00
	$3,150.00	$4,350.00	$1,200.00
Percentage of markup 1,200/4,350 = 27.586%			
Sales	1,937.07	2,675.00	737.93
Inventory, end of period	$1,212.93	$1,675.00	$ 462.07

A frequent source of information for such verification is bank loans outstanding. An examination of the related documents may well establish, in addition to assisting in valuation, the location and ownership of pledged merchandise. Examination of other types of secured indebtedness outstanding at the fire date, such as those of financing, factoring, or warehousing arrangements, may provide similar data.

Quantities of merchandise at a public warehouse should be confirmed and compared with book records. Should any doubt exist concerning the independence of the warehouse, physical examination of the off-location merchandise should be made as soon after the loss as possible. The insured may not always disclose the storing of merchandise at warehouses away from the loss location, whether publicly or privately owned; however, analysis of book accounts may disclose the existence of such storage centers. An examination of the insured's property records may reveal ownership of warehouses, stores, or other buildings used for storage, and these should be physically examined; likewise, if no detailed property records are available, perusal of real estate or personal-property tax bills may produce the desired information. The use of public warehouses would also be disclosed by analysis of supporting documents of the rent, storage, or warehouse expense accounts.

If the insured maintains branch offices or is an affiliate of a group of companies, analysis of branch or intercompany accounts may disclose data about stored merchandise or merchandise on loan. Damaged or destroyed merchandise on the insured's premises may have belonged to branches or other affiliated interests.

The claim representative should seek accounts or subsidiary records that may disclose consigned merchandise, whether in the possession of the insured or others, and the specific location of such merchandise on the date of the loss. Consignors sometimes carry their own insurance. Examination of customers' accounts and correspondence or prior physical-inventory records might reveal the practice of dealing in consigned merchandise. Careful scrutiny of memorandum sales invoices or purchase invoices may expose not only consignment practices but also the practice of holding merchandise on approval or on bailment. If the insured is engaged in foreign trade, information should be sought on the existence of consigned merchandise in foreign countries.

The insured's products may be such as to require finishing at other premises. If the finishing operation is a constant one and the separate inventory records or accounts are not readily available to the claim representative, freight and drayage invoices may reveal similar information. An example of this situation was presented by the case of a small manufacturer whose purchase invoices and freight bills were all checked and found in order, indicating that the merchandise had been purchased and received before the loss. There was, however, a shortage of cartage and drayage bills, which warranted the conclusion that not all the merchandise had been delivered at the insured's premises. Further investigation disclosed that the insured had much of the work done in other shops and that these shops had on hand at the time of the loss large stocks of the insured's merchandise. This development reduced the claim by nearly one-half.

Shipments made to the insured or by the insured under long-term contracts usually raise the question of whether the recording of shipments through billing or invoicing is coincidental with the movement of the goods. Shipments may be received or delivered daily or weekly, affecting immediately the inventory quantities, though billing or invoicing of such merchandise may be done monthly. If the claim representative is not informed of such arrangements, he or she may learn of them from an examination of purchase orders or sales orders. An illustration of such practices is that of billing goods to a customer and holding them for shipping instructions under what is sometimes called "mark, charge, and hold," a procedure not unusual in textile companies.

Comments

While the principles that determine the value of stock on hand have been illustrated briefly in the foregoing sections, varying applications of these principles may have to be made to problems presenting details that have not been discussed. Any set of books may contain unusual entries that must be carefully considered before they are used in preparing the loss statement. The principal difficulties that face the claim representative and an accountant are those presented by the simple question: Do the entries on the books truly represent *all* that has happened? The problem of analyzing a complicated set of reliable records is usually much easier than the problem of substantiating or disproving the authenticity or completeness of records concerning which suspicion has been aroused.

Although any one of the procedures outlined for the determination of stock on hand may be adequate in a specific instance, it is desirable to use, wherever possible, more than one of the methods suggested. The result shown by one procedure may often be either substantiated or disproved by a detailed comparison with the figures resulting from the application of another method.

USE OF ACCOUNTANTS

Books and records are the domain of the accountant; accordingly, the claim representative who is involved in a complicated loss that is to be established through accounting data should be cognizant of any limitations. Accounting has seen great change and development in the past ten or fifteen years. As a result of pressures from the changing business conditions of a highly competitive economy, record keeping is now a complicated art of apportionment, allocation, and distribution of the money results of business transactions, in all of which varying weight is given to established accounting conventions, individual judgment, and generally recognized principles and standards. Simple chronological records of cash transactions have evolved into cost-and-profit determinations by plants, by departments, by products, and by units of product. Cost accounting has grown from the earliest elementary job-cost computations into such techniques as standard costs, process costs, and distribution costs. Specialized systems and machines have been developed for specialized enterprises.

There is a great difference between verifying the book statement of a corner grocery and of a large chain store, and between a similar statement of a small gray-iron foundry and a manufacturer of airplanes. Whenever the accounting involved is beyond the skill and experience of the claim representative, the assistance of a certified public accountant should be secured. The claim representative and accountant, working together, can approach the various problems in a manner calculated to bring into clear focus all the features of the operations of the insured that have a bearing upon the probable amount of loss. Through this approach, the problem can readily be analyzed so as to facilitate an expeditious and equitable adjustment.

QUESTIONS AND PROBLEMS

1. a. Books of account contain many facts of value for the claim representative in adjusting merchandise losses.

Discuss briefly some of these facts of value when the stock is *in sight* and when it is *out of sight*.

b. A book statement of stock value at any particular time is based on starting and ending inventories, sales, purchases, and gross profit. Starting with the last physical inventory on January 1, set up a simple theoretical book statement of the cost value of stock on hand as of June 30th. Use arbitrary figures. The important point is to demonstrate the principle.

2. a. If the theoretical book statement has been set up properly in question 1b, it becomes apparent that the verification of any book statement requires that four components be checked for reliability. What are those components?

b. If a closing inventory is overstated in an annual book statement, how does it affect the gross profit percentage?

c. If the opening inventory is understated, what will be the effect on the gross profit percentage?

3. a. What is gross profit in a merchandising operation? Give an example.

b. What are the three main components necessary to determine the cost of goods sold in a manufacturing operation?

c. What do we mean by markup? Give an example.

d. What is meant by markdown? Give an example. What is meant by markdown percentage? Give an example.

e. What is gross profit percentage? Give an example.

f. What do we mean by the term *turnover* (also called stock turn)?

4. Name six market factors that influence gross profit percentages. *Market factors* is a term used here to distinguish between such things as over- or understating beginning and ending inventories.

5. Following a substantial fire loss in November, 1976, in a hardware supplier's ware-house, it was found that considerable merchandise was either burned out of sight or hopelessly mixed. The claim representative reviewed the perpetual inventory records which had been kept and determined that these records indicated an inventory of $150,000 at the time of the fire. Finding that this insured closed his books once a year on December 31 with the taking of a physical inventory, the claim representative called the firm's accountant and secured the following figures for the year 1975:

Inventory 1/1	$ 60,000
Inventory 12/31	$ 80,000
Purchases	$220,000
Sales	$250,000

The claim representative further determined that purchases in 1976 had amounted to $200,000, with sales of $260,000.

Using the book statement method, compute the amount of inventory at the time of loss. Show all calculations.

6. The A. C. Appliance Store was destroyed by fire resulting in a total loss to stock. Utilizing the insured's books and records, the claim representative ascertains the following:

Last physical inventory (at cost)	$ 50,000
Purchases since last inventory	$ 75,000
Net sales (at selling price) since last inventory	$150,000
Gross profit (margin) percentage	40%

a. Using the book-statement method, determine the actual cash value of the loss. Show all calculations.

b. In arriving at the purchase figures, the claim representative had to start by totaling the purchase invoices. A number of adjustments were made in correcting the sum to reflect properly the value of stock received. Describe four adjustments that were probably made.

21

Bailee Risks

Bailees ordinarily encountered in losses are (1) carriers, (2) warehouse people, (3) processors, (4) contractors, and (5) cleaners and repair people.

Carriers include railroads, truckers, airlines, pipelines, freight forwarders, and express companies.[1]

Warehouse people variously operate tanks, grain elevators, or warehouses for storing property belonging to others.

Processors are generally bleachers, spongers, dyers, finishers, or custom tanners.

Contractors are makers of garments or other articles who receive raw or partly finished materials from customers and work them up into finished products.

Cleaners and repair people may be laundry workers, dry cleaners, rug scourers, or the repairers of shoes, watches, clocks, automobiles, or other property entrusted to them.

CONTRACT OF BAILMENT

Under the contract of bailment, the relation of bailor and bailee begins when the bailor delivers the property into the possession of the bailee and ends when the bailee delivers it to the bailor, or when the bailor sells the property or otherwise is divested of any interest in it.

DELIVERIES

Delivery to the bailee is generally actual, that is, the property is put into the freight car, on the truck, on the loading platform, or into the warehouse, processing, contracting, or cleaning plant. Delivery by the bailee, while generally actual, may be constructive. When the bailee puts the property in the possession of the bailor, and it is removed from the vehicle or premises of the bailee, the delivery is actual. When a carrier bailee notifies the consignee that a shipment has arrived at destination, there is a constructive delivery when the free time expires before the consignee removes the goods. To constitute a constructive delivery, the carrier must, if practicable, give notice to the consignee of the shipment's arrival. When this has been done and the goods are discharged in the usual and proper place, and reasonable opportunity is offered to the consignee to remove them, the liability of the carrier as such terminates.[2]

Ownership of merchandise in a warehouse may be transferred from one bailor to another without physical movement of the merchandise. The warehouse receipt, when passed from one person to another, carries with it title to the property, the delivery of the receipt effecting a delivery of the merchandise.

The claim representative will frequently have to determine the exact time when a delivery was made, in order to decide whether a loss falls under the policy of the bailor making the delivery or under the policy of the bailor accepting it.

---

[1]Marine carriers are not within the scope of this book.

[2]*Becker v. Pennsylvania R. R. Co.*, 96 N.Y. Supp. 1, 5; 109 App. Div. 230, quoting *Tarbell v. Royal Exchange Shipping Co.*, 17 N.E. 721, 724, 110 App. Div. N.Y. 170, 180.

INTEREST OF BAILEE

The bailee has an insurable interest in the property of the bailor and may cover the property by insurance. The insurance may be for the benefit of the bailor, the bailee acting as trustee, or for the benefit of the bailee because of (1) the bailee's lien on the property as security for what the bailor owes for storage or other charges or (2) because of the bailee's liability for loss due to negligence.

LIABILITY OF BAILEE

The liability for loss or damage to property delivered into the bailee's possession by a bailor will depend upon the class to which the bailee belongs and the terms of the contract under which the bailee is holding the property.

A common carrier, for example, is liable for any loss or damage of a bailor's property unless the cause of the loss is one that is exempted in the bill of lading. The Uniform Bill of Lading form used by the railroads sets forth exempted causes of loss in the following provisions:

CONTRACT TERMS AND CONDITIONS
Sec. 1. (a) The carrier or party in possession of any of the property herein described shall be liable as at common law for any loss thereof or damage thereto, except as hereinafter provided.

(b) No carrier or party in possession of all or any of the property herein described shall be liable for any loss thereof or damage thereto or delay caused by the Act of God, the public enemy, the authority of law, or the act or default of the shipper or owner, or for natural shrinkage. The carrier's liability shall be that of warehouseman, only, for loss, damage, or delay caused by fire occurring after the expiration of the free time allowed by tariffs lawfully on file (such free time to be computed as therein provided) after notice of the arrival of the property at destination or at the port of export (if intended for export) has been duly sent or given, and after placement of the property for delivery at destination, or tender of delivery of the property to the party entitled to receive it, has been made. Except in case of negligence of the carrier or party in possession (and the burden to prove freedom from such negligence shall be on the carrier or party in possession), the carrier or party in possession shall not be liable for loss, damage, or delay occurring while the property is stopped and held in transit upon the request of the shipper, owner, or party entitled to make such request, or resulting from a defect or vice in property, or for country damage to cotton, or from riots or strikes.

Tariffs approved by the Interstate Commerce Commission, however, permit common carriers, such as railroads and truck lines, to limit liability on various kinds of shipments in consideration of a lower charge for transportation.

Bailees other than carriers are liable only for loss of the bailor's property in case of negligence, unless the bailee (1) assumes further liability, (2) agrees to keep the property insured, or (3) is liable for loss according to the custom prevailing in the trade.

As stated in the quoted section of the Uniform Bill of Lading, a railroad may be liable as a carrier while transporting a shipment, but only liable as a warehouseman after the shipment has reached its destination and has been put in a freight depot, the free time allowed by the tariff having expired.

BAILOR AND BAILEE INSURANCE

Bailors often carry their own insurance on property that they have delivered to a bailee while the bailee, at the same time, also carries insurance either on the property or on their interest in, or liability to care for it. Bailee insurance is usually effected by use of the trust-and-commission clause. When the bailee covers the property itself, the clause generally reads: ". . . on . . . his own, or held by him in trust or on commission or joint account with others, or sold, but not removed."

When the insurance covers only the bailee's interest in, or liability to care for the property, the typical forms of the clause are:

Building and Contents Form 18 (Ed. Nov. 72)

(a) the insured's interest in similar property owned by others to the extent of the value of labor and materials expended thereon by the insured.

General Property Form FGP-1 (Ed. 12-74)

Coverage C—PERSONAL PROPERTY OF OTHERS: This insurance shall cover for the account of the owner(s) (other than the named Insured) personal property belonging to others in the care, custody or control of the named Insured while (1) in or on the described buildings, or (2) in the open (including within vehicles) on or within 100 feet of the described premises.

Businessowners Policies (701 & 702 Ed. 11-1-75)

1. similar property held by the insured and belonging in whole or in part to others but not exceeding the amount for which the insured is legally liable, including the value of labor, materials, and charges furnished, performed or incurred by the insured.

SMP General Property Form MLB 100 (Ed. 2-71)

PERSONAL PROPERTY OF OTHERS: The insured may apply at each location up to 2%, but not exceeding $2,000, of the limit of liability specified for Coverage B—Personal Property at such location, as an additional amount of insurance, to cover for the account of the owners thereof (other than the named insured) direct loss by a peril insured against to personal property, similar to that covered by this policy, belonging to others while in the care, custody or control of the named insured and only while on the described premises or within 100 feet thereof.

LOSSES IN BAILEE RISKS

Fire, explosion, windstorm, flood, and other perils affect personal property in the possession of bailees in the same way that they affect similar property in the possession of the owner. Therefore, the same methods of determining value and loss are used in adjusting losses on personal property in bailee risks.

But because in bailee risks there are some losses in which both bailor and bailee are interested in the same property, some for which the bailee is liable to the bailor, and others for which he or she is not, it is often necessary not only to determine the value and loss on the bailors' property in bailee risks, but also to obtain evidence showing whether the bailee is interested in it because of charge or expenses, or is liable for the loss, because of negligence or otherwise, to any of the bailors.

In bailee risks the bailee and the bailor may each carry insurance covering the property in bail, or the bailor may carry insurance covering the property, while the bailee carries insurance covering, not the property, but any interest in, and liability to care for, the property. Consequently, it is necessary in many losses to determine whether the loss on a particular article or lot of property should be borne by the insurer of the bailor or of the bailee, or by both, and, if by both, in what proportions.

In bailee risks the character of the property and the way it is received, handled, stored, or delivered may be such as to produce a loss that cannot be determined as falling on any one bailor and that, therefore, must be shared by all bailors, proportionately according to the value of the property belonging to each.

If, for example, ten farmers had each stored in the same elevator 1,000 bushels of wheat of the same grade, making a total of 10,000 bushels in storage, and 2,500 bushels should be damaged as the result of a fire, it would be impossible to determine by which farmer the wheat damaged had actually been stored. Each farmer would be called upon to bear 10 percent of the loss. The character of wheat is such that, when lots of the same grade are poured into the bin of an elevator, they become an inseparable mass. The owner of each lot is entitled to withdraw the same quantity from the bin, but cannot expect to take out the identical grain that was put in. One bushel of wheat of a stated grade is as good as another and can, therefore, be substituted for any other.

In the language of the law, things that can

be substituted for each other in satisfaction of an obligation are *fungible*.

A similar situation exists when two or more purchasers buy for future delivery stipulated quantities of liquid in a tank. If the tank should be punctured by flying fragments from an explosion in nearby property and half of the liquid lost before the holes in the tank were plugged, each purchaser would share in the loss in proportion to the number of gallons of liquid each had bought.

The same situation exists in a warehouse containing bagged sugar, or cases of canned goods, vegetables, fruit, or fish. The bags or cases are concentrated in the warehouse by the producer or a wholesaler who sells lots to retailers or others. When sales are made, warehouse receipts are issued for the lots sold, and, when called for, equivalent quantities are delivered to the purchasers by the producer or wholesaler. The bags of sugar or the cases of canned goods bear no individual marks or numbers and, because one bag or case is as good as another, the most accessible bags or cases are loaded out of the warehouse whenever the holder of a warehouse receipt calls for merchandise. In case of loss, the owners of the sugar or canned goods participate according to the number of bags or cases in the warehouse owned by each.

Sometimes property of different kinds belonging to several bailors is stored in such a manner that when the structure housing it is damaged by fire, windstorm, or other peril, the property is mixed to a degree that would make the cost of separating it more than it would be worth after separation. If corn and wheat belonging to several bailors are stored in adjoining bins and the wall between burns away, the two kinds of grain may be washed together by the hose streams of the firefighters. Each bailor will then own a proportionate part of the mixed mass of wet grain, determined by the relation of the value of the grain to the total value of all the grain just prior to the fire. In legal language, the situation existing after the fire is *confusion of goods*.

In some losses in bailee risks, notably cotton warehouses, the identifying marks on lots of articles of the same kind of property belonging to different bailors are obliterated. A check of the identifiable lots or articles will establish what property of each bailor cannot be found and, therefore, what may be presumed to be among the unidentifiable lots or articles. In such situations each bailor is presumed to own a proportionate part of the unidentifiable salvage according to the same principle that controls when there is confusion of goods.

ADJUSTING REQUIREMENTS

The adjustment of a loss in a bailee risk may require the claim representative to do everything as if the risk were an owner risk, and in addition special investigation and treatment of the following:

1. Ownership of or interest in property held by bailee:

   What was the ownership or interest when the property was delivered to the bailee?

   Had any change taken place prior to date of loss?

2. Possession of bailee property:

   When was the property delivered to the bailee?

   Where was it at the time of loss?

   What quantity is shown by the bailee's records? By the bailor's records?

   What physical evidence confirms or casts doubt upon the showing of the records?

3. Contract between bailor and bailee:

   What was the bailee expected to do with the bailor's property—transport, store, process, fabricate, clean, or repair it?

   How is the contract between bailor and bailee evidenced—by bill of lading, warehouse receipt, written contract, invoice with imprint, ticket, trade custom, or oral statements?

   Does the contract embody any special provision as to the bailee's liability in case of loss?

   For what kind of losses is liability disclaimed? For what kind is it assumed?

   Is the amount of liability limited to a stated sum?

4. Loss and attendant circumstances:

Was the loss one for which the bailee is or is not liable? By reason of law? By reason of contract?

Is there any evidence indicating negligence on the part of the bailee, or of loss or damage caused by the bailor?

5. Acts of bailee and bailor after damage:

Did bailee promptly notify bailor?

Did bailee do what he or she could to minimize damage and deliver whatever was left of the property to bailor?

What did bailor do to protect the property from further damage?

6. Physical conditions in risk after loss:

Can the property of all bailees be identified?

How should any salvage be handled?

7. Bailor and bailee insurance:

What insurance is carried by the bailee and what by the bailor or bailors?

What are the amounts and provisions of each policy?

OWNERSHIP OF, OR INTEREST IN, PROPERTY

When a claim is made by the bailor who delivered the property to the bailee, there is ordinarily no question as to ownership or interest. But if the bailor, after delivering the property to the bailee, sells it but does not remove it from the bailee's premises, there may arise a question as to who owned it or at whose risk it was at the time of loss.

The ordinary routine of investigation begins with checking the record of the bailor's delivery of the property to the bailee. Unless the bailor had sold or agreed to sell the property, or unless some other person asserts ownership or interest, no further investigation is required. But if a sale or an agreement to sell was made, the terms of either must be established by the claim representative, together with any special agreement as to a time at which the risk of loss was to be assumed by the buyer.

POSSESSION BY BAILEE

The time that the property was delivered to the bailee will be evidenced by the date on the bill of lading or warehouse receipt, by the truck ticket, by the book entry, or perhaps by the oral statement of the person who made the delivery or the person who accepted it. In some bailee risks, notably compartment warehouses, it is necessary to know the location of the property at the time of loss. The quantity of the property as shown by the bailor's records should be checked against the quantity shown by the bailee's, and the reason for any difference established. The premises should be inspected, and the property itself, or any remains of it, examined to determine whether the physical evidence corroborates or casts doubt upon the showing of the records. The records of bailor and bailee may be honest and exact, but the property may be missing.

CONTRACT BETWEEN BAILOR AND BAILEE

The purpose for which the bailee holds the bailor's property determines the nature of the bailee's interest in it, and, in some cases, as when property is being hauled by a carrier, the amount of the bailee's liability, because property is often handled by a bailee at a lowered rate based on a low declared value. The purpose is evidenced by bills of lading, warehouse receipts, contracts to process, fabricate, clean, or repair, and other documents of similar nature. The purpose may be evidenced by the fact that the bailee is in possession, and the bailee's duties and liability may be fixed by a custom of the trade. In the absence of a written contract or trade custom, the purpose may have been determined by oral agreement. The contract may be silent as to the bailee's liability; it may provide for an assumption of liability by the bailee for certain kinds of losses or a limitation of liability for others. In many contracts, the bailee agrees to keep the property insured for the benefit of the bailor, sometimes at an agreed low value, sometimes for full value.

In handling bailor and bailee losses, the claim representative must become familiar with the contract between bailor and bailee, examining it if it is in writing; getting statements from both parties to it, if it is oral; and checking with informed persons, if it is governed by a trade custom.

LOSS AND ATTENDANT CIRCUMSTANCES

Investigation of the origin and cause of a loss in a bailee risk should, as in other risks, be directed toward establishing whether the peril causing the loss is insured against by the policy under which claim is made. But in many cases it must go further and establish whether the loss is one for which the bailee is liable by reason of law, contract, or trade custom. If the loss is being handled under insurance effected by the bailee on the property itself and, therefore, for the benefit of the bailor, no special investigation of the bailee's liability need be made. Where claim is made under a bailor's policy, investigation is essential because, if the insurer of the bailor pays the loss for which the bailee is liable, the insurer is subrogated to the bailor's rights and may recover from the bailee.

Except in those losses for which the bailee is liable by law, contract, or trade custom, a bailee is not liable unless negligent. Any suggestion of negligence calls for investigation.

ACTS OF BAILEE AND BAILOR AFTER LOSS

It is the duty of the bailee to give the bailor prompt notice in case of loss and, unless the bailor takes over control of the property, to do what is possible to minimize the damage.

Carriers generally re-cooper packages damaged in transit and deliver them to the consignee. It is their practice to deliver anything that has been damaged unless it has been too badly damaged to be handled.

Warehousers, processors, contractors, cleaners, and repair firms are expected to take all reasonable steps to minimize loss.

When the bailor takes over any property that has been held by a bailee, he or she has the duty to protect the property. Exceptions should be noted on the receipt.

PHYSICAL CONDITIONS IN RISK AFTER LOSS

In addition to the physical conditions ordinarily encountered in owner risks after a loss, there will be found in some bailee risks confusion of the goods belonging to the bailors, and in others, salvage, the ownership of which cannot be determined. Either condition calls for joint action by bailors, bailee, and insurers. In grain elevators and cotton warehouses, claim representatives generally work out salvaging plans with the elevator manager or the warehouser for the benefit of all interests. But in warehouses storing a variety of identifiable property it is necessary to make individual agreements with the owners of each lot.

THEFT OR SURREPTITIOUS REMOVAL

The theft or surreptitious removal from the premises of a bailee of property belonging to bailors is a common occurrence. As long ago as 1869, a commission appointed by Parliament reported on the prevalence of such occurrences in connection with warehouse fires in England. Fires are frequently started in warehouses in order to conceal theft or surreptitious removal of stored property.

CHECK OF INSURANCE

The claim representative who is assigned to any loss in a bailee risk must find out what insurance is carried by the bailor and what by the bailee. The amounts and provisions of each policy should be recorded so that proper treatment will be given to all policies involved. A bailee may be liable for a loss, but the insurer may be reluctant to accept the situation and delay admitting liability for the claims of bailors. When such is the case, the insurers of the bailors should ordinarily pay their policyholders and take subrogation or loan receipts[3] so that they may start proceedings against the bailee and against the insurer.

On the other hand, the bailee may not be liable for the loss but may be carrying insurance that covers the loss of any bailor who is not insured or the excess of loss over the insurance if the bailor is insufficiently insured. A clear and comprehensive record of the insurance will help to bring the loss adjustment to its proper conclusion.

[3]See Appendix M.

BAILOR'S MEASURE OF LOSS

Loss of a bailor is limited to the value of the property and, in case of damage, is measured by the difference between the value of the property before the loss and its value after the loss, not exceeding cost of replacement or repair. If the bailor delivered raw material to the bailee who, by processing it or fabricating it, increased its value, the bailor is entitled to collect on the basis of the increased value because the bailee can require payment for any work done. Labor follows the goods.

BAILEE'S MEASURE OF LOSS

If insurance covers only the bailee's interest, any loss, unless it has been agreed to insure the property or the bailee has negligently caused its loss, will be limited to the unpaid charges earned by handling the property. When these charges are paid, the bailee's insurer is entitled to an assignment and may enforce it against the bailors who owe the charges. A bailee should not be paid a greater sum than would have been collectible from the bailors had no loss occurred.

If the insurance contract contains a trust-and-commission clause that makes it cover the property and does not restrict coverage to the bailee's interest in, or liability to care for, the property, the bailee is entitled to an adjustment based on the cash value of the property at the time of the loss and must account to the bailor for any funds collected.

If the insurance limits the value of the property, the bailee can collect no more than the declared value.

RIGHT OF BAILOR TO INDEPENDENT PAYMENT

The courts have construed the trust-and-commission clause, when used in a policy describing the property, as entitling individual bailors to adopt the bailee's insurance and, if the bailee fails to make claim for their property, to make claim themselves.[4]

4Utica Canning Co., v. Home Ins. Co., 132 N.Y.S. 420 (App. Div. 1909).

PROPERTY IN TRANSIT

When adjusting a loss under the policy of a bailor covering personal property that has been lost or damaged while in the possession of a common carrier and in transit, the claim representative should fix value and loss and have the insured furnish the following papers: (1) the contract of carriage, generally a bill of lading or an express receipt, (2) the freight bill, (3) any original invoice, memorandum, or other document describing the property, (4) copy of the claim made against the carrier and copies of any correspondence relative to it, (5) consignor's verification, and (6) consignee's affidavit. These should be forwarded to the insurer with the proof of loss and the report.

Many policies covering the legal liability of a carrier give the carrier permission to make settlements with shippers or consignees. When dealing with such policies, often the work is confined to auditing the carrier's records.

WAREHOUSE LOSSES

Where a loss in a warehouse is confined to the property of a single bailor that can be identified, examined, or salvaged without difficulty, the adjustment work proceeds as in an owner risk. But when a loss is extensive, the claim representative may have to deal with the property of several bailors and may encounter a situation in which some work must be done for the common good.

If all the property can be identified, any lots that have been mixed should be separated, and a check should be made of all inventories or statements presented by the bailees against all the property involved.

If the property has been damaged in such a way that identification is impossible, the records of the bailors and the bailee should both be checked, and a comparison made between the total of the quantities shown by the records and the total that can be counted, measured, or weighed in the warehouse.

If the loss requires salvage operations, any salvage that can be identified must be credited to the bailor to whom it belongs, or to the insurer that has paid the bailor.

If salvage cannot be identified, it should be sold for account of whom it may concern, and the proceeds apportioned among the bailors interested in it, or their insurers, according to values established.

When the claim representative is called upon to adjust a warehouse loss presenting such a complicated situation, he or she should try to centralize the adjustment of all losses under his or her own charge, or, if such an arrangement is not feasible, cooperate with other interested claim representatives. Joint action for the benefit of all interests is necessary.

When confusion, debris, damaged elevators, exposure to the weather, or other circumstances require expenditures for the common good, it is advisable to develop a master inventory of all property in the warehouse, lotted according to ownerships, so that each lot of property can have charged against it its proper share of any general expense.

Whenever a total loss is paid on a lot of property stored in a warehouse, or whenever a lot is turned over to a salvor to be sold, the claim representative should take up from the insured the warehouse receipt or receipts if any have been issued. Eventually, they should be filed with the insurer. If a loss is adjusted by allowing the insured an agreed amount for damage and if the insured is to keep the property, the warehouse receipt should be left with the insured.

WAREHOUSE CHARGES

When losses in warehouses are handled, charges must be kept in mind, as a warehouser, except in case of negligence, has a lien on any salvage to the extent of the earned charges. Bailors should be notified that before an adjustment is made, they must pay the warehouse charges to the date when the insurer takes over the salvage. Warehouse charges accruing after the salvage has been taken for account of either the insured or the insurer follow the salvage. Warehouse charges are not collectible by bailors, for the same reason that rent is not collectible under a policy insuring stock.

SUBSTITUTIONS

There are times when the burning of the contents of a warehouse gives rise to fraudulent claims for property that was not insured. The owners of the uninsured property compare notes with the owners of the insured property, and if there is a margin between the amount of insurance carried and the value of the property insured, the uninsured owner will frequently prevail on the insured owner to include the uninsured property in the claim. In the case of a cotton warehouse, a policyholder might have sold cotton without canceling the policy, expecting to store other cotton at an early date to be covered by the same policy. If fire occurs while he has no cotton in the warehouse, an uninsured neighbor may prevail upon him to present a claim for the neighbor's cotton. Transactions of this sort are frequently suspected but seldom proved, as the parties tell a prearranged story. The broad coverage of a policy containing the trust-and-commission clause makes it extremely difficult to defeat improper claims of this sort. If the claim representative suspects that a substitution has been made, he or she should examine all purchase records of the insured and, if possible, get access to the bank account and canceled checks. The ordinary warehouse receipt for cotton is issued to the person who stores the cotton. Therefore, the receipt passes from hand to hand without even being endorsed, the final purchaser customarily paying all accrued storage charges. The warehouser has no record which will indicate who owns any particular bale of cotton that has been sold by the bailor who stored it.

In some cases, the claim representative will unearth substitutions made without the knowledge or consent of the insured. Occasionally, persons having access to the warehouse will remove property of good quality, substituting in its place an inferior grade. The substitution will generally be made in the hope of concealing the theft as long as possible. Such substitutions are not numerous and can be discovered only if the fire is extinguished before the property is burned beyond identification.

LOSSES IN PROCESSING PLANTS

Losses in processing plants generally require quick transfer of salvage to other plants where its processing can be completed, or where further damage can be prevented. If there is any question as to the liability of the bailee, or the liability of the bailor's or bailee's insurer, the claim representative should have an agreement executed to provide that the handling of the property shall be without prejudice to the rights of any party involved.

Many processors carry insurance for the benefit of customers, but with a stipulation in the policy that it does not cover property otherwise insured except for the value in excess of the other insurance.

Expenditures due to confusion of goods or made for the common good are treated as in warehouse risks.

Reports covering losses in processing risks should include abstracts or enclose copies of any contracts between bailor and bailee, or should refer to the legal reason or trade custom controlling the bailee's liability.

LOSSES ON CONTRACTOR'S PREMISES

In some contractor risks, the contractor owns none of the material fabricated; in others, the contractor owns part of it. When the contractor owns none, the adjustments follow the same general course as in warehouse losses. Controversy often arises, however, as to the contractor's interest in the goods, the labor, materials, and overhead invested at the time of loss.

In other risks, a contracting operation will be carried on that is subordinate to the regular production of finished goods.

In contracting risks, the contractor should be instructed to notify all bailors of the occurrence of loss and call on them to reveal all details of the insurance they carry.

FUR-STORAGE RISKS, CLEANING AND REPAIR RISKS

As the insurance carried by persons who make a business of storing furs or by laundrymen, cleaners, and repair people is generally

inland marine, and as it is often involved with the off-premises cover of household insurance, losses in such risks require treatment according to any special conditions in the policies and the receipts issued by the bailees.

MISCELLANEOUS

The procedure followed in handling losses on goods in the possession of carriers, warehousemen, processors, contractors, and cleaners should be followed with necessary adaptation to special conditions when customers' goods in factories, stores, or shops are involved. Many manufacturers do special work on goods sent in by other manufacturers, while stores and shops often take in for repair, reupholstering, finishing, or cleaning the furniture, draperies, mattresses, and rugs belonging to customers. If these are destroyed or damaged on the premises, a bailor and bailee situation arises.

When such is the case, the claim representative should see to it that the factory, store, or shop takes steps to protect any remaining property from further damage and, as promptly as possible, (1) make a list of all customers whose property may have been damaged, (2) notify each by letter of the occurrence of the loss, and (3) ask in the letter what insurance the customer may carry, covering the property.

The replies can then be followed up, and the customers can be treated like bailors in any other risks.

CONCLUSION

In all bailee-risk losses, it is the duty of the claim representative to establish the value and loss of the bailor's property, and also the facts indicating whether or not the bailee is liable for the loss or has effected insurance which should bear the loss, even though the bailor carries his or her own insurance.

QUESTIONS AND PROBLEMS

1.a. Ordinarily, when does a contract of bailment begin and when does it end?
   b. When the property is placed on a truck or into a freight car or a warehouse,

delivery is said to be actual. State a situation where delivery would be constructive rather than actual.

c. Railroads, truckers, and other carriers are actually insurers of bailor's property to the extent they are liable as at common law for any loss or damage except as provided in Uniform Bills of Lading or Tariffs approved by the Interstate Commerce Commission. Bailees other than carriers may be liable for damage to the bailor's property in one of four ways. State the four circumstances or ways in which such liability is created.

2. The Riteway Cleaning and Storage Company suffered a serious fire loss at the height of its season. Many rugs were cleaned and stored, others were in the process of being cleaned or awaiting cleaning. The contents were reduced to junk. The cause of the fire was accidental. Riteway has a good broker who provided a policy that covers Riteway's own property and also the property of others while in Riteway's care, custody, and control. As claim representative under a Homeowners policy, how would you handle the loss to your insured's rug?

3. a. An upholsterer's insurance policy covers "the insured's interest in and legal liability for similar property belonging to others." An accidental fire occurs on the upholsterer's premises damaging finished upholstered pieces. What is the bailee's insurable interest in the loss? What is the customer-bailor's insurable interest?

b. Ten Kentucky bluegrass seed farmers bring their seed to a common warehouse where it is stored in a single bin being all of one grade. Part of the seed is destroyed in a fire, and part is salvaged and prorated among the ten farmers in proportion to the amount they put in. What is property like this called?

4. In adjusting bailee losses, the claim representative may be required to do everything normally done as if the risk were an owner risk, and in addition there may be special investigation procedures peculiar to bailee risks. Name five major points particularly applicable to bailee risks and indicate the significance of each point.

5. a. Explain why the claim representative should carefully check any written or oral contracts, custom of the trade, or other documents affecting the bailee-bailor relationship?

b. What is the duty of a bailee to a bailor in event of loss to the bailor's property?

6. A bailee's policy covering a public warehouse contains a trust-and-commission clause making it cover the property but does not restrict coverage to the bailee's interest in, or liability to care for, the property.

a. What adjustment is the bailee entitled to and under what circumstances?

b. If the bailee refuses to make claim for the bailor's property, does the bailor have any rights under the bailee's policy? Explain?

7. a. The claim representative should keep warehouse charges in mind when adjusting losses for bailors. Why?

b. Can the bailor collect warehouse charges he has incurred, under his policy?

8. You have been assigned to adjust a serious though far from total loss in a rug-cleaning and storage plant. Soon after arriving at the premises and obtaining basic information concerning the insured, insurance, property, and circumstances of the loss, you must take three or four important steps. What are they?

22

Condominium Losses

The investigation and adjustment of claims made under condominium policies present the claim representative with relatively new concepts as to what property is covered in a building and for whose interests. The conditions that give rise to these problems are the multiplicity of individual occupants who each own specified areas, or portions of a building, while all of them jointly own other areas or portions.

WHAT IS A CONDOMINIUM?

The word *condominium*, as it pertains to buildings, means that each occupant or tenant owns a unit, a *cube of space*, variously described and defined. In addition to the unit that is owned and occupied, each *unit owner* also owns an undivided share of the common facilities and areas of the building complex including the land, unless the building or buildings are on leased ground. These common areas and facilities may include such things as foundations, main walls, roofs, hallways, corridors, lobbies, stairs, fire escapes, common walls, basements, yards, parking areas, storage spaces, all heat, light, and power lines, ducts and services, air conditioning and incinerating—in other words, all of the real property not owned individually by the unit owners.

Condominiums began gaining popularity in the United States soon after 1961 when federal legislation was enacted and the Federal Housing Authority Model Condominium Act was passed. Each state has subsequently enacted a condominium statute. While these statutes are similar to the FHA Model Act, there are significant differences from one state to another. Therefore, the claim representative should have available the statute of the state in which he or she is working in order to be fully informed on statutory requirements.

TYPES OF CONDOMINIUMS

Residential Condominiums

Originally a condominium was thought of as a *high-rise* apartment building because that is the way their development started. The tax advantages to the unit owner were considerable as both real estate taxes and mortgage interest could be deducted. Furthermore, it was cheaper to buy a condominium than a house, and many of them offer attractive recreational facilities. The high rise usually was located in or near city limits where real estate taxes were becoming immoderate, thus the advantage of a multi-story condominium.

As the condominium idea caught on, the developers built low-rise units, calling them variously *town houses*, of which there are many thousands in the South and Southwest; *duplexes*, *patio* or *garden apartments*, and *plaza homes*. The FHA Model Condominium Statute defines *building* as

> one containing five or more apartments, or two or more buildings, each containing two or more apartments, with a total of five or more apartments for all such buildings, and comprising a part of the property.

Many condominiums are rows or groups of two- to four-unit buildings, each with private entrance but with common recreational facilities and common services. Other condominiums are a series of one-family homes utilizing the same land, recreation, and parking areas.

Resort Condominiums

The resort condominiums are located on islands, along sea coasts, and in lake and ski country. The designs range from groups of dwellings, town houses, to high rise. Many resort condominium units are occupied only during the resort season; some are rented off-season to help defray expenses.

Conversion Condominiums

Thousands of rental apartment houses and hotels, particularly within city limits, have been converted to condominiums, generally for economic reasons. A number of states have passed legislation requiring full disclosure and review before the owner of an apartment house is permitted to convert. The reason is that there have been abuses. Many are old buildings and the mechanical facilities have greatly depreciated, such as piping, wiring, heating, and air conditioning. Some landlords have redecorated and dressed up apartments and areas at a small investment to come out with a high profit on the conversion to a condominium.

Claim representatives, in handling losses on conversions, should be very thorough in their investigation of the cause of loss and in the quality of repair and replacement.

Commercial Condominiums

Gaining in popularity are commercial condominiums, especially for professional offices of lawyers, doctors, and dentists where each owns his or her own unit and all share the telephone-answering and reception service. There are condominium office buildings for business people, and some shopping centers are being developed as condominiums.

LEGAL DOCUMENTS

There are four legal documents to which the claim representative's attention is directed because usually one or more of them will have to be referred to in any but routine small losses. As previously mentioned, the Federal Housing Authority Model Condominium Statute was passed in 1961, and subsequently each state enacted a condominium statute patterned after the FHA Act in whole or with modifications. Each state statute sets the standards for a property to qualify as a condominium. Each state also requires that a *master deed*, a *unit deed*, and the *bylaws* be recorded at the registry of deeds. The fourth legal document of importance is known as the *regulations* and is usually included in the bylaws.

Master Deed (Declaration)

Depending on the state statute, the master deed also may be called the *covenant, charter,* or *deed restrictions*. It is required to be filed with and approved by the proper authorities before committing the land to condominium use and starting construction. The declaration designates many things, the more common being:

1. Description of the land on which the condominium is to be located.
2. Purpose, i.e., residential or commercial.
3. Description of building(s).
4. Description of apartments, number of rooms, etc.
5. Description of common areas and facilities and each unit owner's proportionate interest in them.
6. Type of organization that will manage the condominium.
7. Percentage of votes by unit owners needed to determine whether to repair, rebuild, or sell the property in event of damage or destruction of all or part of the property.

Unit Deed

There is a unit deed for each unit which specifically describes the unit as to size, square feet, the percentage of undivided interest in common areas and facilities, and is subject to easements in favor of other units, and to provisions of the master deed and bylaws, as to the floor plans of the condominium.

Bylaws

The bylaws constitute another document required to be recorded with the master deed. While the master deed runs with the land and deals with how it is to be used and owned, the bylaws set the guidelines by which the unit owners will govern themselves. It concerns itself with such matters as the establishment of the unit owners' board of managers or directors, how many may serve and for what period, and where meetings will be held, who can vote, and what type of organization it will be, i.e., trust, corporation, or association. Bylaws can be very simple in a small condominium or elaborate in one of several hundred or more units. Some bylaws describe such things as methods for collecting assessments; rules for repair work, hiring of personnel, and other operating procedures for the management group. Bylaws are, as a rule, attached to the master deed.

Regulations

Regulations may be part of the bylaws or attached to them. They stipulate the rules of conduct and behavior of the unit owners, such as keeping hallways, stairways, walkways, and other common areas unobstructed; not cooking on terraces without permission; storing bicycles, wagons, scooters, etc., only in permitted areas; providing management with keys to the units; allowing children to play only in designated areas.

CUBE-OF-SPACE CONCEPT

The *cube-of-space* concept is that the unit owner has purchased and has title to a cube of air composed of six sides or surfaces enclosing the bare interior walls, floor, and ceiling of the unit he or she owns. Within the cube of air are those elements owned solely by the unit owner which convert the cube into dwelling quarters. These elements would include such items as *non-load-bearing* partitions, wall and ceiling decorations, floor coverings, plumbing fixtures, appliances, millwork, and cabinetry. All of these accoutrements which outfit the cube of space into dwelling-living quarters may have

been purchased when the building was first erected or from a previous unit owner, or some may have been installed by the present unit owner as improvements and betterments.

Load-bearing partitions, columns, and other structural items which support or reinforce floors, roofs, or ceilings above are *common elements* even though they are within a unit owner's cube of space. Pipes, wires, conduits, and other utilities within each unit are also common elements and facilities, the units being conveyed subject to various easements in favor of other or adjoining units.

Designation of Unit Boundaries

The master deed usually designates the boundaries of each of the units with respect to the floors, ceilings, and the walls, doors, and windows. Not all are the same. One states, for example:

(a) *Floors:* The upper surfaces of the subflooring.
(b) *Ceilings:* The plane of the lower surface of the ceiling joists.
(c) *Interior Building Walls:* The plane of the surface facing such unit of the wall studs.[1]
(d) *Exterior Building Walls, Doors and Windows:* As to walls, the plane of the interior surface of the wall studs;[2] as to doors, the exterior surface thereof; and as to windows, the exterior surfaces of the glass and of the window frames.

Common Areas and Facilities

The master deed describes these in detail.

Percentage of Undivided Interest in Common Areas and Facilities

The master deed usually sets up the undivided interest in common areas and facilities, showing the percentage for each unit by number of unit.

---

[1]MLB-29 (Ed. 7-74) excludes property of any kind contained within the unfinished interior surfaces of the perimeter walls, floors and ceilings of the condominium units except common building elements and certain utilities (see p. 346).
[2]Ibid.

CONDOMINIUM INSURANCE FORMS AND ENDORSEMENTS

The authority for obtaining and maintaining property insurance on the common elements and facilities of the building is delegated to the management association by way of a condominium trust.

The trust agreement spells out the kinds of property insurance, perils to be insured against, what property or properties are to be covered and, frequently, the amount, i.e., 80, 90, or 100 percent of replacement cost. It also provides for the named insured to be the trust, trustees, unit owners, and mortgagees.

Building Insurance

The policies covering common elements and facilities of condominiums are basically building forms tailored to fit the scheme of the condominium concept in which most of the structure is owned in common by the unit owners, while property, real and personal, within the units is owned individually by the unit owners—with the exception of a few common elements mentioned previously.

In examining the building coverage, two policies or forms will be used, MLB-29 and MLB-29A, both Edition of January 1974. The first insures against named perils, the second is all risks of physical loss. Under the form heading:

SMP CONDOMINIUM—ADDITIONAL
POLICY PROVISIONS
MLB-29 (Ed. 1-74)
SMP SPECIAL CONDOMINIUM
PROPERTY FORM
SECTION 1—PROPERTY COVERAGE

there is a Loss Payable Clause which states:

1. Subject in all other respects to the provisions of the Mortgage Clause of this policy, loss, if any, shall be adjusted with the Named Insured but shall be payable to the insurance trustee designated by the appropriate governing body of the Association.
2. Such payment to the insurance trustee shall constitute a complete discharge of this Company's liability under this policy for such loss.

The two important property coverages are to be found under A—Building(s), and B—Personal Property, together with certain exclusions, extensions, and limitations.

COVERAGE A—BUILDING(s): When the insurance under this policy covers buildings, such insurance shall also cover additions and extensions attached thereto; fixtures, machinery and equipment constituting a permanent part of and pertaining to the service of the building; materials and supplies intended for use in construction, alteration or repair of buildings; yard fixtures; detachable building equipment; personal property of the Named Insured, or in which each of the condominium unit-owners has an undivided interest, used for the service or maintenance of the described buildings, including fire extinguishing apparatus, floor coverings and outdoor furniture (but not including other personal property located in lobbies, hallways or in units or rooms furnished by the Named Insured); all while at the described locations.

To complete and to clarify coverage A, an exclusion under Property Not Covered reads as follows:

Under COVERAGE A—BUILDING(s): Property of any kind or description contained within the unfinished interior surfaces of the perimeter walls, floors and ceilings of condominium units, except (1) common building elements and (2) pipes, wires, conduits and other utilities contained within easements appurtenant to the common building elements and within such condominium units.

Before commenting on coverage A it would be well to look at the personal property coverage inasmuch as between A and B the major part of property covered is fairly complete with the exception of limited extensions similar in many respects to those found in the SMP General Property Form.

COVERAGE B—PERSONAL PROPERTY: When the insurance under this policy covers personal property, such insurance shall cover all personal property owned by the Named Insured or in which each of the condominium unit-owners has an undivided interest, including bullion, manuscripts, furniture, fixtures, equipment and supplies not otherwise covered under this policy and shall also cover the Named Insured's interest in personal property owned by others to the extent of labor and materials expended thereon by the Named Insured; all while in or on the described buildings, or in the open, including within vehicles, on the described premises or within 100 feet thereof.

There is one other coverage under MLB-29, though not highly significant. That is Personal Property of Others while in the care, custody, or control of the named insured while on the described premises or within 100 feet thereof. The limit is 2 percent of the limit of liability specified for coverage B—Personal Property but not exceeding $2,000.

Summary of Coverage Under MLB-29. The following summarizes coverage under this policy.

1. Loss is to be adjusted with the named insured and payable to the designated Trustee.
2. Covers the building(s), fixtures, machinery, and equipment, a permanent part of the building(s) and pertaining to its service; yard fixtures, detachable building equipment; personal property in which unit owners have an undivided interest, used for the service or maintenance of the building(s), including floor coverings and outdoor furniture.
   Excluding property within the units other than common building elements.
3. Also covers personal property owned by unit owners as tenants-in-common (jointly) and property of others in the care, custody, or control of the management association.

The claim representative will recognize other provisions, conditions, limitations and extensions in MLB-29, such as coinsurance, deductibles, valuation, replacement cost, and extra expense, all of which are discussed in other chapters.

MLB-29A (Ed. 1-74). The essential purpose of this form is to provide all risks of loss coverage in place of the nine named perils in MLB-29. Coverages under Section I, Property Covered and Section II, Property Not Covered, are the same as under MLB-29. As with almost all risks of loss forms being substituted for similar named peril forms, there are more exclusions and limitations especially as regards perils.

Endorsements. MLB-29B is an endorsement which provides the mechanics by which the association may comply with the statutes, the declarations, the bylaws or requests of the mortgagor/mortgagees to include in the association's policy three categories of property excluded or not insured in either MLB-29 (1-74) or MLB-29A (1-74).

Coverage A Building(s), when designated by an "X" in the box(es) (□) of this endorsement, shall also cover:

□ 1. Fixtures, installations or additions comprising a part of the building within the unfinished interior surfaces of the perimeter walls, floors and ceilings of individual condominium units initially installed, or replacements thereof, in accordance with the original condominium plans and specifications.

□ 2. Fixtures, installations or additions comprising a part of the building within the unfinished interior surfaces of the perimeter walls, floors and ceilings of the individual condominium units initially installed or replacements thereof, in accordance with the original condominium plans and specifications, or installed by or at the expense of the unit-owners.

□ 3. If Other, Describe:

Perhaps the easiest explanation of this endorsement and its purpose is to quote from the Insurance Services Office SMP Manual (revised as of April 1974), page 19:

SMP Condominium Endorsement (Broad Property Coverage) Form MLB 29B, provides coverage for fixtures, installations or additions comprising a part of the building within the unfinished interior surfaces of the perimeter walls, floors and ceilings of individual condominium units, either

a. initially installed, or replacements thereof, in accordance with the original condominium plans and specifications; or

b. initially installed, or replacements thereof, in accordance with the original condominium plans and specifications, or installed by or at the expense of the unit-owners.

Note: SMP Condominium Endorsement Form MLB 29B also makes provision under Item 3 for other building and personal property coverage not adequately covered under Items 1 and 2 above, which are required to be insured under the condominium association SMP policy in accordance with the condominium bylaws and declarations. . . .

Condominium Unit Owner's Insurance

The Homeowners Policy Condominium Unit-Owners Form HO-6 (Ed. 3-74) or HO-6 (Ed. 7-1-75) may be used to insure the interests of unit owners. On occasion, the Homeowners Contents Broad Form, HO-4, is used with the Condominium Unit-Owners Endorsement, for which there is no additional charge. These forms and endorsements are tailored to fit the scheme of the condominium concept.

HO-6 forms cover, in addition to the unit owner's unscheduled personal property, a basic limit of $1,000 as additional insurance on the unit owner's additions and alterations installed in accordance with the original plans and specifications or installed by or at the expense of the unit owner.

1. Unit-Owners Addition and Alterations: This policy covers, for an amount not exceeding $1,000, unit-owners additions and alterations, meaning; fixtures, installations or additions comprising the part of the building within the unfinished interior surfaces of the perimeter walls, floors and ceilings of individual condominium units as

initially installed or replacements thereof in accordance with the original condominium plans and specifications or installed by or at the expense of the unit-owner.

The HO-192 Endorsement which is attached to the HO-4 Homeowners reads slightly differently in that a limit of 10 percent of the coverage on unscheduled personal property may be applied. It is not an additional amount of insurance. HO-192 is an actual cash value form. HO-6 forms are subject to replacement cost coverage.

HO-192 is a named peril form, as are the HO-6 forms. The latter may be converted to all risks of physical loss as respects the unit owner's additions and alterations by attaching endorsement HO-32.

Under the unit owner's additions and alterations provisions of all three forms, the Company's liability is as follows:

(a) If repaired or replaced within a reasonable time after such loss, actual expenses incurred (if any) by the Named Insured, which exceed any recovery for the benefit of the Named Insured for loss or damage to such additions and alterations from any insurance covering the interests of the Unit-Owners collectively of the condominium; or

(b) If not repaired or replaced within a reasonable time after such loss, the actual cash value of the damaged or destroyed additions and alterations, less any recovery for the benefit of the Named Insured for loss or damage to such additions and alterations from any insurance covering the interests of the Unit-Owners collectively of the condominium.

Summary of Coverage Under Unit Owner's Policy. The following list summarizes the property covered under this policy:

1. All property within the boundaries of the unit as originally installed by the developer excluding any common elements.
2. Any variations in original specifications installed at the expense of the developer or unit owner, up to a limit of $1,000.

3. Any additions to the original unit or to the unit as purchased from previous owner.

4. Unit realty, walls, partitions inside the unit including structural units within the unit. Also included are fixtures, millwork, partitions, floor covering, tile, plumbing fixtures, ranges and refrigerators. Also utility pipes, wires, and conduits which are not considered common elements.

The declarations of some condominiums are very specific in stating that the unit owner

shall be deemed to own the walls and partitions which are contained in said owner's respective "apartment space" and also shall be deemed to own the inner-decorated or finished surfaces of the perimeter walls, floors and ceilings, including plaster, paint, wallpaper, etc.

Such a provision in the declarations is probably due to the fact that none of the partitions within the units are load-bearing and therefore are not common elements.

If the foregoing assumption of coverage is correct, there appears to be an overlapping situation between the insurance covering common elements and facilities, and the unit owner's insurance. Both would appear to cover such common elements as load-bearing partitions, pipes, wires, conduits, and other utilities. However, the Other Insurance Clause under "Additional Conditions" makes the Homeowner policy excess over other insurance covering the same property.

3. Other Insurance: If at the time of loss there is other insurance in the name of the condominium association covering the same property covered by this policy, the insurance afforded by this policy shall be excess over the amount recoverable under such other insurance.

Furthermore, MLB forms are primary under General Condition E:

E. Other Insurance: If at the time of loss there is other insurance in the name of a unit-owner covering the same property covered by this policy, the insurance afforded by this policy shall be primary and not contributing with such other insurance.

SUBROGATION

The MLB Condominium forms waive subrogation against any unit owner.

1. The Company waives its right of subrogation against any unit-owner of the described condominium but in all other respects the subrogation provision appearing under "THE FOLLOWING PROVISIONS APPLY TO SECTIONS I and II" remains unchanged.

The Homeowners Condominium policies do not waive subrogation.

INHERENT ADJUSTMENT PROBLEM AREAS

While ISO has endeavored to eliminate overlapping coverages as respects common elements under the Homeowners and MLB Condominium forms and endorsements, there are a few areas in which adjustment problems may develop. The common elements within the units may, by their terms, be covered under both policies. Yet the declaration or master deed may state, for example, that *all partitions* within the unit are owned by the unit owner. If it developed that certain of the partitions were *load-bearing* (common elements), which policy would be called upon to pay for their repair or replacement in spite of the excess clause in the Homeowners and the primary insurance clause in the MLB forms?

Debates are also possible over which partitions are true carrying or load-bearing.

Additional inherent adjustment problems are created when the insurance on the common elements and facilities is on a form not designed for condominiums or improperly designed. A unit owner may have been issued, inadvertently, a Homeowners policy not suitable for a condominium dweller.

Breakage of glass may raise a problem where the declaration or the master deed stipulates that glass breakage in perimeter walls (though a common element) is the responsibility of the unit owner. Large Thermopane doors are very expensive and can be broken by other than named perils in MLB-29. Form MLB-29A insures against glass breakage only for perils similar to MLB-29 and then puts a limit of $50 per plate and $250 per occurrence. The Homeowners policy of the unit owner, under additions and alterations, covers within the unfinished interior surfaces of the perimeter walls. The declarations may define the unit boundaries "and as to windows, the exterior surfaces of the glass and of the window frames."

Again, the adjustment of condominium losses must be preceded by careful examination of the declaration and unit deed, the policies of the unit owner and of the management association covering common elements and facilities.

GUIDELINES FOR CLAIM REPRESENTATIVES

I. Insurance—the management association (trust).
   A. Policy form number and edition date.
   B. Is the form tailored for a condominium?
   C. What property is covered?
      1. Common elements and facilities in which each unit owner has an undivided interest?
      2. Is it endorsed to include fixtures, installations, or additions comprising part of the building located within individual condominium units, which are initially installed or subsequently replaced according to original plans and specifications?
      3. Same as B above but including such property installed by or at the expense of the unit owners?
      Note: Examine state statute and declarations to determine if there is a requirement to cover property described in B and C above and whether at replacement cost new or actual cash value.

4. Is there an exclusion of property within condominium units, except common elements (bearing walls, columns, and other supports, etc.) and conduits, piping, wiring and other utility service?
5. Is personal property of the management association covered, i.e., office equipment, furniture, and supplies? Other?
6. Is any property covered away from the described premises? Limitations?
7. Is business personal property of others covered, i.e., leased, consigned or concession property? Limitations?
8. Any question of coverage on motor-driven vehicles on premises, not licensed for the highway but used for the service of the premises?
9. Check Building and Personal Property Covered as well as Property Not Covered, to determine if there is for any of the following and to what extent:
   a. Trees, shrubs and plants.
   b. Newly acquired buildings, additions and extensions to existing structures; on or off premises.
   c. Swimming pools, sauna baths, diving boards, etc.
   d. Piers, wharves, docks, retaining walls, walks, tennis courts, or paved surfaces.
   e. TV antennas.
   f. Storage and recreation buildings, cabanas, storage sheds of unit owners.
   D. Is the loss adjustment subject to:
      1. Replacement cost? Is it a limited coverage or full replacement? Is it included in the condominium policy or added by endorsement? Does it exclude certain property from replacement cost?
      2. Actual cash value? What is the basis of the valuation?
      3. Is there coinsurance?

4. Is there an Agreed Amount Endorsement? Did the loss occur prior to expiration date on endorsement?
E. Is there extra expense over normal expense coverage during period of restoration?
F. What deductibles are there?
G. Establish name and interest of loss payees.
II. Insurance—condominium unit owners.
A. Policy form number and edition date.
B. Is the form itself tailored for a condominium, or is it a Homeowners tenant form, such as HO-4 with a Condominium Unit-Owners Endorsement?
C. What property is covered that is generic to a condominium?[3]
1. Does it cover building items within the unit, or subsequently installed by or at the expense of the unit owner, including such items as—
a. Wall and ceiling decorations or treatment as paneling, etc.?
b. Floor coverings as rugs, vinyl, etc.?
c. Partitioning, non-load-bearing?
d. Cabinets, cupboards, plumbing, cooking, and lighting fixtures, millwork, etc.?
2. Has the policy limit on unit owner's Additions and Alterations coverage been increased by endorsement?
3. Has endorsement HO-32 been attached, converting the specified peril form to all risks of physical loss?
D. What deductibles are there?
E. Establish name and interest of mortgagee or loss payee.

EXAMINATION OF LEGAL DOCUMENTS

The claim representative should have access to copies of the following legal documents

for examination of each one that is relevant to the particular loss being handled.[4]

> Master deed (declaration)
> Unit deed
> Bylaws
> Regulations
> State statute
> City or county ordinances or laws

Each condominium unit owner generally has available copies of the first four documents. On routine losses contained within the unit and where loss or damage is confined solely to the unit owner's property, there is generally no occasion to scrutinize the legal documents.

When a loss involves property within the unit owned by the unit owner, and also property classified as "common elements and facilities" in which each unit owner has an undivided interest, the first three legal documents as well as the unit owner's insurance policy and that of the management association should be examined.

When a loss involves only the common elements and facilities, or, in addition, one or more units, then it would be well to examine all six legal documents listed above. *State statutory provisions override both insurance policy provisions as well as any contained in the declaration, unit deed, and bylaws.*

Examination of principal legal documents is usually done to disclose one or more of the following:

1. Date and purchase price by original unit owner or date and purchase price by present owner if not the original.
2. How are the horizontal and vertical boundaries defined in the declaration or master deed?
   a. To the surface of the studs in walls and joists above.
   b. To the unfinished floor below.
   c. To the unfinished surface of the perimeter walls and ceiling.
   d. To the inside or outside of glass in exterior walls.
   e. Other definitions.

---

[3]See p. 348.

[4]See p. 344 for the description and contents of these documents.

3. Plans and specifications of original fixtures, installations, or additions comprising part of the building within the unit of the insured unit owner.
   a. Any replacements of above by the insured unit owner.
   b. Any fixtures, installations, or additions comprising part of the building installed by or at the expense of the unit owner not in original plans and specifications.
4. Has unit owner arranged with management association to cover any additions or installations made by the unit owner, or has unit owner provided for same under the Homeowners policy?
5. Basis on which insurance on common elements and facilities is to be valued. By law or by trust agreement?
   a. Actual cash value with coinsurance.
   b. Agreed amount. What is expiration date?

DETERMINATION OF LOSS AND DAMAGE

Within a condominium there will be two classes of property involved in most losses.

1. Unscheduled personal property.
2. Real property (building, fixtures, etc., comprising part of the building, additions and alterations installed by or at the expense of the unit owner).

Unscheduled Personal Property

The investigation and adjustment of a loss to personal property in a condominium will be little different from that in any dwelling occupancy and is discussed in detail in Chapter 16, "Personal Property in Use." Any variances will be reflected in policy provisions, deductibles, limitations, definition of premises as respects theft losses, etc., of the particular unit owner's insurance.

The management association has no interest in the unit owner's unscheduled personal property within the unit.

Real Property

Within the boundaries of the units, in addition to the personal property of the unit owner, there is real property, i.e., property which is a permanent part of the building either structurally, decoratively, or as fixtures, etc.

Part of this real property is owned by the unit owner. This real property generally is the non-load-bearing partitions forming the rooms and closets; the plaster, dry-wall, decorations and paneling on those partitions; tiling on floors and walls; doors, trim, cabinetry and other millwork; plumbing fixtures; cooking and refrigerating appliances; and floor coverings to the extent they are construed to be a part of the building, such as glued-down carpeting over a rough floor.

The plumbing pipes, electric wiring, air-conditioning conduits, and other utility type services would all seem to be common building elements according to the MLB-29 and MLB-29A forms.[5] These items are in the perimeter walls, common and load-bearing walls, and in floors and ceilings, and constitute *common elements.* Their extension into the partition walls of the units would seem to make them *appurtenant* to the common elements and covered under the MLB forms.

Another area where opinions can differ, as no clear line is drawn, is the question of load-bearing partitions. Since they support floors above, the units above have an interest in them, and this could establish an undivided interest of *all* unit owners in *all* load-bearing walls and in *all common walls,* i.e., those separating one unit from the other.

So there are two separate insurable interests in the real property within the condominium units: the unit owner, whose interests are covered under the individual Homeowners policies, and *all* unit owners jointly whose interests are protected under the policy covering common units and facilities.

Preparation of Estimates

The claim representative, or representatives, should prepare or have prepared an estimate of the cost of repairing or replacing *all* real property:

[5]See p. 347.

1. Estimate cost to repair or replace common elements within the units to include principally:
   a. Common walls between units.
   b. Other load-bearing partitions.
   c. Wiring, piping, and conduits within walls and ceilings.
2. Estimate the cost to repair or replace the unit owner's real property including primarily:
   a. Fixtures, installations, or additions as initially installed, or
   b. Replacements thereof in accord with original condominium plans and specifications, or
   c. Installed by or at the expense of the unit owner.
3. Establish depreciation on above in event repairs and replacement are not done within a reasonable time after the loss, as recovery will be based on actual cash value.
4. Check declaration or master deed to determine unit owner's responsibility for glass doors or windows in exterior walls, as some boundary descriptions of units go to exterior surface of glass, others to the interior surface.

Additional Living Expense (Homeowners Policy)

The claim representative should establish additional living expense in the customary way.[6]

Extra Expense (MLB-29 and MLB-29A)

The claim representative should determine if this limited coverage is applicable in order to continue as near as practicable the normal operation of the condominium during the period of operation.

Application of Coverage to the Loss

Example 22-1, the application of coverage and the allocation of deductibles in a loss to the building which involves both the Association's insurance and that of two unit owners, was prepared by Robert L. Lusk, Consultant to the Property Loss Research Bureau (PLRB). It appears in a Bureau publication entitled *Condominium Insurance Coverage–1974*, and is available through the PLRB at the Chicago headquarters.

[6]See Chap. 25, "Business Interruption, Extra Expense, and Additional Living Expense."

EXAMPLE 22-1

This is a loss that involves two condominium units and also the common elements. The Association carries MLB 29(I-74) and MLB 29B-2. These policies cover the common elements as well as the units. There are no coinsurance problems; the loss is $2,900; deductible, $1,000. Unit owners carry HO-6 with $100 deductible. Loss is confined to building, not to personal property.

Step 1. Determine repairs to each interest.

Repairs to laundry room and halls (Association)	$1,500
Repairs to unit 525	600
Repairs to unit 526	800
Total repairs	$2,900

Step 2. Allocate deductible of $1,000 in Association policy to each interest involved in the loss on a loss-to-loss basis.

Association	$1,500	$1500/2900 \times 1000 =$	$ 517.24
Unit 525	600	$600/2900 \times 1000 =$	206.90
Unit 526	800	$800/2900 \times 1000 =$	275.86
	$2,900		$1,000.00

EXAMPLE 22-1 *(continued)*

Step 3. Determine payment by *primary* insurance.

MLB Is Primary	Loss		Deductible		Primary Pays
Pays on Association loss	$1,500	–	$ 517.24	=	$ 982.76
Pays on 525	600	–	206.90	=	393.10
Pays on 526	800	–	275.86	=	524.14
	$2,900		$1,000.00		$1,900.00

Step 4. Determine *excess* loss. In this situation where there is adequate insurance under the Association policy, the only *excess* loss to be assumed (in part) by the unit owner's HO-6 policies is the allocated deductible.

Association, of $517.24 assigned to "common" elements expense.
Unit 525, of $206.90 assigned to that unit's HO-6 policy.
Unit 526, of $275.86 assigned to that unit's HO-6 policy.
Excess over liability of MLB cover, $1,000.

Step 5. Determine payment to be made by HO-6 policies.

	Loss	Amount Recoverable	Excess	Deductible	Claim
Unit 525	$ 600	$393.10	$206.90	$100	$106.90
Unit 526	800	524.14	275.86	100	175.86
	$1,400	$917.24	$482.76	$200	$282.76

Step 6. Recapitulation.

Association—MLB Policies—Step 3	Pays	
As primary	$982.76	
On unit 525	393.10	
On unit 526	524.14	
Total MLB		$1,900.00

Unit Owners—HO-6 Policies—Step 5		
On unit 525	$106.90	
On unit 526	175.86	
Total HO-6		282.76
Total paid by insurers		$2,182.76

Unit Owners Pay Their Deductible—Step 5		
Unit-owner 525	$100.00	
Unit-owner 526	100.00	
Total		$ 200.00

Association Common Expenses—Step 2		
(Absorbed by all unit owners of condominium)		$ 517.24
Grand total		$2,900.00

Comment by PLRB: Net deductibles total $717.24 ($517.24 + $100 + $100) rather than $1,000 + $100 + $100 because the amount of the deductible under the primary insurance becomes a part of the *excess of loss over the amount recoverable under such other insurance.* That amount not charged to common expenses is partially reimbursed under the HO-6 forms (Step 5).

QUESTIONS AND PROBLEMS

1. **a.** What is a condominium?
   b. Name two types of condominiums.
2. There are four legal documents, one or more of which may be of importance in adjusting a loss on a condominium. What are the names of these legal documents? Briefly state the general purpose of each.
3. What is a conversion condominium?
4. What constitutes the insurable interest of the unit owner?
5. What is the cube-of-space concept?

6. Authority for obtaining insurance on the common elements and facilities of a condominium is delegated to the management association, entity or individual, depending on the management structure. Tell briefly what these common elements and facilities consist of which are covered under the policy.
7. Summarize in general the coverage under a unit owner's condominium policy.
8. Why is it important on condominium losses to check state statutory provisions pertaining to condominiums?

Automobile—
Physical Damage

The purpose of this chapter is to present the basic guidelines that will enable claim representatives to enter into the investigation and adjustment of first-party automobile physical-damage claims with some assurance. Legal aspects are limited to those germane to this particular policy coverage, avoiding any involvement with the legal liability coverage.

Most insurers of automobiles have their own claim training and procedure manuals that express individual company attitudes toward claim handling and toward policy interpretations. The majority either provide the various appraisal and other claim forms or state preferences for them.

In order to adequately present policy coverage, conditions, and provisions, the Family Automobile Policy (FAP) is used in the following discussion, as it contains the basic principles underlying all automobile insurance policies.

AUTOMOBILE INSURANCE POLICIES

While there has been a general standardization of coverages, conditions, and provisions of automobile policies, the majority of insurers design and draft their own. Typical examples of a relatively recent trend toward writing simplified, easy-to-read policies are the *Plain Talk Car Policy* of Sentry Insurance Company and the *Century II Auto Policy* of Nationwide Insurance Company. These and other individual company policies resemble the FAP.

Basically there are two types of automobile insurance policies: (1) those covering private passenger automobiles and (2) those covering business or commercial vehicles.

Most owners of private passenger automobiles are insured under the Family Automobile Policies which are marketed under that name or policies with similar coverage under a name of the individual insurer's selection. A few private passenger automobiles are covered under the Special Automobile Policy (SAP) which is a somewhat limited contract compared to the FAP. The Basic Automobile Policy (BAP) is used primarily for business vehicles but also for some private passenger automobiles for special-purpose use, such as assigned risks and non-owned automobiles. The Comprehensive Automobile Policy (CAP), primarily a broad liability policy, is used for commercial vehicles and usually in conjunction with another policy.

THE FAMILY AUTOMOBILE POLICY—PHYSICAL DAMAGE

Similar to most property insurance policies, a *Declaration* page is attached to the FAP setting forth information as to the name of the insured, occupation and employment; producer, inception and expiration dates (12:01 A.M.); year, make, model, and identification of the vehicle or vehicles; coverages, limits of liability, and amount of deductibles.

Who Is Insured—Owned Automobile

As respects an owned automobile, the policy insures the insured named in the Declarations and any resident of the same household.

The policy also insures any other person who is *using* or *operating* the automobile with the permission of the insured named in the policy; and any other person or organization but only with respect to his or its liability because of acts or omissions of one of the above described insureds.

Who Is Insured—Nonowned Automobile

As respects a nonowned automobile, the policy insures the insured named in the Declarations and any relative, but only as respects a private passenger automobile or trailer with permission of its owner. It also insures any other person or organization but only with respect to his or its liability because of acts or omissions of one of the above described insureds.

Named Insured Versus the Insured

The *named insured* is the individual named in the Declarations and the spouse if a resident of the same household. The *insured* is a person or an organization described under "Persons Insured." A *relative* must be a resident of the same household as the named insured.

What Vehicles Are Covered?

The policy covers *owned* and *nonowned* automobiles; *temporary substitute* automobiles; *private passenger* and *farm* automobiles; and *trailers*. These vehicles are defined briefly below. The claim representative should examine the automobile policy to be certain that coverage is afforded the vehicle involved.

Owned automobile is (1) a private passenger, farm, or utility automobile described in the policy for which a specific premium charge indicates that coverage is afforded and (2) a trailer owned by the insured on the effective date of the policy and described

therein. Also it is any vehicle as described above which was acquired *by the named insured* during the policy period if it replaces *owned automobile*, or if the Company insures all of the *owned automobiles* of the insured on date of such acquisition and is notified by the insured during the policy period or within 30 days after acquiring the automobile. A temporary substitute is also covered under *owned automobile*.

Nonowned automobile is an automobile or a trailer that is not owned by or furnished for the regular use of the named insured or any relative except as a temporary substitute automobile. (Check individual state provisions.)

Temporary substitute automobile is any automobile or trailer that is not owned by the named insured, while being temporarily used with the permission of the owner as a substitute for the *owned automobile or trailer* withdrawn from normal use because of its breakdown, repair, servicing, loss, or destruction.

Private passenger automobile is a four-wheel private passenger, station wagon, or jeep-type automobile.

Farm automobile is a truck-type automobile of load capacity of 1,500 pounds or less not used for business or commercial purposes other than farming.

Trailer is one designed for use with a private passenger automobile. It may be used for business or commercial purposes as long as it is in use with a private passenger, farm, or utility automobile but not as a home, office, store, display, or passenger trailer.

All the above definitions should be read in their entirety, not individually, before deciding whether a vehicle is or is not covered.[1]

Limit of Liability

The limit of liability for loss shall not exceed the actual cash value of the property or any part thereof, nor what it would cost to repair or replace, at the time of loss, with like kind and quality but in no event more than the limit of liability stated in the Declaration as respects the owned automobile.

[1]See also Exclusions, p. 359.

The limit for loss to personal effects is $100 in any one occurrence, and $500 to any trailer not owned by the named insured.

Other Insurance

If there is other insurance, the policy will be liable for no greater amount than its pro rata proportion of the loss based on the applicable limits of liability of all valid and collectible insurance. The FAP insurance shall be excess over any other valid and collectible insurance as respects a temporary substitute automobile or a nonowned automobile.

Conditions and Provisions

Conditions set forth in the automobile policies as respects physical damage are similar to those in most other property insurance policies.

Notice of loss must be given to the insurer providing specified information regarding the accident. Insured's duties in event of loss are spelled out, proof of claim is required, and, in event of failure to agree on the amount of loss, provisions are made for the insured or the insurer to demand an appraisal. There are also *subrogation, assignment*, and *cancellation* clauses.

The following Conditions and Provisions in the Family Automobile Policy are of significant importance to the claim representative in the handling of automobile physical damage claims.

Two or More Automobiles

When two or more automobiles are insured hereunder, the terms of this policy shall apply separately to each, but an automobile and a trailer attached thereto shall be held to be one automobile as respects limits of liability under Part I (Liability) of this policy, and separate automobiles under Part III (Physical Damage) of this policy, including any deductible provisions applicable thereto.

Assistance and Cooperation of the Insured

The insured shall cooperate with the company and, upon the company's request, assist in making settlements, in the conduct of suits and in enforcing any right of contribution or in-demnity against any person or organization who may be liable to the insured because of bodily injury, property damage or loss with respect to which insurance is afforded under this policy; and the insured shall attend hearings and trials and assist in securing and giving evidence and obtaining the attendance of witnesses. The insured shall not, except at his own cost, voluntarily make any payment, assume any obligation or incur any expense other than for such immediate medical and surgical relief to others as shall be imperative at the time of accident.

Insured's Duties in Event of Loss

In the event of loss the insured shall: (a) protect the automobile, whether or not the loss is covered by this policy, and any further loss due to the insured's failure to protect shall not be recoverable under this policy; reasonable expenses incurred in affording such protection shall be deemed incurred at the company's request; (b) file with the company, within 91 days after loss, his sworn proof of loss in such form and including such information as the company may reasonably require and shall, upon the company's request, exhibit the damaged property and submit to examination under oath.

Payment of Loss

The company may pay for the loss in money; or may repair or replace the damaged or stolen property; or may, at any time before the loss is paid or the property is so replaced, at its expense return any stolen property to the named insured, or at its option to the address shown in the declarations, with payment for any resultant damage thereto; or may take all or such part of the property at the agreed or appraised value but there shall be no abandonment to the company. The company may settle any claim for loss either with the insured or the owner of the property.

No Benefit to Bailee

The insurance afforded by this policy shall not inure directly or indirectly to the benefit of any carrier or other bailee for hire liable for loss to the automobile.

While the wording of many conditions and provisions of the automobile policy is not identical to that in insurance policies covering real and other personal property, as discussed in earlier chapters, in tenor they are much alike. It is recommended that the claim representative review Chapter 3.

Coverages

Collision. The policy covers, in excess of any deductible, damage caused by collision to the owned or nonowned automobile. *Collision* is defined as:

Collision of an automobile covered by this policy with another object or with a vehicle to which it is attached or by upset of such automobile.

Most companies waive deductibles when the collision involves another automobile covered in the *same* company.

Comprehensive (Excluding Collision). This is an all risks of physical loss coverage, with a few exclusions, including collisions, to owned and nonowned automobiles.

Breakage of glass and loss caused by missiles, falling objects, fire, theft or larceny, explosion, earthquake, windstorm, hail, water, flood, malicious mischief or vandalism, riot or civil commotion, or colliding with a bird or animal, shall not be deemed to be loss caused by collision.

Personal Effects. Personal effects of the named insured or a relative, damaged by the perils of fire or lightning while in or upon the owned automobile, are covered. This includes apparel and other personal effects.

Supplemental Payments. The FAP will reimburse the *insured* for transportation expenses incurred during a period *beginning* 48 hours after a covered theft of the entire automobile is reported to the Company *and the police*, and *ending* (1) when it is returned to use or (2) when the Company pays the loss.

The limit per day of expenses is $10, and the aggregate limit is $300 but may be increased by endorsement.

General average and salvage charges the insured is legally liable for, as to the automobile being transported, are also covered.

Towing and Labor Costs. Towing and labor costs necessitated by the disablement of the owned or of any nonowned automobile are covered provided the labor is performed at the place of disablement.

Exclusions

This policy does not apply under Part III:

(a) to any automobile while used as a public or livery conveyance;

(b) to loss due to war;

(c) to loss to a non-owned automobile arising out of its use by the insured while he is employed or otherwise engaged in the automobile business;

(d) to loss to a private passenger, farm or utility automobile or trailer owned by the named insured and not described in this policy or to any temporary substitute automobile therefor, if the insured has other valid and collectible insurance against such loss;

(e) to damage which is due and confined to wear and tear, freezing, mechanical or electrical breakdown or failure, unless such damage results from a theft covered by this policy;

(f) to tires, unless damaged by fire, malicious mischief or vandalism, or stolen or unless the loss be coincident with and from the same cause as other loss covered by this policy;

(g) to loss due to radioactive contamination;

(h) under coverage D, to breakage of glass if insurance with respect to such breakage is otherwise afforded.

INVESTIGATION

Unfair Claim-Handling Practices

Claim representatives should review Chapter 2 on this subject and should have in their possession, or be familiar with, legislation enacted in the state in which they are doing business. Regulatory provisions in some state statutes are quite rigorous, and companies and their representatives who are in violation may be subject to severe penalties.

Waiver and Estoppel

This subject is discussed in Chapter 7. The claim representative should review these two kindred doctrines.[2]

There are a number of circumstances under which an owned or a nonowned automobile may sustain a loss for which there is no liability. The claim representative must be on guard so as not to extinguish any right the insurer may have otherwise possessed. To avoid committing the insurer to a claim which might under other circumstances be declined, the coverages and the exclusions should be committed to memory or kept available for frequent reference purposes.

Examples of situations that might give rise to doubt as to liability under the policy include the following, although each insurer may have its own interpretation.

1. An automobile being used as a school bus consistently and making a fare charge.
2. Damage caused by mechanical breakdown, such as a defective hood latch allowing the hood to fly back violently and break the windshield.
3. The age of the driver falsified.
4. Owned automobile being driven by a garage mechanic while looking for parts to make repairs.
5. Insured's child using car to commit a felony.
6. Owned automobile being driven by named insured's friend while visiting for the day and without named insured's permission.

Verification of Coverage

When a claim is assigned, verifying coverage should be standard procedure as one of the first steps in the investigation and before any action is taken that might inadvertently commit the insurer to a loss for which it is not liable or for which there is no coverage. The original policy, a daily report, or a copy of the policy and its endorsements should be reviewed. Details[3] of the investigation of the insurance coverage are discussed at length in Chapter 7.

Identification of Vehicle

The vehicle for which damage is claimed must be identified as an owned vehicle described in the policy or as a nonowned vehicle covered under the policy. Identification should include the VIN (vehicle identification number), which supplies serial number, make, model, year, body style, engine identification, etc.

The VIN on automobiles 1968 or later is located at the lower left-hand corner of the windshield and can be read from the exterior of the vehicle.

A full explanation is required if the involved vehicle is not owned or one recently acquired by the insured.

Interviewing Insured

When interviewing the insured, the claim representative should establish the existence of any liens, mortgages, or other encumbrances. Those not shown in the policy should be checked with the lienholder for *other insurance* and the amount of lien. A brief history of the vehicle is desirable, such as when and from whom purchased, cost and method of payment, and whether new or used. While the insured is being interviewed, the facts concerning the accident or loss should be obtained.[4]

Facts of the Loss Occurrence

On any but very minor claims, a written statement from the insured is advisable while events still are fresh in mind. The statement should be signed by the insured and witnessed by the claim representative. It should contain only factual information, avoiding opinions and conclusions insofar as it is possible.[5]

Collision or Upset. Generally, if the loss resulted from collision or upset, most of the following facts should be thoroughly uncovered by the claim representative.

1. Kind of loss.
2. Property involved.
3. Date, time, and place of accident.

---

[2]See pp. 80–82.
[3]See pp. 92–97.

[4]See pp. 83–86.
[5]See pp. 84–85.

4. Driver of insured's vehicle—name, address, age, employment, and driving experience.
5. Point of departure and destination of vehicle.
6. Weather and road conditions.
7. Traffic conditions.
8. Traffic lights or signs at location.
9. Speed of insured's vehicle.
10. Description of other vehicle if involved.
11. Driver of other vehicle, name, age, address, employment, and driving experience.
12. Speed of other vehicle if known—or approximate.
13. Point of impact of vehicles; all objects struck, and coming-to-rest position.
14. Photographs.
15. Report of local or state police.
16. Any arrests or summons served.
17. Diagram of accident.
18. Names, addresses of witnesses.
19. Any facts that indicate subrogation possibilities against a third party or against the insured.
20. If towed from scene, by whom and by what authority.
21. Present location of damaged vehicle.
22. Location and description of all resultant damage and all prior damage.

Total Theft Losses. In handling total theft losses it is assumed that the claim representative has *verified coverage* and *identified the insured and the vehicle*. Total thefts may be *recovered* or *unrecovered*. While a written statement is being taken from the insured and any others who have knowledge of the theft, the following information should be obtained.

1. Identify the insured or the person who had custody of the vehicle just prior to the theft.
   a. Name, age, residence, and occupation.
   b. Was car being used with insured's permission?
   c. For what purpose?
2. Exact location where theft occurred.
3. Give full physical description of vehicle as to color, dents, missing parts, broken glass, paint and tire condition. Such data will be helpful to the police and the National Automobile Theft Bureau.
4. Obtain full details of events leading up to the theft and after.
5. When were police notified? By whom, where, by phone or in person? Name of officer?
6. Does insured intend making claim under Supplemental Payments section of the FAP, or under Loss of Use by Theft-Rental Reimbursement of the SAP? Inform insured of the availability of this coverage.

The *National Automobile Theft Bureau*, a voluntary, unincorporated, nonprofit association, has for one of its objectives the investigation of suspicious fire, theft, and fraud vehicle losses. The Bureau maintains a computerized stolen-vehicle file for North America thefts. The Bureau's Operational Manual is available to all member companies as are the numerous forms used. If the insurer is a member of the NATB, it is recommended that the Bureau's Form 200 be sent as soon as practicable to the nearest office of NATB. A questionnaire sent the insured by one insurer, Affidavit of Vehicle Theft (Appendix F), also provides an opportunity, via the U.S. Postal Service, to bring in a federal agency in a fraud case.

Suspicious Fire Losses to Vehicles. If what the claim representative finds during the investigation of a vehicle fire shows it to be legitimate, all that remains, as a rule, is to evaluate the damage. But if what is learned indicates possible incendiarism, there is usually much more investigating to be done. It is recommended that Chapter 10, "Arson Investigation and Detection," be reviewed in its entirety, with special attention to Did Insured Have a Motive?, Burden of Proof, Protecting the Investigation, Preservation of Evidence, and Analysis of Proof of Arson Requirements in Selected States.

Verification of coverage and identification of the vehicle is presumed to have been made by the claim representative. If the insurer is a member, the NATB should be notified as soon as possible.

Since the claim representative is usually one of the earliest on the scene, the NATB recommends the following steps to preserve evidence for consideration by the police, fire marshal, NATB agent, or other professional investigators later on.

1. Photograph the remains of the vehicle, and locate it with respect to landmarks such as roads, intersections, houses, street lamps, etc. Describe the terrain and make a sketch.
2. Search the area for glass or metal containers that may have contained flammables. Look for spare tires, tools, and other accessories the owner may have hidden to pick up later.
3. Check for footprints or related signs. Locate tire marks of the burned vehicle and *other automobiles.* Someone may have picked the owner up after the burning.
4. Preserve any containers, gas caps, siphon hose, burned matches, and other physical evidence. Avoid obliterating fingerprints. Label all items showing time, date, and location where found.
5. Soil samples from beneath the vehicle and wheels should be placed in airtight containers for laboratory tests to reveal any flammable liquids.
6. Contact witnesses in the area to fix the time and date of the fire. Get their story in detail as to whom they saw, other cars, what part of car was first seen burning, color of smoke, attempts to extinguish fire, etc.
7. If the salvage was removed before the arrival of the claim representative, interview the wrecker driver as to conditions found.
8. Interview any law enforcement official who may have made an investigation.
9. Check with fire department and police records.

To qualify for a NATB special investigation, the member insurer's investigation should reveal at least one of the following:

1. Evidence of serious mechanical failure of the automobile prior to the fire.
2. Discrepancies in statements between the insured and witnesses.

3. Previous automobile fire loss suffered by the insured.[6]

The insured, the driver, and any witnesses to the fire should be interviewed and their written statements taken. The manner of the person taking the statements or the type of questions asked should not arouse suspicion that the fire is believed of incendiary origin. The insured or the driver should be asked questions as to places visited; destination at the time of fire; where and when fire was first discovered; and what effort was made to extinguish it. How did the insured or driver get home after the fire, and who was notified?

Windstorm, Hail, and Flood Losses. These losses are covered under the Comprehensive portion of the policy. Generally, once coverage has been established and the occurrence verified, the major concern of the claim representative is evaluating the damage.

EVALUATION OF DAMAGE TO VEHICLES

Estimating the cost to repair damage to an automobile involves the four basic elements for estimating all property damage, i.e., *labor, material, overhead, and profit.* Garages and body shops generally lump labor, overhead, and profit together. The starting point is wages, to which overhead and profit, as much as 100 percent, is added. The sum total becomes an *hourly rate.* As in any business, pricing structures vary depending on the competition in the particular area.

Material charges will vary according to whether the parts are new or used, the latter being known as *LKQ parts,* and whether the parts are interchangeable. This is an important consideration because the policy stipulates *like kind and quality.* Some makes of cars, manufactured by the large companies, have a number of common body parts interchangeable from one make to another.

---

[6]NATB Manual for the Investigation of Automobile Fires.

Individual Insurer's Procedure

Estimates are prepared by a garage or body shop, an employee of the insurer (staff appraiser), or an independent appraiser who is paid for each estimate. The procedure for obtaining estimates and deciding who will make them is a matter of the individual insurer's procedural practice. Some use a *fast-track* or *telephone adjustment* method to process small claims. They will accept an estimate from a single source subject to verification of labor and material charges on claims of up to $100 or $150. On claims ranging from $150 to $300, a staff appraisal is accepted, or estimates from two other sources will be accepted and the loss paid on the lower one subject to review and analysis of both estimates. Where damage appears greater than $300, a staff appraiser or an independent appraiser may be assigned. Each insurer establishes its own categories of size of loss and procedure for handling.

Checking Estimates

Field claim representatives, when they are *assigned* to a vehicle loss, generally are charged with the responsibility of reviewing and checking estimates regardless of who made them. It is presumed they have been introduced to and are familiar with Flat-Rate Manuals (Crash Books). These manuals contain parts, prices, and hours of labor for operation (also Parts and Labor Manual).

The parts prices are actual factory releases and are the prices to be charged to the customer. Labor time shown has been established under actual average shop conditions, and the operations include the necessary steps to perform required work.

Replacement Panels. A replacement panel may be a *full panel*, a *partial panel*, or it may be a *partial repair patch*. Of the three, only the full panel is a factory item; the other two are products of outside manufacturers.

Overlap and Included Operations. *Overlap* is the full flat-rate labor allowance of two closely associated operations when, as a practical matter, the labor incident to one operation materially decreases the amount of labor necessary to perform the second operation. Whether intentional or not, the possibility of overlap charges appearing in an estimate is considerable.

An example of overlap would be for the removal and replacement of a Ford fuel tank. The flat-rate time is 1.2 hours. This rate assumes that this is the only damage and *all* operations necessary to remove and replace the tank are included in the rate. This is true in every *remove and replace* rate in the Flat-Rate Manual. If the frame of the automobile, in this illustration, was also damaged, the fuel tank would have to be removed and replaced regardless of the damage to it. Thus, this operation is included in the flat-rate time of 30 hours to remove and replace the frame, and hence, an additional labor charge of 1.2 hours is overlap.

An example of *included operations* would be removing a fender. Other components (headlights, trim, etc.) have to be removed and replaced. No additional labor is warranted as it is an included operation in the Flat-Rate or Parts and Labor Manuals.

Partial Losses

Check specifications, i.e., what work has to be done.

1. Can the part be repaired rather than replaced?
   a. Exterior metal parts.
      (1) Roughing.
      (2) Aligning.
      (3) Bumping.
      (4) Metal finishing.
      (5) Welding and brazing.
      (6) Can LKQ parts or rebuilt parts be used?
   b. Fiberglass.
      (1) Repairable by competent artisan?
      (2) Replace part or all of section.
      (3) Consider fiberglass boat repair firm.
   c. Painting.
      (1) Will spot painting or blending do the job?
      (2) Will painting a panel or other section match?

(3) Will putty or plastic filler fill the low spots?

(4) Complete paint versus depreciation?

d. Frame damage.

(1) Can it be straightened in a frame machine if a sag, sway, or diamond?

(2) Can damage be cut out, new put in, and welded?

(3) Can weakened welds be opened and rewelded?

e. Windshields—when to replace.

(1) When the glass on either side of the sandwich is shattered or cracked.

(2) When there is a star break through the glass and there are radiating cracks.

(3) When windblown sand reduces vision.

(4) When small fractures are in a critical area (the area cleaned by the normal sweep of the wiper blades—not the return position).

f. Windshields—when not to replace.

(1) When small cracks are in noncritical area.

(2) When damage due to improper mounting is covered under new-car warranty.

(3) When damage is obviously old and done prior to policy effective date. Old cracks show discoloration as a rule.

g. Fabric roof covers.

(1) Can minor dents in roof be bumped out without removing vinyl cover?

(2) If necessary to straighten roof panel only, can vinyl cover be partially or fully removed and replaced?

(3) Is roof vinyl or simulated by special paint?

(4) Can little bubbles, tears, and wrinkles be repaired?

h. Items usually not repairable.

(1) Safety items, if damaged, must be replaced (steering, front suspension, and brake systems).

(2) Plastic parts.

(3) Tires.

(4) Chrome parts.

(5) White metal.

(6) Cast or forged parts.

2. Is operation necessary as a result of occurrence?

a. Are repairs to *old damage* included?

b. Does damage seen in photographs track with specifications?

c. Do the specifications include items of repair unrelated to the damage as related by eyewitnesses, police reports, etc., such as wheel alignment, balancing tires, transmission, engine work?

3. Is there apparent overlapping of repairs?

Total Losses

Total losses to insured vehicles fall into three categories: (1) the obvious total loss by collision, fire, flood, or some other peril insured against, (2) the constructive total loss in which repairs plus salvage exceed ACV, and (3) loss by theft and the whereabouts unknown to the named insured.

Most automobile coverages are written with the limit of liability being the *actual cash value*. Literally, this means what the vehicle is worth in cash, or the amount of money it would take to obtain a replacement automobile of like kind and quality and in the same physical condition at the time and place of the loss.

Comparative Method. The usual and most practical approach for evaluating a total loss is the *comparative method*. The principle behind this method is to establish as nearly as possible the value of an automobile of the same make, model, and year, with the same equipment and in the same condition in every way as the one on which total loss is claimed. The following are some of the information the claim representative should ascertain by personal inspection if vehicle is available, by talking to the named insured or others familiar with the automobile, by examining photographs the insured may offer, and from an appraiser's report if one has been made.

1. Make of vehicle, year, model, and body style.
2. Engine—number of cylinders, size and condition.
3. Transmission type; power brakes, steering, windows, seats.
4. Radio, heater, air conditioning.
5. Mileage.
6. General all-round mechanical condition.
7. Condition of paint, glass, roof, and upholstery.
8. Body condition, dents, scratches, any old damage.
9. Tires, type, premium, first line, recaps, etc.
10. Special equipment, e.g., CB radio, cassette stereo player, telephone, etc.

Possessing the foregoing information, the claim representative should be able to approximate the actual cash value of the insured's vehicle as it existed at the time and place of the loss. Three sources can be used.

1. *Guide Books.* Depending on the name of the Guide Book, each make and model automobile usually will have two prices. They are either "wholesale" and "retail," or "high" and "low" books. Guide Books are only a guide. Settlement of a loss is seldom concluded solely on the basis of the figures in these books. Additions or subtractions have to be made depending on whether the "total loss" vehicle was in better condition or not as good a condition as the vehicle listed in the "the book," and on whether it had more or less equipment.
2. *Dealer Quotations.* Claim representatives should keep a list of reliable dealers in both new and used cars, including addresses, telephone numbers, and names of *sales managers* inasmuch as all dealings are best done with them. These sales managers are usually glad to make quotations as it provides possibilities of a sale. The specifications of the car (including its condition and equipment) you are attempting to locate should be furnished the sales manager with the authority of the insured.

If possible, two or three used car dealers should be visited or called. On each quotation the equipment, mileage, and condition of the vehicle should be compared with the total-loss vehicle. As with Guide Book values, additions and subtractions should be made for better or poorer condition of the total-loss vehicle and for more or less equipment.

3. *Newspaper Ads.* Classified advertising will be found helpful in locating comparable vehicles. The ads to be looked for are those of private individuals, not dealers. If a similar vehicle is advertised, the claim representative can make inquiry by phone as to the (a) equipment and condition of vehicle, (b) bottom price, and (c) location of vehicle.

If the vehicle sounds comparable to the total loss vehicle, arrangements can be made to inspect it or have an appraiser make an inspection.

State regulation (Unfair Claim Settlement Practices): Where state statutes or insurance department ruling requires that total loss evaluation be done in a prescribed manner, insurers follow those requirements.

Sales taxes: Applicable laws pertaining to the adding of sales tax to total loss settlements should be checked.

Current-Year Method. Some insurers, seeking a fair method for evaluating total-loss vehicles that are of current-year purchase (frequently only a few months old), have developed depreciation formulas when no value is listed in the Guide Books. These formulas are usually based on the dealer's itemized invoice, including optional equipment, and receipts for subsequently installed equipment; an appraiser's report, or statements of new car sales managers with whom a "price" has been negotiated without commitment. From one or the other of these a depreciation rate per mile of use is deducted. For example, one insurer estimates the first-year depreciation at 24 percent and an average mileage of 15,000 miles. The depreciation rate per mile is $24 \div 15,000 = .0016$. This factor multiplied by the agreed replacement cost gives the *cents* depreciation per mile. If a car had 4,000 miles at the time of loss and the agreed replacement cost was $6,000, the depreciation to be deducted would be .0016 × $6000 × 4000 = $384.

NONWAIVER AGREEMENT

Guarding against waiver or estoppel is discussed in Chapter 7 and applies to the investigation of all property losses.[7]

AUTHORIZATION TO REPAIR

Most losses are partial, and after an agreed cost of repair is reached, the repairer will need verbal or written authorization to make the repairs. Such authorization is obtained from the insured or his or her legal representative. To confirm that the insured gave

[7]See p. 80. See also Appendix L.

instructions to make repairs a form similar to the one illustrated may be used but only when the insured is willing to have the repairs made by the shop that made the estimate on which the loss was agreed. Claim representatives should be cautioned not to recommend a specific repair firm, unless requested by insured under a state statute.

SUBROGATION

The general principles of subrogation set forth in Chapter 9 are equally applicable to automobile physical damage losses. Special attention should be given to such matters as:

1. A volunteer payee has no right of subrogation.
2. How the release of a tort feasor prior to a loss and subsequent to a loss affects the rights of the insured and the insurer.

AUTHORIZATION TO REPAIR

Claim File 23-455

To _____ Parkway Auto Repair Company _____ Date April 7, 1977

Address _____ 203 Henry Street East

City Chicago _____ State Illinois

You are authorized to repair my:

1976	Chevrolet	C55 001514	00122 554
Year	Make	Identification No.	Motor No.

on the basis of your estimate of the cost of repairs or replacements.

It is understood by the undersigned that in carrying out these instructions you are acting solely for the undersigned and not for the insurance company, or for any of its representatives.

_____ Jack Perl _____ Signed _____ Marie W. Winter _____
Witness   Owner

3. Notification to the wrongdoer.
4. Use of subrogation and loan agreements.
5. Use of attorneys.
6. Reporting to the insurer.

The key to successful subrogation, where one or more vehicles are involved, rests with the claim representative's early investigation and obtaining of the facts of the occurrence.[8] Not infrequently, where liability is clear, the insurer of the other vehicle(s) will come forward and make full payment. In other situations the claim representative will have to seek out the driver and occupants of the other vehicle(s), take statements, interview witnesses, check police reports, and talk to the claim representative(s) of the other insurers. Such claim representatives should be invited to inspect the damaged vehicle prior to having repairs made to avoid later allegations that the repair cost is excessive.

Generally an individual insurer's procedure for handling subrogation cases is clearly established and should be followed. Most reputable insurers frown on the dumping of questionable or partially investigated subrogations claims on lawyers with the hope of *getting something out of the case.*

NATIONWIDE INTERCOMPANY ARBITRATION AGREEMENT

This agreement, signed by most insurers of automobile physical damage, applies to any physical damage and plate glass damage subrogation claims not in excess of $2,500. There is also a provision for arbitration of any controversy as to policy coverage and interpretation, or any claim involving an amount in excess of $2,500, *if the parties give prior consent.* This and certain special arbitration agreements are too detailed and extensive for reproduction here. They are available from most insurers.

SALVAGE

As respects insured vehicles that have been damaged, salvage is the remaining value. Salvage of vehicles generally falls into one of three categories.

[8]See pp. 127–131.

1. Rebuilding Value. Frequently the cost of repairing a vehicle exceeds its actual cash value. The insured is paid the value and the insurer disposes of the remains. There are many individuals operating garages, service stations, or body shops who pay a fair price for a constructive total loss. Then in their spare time they repair the vehicle with used parts or interchangeable parts, eventually restoring it to sell at a profit. Many are on the lookout for certain makes, models, and years of vehicle.

2. Parts Value. Many total-loss vehicles are put into yards and their parts sold. Many of these yards are well organized and the owners belong to associations covering many states. These associations communicate by wire service and provide spare parts to each other for sale to customers.

3. Junk Value. The third classification of salvage is, as its name implies, pure junk not even worth parts, except perhaps tires, battery, and a radio or cassette player. The balance is cut up and crushed, or the metal is ground up into a granulated composite.

Methods of Selling Salvage

As with other procedures in the handling of automobile physical damage losses, the claim representative's actions in disposing of salvage are strictly subject to the individual insurer's instructions. There are a number of methods by which salvage is sold, of which the following four are most common.

1. Salvage Disposal Pools. Independently owned firms which tow in damaged vehicles and exhibit them for sale in a protected area. Bid forms are obtained at the pool by potential buyers. A set fee is charged for this service in addition to a towing charge to bring the vehicle to the pool. These firms normally pay outstanding towing and storage charges when they pick the vehicle up, adding these to their invoice.

2. Auction-Type Sale. A variation of the salvage disposal pool with the vehicle being auctioned off to the highest bidder at the time of sale. Sales are held on a regularly scheduled basis. The company reserves the right to reject any and all bids. This type of disposal requires attendance by a company representative.

3. Contract Salvage Sale. The sale of vehicles to one specified buyer in an area via a written contract. Recovered thefts with little or no damage are usually excluded from the contract. Contracts are based on a percentage of the actual "pre-accident" value of the vehicle.

4. Sale by Sealed Bid. By this method bid cards are sent to buyers who are advised of the identity and location of the vehicle. Sale is to the highest bidder.

Salvage Left With the Insured

The claim representative is cautioned when leaving salvage with the insured to put the insured on notice that the vehicle is subject to any lien or mortgage that may exist, and that title and ownership remain with the insured.

Any lienholder should also be notified so as to protect any existing interest.

Title and Registration

It is important that a clear title is available for the buyer of the salvage. Title should not pass to the buyer until a certified check is received. Verification of registration is of special importance in some states. A "salvage title" should be obtained prior to exhibiting the salvage for sale.

Odometer (Mileage) Statement Laws (Federal Law 15, VSCS, Sections 1981-1991)

Under this law it is illegal for anyone to tamper with an odometer in a car for the purpose of showing less than the actual mileage. Also, it is required that the owner of a car furnish the buyer of the car an odometer (mileage) statement (see Appendix F).

If an odometer is repaired or replaced, and the resulting mileage shown is not accurate, written notice must be attached to the left door frame of the vehicle by the owner or his agent. The notice must show the actual mileage at the time of repair or replacement and the date of such repair or replacement. The odometer must be adjusted to zero.

PROOF OF LOSS

See Appendix C, Statement in Proof of Loss, Including Subrogation and Satisfaction Agreements.

REPORTS TO INSURERS

Chapter 28 discusses in considerable detail the structure of reports to insurers. Automobile physical damage reports would follow the same general format.

Many insurers prefer short, handwritten reports on routine, uncomplicated losses. Where the loss involves a substantial amount of money or is complicated as to cause, subrogation, or policy coverage, *topical headings* are more desirable. The following guide is suggested.

1. Coverage.
   a. Type of policy, endorsements, deductible.
   b. Liens or mortgages.
   c. Agency.
2. Insured and/or owner.
   a. Identify by name, sex, age, driving experience.
   b. Address.
   c. Employment.
3. Identity and description of vehicle.
   a. License No., State, VIN.
   b. Description as to make, model, body style, color, etc.
4. Facts of accident.
   a. Time, date, location, weather conditions.
   b. Driver's name, address, phone number, age, employment.
   c. Witnesses.
   d. Other vehicle, occupants, driver, etc.
   e. Diagram, photos, statements.
   f. Police reports.
5. Loss evaluation, settlement.
   a. Estimates, appraisals, loss of use, salvage, towing, rental, storage.
   b. Basis of settlement, depreciation, etc.

6. Subrogation—tort, contract, or warranty.
   a. Disposition or recommendation.
7. What remains to be done.

QUESTIONS AND PROBLEMS

1. Under a Family Automobile Policy (FAP) with respect to an owned automobile, the son of the named insured tells a neighbor friend to drive the family car to town and get some parts he needs to fix a motorcycle he is working on. The friend is a hot-rodder, and en route to town he is involved in an accident. He is given a ticket for reckless driving. Damage to the other car is $500. The damage to the insured's car is $1,000. Will the insured's FAP cover the damage to either automobile? Explain your answer.

2. Company cars are furnished to salespersons of a large organization. They use the cars for business purposes primarily. The car is kept garaged at the employee's home nights and weekends if not in use. The company services the cars and furnishes gasoline and oil. One employee also has a personal automobile which is covered by a Family Automobile Policy (FAP). On a weekend pleasure trip with the family, the employee uses the company car, which is not prohibited, and runs into a tree damaging the car to the extent of $500. Will the employee's FAP pay for the damage to the company car?

3. There are three limits of liability for physical damage coverage under an automobile policy, the lowest of which is the maximum amount the policy will pay. What are they?

4. The insured, under a Family Automobile Policy, runs into a tree alongside a country road. Damage is slight but the car cannot be driven. The insured leaves the car and hitches a ride home. The next day he reports it to the insurer who sends a claim representative to meet the insured at the scene. During the night the car has been stripped of tires, radio, battery, and other parts. Discuss coverage under FAP.

5. An insured, driving on a back road one dark night, collides with a cow causing damage to the car. Would the damage be covered under the collision portion of FAP or under the comprehensive? Explain your answer.

6. What does VIN stand for? Where would you look for it on an automobile?

7. A collision involving your insured's automobile and a truck is reported. As claim supervisor for the insurer, you send a trainee claim representative to make an investigation and obtain the facts. State at least ten points of information or actions you would instruct your representative to cover in addition to date, time and place of accident, and photographs.

8. You are taking a written statement from the insured who has reported an unrecovered stolen car under an FAP policy. Briefly outline the information that you would want to include in the statement.

9. Flat-Rate Manuals, Parts and Labor Manuals, etc., contain parts, prices, and hours of labor for various operations. In application of these manuals, what do we mean by overlap? Give at least one example of overlap.

10. What is the underlying principle of the comparative method for evaluating total losses to automobiles?

11. If a total-loss vehicle is available for inspection, outline in general the data you would note from the inspection and from interviewing the insured in order to develop a value by the comparative method.

12. There are three sources used to develop a value by the comparative method. What are they?

13. Some insurers use a current-year method to evaluate total losses when the particular vehicle has not yet been listed in a Guide Book and the vehicle is only a few months old and has a low mileage on the odometer. Explain the method briefly.

14. The Nationwide Inter-Company Arbitration Agreement applies to what situations?

24

Floods, Mudslides, and FAIR Plans

The flooding of homes and business establishments takes place when rivers, streams, and creeks overflow their normal banks following heavy rains or spring thaws. The water may rise gradually, giving the exposed property owners warning, or sudden cloudbursts may cause flash flooding with no advance warning.

Dams, large and small, have a history of many failures for various reasons, causing the flooding of lowlands, frequently with little or no warning. The cost in lives and property over the years became so alarming that in 1966 Congress passed a bill ordering the Army Corps of Engineers to inspect every dam in the country and report to Congress within two years on the results and submit safety recommendations.

Coastal areas, particularly along the Atlantic and Gulf coasts, are subject to inundation in hurricane seasons. The flooding may occur gradually as tide-waters reach several feet above normal, or where heavy wave action and high water lash a shoreline, undermining foundations, battering walls, and not infrequently leaving no trace of the building(s).

NATIONAL FLOOD INSURANCE ASSOCIATION (NFIA)

For many years Congress periodically gave consideration to a national flood insurance plan, usually with greater concern following a year of serious flood damage in various parts of the country. The U.S. Department

of Housing and Urban Development (HUD) undertook a study for a national flood insurance program in 1966 and, working with members of the insurance industry, developed a plan for limited flood coverage. The National Flood Insurance Program is designed to provide federally subsidized flood insurance to property owners in flood areas, mudslide areas, or flood-related erosion-prone areas. In return for the availability of flood insurance, communities must adopt and administer flood-plain-management regulations that protect new construction from future flooding. These prerequisites have to do with a community establishing measures to minimize damage from flooding. Such communities must cite their legal authority to regulate land use; summarize codes, ordinances, or regulations already taken to reduce property damage; submit maps outlining areas that are flood-prone; provide a history of floods in the area; report on steps taken to control floods; and show that measures have been taken to regulate new construction through building permits, subdivision regulations, and location restrictions.

The program is administered by the National Flood Insurance Association (NFIA) whose members include qualified private insurance companies licensed to write property insurance under the laws of any state and formed specifically to provide flood insurance. One insurer is appointed as a servicing company, usually on a statewide basis, to disseminate information to the public, appoint qualified adjusters, and supervise and process the adjustment of claims for loss payments.

An Emergency Flood Program amendment in 1970 enabled property owners to obtain *limited* flood insurance in communities for which no actuarial rate had yet been determined. To participate, the communities are required to have a land-use-and-control authority. The emergency program originally was for two years but was extended until 1976. It gives a community time to develop and put into effect the prerequisites of the FIA (Federal Insurance Administration) and during that period to enjoy some protection. Maximum rates and coverage depend on whether the community qualifies for the *regular* or the *emergency* program.

NFIA INSURANCE POLICIES

There are two NFIA flood insurance policies covering property.

1. Dwelling Building and Contents Form.
2. General Property Form.

The first covers residential buildings of one to four families, and the contents of such residences. The second covers the buildings and contents of properties occupied for commercial, manufacturing, or farming purposes.

The two forms are identical in most respects with the exception of "Property Covered" and "Property Not Covered"; a Loss Payable Clause applicable to the contents item in the General Property Form; and the Replacement Cost Provisions[1] for a Single Family Dwelling Structure under the Dwelling Building and Contents Form.

The policies are complete when they have attached to them the Applications and Declarations. The General Conditions and Provisions follow closely those of the 1943 New York Standard Fire Policy and also include Pair and Set, Property of Others, Alterations and Repairs, and Liberalization clauses. Careful attention should be paid to the

Other Insurance clause as it relates to "Excess" insurance.

There is a Statutory Provisions clause which reads as follows:

Statutory Provisions—Any terms of this policy which are in conflict with the statutes of the State wherein the property is located are hereby amended to conform to such statutes, except that in cases of conflict with applicable Federal law or regulation, such Federal law or regulation shall control the terms of this policy.

Claim representatives should be familiar with these various conditions and provisions which are examined in Chapter 3.

Insuring Clause Under NFIA policies

The insuring clause in the two flood forms is identical. It also is patterned after the New York Standard Fire Policy insuring clause with a significant difference. *These flood forms do not cover the peril of removal.* They do cover pro rata for 30 days at proper locations to which property shall necessarily be *removed* to protect it. Most property insurance policies include the *direct loss by removal of the property covered from the premises endangered by the perils insured against.* Although the NFIA policies exclude loss resulting from neglect of the insured to use reasonable means to save and preserve the property *at the time and after* the occurrence of the flood, they do not specifically cover loss to the property *occasioned* by its removal. Also, the policy is silent as to who will bear the expense incurred to remove property endangered if done by the insured to avoid the charge of neglect.

Definition of *Flood*

The NFIA policies define *flood* in the following terms:

Wherever in this policy the term "flood" occurs, it shall be held to mean
A. A general and temporary condition of partial or complete inundation of normally dry land areas from:
1. The overflow of inland or tidal waters.

---

[1] Neither policy contains a coinsurance clause.

2. The unusual and rapid accumulation or runoff of surface waters from any source.
3. Mudslides (i.e., mudflows) which are proximately caused or precipitated by accumulations of water on or under the ground.

B. The collapse or subsidence of land along the shore of a lake or other body of water as a result of erosion or undermining caused by waves or currents of water exceeding the cyclical levels which result in flooding as defined in A-1 above.

An amendment in 1969 added A-3, mudslides, i.e., mudflows which occur when soil combined with water from above or below ground forms a plasticized flowing mass capable of causing damage to buildings and contents in the path. Another amendment was added in 1973 to include B in the definition.

Perils Excluded

As in all property insurance contracts, the peril or *perils covered* must be read in conjunction with *perils not covered*. The NFIA policies are quite explicit in Perils Excluded as shown below:

This Company shall not be be liable for loss:
A. By (1) rain, snow, sleet, hail or water spray; (2) freezing, thawing or by the pressure or weight of ice or water, except where the property covered has been simultaneously damaged by flood; or (3) water, moisture or mudslide damage of any kind resulting primarily from conditions, causes or occurrences which are solely related to the described premises or are within the control of the insured (including but not limited to design, structural or mechanical defects, failures, stoppages or breakages of water or sewer lines, drains, pumps, fixtures or equipment, seepage or backup of water, or hydrostatic pressure) or any condition which causes flooding which is substantially confined to the described premises or properties immediately adjacent thereto;
B. Caused directly or indirectly by (1) hostile or warlike action in time of peace or war, including action in hindering, combating or defending against an actual, impending or expected attack, (a) by any government or sovereign power (de jure or de facto), or by any authority maintaining or using military, naval or air forces, or (b) by military, naval or air forces, or (c) by an agent of any such government, power, authority or forces, it being understood that any discharge, explosion or use of any weapon of war employing nuclear fission or fusion shall be conclusively presumed to be such a hostile or warlike action by such a government, power, authority or forces; (2) insurrection, rebellion, revolution, civil war, usurped power, or action taken by governmental authority in hindering, combating or defending against such an occurrence;
C. By nuclear reaction or nuclear radiation or radioactive contamination, all whether controlled or uncontrolled, or due to any act or condition incident to any of the foregoing, whether such loss be direct or indirect, proximate or remote, or be in whole or in part caused by, contributed to, or aggravated by the peril insured against by this policy;
D. By theft or by fire, windstorm, explosion, earthquake, landslide or any other earth movement except such mudslide or erosion as is covered under the peril of flood;
E. Caused by or resulting from power, heating or cooling failure, unless such failure results from physical damage to power, heating or cooling equipment situated on premises where the property covered is located, caused by the peril insured against;
F. Occasioned directly or indirectly by enforcement of any local or state ordinance or law regulating the construction, repair or demolition of building(s) or structure(s);
G. Caused directly or indirectly by neglect of the Insured to use all reasonable means to save and preserve the property at the time of and after an occurrence of the peril insured against by this policy.

A few comments with respect to some of these excluded perils may be helpful.

The exclusion of loss under peril C applies whether or not the peril of flood, as defined, is in any way responsible for the loss, either causing, contributing to or aggravating it.

Under D, theft would include looting at the time of and after the flood, as defined. Loss caused by fire or explosion, though set in motion by flood, as defined, would not be covered. While loss by earthquake is excluded, if the earthquake ruptured a dam, damage by a resultant flooding would be covered. Loss by windstorm is not covered, but where wind causes high waves on bodies of water, or wind raises tidewaters and flooding results, that loss by flood is covered.

Under E, for such loss to be covered the equipment damaged by flood must be situated on the premises where the property is located.

As has been previously stated, the NFIA policies do not include the peril of *removal* found in most property and standard fire insurance policies. Under G, the insured has an obligation to use all reasonable means to save and preserve the property at the time of, and after, the occurrence.

The danger of our larger rivers reaching flood stage often increases at points downriver as the runoff water from large areas upriver accumulate. The runoff may be from heavy rains over a long period or from spring thaws. Authorities maintain constant watch, take precautionary steps, such as sandbagging, opening dams and floodgates, and keeping the public informed hourly. Storekeepers in the communities that are threatened, particularly those with basement sales and stockroom areas, and especially if no insurance is carried, move stocks and often fixtures and equipment to higher levels. Whether they move them from basement to first floor, to second floor, or to other buildings for safety, is contingent on the seriousness of the flood threat (i.e., the probable depth the water will be after it reaches the premises), the facilities, judgment, and diligence of the owner.

Much stock can be damaged in the hurry and confusion of handling it. Some stocks, like hardware, may suffer no injury. Others, like soft goods, men's wear, and ladies' wear, are subject to soilage. Light house furnishings may be scratched or marred. *Damage* resulting from the handling and removal of the property is not covered under the policy. However, in some floods it may take many days for the water to recede. If the property that was removed to upper floors is damaged by dampness, mold, or foul odors from floodwaters in the premises, that is direct damage and is within the policy coverage.

A similar situation could occur in residences where clothing, furnishings, and other personal property are moved to upper floors for safety but later injured by dampness, mold, or foul odors.

Expenses incurred by the insured to move and preserve the property from loss by flood that ultimately reaches the premises and partially or totally inundates it would not be covered under the policy according to the NFIA interpretation. Indemnification is not provided until the property is *directly* damaged by flood. The reasoning is understandable in view of the widespread catastrophic character of floods and the impossibility of determining actuarial rates for what could amount to monumental aggregate expenses in a single flood. In this respect there is an important difference between flood policies and most other property insurance policies. In fire losses, for example, the expenses incurred to move and protect property from loss and to separate the damaged from the undamaged in order to minimize the loss under the policy are reimbursable though seldom specifically covered.

Property Covered—Dwelling Building and Contents Policy

Policy provisions regarding property covered and property not covered under the NFIA Dwelling Building and Contents Policy follow.

PROPERTY COVERED

A. Dwelling: The term "dwelling" shall mean a residential building designed for the occupancy of from 1 to 4 families and occupied principally for dwelling purposes by the number of families stated herein.

When the insurance under this policy covers

a dwelling, such insurance shall include additions in contact therewith; also, if the property of the owner of the described dwelling and when not otherwise covered, building equipment, fixtures and outdoor equipment, all pertaining to the service of the described premises and while within an enclosed structure located on the described premises; also, materials and supplies while within an enclosed structure located on the described premises or adjacent thereto, intended for use in construction, alteration or repair of such dwelling or appurtenant private structures on the described premises.

The Insured may apply up to 10% of the amount of insurance applicable to the dwelling covered under this policy, not as an additional amount of insurance, to cover loss to appurtenant private structures (other than the described dwelling and additions in contact therewith) located on the described premises. This extension of coverage shall not apply to structures (other than structures used exclusively for private garage purposes) which are rented or leased in whole or in part, or held for such rental or lease, to other than a tenant of the described dwelling, or which are used in whole or in part for commercial, manufacturing or farming purposes.

B. Contents: When the insurance under this policy covers contents, such insurance shall cover all household and personal property usual or incidental to the occupancy of the premises as a dwelling—except other property not covered under the provisions of this policy, and any property more specifically covered in whole or in part by other insurance including the peril insured against in this policy; belonging to the Insured or members of the Insured's family of the same household, or for which the Insured may be liable, or, at the option of the Insured, belonging to a servant or guest of the Insured; all while within an enclosed structure located on the described premises.

The Insured may apply up to 10% of the amount of insurance applicable to the contents covered under this policy, not as an additional amount of insurance, as follows:

(a) If not the owner of the described premises, to cover loss to improvement, alterations, and additions to the described dwelling and

appurtenant enclosed private structures as described above.

(b) If an individual condominium unit owner of the described premises, to cover loss to the interior walls, floors, and ceilings that are not otherwise covered under a condominium association policy on the described dwelling and appurtenant enclosed private structures as described above.

This Company shall not be liable for loss in any one occurrence for more than:

1. $500.00 in the aggregate on paintings, etchings, pictures, tapestries, art glass windows and other works of art (such as but not limited to statuary, marbles, bronzes, antique furniture, rare books, antique silver, porcelains, rare glass or bric-a-brac);

2. $500.00 in the aggregate on jewelry, watches, necklaces, bracelets, gems, precious and semi-precious stones, articles of gold, silver or platinum and furs or any article containing fur which represents its principal value.

C. Debris Removal: This insurance covers expense incurred in the removal of debris of or on the dwelling, appurtenant enclosed private structures or contents covered hereunder, which may be occasioned by loss caused by the peril insured against in this policy.

The total liability under this policy for both loss to property and debris removal expense shall not exceed the amount of insurance applying under this policy to the property covered.

PROPERTY NOT COVERED

This policy shall not cover:

A. Accounts, bills, currency, deeds, evidences of debt, money, securities, bullion, manuscripts or other valuable papers or records, numismatic or philatelic property.

B. Fences, retaining walls, seawalls, outdoor swimming pools, bulkheads, wharves, piers, bridges, docks; other open structures located on or partially over water; or personal property in the open.

C. Land values; lawn, trees, shrubs or plants, growing crops, or livestock; underground structures or underground equipment, and those portions of walks, driveways and other paved surfaces outside the foundation walls of the structure.

D. Animals, birds, fish, aircraft, motor vehicles (other than motorized equipment pertaining to the service of the premises and not licensed for highway use), trailers on wheels, watercraft including their furnishings and equipment; or business property.

DEDUCTIBLES

A. With respect to loss to the dwelling, appurtenant enclosed private structures or debris removal covered hereunder, this Company shall be liable for only the amount of loss in any one occurrence which is in excess of (a) $200. or (b) 2% of the amount of loss to the dwelling, whichever is the greater.

B. With respect to loss to contents or debris removal covered hereunder, this Company shall be liable for only the amount of loss in any one occurrence which is in excess of (a) $200. or (b) 2% of the amount of loss to the contents, whichever is the greater.[2]

The following comments cover the major provisions that are relevant to the peril of flood as defined in the policy.

A. Dwelling. Occupancy is limited to four families. The policy covers the dwelling and, if the property of the owner and not otherwise covered, building equipment, fixtures and outdoor equipment, all pertaining to the service of the premises; materials and supplies for construction, alteration, and repair of the dwelling or private structures are all covered *while within an enclosed structure on the described premises.* This would eliminate property in the open subject to floating or washing away in a flood.

Property in the open under a carport would not be *within an enclosed structure.* Property in an enclosed storage room or compartment built into a carport *would be within an enclosed structure.*

Ten percent of the amount of dwelling insurance may be allocated and applied to loss on appurtenant private structures located on the premises. This provision does not apply to structures rented or held for rent to other than a tenant of the dwelling; nor to private structures used in whole or in part for commercial, manufacturing, or farming purposes. There is at present no unanimity on whether a utility shed not attached or anchored permanently to some type of foundation would be considered a structure or personal property. It was the majority opinion polled at the closed session of the 1975 PLRB Loss Managers' Conference in Denver, Colorado, that a utility shed qualified as an appurtenant private structure.

B. Contents. The significant provision applicable to this coverage is that all of the property described is covered *while within an enclosed structure located on the described premises.* If the insured is not the owner of the dwelling, 10 percent of the amount of contents insurance may be allocated and applied to improvements, alterations, and additions to the dwelling, and to appurtenant *enclosed private structures.* If the insured is an individual *condominium* unit owner, 10 percent of the amount of the insurance on contents may be allocated and applied to cover loss to interior walls, floors, and ceilings not otherwise covered under a condominium association policy.

Other provisions under Contents pertain to limitations on specific items and kinds of personal property.

C. Debris Removal. The expenses are covered to remove debris *of or on the dwelling, private structures, and contents.* Debris would include mud and silt. Unlike most other debris removal clauses, the policy covers the removal of all debris from the peril insured against; not limited to debris of the property covered.

Property Not Covered

The description of *property not covered* is clearly set forth.

[2]Standard Flood Insurance Policy (Issued Pursuant to the National Flood Insurance Act of 1968, or Any Acts Amendatory Thereof), Insurance Companies Members of National Flood Insurers Association, Arlington, Virginia, "Dwelling Building and Contents," NFIA-1 (Ed. 7-74).

Deductibles

Debris removal as a result of floods and mudslides can be considerable. The policy provides for a deductible of $200 or 2 percent of the amount of insurance, whichever is greater. This deductible applies *separately* to the dwelling coverage and separately to the contents coverage.

Replacement Cost Provisions

The provisions under this coverage run parallel in most respects to those under the Homeowners and similar policies.

1. The provisions apply only to a single family dwelling.
2. To qualify for full replacement cost, the whole amount of insurance must be either 80 percent or more of the full replacement cost of the building structure, or *the maximum amount of insurance available under the NFIA Program.* This is another way of stating that if the maximum amount of insurance available under the NFIA Program is carried on a single family dwelling, the insured qualifies for full replacement cost with no deduction for depreciation, even though the amount of insurance carried is not equal to 80 percent of the replacement cost of the building structure.

Property Covered—General Property Policy

Below is a description of property covered and property not covered under the NFIA General Property Form.

PROPERTY COVERED

A. Building: When the insurance under this policy covers a building, such insurance shall include additions and extensions attached thereto; permanent fixtures, machinery and equipment forming a part of and pertaining to the service of the building; personal property of the insured as landlord used for the maintenance or service of the building including fire extinguishing apparatus, floor coverings, refrigerating and ventilating equipment, all while within the described building; also materials and supplies while within an enclosed structure located on the described premises or adjacent thereto, intended for use in construction, alteration or repair of such building or appurtenant private structures on the described premises.

When the insurance under this policy covers a building used for residential purposes, the insured may apply up to 10% of the amount of insurance, applicable to such building, not as an additional amount of insurance, to cover loss to appurtenant private structures (other than the described building and additions and extensions attached thereto) located on the described premises. This extension of coverage shall not apply to structures (other than structures used exclusively for private garage purposes) which are rented or leased in whole or in part, or held for such rental or lease, to other than a tenant of the described building, or which are used in whole or in part for commercial, manufacturing or farming purposes.

B. Contents: When the insurance under this policy covers contents, coverage shall be for either household contents or other than household contents, but not for both.

1. When the insurance under this policy covers other than household contents, such insurance shall cover merchandise and stock, materials and stock supplies of every description; furniture, fixtures, machinery and equipment of every description all owned by the insured; improvements and betterments (as hereinafter defined) to the building if the insured is not the owner of the building and when not otherwise covered; all while within the described enclosed building.

2. When the insurance under this policy covers household contents, such insurance shall cover all household and personal property usual or incidental to the occupancy of the premises as a residence—except animals, birds, fish, business property, other property not covered under the provisions of this policy, and any property more specifically covered in whole or in part by other insurance including the peril insured against in this policy; belonging to the In-

sured or members of the Insured's family of the same household, or for which the Insured may be liable, or, at the option of the Insured, belonging to a servant or guest of the Insured; all while within the described building.

The Insured, if not the owner of the described building, may apply up to 10% of the amount of insurance applicable to the household contents covered under this item, not as an additional amount of insurance, to cover loss to improvements and betterments (as hereinafter defined) to the described building.

The Insured, if an individual condominium unit owner in the described building, may apply up to 10% of the amount of insurance on contents covered under this policy, not as an additional amount of insurance, to cover loss to the interior walls, floors, and ceilings that are not otherwise covered under a condominium association policy on the described building.

This Company shall not be liable for loss in any one occurrence for more than:

(a) $500.00 in the aggregate on paintings, etchings, pictures, tapestries, art glass windows and other works of art (such as but not limited to statuary, marbles, bronzes, antique furniture, rare books, antique silver, porcelains, rare glass or bric-a-brac);

(b) $500.00 in the aggregate on jewelry, watches, necklaces, bracelets, gems, precious and semi-precious stones, articles of gold, silver or platinum and furs or any article containing fur which represents its principal value.

3. When the insurance under this policy covers improvements and betterments, such insurance shall cover the Insured's used interest in improvements and betterments to the described building.

(a) The term "improvements and betterments" wherever used in this policy is defined as fixtures, alterations, installations, or additions comprising a part of the described building and made, or acquired, at the expense of the Insured exclusive of rent paid by the Insured,

but which are not legally subject to removal by the Insured.

(b) The word "lease" wherever used in this policy shall mean the lease or rental agreement, whether written or oral, in effect as of the time of loss.

(c) In the event improvements and betterments are damaged or destroyed during the term of this policy by the peril insured against, the liability of this Company shall be determined as follows:

(1) If repaired or replaced at the expense of the Insured within a reasonable time after such loss, the actual cash value of the damaged or destroyed improvements and betterments.

(2) If not repaired or replaced within a reasonable time after such loss, that proportion of the original cost at time of installation of the damaged or destroyed improvements and betterments which the unexpired term of the lease at the time of loss bears to the period(s) from the date(s) such improvements and betterments were made to the expiration date of the lease.

(3) If repaired or replaced at the expense of others for the use of the Insured, there shall be no liability hereunder.

C. Debris Removal: This insurance covers expense incurred in the removal of debris of or on the building or contents covered hereunder, which may be occasioned by loss caused by the peril insured against in the policy.

The total liability under this policy for both loss to property and debris removal expense shall not exceed the amount of insurance applying under this policy to the property covered.

PROPERTY NOT COVERED

This policy shall not cover:

A. Accounts, bills, currency, deeds, evidences of debt, money, securities, bullion, manuscripts or other valuable papers or records, numismatic or philatelic property.

B. Fences, retaining walls, seawalls, outdoor swimming pools, bulkheads, wharves, piers, bridges, docks; other open structures located on or partially over water; or personal property in the open.

C. Land values; lawn, trees, shrubs or plants, growing crops, or livestock; underground structures or underground equipment, and those portions of walks, driveways and other paved surfaces outside the foundation walls of the structure.

D. Automobiles; any self-propelled vehicles or machines, except motorized equipment not licensed for use on public thoroughfares and operated principally on the premises of the Insured; watercraft or aircraft.

E. Contents specifically covered by other insurance except for the excess of value of such property above the amount of such insurance.

DEDUCTIBLES

A. With respect to loss to the building or debris removal covered hereunder, this Company shall be liable for only the amount of loss in any one occurrence which is in excess of (a) $200. or (b) 2% of the amount of loss to the building, whichever is the greater.

B. With respect to loss to contents or debris removal covered hereunder, this Company shall be liable for only the amount of loss in any one occurrence which is in excess of (a) $200. or (b) 2% of the amount of loss to the contents, whichever is the greater.[3]

The following comments concern those major provisions which are most relevant to the peril of flood, as defined in the policy.

A. Building. The description of building coverage is similar to that found in general property forms that insure against fire and extended coverage perils, except that yard fixtures and other than real property are not covered if in the open. Such items must be within a fully enclosed structure, thus avoiding claims for materials, supplies, and other personal property being washed away or floating away in a flood.

[3] Standard Flood Insurance Policy (Issued Pursuant to the National Flood Insurance Act of 1968, or Any Acts Amendatory Thereof), Insurance Companies Members of National Flood Insurers Association, Arlington, Virginia, "General Property," NFIA-8 (Ed. 7-74).

If the building is occupied as an apartment house or for other residential purposes, 10 percent of the insurance on the building may be allocated and applied to loss to appurtenant private structures on the premises. This extension does not apply to structures (other than private garages) rented or leased to other than a tenant of the described building, nor to structures used in whole or in part for commercial, manufacturing, or farming purposes.

B. Contents. Coverage under this form may be for household contents *or* other than household contents; *not for both.* The significant provision applying to the contents is that all of the property described is covered *while within the described enclosed building*, not in the open. When the insurance covers on household contents, the insured, if not owner of the building, may allocate and apply 10 percent of the amount of contents insurance to cover improvements and betterments to the building.

If the insured is an individual condominium unit owner, 10 percent of the amount of the insurance on contents may be allocated and applied to loss to interior walls, floors, and ceilings not otherwise covered under a condominium association policy.

The same limitations are stated on specific property under 2(a) and 2(b) as are stated under the Dwelling Building and Contents Form.

Improvement and Betterment Provisions. Improvements and betterments are covered under the insurance of other than household contents (B-1). This is an optional coverage up to 10 percent of contents insurance, as explained above under household contents. Section 3 outlines the formula for loss determination on improvements and betterments. It follows the formula which is set out in most policies covering improvements and betterments.

C. Debris Removal. This clause is similar to that under the Dwelling Building and Contents Form.

Property Not Covered

The description of *property not covered* is clearly set forth.

Deductibles

This clause is similar to that under the Dwelling Building and Contents Form.

General Conditions and Provisions

The general conditions and provisions of the Dwelling Building and Contents Form and the General Property Form are the same except for a Loss Payable Clause in the latter.

NFIA CLAIM-HANDLING RULES AND REGULATIONS

The NFIA designates a member insurer as a servicing company for a specified territory, state, or area. The servicing company transacts the business, collects premiums, and pays losses. The NFIA also provides a comprehensive *Claim Managers Manual* for each servicing company.

The *Claim Managers Manual* encompasses all the claim-handling procedures, beginning with the receipt of notice of loss, assignment to a claim representative, file makeup, coding, reports to NFIA, the handling of coverage questions, supervision of claim representatives, approval of payment, issue of NFIA drafts, closing of files, and forwarding to NFIA. The servicing company's claim department, in effect, handles claims as though they arose under one of the company's own policies, but follows the procedures laid down by NFIA.

Qualified Flood Claim Representatives

Qualified claim representatives include those of insurers and independent adjusters. The NFIA manual specifies qualifications of claim representatives as follows:

1. Individual adjusters should have at least two years of property loss adjustment experience involving the adjustment of wind or combination of wind and water losses.

2. Otherwise, at least five years' experience adjusting property losses.
3. Adjusters must be capable of preparing their own estimates up to $2,500 and validating *all* contractor's estimates.

Claim Forms of NFIA

The following snapout forms are provided by NFIA for use on their losses: Notice of Loss, Preliminary Report, Worksheet—Contents—Personal Property, Worksheet—Building, Adjuster's Report, and Proof of Loss. See Appendix P for several of these forms.

Briefing Adjusters

The servicing offices are required to brief qualified adjusters in handling the NFIA flood claims.

FLOOD DAMAGE VERSUS WIND DAMAGE

When there is mixed wind and flood loss damage to properties, as frequently occurs in hurricanes along the Atlantic and Gulf coasts, there is the difficult task of separating one from the other. If, however, a single multi-peril policy includes loss by flood, all of the damage is covered and separation is not usually needed. But most property insurance policies *exclude* loss caused by, resulting from, contributed to, or aggravated by flood, surface water, waves, tidal water or tidal wave, overflow of streams or other bodies of water, or spray from any of the foregoing, all whether driven by wind or not.

The NFIA claim procedures provide for *separate claim representatives* to handle losses of mixed wind and water damage. The Worksheets have a column for known wind loss, one for known flood loss, and a third column for the gray-area loss, i.e., loss and damage that the claim representatives either cannot agree upon as to cause or are of the opinion that the cause cannot be separated. (See NFIA Worksheets, Appendix P.)

Arbitration

In those cases where the claim representatives cannot agree on how the damage by wind and water is to be separated, the NFIA will recognize binding arbitration by the appointment of a third, disinterested party to act as sole arbitrator. The arbitrator is to be chosen by the two claim representatives involved from a panel of qualified adjusters designated by the AIA-PCS, PLRB, NAII, or any qualified expert mutually acceptable to the NFIA and the windstorm insurer and on the scene of the loss.

ACTION OF FLOODWATERS

River waters can rise gradually, inundating structures partially or completely. They can recede quickly, but in some cases remain at a flood level for several days, then recede gradually. When rivers overflow, there also may be strong currents. Floating contents of buildings, or property in the open, along with other river debris, can pound and batter walls inside and outside a structure.

High waves along the coast, aided by high winds, batter, scour, wash away sand and earth around foundations, columns, piers and other supports, eventually causing a structure to collapse or even float out to sea. Often the lower portion of a structure will be gutted by water and wave action, while the upper stories show little or no damage.

Hydrostatic pressure from groundwater percolating through soil may force water through foundation walls and cracks in concrete floors, sometimes lifting large areas of concrete floor slabs and flooding the basement. Sanitary sewers, filled to capacity, back up through toilet bowls, sinks, and tubs. Capped floor drains may burst from the pressure of water.

Pollution in floodwaters from raw sewage contaminates everything it reaches, both building and contents. Sometimes tanks containing crude oil, fuel oil, and other contaminating liquids have their piping ruptured or are floated from their anchorage, battered, and opened to empty their contents over the flooded area.

EFFECTS OF FLOODWATERS ON BUILDINGS AND CONTENTS

How badly buildings and their contents can be damaged during floods depends on several

conditions,[4] some of which are beyond control.
1. Inherent damageability of material.
2. Extent of wetting, i.e., sprayed, dampened, submerged, partially or completely.
3. Length of time submerged or exposed.
4. Pollutants in water (oils, sewage, chemicals, salt).
5. Debris in water.
6. Wave and current action of water.
7. Weather during and immediately following the flood.
8. Availability of salvors and repair services.
9. Promptness of action in attending to property after the waters recede.

Local Building Ordinances

Most communities have a building department and ordinances and laws to regulate construction. Following a flood, the department becomes very conscious of its responsibilities and not only will enforce any existing building code or ordinances but may elect to establish new emergency regulations in the interest of the safety of the citizens.

Damaged buildings are usually inspected for safety, and, not infrequently, when the claim representative arrives at the premises, a notice of condemnation will be found on the building. Sometimes these notices are placed there, following an early mass inspection tour, as a precaution with a more careful and detailed inspection to follow. Condemnation of any buildings should be discussed with local authorities.

Local and state boards of health are usually quite active following a flood to make certain there are no violations of the laws and to prevent sickness and eliminate any unsanitary conditions that would endanger the health of the community.

As soon as practicable, the claim representative should establish rapport with these departments and maintain communications so as to be informed at all times of any requirements relevant to the handling of loss adjustments on buildings and on contents.

[4]The Property Loss Research Bureau has prepared an excellent booklet on this subject called *Flood Adjuster's Handbook*.

Building Materials—Effects of Flooding

Wood Products. Air-dried lumber contains 12 to 15 percent moisture by weight, and that is approximately the moisture content of wood in the average home. It is less during heating seasons and increases slightly in summer months.

Unprotected wood wet down or submerged absorbs moisture in the cells and expands mostly *across* the grain. The manner in which it is attached will influence to some degree how much it will twist and warp. Finished floors, edge-grain in particular, having little or no room to expand sideways, will ridge and cup along the edges of each piece producing a washboard effect. Serious expanding can occur when the floors are submerged. Large areas of finished flooring may be thrust upward in mounds or waves, sometimes lifting joists with them.

Interior grades of plywood on subfloors and on sidewalls delaminate. Veneers come loose on doors, cabinetry, and wall paneling. Exterior-type plywood, with waterproof glues, will withstand short periods of submersion, but on prolonged submersion they also tend to delaminate.

It is usually good practice not to write up specifications of an estimate on repairing or replacing wood timbers or woodwork until a sufficient drying out time has passed to be certain what work is necessary.

Plaster and Lath. A characteristic of gypsum plaster is that it can be saturated with water to the point of being plastic, but upon slowly being dried out it returns to its original hardness. There is no better example of gypsum plaster's ability to withstand the effects of wetting than that contained in the Gypsum Association's report on the Topeka flood of 1951. Two motels were submerged under 8 feet of water for five days. Less than six weeks after the waters receded, both motels were back in business with no repairs needed to the plaster walls.

The drying-out process must be controlled with a modest amount of heat and good circulation of air. Old-type dry wood lath may swell enough to break the back key of the plaster, in which case replacement is usually needed. Some types of paperbacked metal lath do not hold up as well as heavier types, and in some cases rust may set in.

Plaster ceilings do not withstand submersion as well as sidewall plaster and will usually have to be replaced.

Preparing specifications for repair and replacement of lath and plaster should be postponed until it is clear as to what has to be done.

Gypsum Drywall. Drywall is a core of gypsum plaster between two layers of paper. It comes 3/8-, 1/2-, and 5/8-inch thick, and in sheets 4 feet by 8 feet, 9 feet, 12 feet, and 14 feet. When submerged, gypsum board, or Drywall, is greatly weakened as the gypsum and paper softens. Frequently it will survive submersion for short periods. Delamination of the paper occurs *after* it dries out.

Tests are recommended before drafting specifications for repair or replacement. Nailing should be carefully examined to see that the Drywall did not pull away when wet.

As with plaster and lath, Drywall on ceilings does not hold up well when submerged. It tends to buckle and pull away from the nailing.

Insulation and Fiberboards. Building products like Celotex, insulation board, Masonite, or hardboard, and other composition boards, whether in sheet form or as tile, do not weather submersion very well. They absorb water and tend to buckle and warp unless heavily impregnated with asphalt or similar water-resistant materials. Careful examination should be conducted after a flood to determine what repairs or replacement are indicated.

Wall Tile. Ceramic wall tile applied over metal lath and plaster tends to hold up well following submersion. Much will depend on the quality of workmanship and type of backing cement or adhesive.

The same tile applied over Sheetrock W-R Gypsum wallboard, which is nominally water-resistant, will usually not stand up under flooding due to the adhesives and the gypsum and paper backing of the wallboard.

Painting and Wallpapering. Painted walls, ceilings, and woodwork, and wallpapered areas usually require complete redecorating. Water blisters may show up on the walls and ceilings as water soaks through from the backside of plaster or woodwork. All redecorating should be put off until the premises are thoroughly dried out, which may be long after the claim representative has left the scene.

Electric Wiring and Fixtures. Larger communities, by ordinance, require complete rewiring after a flood to avoid a fire hazard. The more expensive fixtures may be salvaged and rewired. Where there is no ordinance or building regulations that compel the rewiring, a reliable electrical contractor should be engaged to completely inspect the system, test it, and make recommendations for repairs or replacements.

Plumbing. Plumbing pipes and fixtures usually are not damaged by mere submersion. Unless they have been injured by debris, or pipes have been broken or dislocated, very little is necessary to restore them to their original condition. They will need testing by a competent plumber, and the fixtures will require cleaning.

Heating Systems. Furnaces of all types that have been submerged will have to be thoroughly tested by competent heating engineers or contractors. Generally the burner units, electrical wiring, motors, fireboxes, and all other operational parts will need taking down, examining, and repairing or replacing. Insulated jackets will have to be reinsulated.

Eliminating Mud and Pollution

River flooding frequently leaves a layer of mud and silt from a fraction of an inch thick to several inches thick on lower floors and contents. Seacoast flooding may leave inches to feet of thick sand accumulations. Shoveling and hosing down is the most common

method of getting rid of it. Furnishings such as sofas, tables, bedsteads, and carpeting are taken out and hosed down before being sent to the cleaning establishments if warranted.

Where sanitary sewers have backed up, polluting the premises, it may be necessary to call in professional cleaners and decontaminators. Deodorizing and disinfecting also can be done by professional services which are available in most parts of the country.

Contents—Effects of Flooding

What household effects can be salvaged and what must be considered worthless is a matter of good judgment. Unlike building materials, household items are things that almost everyone is familiar with.

If cleaning and repair services are available, they should be brought in to take care of items that show any indication that cleaning or repairing will restore them to useful condition.

Appliances such as washers, dryers, refrigerators, freezers, and ranges that have been submerged and coated with mud and silt must be examined carefully to determine whether they are worth saving. This should be done by a reputable servicing firm. Radios and television sets should be handled in the same manner. When it is necessary to wait several days for repair services, consideration should be given to hosing down and wiping off heavy appliances, and setting them aside to dry.

Mercantile and Manufacturing Stocks

Stocks of manufacturers—raw, in process, and finished—also stocks of merchandise should be handled as discussed in Chapters 17 and 19.

ADJUSTMENT PROCEDURE

The procedure for handling claims on buildings and personal property in flood losses is little different from that in handling losses caused by many other perils. Also procedures for the investigation of the insured, the insurance, and the property; the checking of claims; and salvaging are all treated in earlier specific chapters.

Reports

The claim representative is required to submit to the servicing company office the NFIA Preliminary Report of Inspection and Estimate Form within ten days after receipt of assignment.

The final report may be submitted to the servicing company office on NFIA Adjuster's Report form (Appendix P). In cases where the claim representative thinks a narrative report is warranted, the NFIA Narrative Report Captions should be used.

FAIR PLANS

Background

The purpose of FAIR (fair access to insurance requirements) Plans is to provide a means of writing fire insurance on risks (real and personal property) unable to secure coverage in the normal insurance market. These plans had their birth following the riots of the mid-1960s, beginning with the Watts outbreak in 1965. Insurers had up to that time been including the Peril of riot and civil commotion in their policies for little, if any, rate consideration. This resulted in the insurers having to pay losses in excess of 100 million dollars without having received any specific premium. While the losses were paid, it was obvious that some reform in underwriting, selection, and rating was necessary.

In 1968, property owners located in urban core areas of most major cities were finding it extremely difficult to secure fire insurance.

A National Advisory Panel appointed by President Johnson warned in January of 1968, that the revitalization of the Nation's cities would be impossible without fair access to property insurance. It then set forth its recommendations, including the establishment of FAIR Plans (fair access to insurance requirements) to resolve the key question of availability of coverage in urban areas.

These recommendations, essentially, were mandated by Congress in the Urban Property Protection and Reinsurance Act of 1968 authorizing Federal and State Governments to form a new reinsurance partnership with the insurance industry. Under this arrangement urban property owners would have fair access to insurance as prerequisite for obtaining building rehabilitation loans vital to the preservation of the Cities. Insurance companies, in turn, would be protected against catastrophic losses from riots through reinsurance purchased from the Federal Government.

The legislatures in most States where urban areas evidenced the need for revitalization responded to the Federal mandate by enactment of legislation which qualified them for participation. The result was the formation by the insurance industry of various Associations (Facilities) to implement the FAIR Plan Programs in accordance with guidelines specified by the legislatures and under regulatory supervision of the Insurance Commissioners. One notable exception to this is Louisiana where the industry-supported FAIR Plan does not qualify for riot reinsurance.

Enabling State legislation in some instances ties the term (life) of the Plan to the expiration of the Urban Property Protection and Reinsurance Act of 1968 (Public Law 90-448).[5]

In April, 1975, President Ford signed into law Public Law 94-13 extending the Urban Property Protection and Reinsurance Act of 1968 to April 30, 1977.

FAIR Plans, by state legislation, are mandatory "facilities" (pools) and require participation by all insurers writing basic property insurance in the state. Exceptions include Indiana, Iowa, and Kansas, where participation is voluntary. Losses and operating expenses are shared by "facility" member companies on the basis of premium volume. The plans are not subsidized by state or federal moneys.

Qualification for insurance excludes any environmental considerations, such as location in hazardous areas. Properties are inspected free, and if there appears to be no faulty construction, defective wiring or heating, deterioration, poor or hazardous housekeeping, overcrowding, or accumulation of

---

[5] E. L. Lecomte, General Manager of Massachusetts and Rhode Island FAIR Plans, in a talk delivered before the National Association of Independent Insurance Adjusters, October, 1974, New York, N.Y.

rubbish or flammable materials, the property generally qualifies. Not all state plans are alike.

The limited underwriting standards in such plans greatly mitigate any actuarial approach and intensify the moral hazards. One effort to partially overcome such handicaps is the requirement that the amount of insurance on a risk have some reasonable relation to the actual cash value of the property.

The plans insure against the basic perils of fire, extended coverage, and vandalism and malicious mischief. Some include sprinkler leakage or time element coverage. Homeowners coverage is available through the Massachusetts and Rhode Island FAIR Plans. Generally speaking, insurance is provided at standard rates and on standard policy forms. There are presently 28 FAIR Plans operating in 26 states, the District of Columbia, and the Commonwealth of Puerto Rico.

To gain some idea of the magnitude of these programs, insuring property principally in the inner-city and hard-core areas, it is to be observed that in 1974 approximately 640,000 policies were issued, generating written premiums of 110 million dollars. Since inception in 1968, average loss ratios approach 100 percent and combined loss and expense ratios are well over 100 per cent.

At present 16, or more than half, of the FAIR Plans operate as syndicates. The states in which syndicate operations are to be found accounted for 90 percent of all FAIR Plan premiums in 1974. These are high-population states with the country's largest cities, all of which have the usual inner-city problems. The remaining 12 FAIR Plans operate under a single or multiple servicing carrier modus. In this latter configuration the FAIR Plans accept applications and premiums and provide administrative and accounting services; thereafter, policy approvals are funneled to the servicing carrier(s) who issue policies and adjust losses. The syndicate plans function as a Company (insurer), accepting applications and premiums; providing for inspections; and performing all accounting, underwriting, and claims services.

Claim Handling

The inherent problems artificially generated by the formation of the FAIR Plans make it essential that close supervision of the handling of claims be given priority. When the loss dollar exceeds the premium dollar, as it does in a number of states, experienced claim representatives are in high demand.

The FAIR Plan claim departments in a syndicate-type operation have the responsibility of appointing qualified claim representatives to handle losses and designate what builders, salvors, accountants, attorneys, arson investigators, and other experts are to be used. The claim representatives receive their assignments from the claim department of the FAIR Plan, and report to and confer with that department.

Because of the value and loss peculiarities as well as other sophistications which may be associated with properties insured in the FAIR Plans, a high level of experience and degree of expertise is sought in individuals, whether staff or independent adjusters, who supervise and/or handle plan losses.

Loss personnel must have a complete knowledge and understanding of the "indemnity concept" as well as of the various measures of Cash Value (see Chapters 14, 16, and 17).

Additionally, the underwriting philosophies of the plans concerning cash value, which differs somewhat from the normal insurance market, must be fully understood. Thus, where permitted by law, in those states following the "Broad Evidence Rule," the plans will seek to establish "reasonable insurable values" (amounts of insurance) which afford indemnity and simultaneously avoid the inherent risks associated with economic waste.

In many instances the age and type of construction of buildings insured in the plans will generate unusual repair problems or considerations. This mandates that those involved in adjustments be particularly knowledgeable about construction, the different qualities of building materials, and workmanship. (Review Chapter 14, "Buildings and Structures.")

Properties insured in the plans are highly

susceptible to loss by vandalism and malicious mischief, riot and civil disorder, as well as arson. Therefore, the adjuster must be meticulous in investigating the origin of loss. In the absence of coverage, vandalism and malicious mischief damage must be separated from that caused by other insured perils. Losses from prior casualties, covered or not, must be identified and segregated. *Claims for damage from riot and civil disorder must be totally documented in accordance with the Federal Insurance Administration's Claim Procedure* to assure a successful reinsurance recovery by the plan's membership. Origins of loss which are of a suspicious or incendiary nature must be immediately brought to the attention of the plans's claim department. The adjuster must determine from the plan precisely what action is to be taken to produce the most favorable results without exposing the plan to legal involvement or to embarrassment.

BEACH PLANS

Another type of pooling facility is the Beach Plan. Beach Plans are found in seven seacoast states. Four states—Alabama, Louisiana, Mississippi, and Texas—are hurricane-exposed Gulf states; two states—North Carolina and South Carolina—are hurricane-exposed East Coast states, and Florida is exposed on both Gulf and East coasts.

The function of the Beach Plans is to provide access to insurance which is difficult or impossible to obtain in the normal insurance market. Membership of insurers writing fire and extended coverage is mandatory in all of the above-mentioned states, except Alabama where it is voluntary. Standard fire and extended coverage policies for both habitational and commercial properties are written at standard (bureau) rates in most of the Plans.

Beach Plans operate much like the FAIR Plans. Adminstrative, accounting, and underwriting services are performed by the plan's staff; policies are issued and losses adjusted by the servicing carriers, except in Florida and Texas where the plan's staff makes the loss assignments.

QUESTIONS AND PROBLEMS

1. The National Flood Insurance Program was established under the National Flood Insurance Act of 1968. It is underwritten by the National Flood Insurance Association (NFIA). Members include insurance companies cooperating with the Federal Insurance Administration (FIA). What are the main functions of the member insurance companies of NFIA in the program?

2. There are two NFIA flood insurance policies. State the title of each and tell in general what each policy is designed for.

3. The insuring clause in the two flood policies is approximately the same as the 1943 New York Standard Fire Policy except for the substitution of the word Flood in place of Fire and Lightning and except for Removal. Explain the essential difference between Removal in the flood policies, and Removal in the New York Standard Fire Policy and most other property insurance policies.

4. The NFIA policy definition of Flood includes mudslide (mudflows) and erosion. As closely as you can, give the NFIA definition of Flood, which encompasses all three of the above.

5. Personal property in the open is not covered under the flood policies. What is the reason for this? What about property in a carport storage room if fully enclosed? Is that covered?

6. Most property insurance policies limit the removal of debris to the debris of the property covered. How does the Debris Removal clause in the flood policy differ?

7. What are the NFIA qualifications for claim representatives to handle flood losses?

8. Under what circumstances would there be coverage for seepage through foundation walls or through basement floors due to hydrostatic pressure?

9. What are the deductibles under the flood policies? How do they apply?

10. What is the essential difference in the Replacement Cost provisions of the Dwelling Building and Contents Flood Policy and the Replacement Cost provisions of most other property policies—HO for example?

11. In the words *FAIR Plan* what do the letters *F A I R* stand for? Briefly, and in your

own words, explain how and why FAIR Plans were established.

12. In almost all states, by legislation, FAIR Plans are mandatory "pools."

  a. Explain briefly.

  b. Are the plans subsidized by state or federal moneys?

13. Are the FAIR Plan insurance policy forms standard or designed specially for the risks covered? Are the rates standard rates?

14. Most properties covered under FAIR Plan insurance are located in the inner cities and frequently in what are called "hard core" areas. They are usually old buildings showing wear and tear from use and inadequate maintenance. Many show obsolescence as to construction, layout, and occupancy design. Considering these circumstances, discuss some of the problems that experienced claim representatives are faced with.

25

Business Interruption, Extra Expense, and Additional Living Expense

Insurance covering the earnings of manufacturing plants, mercantile establishments, service organizations, and other income-producing risks is variously called *business interruption, use and occupancy, gross earnings, income* or *prospective earnings* insurance. In England it is called *loss of profits* insurance.

The purpose of business interruption insurance is to pay the policyholder in case of a covered loss, subject to the limitations stated in the form, what the business would have earned had no loss occurred.

When a place of business is damaged by a covered peril, it suffers a partial or total loss of income during the period required to repair the realty and to repair or replace the personal property involved. During this period of restoration, certain fixed overhead charges may continue. Standard business interruption insurance policies cover these fixed charges and also the net profit to the extent they would have been earned had there been no interruption. In other words, indemnity under the policy is limited to the *actual financial loss sustained*.

FORMS

The withdrawal in every rating territory of the two-item forms and their replacement with the gross earnings forms is an important development resulting from longstanding ef-

forts in the industry to reduce the number of and simplify previously existing forms that often confused agents, underwriters, insureds, and claim representatives.

Two-item forms are still preferred by some mercantile and manufacturing insureds. These forms are usually special filings by such insurers as those writing Highly Protected Risk or Superior Risk policies.[1] The two forms now ordinarily used are the Gross Earnings Form 3, for mercantile or nonmanufacturing risks, and the Gross Earnings Form 4, for manufacturing or mining risks. Each of these forms can have attached, subject to a minimum coinsurance requirement of 80 percent, either the Ordinary Payroll Exclusion Endorsement, or the Ordinary Payroll—Limited Coverage Endorsement.

Another form that has been simplified for small mercantile, nonmanufacturing businesses, known as the Earnings Form, is likewise available in most states.

Form MLB-140 (Ed. 5-69) is a Gross Earnings Endorsement under the Special Multi-Peril Program (SMP). It covers loss resulting directly from necessary interruption of business caused by damage or destruction of real or personal property (except finished stock). Form MLB-141 is an Ordinary Payroll Exclusion Endorsement. Form MLB-142 is

[1]See p. 27.

the Ordinary Payroll—Limited Coverage Endorsement.

Special Multi-Peril Form MLB-143 (Ed. 5-69) is a Loss of Earnings Endorsement patterned after the gross earnings forms with special provisions and limitations. It is designed for the small to medium-size mercantile and manufacturing risks.[2]

The Businessowners Policies (MLB-700 and MLB-701 Ed. 12-75) cover loss of income. This simplified coverage is also similar to a Gross Earnings Form and covers the *reduction in gross earnings less charges and expenses which do not necessarily continue during the interruption of business.* It also covers the reduction in rents, less noncontinuing charges and expenses.

GROSS EARNINGS FORMS

The Gross Earnings Business Interruption Form 3 for *mercantile and nonmanufacturing* risks, and its counterpart for *manufacturing risks,* Form 4, differ basically in the Resumption of Operations Clause and in the definition of *gross earnings.* Loss resulting from damage to or destruction of finished stock is not covered under the manufacturing form.

Insuring Clause

The insuring clause embodied in the gross earnings forms states:

This policy insures against loss resulting directly from necessary interruption of business caused by damage to or destruction of real or personal property by the peril(s) insured against, during the term of this policy, on premises occupied by the Insured and situated as herein described.

In the event of such damage or destruction this Company shall be liable for the ACTUAL LOSS SUSTAINED by the Insured resulting directly from such interruption of business, but not exceeding the reduction in Gross Earnings less charges and expenses which do not necessarily continue during the interruption of business, for only such length of time as would be

required with the exercise of due diligence and dispatch to rebuild, repair or replace such part of the property herein described as has been damaged or destroyed, commencing with the date of such damage or destruction and not limited by the date of expiration of this policy. Due consideration shall be given to the continuation of normal charges and expenses, including payroll expense, to the extent necessary to resume operations of the Insured with the same quality of service which existed immediately preceding the loss.

The interruption to the insured's business must *necessarily* be caused by damage to or destruction of real or personal property *on the premises occupied by the insured situated as described in the policy.*

In adjusting practice, the contract is treated as including loss sustained when business is *not suspended* but when any damage to the property causes an increase in the cost of operation.

Actual Loss Sustained. The Gross Earnings Form, like all standard business interruption policies of insurance, limits liability to "actual loss sustained." This is founded on the principle of indemnity. If an insured was operating at a net loss prior to the interruption, the continuing expenses during a suspension must exceed the projected operating loss during that period had there been no interruption. Otherwise the insured cannot collect under the contract.

The term *actual loss sustained* means the loss of net profit the insured will sustain, plus the amount that will have to be paid out of pocket because of the charges and expenses to be met while the business is suspended, less any expense saved. The result will be the reduction of earnings. The reduction must be the result of a total or partial suspension of business caused by the destruction of, or damage to, the property described in the policy by a peril insured against.

An exact determination of actual loss sustained would require exact knowledge of what the insured would have earned, had there been no casualty, as well as of what was earned after it occurred. It is often possible to be sure that after the casualty the insured earned nothing, or earned a definite sum of money, but what would have been earned if there had been no casualty is almost always a matter of speculation. In most instances, however, it can be reasonably approximated.

In practice, claim representatives treat actual loss sustained on the basis of (1) sales lost and (2) sales made at increased cost. On sales lost, the full amount of the earnings that would have been made is lost with the sales unless there is some saving on expense. On sales made at increased cost, the earnings lost are measured by the increased cost. Expense incurred for the purpose of reducing the loss under the policy is not treated as actual loss sustained but as a separate subject of insurance because of its freedom from contribution requirements.

Production may be temporarily interrupted in a manufacturing plant without loss of sales. Sales might be made through existing excess stock. Consequently there may be no actual loss sustained.

The business interruption policy will not do more for the insured than the business would have done had there not been an interruption of the operations.

Reduction in Gross Earnings. *The reduction in gross earnings less charges and expenses which do not necessarily continue during the interruption* is the basic measure of loss to the insured. It is also a limit of liability to the insurer. Methods of measuring the reduction are discussed later.

Period of Interruption. The actual loss sustained or the reduction in gross earnings less charges and expenses that do not necessarily continue are covered for only the time required, with due diligence and dispatch, to repair or replace the damaged property. This includes both real and personal property on the premises occupied by the insured. There is no *requirement* that the property be repaired or replaced; the policy merely covers the loss during the time it *could* with due diligence and dispatch be repaired or replaced.

If the insured elected to move or go out of business he or she would still collect the actual loss sustained. This is variously call the *period of indemnity,* the *period of interruption,* and the *period of suspension.*

The time period during which loss is covered is not limited to the expiration date of the policy. If the loss occurred a few days before expiration and six months was required to restore the property, the reduction in gross earnings, less charges and expenses that do not necessarily continue, is covered though the policy has expired.

Due Diligence and Dispatch. The words "due diligence and dispatch" as used in the form have no precise meaning. Claim representatives generally agree that a reasonable time to obtain estimates from contractors, perhaps to have architects draw up plans if necessary, and to prepare the claim is part of the period of suspension. The time for taking of inventories, replacing machinery and equipment, and in the case of a mercantile risk, replacing stock and fixtures, if done within a reasonable period, must be considered to meet the "due diligence and dispatch" requirement.

Delays resulting from the insured's inability to obtain specialized or custom-made equipment or machinery are also covered.

Delays due to abnormal weather conditions, such as blizzards, floods, or freezing, are matters beyond the control of the insured. Delays in obtaining building materials or machinery and equipment caused by strikers *away* from the premises are covered. Under these circumstances it is possible to incur a substantial business interruption loss, although the property damage may be relatively minor.

When the time to repair or replace the property is delayed by disagreement between landlord and tenant, the insurer can hardly be held liable. Likewise, when the delay in time results from the arbitrary actions of an unreasonable insured pressing for excessive payment, the additional time should not be considered part of the period of interruption covered by the policy.

Resumption of Operations Clause

The insured, under all forms of business interruption insurance policies, is required to do everything reasonable to reduce the loss. The gross earnings forms stipulate this condition under the Resumption of Operations Clause:

> It is a condition of this insurance that if the Insured could reduce the loss resulting from the interruption of business, (a) by complete or partial resumption of operation of the property herein described, whether damaged or not or (b) by making use of merchandise or other property at the location(s) described herein or elsewhere, such reduction shall be taken into account in arriving at the amount of loss hereunder.

If the insured could reasonably be expected to continue operating at the location described, partially or completely, he or she will be expected to do so. If the insured could so operate but does not, the loss will be adjusted as though he or she had.

Furthermore, the insured will be expected to use merchandise or other property, both real and personal, at the described location or elsewhere.

The Manufacturing Form adds the condition:

> (c) by making use of stock (raw, in process or finished) at the location(s) described herein or elsewhere, such reduction shall be taken into account in arriving at the amount of loss hereunder.

All the foregoing is contingent upon whether by so doing the insured could reduce the loss resulting from the interruption of the business. This condition of the policy requires prompt and open discussion between the insured and the claim representative in order to determine what kind of property is available and could be utilized to reduce the loss. Careful estimates of the situation are frequently needed to justify the use of other property or other facilities.

Expenses to Reduce Loss Clause

Expediting expense and *extra expense* are the terms most often used by the claim representative in referring to *expenses to reduce the loss.* The policy stipulates:

> This policy also covers such expenses as are necessarily incurred for the purpose of reducing loss under this policy (except expense incurred to extinguish a fire), but in no event shall the aggregate of such expenses exceed the amount by which the loss otherwise payable under this policy is thereby reduced. Such expenses shall not be subject to the application of the Contribution Clause.

This clause has two conditions of considerable importance in the adjustment of a loss: (1) The amount of such expenses which is recoverable by the insured is limited to the amount by which the loss is reduced. (2) The coinsurance provisions do not apply to extra expense incurred to reduce the loss.

Gross Earnings Clause—Mercantile Form

The policy definition of *gross earnings* is the key to determining the amount of insurance to comply with the coinsurance requirement and also for the measurement of loss, inasmuch as it is the reduction in gross earnings that the policy covers.

The Mercantile Form states:

> For the purposes of this insurance "Gross Earnings" are defined as the sum of (a) Total net sales, and (b) Other earnings derived from operations of the business,
> less the cost of: (c) Merchandise sold, including packaging materials therefor, (d) Materials and supplies consumed directly in supplying the service(s) sold by the Insured, and (e) Service(s) purchased from outsiders (not employees of the Insured) for resale which do not continue under contract.
>
> No other costs shall be deducted in determining Gross Earnings.
>
> In determining Gross Earnings due consideration shall be given to the experience of the

business before the date of damage or destruction and the probable experience thereafter had no loss occurred.

Net sales are usually considered gross sales less returns, allowances, discounts, freight out, and bad debts. These items, being related to sales, are ones for which the insured could not normally sustain a loss.

Other earnings derived from the operation of the business would include such things as income from leased departments and interest on charge accounts.

Merchandise sold needs no explanation except that it is in terms of *cost of goods sold* including packaging materials for the merchandise.

Materials and supplies consumed directly include those items the consumption of which is immediate, such as wrapping materials and packing materials. In a service organization such as a motel these items would be soaps, fuel, cleaning compounds, broken dishes, stolen silverware, and guest supplies.

Services purchased from outsiders for resale which do not continue under contract might be a reupholstery service for a department store; installation of carpeting and other floor coverings; rug cleaning; and reconditioning and storage of furs.

Since no other costs shall be deducted in determining gross earnings, it is apparent that full payroll is included. Ordinary payroll may be excluded by endorsement or it may be limited by endorsement to 90, 120, 150, or 180 days.

Gross Earnings
Clause—Manufacturing Form

One of the basic differences between the Gross Earnings Form for mercantile risks and the Gross Earnings Form for manufacturing risks is in the definition of *gross earnings*. This is due to the nature of the two types of operation.

A mercantile business exists by purchasing stocks of merchandise for resale. The difference between the cost of the goods purchased and the selling price is the gross earnings.

A manufacturer converts so-called raw stock into salable merchandise. The net sales value of his production is his income. The cost of raw materials and supplies necessary to produce the finished stock is deducted from his net sales to determine his gross earnings.

The Gross Earnings Form 4 for manufacturing risks defines *gross earnings* as follows:

> For the purpose of this insurance Gross Earnings are defined as the sum of:
> (a) Total net sales value of production,
> (b) Total net sales of merchandise, and
> (c) Other earnings derived from operations of the business, less the cost of:
> (d) Raw stock from which such production is derived,
> (e) Supplies consisting of materials consumed directly in the conversion of such raw stock into finished stock or in supplying the service(s) sold by the Insured,
> (f) Merchandise sold, including packaging materials therefor, and,
> (g) Service(s) purchased from outsiders (not employees of the Insured) for resale which do not continue under contract.

Important to note here is the term *sales value of production*.[3]

The Manufacturing Form logically distinguishes between the finished stock produced by the insured and any *merchandise* purchased for resale. The sales of each are determined, and the cost of each is computed for value and loss purposes.

Contribution Clause

The standard gross earnings forms are generally written subject to a Contribution (Coinsurance) Clause which reads:

> In consideration of the rate and form under which this policy is written, this Company shall be liable, in the event of loss, for no greater proportion thereof than the amount hereby covered bears to the Contribution (Coinsurance) percentage specified on the first page of this policy (or endorsed hereon) of the

[3]See p. 415.

Gross Earnings that would have been earned (had no loss occurred) during the 12 months immediately following the date of damage to or destruction of the described property.

It is important to note that the basis for determining the amount of insurance required is the *twelve months immediately following the date of loss.* It is not the twelve months prior to the loss.

Finished Stock Clause—Manufacturing Form

The Gross Earnings Manufacturing Form excludes *any loss resulting from damage to or destruction of finished stock* and for the time required to reproduce such finished stock. Business interruption insurance policies are concerned only with the *prospective, future earnings* of a business. Finished stock is stock which was produced before the loss occurred. Coverage under the contract is for the sales value of production which is prevented as a result of interruption in the insured's operations.

Interruption by Civil Authorities Clause

The gross earnings forms stipulate:

This policy is extended to include the actual loss sustained by the insured, resulting directly from an interruption of business as covered hereunder, during the length of time, not exceeding 2 consecutive weeks, when, as a direct result of damage to or destruction of property adjacent to the premises herein described by the peril(s) insured against, access to such described premises is specifically prohibited by order of civil authority.

Before the widespread city rioting in 1967, this clause read:

This policy is extended to include the actual loss as covered hereunder, during the period of time, not exceeding 2 weeks, when as a direct result of the peril(s) insured against, access to the premises described is prohibited by order of civil authority.

The newer wording requires that the order prohibiting access be a direct result of damage to or destruction of property adjacent to the described premises by a covered peril. The words *adjacent to* are held to mean nearby, not distant.

Coverage for loss under these and other civil authority clauses is subject to the individual insurer's interpretation and dependent upon each fact, situation, and circumstance.

Special Exclusions Clause

The following three exclusions are stipulated in the forms, each being considered a consequential rather than a direct loss:

This Company shall not be liable for any increase of loss resulting from:
(a) enforcement of any local or state ordinance or law regulating the construction, repair or demolition of buildings or structures; or
(b) interference at the described premises, by strikers or other persons, with rebuilding, repairing or replacing the property or with the resumption or continuation of business; or
(c) the suspension, lapse or cancellation of any lease, license, contract or order unless such suspension, lapse or cancellation results directly from the interruption of business, and then this Company shall be liable for only such loss as affects the Insured's earnings during, and limited to, the period of indemnity covered under this policy;
nor shall this Company be liable for any other consequential or remote loss.

The exclusion for loss caused by enforcement of local or state ordinances regulating construction is similar to that found in the New York Standard Fire Policy and discussed in Chapter 3.

Any delay in restoring the property caused by interference *at the described premises* by strikers or other persons is not covered. Delays caused by strikers away from the premises would be covered, as the exclusion is worded.

Loss resulting from the cancellation of any lease, license, contract, or order as a direct result of the interruption does not extend beyond the period of suspension. In other words, the insurer is liable only for the actual loss sustained during the time required to repair or replace the damaged property.

Special Limitation. The following special limitation is also stipulated:

> Limitation—Media for Electronic Data Processing: With respect to loss resulting from damage to or destruction of media for, or programming records pertaining to, electronic data processing or electronically controlled equipment, including data thereon, by the perils insured against, the length of time for which this Company shall be liable hereunder shall not exceed:
> (a) 30 consecutive calendar days; or
> (b) the length of time that would be required to rebuild, repair or replace such other property herein described as has been damaged or destroyed,
> whichever is the greater length of time.

Definitions

The Gross Earnings Manufacturing Form defines *raw stock, stock in process, finished stock, merchandise,* and *normal* as follows:

> The following terms wherever used in this policy shall mean:
> (a) "Raw Stock": material in the state in which the Insured receives it for conversion by the Insured into finished stock.
> (b) "Stock in Process": raw stock which has undergone any aging, seasoning, mechanical or other process of manufacture at the location(s) herein described but which has not become finished stock.
> (c) "Finished Stock": stock manufactured by the Insured which in the ordinary course of the Insured's business is ready for packing, shipment or sale.
> (d) "Merchandise": goods kept for sale by the Insured which are not the product of manufacturing operations conducted by the Insured.
> (e) "Normal": the condition that would have existed had no loss occurred.

Alterations and New Buildings Clause

The gross earnings forms stipulate:

> Permission granted to make alterations in or to construct additions to any building described herein and to construct new buildings on the described premises. This policy is extended to cover, subject to all its provisions and stipulations, loss resulting from damage to or destruction of such alterations, additions or new buildings while in course of construction and when completed or occupied, provided that, in the event of damage to or destruction of such property (including building materials, supplies, machinery or equipment incident to such construction or occupancy while on the described premises or within one hundred (100) feet thereof) so as to delay commencement of business operations of the Insured, the length of time for which this Company shall be liable shall be determined as otherwise provided herein but such determined length of time shall be applied and the loss hereunder calculated from the date that business operations would have begun had no damage or destruction occurred.

This is an important coverage to an insured who, while altering or adding to an existing building or constructing an entirely new building, sustains a loss which results in a delay in commencing operations. The policy covers the loss of gross earnings from the date operations *would have begun* had there been no interruption.

There are other clauses common to both the mercantile and the manufacturing gross earnings forms which have been discussed in earlier chapters and which are found in many of the standard property insurance forms.

Ordinary Payroll

Under the definition of *gross earnings* in the contract, full payroll is covered. If the insured wishes to exclude or limit ordinary payroll, as distinguished from the payroll for executives and important employees, two endorsements are available. The Ordinary Payroll Exclusion Endorsement for use with Forms 3 and 4 stipulates:

In consideration of the rate charged and substitution of the following Contribution Clause in lieu of the Contribution Clause contained in the form attached to this policy, this Company shall not be liable for any ordinary payroll expense as hereinafter defined.

Contribution Clause: In consideration of the rate and form under which this Policy is written and this endorsement, this Company shall be liable, in the event of loss, for no greater proportion thereof than the amount hereby covered bears to 80.....% of the Gross Earnings that would have been earned (had no loss occurred) during the 12 months immediately following the date of damage to or destruction of the described property, less the same percentage of ordinary payroll expense for that 12 months period.

Definition of Ordinary Payroll Expense: The entire payroll expense for all employees of the Insured, except officers, executives, department managers, employees under contract and other important employees.

All other provisions and stipulations of this policy remain unchanged.

Ordinary payroll is usually considered that payroll which could be eliminated in event of a long period of interruption. The language of the endorsement as to the amount of insurance to be carried is clear.

The intent of what losses should be paid is also clear. The question of which employees on the insured's ordinary payroll should be retained in case of interruption is a matter of judgment and subject to adjustment. In some instances the insured is bound by union rules. During a brief suspension of a day or a few days, certain ordinary payroll employees may be *other important employees* under the definition of ordinary payroll expense.

In computing the amount of insurance required under the Payroll Exclusion Endorsement, all ordinary payroll including social security taxes, unemployment tax, compensation insurance, and other variable charges related to payroll are deducted from the gross earnings as defined in the contract. The coinsurance percentage applied to the amount so determined will determine the insurance required.

The Ordinary Payroll—Limited Coverage Endorsement is available to those insureds who want short-period (90, 120, 150 or 180 days) ordinary payroll coverage. It reads as follows:

In consideration of the rate charged and substitution of the following Contribution Clause in lieu of the Contribution Clause contained in the form attached to this policy, the liability of this Company for the ordinary payroll expense, as hereinafter defined, is limited to such expense which must necessarily continue during the interruption of business for not exceeding 90*......... consecutive calendar days immediately following the date of damage to or destruction of the described property.

Contribution Clause: In consideration of the rate and form under which this policy is written and this endorsement, this Company shall be liable, in the event of loss, for no greater proportion thereof than the amount hereby covered bears to 80.....% of the Gross Earnings that would have been earned (had no loss occurred) during the 12 months immediately following the date of damage to or destruction of the described property, less the same percentage of ordinary payroll expense for the portion of that 12 months period which follows the 90*......... days specified above.

Definition of Ordinary Payroll Expense: The entire payroll for all employees of the Insured, except officers, executives, department managers, employees under contract and other important employees.

All other provisions and stipulations of this policy remain unchanged.

The amount of insurance required under the Limited Payroll Endorsement is computed as under the Payroll Exclusion Endorsement except that the amount of ordinary payroll and related charges to be deducted from gross earnings will be the or-

*The 90-day limit may be increased to 120, 150, or 180 days.

dinary payroll for the number of days selected under the limited coverage.

One advantage of the gross earnings forms is that the amount of insurance is blanketed over net profit, continuing operating expenses, and payroll. The insured therefore has latitude for careful consideration of the extent to which he will make claim for his ordinary payroll in situations where other expenses may have been underestimated.

GROSS EARNINGS OF SERVICE RISKS

All business is broadly classified into mercantile, manufacturing, and service risks. The Gross Earnings Form was first designed for mercantile businesses, specifically retail and wholesale firms. It was readily adapted to manufacturing risks, as previously mentioned, by altering the definition of gross earnings and also the Resumption of Operations Clause.

Service risks are those that primarily sell service. Such risks include hospitals, bowling alleys, hotels and motels, restaurants, theatres, laundries, and dry cleaners. The 1953 definition of *gross earnings* in Form 3 "was designed to end the 13-year old controversy over the items of costs and expenses properly deductible from sales income for purposes of the application of the Contribution Clause, for service business."[4] It added:

(d) *Materials and supplies consumed directly in supplying the service(s) sold by the Insured*, and

(e) Service(s) purchased from outsiders (not employees of the Insured) for resale which do not continue under contract.

Supplies consumed in the sale of services of some businesses would not be questioned. For example, stationery, soap, fuel, stolen articles, and broken dishes in a motel or hotel would reasonably fall into the category of consumed supplies.

AGREED AMOUNT ENDORSEMENT

The Contribution Clause in the gross earnings forms[5] limits the insurer's liability to that proportion of any loss which the amount of insurance bears to a specified percentage of the gross earnings *that would have been earned during the twelve months following the date of the loss.* The income and gross profit of most businesses do not continue the same from one year to the next. As a result, and especially in a period of inflation or normal growth of a business, application of the Contribution Clause in event of loss frequently will penalize an insured.

The Agreed Amount Endorsement, available for most mercantile and nonmanufacturing risks in all jurisdictions and for manufacturing risks in a number of jurisdictions, will prevent the insured from being penalized on any loss up to the amount of insurance. To accomplish this the endorsement suspends the Contribution Clause in the form from the date of the endorsement to its expiration date (one year), or to the expiration date of the policy, whichever is first.

The insured must file a satisfactory statement of the business-interruption values with the rating bureau at inception of the endorsement and annually thereafter. Failure to do this will render the agreed amount clause void and reinstate the contribution clause. It is important, therefore, that the claim representative verify that values have been filed as and when required.

The endorsement, in some states, contains the equivalent of the full reporting clause in the stock reporting forms. It limits liability to that proportion of the loss which the business-interruption value reported (to the bureau) bears to the *actual* business-interruption value for the year specified. Consequently, in those jurisdictions where the endorsement contains such a provision, it is most important that actual values for the period specified in the endorsement be carefully determined.

---

[4]Henry C. Klein, *Business Interruption Insurance*, The Rough Notes Company, Inc., Indianapolis, Ind., 1964.

[5]See p. 391 for a discussion of the Contribution Clause.

PREMIUM ADJUSTMENT ENDORSEMENT

The intent of this endorsement is to convert the insurance provided by the Gross Earnings Form, to which it is attached, into a premium adjustment form. The premium becomes provisional.

The insured is required to submit reports on prescribed forms, on the effective date of the endorsement, showing the gross earnings as defined and covering the latest preceding fiscal year for which such figures are available. Then, within 120 days after the close of each succeeding fiscal year, a similar report is to be filed covering the preceding fiscal year.

The coinsurance provisions are not eliminated by this endorsement nor is the amount of insurance increased according to values reported. The practical effect of the endorsement is to permit the insured to set the insurance sufficiently high to avoid application of the Contribution Clause in the event of a partial loss. The premium is adjusted downward annually in accord with the actual gross earnings during the year.

As in the Agreed Amount Endorsement, the insurer's liability is limited to that proportion of any loss which the last reported business-interruption value bears to the actual value during the period covered by such report. It is a necessary function of the claim representative to check the last reported value very carefully.

Insurance under the endorsement is excess over any other insurance not written on the same plan, terms, conditions, and provisions.

BLANKET BUSINESS INTERRUPTION INSURANCE

When two or more plants of the same ownership contribute materials to or are otherwise dependent upon one another, the business interruption insurance may be written to blanket the operations at all locations. If some or all plants are independent of one another, the business interruption insurance may still be written blanket.

CONTINGENT BUSINESS INTERRUPTION INSURANCE

When the property of a manufacturer or mercantile business, not owned by the insured, is damaged by a covered peril and as a result the insured's operations are interrupted, the insured can be protected from loss by contingent business interruption insurance.

Contributing contingent business interruption insurance protects those insureds whose operations are wholly or partly dependent for materials or supplies on other non-owned businesses which if damaged would cause an interruption of the insured's business and a resultant loss of earnings.

Recipient contingent business interruption insurance protects an insured from loss of earnings when the property of a customer (recipient) of the insured sustains damage resulting in an interruption of the insured's operations.

EXTENSION OF PERIOD OF INDEMNITY

The standard business interruption insurance policies limit the period of indemnity to the length of time that would be required with the exercise of due diligence and dispatch to rebuild, repair, or replace the part of the property described that has been damaged or destroyed. Very often the insured's business continues to show a loss of earnings for an extended period following complete restoration of the physical property. Customers have taken their trade elsewhere and, in many cases, weeks or months may go by before they are regained. Seasonal businesses are especially vulnerable to continued loss of income following restoration of the physical property. Examples are seasonal hotels, canneries, toy manufacturers, mercantile risks that depend heavily on Christmas trade, and clothing manufacturers who begin cutting months before the beginning of the season for which the clothing is intended. If there is an interruption of operations in such risks just prior to, or even during the seasonal period, the insured may continue to lose income for all or the balance of the season, depending upon when the physical restoration is completed.

To illustrate, a seasonal hotel is damaged by fire and as a result is unable to open until the normal season is half over. The income during the balance of the season may be considerably below the income anticipated based on the previous year's experience because of cancellations due to the fire and general customer reactions. The loss of earnings on the diminished income after physical restoration and until normal business resumes (probably the end of the season in this example) is covered under the Endorsement Extending the Period of Indemnity, which provides as follows:

In consideration of $.......... additional premium, this policy is extended to cover the Actual Loss Sustained by the Insured resulting directly from the interruption of business, as covered by this policy for such additional length of time as would be required with the exercise of due diligence and dispatch to restore the Insured's business to the condition that would have existed had no loss occurred, commencing with the later of the following dates:

The date on which the liability of this Company for loss resulting from interruption of business would terminate if this endorsement had not been attached to this policy; or

The date on which repair, replacement or rebuilding of such part of the building(s), structure(s), machinery, equipment, or furniture and fixtures of the property herein described as has been damaged or destroyed is actually completed; but in no event for more than .... consecutive calendar days from said later commencement date.

This extension of time may be purchased in units of 30 days and is subject to the terms and conditions of the policy including the Contribution Clause.

EARNINGS INSURANCE FORM

This business interruption insurance form is patterned after the Gross Earnings Form 3. It is designed for small mercantile and non-manufacturing risks. There is no contribution clause in this form but there is a provision limiting recovery to 25 percent of the amount of the policy in any 30 consecutive calendar days. In some states this limit, at the insured's option, may be 16⅔, 25, or 33⅓ percent. The insuring clause reads as follows:

When this policy covers EARNINGS, This Company shall be liable for the ACTUAL LOSS SUSTAINED by the Insured resulting directly from necessary interruption of business caused by damage to or destruction of real or personal property by the peril(s) insured against, during the term of this policy, on the premises described, but not exceeding the reduction in Earnings less charges and expenses which do not necessarily continue during the interruption of business, for only such length of time as would be required with the exercise of due diligence and dispatch to rebuild, repair or replace such part of the property herein described as has been damaged or destroyed, commencing with the date of such damage or destruction and not limited by the date of expiration of this policy. Due consideration shall be given to the continuation of normal charges and expenses, including payroll expense, to the extent necessary to resume operations of the Insured with the same quality of service which existed immediately preceding the loss.

This Company shall not be liable for more than the percentage specified on the first page of this policy (or endorsed hereon) of the amount specified for this item in any 30 consecutive calendar days.

Earnings is defined as the sum of: (1) total net profit, (2) payroll expenses, (3) taxes, (4) interest, (5) rents, and (6) all other operating expenses earned by the business.

The Earnings Insurance Form, like the Gross Earnings Form 3, contains clauses covering resumption of operations, expenses to reduce loss, interruption by civil authority, and special exclusions. These and other clauses common to both forms are discussed in the preceding pages.

The 25 percent monthly limitation assumes that in most instances the time to rebuild would not exceed four months. Also, in order for the insured to recover in full for 30 consecutive days in the peak season, he or she must carry insurance equal to four times the net profit and the necessarily continuing operating expenses for those peak season 30 days.

The insured recovers the actual loss sustained *or* the net profit and necessarily continuing expense, whichever is less. Any excess over and above the 25 percent monthly limitation cannot be carried over into the next 30 consecutive days. If the period of interruption extends beyond 120 days, then any accumulated excess is carried over, subject to the percentage limitation.

EFFECTS OF PERILS

Fire, explosion, windstorm, or other peril may destroy a manufacturing plant and cause a total suspension of its business. In some plants the design is such that all material must move through a single building or process, a *bottleneck*. In such a plant the destruction of the building or the disabling of the process makes it impossible to continue operations and may, therefore, cause a *total suspension* of business.

On the other hand, the peril may damage rather than destroy the building, equipment, stock in process of manufacture, or raw stock of a plant in such a way as to prevent full operation of the property but still permit some production. In this case there will be only a *partial suspension*.

In similar fashion, the destruction of a mercantile risk will produce a total suspension of business while damage to it may permit some sales to continue and, therefore, cause only partial suspension.

BUSINESS-INTERRUPTION LOSSES

Following the destruction of a manufacturing plant there is an immediate ending of production. Unless there is a reserve of finished stock outside the area of destruction, there will be no more sales. If there is a reserve, sales will end when it has been exhausted. When sales end, income ceases, and until the plant is rebuilt or the manufacturer purchases or leases a new one, or arranges to have the product made in other plants, there will be a total suspension of business.

Many costs, charges, and expenses necessary to the operation of the business will not continue. Payments for materials, supplies, and power, ordinary payroll, compensation insurance premiums, and payroll taxes for labor that is laid off are examples. But other charges and expenses will continue for varying amounts and periods of time. Skilled employees, for example, may hold contracts under which they must be paid, perhaps for six months or a year. Interest on indebtedness will continue, as will taxes on real estate, at least in part. In some instances a basic daily, weekly, or monthly charge on a power contract continues, and in others a similar charge on royalties. Salespersons away from headquarters may have to be paid the expense of traveling home, and some office employees must be retained for accounting work and to look after collections or other details.

Stockholders or owners will lose the profits the business had been making.

Following damage to a plant, as contrasted with its destruction, it may be possible for the manufacturer to put the property in operating condition in a short time and suffer nothing more than reduced production or an increase in the cost of producing with a moderate loss of profit until full operations are resumed. If resourceful, the insured may even make up delayed production by renting temporary quarters or additional equipment, or by running overtime after the plant has been put in order. In such a case, the loss will be no more than the extra expense incurred as a result of the delay and the emergency measures.

The destruction or damage of mercantile risks produces losses that differ in detail, but not in principle, from those occurring in manufacturing risks.

Generally speaking, the amount of any business-interruption loss is measured by the adverse effect of the destruction or damage of the property on the succeeding operating statements of the business, not necessarily on the first one made after the loss.

Loss resulting from order of civil authority prohibiting access to the premises can be no greater than the gross earnings on the sales that would have been made if the public had been admitted. Generally, it is less. In some instances the business will lay off sales personnel or otherwise reduce expenses while customers are denied access to the premises. In others, customers will, after prohibition of access has been ended, come in and buy practically all that they would have bought during the period of prohibition as well as afterward.

Circumstances That Determine Amount of Loss

The amount of a business-interruption loss is determined by:

1. The damage to the property described in the policy, or the order of civil authority, prohibiting access to the premises, and the effects of the damage or of the order on the sales, production, or the cost of operating the business.
2. The rate at which the business had been selling or producing before the loss, and the probable rate at which it would have sold or produced after the loss.
3. The time required, with the use of due diligence and dispatch, to rebuild, repair, or replace the property, or the time for which available materials or other controlling circumstances would have permitted operations.
4. The expenses that can be discontinued while the business is suspended.
5. The possibility of continuing business at an expense that will permit earning more than direct costs of operation.

Methods of Adjustment

Two basic methods of adjustment are used for business-interruption losses: (1) the forecast method and (2) the workout method. Details of the two are variously combined in many adjustments.

When the *forecast* method is used, the claim representative, shortly after the occurrence of the loss, estimates the business-interruption value and the amount of loss and tries to agree with the insured upon:

1. The probable earnings, had there been no loss, for the twelve months following date of loss.
2. The period of the suspension.
3. The sales or production that will be lost during the suspension.
4. The charges and expenses that will not continue during the suspension, or
5. The increased cost of producing or selling during the period necessary to restore the property, and/or
6. The amount that should be spent to reduce loss under the policy.
7. The amount for which the insurer would be liable under the policy if no expenditures were made to reduce loss.

If the ordinary payroll is covered, estimates and efforts to agree also include:

8. The amount of ordinary payroll expense that determines how much insurance should be carried on payroll to satisfy contribution requirements.
9. The ordinary payroll expense necessary to resume operation that would have been earned if no loss had occurred.

When the *workout* method is used, the claim representative authorizes the insured to:

1. Replace, repair, or recondition the property as soon as possible, resume or continue operation, and when restoration has been completed, present claim for the difference between the probable gross earnings that would have been earned, had no loss occurred, and the actual gross earnings resulting from operations during the period of restoration, and/or
2. Make expenditures necessary to reduce loss and contrast the amount spent with the sum for which the insurer would have been liable if the amount had not been spent.

The objectives, when either method is used, are satisfactory agreements upon the following factors:

1. The amount of the year's probable earnings that will determine whether or not

the operation of the Coinsurance or Contribution Clause will reduce the liability under the insurance.

2. The actual loss sustained, which may be
   a. The margin between selling prices and direct costs of the sales lost, less any charges and expenses that do not continue.
   b. The increased cost of producing or selling.
3. The expense, if any, necessary to reduce loss under the policy.
4. The amount by which the loss under the policy will be or was reduced by the expense.

Required Investigation

It may be necessary to find the answer to any of a series of questions. Answers to some can be made with certainty if investigation is thorough, but to others they can be nothing more than opinions of what is probable. As the following questions are phrased, they apply to losses that the claim representative plans to consider by the forecast method before the property has been rehabilitated.

1. When, how, and to what extent was there destruction of or damage to any building, structure, piece or group of equipment, lot of stock or supplies, or other property described in the policy?
2. How and in what degree will the destruction or damage suspend business and reduce the income that the insured expected to receive from it or increase the cost of operating it?
3. What circumstance or combination of circumstances will determine the length of time following the casualty during which the insurer will be liable for the loss?
   a. The time which, with the exercise of due diligence and dispatch, would be required to rebuild, repair, or replace buildings and equipment.
   b. The time for which the damaged or destroyed raw stock would have made operations possible.
   c. The time required to replace or restore the damaged or destroyed raw stock.
   d. The time required to replace or restore to the same state of manufacture in which it stood at date of loss any destroyed or damaged stock in process of manufacture.
4. Will any circumstance not covered by the insurance delay resumption of business at normal cost?
5. Will the insured suffer loss due to reduced income or increased cost of operation or a combination of the two during the entire time required to rehabilitate the property?
6. What should be done by the insured to shorten the time and what should be the cost?
7. What was the experience of the business before the date of the casualty, and what would have been its probable experience after that date had the casualty not occurred?
8. What loss of earnings will the insured probably sustain during the period of rebuilding, repairing, or replacing if the work is done during ordinary working hours?
9. To what extent can the probable loss be reduced by intelligent use of overtime or by other expediting expenditure?
10. What part of the loss is not covered by the policy?
11. For what part of the loss is the insurer liable after allowing for contract exclusions or contribution requirements?

In losses that are to be adjusted by the workout method, the questions to be answered are of the same import, but they will be asked, after the property has been rehabilitated, about what has occurred and what has been done instead of what might occur and what should be done.

PROCEDURE

Procedure should include (1) getting the insured's story, (2) discussion and explanation, (3) examination and listing of policies, (4) inspection of the property, (5) inquiry into date, time, and cause of loss, (6) approval of efforts to resume operations, (7) authorization of expense necessary to reduce loss,

(8) choice of method of adjustment, (9) preparation for adjustment, (10) audit or development of claim, (11) fixing by agreement or appraisal the amount of the business-interruption value and the amount of loss, (12) applying the terms of the policies and determining the amount for which any insurer is liable, and (13) reporting to the insurer or insurers.

The Insured's Story

The claim representative should get the insured's story, asking how the destruction or the damage of the property will affect production, cost of operating, or sales; what, if anything, can be done to reduce the loss; and how resumption of operations and restoration of the property can be accomplished in the shortest possible time. Prompt contact with the insured is essential in situations requiring emergency measures to expedite resumption.

In minor losses, the story is short and informal. The insured points out the damage to building, or the damaged machines if a manufacturer, or the damage to building, or the damaged fixtures, stock, or store section if a merchant, and gives any knowledge or opinion of how the damage will affect production, sales, or costs and how to restore the property with the least loss of time.

In large and complicated losses, the controlling person in the insured's organization, the responsible associates and employees, the producer, and the public adjuster, if one has been employed, should join in the discussion by which the story is developed.

If the property has been destroyed or severely damaged, the insured should be questioned about the possibilities of acquiring other property in which to resume business. If it has been damaged but offers possibilities of early repair, methods of repair should be discussed.

The insured's opinion on the possibility of reducing loss by expenditures for emergency installations or repairs, overtime work, or the services of friendly competitors who will make the insured's products or supply goods that can be sold should be asked for and considered.

Discussion and Explanation

Discussion will reveal the attitude of the insured, whether he or she is cooperative or otherwise, and will aid the claim representative in estimating the insured's ability. It will also inform the claim representative of the problems that will be presented in the adjustment and the necessity of preparing to cope with them.

The claim representative should learn how to present in language that claimants will readily understand the purpose of business interruption insurance and how it operates. Many uninformed claimants expect payments for the daily, weekly, or monthly averages of net profits and fixed charges instead of for the lost gross earnings on sales or production out of which the charges would have been paid and the profit made, or the increased cost of operating, if volume can be maintained.

If the insured, following a total suspension of business, offers to prepare a statement of gross earnings computed according to the averages of experience, he or she may be asking too much or too little, depending upon what loss of production or sales is probable. If the business is the same from month to month, a claim on the basis of the averages will be in order, but if the business fluctuates, the claim will be too high if the suspension occurs during low-volume days, weeks, or months, or too low if during high-volume periods.

There are three kinds of business-interruption losses: (1) loss due to reduction of sales or production, (2) loss due to increased cost of producing or selling, and (3) loss due to expenditure made for the purpose of reducing loss. After learning the facts of the situation and which kind of loss the insured will sustain, the claim representative should explain, unless the insured has thorough understanding of the contract or is being assisted in the adjustment by an informed and competent adviser, the purpose of the contract and how the claim should be prepared so that the purpose will be fulfilled. Explanation should be made, as far as possible, in nontechnical language, but the claim representative must be prepared at any time to use the exact words of the form, if the insured seems to be doubtful of the explanation, and to point out their application to the matter being discussed.

As standard forms now specifically provide that expense necessarily incurred for the purpose of reducing loss is not subject to contribution and is collectible to the extent that it does not exceed the amount by which the loss under the policy is reduced, it is easy to persuade the insured to make special installations or unusual purchases, or to arrange for overtime operation when these will reduce loss.

The necessity of examining the books and records of the business should be explained in connection with the provision in the contract that the amount of insurance that should be carried and the amount of any loss are both to be determined after giving due consideration to the experience of the business before the loss and the probable experience after the loss.

Examination and Listing of Policies

Examination and listing of the business interruption policies will inform the claim representative on the coverage and amount of the insurance. If there is coverage under both items of a two-item form, the amount under each item should be listed separately. There are today very few nonconcurrencies in business interruption policies because standard forms are generally used.

In serious losses, examination should be made not only of the business interruption policies but also of all other policies covering building, contents, rents, lease-hold, extra expense, or profits and commissions. Policies covering stock should be particularly examined for market-value or selling-price provisions. All policies covering the property should be examined for debris removal clauses.

Unless the claim representative is informed about all insurance covering in or on the property, it will not be possible to make an equitable allocation of any expense that may be incurred for the common good.

Inspection of Property

In ordinary losses, inspection follows a simple routine. The claim representative identifies the property, sees the physical evidence of its damage by a peril insured against, and notes how the damage will curtail production, reduce sales, or increase operating costs. At the same time he or she sees what, if anything, is being done or should be done to resume operations or use of the part of the property that was affected.

In serious losses, inspection must be directed according to circumstances. In some, it should be repeated at intervals as the work of restoring the property progresses.

The following outline gives some general idea of how inspections may be made in order to establish the facts or show the probabilities that are proved or indicated by the appearance of the property.

Identification. The property in which operation will be suspended or made more expensive should be checked against the description in the policy.

Location of Damage. The structure, equipment, or stock that was damaged should be determined as being within or outside the area covered by the policy.

Cause, Extent, and Degree of Damage. The evidence of fire, explosion, wind, or other peril insured against should be noted, also any evidence of electrical injury, collapse, flood, or other peril not insured against. If there is evidence of damage caused by both kinds of perils, it should be noted whether (1) the damage done by each kind of peril can be definitely determined or (2) the damage done by both kinds of peril is so mixed that the damage done by each kind cannot be definitely determined.

The extent and degree of damage should be noted, and the repairs or reconditioning necessary to restore structure, equipment, or stock to tenantable or usable condition visualized.

Effect of Damage on Operations. The effects of the damage on the use of the property should be noted, whether it has necessitated the shutting down of the plant or the closing of the store, or has affected only part of the property, permitting operations to continue in the rest.

The effect on the business of the impaired usefulness of the property should be noted as (1) curtailment of production, (2) loss of sales, (3) increased cost of operation.

Possibilities of Resuming Operation. Physical conditions pointing toward temporary or permanent repairs should be noted, also those indicating whether it will be advisable to remove operations in whole or in part to another location.

The time necessary to make repairs should be estimated according to the condition noted.

General Condition of Property. The general condition of the property should be noted—its suitability and its capacity. Particular attention should be given to evidences of use or idleness prior to the date of loss.

When inspecting property that has been damaged rather than destroyed, the claim representative should give special attention to the sections of the building, the pieces of equipment, or the lots of stock affected. Their importance in the operation of the business should be ascertained, the way in which the damage has impaired their usefulness should be noted, and, if their appearances do not clearly indicate what should be done to repair or recondition them, arrangements should be planned for any necessary examinations or tests.

Inspection of stocks on hand is sometimes important. An undamaged reserve of finished stock will permit sales to continue while productive facilities are being repaired. On the other hand, a shortage of raw materials may be the factor limiting the period of the loss rather than the length of time needed to restore the damaged property.

In large properties, important sections may be undamaged. Inspection of these sections will inform the claim representative on the general condition of the property, its capacity, its use, and its housekeeping.

Determining Date, Time, and Cause of Loss

Inquiry into the date, time, and cause of loss should be made in the same way as when a property loss is being adjusted. It seldom needs to go further.

As part of an inquiry, the claim representative should determine whether the building, equipment, or other property, the destruction or damage of which has caused the interruption of production, sales, or services of the business, is the property described in the policy or a part of it. With two exceptions, the insurer will only be liable for loss of earnings under a business interruption policy if the loss results from the destruction or damage of the property described in the policy, that is, the buildings, equipment, supplies, or stock that make up the physical risk.

Exception one is when loss results from the order of a civil authority prohibiting access to the premises as provided for in the policy.

Exception two is when the policy has been endorsed to include the hazard of interruption of power or other service received from a source outside the risk and when there has been an outside interruption of the service caused by a peril insured against.

In some losses, circumstances other than the destruction of, or damage to, the property contribute to the interruption of business and in doing so cause an added amount of loss for which the insurer is not liable. Weather, transportation difficulties, and material shortages are the circumstances most commonly encountered. There are losses during hurricanes involving plants that carry windstorm insurance in which the situation is confused because floods that precede the hurricanes wash out bridges, roads, or railroads serving the plants. The plants are then damaged by wind. The loss of business suffered because of the time required to replace the bridges or repair the roads or railroads is not caused by windstorm and, therefore, is not covered by the insurance. Only the loss during the time required to repair the windstorm damage to the property, without taking into account the time required to repair the bridges, roads, or railroads, is covered.

A heavy loss of income was suffered by an interstate fairgrounds organization as a result of a hurricane. Some damage was done to the buildings, but the fair was held on schedule with practically all its usual space open to the public. The attendance, however, was slim. Many persons who ordinarily visited the fair did not do so, some because of the risky condition of the highways, many of which were obstructed by fallen trees and power lines; others, because there was need for them to stay at home and get their own damaged property in order.

Retail sales are affected by weather conditions. Shoppers often are inclined to avoid going to stores on rainy days. Transportation difficulties and strikes prevent the receiving and shipping of materials and products. Shortages of raw materials may make full operation of the plants using them impossible.

Loss due to order of civil authority prohibiting access to the premises is generally limited to two weeks. The claim representative should learn the exact terms of any order issued because of which a loss is claimed.

Approval of Efforts to Resume Operation

It is incumbent upon the insured to do what is reasonable to reduce the loss or otherwise expect to bear the part of it that might have been averted.

If the damage to the property has been slight there may be resumption of complete operation with little delay. If the damage has been severe, resumption will generally be a step-by-step process.

Efforts to resume business must be guided by circumstances. If the property has been destroyed and there is reason to believe that business can be resumed and operated at a profit in other quarters, the insured should be aided in acquiring a new location. If the property has been damaged, consideration should be given to temporary repairs, installations, or arrangements to reduce the period of suspension and thereby reduce any

decrease of production or sales. Temporary roofs, emergency power lines, rented motors, and the substitution of manpower for disabled mechanical operations are the usual means of shortening suspension. Sometimes, however, immediate permanent repairs are preferable to temporary work.

While the business-interruption loss and the property loss are usually covered by separate insurance contracts, they should, if possible, be handled by cooperating claim representatives unless they are handled by the same claim representative. Cooperation is particularly necessary at the beginning of the adjustment when it must be decided whether permanent repairs should be made at once or should be preceded by temporary repairs. When permanent repairs are authorized, there should be a clear understanding that they are to (1) take the normal course and be paid for at regular prices and wage rates or (2) be expedited in order to reduce the period of business interruption and, therefore, paid for at premium prices necessary to get quick deliveries of materials and at overtime labor rates for crews working for more than regular hours. The insurers who cover the property will be liable for cost of repairs at regular prices. The insurers who cover business interruption will be liable for the premium, or excess cost of material, and for overtime, to the extent that they reduce the loss.

Expense to Reduce Loss

Expense to reduce loss is in many instances specifically authorized by the claim representative. In such instances it is necessary to check only the correctness of the amount. He or she may have authorized the expenditure of a definite sum in dollars. If so, the check is easy. On the other hand, the claim representative may have authorized certain work to be done, requiring expenditures for materials and labor. When such is the case, the check to see whether the expenditures are reasonable is a bit more difficult. Items of expense not specifically authorized must be scrutinized to determine whether they are necessary and must be contrasted with the amount by which loss under the policy was reduced because of the expense.

The claim representative is well advised to use care in authorizing the insured to proceed with temporary or permanent repairs, to purchase outside services, to arrange for temporary operations, or to take other steps intended to reduce the loss. There have been embarrassing situations where the insured, innocently following instructions, has incurred considerably more expense than the amount by which the loss was reduced. The authorization should be directed to specific expediting measures and expenditures, and if there is any question of future misunderstanding, the instructions or agreement should be reduced to writing.

The claim representative in consultation with the insured, who knows the business better than anyone, should study the probable ultimate effect any expenditure will have in reducing the loss under the policy.

In some instances the loss sustained by reason of a suspension or threatened suspension of sales due to destruction or damage of the property will be measured by the excess cost of buying from outsiders materials that the business would normally produce for its own use.

Structural additions, alterations made, or equipment purchased to reduce business-interruption loss may have a useful value to the insured after the loss has ended, or a selling value of more than the cost of removal. If so, proper credit should be taken in the business-interruption loss for the useful or salvage value of these items.

Expenses incurred to reduce the loss are covered to the extent that they do not exceed the amount by which the loss *under the policy* is reduced. When the insured is seriously underinsured, care must be exercised in testing the advisability of authorizing expense to reduce the loss. Such expense cannot exceed the recoverable loss under the policy. As previously stated, expense incurred to reduce the loss is not subject to application of the Contribution Clause.

Example 25-1 illustrates a situation in which continuing a partial operation during the period of interruption resulted in a greater loss than a total suspension of operations would have. Assume under this particular Gross Earnings Form that the insured is a coinsurer for 40 percent because of insufficient insurance.

Choice of Method of Adjustment

In the following situation the circumstances clearly indicate that the claim representative should use the forecast method of adjustment:

1. When the insured wishes to make alterations in the property while doing the repair work necessary to resume full operation.
2. When the insured wishes to delay the repairs to suit his convenience, or make them in such a way that the time taken will exceed the time that would be required with the exercise of due diligence and dispatch to complete them.

In other situations, the choice of method is generally a matter of speculation. In many, the claim representative has no choice, as the insured will not make claim until the property has been restored and then account for the experience during the period of restoration.

Preparation for Adjustment

In the majority of small and moderate sized losses, no special preparation is necessary before discussing figures with the insured and trying to make an adjustment. Ordinarily the claim representative inspects the property, considers the claim, looks at a profit and loss statement and the daily, weekly, or monthly record of sales, and offers the figures he or she is willing to agree upon.

In difficult and large losses, extensive preparation is necessary before the claim representative can discuss the claim intelligently, or make an equitable offer of settlement. Preparation may include any of the following:

1. Gathering information on the period of suspension or the period of operation at increased cost.
2. Examination of the insured's records.
3. Market survey.

EXAMPLE 25-1   A Partial Operation Fails to Reduce the Loss Under the Policy

I. Total suspension during period of interruption

Projected sales for the period	$75,000	
Cost of merchandise sold (66⅔%)	50,000	
Gross earnings projected	$25,000	
Less abated expenses:		
Rent, heat and light ⎫		
Miscellaneous ⎬	15,000	
Payroll ⎭		
Business-interruption loss	$10,000	
Coinsurance application limits insurer's liability to:		
60% × $10,000		$6,000

II. Partial operation during period of interruption

Actual sales during period	$45,000	
Cost of merchandise sold (66⅔%)	30,000	
Gross earnings by partial operation	$15,000	
Projected gross earnings less actual sales:		
$25,000 − $15,000 = $10,000		
Less abated expenses:		
Payroll ⎫	2,000	
Miscellaneous ⎬	$ 8,000	
Coinsurance application limits insurer's liability to:		
60% × $8,000		$4,800
Add expenses incurred to reduce the loss (not subject to coinsurance):		
Air freight ⎫		
Travel for buyer ⎬	3,200	
Advertising ⎪	$8,000	
Temporary repairs ⎭		
Insurer's liability limited to actual loss under the policy		
during total suspension		$6,000

4. Investigation of causes, other than market conditions, of any loss for which the insurer is not liable.

The foregoing list is not intended to be all-inclusive. An unusual loss may demand unusual preparation in studies of physical conditions, labor relations, quotas, allocations, regulations of governmental authorities, and other subjects.

Period of Suspension. Preparation for discussing the time during which loss for which the insurer is liable should cover the circumstances controlling the specific case at hand. The circumstances are usually (1) rebuilding, repairing, or replacing, (2) availability of stock, (3) availability of raw stock, (4) availability of stock in process, and (5) availability of merchandise. Occasionally, there are others, such as (6) abnormal economic conditions, (7) governmental order or regulation, and (8) unusual conditions in the environment.

Rebuilding, Repairing, or Replacing. When the period necessary to rebuild, repair, or replace is to be fixed by agreement before restoration is made, the damage should be surveyed and the best method of restoring the property to its full usefulness agreed upon. The length of time necessary to do the work should then be estimated. If the claim representative feels competent to estimate the time with a reasonable degree of accuracy, he or she may prepare to work out an agreement with the insured. In large or otherwise unusual losses, however, the time is best estimated by a competent builder, engineer, or other expert.

Consideration should be given to the possibility of restoring normal operation in a shorter time than would be necessary to re-create the structures and equipment exactly as they existed before they were destroyed or damaged. Good planning may produce for the insured an improved combination of design and construction that will not only permit speedier resumption of operation than if the old setup were restored, but will also make for greater usefulness and reduce cost of operating.

In serious losses, the restoration of the buildings usually requires more time than other work necessary to restore operations, as equipment can generally be put in order, raw stock reconditioned or replaced, and new merchandise obtained before repairs to the buildings can be completed. A building of ordinary design built of materials readily available can be restored in less time than an unusual structure containing materials that are difficult to find and that cannot be promptly delivered. Rain, snow, high winds, and extremes of heat or cold retard building work. Any time estimate must give consideration to the season of the year in which restoration is to be made and the weather conditions that are to be expected.

The time required to replace or repair machinery will depend upon the ability of the manufacturers or dealers to deliver new machines or to supply parts, also upon the availability of labor sufficiently skilled to make installations or repairs.

Standard machines that are carried in stock by the manufacturers—sewing machines and motors, for example—can be quickly replaced, and any spare parts needed for repairing them are ordinarily obtainable upon request. Specially made machines, such as steam hammers, machines used for producing paper and linoleum, machines made in foreign countries, and some of the complicated, patented machines, such as linotypes and monotypes, generally require a long time to replace or repair. Occasionally, the maker of a patented machine that has been damaged will be reluctant to supply repair parts.

In one unusual business-interruption claim, a serious loss of production was caused by the destruction of a large, specially made machine that had produced composition shingles, a third of the plant's output. A

new machine was promptly ordered, but the adjusters found that the manufacturer was so inadequately equipped that the plant could produce only two machines in a year and, therefore, could not deliver the needed machine in less than six months.

When ore or coal bridges or similar heavy and specially built mechanisms are involved, it is highly important that any drawings or other engineering data relative to the design, workmanship, or operation of the mechanism be located and made available for study discussion.

Fixtures and equipment present the same situations as machinery. Typewriters, adding machines, calculators, and other business machines are ordinarily carried in stock and can be replaced promptly, while counters, partitions, shelving, cabinets, and similar fixtures that have been built to order may require considerable time to replace.

Availability of Stock. Stock is an occasional factor in the period of loss. In manufacturing risks, raw stock and stock in process affect the period; in mercantile risks, the stock in the premises affects it.

When damage necessitates the rebuilding or repairing of buildings or equipment, the loss period ends with the date on which, with the use of due diligence and dispatch, restoration could have been completed, unless (1) operating efficiency was restored prior to that date, (2) the available supply of raw stock, whether on hand or possible of acquisition, would have forced a shutdown at an earlier date, or (3) replacement of stock in process in manufacturing risks, or of stock on hand in mercantile risks, requires additional time.

Availability of Raw Stock. Because of the actual loss sustained limitation, business-interruption loss is limited, in case raw stock is destroyed or damaged, to (1) the time for which the damaged or destroyed raw stock would have made operations possible or (2) the time required, with the exercise of due diligence and dispatch, to replace or restore the damaged or destroyed raw stock.

The claim representative should determine, when handling a loss in a manufacturing risk involving the destruction or damage of raw stock, the length of time during which the raw stock on hand would have permitted the plant to operate, and also the time required to replace the raw stock, if destroyed, or recondition it for use, if damaged.

If raw stock on hand would have permitted only 90 days of operation, and it was destroyed or damaged and could not be replaced or reconditioned in less than 120 days, the maximum period of loss would be 90 days.

On the other hand, if buildings and machinery could be repaired in 20 days, but all raw stock had been destroyed and none could be had until the end of 30 days, the business-interruption loss would continue for 30 days.

Availability of Stock in Process. No specific provision is made in the form for loss caused by damage to or destruction of stock in process. As with raw stock, the actual loss sustained limitation, by implication, covers the time to restore stock in process.

If stock in process of manufacture has been damaged or destroyed, additional time is allowed to replace it or restore it to the same state of manufacture as that existing before loss. The additional time begins with the ending of the period required to restore buildings and machinery to operating condition. If the entire plant must be used to restore the stock in process, the loss during the time will be equivalent to a total suspension; if a part only, to a partial suspension.

Replacement of stock does not ordinarily play a serious part in a manufacturing loss unless it involves raw stock of a seasonal nature, destroyed early in the operating period.

Availability of Merchandise. Merchandise is stock purchased for resale. In mercantile losses the buying, assembling, receiving, tagging, marking, and placing in bins, on shelves, in showcases, or on counters of the various lots of merchandise may be a time-consuming process. Occasionally the loss period has to be extended beyond the time to repair the building and replace fixtures and equipment, to allow for complete replacement to merchandise.

Abnormal Economic Conditions. Abnormal economic conditions sometimes cause delays in obtaining materials and equipment. Long-term strikes at the supplier's premises, or if a supplier is heavily back-ordered, may involve delays beyond the insured's control. Such delays are covered, subject to policy conditions.

Governmental Order or Regulation. Problems involving *priorities* on materials are more common in wartime. In many situations, inability to obtain priorities severely increases the period of suspension and consequently the amount of loss under the policy. This may be particularly troublesome where machinery and building materials, such as steel, are hard to obtain.

Unusual Conditions in the Environment. Where construction is delayed because of heavy local rains, flooding, or winter snows and freezing, as long as the insured has used due diligence, such delays are covered in determining the period of suspension.

Delays in rebuilding, repairing, or replacing, caused by strikers at the described premises, are specifically excluded in the form.

Delays due to disputes of tenant and landlord, one of whom is the insured, are not covered. It is doubtful that arbitrary and unreasonable actions on the part of the insured, resulting in delays, would be covered.

Checking During Workout Adjustment.
When the loss period is to be fixed by the actual time taken in restoring the property, little checking of it is done in ordinary losses of moderate size. But when a serious loss is being adjusted by the workout method, the claim representative should generally employ a builder or an engineer to keep in touch with the work of restoration and should instruct that person to suggest to the insured at any time how the speed of the work can be increased. When the period is to be fixed by the time actually taken in making replacements or repairs, the claim representative and the builder or engineer should make prompt surveys of any damaged structures or equipment, determine what structures or equipment will control the period of the loss, and urge the insured to order promptly the materials necessary for replacement of the parts needed to make repairs.

If the situation warrants it, the insured should be asked to send the purchasing agent to buy the necessarry materials or articles, possibly followed up by a representative to expedite delivery.

If the insured is a person of integrity and ability, the actual replacement or repair of the property will fix with accuracy the period of the loss, unless delays occur from causes for which the insurer is not liable, and circumstances make it difficult to determine what part of the time should be charged to these delays.

Examination of Records. Records are examined for the experience of the business before the loss and, when a loss is being adjusted by the workout method, for the experience during the workout period, sometimes even afterward.

In minor losses, the claim representative seldom does more than look at the last profit and loss account, the monthly record of sales, and the accounts showing the expenses. In serious losses, all records are given a thorough examination. *The assistance of an accountant is advisable on most of the larger losses.*

Records, as considered by the claim representative, may roughly be classed as financial, property, quantity, operating, and statistical. They include books of account, inventories, production records, cost accounts, orders on hand, contracts, and budgets. No attempt is made to enumerate all of them.

Entries made before a loss in the books of account register the income and expenses that determine the past operating profit or loss of the business. The daily, weekly, or monthly entries for a given period will, if compared with those of comparable previous periods, show the trends of the business. Forecasts of probable experience are, in many instances, based upon the trend of the business before the loss, as shown by the records, and modified according to the prospects of future supply, demand, and cost of operation.

Entries made after the loss will show expenses actually paid and, if suspension of business has not been total, also income received, increase or decrease of inventories, and profit or loss.

Inventories, physical or perpetual, will show by comparison, when those of different dates are available, whether materials or finished goods on hand increased or decreased in quantity or value between inventory dates.

Production records for periods prior to a loss can be compared with those for the period after the loss to show whether there has been a loss in unit volume.

Cost accounts are summaries of experience in past periods and are sometimes useful in estimating the cost of future production.

Budgets show the insured's expectations of dates of preparation and are to be considered when forecasts are being made.

Orders on hand or contracts under which the insured is producing are indications of probable experience. Forecasts should be checked against productive capacity, materials, and labor available.

During periods of government or trade allocations or quotas, records covering either are highly important.

The insured cannot be required to produce income tax returns for examination. In many instances, however, they will be produced when requested. In asking for them, the claim representative should make it clear that he or she is not demanding them and that the insured is under no obligation to produce them.

Survey of Market Conditions. In losses involving large amounts based on future sales, it is advisable to make a survey of market conditions before estimating the probable experience of the business had no loss occurred. In stable periods, the survey seldom needs to go further than the market pages of the daily papers. Often, an inquiry directed to a single well-informed person or organization suffices. In periods of change, however, the survey may require the examination of trade papers, market statistics, and published reports of corporations in the same line of business, as well as consultation with persons of recognized authority.

In some instances, the claim representative can make an effective survey; in others, particularly when insured and claim representative are in serious disagreement, a survey made by an expert will carry more weight.

The general objectives of a survey are to collect and present the facts and authoritative opinions that will indicate whether it is probable that, during the period covered by the claim,

1. The insured would sell, or be justified in producing for sale, as many units of stock as the number on which claim is based and would receive for them the prices claimed,
2. Sufficient materials and labor would be available to support the rate of operation, in the case of manufacturing, or sufficient stock would be available to support the rate of selling, in the case of merchandising,
3. Prices and costs in the period would tend to be what the insured claims.

Summaries and forecasts of general conditions are made by industrial engineers, business consultants, other specialists, and business bureaus. Many are printed, distributed, and quoted from in the daily newspapers. Trade papers and magazines print similar information for the various trades and industries. The federal government prints reports reflecting market prospects. Among these are estimates of acreages of grain, cotton, and tobacco planted, reports of crop prospects or yields, reports of merchandise imported, and reports showing inventories of the more important commodities. The Federal Reserve Banks issue reports on sales and inventories of various kinds of businesses in their respective districts.

The possession of a properly made survey will increase the claim representative's information on probabilities. It can often be used most effectively with the insured, particularly if it shows the sales, inventories, or volume of production of other organizations in the same industry.

Audit or Development of Claim

Although business interruption insurance has been written for over 100 years and the forms have been revised from time to time as problems of coverage and adjustment became better understood, underwriters have never tried to incorporate into them any specific requirements with which the insured must comply in case of loss. There is a general statement in current forms that, whether for the purpose of ascertaining the amount of loss sustained or for the application of the Contribution Clause, due consideration shall be given to the experience of the business before the loss and the probable experience thereafter, had no such loss occurred.

In the absence of specific requirements, business-interruption losses are adjusted in the same general way as are losses under policies covering real or personal property. In some instances, claims are prepared in varying degrees of detail and presented to the claim representatives. In others, no formal claim is made, as the insured invites the claim representative to discuss the situation, opens the books for examination, and tries to agree upon the amount for which the insurer is liable.

The amount of the insurer's liability under any business interruption policy containing a contribution clause will be determined by the following factors:

1. The business-interruption value.
2. The amount of loss sustained.
3. The amount of any expense that has reduced the loss under the policy.
4. Other insurance.

In support of the first three factors, claim representatives expect the insured to show from entries in the books, orders on hand, or the opinions of market observers that the figures are reasonable. In support of the last, policies or binders are expected to be tendered for examination.

The work of auditing or developing a claim calls for (1) consideration by the claim representative of figures presented by the insured and the circumstances of the loss and

(2) agreement upon a business-interruption value and an amount of loss that are probable in the light of past experience and the future prospects that existed when the loss occurred, or of the actual experience after the loss. Expense incurred to reduce loss is generally a matter of record. The amount by which the loss was reduced is, however, often a matter of estimate.

Experience before the loss is generally accepted as the best guide to probable experience had no loss occurred. But it is not always so. A plant that has been running at less than capacity may unexpectedly pick up a large order that will make its future more promising than its past indicates. On the other hand, a plant that has been running at capacity may experience a sudden loss of business due to a decrease in demand for its product.

Business-Interruption Value

Ordinarily, a business-interruption loss is adjusted within a short time after the casualty. When such is the case, the business-interruption value will be fixed by agreement between the insured and the claim representative following their consideration of the earnings of the business for the twelve months before the loss and the probable earnings for the twelve months after date of loss, had the loss not occurred. The only business records available will be those covering operations prior to the loss. Occasionally, however, adjustment will be delayed, and the twelve months after the loss will go by before it is disposed of. In this case, the actual experience of the business after the loss will be available. By modifying the actual experience to allow for handicaps imposed by the aftereffect of the loss, for additions to capacity installed or brought into operation, or for reductions due to causes other than the casualty, a reasonable agreement should be possible.

Business-interruption value is generally estimated and agreed upon after making an examination of the latest profit and loss account, and the sales record for the 24 months before the loss, sometimes after making or getting a survey of market conditions.

A profit and loss account for the year, or last fiscal period, preceding the loss will show the experience of the business before the loss, its sales, costs, profit made, or loss sustained.

A word of caution is advisable in connection with any profit and loss statement based on the inventory of stock made after the loss for the purpose of adjusting the property loss. Self-interest may lead the insured to include in such an inventory all the damaged stock in order to increase the claim, and to omit the undamaged stock, which, if included, would increase the sound value and reduce the insurance collection because of coinsurance or contribution requirements. In making such an inventory, the insured's tendency may be to put high values on badly damaged stock and low values on sound or slightly damaged stock, thereby producing an inventory that shows a high percentage of damage, tending to increase the claim, and a higher value than a normal inventory taken on the same date would have shown, had no loss occurred. If, therefore, a profit and loss statement uses it as a closing inventory, it will, because it is disproportionately high in proportion to the opening inventory, make the account show a higher than actual profit.

The regular profit and loss account for the last fiscal or calendar year is, in many cases, a more reliable guide to the experience of the business before the loss. The inventories used in making the account are generally on a comparable basis.

The month-to-month record of sales for the 24 months before the loss will show whether the trend of sales was upward or downward. In most losses, the business-interruption value is estimated by making up a probable profit and loss account for the 12 months after the loss, showing as sales for the period the sales for the 12 months before the loss, increased or decreased by the percentage by which those sales exceeded or fell short of the sales of the preceding 12 months.

In some instances, the experience for the 12 months before the loss will not indicate the probable experience, had there been no loss. If the rate of operating or selling has changed during the period, if orders in hand have materially increased or decreased, if the physical arrangements of the premises have been changed, or if the insured has raised or lowered prices, a better estimate of future sales can be made from the sales figures of the three or four months before the loss than from those of the full year preceding it.

Any experience before the loss should be considered in the light of general business conditions before being accepted as the best guide to probable future experience. In periods of business change, general market conditions are sometimes better indications of the insured's future prospects than is the business record. Sometimes, prospective changes are indicated by happenings in the business itself. In some instances, an increased wage scale, reducing profits, will have been agreed upon prior to the loss, to become effective within the year after the loss. In others, the insured will have made new contracts for materials at prices above or below those current at the time of the loss. An inquiry into special conditions affecting the insured's future, or a market survey of general conditions affecting the future of all similar businesses, is at times advisable.

In connection with new businesses that have no past experience, or businesses that have radically changed their methods of operation, the best forecast of earnings for the 12 months following date of any loss will be one based on market demand, productive capacity, contracts and orders in hand, and material and labor available.

Profit and Loss Statement

Sometimes called the *income statement* or *operating statement*, the *profit and loss statement* is the most important accounting record to the claim representative in developing or checking a business-interruption claim. It has been referred to as a moving picture of a business because it shows the flow of capital and stock, in and out, over an accounting period—generally a fiscal year.

It records the sales, the cost of sales, the expenses to operate, and the net profit or net loss. It shows to what extent expenses are being earned. Every income and expense account balance is shown on the profit and loss statement.

From this statement the claim representative can determine the gross profit and the insurable value, as well as the percentage relationship to net sales of gross profit, net profit, and various expenses. These figures are helpful in projecting the probable loss during the period of suspension, and also for projecting the gross earnings for the 12 months following the date of loss to see whether the amount of insurance meets any Contribution Clause requirements.

Rearranging Profit and Loss Statement. *Gross profit*, an accounting term, is the difference between total sales and the total cost of goods sold within a specified period. *Gross earnings* is an insurance term applicable to the business interruption insurance form. The terms are similar in meaning but not identical inasmuch as gross earnings, for coverage purposes, is specifically defined in both the mercantile and manufacturing forms. The gross earnings is the basis on which the required amount of insurance is determined.

There are differences between the accountant's treatment of certain items in the profit and loss statement and the treatment required by the definition of gross earnings in the business interruption insurance form. The claim representative must rearrange the differences to determine insurable value under the policy.

Value of Mercantile Operation

Under the Gross Earnings Form the definition of "gross earnings" is specified as the sum of:

(a) Total net sales, and
(b) Other earnings derived from operations of the business, less the cost of:
(c) Merchandise sold, including packaging material therefor,
(d) Materials and supplies consumed directly

in supplying the service(s) sold by the Insured, and

(e) Service(s) purchased from outsiders (not employees of the Insured) for resale which do not continue under contract. No other costs shall be deducted in determining Gross Earnings.

Net Sales. Deductions from gross sales to determine net sales would include discounts to customers, bad debts, commissions, returns and allowances, freight and express out, and any other item not actually received or retained by the insured as income. These are all items on which the insured could not sustain a loss. See Example 25-2.

EXAMPLE 25-2

Gross sales	$ ____	
Deduct:		
Returns and		
allowances	$ ____	
Discounts	____	
Bad debts	____	
Freight out.............	____	____
Net sales	$ ____	

Other Earnings. Other earnings include any other revenue such as rent from portions of the described premises, gross earnings from leased departments, or interest on charge accounts.

Cost of Merchandise Sold. The cost of merchandise sold is the merchandise inventory on hand at the beginning of the accounting period, plus merchandise purchased (less discounts plus freight in), less the merchandise inventory at the end of the accounting period. See Example 25-3.

EXAMPLE 25-3

Merchandise inventory		
beginning........................	$ ____	
Merchandise purchased	$ ____	
Less purchase discount ...	____	____
Plus freight in	____	____
Merchandise available for sale	$ ____	
Deduct inventory ending	____	
Cost of merchandise sold.............	$ ____	

By definition, the cost of merchandise sold includes all packaging material used in the sale of the merchandise during the accounting period.

Materials and Supplies Consumed in Service Rendered by Insured. The deduction for materials and supplies in the service rendered by the insured applies to businesses part or all of whose operation consists in selling service.[6]

Services Purchased From Outsiders for Resale. This deduction is for purchased services which in the event of loss would not continue since they are not under contract.

An illustration of a profit and loss account for a mercantile operation is shown in Example 25-4. The business-interruption value computed from this account is shown in Example 25-5.

Value of Manufacturing Operation

Gross earnings under the Manufacturing Form is defined as the sum of:

(a) Total net sales value of production,
(b) Total net sales of merchandise, and
(c) Other earnings derived from operation of the business, less the cost of:
(d) Raw stock from which such production is derived,
(e) Supplies consisting of materials consumed directly in the conversion of such raw stock into finished stock or in supplying the service(s) sold by the Insured,
(f) Merchandise sold, including packaging materials therefor, and
(g) Service(s) purchased from outsiders (not employees of the Insured) for resale which do not continue under contract.

No other costs shall be deducted in determining Gross Earnings.

The definition combines mercantile and manufacturing operations to accommodate businesses that manufacture articles for sale and also purchase some merchandise for resale.

[6]See p. 395.

EXAMPLE 25-4   A.B.C. Merchandise Company Profit and Loss Account
Jan. 1 to Dec. 31, 1977

Sales			$910,000
Less			
Returns and allowances		$ 3,000	
Cash discounts		7,000	10,000
Net sales			$900,000
Cost of goods sold:			
Inventory Jan. 1, 1977		$ 50,000	
Purchases	$600,000		
Freight inward	2,000		
	$602,000		
Returns	$2,000		
Discounts	5,000	7,000	595,000
Merchandise available for sale		$645,000	
Less inventory, Dec. 31, 1977		45,000	
Cost of goods sold			600,000
Gross profit on sales			$300,000
Expenses:			
Salaries		$160,000	
Payroll taxes		8,000	
Rent		50,000	
Supplies, wrappings, etc.		2,000	
Postage, etc.		1,000	
Telephone and telegraph		10,000	
Depreciation on furniture and fixtures		20,000	
Bad debts		1,000	
Advertising		19,000	
Delivery expense		6,000	
Taxes, licenses, etc.		1,000	
Insurance premiums		2,000	
Total expenses			280,000
			$ 20,000
Other income:			
Sublease (corner store)		$ 200	
Vending machines		800	1,000
Net income for the year			$ 21,000

The major difference in the definitions of gross earnings in the manufacturing form and the mercantile form is that the former introduces two new terms: (1) *sales value of production* and (2) *raw stock* from which such production is derived. Discussion here will be confined to these differences, and appropriate comment will be made with reference to consumable materials.

Sales Value of Production. The principal operation of a mercantile concern is to purchase merchandise for resale. It is assumed that the profit is earned when the goods are sold. In most cases the business-interruption loss can be related to lost sales during the suspension period.

In a manufacturing operation, the finished stock that is sold has been converted from raw materials by the manufacturer. It is assumed that the profit has been earned when the product is manufactured. Thus the form uses the term "sales value of production" and excludes any loss of earnings re-

EXAMPLE 25-5 A.B.C. Merchandise Company Business-Interruption Value

Sales			$910,000
Less:			
Returns and allowances		$ 3,000	
Cash discounts		7,000	
Bad debts		1,000	11,000
Net sales			$899,000
Cost of goods sold:			
Inventory, Jan. 1		$ 50,000	
Purchases	$600,000		
Freight inward	2,000		
	$602,000		
Returns	$2,000		
Discounts	5,000	7,000	595,000
Merchandise available for sale		$645,000	
Less inventory Dec. 31		45,000	
Cost of goods sold			600,000
Gross profit on sales			$299,000
Deduct: supplies, wrappings, etc.			2,000
			$297,000
Other income:			
Sublease (corner store)		$ 200	
Vending machines		800	1,000
Gross earnings and value			$298,000

Note: Bad debts are deducted from sales, as they are money never received. Supplies and wrappings are deductible by definition as consumable items. Transposition of these items does not change the "net income."

sulting from damage to or destruction of "finished stock" or for the time required to reproduce finished stock. An insured can protect this value by attaching a "selling price" clause to the physical damage contract. Business-interruption insurance coverage is based on indemnifying the insured against loss of production facilities. In most cases the business-interruption loss can be related to the sales value of *production prevented* during the suspension period.

The projected sales value of production has to be demonstrated. In the majority of cases it can be established from previous actual sales, current orders, production forecasts, or budgets. However, overproduction, economic conditions, changes in style, models, and other factors that tend to depress or increase the normal or anticipated selling prices must be considered in determining the sales value of production.

In computing the business-interruption value, the sales value of production must be projected for 12 months following the date of loss. If the operating statement for a prior period is used as the basis for this projection, care must be taken to adjust "sales" to "sales value of production." This is done by deducting the beginning inventory of finished goods at the selling price and adding the ending inventory of finished goods at the selling price to the net sales.

Likewise, the cost of raw stock consumed in production must be accurately determined. This is done by adding the beginning inventory of goods in process and deducting the ending inventory of goods in process from the raw materials which were put into production. In this fashion the raw stock consumed is properly related to the sales value of production.

Raw Stock. Raw stock is defined as "material in the state in which the insured receives it for conversion by the insured into finished stock." In the determination of gross earnings, the cost of raw stock, from which production is derived, is deducted.

Recovery for loss resulting from damage to or destruction of raw stock is limited to the length of time during which such raw stock would have made operations possible or to the length of time necessary to replace or restore the raw stock, whichever is less. This is not so stated in the contract but conforms with the policy limitation of "actual loss sustained."

Stock in Process. Stock in process is, by definition, raw stock which has had some operation performed on it toward its conversion into a finished product. It consists of the inventory of material and manufacturing costs of work in process, whereas finished goods is the inventory of the completed or finished product of the plant.

Supplies Consisting of Materials Consumed. In a manufacturing operation many supplies and materials are consumed directly in the conversion of raw stock into the finished product. Common examples are expendable machine and tool accessories, welding rods, sand and emery paper, water, lubricants, gasoline, and oil. Some claim representatives are of the opinion that small hand tools that wear out rapidly may fall into this classification.

An illustration of a profit and loss account for a manufacturer is shown in Example 25-6. A schedule of cost of goods sold is shown in Example 25-7. The computation of the business-interruption value from this account is shown in Example 25-8.

Deducting the opening inventory of finished stock at selling price and adding the closing inventory of finished stock at selling price has the effect of adjusting "sales" to the

EXAMPLE 25-6 A.B.C. Manufacturing Company
Profit and Loss Account
Jan. 1 to Dec. 31, 1977

Sales (less returns and allowances)		$650,000
Less cash discounts		5,000
Net sales		$645,000
Cost of goods sold (see Schedule, Example 25-7)		425,000
Gross profit on sales		$220,000
Selling expenses:		
Salespersons' salaries	$52,000	
Payroll taxes	2,150	
Sales office rent	5,000	
Depreciation, furniture and fixtures	350	
Advertising	9,500	
Miscellaneous expense	11,000	80,000
		$140,000
Administrative expenses:		
Office rent	$ 6,500	
Office salaries	30,000	
Payroll taxes—general	1,100	
Bad debts	500	
Telephone and telegraph	3,500	
Interest expense	500	
Heat, light	800	
Depreciation, furniture and fixtures	200	
Taxes	4,200	
Insurance	800	
Miscellaneous expense	16,900	65,000
Net income for the year		$ 75,000

EXAMPLE 25-7 A.B.C. Manufacturing Company
Schedule of Cost of Goods Sold
Jan. 1 to Dec. 31, 1977

Inventory of finished stock, Jan. 1			$ 79,000
Inventory of stock in process, Jan. 1		$ 4,000	
Materials:			
Inventory, raw materials, Jan. 1	$ 11,500		
Purchases	141,500		
Freight inward	1,200		
	$154,200		
Less returns $1,200			
Cash discounts 1,000	2,200		
	$152,000		
Less inventory Dec. 31	12,500		
Raw materials used		139,500	
Direct labor		170,500	
Manufacturing overhead:			
Indirect labor	$ 42,500		
Payroll taxes	4,100		
Insurance, factory	400		
Taxes, factory	4,500		
Heat, light, and power	4,800		
Repairs and maintenance	5,200		
Depreciation, building	4,500		
Depreciation, machinery	8,000		
Supplies used in production	5,000		
Supplies, shipping	6,000		
Total manufacturing expense		85,000	
		$399,000	
Less inventory of stock in process, Dec. 31		8,000	391,000
Cost of goods manufactured			$470,000
Less inventory of finished stock, Dec. 31			45,000
Cost of goods sold			$425,000

EXAMPLE 25-8 A.B.C. Manufacturing Company Business-Interruption Value

Sales (less returns and allowances)		$650,000	
Less:			
Bad debts	$ 500		
Cash discounts	5,000	5,500	
Net sales		$644,500	
Less finished stock inventory, Jan. 1, at selling price (153% of $79,000) ..		120,870	
		$523,630	
Add finished stock inventory, Dec. 31, at selling price (153% of $45,000)		68,850	
Sales value of production		$592,480	100.0%
Materials:			
Raw materials used (see schedule of cost of goods sold) ...	$139,500		
Supplies used in production and shipping	11,000		
	$150,500		
Add stock-in-process inventory, Jan. 1	4,000		
	$154,500		
Less stock-in-process inventory, Dec. 31	8,000	146,500	
Business-interruption value		$445,980	75.3%

"sales value of the production" for the accounting period. Conversion of the finished-stock inventory from cost to selling price is effected by applying the ratio of "sales" ($650,000) to "cost of goods sold" ($425,000), or 153 percent, to the cost inventory.

Bad debts have been deducted from sales. Supplies consumed directly have been added to the materials used in production. Raw stock consumed in production has been determined after adjusting for variation between beginning and ending work in process.

Worksheets

A convenient business-interruption worksheet has been standardized for computing the gross earnings of either mercantile or manufacturing risks. Complete instructions for its use are given, with explanatory notes. A copy is shown in Appendix Q.

Ordinary Payroll

Ordinary payroll has not been deducted in the foregoing examples.[7]

Determination of Loss

The gross earnings forms cover actual loss sustained, "not exceeding the reduction in Gross Earnings less charges and expenses which do not necessarily continue during the interruption of the business." The reduction of gross earnings may be the result of sales lost or sales made at increased cost.

Sales Lost. When a manufacturing or mercantile risk is destroyed and the manufacturer or merchant has no other plant or store to which the business can be transferred, or if a manufacturer cannot continue it by using the facilities of friendly competitors, there will be a total suspension of business. All sales that would have been made from the use of the property from the time the risk was destroyed until it is rebuilt will be lost. In such a situation, the actual loss sustained

by the merchant or manufacturer will be the net profit that would have been made, plus the continuing expenses that will have to be paid out during the interruption. Another way of stating it is to say that the insured will lose the amount that would have been received from the sales, less what will not have to be spent because of not producing or operating.

Loss of sales may begin immediately after the destruction of the property, or may not begin until some future date. If a retail store, or a manufacturing risk that has no reserve of finished stock, is destroyed, loss of sales will begin at once. If, however, a manufacturing plant carries a reserve of finished stock in a warehouse or other premises that escape destruction, there may be no loss of sales for several weeks followng the casualty. If a plant produces in one season and sells in another, its destruction during the producing season will cause a loss of sales beginning with the selling season.

Loss of sales, caused by interruption of business for which the insurer is liable, is covered, even if the sales lost would not, in due course of the business, have been made during the period when the property was disabled.

When a loss is to be adjusted by the forecast method, the information ordinarily considered as indicating the probable dollar volume of sales that will be lost includes the daily, weekly, or monthly record of sales before the loss, contracts, orders in hand at the date of loss, and, sometimes, inquiries. Occasionally, a market survey is in order. All this information has been discussed in the preceding section on business-interruption value.

When a loss is being adjusted by the work-out method and there has been a loss of sales during the period of restoration, or a loss of production during the period that will be registered at a later date by a loss of sales, the information indicating probable dollar volume of sales that would have been made had the loss not occurred will be the same as that listed in the preceding paragraph. If, however, the loss involves a manufacturing plant, it is necessary to consider what the plant

---

[7]For a discussion of ordinary payroll endorsements, coverage, and definition, see p. 393.

would have produced during the period. Information indicating probable unit production includes production records, plant capacity, and labor available. From what would probably have been sold or produced there will be deducted what was actually sold or produced. The remainder will be the immediate or future sales loss, except in those situations when the insured can, in one way or another, make up the lost production in time to meet sales demand.

Ordinarily it is agreed that the loss of sales shall be determined by setting up the dollar value of the sales, or the sales value of production, that would probably have been made during the period when the property was being restored, and deducting the dollar value of the actual sales, or the actual sales value of production during the period, as the case may be. In setting up probable sales or production, the conventional procedure is to set up the sales or production for the same months in the year preceding the loss, and to increase or decrease them according to the trend shown by the monthly records of the business. This procedure, however, is not in order when market changes or other factors indicate a change of trend.

When, as a result of damage to a risk, there is a total or partial suspension of business, the accepted practice under the forecast method is to estimate and agree upon the dollar volume of sales that will be lost for the days, weeks, or months during the period necessary to restore the property; or, under the workout method, after operations have been restored, to examine the records of the business and make an agreement based on what they show. Business may be totally suspended for a week, may be running at half capacity the next week, at three-fourths the following week, and thereafter at full capacity.

In any manufacturing plant, maximum productive capacity is determined by equipment, arrangement, space, and labor available. If, in connection with a busy plant, claim is made for increased future production, inquiry should be directed into the capacity of the plant.

In connection with new businesses that have no history, probable experience is indicated by such circumstances as capacity, orders in hand, and market prospects.

When a plant is working on a quota and cannot sell more in a year or other given period than the number of units allotted to it for production, and production is interrupted but later resumed, there will ordinarily be no loss of sales. Its loss will, therefore, be the increased expense of operating.

Following a short interruption of business, it may be impossible to determine whether there has been or will be any loss of sales; the shorter the interruption, the harder it is.

Loss According to Sales Lost. The language used in the gross earnings forms lays stress on reduction in gross earnings less charges and expenses which do not necessarily continue. A real understanding of the measure of loss will be made easy for a claimant if the claim representative explains that the loss is that part of the income on lost sales out of which the insured would have paid the fixed charges and made a profit. In other words, it is the margin (gross earnings) in the lost sales dollar over the cost of the sales. In the case of a merchant it is the margin over the present cost value of the merchandise. In the case of a manufacturer it is basically the margin over the cost of materials and supplies used in production of finished goods. Because the insurance covers this margin, the amount of insurance collectible in case of loss depends upon the dollar volume of sales lost less any reduction that can be made in expense. The amount follows the ups and downs of the sales and, therefore, when contribution requirements are fulfilled, gives the insured protection during peak periods when sales exceed daily or weekly average, while during low periods, when sales are less than average, no more is collectible than the amount that would have been received as margin had the sales actually been made.

Under a gross earnings form *with ordinary payroll exclusion*, assume that selling price, costs, and margin over costs of a manufacturer producing a household appliance are as shown in Example 25-9.

EXAMPLE 25-9

Selling price. $10
Material. $5
Ordinary labor. 3   8
Margin over cost. . . . . $ 2

If the manufacturer's business should be suspended and production and sales interrupted, the loss would be at most $2 for each appliance that was prevented from being made and sold. The manufacturer would fail to receive the $10 the purchaser would have paid for the appliance, but would not spend the $5 for material and might not spend the $3 for labor. Even if the manufacturer elected to pay the payroll, the insurer's loss would be limited to $2 because the endorsement precludes payment of ordinary payroll.

A study of the books might show that, of the $2 margin, $1.25 went to pay administrative and selling expenses and $.75 was left over as profit before income taxes. The administrative expenses would continue during the suspension. The selling expenses would probably discontinue. In such a situation the manufacturer's loss for each appliance not made and sold would be properly accounted for as shown in Example 25-10.

EXAMPLE 25-10

Margin over cost	$2.00
Less expenses discontinued:	
Selling expense	.25
Loss	$1.75

If the suspension covered a month during which 10,000 appliances would have been produced and sold, the business-interruption loss would be $10,000 \times \$1.75$, or $17,500. If in a month when 2,500 would have been produced and sold, it would be $2,500 \times \$1.75$, or $4,375. Expressed as a percentage of selling price the rate of loss would be $1.75/\$10.00$, or 17.5 percent of sales lost, as shown in Example 25-11.

If the loss involved the month when 10,000 appliances would have been sold, the amount of $17,500 to be paid by the business interruption insurance would compare with what the business would have done, had there been no interruption, as shown in Example 25-12.

The insured should accept the offer of $17,500 and be glad to do so.

If the loss involved the month when 2,500 appliances would have been sold, the amount of $4,375 to be paid by the business interruption insurance would compare with what the business would have done, had there been no interruption, as shown in Example 25-13.

The claim representative offering the insured $4,375 might be given the answer that salaries, rent, and other fixed overhead for each month in the year averaged $5,000, and that the net profit averaged $2,500, making a total of $7,500. If only $4,375 insurance money was to be collected, the insured would suffer a deficit of $3,125 on the month's operation.

The answer to the insured should be that, if there had been no interruption of business, the accounts for the month would have shown the same deficit (see Example 25-14).

It is thus clear that, by paying the insured $4,375, the policy is doing what the business would have done had it not been suspended.

Sales Made at Increased Cost. In some instances the actual loss sustained by the insured will be the increased cost of producing or selling. There will be no reduction in the unit volume of sales, but each unit will cost more than if there had been no casualty, and the net profit for the period of the suspension will be reduced by the amount of the increase in the cost.

In losses of this kind, the situation is sometimes complicated by inability to determine exactly how many units would have

EXAMPLE 25-11

	Quantity	Price	Sales	Rate, %	Loss
High month	10,000	$10	$100,000	17.5	$17,500
Low month	2,500	$10	25,000	17.5	$ 4,375

EXAMPLE 25-12

Sales		$100,000
Materials	$50,000	
Labor	30,000	80,000
Margin earned for month		$ 20,000
Selling expenses abated for		
month, 10,000 appliances @ 25¢		2,500
Available for charges and profit ..		$ 17,500

EXAMPLE 25-13

Sales		$25,000
Material	$12,500	
Labor	7,500	20,000
Margin earned for month		$ 5,000
Selling expenses for month,		
2,500 appliances @ 25¢		625
Available for charges and profit ...		$ 4,375

EXAMPLE 25-14

Sales		$25,000
Material	$12,500	
Labor	7,500	20,000
Margin earned for month		$ 5,000
Average per month of salaries, rent,		
and other fixed overhead		5,000
Average per month of net profit ...		2,500
		$ 7,500
Less margin earned for month,		
as above		5,000
Deficit before selling		$ 2,500
Selling expenses for month,		
2,500 appliances @ 25¢		625
Deficit for month		$ 3,125

been produced or sold had there been no casualty. In this case, the number of units becomes a matter of opinion and must be fixed by agreement.

If, following a casualty, operations are resumed, the cost of the sales made after the casualty must be determined and contrasted with what would have been their cost had they been made in the normal operation of the premises without a casualty. The loss on such sales will be the increased cost of producing them, not exceeding what would have been the insurable margin on the sales in normal operations.

EXAMPLE 25-15

Sales		$10,000
Cost of sales:		
Materials consumed ...	$6,000	
Direct labor	2,250	8,250
Margin		$ 1,750

Assume, for example, that the insured's normal operations were as shown in Example 25-15 (with ordinary payroll excluded). The insurable margin of sales would be

$$\frac{\$1,750}{\$10,000}, \text{ or } 17.5 \text{ cents per sales dollar}$$

If operations after the casualty resulted in an increased cost per sales dollar of 10 cents, the insured could claim the 10 cents under the business interruption insurance. But, if the increased cost was 20 cents, the insured could claim only the 17.5 cents that would have been made, had no casualty occurred.

Caution. An effort to shortcut the computation of a partial suspension loss, being adjusted by the workout method, by multiplying the loss of sales by the insurable margin that existed in the sales dollar before the loss may result in a serious understatement of the loss. The reason is that the insurable margin in the sales after the loss may be much less than in the sales before, because of increased costs of producing or selling due to the loss. Under the workout method an equitable adjustment of a partial suspension loss can be made only by setting up a projected profit and loss account for the period of the suspension and comparing its showing with an actual profit and loss account for the same period, giving consideration to any factors, other than the casualty, that may have affected the showing of the actual account.

Noncontinuing Charges and Expenses. Because the gross earnings forms limit loss to the reduction in gross earnings less charges and expenses which do not necessarily continue during the interruption, an examination of typical charges and expenses is important. It will aid in determining whether the various expenses should or should not continue.

Advertising. Under contract that requires stipulated payments, even though the business may be totally suspended by a covered peril, advertising is an expense which generally continues. Advertising not under contract can usually be discontinued, although a certain amount may be necessary to the extent that the insured will "resume operations—with the same quality of service which existed immediately preceding the loss." The expenditure may be continuous throughout the suspension if it is relatively short, or it may be discontinued during a long suspension but incurred again prior to the reopening and return to business.

Advertising in excess of normal may become an extraordinary expense in reducing the loss should the insured elect to conduct a sale during the suspension.

Amortization. Amortization is a continuing expense where the insured purchases or improves property used in operations and amortizes expenditures over a period of years. In any statement of a business-interruption loss, amortization may properly appear as a continuing charge, or it may disappear as a charge and be included in the net-profit item.

Bad Debts. Bad debts are uninsurable, as they are moneys never received. While treated as an expense by most accountants, they should be deducted from sales for business-interruption purposes.

Charge for Credit Information. Charge for credit information is a continuing charge when secured on the basis of a minimum payment for reports, not exceeding a certain number, the minimum payment covering a definite period of time, whether or not the business operates.

Collection Expense. The expense of collection by an outside agency is not usually a continuing expense unless contracted for.

Depreciation. Depreciation is a continuing expense provided the depreciation shown in the profit and loss account is an accurate estimate of the wear and tear on the property described in the business-interruption contract. The amount of depreciation shown in the account may properly be treated in the case of loss as a continuing charge, and if half the property were destroyed, half the charge would be ended and half would continue. In accounting practice, however, depreciation is often an arbitrary write-off, generally the largest write-off that the income tax authorities will permit. Consequently, in the computation of a business-interruption loss, an adjustment of the depreciation entry in the profit and loss account to the actual depreciation experienced by the property may be necessary. If actual depreciation is less than the amount written off as depreciation, the excess should be added to net profit. If the entire property, real or personal, is destroyed, the depreciation is a noncontinuing expense. It was earned prior to the suspension and could not possibly exist subsequent to destruction of the property.

Commissions. Commissions may be a continuing expense or not, depending on circumstances. The authors believe that, except for salespersons' commissions, they should be treated as costs and shown in the accounting for business-interruption value as reducing the amount received, or to be received, from the sale of goods. The expenditures are made only when sales are made; they can never be lost and, therefore, whether treated as costs or as expenses, can never be the subject of claim under the policy.

Commissions paid to outsiders are normally treated as costs. If there are no sales, no commissions are paid out. Salespersons, however, are often compensated on a commission basis but are closely attached to the business and essential to its success. They are, in such instances, key employees, and their prospective commissions should be treated in the same way as the salaries of other key people. In the case of suspension of business, they will be paid according to their normal earnings in order to hold them.

Donations. Donations made regularly to normally supported charities are generally treated as necessary continuing charges.

General Expenses. General expenses is an item frequently shown in a profit and loss account and often is a catchall for miscellaneous expenses with no breakdown. The only way to determine whether these expenses can be discontinued, and to what extent, is to examine each account and identify it.

Heat, Light, and Power. When heat, light, and power are secured under contract, they are continuing expenses to the extent they are not cancellable. When not under contract, whether purchased from the outside or provided by the insured, they generally can be reduced and sometimes discontinued.

Insurance Premiums. Insurance premiums for property, liability, and life insurance are generally continuing expenses. When the building or machinery is not replaced, the automatic reinstatement provision under most property policies may entitle the insured to a pro rata return premium for the unexpired term.

Interest on Bills Payable. Interest on bills payable, including interest on bank loans from others, is generally a continuing expense.

Maintenance. Maintenance of buildings is a continuing expense unless they are damaged or destroyed. In the latter case maintenance ceases. In partial damages to buildings maintenance of the damaged portion usually discontinues. Circumstances of each case will govern.

Maintenance of machinery and equipment diminishes substantially when the machinery and equipment become idle. Maintenance ceases when the property is destroyed.

Professional Services. Such professional services as those of lawyers, accountants, and special consultants are items of expense usually under contract. If so, they may not be discontinued depending upon the contract provisions and the length of the suspension.

Memberships and Dues. Memberships in and dues payable to trade organizations are continuing expenses.

Rent. In a serious loss, rent does not continue if there is a lease with a clause that provides for abatement when the premises are made untenantable by fire, windstorm, or other peril. In the absence of such a clause, the insured may have to continue paying rent even though the property is completely destroyed. The answer to continuance of rent will depend upon the findings in each instance.

Royalties. Royalties that must be paid whether or not there are sales of production are a continuing expense. Otherwise, if paid on the basis of production, they may be discontinued.

Salaries. Salaries of employees under long-term contracts or employees who are too valuable to lose are properly continuing charges during a period of suspension if the employees are kept functioning in their positions or are sent home to remain idle until resumption of business. If, however, they can be transferred to other work for which they will be compensated, their salaries will not be continuing charges. For example, if, after a loss in which buildings and contents and business interruption were covered by insurance, operating employees were transferred to repair work for which they were paid out of funds received from the insurance covering building and contents, their salaries, to the extent that they were paid out of such funds, would cease to be continuing expenses.

Taxes. Taxes on property are seldom abated because of its loss or damage until the next tax year, and such taxes are, therefore, continuing charges in most losses. Sales taxes are not treated as charges but are shown as a deduction from sales. Income taxes, whether federal or state, are payable by the insured out of net profit and should not appear in any statement of a business-interruption loss.

In considering any charge or expense for which claim is made, the claim representative should apply two tests: Would it have been earned had no casualty occurred? Must the insured pay it after the casualty? If answers to both questions are "yes," it is payable as part of the business-interruption loss.

If a business has been making net profit, it has been earning all its charges and expenses, for there can be no net profit unless income exceeds outgo. If facts in hand indicate that this probable experience of the business after a casualty would be no less successful than its experience before, the inference that it would have continued to earn its charges and expenses is justified. Charges or expenses incurred under contracts or because of legal requirements will continue according to the terms of the contracts or the provisions of the laws under which they were incurred. An officer or employee under yearly contract will have to be paid a salary until the expiration of the contract, while taxes on real and personal property will have to be met until relief is given by operation of law.

Telephone and Telegraph. Telephone and telegraph charges continue without much reduction during short suspensions. In fact, such charges may increase as an expense to reduce loss. However, in a long suspension, expenses of this type tend to be reduced substantially even when incurred in connection with restoring the property or reordering materials, supplies, and merchandise.

Suspension of Operations, Effect on Sales

In some instances, damage to a manufacturing plant causes a suspension of operations that is followed by loss of production and consequent loss of sales. In others, production will be deferred without any loss of sales, but generally with some increase in the cost of operating.

Some plants carry no reserve of finished goods and, if they do not produce, have nothing to sell. Others carry a reserve and, if operations are suspended, may be able to fill all orders out of the reserve until repairs have been made and production resumed.

It is part of the claim representative's task to determine in any case involving a suspension of operations whether the suspension will produce a loss of sales, will only defer sales, or will have no effect on sales.

In some industries production is seasonal and the sales value of finished goods is limited by the quantity of raw material available. Consider the position of a plant that has bought its year's supply of raw material and arranged its operating schedule to work up the material in twenty-five weeks. Assume that the raw material will produce 50,000 units of finished goods. The buildings and equipment of the plant are damaged by fire, but without damage to raw material, stock in process, or finished goods. Operations are suspended for four weeks, after which they are resumed and continued to conclusion. The plant will finish its production four weeks later than had been planned, but there will be no loss of sales. The business-interruption loss will be the additional cost of the longer period of operation.

Many losses involve suspension of operations without immediate loss of sales, and it is impossible to determine with any certainty what effect the loss of production will have on future sales. Such losses generally occur in plants that carry reserves of finished goods. While operations are suspended, the reserve diminishes from day to day as goods are shipped, and the question arises, "Will there come a time in the future when the reserve will be exhausted and orders, which ordinarily could have been filled, will be lost?" The answer to the question is never positive, because no one can be sure about future events. The answer must follow the stipulation in the policy and be made after giving consideration to "the experience of the business before the loss and the probable experience thereafter." Probable experience is a matter of opinion, over which the insured and claim representative may honestly differ after considering the evidence in hand and trying to visualize all the circumstances that may affect the experience after the loss. Compromise of differing opinions is often necessary if agreement is to be reached.

The ordinary guides followed in trying to find an answer to the question of how suspension of operations may affect future sales are production and shipping records, inventories of finished goods on hand, and capacity of the plant.

Production records before the loss may show a rate of operations at 100 percent of capacity or some lesser percentage. Shipping records may show that goods are being shipped faster than they are produced or at the same rate, or at a lower rate. Inventories will rise, remain stationary, or fall, depending upon whether production is greater than shipments or at the same rate, or shipments are greater than production.

Conclusions are ordinarily drawn from a study of the records covering operations before the loss and may be stated as follows:

1. If production was outrunning shipping and periodic inventories of finished goods were increasing, it is probable that a suspension of operations, unless prolonged, will not result in a loss of sales.
2. If production and shipping were proceeding at the same rate and periodic inventories of finished goods were not increasing or decreasing, it is probable that a suspension of operations will result in a loss of sales.
3. If shipping was outrunning production and periodic inventories of finished goods were decreasing, it is highly probable that a suspension of operations will result in an equivalent loss of sales.

Any showing of the records must be weighed against evidence of plant capacity. When a plant is running at capacity and has orders in hand, or has established a market that warrants capacity operation in the future, it is probable that any suspension of operations will result in a loss of sales equivalent to the loss of production. But if it is running at less than capacity, there may be a possibility of expanding operations and by doing so make up what would have been produced during the period of suspension, thus avoiding any loss of sales.

Loss When Production Is Deferred

When there is a suspension of operations without loss of sales because production has been deferred but not lost, the insured may actually sustain a loss or may not.

Consider the case of the plant, referred to in the preceding section, that bought its year's supply of raw material and planned to work it up into finished goods in 25 weeks. Because of a fire, it did not complete its operations until the end of 29 weeks. There was no loss of sales. The plant produced the 50,000 units that it had planned to produce and sold them for the same amount it would have sold them for if they had been ready

four weeks earlier. But the profit and loss account will show a greater cost of sales and, therefore, a smaller net profit than it would have shown had operations been completed in the 25 weeks that would have sufficed had there been no fire. Certain expenses that should have run for only 25 weeks necessarily ran for 29 weeks and were, therefore, greater. In such a case, the business-interruption loss is the difference between the net profit that would have been earned had the plant operated normally for 25 weeks as planned, and the actual net profit earned after operating 29 weeks. This difference should be equivalent to the increased cost of maintaining the plant for 29 weeks as contrasted with 25 weeks.

If a plant is running at less than capacity but is producing all the finished goods that can be sold, failure to produce for three or four days may do no more than reduce slightly the inventory of finished goods on hand. The reduction can be made up without extra cost by using the idle capacity and the insured will be as well off as though the shutdown had not occurred.

Conflict of Covers

Rent or rental value, profits and commissions, extra expense insurance, or insurance covering stock at its selling price may create, if carried by the insured, conflict of covers on the property described in the business interruption contract. When the business interruption contract is endorsed to permit the carrying of rent insurance, there will be no conflict between two covers. If extra expense insurance is subject to the proviso that it is excess insurance, it will not conflict with the business interruption insurance coverage of expense to reduce loss. But to date there is no accepted way of obviating the conflict of mercantile risks between business interruption insurance and profits and commissions insurance, or selling price insurance covering stock.

Appraisals

Business-interruption losses are seldom appraised for at least two reasons: (1) Questions of probable earnings for the 12 months following the loss and during the period of interruption are matters of opinion which are usually compromised. (2) The time element is also generally a matter of opinion of builders, machinists, and other experts, while determining the loss of earnings from the books requires an expert accountant. A single appraiser for the insured and an umpire, both qualified as builder, machine expert, and CPA, would be almost impossible to find.

Reports and Statements of Loss

Underwriters expect reports that will cover various combinations of (1) insurance, (2) insured, (3) risk, (4) cause and extent of damage to the property, (5) degree of suspension, (6) survey, (7) efforts to resume operations, (8) amount of property loss, (9) choice of method of adjustment, (10) preparation for making the adjustment, (11) claim, and (12) adjustment. It is rarely necessary to report on all subjects.

Statements of loss should go into sufficient detail to show how amounts agreed upon were established. A statement of loss should always show, immediately following the heading, the type of business interruption form; the number of the form; the percentage of the Contribution Clause; and to what extent ordinary payroll is included. Also note any special endorsements that have a bearing on the adjustment.

The statement should also always include:

1. The projected business-interruption value for the 12-month period immediately following the date of loss.
2. The basis for the projection of value as it relates to past performance of the business supported by sales or production trend figures.
3. A brief résumé of the property involved, its location in the risk, and the extent of damage resulting in a suspension of the business or an increased cost of operating. The amount of damage to each class of property should be stated.
4. If an order of civil authorities resulted in an interruption of operations, a brief statement should be made of its effect in lieu of 3 above.
5. The length of the period of suspension, whether partial or total, how determined, and whether estimated or based on workout.
6. How the amount of loss agreed upon was computed.
7. Whether a Contribution Clause or a deductible limited the insurer's liability.
8. Details of expense incurred to reduce loss.
9. A demonstration of what the loss would have been had expense not been incurred to reduce loss.
10. A proration of the loss among insurers.

Final papers should include a copy of the claim, if any formal claim was made, also any estimates of builders, engineers, or other experts concerning the time necessary to restore operating conditions in the property. If an accountant was employed, his or her report should be included. Copies of any market survey, charts, or graphs should be included.

Typical Situations

The exhibits of "Statement of Loss" in Examples 25-16 to 25-18 represent typical business-interruption losses.

EXTRA EXPENSE INSURANCE

Business interruption insurance covers the insured's *loss of earnings*, subject to the policy provisions, resulting from an interruption of operations by a covered peril. Extra expense insurance covers all extra expense incurred by the insured in order to continue as nearly as practicable the normal operation of the business. It does not cover loss of earnings or loss of income.

While the business interruption insurance forms cover "expense to reduce loss," such expense is limited to the extent to which it reduces loss *under the policy*. In many situations the insured may be required to spend substantially more than permitted under the business interruption insurance to continue normal operations.

EXAMPLE 25-16   Statement of Loss: The General Merchandise Store

Any Town, United States
Fire—January 21, 1976
GAB File 50005-70007

Fire loss. Total destruction of building and contents. Temporary location obtained but incurred expense did not reduce loss. Contribution Clause not complied with. Insurance $40,000.00; value $90,757.81; loss $28,876.38; claim $25,453.57.

		Value	Loss	Claim
Business Interruption Form 3-19C, Gross Earnings Form— *50% Contribution, Retail Merchandise Store.*				
Business-Interruption Value for year ending 1-21-77 based on actual experience for fiscal year ended 12-31-75 and projected:				
Gross sales		$336,601.48		
Less:				
Returns and allowances	$ 658.62			
Bad debts	32.93			
Sales tax	6,600.02	7,291.57		
Net sales		$329,309.91		
Less:				
Merchandise	$239,414.63			
Freight in	1,671.02			
Consumable supplies	168.41			
	$241,254.06			
Deduct purchase discount	2,701.96	238,552.10		
Gross earnings and value		$ 90,757.81	$90,757.81	
Other expenses		77,092.45		
Net profit projected		$ 13,665.36		
Insurance in force	$ 40,000.00			
Insurance required (50%)	45,378.90			

Circumstances of Loss

Fire originating in adjacent building destroyed six buildings and contents including insured's.

The entire loss was estimated at $400,000.00. The amount of physical damage to insured's property was:

Building	$ 40,383.16
Contents	47,709.44
Total physical loss to insured	$ 88,092.60

Loss as Determined

The insured decided to build a larger and more modern building. Estimated time to replace the building as it was, was obtained from two general contractors, on basis of which the suspension period was agreed to 6⅓ months or until 8-1-76.

The insured purchased an old garage building on a side street and reconditioned it sufficiently to resume business one week after the fire. To attract customers, prices were greatly reduced. On the basis of the temporary location, the Reduction in Gross Earnings plus Extraordinary Expenses amounted to $43,728.82.

EXAMPLE 25-16   Statement of Loss: The General Merchandise Store *(continued)*

	Value	Loss	Claim

Since the incurred Extra Expenses did not reduce loss, claim was computed on a total suspension basis.

The calculated lost sales were projected on basis of previous experience for the same weeks of the year, since there is great seasonal variance.

The monthly projection is—

1-21-76 to 2-1-76	$ 3,402.22		
February	19,443.20		
March	31,612.20		
April	22,602.05		
May	24,361.24		
June	31,436.42		
July	26,712.60		
Lost gross sales	$159,569.93		
Less:			
Returns and allowances	$ 312.23		
Bad debts	15.61		
Sales tax	3,128.82 3,456.66		
Net sales	$156,113.27		
Less:			
Merchandise	$113,417.47		
Freight in	896.50		
Consumable supplies	79.90		
	$114,393.87		
Deduct purchase discount	1,305.23 113,088.64		
Reduction in gross earnings	$ 43,024.63		
Less noncontinuing expenses:			
Salaries—manager & assistant manager	$ 4,249.26		
Advertising	4,479.48		
Repairs and maintenance	136.22		
Depreciation	373.57		
Light, heat & water	780.49		
Postage & office supplies	155.52		
Employees payroll expense	2,619.85		
Licenses & dues	94.22		
Travel expense	118.45		
Telephone & telegraph	42.21		
Garage & warehouse rent	606.61		
Interest	174.96		
Car expense	291.32		
Miscellaneous expense	26.09 14,148.25		
Reduction in gross earnings Less noncontinuing expenses	$ 28,876.38	$28,876.38	
Companies' liability under operation of 50% Contribution Clause is—$40,000.00/$45,378.90 of $28,876.38, or			$25,453.57
Value, loss, and claim	$90,757.81	$28,876.38	$25,453.57

General Adjustment Bureau, Inc., Any Town, United States
John Doe, Adjuster

EXAMPLE 25-17   Statement of Loss: The Ladies Footwear Manufacturing Company

Any Town, United States
Tornado—April 25, 1976
GAB File 50005-80012

Claim for Extraordinary Expenses only. (Insured had to make up production to hold national accounts.) Detailed calculations of incurred extra expenses. Demonstration of savings shows detailed noncontinuing expenses as projected. Contribution Clause complied with. Insurance $1,400,000.00; value $1,278,206.29; loss $26,048.07; claim $26,048.07.

		Value	*Loss*

Business Interruption Form 4-19C, Gross Earnings Form—90% Contribution, Ordinary Payroll Exclusion, Ladies Shoe Manufacturing.

Business Interruption Value for year ending 4-25-77 based on actual experience for two prior fiscal years and projected.

Gross sales		$7,705,751.90	
Less:			
Discounts allowed	$ 19,363.78		
Returns & allowances	6,293.67		
Commissions to outsiders	56,643.06	82,300.51	
Net sales		$7,623,451.39	
Less:			
Raw materials	$3,623,556.30		
Consumable supplies	35,395.10		
Packing & shipping supplies	36,601.58		
Freight in	110,371.82		
Royalties (per pair of shoes)	91,684.48		
	$3,897,609.28		
Deduct purchase discount	74,721.72	3,822,887.56	
Gross earnings		$3,800,563.83	
Less exclusion:			
Ordinary payroll	$2,320,568.94		
Ordinary payroll taxes, insurance, etc.	201,788.60	2,522,357.54	
Value		$1,278,206.29	$1,278,206.29
Other expenses		1,033,312.87	
Net profit projected		$ 244,893.42	
Insurance in force	$1,400,000.00		
Insurance required (90%)	$1,150,385.67		

Circumstances of Loss

A tornado struck plant at 3:11 P.M. on Tuesday, April 25, 1976. About 5,000 sq ft of roof structure, consisting of bar joists, steel decking, insulation and tar and gravel roof, was ripped loose, then carried, by bouncing diagonally across the 50,000 sq ft of roof area. It swept with it all ventilators, the Cyclone cleaning system air conditioning cooler tower, and two poles carrying three electric lead-in transformers. Wherever the mass of roof debris bounced, it tore loose roofing and insulation. In two places it bent the bar joists to the point they were pulled off their supporting columns.

Six inches of rain fell in three hours. Steel bins containing lasts and supplies were filled with water. A portion of the roof over finished stock and last storage was blown away. Some shoes were found six blocks away. Over 20,000 lasts were damaged or destroyed. All machinery and equipment was wet and/or infiltrated with blown debris. The amount of physical damage was as follows:

EXAMPLE 25-17 Statement of Loss: The Ladies Footwear Manufacturing Company (continued)

	Value	Loss
Building	$ 127,611.16	
Machinery, equipment, & lasts	53,796.64	
Stocks and supplies	59,988.92	
Total physical damage	$ 241,396.72	

Loss as Determined

The tornado caused a total shutdown. Early estimates indicated a total suspension of 30 days to rebuild cleaning system and repair building. Replacement of lasts, to be made by three different companies, was estimated at 60 days.

Insured's commitments to several national firms had to be met or contracts canceled.

Through most excellent cooperation of general and subcontractors, last makers and competitors, production resumed on Monday 5-1-76. Restoration and temporary work were scheduled on 24 hours per day, including Saturday and Sunday. Open building areas were closed off. Machinery shifted. A very crude blower system was installed. Portable electrical transmission units rented. Strategic lasts were both borrowed and modified.

Excepting one customer, all agreed to delayed deliveries if most urgent items were furnished. Work schedule was on this basis. A new customer was acquired to offset the one that canceled.

By scheduling daily overtime and Saturdays, the sales value of production was made up. Loss was confined to incurred Extra Expenses, which reduced loss under the policies.

Extraordinary Expenses

J. E. Lukes Company—temporary blower		$	1,726.52
Coral Bros. Company—crane rental			217.46
Staley Company—portable electrical equipment rental			300.00
Jones Company—temporary wiring and floodlights rented			131.93
Wirtz Construction Company— temporary repairs			196.53
Nelson Lumber Company—materials for temporary repairs			127.68

Premium Labor of Plant Employees

4-25-76 to 5-1-76 salaries	$	3,330.40	
Less normal straight-time salaries		2,220.00	1,110.40
4-25-76 to 5-1-76 hourly wages	$	4,340.10	
Less normal hourly wages		3,525.51	814.59
Payroll taxes & insurance			115.69
Saturdays worked 6-3-76 hourly wages	$	10,221.98	
Less straight time		5,738.84	4,483.14
6-10-76 hourly wages	$	9,901.40	
Less straight time		5,783.11	4,118.29
6-17-76 hourly wages	$	9,361.30	
Less straight time		5,290.89	4,070.41
Payroll taxes and insurance			713.59

EXAMPLE 25-17   Statement of Loss: The Ladies Footwear Manufacturing Company *(continued)*

			Value	*Loss*
Extra Production Costs				
Extra outside labor for hauling to				
temporary storage space.—		$ 333.22		
Extra handling labor, four days—		297.35		
Premium costs on 9 styles of lasts with				
normal costs of $166,743.27—		6,967.70		
Premium costs on 4 styles of lasts with				
normal costs of $24,858.40—		1,447.60		
		$ 27,172.10		
Deductions:				
Salvage value of temporary materials	$ 138.00			
Normal Saturday premium labor—				
Maintenance Department	973.67			
Credit on unused materials	12.36	$ 1,124.03		
Total extraordinary expenses		$ 26,048.07		$26,048.07
Value and loss			$1,278,206.29	$26,048.07

Note: Application of 90% contribution does not reduce claim.

Demonstration of Savings Through Incurrence of Extraordinary Expenses

Except for the expense of temporary repairs, premium labor, special handling of lasts and extra labor, a total suspension could have occurred to 5-25-76 or 22 workdays, with partial operations, estimated to average 70% of normal, until 6-8-76 or 10 more workdays. The average production per workday in May was 9,035 pairs selling at $2.910. The average in June was 11,012 per day with average selling price at $2.980. Lost gross sales could have been:

22 × 9,035 × 2.910 or	$ 578,420.70
5 × (30% × 9,035) × 2.910 or	39,437.78
5 × (30% × 11,012) × 2.980 or	49,223.64
	$ 667,082.12

The prevented gross earnings less ordinary payroll expense would be— $1,278,206.29/$7,705,751.90 of $667,082.12, or — $ 110,653.51

Less estimated noncontinuing expenses:

Salaries	$ 1,110.40	
Electricity	1,659.79	
Water	221.30	
Repairs	164.82	
Maintenance	1,947.34	
Truck expense	862.44	
Telephone & telegraph	175.63	
Factory & office supplies	133.68	
Salesman's expense	684.70	
Travel	261.41	7,221.51
		$ 103,432.00
Claim allowed		26,048.07
Savings		$ 77,383.93

90% Contribution Clause complied with.

General Adjustment Bureau, Inc., Any Town, United States
John Doe, Adjuster

EXAMPLE 25-18   Statement of Loss: The Pharmacy Shoppe

Any Town, United States
Fire—February 5, 1977
UAC File 017P5071

Fire loss: On February 5, 1977, 0645 hrs, a fire occurred involving the snack shop section of the premises, causing extensive damage to the restaurant fixtures, and heavy smoke and heat permeated the drug section rendering the contents a total loss and damaging the fixtures and building. Contents loss $25,191.18. Building loss (Gross) $14,127.00.

		Value	Loss
Business Interruption			
Value for the year following date of loss calculated from operating records from the inception of the business:			
October 22, 1976 through February 5, 1977 and projected:		$175,954.00	
Gross sales		$175,595.00	
Less:			
State sales tax	$ 4,947.83		
Returns and allowances	902.64		
Bad debts	1,451.62		
Total	$ 7,302.09		
Net sales		$168,651.91	
Less:			
Cost of merchandise sold		102,304.93	
Gross earnings on sales		$ 66,346.98	
Add:			
Other income		2,400.00	
Gross earnings and value		$ 68,746.98	$68,746.98
Less:			
All other expenses		46,136.90	
Net profit as projected		$ 22,610.08	
Insurance required (50%)	$34,373.49		
Insurance in force	37,500.00		

Business Interruption Form 3-19G, Gross Earnings Form—50% Contribution, Insurance $37,500, pharmacy and luncheon.

		Value	Loss
Contents loss	$25,191.18		
Building loss	$14,127.00		
Suspension period	75 days		
Sales prevented:			
February 5-28, 1977		$ 12,568.15	
March 1977		14,662.84	
April 1-20, 1977		9,775.23	
		$ 37,006.22	
Less sales deductions:			
State sales tax	$ 1,040.98		
Returns and allowances	189.84		
Bad debts	304.93		
Total	$ 1,535.75	1,535.75	
Net sales prevented		$ 34,470.47	
Less:			
Cost of merchandise sold		21,516.53	
Gross earnings (sales) prevented		$ 13,953.94	
Add other income prevented		504.76	
Gross earnings prevented		$ 14,458.70	

EXAMPLE 25-18   Statement of Loss: The Pharmacy Shoppe *(continued)*

		Value	Loss
Less noncontinuing expenses:			
Wages (50% Continues)	$ 1,730.04		
Rent	973.63		
Payroll taxes	339.09		
Depreciation (50% Continues)	438.89		
Total	$ 3,481.65	3,481.65	
Reduction of gross earnings, after abatements		$ 10,977.05	$10,977.05
Value and loss		$68,746.98	$10,977.05

Note: Contribution Clause is inoperative. No deductible applies. Loss inspected February 5, 1977.

Underwriters Adjusting Company
Any Town, United States
John Smith, Adjuster

Where both business interruption insurance and extra expense insurance are carried by the insured, the latter is excess and does not contribute with the business interruption insurance provided the form so specifies. If there is no provision making the extra expense insurance excess, it is specific coverage and the business interruption insurance is blanket.

Period of Restoration. The length of time for which the coverage applies is the "period of restoration" which is equivalent to the "period of suspension" in the business interruption forms.

Definition of Extra Expense. All extra expense forms, though not identical in wording, make clear that the coverage is for extra expense incurred over and above the normal expense for the loss period had no damage occurred. The definition used in the Uniform Standard New England Form, TE-8 (11-66), reads:

The term "Extra Expense," wherever used in this form, is defined as the excess (if any) of the total cost incurred during the period of restoration chargeable to the operation of the Insured's business, over and above the total cost that would normally have been incurred to conduct the business during the same period had no damage or destruction occurred. Any

salvage value of property obtained for temporary use during the period of restoration, which remains after the resumption of normal operations, shall be taken into consideration in the adjustment of any loss hereunder.

Uniform Standard Form 19K (Ed. 10-69) is a Combined Business Interruption and Extra Expense Insurance Form. It is a Gross Earnings Form for mercantile, nonmanufacturing, and manufacturing risks.

Limit of Liability. The insured's recovery for extra expense incurred is limited to specified monthly percentages of the amount of insurance during the period of restoration. The period for which these monthly percentages apply can be more than but not less than three months, and no more than 40 percent of the amount of the policy is to be allocated to any one month.

Commonly used limits are: 40 percent when the period of restoration is not in excess of one month, 80 percent when the period of restoration is in excess of one month, but not in excess of two months, and 100 percent when the period of restoration is in excess of two months.

These limits are not monthly limits. They merely set forth the percentage of the amount of insurance that may be used for the period specified. For example, only 40 percent may be used if the period of restoration is less than one month. The insured may spend 60 percent of the amount of insurance in that month, but if the period of restoration is only one month, only 40 percent can be recovered.

If the period of restoration is two months and the insured only incurs extra expense of 20 percent in the first month, he may still spend another 60 percent of the amount of insurance in the second month because his limit is 80 percent for a two-month period. A month is, by definition, 30 days.

Other provisions of the extra expense forms are self-explanatory.

ADDITIONAL LIVING EXPENSE

Homeowners policies, and those with the broad forms attached, cover additional living expense (ALE). This is the *necessary increase* in living expense resulting from loss by a covered peril, and incurred by the insured, to continue the normal standard of living of the named insured's household.

The wording of ALE coverage is not identical in all forms. For example, the New York Homeowners policy requires that the described dwelling or appurtenant private structures be "untenantable" to activate coverage. However, the following conditions are common to all forms:

1. The increase *must be necessary*.
2. It *must result from loss by a covered peril*.
3. It *must be incurred by the named insured* (not necessarily spent—but obligated to pay).
4. It must be incurred for the purpose of continuing as nearly as practical the insured's *normal standard of living, prior to the loss*.
5. The period for which this coverage applies is
   a. The time to repair or replace the property with due diligence or
   b. Until the named insured's household becomes settled in permanent quarters.
   c. For not exceeding two weeks when access to the premises is prohibited by order of civil authority.

When Coverage Operates

ALE coverage operates when all or part of the insured's home or apartment is not habitable. For example, fire, confined to a kitchen, may require the insured to incur *additional* eating costs during the repair period because he and his family use restaurants. Another example: The entire house or apartment is made uninhabitable by a covered peril, and the insured's household must take temporary residence in another apartment or house or in a motel or hotel.

When access to the premises, though undamaged, is prohibited by order of civil authority as a result of a covered peril, ALE operates for not exceeding two weeks. The order may be oral or written. Physical barricading of the entry to the street or area is also sufficient.

If the insured moves out voluntarily merely because of the threat of damage by a covered peril such as hurricane, tornado, or fire, there is no coverage.

If, on first inspection of the loss, it appears that ALE coverage will be activated, it is important to explain to the insured what its purpose is, how it is computed, and the limits. To overlook the situation may result in presentation of an excessive claim at a later date—one which will be difficult to adjust. The claim representative should try to agree on the time period. This will give a clue to whether the insured should seek temporary quarters in a motel or hotel, or should rent a house or apartment. Discuss with the insured normal expenses prior to the loss, such as mortgage costs, weekly food costs, utilities, heating, transportation, laundry, and cleaning, etc. Have an understanding, as nearly as practical, on which expenses will increase and which are apt to decrease or discontinue entirely. When specific agreements are possible, reduce them to writing.

During the time the property is being repaired or replaced, the claim representative should make periodic progress checks and inquire of the insured how expenses are running.

An illustration of the computation of loss is shown in Example 25-19.

EXAMPLE 25-19

Item (Two Months)	(1) Repair Period Expense	(2) Same Period, Normal Expense	(3) Abated or Reduced Expense	(4) Gross Over Normal Expense
Motel	$ 225.00			$225.00
Mortgage	160.00	$160.00		
Taxes (realty)	100.00	100.00		
Electricity	3.00	12.00	$ 9.00	
Telephone	20.00	10.00		10.00
Meals	600.00	400.00		200.00
Laundry and cleaning	60.00	35.00		25.00
Gas and oil	50.00	30.00		20.00
Garbage disposal		10.00	10.00	
	$1,218.00	$757.00	$19.00	$480.00
			Expenses reduced	19.00
			Total claim	$461.00

The additional living expense coverage also provides for the fair rental allowance of any portion of the described dwelling or appurtenant private structures, rented or held for rental, for a period necessary to restore same to a tenantable condition, *less* any charges or expenses that do not continue. In other words, what the insured can recover is only the *actual loss sustained*.

The coverage also implies that, on any portion held for rent, there must be a reasonable probability that it could have been rented during the period rather than a hope to rent it. Otherwise there would be no loss of rental value.

QUESTIONS AND PROBLEMS

1. a. Basically, there are two methods of adjusting a business-interruption loss. Sometimes they are used in combination; at other times they are used individually. What are the two methods and, generally, under what circumstances are they used? b. Under each method, the claim representative endeavors to reach an agreement with the insured on specific performances or factors in order to produce equitable results. Under each method state in general terms those specific performances or factors.

2. Immediately after a fire loss at the Sellcheap Shirt Store the claim representative handling the business-interruption claim was faced with the following situation. Coverage was afforded under a Gross Earnings Form 3. The claim representative felt that it would take 90 days before operations could be resumed, and a preliminary inspection of the insured's books indicated a coinsurance penalty of 40 percent. When the insured was advised of this, he exerted pressure on the claim representative to authorize an expense of $7,000 to resume partial operation during the 90-day period. In reaching a decision the claim representative made the following assumptions: (a) That sales for the 90-day period of interruption would have been $90,000 with the cost of merchandise sold being 66⅔ percent for a projected gross earnings figure of $30,000. Abated expenses were estimated at $15,000. (b) Sales during the proposed partial resumption of business were estimated at $60,000. Abated expenses were estimated at $5,000.

Should the claim representative authorize the expense of $7,000 in order for the insured to resume partial operations? Explain your answer and show all calculations.

PROBLEM 6

Profit and Loss Statement
for a Department Store Company—12 Months

A.	Gross sales			$400,000
B.	Less: returns and allowances			20,000
C.	Net sales			$380,000

Cost of Merchandise Sold:

D.	Inventory—beginning of year		$ 80,000	
E.	Add: Purchases	$300,000		
F.	Freight and express in	4,000	304,000	
			$384,000	
G.	Deduct: Inventory—end of year		90,000	
			$294,000	294,000
H.	Gross profit* on sales			$ 86,000
I.	Leased departments rental income			2,900
J.	Gross profit* on sales and leased departments			$ 88,900

Selling, General and Administrative Expense:

K.	Advertising	$ 3,000	
L.	Stationery	250	
M.	Depreciation—fixtures and equipment	3,500	
N.	Dues and donations	150	
O.	Heat, light, and power	2,000	
P.	Insurance	1,400	
Q.	Legal and accounting	70	
R.	New York Office expense	2,000	
S.	Office expense	500	
T.	Rent	3,000	
U.	Wrapping and packaging supplies	1,100	
V.	Salaries and wages	50,000	
W.	Taxes—payroll, compensation	1,000	
WA.	Taxes—personal property	300	
X.	Telephone and telegraph	200	
Y.	Travel expense (buyers)	1,500	
		$ 69,970	69,970
	Operating income		$ 18,930

Other Income:

Z.	Discounts Earned	$ 6,000	
AA.	Rent Income	150	6,150
			$ 25,080

Other Deductions:

AB.	Bad debts	$ 300	
AC.	Interest expense	1,500	
			1,800
AD.	Net profit before Federal Income Tax		$ 23,280

Gross profit is an accounting term and the term does not appear in a business interruption statement.

3. The Alpha Merchandise Company was severely damaged by fire on December 18, 1976. In addition to other insurance, Alpha carried a business interruption Gross Earnings Form 3.

a. What is the purpose of carrying business interruption insurance?

b. The Gross Earnings Form refers to due diligence and dispatch to rebuild, repair, or replace property damaged or destroyed. Alpha decides not to rebuild. Is it entitled to recover under the policy? Explain.

c. Alpha's policy expired on January 1, 1977. It would take six months before Alpha was able to resume operations. Explain the effect of the policy expiration on the adjustment of the claim.

d. Certain expenses were incurred by Alpha in moving into another building. This move enabled Alpha to resume operations six weeks earlier than it would have if it had not moved. Name one condition of considerable importance in the adjustment of the claim for such expense.

4. a. Under definition of *gross earnings* in the mercantile form give an example of "materials and supplies consumed directly in supplying services sold by the insured." Also, give an example of "services purchased from outsiders for resale."

b. A mercantile operation is one in which merchandise is bought for resale, the difference being, in general terms, the gross profit. The profit is earned when the sale is made. In a manufacturing gross earnings form, what is meant by "net sales value of production"? Explain the essential difference between the mercantile and the manufacturing operation. Why is finished stock excluded under the manufacturing form?

5. a. Briefly explain the importance of the "profit and loss statement" (operating statement) to the claim representative in adjusting business-interruption losses.

b. *Gross profit* is an accounting term; *gross earnings* is an insurance term applicable to business interruption insurance. Explain the similarity or difference.

c. Name four probable deductions necessary to reduce *gross sales* to *net sales*.

6. There are differences between the accountant's treatment of certain items in a profit and loss statement and the treatment required by the definition of gross earnings in the business interruption form. Bearing these differences in mind, rearrange the Profit and Loss Statement for a Department Store Company to establish the business-interruption value for 12 months under a mercantile gross earnings form. Your rearrangement should not change the *net profit*. Each item in the profit and loss account is identified by a letter or a combination of two letters. Show the corresponding letter or combination of two letters for each item.

7. A loss at Furniture Mart, Inc., is reported to you under a $25,000 Gross Earnings Business Interruption Form 3 written with a 50 percent coinsurance clause. You and the insured agree that sales and expenses for the one-year period following the loss would have been identical to those for the preceding year. He furnishes you with a Furniture Mart, Inc., Financial Statement (see page 438).

As a result of the fire, Furniture Mart was out of business for three months. Assume that for both income and expense items the figures for three months would be exactly 25 percent of the annual figures.

a. Compute the business-interruption value for the year following the loss.

b. Compute the actual loss sustained by the insured for the three-month period, assuming that salaries must necessarily continue since they are all for members of the insured's family and important employees. The other expense items are discontinuing.

c. Assume that the insurance policy was only in the amount of $15,000. Compute the recovery under the policy. Show all computations.

8. The gross earnings forms limit loss to the reduction in gross earnings less charges and expenses which do not necessarily continue during the interruption. Discuss very briefly whether the items on page 438 would generally be *continuing charges, noncontinuing charges,* or *might be either* under certain circumstances.

a. Advertising under contract.
b. Advertising not under contract.
c. Amortization of machinery and equipment.
d. Bad debts.
e. Expense of collection by an outside agency not under contract.
f. Sales commissions to outsiders.
g. Donations regularly made to normally supported charities.

h. Heat, light, and power under contract.
i. Insurance premiums for property, liability, and life insurance.
j. Interest on bills payable.
k. Professional services.
l. Membership and dues.
m. Realty taxes, sales taxes, income taxes.

9. Some forms that include additional living expense (ALE) agree to pay the necessary increase in living expense if the "premises"

PROBLEM 7

Furniture Mart, Inc., Financial Statement

Closing inventory		$ 40,000
Sales		85,000
Expenses:		
Salary of principal	$12,000	
Salary of bookkeeper	8,000	
Salary of sales people	10,000	
Rent	4,000	
Electricity	500	
Telephone and advertising	500	
Purchases	50,000	
Opening inventory	30,000	
Returns by customers	5,000	
	$120,000	
Operating profit	5,000	
		$125,000

PROBLEM 10

Additional Living Expense Claim

	Claimed Incurred Expense for Two Months	Normal Expense for Two Months
A. Mortgage payment	$ 400	
B. Motel (2 mos. @ $200)	400	
C. Realty taxes on home	200	
D. Meals outside (incl. tips)	1,200	
E. Telephone bills	50	
F. Laundry at motel	100	
G. Transportation:		
School transportation	50	
Insured's bus fares to work		
44 days @ $2.00	88	
H. Garbage collection	10	
	$2,498	$

are rendered *untenantable*. The 1976 Homeowners—2, Broad Form says if the residence premises are rendered *uninhabitable*. There is no practical distinction between the two as the intent of coverage is the same.

a. An insured, consisting of mother, father, and two teenagers, lives in a three-bedroom, two-bath, ranch-type home. The kitchen is badly damaged by fire, making it necessary to replace cabinets, range, refrigerator, and other appliances. Fortunately, due to the layout, the balance of the house is undamaged except for necessary airing out of rooms. Insured insists on moving to a motel for the three weeks it is estimated to restore the kitchen. How would you handle the situation?

b. Assume the opposite situation where the kitchen was left practically intact but the rest of the house was untenantable for a month. How would you handle that situation?

10. As a result of hurricane damage, an insured's home is rendered untenantable for two months while the premises are being restored. Insured and spouse with their three teenage children move into a motel and file a claim under the Homeowners policy. See the Additional Living Expense Claim on page 438.

As claim representative, discuss with the insured policy coverage of *necessary increase* in living expense with regard to each item. On the basis of your conversation, analyzing each item of claim, insert and explain a hypothetical "normal expense" (if any) for each item to establish a hypothetical overall loss.

Rents, Rental Value, and Leasehold

Rent, rental value, and leasehold insurance may cover (1) rents actually received or paid, (2) rents receivable from premises ordinarily rented but temporarily vacant, (3) the value to owners of premises that they occupy, or (4) the value to lessees of the use or possession of the premises that they hold under the lease.

RENTS, RENTAL VALUE, AND LEASEHOLD AS SUBJECTS OF INSURANCE

Rents and rental value are covered by forms, some of which cover only occupied or rented portions of a building, others of which cover all portions, whether occupied or vacant. Leasehold interests are covered by a variety of standard and specially drafted forms.

EFFECTS OF PERILS INSURED AGAINST

If rented or subrented premises are damaged and rendered partly untenantable, the owner or lessee will, in many cases, suffer some loss of rental income. In similar situations, an owner-occupant or a lessee-occupant will suffer some loss of use of the premises. If such premises are destroyed or so badly damaged as to be rendered wholly untenantable, the owner may lose the entire rental income during the period required to rebuild or restore, and the lessee may lose a valuable lease due to its cancellation.

Rent Insurance

Rent insurance was devised to indemnify an owner for the loss of rent that would be sustained if the building were damaged or destroyed by a peril insured against, and the tenant, by reason of the damage or destruction, was, thereafter, relieved from the obligation to pay rent. It has, in recent years, been greatly liberalized, and the owner may now collect under it even though the tenant is obligated to continue paying rent. The insured, however, may not collect from both.

Under the common law a tenant is not relieved by damage or destruction of the property from paying the rent agreed upon. Most of the states, however, relieve the tenant, by statute, from the obligation to do so.

FIRE CLAUSE IN LEASES

Agreements between landlord and tenant are usually in writing and are called *leases*. Leases now in use generally contain a *Fire Clause*, which fixes the rights and duties of both lessor and lessee in case of fire. The following fire clause is similar to most fire clauses.

It is further agreed that in case the building, or buildings, erected on the premises shall be partially damaged by fire the same shall be repaired as speedily as possible at the expense of the lessor. In case the damage shall be so extensive as to render the demised premises wholly untenantable, the rent shall cease until such time as the building shall be put in complete repair; but in case of total destruction of the premises by fire, or otherwise during the time hereby demised, the rent shall be paid up to the time of such destruction and then and from thenceforth, this lease shall cease and come to an end.

Under the terms of this fire clause, the tenant, in case of partial damage, is relieved from paying rent after the premises have been rendered untenantable until such time as the fire damage has been repaired. The owner will suffer a loss of rent during this period. In case of total destruction the tenant is relieved from any further obligation to pay rent.

Present-day rent forms disregard any obligation of a tenant to pay rent. They stipulate that if the premises or any part of them be rendered untenantable by a peril insured against during the term of the policy, the insurer shall thereupon become liable for the rental value of such untenantable portions. They do not require the owner to prove that rent cannot be collected from the tenant while the premises are under repair.

RENTAL VALUE INSURANCE

Rental value insurance was devised to protect an owner who occupies the premises and may be ousted by their destruction or damage, making it necessary to rent temporary quarters until the property can be rebuilt or repaired and again be tenantable. This form of insurance has, however, been extended to cover vacant premises or parts of them because a prospective tenant might appear at any time who would lease the vacant space.

Rent and Rental Value Insurance Combined

Insurance covering the rents of occupied parts of a building and the rental value of vacant parts is often combined in a single form.

MEASURE OF LOSS

The measure of loss under a rent or rental value policy is the amount of rent or rental value lost because the premises, in whole or in part, have been rendered untenantable by one of the perils insured against. It is stipulated in practically all forms that the loss shall be computed from date of destruction or damage and shall not continue for any greater length of time than would be required with the exercise of reasonable diligence and dispatch to make the premises again tenantable. The additional time that might be necessary to find a new tenant is not covered. Practically, the measure of loss is determined by the period required under normal conditions to repair the premises and by the rate of rent paid or the rate of rental value. Rent and rental value are generally defined as determined rents or rental value, less charges and expenses that do not necessarily continue after the casualty.

ADJUSTMENT FACTORS

The majority of rent or rental-value forms incorporate the principle of coinsurance or average, based on the rent or rental value for some stipulated period, such as 12 months following the date of loss. In some forms the period stipulated is the number of months that would normally be required to rebuild the building in case of total loss. It is necessary, therefore, in the adjustment of most rent or rental-value losses to establish three factors:

1. The length of time that normally would be required to repair or rebuild the premises.
2. The weekly or monthly amount of rent paid, or the weekly or monthly rental value of the portion or portions of the premises damaged and the charges and expenses that do not necessarily continue.
3. The total amount of the rent, or the total rental value of the entire premises for the length of time on which coinsurance or average is based.

HOW ADJUSTMENT FACTORS ARE DETERMINED

The length of time normally required to restore the premises may be determined by three methods: (1) estimated with or without the help of a builder, (2) fixed by allowing the actual repairs to be made and accounting for the time, (3) in case of disagreement, appraised.

If separately rented, or valued, sections of a structure are involved, the time necessary to restore each should be determined separately. The rate of rent to be paid can be determined from the lease. Some leases obligate the tenant to pay a certain amount monthly or quarterly and, in addition, to pay certain fixed charges, such as taxes or interest on a mortgage. Many mercantile leases also obligate the tenant to pay a percentage of the sales made. Occasionally premises are occupied by short-term tenants who do not execute leases. The rate of rent in such cases must be determined from the statements of the owner and the tenant, from the books, or from the cancelled checks of the tenant. The monthly or annual rental value of a building occupied by its owner is to be determined by comparing the building with others of like size and occupancy that are occupied by rent-paying tenants in the same, or similar, neighborhoods. The opinions of active real estate rental agents may be sought as guides in such cases. The monthly rate of rent or rental value, multiplied by the number of months specified, will fix the basis of coinsurance or average.

UNSETTLED QUESTION

Does the contract of rent insurance allow that, to the time that would be required with the use of ordinary diligence to repair the premises, there should be added the time which would be required for the adjustment of the loss on the structure rented or occupied? This question has been responsible for much controversy. Until it has been settled either by adjudication or by clarification of the form, the logical answer seems to be that a reasonable time for the adjustment of the property loss should be added to the time that would ordinarily be required to make the repairs. Under present conditions, practically all property on which rent insurance is carried is also protected by insurance on

the property itself. It is reasonable to suppose that the work of repairing a structure will not ordinarily be started until the estimated cost of the necessary repairs has been determined. Such determination ordinarily completes the adjustment of the loss under the policies on the building.

APPRAISALS

As a rule, appraisals of rent and rental-value losses are satisfactory. It is usually the time element that makes appraisal necessary. When a rent loss is appraised because of disagreement as to the length of time required to make repairs, the problem for the appraisers is one of building repair. Good builders are competent to appraise such losses. If a rental-value loss should require appraisal because of disagreement over the monthly rate of rent to be allowed, the claim representative might find it wise to nominate a real estate agent as the insurer's appraiser, rather than a builder.

FINAL PAPERS

Final papers should include a statement of the monthly rate of rental applying to the building, if it is rented to a single tenant, or a list of the separately rented premises and the monthly rate of rent for each. The claim representative should also enclose a statement showing the estimated time required for repairing each separately rented section. If outside help is required to determine rental value, the report of the person employed should accompany the proof of loss.

LEASEHOLD INTEREST

Leasehold interest insurance may be written to protect the interest of a lessee arising under any of the following conditions:

1. If the rental value of the premises is greater than the rent paid by the lessee.
2. If the lessee is subletting the premises, or any part of them, at a profit.
3. If the lessee has paid a bonus for the lease.
4. If the lessee has installed improvements that have become the property of the owner.

5. If the lessee is in possession under a lease that does not provide for cancellation or abatement of rent in case of fire.

Under condition 4, the interest of the lessee may also be covered under an *improvements and betterments* form.[1]

EFFECTS OF DAMAGE ON INTEREST OF LESSEE

The terms of a lease determine what will be the effect of damage or destruction of the property upon the interest of the lessee. If the lease provides for cancellation, the lessee, in case of serious damage, may lose the entire interest. If a casualty occurs but the damage is not sufficient to cancel the lease, the lessee may suffer a daily or monthly loss until the premises have been restored. The same kind of loss may also be suffered by a lessee if it is specifically provided that the lease shall continue, regardless of how seriously the premises are damaged.

FORMS

Leasehold insurance is written under two kinds of forms, devised to cover the interest of a lessee under a lease (1) that may be canceled by destruction or damage of property, (2) that may not be canceled.

Forms of the first kind cover the full interest of the lessee in the lease. Those of the second insure against the loss that the lessee may expect to sustain while the premises are untenantable as the result of fire. The second kind of form is generally written on a one-year basis.

Forms of the first kind provide that, in case the lease is canceled, a payment shall be made that is theoretically or actually equivalent to the value of the leasehold interest. This interest ordinarily diminishes in value from month to month as the lease approaches expiration. The forms, therefore, provide that the insurance in force shall be reduced monthly by a specific sum. These forms generally incorporate a provision for

proportionate payment in case of loss that does not involve cancellation of the lease.

Forms of the second kind are similar in their intent to rent or rental value forms. A lessee in possession under a lease that does not provide for cancellation or abatement of rent in case of fire can also be insured under a properly written rental value form.

CANCELLATION OF LEASE

A lease may be subject to cancellation in case of fire because of a specific condition in the lease itself, known as a *fire clause*. In some states, a lease that does not specifically provide that it shall continue in case of fire may be canceled under the state law. A fire clause commonly used provides for a termination of the lease in case the building is substantially destroyed, but there are a number of other fire clauses quite different in their provisions. Some provide for termination in case the building cannot be repaired within a certain period of time following damage by fire; others, that the lease shall terminate if the owner decides to rebuild. In a few leases there is a modernized clause that includes other casualties as well as fire.

MEASURE OF LOSS WHEN LEASE IS CANCELED

If a lease is canceled, the lessee suffers a loss measured by the value of his or her interest. This value will be determined by (1) the unexpired term of the lease, (2) the rent to be paid by the lessee, (3) the bonus, if any, paid for the lease and/or the amount, if any, spent for improvements, (4) the returns expected in use of the premises, or subrentals to be collected.

Excess of Rental Value Over Rent Paid

If the rental value of the premises is greater than the rent paid by the lessee, the value of the leasehold interest is ordinarily estimated as being the difference between the rental value and the rent to be paid for the unexpired term of the lease, less proper reduction

[1] Losses on improvements and betterments and losses involving the liability of a lessee to repair or rebuild in case of fire are discussed on p. 202.

to determine present worth. See Example 26-1.

Subletting

If the lessee is subletting the premises or any part of them at a profit, the value of the leasehold interest is ordinarily estimated as the difference between the total rent fixed by subleases in force at the time of the fire and the total rent payable by the lessee for the

premises sublet, less maintenance and operating charges for the unexpired term of the lease. See Example 26-2.

Bonus Paid for Lease

If the lessee has paid a bonus for the lease, the value of the leasehold interest is ordinarily estimated as being the portion of the bonus that would be apportioned to the unexpired term of the lease. See Example 26-3.

EXAMPLE 26-1

A lessee in possession of premises under a 20-year lease pays a monthly rental of $1,000. At the beginning of the eleventh year of the lease the growth of the neighborhood has reached a stage where leases of similar premises are being made on the basis of $2,000 a month. At this time the lease is canceled by fire. In the absence of unusual conditions, the value of the leasehold on a 4% basis, interest compounded semiannually, will be as follows:

Monthly rental value	$ 2,000
Monthly rent	1,000
Excess	$ 1,000
Remaining term of lease, 120 months at $1,000	$120,000
Present worth at 4% of 120 monthly payments, 83.14% of $120,000	$ 99,768

EXAMPLE 26-2

A lessee in possession of premises under a lease that has 5 years to run sublets the premises at a total rent of $15,000 a year payable monthly. He pays the owner a net rent of $7,500 a year in monthly installments and pays taxes on the property of $1,500 a year. The lease is canceled by fire. The value of the leasehold interest, in the absence of unusual conditions, will be determined as follows:

Total annual rent, fixed by subleases		$15,000
Annual rent payable	$7,500	
Taxes, yearly	1,500	
Fuel and janitor, yearly.	2,500	11,500
Annual profit		$ 3,500
Remaining term of lease 5 years at $3,500		$17,500
Present worth at 4% of 60 monthly payments, 90.8% of $17,500		$15,890

EXAMPLE 26-3

A purchaser pays $10,000 for a lease that has 10 years to run and becomes the lessee of the premises. At the end of 2 years, the lease is canceled by fire. The value of the leasehold interest, in the absence of unusual conditions, will be estimated as follows:

Full term of lessee's interest	10 years
Bonus paid	$10,000
Amount of bonus apportioned to each year of lessee's interest, $10,000 ÷ 10	$1,000
Unexpired term of lease	8 years
8 years at $1,000	$8,000

In this case there is no deduction, as no future savings or profits are being considered.

Improvements

If the lessee has installed, at its own expense, improvements that have become the property of the owner, the value of this part of the leasehold interest is ordinarily estimated as being the amount of the expense that would be apportioned to the unexpired term of the lease.

Any calculation when improvements are involved is based on the same principle as that which governs when the interest of a lessee has been acquired by payment of a bonus.

The value of a leasehold interest may arise through a combination of conditions. For example, a lessee may install improvements and also experience a decided rise in the rental value of the premises. Under such conditions, the value of the lessee's interest will be determined by the amount of the expenditure and also the excess of rental value. In other cases, a lessee may pay a bonus for possession, make improvements, and, after doing so, sublet.

MEASURE OF LOSS WHEN LEASE CONTINUES

If leased premises are damaged by a fire that prevents the lessee from using them or from collecting subrentals, but the lease remains in force, the loss suffered by the lessee will be determined by (1) the length of time the premises are out of use, (2) the terms of the lease providing for abatement or continuance of rent, (3) the nature of the lessee's interest, (4) the terms of any subleases providing for abatement or continuance of rent.

Excess of Rental Value Over Rent Paid

If the rental value is greater than the rent paid, and the rent abates in case of fire, the lessee's loss will be the difference between the two for the period of time necessary to restore the premises. If the rent does not abate, it will be the full rental value for the period. See Example 26-4.

Subletting

If the lessee is subletting at a profit and the rent, expense, and subrentals abate in case of fire, the loss will then be the difference between the sum of the rent and expenses, and the aggregate of the subrentals for the period of time necessary to restore the premises. See Example 26-5.

Subletting With No Abatement From Lessor

If the lessee is subletting at a profit and the rent and expense do not abate, but the subrentals do, the loss is the full amount of the

---

EXAMPLE 26-4

If the rent abates,	
Monthly rental value	$ 500
Monthly rent paid.	350
Difference	$ 150
Time necessary to restore property, 5 months; 5 months at $150.	$ 750
If rent does not abate, monthly rental value.	$ 500
Time necessary to restore property, 5 months; 5 months at $500	$2,500

EXAMPLE 26-5

Aggregate monthly subrentals		$750
Monthly rent.	$500	
Monthly expense.	100	600
Difference.		$150
Time necessary to restore property, 5 months; 5 months at $150.		$750

EXAMPLE 26-6

Bonus paid for lease...	$10,000.00
Unexpired term of lease at time bonus was paid............................	10 years
Proportion of bonus apportioned to each month,1/120 or......................	$ 83.33
Time necessary to restore property, 5 months; 5 months at $83.33..............	$ 416.66

subrentals. An example illustrating this self-evident proposition is unnecessary.

Bonus Paid for Lease

If lessees pay a bonus or improve the property at their own expense, their loss will be such proportion of the bonus, or cost of improvements, as will be apportioned to the time necessary to restore the property. See Example 26-6.

When a bonus or the cost of improvements is apportioned, the apportionment should be made over the number of months remaining in the lease at the time the bonus was paid or improvements made.

The loss suffered by a lessee whose lease continues may involve, at the same time, increased rental value, bonus, and improvements, or bonus, improvements, and subrentals. When more than one element of loss is to be considered, the elements should be determined separately.

ADJUSTMENT FACTORS

The adjustment of a leasehold loss may call for the determination of three or more of the following factors:

1. *Rent paid by lessee.* The rent to be paid by the lessee is usually stipulated in the lease, which should be examined. If claim is made for an amount different from that stipulated, the claim representative should ask for supporting evidence, such as canceled checks, receipts, or entries in books of account.
2. *Term of lease.* The term of the lease is to be taken from the lease itself. If the lease contains an option of renewal, the language of the option should be carefully studied.
3. *Provision in case of fire.* The effect that a fire may have on the lease will generally

be stipulated in a clause in the lease, often headed Fire Clause. If there is no provision in the lease, the state law should be looked up. The Fire Clause is generally copied in the policy form with a warranty that it shall not be changed without notice to the insurer. The form should be compared with the lease.

4. *Bonus paid.* The amount and date of payment of any bonus are both necessary items in the adjustment of a leasehold loss. Written evidence, such as canceled checks, contracts, and book entries, should be asked for.
5. *Improvements.* The amount expended and the date of installation of improvements should be established. Bills, plans, specifications, and canceled checks are pertinent evidence. If a purchaser of a lease pays for improvements made by the lessee who sold it the payment should be treated as a bonus.
6. *Cost of operation, taxes, charges, expense of maintenance.* The items in this heading should be taken from books of account or substantiated by canceled checks.
7. *Subrentals.* Subleases should be examined. If subtenants are in possession under oral rent agreements, their statements should be taken for comparison with the items of the claim.
8. *Rental value.* Rental value is a matter of estimate. Comparisons of floor areas, space, and location should be made with those of other properties rented. The rental value claimed should not exceed current rentals paid for similar property in equally desirable neighborhoods. In case of doubt, a competent renting agent should be consulted. Rental value may be appraised in case of dispute.
9. *Time necessary to restore the property.* The time necessary to restore the property

is to be determined by agreement, using the help of a builder if necessary, or by appraisal.

PRACTICAL CONSIDERATIONS

A tentative theoretical value of a lessee's interest may be based on the assumption that conditions prevailing at the time the value is calculated will persist throughout the term of the lease. Such a value of a lessee's interest under a long-term lease should be checked against estimates obtained from real estate operators who are familiar with rental conditions. The longer the lease, the more uncertain will be the actual value as contrasted with the theoretical. The best test of value is the offer a competent tenant or operator will make for a similar lease.

The value of a leasehold extending over 20 years may be tremendously enhanced by a change in traffic routes, or by the coming into the neighborhood of owners, tenants, or types of business that tend to make it more desirable. On the other hand, a decline in the importance of the neighborhood or the increasing obsolescence of the particular building under lease may in a few years destroy, or at least depreciate, the value of the lessee's interest.

FINAL PAPERS

Final papers should include originals or copies of any estimates of the damage to the property, or the time necessary to restore, together with reference to the evidence from which the other factors of loss were determined. If rental value, or the probable price for which the lease could have been sold, was estimated by an expert, the estimate should be made a part of the papers submitted for determination of the loss.

QUESTIONS AND PROBLEMS

1. a. Distinguish between the terms *rent insurance* and *rental value insurance* as to their purpose.
b. Most lease agreements contain a fire clause. What, in general, does the fire clause provide?

c. The measure of loss under rental insurance and rental value insurance is defined in each policy and is very much the same in both forms. In your own words, give a definition or formula to measure the loss as to time and amount.
2. Most rental or rental value forms contain the principle of coinsurance, based on the rent or rental value for a stipulated period. In some forms the period stipulated is the number of months that would normally be required to restore the building in case of a total loss. The claim representative must establish three factors. What are they?
3. a. Lessees may lease an entire building and then sublease the various parts, in some instances occupying a portion themselves. Other lessees lease a part of a structure and sublease part or parts of their leased premises.

Assume the Long Row Office Building leased a building which was so badly damaged by fire that the cancellation clause operated terminating the lease. Assuming no bonus had been paid for the lease, state four factors you would consider in measuring the loss to the lessee's interest.
b. A lease, by virtue of growth in the neighborhood, inflation, etc., has a value of $2,000 per month whereas at its inception 10 years ago the value was $1,000 per month. With 10 more years to run, fire cancels the lease. The excess value is 120 months at $1,000, or $120,000. State in general terms the basis on which you would adjust the excess value with the insured.
4. A purchaser pays a bonus of $20,000 for a lease that has 10 years to run. At the end of three years, the lease is canceled by fire. In the absence of unusual conditions, what is the value of the leasehold interest? Show all calculations.
5. Insured leases a building for $500 per month. The rental value is $800 per month.
a. If the rent abates and it requires 6 months to restore the building for occupancy, what is the lessee's measure of loss?
b. If rent does not abate? Show all calculations.

27

Application of Insurance, Contribution, and Apportionment

A policy may stipulate (1) the extent of the *application* of the insurance, (2) the *contribution* to be made by the insurer in case of loss, and (3) the *proportion* of the loss for which the insurer shall be liable if there is other insurance.

APPLICATION OF INSURANCE

A policy will apply in full to any loss that does not exceed the amount of the policy, unless its terms state otherwise. Some policies limit the extent to which the insurance will apply by describing the subject matter as the loss in excess of a stated amount or in excess of the amount collectible under other insurance. Others accomplish the same result by describing the property and adding clauses limiting the extent of the application of the insurance in case of loss. All such policies are *excess policies*. The clauses referred to are *excess clauses*.

In still other policies, *deductible clauses* provide for the deduction of a stipulated amount from any loss.

Some policies contain *franchise clauses* providing that there shall be no liability unless loss exceeds a stipulated amount or a stipulated percentage of the value involved.

Exclusion clauses are embodied in some policies, excluding from their coverage property specifically described, foundations for example, or property otherwise insured.

Policies sometimes limit liability on named articles, or at specified locations, or for any one loss.

CONTRIBUTION BY INSURER

The contribution, that is, the payment to be made by the insurer in case of loss, may be affected by a variety of limitation clauses such as the *three-fourths-value clause*, the *average clause*, known also as the *contribution clause*, the *coinsurance clause*, or the *pro rata distribution clause*. Under a three-fourths-value clause, the insurer pays the full amount of any loss that does not exceed three-fourths of the value of the property covered by the insurance; under the other clauses, the full amount, if enough insurance is carried, but only part, if the insurance is insufficient.

PROPORTION

When two or more policies insure the same interest against the same peril and cover the same property, the insurer writing each is liable for a proportion of any loss.

Sum for Which Insurer Is Liable

When the value of the property and the loss on it have been determined, the sum for which any insurer involved is liable is fixed by the terms of its contract, unless they are ambiguous or in conflict with the terms of any other contracts that also cover the loss.

If only one policy is involved, the claim representative must compute the sum for which the insurer is liable according to such limitations of liability as its terms provide. If more than one policy is involved and each is liable for part of the loss, the claim representative must compute the amount for which each is liable.

When the terms of policies are not ambiguous or in conflict, the problems of contribution and apportionment are simple. In such instances, the claim representative is expected to apply the terms of the policies properly and make arithmetically correct computations of the sum for which any insurer is liable. But when the terms are ambiguous or conflicting, the problems they present should be submitted to the interested insurers, unless methods of solution have been established by law, custom of the business, or adopted by the interested insurers, such as are registered in the Guiding Principles.[1]

EXCESS CLAUSES

Excess clauses provide that the insurance shall not attach until the loss to the property exceeds a stated amount, or exceeds the amount collectible from other insurance covering the same property.

The Excess Clause in the Multiple Location Reporting Form A is cited as an example of a pure *excess clause* because credit is given, in computing premium, for the amount of the specific insurance covering the same property and peril.[2]

Other insurance clauses in property policies may contain excess provisions, but if they are not pure excess clauses they may be set aside by the courts if their operation does not indemnify the insured.[3] The reason becomes obvious where the insured has two policies of insurance, each containing excess provisions.

DEDUCTIBLE CLAUSES

Deductible clauses stipulate that a specified sum or percentage shall be deducted from the amount of loss to the property. The deductible may apply to loss at each structure or location, or to loss in each occurrence.

There are *straight* deductibles that specify deduction of a flat amount. There are diminishing, or *disappearing*, deductibles that are gradually consumed as the loss increases and disappear when the loss reaches a prescribed amount.

Disappearing Deductibles

The Loss Deductible Clauses 1 and 2, under some Homeowners forms currently used and under the SMP MLB-100 (Ed. 2-71), are classic examples of the diminishing or disappearing deductible. Loss Deductible Clause 1 reads:

> Applicable only if so stated in the Declarations: With respect to loss by windstorm or hail to buildings, structures or personal property in the open, this Company shall be liable only when such loss in each occurrence exceeds $50. When loss is between $50 and $500 this Company shall be liable for 111% of loss in excess of $50 and when loss is $500 or more, this loss deductible clause shall not apply. This loss deductible clause shall not apply to Coverage D (Additional Living Expense).

This deductible applies only to loss by the perils of windstorm and hail to buildings, structures, and personal property in the open. It does not apply to personal property inside a structure or under cover. Also, it applies to the aggregate loss in each occurrence. Computation under the clause would be:

Loss to garage	$200
Deductible	50
	$150

$150 \times 1.11 = \$166.50$

When the loss exceeds $500, the operation of the clause causes the deductible to disappear.

---

[1]See pp. 459-497.
[2]See p. 276 for discussion of its application.
[3]Also set aside when in conflict with the Guiding Principles.

Loss to garage	$501
Deductible	50
	$451

$451 \times 1.11 = \$500.61$

Liability under the policy	$501

Loss Deductible Clause 2 reads:

Applicable only if so stated in the Declarations: With respect to loss by any of the perils insured against other than:

(a) fire or lightning, or
(b) windstorm or hail to buildings, structures or personal property in the open,

this Company shall be liable only when such loss in each occurrence exceeds $50. When loss is between $50 and $500 this Company shall be liable for 111% of loss in excess of $50 and when loss is $500 or more, this loss deductible clause shall not apply. This loss deductible clause shall not apply to Coverage D (Additional Living Expense).

No more than one deductible amount shall apply in event of loss by windstorm or hail arising out of any one occurrence.

This deductible applies to loss by covered perils other than fire or lightning, and also windstorm or hail to buildings, structures, or personal property in the open.

Since no more than one deductible *amount* shall apply to loss by windstorm or hail in any one occurrence, it is necessary to make two calculations to determine which deductible application produces the *smaller* amount.

Assume loss to building	$300
Assume loss to contents	$400

First, apply Loss Deductible Clause 1 to the building loss:

Building loss	$300.00
Deductible	50.00
	$250.00

$250 \times 1.11 = \$277.50$

Contents loss	400.00
Liability under the policy	$677.50

Second, apply Loss Deductible Clause 2 to contents loss:

Contents loss	$400.00
Deductible	50.00
	$350.00

$350 \times 1.11 = \$388.50$

Building loss	300.00
Liability under the policy	$688.50

The insured collects the lesser amount, $677.50.

In most states, deductibles are mandatory and apply to all perils; in others, only the disappearing windstorm and hail deductible is mandatory; while in a few states deductibles are still optional.

Straight Deductibles

Sometimes called *flat deductibles*, this type merely requires the deduction of a stipulated amount from the loss regardless of the size of the loss. The computation under the clause would be:

Loss	$600
Deductible	50
Liability under the policy	$550

Deductible and Limit of Liability

Occasionally a claim will be received that is subject to both a deductible and a *limit of liability applying to the property involved*. This presents no problem if the loss is covered by certain inland marine forms, such as that of the Outboard Boat Policy. Under that policy the deductible clause states that it applies to the loss or to the limit of liability *whichever is less*. However, the Homeowners and most other policies simply state that the deductible applies *to the loss*. This is interpreted here to mean the *insured's loss* to property covered.

Occasionally, a claim is submitted which involves both a deductible and a limit of liability applying to *specified* property. In this type of situation, three steps must be considered. The payment is based on the lowest amount. These steps are:

1. Actual cash value loss.
2. Actual cash value loss less the applicable deductible.
3. Actual cash value loss of property not subject to a limit of liability plus the limitation on property subject to a limit.

See Examples 27-1 and 27-2 for specific illustrations.

EXAMPLE 27-1

Theft loss under HO-5 policies involving $150 in cash and $250 in personal property. There is a limit of liability of $100 on money.

1. The company is never liable, under any circumstances, for more than the actual cash value, which is $400.
2. On losses under $500, the company is not liable for more than 125% of the excess over $100.

Loss	$400	
Deductible	100	
Difference	1.25 × $300	$375

3. When an item, such as money, is subject to a policy limitation, the maximum liability cannot total more than 100% of loss on unlimited items plus the amount of limitation on limited items.

100% of personal property	$250	
Limitation on money	100	
Total	$350	$350

In this example the lowest amount is $350, and that would be the amount payable to the insured.

EXAMPLE 27-2

Claim under an HO form involving $125 in money and $25 in personal property.

1. The company is never liable for more than the actual cash value, $150.
2. The company is not liable for more than 111% of the excess over $50.

Loss	$150	
Deductible	50	
Difference	1.11 × $100	$111

3. The maximum liability cannot total more than 100% of loss on unlimited items plus the amount of limitation of liability on limited items.

100% of personal property	$ 25	
Limitation on money	100	
Total	$125	$125

In this example the lowest amount is $111, and that would be the amount payable to the insured.

Percentage Deductibles

The deductible in some insurance coverages, notably earthquake, requires a deduction from the loss of a percentage of the value of the property. The amount is frequently 5 percent but may be more or less depending on susceptibility. For the claim representative, the problem in application is one of obtaining an agreement on value, particularly if the form uses the term *actual value* or *actual cash value*.

EXCLUSION CLAUSES

The clauses excluding coverage on such things as foundations below the level of the basement or other lowest floor, or excluding yard stocks, motor vehicles, bituminous coal, or other property, need no discussion. The loss on such excluded property should not be included in the claim.

The essential language of the type of exclusion clause referring to other insurance is:

This policy does not cover property otherwise insured.

The clause is not ordinarily noted in the computation of loss but is referred to in the claim representative's letter reporting on the adjustment, usually by the statement that certain property in the premises was otherwise insured and that the loss on such property was borne wholly by the other insurance.

The Homeowners policies, under Coverage C—Unscheduled Personal Property, stipulate:

This coverage does not include ... property which is separately described and specifically insured in whole or in part by this or any other insurance.

This is interpreted as an exclusionary clause or provision of the policy. It is not an other-insurance clause or an excess clause. Problems have arisen in connection with the intended meaning of "separately described and specifically insured." If the insured has a Personal Articles Floater, the items described and specifically insured in the floater are excluded from coverage under Unscheduled Personal Property in the Homeowners. Should the amount of insurance on any item scheduled be insufficient to cover the loss to the item, the insured cannot look to the Unscheduled Personal Property coverage for the excess.

Receipts from bailees such as cleaners and furriers, or from common carriers, on which a *limitation of liability* is stated should not be confused with insurance, even if the insured has paid extra to have the limit increased. Also, insurance on household effects taken out with a moving concern is not considered to come within the wording of "property which is separately described, and specifically insured." To comply with such wording, each item must be described and have a specific amount of insurance placed upon it.

LIMITATION OF AMOUNT

Policies that cover groups of property in which units are alike in kind but vary greatly in value often limit the amount of insurance that shall apply to any one unit, or the maximum amount for which the unit may be valued in making a claim. Policies covering livestock may limit the amount collectible for loss of any one animal; policies covering an architect's plans, the amount for any one set of plans; policies covering photographic negatives, the amount for any one negative. Policies insuring merchants and manufacturers, and including in their coverage the personal property of employees, officers, or partners, often limit the amount covering the property of any one of such persons. Many floater policies and all general cover or reporting form policies limit the amount covered at any one location. Some large blanket policies limit the amount to be paid as the result of any one fire, explosion, windstorm, or other casualty.

Specific computations which show how these limitations operate seem unnecessary. Claims for livestock, architect's plans, or photographic negatives must necessarily be supported by inventories showing unit values. If any unit is entered in the inventory for more than the limit stated in the policy, the entry should be noted and the excess

deducted from the total of the inventory. Claims for personal property of employees, officers, or partners are likewise supported by lists showing their names and the amount of loss sustained by each. These lists should be treated in the same way as the inventories just referred to.

The operation of a limit at a location or as the result of a single casualty should be self-evident.

THREE-FOURTHS-VALUE CLAUSE

The three-fourths-value clause reads:

It is understood and agreed to be a condition of this insurance that, in the event of loss or damage by fire to the property insured under this policy, this company shall not be liable for an amount greater than three-fourths of the actual cash value of each item of property insured by this policy (not exceeding the amount insured on each such item) at the time immediately preceding such loss or damage; and in the event of additional insurance—if any is permitted hereon—then this company shall be liable for its proportion only of three-fourths of such cash value of each item insured at the time of the fire not exceeding the amount insured on each such item.

The operation of the clause will reduce the insurer's payment if the property covered by the item is insured for more than three-fourths of its value, and the loss exceeds such three-fourths; otherwise it will not. Computations because of the clause should be substantially as shown in Example 27-3.

EXAMPLE 27-3

Item 1, $2,000 insurance
Agreed sound value $2,500
Agreed loss $2,275
Less one-fourth for three-
  fourths-value clause   625
Insurer pays $1,875

COINSURANCE, CONTRIBUTION, AND AVERAGE CLAUSES

The purpose of a coinsurance, contribution, or average clause is to limit the liability of an insurer to the amount for which it would be liable if an inadequate amount of insurance were carried on the property.

An insurer writing a policy that does not contain one of these clauses may, in case of serious underinsurance, be called upon to pay the full amount of its insurance when only a small part of the property has been destroyed.

The Coinsurance Clause (Form 18) states:

In consideration of the rate and (or) form under which this policy is written it is expressly stipulated and made a condition of this contract that the Insured shall at all times maintain contributing insurance on each item of property covered by this policy to the extent of at least the percentage specified on the first page of this policy of the actual cash value at the time of the loss and that failing to do so, the Insured shall to the extent of such deficit bear his, her or their proportion of any loss.

In the event that the aggregate claim for any loss is less than 2% of the total amount of insurance upon the property described herein at the time such loss occurs, the Insured shall not be required to furnish any inventory of the undamaged property to establish the actual cash value referred to in the Coinsurance Clause provided, however, that nothing herein shall be construed to waive the application of the Coinsurance Clause.

If this policy be divided into two or more items, the foregoing conditions shall apply to each item separately.

Note that this is a *requirement* that the insured is to maintain *contributing insurance*.[4]

---

[4]The distinction between the use of *contributing insurance* and *insurance* in the Coinsurance Clauses has no particular significance in the application of the two clauses.

If the insured fails to comply with this requirement, he or she will become a coinsurer to the extent of the deficit.

The Coinsurance Clause used in the Southeast reads very similarly to the Form 18 clause:

It is a part of the conditions of this policy, and the basis upon which the rate of premium is fixed, that the Insured shall at all times maintain insurance on each item of property insured by this policy of not less than ( ) per cent of the actual cash value thereof, and that, failing so to do, the Insured shall be an insurer to the extent of such deficit, and in that event shall bear his, her or their proportion of any loss.

The operation of either of these clauses will reduce the insurer's payment when both the amount of the insurance and the amount of the loss are less than the stipulated percentage of the value of the property. The effect of the clause (using 80 percent) is shown in Examples 27-4 to 27-6.

The Pacific Fire Rating Bureau Average Clause, used on the West Coast, states:

It is expressly stipulated and made a condition of the contract that, in event of loss, this company shall be liable for no greater proportion thereof than the amount hereby insured bears to . . . . per cent (. . . . . %) of the actual cash value of the property described herein at the time when such loss shall happen, nor for more than the proportion which this policy bears to the total insurance thereon.

Like the preceding clauses, this clause will reduce payment when both the amount of the insurance and the amount of the loss are less than the stipulated percentage of the

---

EXAMPLE 27-4

Item 1, $5,000 insurance				
Agreed sound value	$7,500			
Agreed loss		$5,000		
Insurance required by 80% coinsurance clause	6,000	would pay	$5,000.00	
Insured a coinsurer	1,000	contributes	833.33	
Insurance carried	$5,000	pays	$4,166.67	

EXAMPLE 27-5

Item 1, $5,000 insurance
Agreed sound value..... $6,000
Agreed loss $4,000

80% of value........... $4,800
Insurance, $5,000 pays $4,000
   80% coinsurance clause does not reduce
   amount to be paid. Insurance exceeds 80% of
   value.

EXAMPLE 27-6

Item 1, $5,000 insurance
Agreed sound value..... $7,500
Agreed loss.................. $6,500

80% of value........... $6,000
Insurance, $5,000 pays $5,000
   80% coinsurance clause does not reduce
   amount to be paid. Loss exceeds 80% of value.

value of the property. The effect of the clause (using 80 percent) would be as in Examples 27-7 to 27-9.

Because the purpose of coinsurance, contribution, and average clauses is the same, a contribution clause or an average clause is often erroneously referred to as a coinsurance clause. Such an erroneous reference has been imprinted on many forms.

In the great majority of losses the operation of a coinsurance clause will produce the same payment as the operation of a contribution clause or an average clause of the same percentage. In all losses involving only one policy or several concurrent policies, payment will be the same under the policy or policies no matter which clause is used. But in losses involving policies that are not concurrent, the payment under any policy that contains a coinsurance clause, and that also covers more property than another, may be greater than would be the case if it contained an average or contribution clause. Because such instances are seldom encountered, many underwriters are unaware of the difference between the effects of the coinsurance clause and of the contribution or average clause in these cases.

The occasional difference results from the difference in the stipulation of the clauses. The coinsurance clause stipulates that,

EXAMPLE 27-7

Item 1, $5,000 insurance
Agreed sound value... $7,500
Agreed loss $5,000

80% of value............... $6,000
Under operation of 80% average clause insurance
   pays 5,000/6,000 of $5,000, or $4,166.66

EXAMPLE 27-8

Item 1, $5,000 insurance
Agreed sound value... $6,000
Agreed loss $4,500

80% of value $4,800
Insurance, $5,000 pays.............. $4,500
Operation of 80% average clause does not reduce
   amount to be paid. Insurance exceeds 80% of
   value.

EXAMPLE 27-9

Item 1, $5,000 insurance
Agreed sound value.......... $7,500
Agreed loss........................ $6,500

80% of value $6,000
Insurance, $5,000 pays.............. $5,000
Operation of 80% average clause does not reduce
   amount to be paid. Loss exceeds 80% of value.

unless an amount of insurance not less than a stated percentage of the value of the property is in force under the policy or policies at the time of loss, the insured must bear part of it. The average clause stipulates that the loss under the policy shall not be of greater proportion than its amount bears to a stated percentage of the value of the property.

In some losses under nonconcurrent policies, the coinsurance clause in a policy covering more property than another will not limit the insurer's liability as intended. Consider the liability of an insurer under a blanket policy, containing a 100 percent coinsurance clause and covering two buildings of equal value. The amount of the blanket policy is one-half of the value of both buildings. If there is no other insurance and if either building is destroyed, the blanket policy will pay a 50 percent loss. But if there is also a specific policy on one building for 100 percent of its value, and the other building, on which the blanket policy is the only insurance, is destroyed, the blanket policy, according to the holding of the courts, must pay, not a 50 percent loss, but a 100 percent loss. This is not what the insurer intended when the policy was written. It is harsh treatment of the blanket policy, but it is in accordance with the language of the coinsurance clause.

The insurance maintained on the two buildings, to follow the language of the Coinsurance Clause, is the sum of the amounts of the blanket and specific policies. The requirements of the clause have been fulfilled and, consequently, the blanket policy must pay the full loss.

The situation has been considered by at least one court of final jurisdiction. Its opinion includes the following:

> The defendants appealing contend that the provision for coinsurance could be satisfied only by insurance covering the whole property the same as did their policies. The question presented is not free of difficulty. It is entirely different from a question of concurrent insurance. A provision for concurrent insurance is a privilege extended to the insured which, as usually framed, results in a forfeiture of the policy if the insured exceeds the privilege. A provision for coinsurance is an obligation imposed upon the insured to keep a specific amount or a percentage of additional insurance in force; and if he fails to do so he becomes a coinsurer to the extent of the omitted insurance. There was no requirement that the insurance be concurrent; that is, that it cover all of the property covered by the policies containing the coinsurance clause. The policies did provide that when the requirement of coinsurance was in a policy covering two or more items the requirement for coinsurance should be construed as applying separately to each item of the policy. The construction which we are required to adopt is one favorable to the plaintiff and one which will afford it indemnity rather than put it to a loss. . . .

In view of the rule of construction favorable to the insured, the uncertainty of the precise application of the language of the coinsurance clause, and the disfavor with which the law regards provisions for coinsurance the trial court properly held that the condition as to coinsurance was satisfied.[5]

On the other hand, the contribution clause and the average clause never fail to limit the liability of a policy. They stipulate that the policy shall not be liable for a greater proportion of the loss than the amount of the policy bears to the stipulated percentage of the value of the property. It is, therefore, impossible for the existence of another policy to make a policy containing one of those clauses pay more than it would pay if it were the only insurance.

The situation was considered by the New York courts in cases brought by one Buse against three companies. The opinion in these cases tends to be misleading because the court refers to the policies as "full coinsurance" policies. Fortunately, however, the language of the opinion was that of the New York Standard Average Clause.[6]

> The contribution has been provided for by the coinsurance clause attached, which fixes the liability of the company for the proportion of loss or damage which the face of the policy bears to 100 per cent of the actual cash value of the property.[7]

The word coinsurance should read "average." Even our courts are under the impression that coinsurance and average are synonymous terms.

From here on, the term "average clause" will be used to include all forms of contribution clauses that have the effect of average clauses.

Examples will be set up according to the form in which most of the adjustment organizations present situations involving nonconcurrent policies. Thus, a situation in which two items of property are covered (1)

---

[5]*Northwestern Fuel Co. v. Boston Ins. Co.*, 131 Minn. 19, 154 N.W., 513, 46 Ins. L.J. 715, *Joyce on Insurance*, Vol. 4, p. 4184, sec. 2496a.
[6]Now the New York Standard Coinsurance Clause.
[7]*Buse vs. National Ben Franklin et al.*, 160 N.Y. Supp. 576, 48 Ins. L.J. 404; *affirmed*, 123 N.E. 858 (N.Y. Ct. of Appeals).

by a specific policy on each and also (2) by a blanket policy covering both, is stated and set up in Examples 27-10 to 27-12.

The owner of a manufacturing plant holds four policies, or groups of policies. One covers his building for $100,000; another, his equipment for $150,000; the third, his stock for $200,000; and the fourth, all real and personal property for $500,000. The policies on building, equipment, and stock contain 80 percent average clauses; the policy or policies covering all real and personal property, the 100 percent average clause. He suffers a loss. The agreed figures are shown in Example 27-10. In reporting to the insurers on any question of apportionment or in summarizing an adjustment, the claim representative would set up the situation as shown in Example 27-11. The apportionment would be shown in another paragraph.

Consider the situation previously presented of the two buildings of equal value.[8] See Example 27-12.

WAIVER OF INVENTORY AND APPRAISEMENT CLAUSE

The following clause, or one with similar language, is generally made a part of coinsurance, contribution, and average clauses:

In the event that the aggregate claim for any loss is both less than $10,000 and less than 5% of the total amount of insurance upon the property described herein at the time such loss occurs, no special inventory or appraisement of the undamaged property shall be required, provided, however, that nothing herein shall be construed to waive application of the first paragraph of this clause.

If the insurance under this policy be divided into two or more items, the foregoing shall apply to each item separately.

The practical effect of this clause is to relieve the insured of the trouble and expense of making an inventory of undamaged personal property, or making an evaluation of the building(s), on small losses, to determine whether the coinsurance requirement

[8]See p. 454.

EXAMPLE 27-10 Agreed Figures

	Value	Loss
Buildings	$250,000	$ 10,000
Equipment	375,000	30,000
Stock	500,000	100,000

has been met. It *does not waive* the application of the coinsurance clause. The claim representative is free to make an inventory or appraise the building(s) if he or she so wishes. If the claim representative determines that the amount of insurance does not meet the requirements—that the insured is actually a coinsurer—he or she can determine the insurer's limit of liability accordingly.

Pro Rata Distribution Clause

A typical pro rata distribution clause reads:

It is a condition of this policy that the amount insured hereunder shall attach in or on each building, shed and other structure and/or place in that proportion of the amount hereby insured that the value of the property covered by this policy in or on each said building, shed and other structure and/or place shall bear to the value of all the property described herein.

If several locations are involved, the sound value and loss at each should be ascertained, after which payments may be determined as in Examples 27-13 and 27-14.

100 Percent Average Clause and Pro Rata Distribution Clause Compared

While the 100 percent average clause effects a pro rata distribution of the insurance, the pro rata distribution clause does not require 100 percent insurance to collect in full certain losses that may occur. As shown by Example 27-14, if the loss at one or more locations is less than the insurance attaching, the loss may be collected in full although the insurance is less than the aggregate value. Under the 100 percent average clause no loss may be collected in full unless there is 100 percent insurance.

EXAMPLE 27-11   Summary

	Value	Loss	Insurance		
Buildings	$ 250,000	$ 10,000	$100,000	80%	
Equipment	375,000	30,000	150,000	80% } $500,000 100%
Stock	500,000	100,000	200,000	80%	
	$1,125,000	$140,000	$450,000		

EXAMPLE 27-12   Apportionment

	Value	Specific Insurance	Blanket Insurance	Loss
Building A	$50,000	Nil		$50,000
Building B	50,000	$50,000 }	$50,000	Nil

1. If the blanket policy contains a 100% coinsurance clause, the insurer writing it will pay $50,000, because the insured has insurance amounting to 100% of value.
2. If the blanket policy contains a 100% average clause, the insurer writing it will pay

$$\frac{\$50,000}{100\% \text{ of } \$100,000} \times \$50,000, \text{ or } \$25,000$$

EXAMPLE 27-13

Insurance	$10,000.00
Agreed sound value, all locations	$12,000.00
Sound value at location of loss	$5,000.00
Loss	$5,000.00
Insurance attaching 5,000/12,000 of $10,000	$4,166.66
Payment to be made	$4,166.66

EXAMPLE 27-14

Insurance...........................	$10,000
Agreed sound value, all locations........	$12,000
Sound value at location of loss...........	$5,000
Loss	$2,500
Payment to be made	$2,500

SPECIFIC, BLANKET, AND FLOATING INSURANCE

Specific Insurance

The term *specific* as it is usually applied to insurance is, unfortunately, relative rather than absolute, there being no authoritative definition of specific insurance. A policy covering a single building, a single machine, or a single bale or lot of merchandise is certainly specific. But by common usage a policy that covers in a single item all of the machinery or all of the stock in given premises is spoken of as specific, in contrast to one that covers in a single item both machinery and stock. Insurance covering at one location is also considered specific in contrast to insurance covering at several locations, as is also insurance covering a single ownership, that of a bailor, for instance, in contrast to insurance containing the trust-and-commission clause and covering in the name of the bailee the property of several bailors. Under a specific policy containing a coinsurance, contribution, or average clause the sound value of the property covered must be determined separately if other insurance of broader coverage is also involved.

Blanket Insurance

When two or more items of property ordinarily insured separately are insured under a single item or when property at two or more locations is so insured, the insurance is termed *blanket*. As the word blanket indicates, the insurance covers the entire property, and if the policy does not contain an average or coinsurance clause, it may be called upon to cover wherever protection is needed. In adjusting a loss under blanket insurance subject to an average, a coinsurance, or a pro rata distribution clause the sound value of all property covered must be determined, even though the loss may be confined to a part of the property that is also covered by specific insurance.

Floating Insurance

Floating insurance covers the property described at any place within the boundaries specified. Floaters are sometimes described as *general* or *limited* floaters, according to the breadth or narrowness of the coverage, a general floater covering at any location within an area, and a limited floater being restricted to specific locations within the area. The terms *general* and *limited* are, of course, relative. In some floaters it is stipulated that liability in any one location is limited to a given amount; in others there is no such stipulation. The sound value under a floater includes all insured property within the geographic boundaries specified in the floater at the time of loss.

APPORTIONMENT

Apportionment is the act or the result of computing and assigning to each of two or more policies insuring the same property its proportion of the amount of the insurance loss. When the policies insure the same interest against the same peril and cover the same property under the same terms, each policy, in case of loss, is liable for its pro rata share. The provision for the pro rata liability in the 1943 edition of the New York Standard Policy reads:

> This Company shall not be liable for a greater proportion of any loss than the amount hereby insured shall bear to the whole insurance covering the property against the peril involved, whether collectible or not.

When policies separately insure different interests in the same property, the principle of pro rata liability does not govern. As an example, two persons who own each an individual half interest in a building may hold separate policies covering the two half interests, one for $2,500, the other for $500. A loss of $500 occurs. In the absence of coinsurance or average clauses, the policy held by each half owner pays half of the loss, or $250.

The principle of pro rata liability does not govern when both ordinary and excess insurance are involved, but does govern when any of several concurrent policies is not collectible because of breach of warranty or other reason.

When several policies cover all of the property described in each and are subject to the same provisions and clauses affecting contribution and apportionment, the policies are said to be concurrent. In case of loss under concurrent policies, apportionment is a simple operation. When, however, some of the policies cover more or less property than the others, but each covers some property covered by all others, or when the provisions and clauses affecting contribution and apportionment are not the same in all policies, the policies are said to be nonconcurrent.

In case of loss under nonconcurrent policies, apportionment may be a highly complicated operation.

Because policies may be specific, blanket, or floating, according to their description of the property covered and of its location, property covered by a specific policy may also be covered by blanket or floating policies that cover other property as well. In such instances the policies are nonconcurrent as to coverage. And because of rate differentials or other reasons, policies covering the same property may be written, some with average or coinsurance clauses, some without, or all with such clauses but with different percentages stated in the clauses. In such instances, the policies are nonconcurrent as to clauses. In other instances, policies are nonconcurrent both as to coverage and as to clauses. In some losses under nonconcurrent policies, the terms of the policies will be such that an apportionment can be made that is legally sound and mathematically correct, but in many, the terms in each policy are in conflict with those in the others, and any apportionment must be to some extent arbitrary.

Prior to 1934, a number of rules for the solution of apportionment problems arising under nonconcurrent fire policies had been formulated by claim representatives or laid down by the courts. There was, however, no countrywide acceptance of them, and as a result many acrimonious controversies arose over apportionments in which the insured was the suffering bystander while the insurers wrangled among themselves, each contending for the use of the rule under which its share of the loss would be the smallest. Thoughtful underwriters, loss men, and claim representatives realized that these controversies were harmful to public relations.

In 1934, rules approved by the National Board of Fire Underwriters, although not binding on insurers, reduced controversies to a minimum. Minor changes in the rules were made in 1942. Acceptance of the rules was general throughout the industry.

The occasional overlapping of fire, inland marine, and casualty coverages produced so many problems of apportionment that the National Board of Fire Underwriters, the Inland Marine Underwriters Association, and the Association of Casualty and Surety Companies made a number of agreements among themselves concerning the manner in which losses presenting problems of overlapping coverages should be apportioned. These agreements were given the title Agreement of Guiding Principles. Companies indicated their acceptance of these principles by signing an agreement to adopt the rules of apportionment. These rules supplemented those of the National Board of Fire Underwriters (now the American Insurance Association).

THE GUIDING PRINCIPLES

The changing concept of underwriting from traditional *casualty* and *fire* lines to mul-

tiple-line underwriting resulted in numerous overlapping coverage conflicts. By 1955 all state licensing changes had been completed, permitting any insurer to write all types of insurance except life insurance.

With regulatory restrictions removed, we enter into a new era of insurance business. Multiple Peril underwriting is now an actuality and competition is even keener than before. During these formative years, policies are constantly undergoing change to provide a contract more saleable to the insured. And yet, we cannot overlook the fact that no matter how much we broaden or alter policies, the economic position of the insured still dictates the extent of his purchases. As a consequence of this competitive spirit and underwriting change, greater complexities of interlocking coverages have been developing.

The problems encountered were discussed by representatives of the various trade associations. They came to the conclusion that joint action was necessary because the coverages of the new policies crossed and recrossed the old jurisdictional lines. The prevailing agreements were not applicable to resolve many of the new overlapping situations. A sub-committee, selected from the membership of the Association of the National Board of Fire Underwriters, and the Inland Marine Underwriters Association, was assigned the task of reviewing the overall program of Guiding Principles. It was the hope of the sub-committee that possibly one basic philosophy could be drafted and applied to all problems of overlapping coverage. With this as a goal, they set to work on June, 1959. As the work progressed, representatives of the National Bureau of Casualty Underwriters and Surety Association of America were invited to assist in the project. In addition, the National Automobile Underwriters Association and others were consulted.[9]

The purpose of the Guiding Principles is to attempt to resolve these conflicts of over-

---

[9]B. R. Lothgren, former executive assistant at the Western Departmental Office, General Adjustment Bureau, Inc., and chairman of the subcommittee on Overall Guiding Principles.

lapping coverages. Recognizing that disputes over apportionments are against the interests of both insureds and insurers, the industry has set down these Principles which, it is hoped, will eliminate most of them. The associations that participated in the program for developing the principles have advised their members and subscribers to adopt them. Adherence to the principles is on a voluntary basis, and there are no signatories.

The Guiding Principles supersede all other apportionment rules for overlapping coverage, including those promulgated in 1934 by the National Board of Fire Underwriters. They apply to first-party overlapping coverage situations involving fire, casualty, and inland-marine policies. The effective date of the Guiding Principles was November 1, 1963.

The complete text of the Guiding Principles follows. It contains interpretations, explanations, and illustrative examples.

THE GUIDING PRINCIPLES

FOREWORD

Under practices predating these Guiding Principles, where an overlap in coverage existed between or among policies in the casualty, fire or inland marine classifications of insurance, each such classification participated as a group in the adjustment (subject to extent of available insurance and limiting conditions) without regard to the number of policies involved under each classification.

With the advent of multiple-line policies[1] which cross and re-cross jurisdictional lines, the Associations recommending these Guiding Principles have concluded that, excepting overlap between boiler-machinery policies with any other classification on insurance[2], it is no longer practical to group policies by "segments" of the industry; rather that each policy should contribute as an individual policy unless it be concurrent[3] with another policy or policies, in which instance such **group of concurrent policies** should contribute as if it were a single policy, subject to the Specific Principles and General Conditions contained herein.

However, retention of the classification concept **is** necessary to determine under which of the Principles certain overlaps are apportioned; namely, casualty, fidelity,[4] fire, inland marine; casualty-casualty, fire-fire, inland-inland. For this purpose, and not to determine concurrent policies, the component coverages found in multiple-line policies should be identified on the basis of their traditional underwriting classification; i.e., the burglary and theft coverages of homeowners policies are casualty; the all-risk personal property coverage found in certain homeowners policies is inland marine.

---

[1] Wherever the term *policy* is used, it shall be construed to include fidelity bonds, certificates or certifications of insurance.
[2] See boiler-machinery Illustrative Problems, pp. 478-488.

[3] See Definitions, p. 497.
[4] Fidelity wherever used in these Guiding Principles shall not include surety or public official statutory or qualifying bonds.

GUIDING PRINCIPLES

for

OVERLAPPING INSURANCE COVERAGES

(Superseding All Guiding Principles of Prior Date)

THE PURPOSE

WHEREAS from time to time disputes arise in the adjustment and apportionment of losses and claims because of overlapping coverages, which disputes require litigation or arbitration, and

WHEREAS the occurrence of such disputes is against the interests of the insuring public and the companies, and

WHEREAS it is desirable to lay down certain Principles for the elimination of these disputes,

THEREFORE BE IT RESOLVED that the Association of Casualty and Surety Companies, the Inland Marine Underwriters Association, the National Automobile Underwriters Association, the National Board of Fire Underwriters, the National Bureau of Casualty Underwriters and the Surety Association of America recommend to their respective members and subscribers their concurrence in adopting the following Guiding Principles, effective as to losses and claims, other than losses and claims involving retrospective[1] rated policies, occurring on and after **November 1, 1963.**

Note: When retrospective rated boiler-machinery--fire policies overlap, these Guiding Principles **do** apply.

THE PLAN

These Principles provide for the equitable distribution of available insurance. As among insurance companies, the "other insurance" clause(s) which is (are) contained in a policy(ies) of insurance, and which may include an excess provision[1], shall be set aside and be inoperative to the extent that it is (they are) in conflict with the purpose of these Principles. Otherwise, these Principles will not change coverage or other conditions under any policy(ies) of insurance.

Further, the application of these Principles shall in no event operate to reduce recovery to the insured below that which would have been obtained under any policy or policies covering the risk.

PART I

THE PROCEDURE

Dealing with first-party property losses and claims, except those situations more specifically provided for in Part II (Specific Principles — casualty-casualty, fire-fire and inland-inland) and the General Conditions.

[1] See Definitions.

GENERAL PRINCIPLES

1. Insurance covering same property and same interest:

A. Insurance covering a specifically described article or object, whether or not for an express amount, at a designated location[1] shall be primary to any other insurance.[2] (See Notes 1 and 2)

B. Insurance covering a specifically described article or object, whether or not for an express amount, without designation of location shall be excess as to "1-A" but primary as to any other insurance.[2] (See Notes 1 and 2)

C. Insurance covering a specifically described group or class of related articles or objects, whether or not for an express amount, at a designated location shall be excess as to "1-A" and "1-B" but primary as to any other insurance.[2] (See Notes 1 and 2)

D. Insurance covering a specifically described group or class of related articles or objects, whether or not for an express amount, without designation of location shall be excess as to "1-A," "1-B" and "1-C" but primary as to any other insurance.[2] (See Notes 1 and 2)

E. Insurance covering at a designated location and not specific as to an article or object or as to group or class of related articles or objects shall be excess as to "1-A," "1-B," "1-C" and "1-D" but primary as to any other insurance.[2] (See Notes 1 and 2)

F. Insurance without designation of location and not specific as to an article or object or as to group or class of related articles or objects shall be excess to "1-A," "1-B," "1-C," "1-D" and "1-E."

However, as between insurances without designation of location and not specific as to an article or object or as to group or class of related articles or objects, the policy for the more limited purpose[1] (other than peril) to which the insurance applies shall be primary.[2] (See Notes 1 and 2)

G. Two or more policies providing coverage as set forth in "1-A" through "1-F," respectively, shall be contributing. Contribution shall be as follows:

(1) Whether or not deductibles are involved, contribution shall be on the basis of the Limit of Liability Rule[3] except that, in the event there is an area of common coverage under two or more policies and separate coverage under any one or more such policies, the policy or policies affording separate coverage shall respond first to that loss it alone covers and the remainder of its limit of liability shall contribute to the common loss on the basis of the Limit of Liability Rule.

(a) When one of the policies is subject to a deductible, the amount of loss in excess of the deductible will be considered as the common loss. The policy(ies) without a deductible shall first respond to the loss which it alone covers to the extent of its limit of liability, thereafter the remainder of its limit of liability will contribute with the other insurance to the common loss on the basis of the Limit of Liability Rule.

(b) When two deductibles are involved, the amount of loss in excess of the higher deductible will be considered as the common loss. The differential between the higher and lower deductible shall be assessed to the limit of liability of the policy(ies) subject to the lower deductible The remainder of its limit of liability will contribute with the insurance subject to the higher deductible to the common loss on the basis of the Limit of Liability Rule. Where there are more than two deductibles, the same procedure shall apply.[2] (See Notes 1 and 2)

Note 1. In overlapping situations involving boiler-machinery policies, classifications "1-C," "1-D," "1-E" and "1-F" shall not consider other insurance primary. Therefore, losses will be apportioned in accordance with General Principle 1-G

Insurance effected on a specifically described article or object as defined in General Principles 1-A and 1-B shall be primary to the boiler-machinery policy. However, a building is not construed in overlapping situations involving boiler-machinery policies as a specifically described "article" or "object."

Note 2. In overlapping situations involving burglary policies the term "article" or "object," wherever used in these Principles, is not construed to include buildings or structures.

[1] See Definitions.
[2] See Illustrative Problems.
[3] See General Condition 2.

General Principles

2. Insurance covering same property and different interests:

A. Bailee's customers insurance shall be primary to other insurance effected by the same named bailee-insured.   (See General Condition 8)

B. Insurance secured by a custodian covering property belonging to others shall be primary to any other insurance.   Where there is more than one custodian, the insurance of the custodian in possession of the property shall be primary.   (See General Condition 8)

> **Note:** Bankers and brokers blanket bonds, and fidelity, burglary, theft and jewelers block insurance providing coverage on property "held by the insured in any capacity whether or not the insured is liable for the loss thereof," or with equivalent verbiage, are not construed as insurance covering "different interests" and are not bailee's customers insurance or insurance secured by a custodian covering property belonging to others.

Exceptions:

General Principle (2-B) shall not apply:

(1) when the custodian's insurance is afforded under a policy provision containing the words "property for which the insured is liable," ". . . . . .may be liable," ". . . . . .is legally liable," or equivalent verbiage;

> **Note:** For the purpose of these Guiding Principles the above verbiage is construed to provide liability coverage.

(2) when the owner and custodian of the property have stipulated otherwise by written agreement prior to the loss.

C. Contents policies insuring at the place of the loss and covering "employees'," "partners'" or "executives'" personal property, except in 2-B-(1) above, shall be primary to any off-premises coverage available under the employee's insurance. However, insurance covering a specifically described article or object, whether or not for an express amount, shall be primary.

D. Coverage for property "used" or "worn" by the insured, for property of servants or guests, and insurance afforded by the "physical damage to property" coverage, shall be primary to any available insurance in the name of the owner of the involved property, except insurance covering a specifically described article or object, whether or not for an express amount, shall be primary.

E. Installment-Sales or Deferred-Payment Merchandise Insurance:

(1) Evidence of insurance issued by a vendor to a vendee under the provisions of a dual-interest policy specifically or generally describing the article or articles and their values individually or in total as invoiced under a conditional-sales contract shall be deemed to be insurance on specifically described property.

(a) Above-described insurance shall be primary when overlapping with other contents policy(ies).

(b) Above-described insurance shall contribute on the basis of the Limit of Liability Rule when overlapping with insurance expressly describing an article(s) or object(s) whether or not an express amount of insurance applies to each such article(s) or object(s).

(2) When no such evidence of insurance has been issued, the dual-interest policy shall be deemed to be blanket floating insurance.

(a) Above-described insurance shall be excess to other contents insurance in those cases where loss occurs at the location shown in the contents policy.

(b) Above-described insurance shall contribute on the basis of the Limit of Liability Rule when overlapping with a floater policy.   It is to be noted that the ten percent (10%) optional extension of the fire policy is floater coverage.[2]

---

[2]See Illustrative Problems.

GENERAL CONDITIONS

As to General Principles 1 and 2, and any additional Principles or amendments as may hereafter be adopted, it is AGREED that:

1. To provide the greatest recovery to the insured, the insurance declared to be excess or non-contributing under the governing Principle shall not include, in applying any coinsurance, average, or distribution clause(s) contained in any policy(ies), the value or loss on property covered under the insurance declared to be primary. However, it shall include any excess value not covered by the primary insurance and the loss unrecoverable under the primary insurance.

   When a coinsurance (not reduced rate contribution or average) clause is present in any or all policies, it shall be applied as if it were a reduced rate contribution or reduced rate average clause[2]. However, if by this procedure the insured collects less than he would collect under the terms of the coinsurance clause, the coinsurance clause shall be applied as such.

2. "Contribution," unless otherwise as specified in General Principle 1-G, shall be on the basis of the applicable limit of liability under each respective policy or group of concurrent policies as though no other insurance existed, and the limit separately determined under each policy or group of concurrent policies shall be the smallest of the following:

   (a) the amount of insurance,
   (b) the amount of loss, or
   (c) the amount payable after applying any policy limitation(s).

   The limits so determined of all policies or groups of concurrent policies herein declared contributing shall be added and, if the total amount exceeds the whole loss, each policy or group of concurrent policies shall pay such proportion of the loss as its limit bears to the sum of all the limits, but if the sum of the limits of liability is less than the whole loss, then each policy or group of concurrent policies shall pay its limit of liability. The determined liability of a group of concurrent policies shall be apportioned pro rata among the policies of the group.

3. Insurance covering property both scheduled and blanket, or both specific as to location and floating, shall be deemed to insure each item or portion separately, and the loss shall be apportioned in accordance with the Principle applying to each item or portion declared to be separately insured.

   In applying such Condition:

   A. Extensions of coverage in the name of the same insured, whether optional, those creating additional insurance, or based upon a percentage of the principal building or contents policy(ies), whether "permitted" or not, and without reference to inception date, shall be considered as excess to any specific coverage applying to the involved property. However, in the absence of specific insurance, the extensions shall be considered as:

   (1) Blanket insurance for on-premises losses.

   Examples:
   Private structures.
   Rental value.
   Additional living expenses.
   Improvements and betterments.
   Replacement cost coverage.
   Debris removal.

   (2) Floater insurance for off-premises losses.

   Examples:
   Contents while "elsewhere."
   Property removed for preservation from damage caused by the perils insured against.
   Livestock, farm and dairy produce while "elsewhere."

[2]See Illustrative Problems.

General Conditions

4. When the owner of a building is also the owner of the contents of the building and any overlapping coverage exists involving items of building equipment and fixtures essentially in the nature of **real** property, the building policy(ies) shall be primary.

> **Examples:** Covered under building policy(ies).
> Antennae and Towers—TV, detached—**not** affixed[1] to the building or to an outbuilding.
> Porandas—demountable screened enclosures.
> Readily removable equipment and fixtures that are included in the realty mortgage.
> Wall-to-wall carpeting only when included in the realty mortgage.

> **Note:** The building policy(ies) shall include, whether in position or stored on the premises, storm doors, storm sash, shades, blinds, wire screens, screen doors and awnings.

5. When the owner of a building is also the owner of the contents of the building and any overlapping coverage exists involving items of building equipment and fixtures essentially in the nature of **personal** property, the contents policy(ies) shall be primary, except when such items are included in the realty mortgage, in which event the policy(ies) covering building shall be primary.

> **Examples:** Covered under contents policy(ies).
> Antennae and Towers—TV, affixed[1] to the building or to an outbuilding.
> Fuel.
> Laundering machines whether or not attached to the realty.
> Portable air-conditioning and ventilating units.
> Refrigerators.
> Stoves.
> Wall-to-wall carpeting when not included in the realty mortgage.

6. Tenant's improvements and betterments insurance shall be primary to building insurance when the insured is owner and occupant of a co-operative apartment. However, the tenant's insurance shall first be made available to the loss on his own property and to property not otherwise insured.

7. The Principle specifically providing the basis of apportionment shall prevail over any Principle more general in scope.

8. Where a bailee's policy(ies) covers his own property, as well as property of others, the bailee's policy(ies) shall first be made available to the loss on the bailee's own property and to property not otherwise insured. Such claim or claims will be adjusted subject to all policy conditions affecting the adjustment, except that value and loss of otherwise insured property shall be deleted from the adjustment.

A second statement of loss should then be prepared by the adjuster including all values and loss covered by the terms of the bailee's policy(ies) as written to determine the maximum liability under the policy.

Distribution should then be made

(a) to the loss on the bailee's own property and to the loss on otherwise uninsured interests,

(b) to the otherwise insured interests for the difference, if any, up to the maximum liability under the bailee's insurance.

While right of action under subrogation is retained by the bailors' insurers, the inclusion of the bailee insurer's name in any action against the bailee is contrary to the intent of these Principles.

Claim filed by other insurers with the bailee insurers after payment or advance to owners shall be recognized to the same extent as if directly presented by the owner through the bailee in order to fulfill the purpose of these Principles, except where the bailee insurer may have certain facts in connection with a specific claim that justify reimbursement in a sum less than the amount paid by the bailor insurer.

9. Differences of opinion respecting the application or effect of these Principles shall be submitted for arbitration in the manner determined by the participating Associations. Payments of loss, or advances under loan agreements, or otherwise, shall be without prejudice to the rights of the insurers under these Principles.

[1]See Definitions.

ILLUSTRATIVE PROBLEMS

The following Illustrative Problems are for guidance purposes only and are not intended to limit the scope of the Principles.

General Principle 1-A

This applies to insurance written to cover an individual article or object, whether or not for an express amount, **at a designated location,** such as:

> Neon Sign
> Picture
> Stained-Glass Window
> Plate of Glass
> Manuscript or Valuable Paper

Illustrative Problem (1) — $1,200 loss to a plate of glass.

Coverage

Casualty (glass) policy covers replacement cost of glass   **(Open)**
Fire and extended coverage insurance—
Building (subject to 80% coinsurance clause) $25,000.00

Property	Value	Loss
Plate of glass	$ 1,200.00	$1,200.00
Building (exclusive of plate of glass)	28,800.00	None
	$30,000.00	$1,200.00

Solution

Entire loss to plate of glass is assessed the casualty policy.

◊   ◊   ◊   ◊

Illustrative Problem (2) — $1,200 loss to a plate of glass and $200 boarding-up charge.

Coverage

Casualty (glass) policy covers replacement cost of glass ....   (Open)
Boarding-up charge $75.00
Fire and extended coverage insurance — Building (subject to 80%
coinsurance clause) $25,000.00

Property	Value	Loss
Plate of glass	$ 1,200.00	$1,200.00
Boarding-up charge	—	200.00
Building (exclusive of plate of glass)	28,800.00	
	$30,000.00	$1,400.00

Solution

Casualty policy is primary insurance. However, policy has a $75.00 limitation on boarding-up charge. Therefore, claim under each type of insurance is:

Primary insurance — plate glass casualty policy

Plate of glass $1,200.00
Boarding-up charge 75.00

                                        $1,275.00

Excess insurance — fire and extended coverage policy

Boarding-up charge ($200 less $75) 125.00

         Total recovery $1,400.00

Note: If metal stripping or obstruction removal is involved, the solution would parallel the above. Debris removal is charged under fire policy and is not to be confused with removal of obstruction.

General Principle 1-A

Illustrative Problem (3) — $100 loss to a neon sign.

Coverage

Inland marine neon sign policy subject to 100% coinsurance clause and $10 deductible clause	$125.00
Fire insurance — Building (subject to 90% coinsurance clause)	$25.000.00

Property

	Value	Loss
Neon sign	$ 150.00	$100.00
Building (exclusive of the neon sign)	30,000.00	None
	$30,150.00	$100.00

Solution

Primary insurance

Inland marine policy — application of 100% coinsurance clause

$125.00/$150.00 of $100.00 or	$83.33
Less deductible	10.00
Claim under primary insurance	$73.33

Excess insurance

	Value	Loss
Building, including neon sign	$30,150.00	$100.00
Less value covered by the primary insurance	125.00[4]	
Less amount paid by the primary insurance		73.33[4]
Excess value and loss	$30,025.00	$ 26.67

Application of 90% coinsurance clause is $25,000.00/$27,022.50 (90% of $30,025.) of $26.67 or $24.67

Total claim under each policy is:

Inland policy	$73.33
Fire and extended coverage policy	24.67
Total claim	$98.00

[4]See General Condition 1.

◊ ◊ ◊ ◊

General Principle 1-B

This applies to insurance written to cover **an individual article or object,** whether or not for an express amount, without designation of location, such as:

Fur Coat
Diamond Ring
Camera
Animal
Bulldozer

Illustrative Problem (1) — Total loss to a fur coat (off-premises).

Coverage

Inland marine policy

Scheduled fur floater	$ 500.00
Fire insurance — household contents form (10% applicable to property away from premises)	$5,000.00

Property

	Value	Loss
Fur coat	$500.00	$500.00

Solution

Entire loss to fur coat is assessed to inland marine policy.

General Principles 1-B - 1-E and General Condition 1

Illustrative Problem (2)

Coverage

Household contents policy		$5,000.00
Personal property floater or homeowners MIC 5		8,500.00
Unscheduled personal property	$7,500.00	
Scheduled property — picture	1,000.00	

No credit or pickup endorsement

Fire loss — on-premises

Property	Value	Loss
Picture	$ 1,500.00	$1,500.00
Unscheduled personal property	15,000.00	6,000.00
	$16,500.00	$7,500.00

Household contents policy insures all personal property at a designated location, whereas the personal property floater covers separately on unscheduled personal property and on scheduled property. Policies are not alike in coverage. Therefore, loss is distributed in accordance with Principles 1-B, 1-E and General Condition 1.

Primary insurance

Step 1 — Application of Principle 1-B

Personal property floater covering scheduled property without designation of location is primary to the household contents policy.

Recovery from scheduled property coverage is $1,000.00

Step 2 — Application of Principle 1-E

Household contents policy covering all personal property at a designated location is primary to the unscheduled personal property floater.

In accordance with General Condition 1, the amount not recovered from the scheduled personal property floater is assessed to the household contents policy.

Excess loss to scheduled property is $500.00

As the household contents policy insures at a designated location, it is primary to the unscheduled personal property floater coverage as respects loss sustained to unscheduled personal property. The household contents policy, therefore, is charged, in addition to the excess loss to scheduled personal property, with the loss to unscheduled personal property to the extent of the difference between $500. which has been paid on excess loss to scheduled property and the amount of its policy. Amount paid on unscheduled personal property is ($5,000.00 less $500.00 or) $4,500.00.

Total payment under household contents policy is:

Scheduled property	$ 500.00
Unscheduled personal property	4,500.00
	$5,000.00

Step 3 — Application of General Condition 1

"To provide the greatest recovery to the insured, the insurance declared to be excess or non-contributing under the governing Principle shall not include, xxx the value or loss on property covered under the insurance declared to be primary. However, it shall include only excess value not covered by the primary insurance and the loss unrecoverable under the primary insurance."

The amount of unscheduled personal property not recovered from the primary insurance is $1,500.00 ($6,000.00 less $4,500.00). This sum is assessed the unscheduled personal property floater.

Total claim under each policy is:

Household contents

Scheduled property	$ 500.00	
Unscheduled personal property	4,500.00	$5,000.00

Personal property floater

Scheduled property	$1,000.00	
Unscheduled personal property	1,500.00	2,500.00
		$7,500.00

General Principle 1-C

This applies to insurance written to cover a specifically described group or class of related articles or objects, whether or not for an express amount, **at a designated location,** such as:

Stained-Glass Windows
Silverware
Trophies
Antiques

Illustrative Problem (1) — Loss to antiques in dealer's premises.

Coverage

Inland marine — fine arts dealer's policy covering blanket on antiques . . . . $ 5,000.00
Fire insurance — contents 90% coinsurance clause 20,000.00

Property	Value	Loss
Antiques	$ 5,000.00	$1,500.00
Other contents	30,000.00	None
	$35,000.00	$1,500.00

Solution

Entire loss to antiques is assessed the inland marine policy.

◊   ◊   ◊   ◊

Illustrative Problem (2) — Loss to stained-glass windows and building.

Coverage

Inland marine fine arts policy covering stained-glass windows . . . . $ 10,000.00
Fire and extended coverage insurance —
    Church building subject to an 80% coinsurance clause 100,000.00

Property	Value	Loss
Stained-glass windows	$ 10,500.00	$10,500.00
Church building (other than stained-glass windows)	157,000.00	5,000.00
	$167,500.00	$15,500.00

Solution

Primary insurance — inland marine (fine arts policy)

Loss to stained-glass windows is assessed the inland marine policy to the extent of its policy limits.

Excess insurance — fire and extended coverage (building policy)
Balance of loss is assessed to the building policy as follows:

Building including stained-glass windows	$167,500.00	$15,500.00
Less value covered by the primary insurance	10,000.00[4]	
Less amount paid by the primary insurance		10,000.00[4]
Excess value and loss	$157,500.00	$ 5,500.00

Application of 80% coinsurance clause is:
    $100,000.00/$126,000.00 (80% of $157,500.00) of $5,500.00 or $4,365.08

Claim under each policy is:
    Inland marine policy $10,000.00
    Fire and extended coverage policy 4,365.08

    Total claim $14,365.08

---

[4]See General Condition 1.

General Principle 1-C

Illustrative Problem (3) — Loss to stock.

Coverage

Stock	$ 5,000.00 — no coinsurance
Contents	10,000.00 — no coinsurance

Property

Loss to stock	$ 1,000.00

Solution

Stock loss is less than the amount of specific stock coverage; therefore, entire loss assessed to the specific stock policy.

◊ ◊ ◊ ◊

Illustrative Problem (4) — Loss to stock.

Coverage

Stock	$ 5,000.00 — 80% coinsurance
Contents	10,000.00 — 80% coinsurance

Property

	Value	Loss
Stock	$ 10,000.00	$ 1,000.00
Furniture and fixtures	7,500.00	nil
	$ 17,500.00	$ 1,000.00

Solution

Primary insurance — stock

Application of 80% coinsurance clause under policy insuring specific on stock is:
$5,000.00/$8,000.00 of $1,000.00 or $625.00

Excess insurance — contents

	Value	Loss
Contents	$ 17,500.00	$ 1,000.00
Less value covered by the primary insurance	5,000.00	
Less amount paid under the primary insurance		625.00
Excess value and loss	$ 12,500.00	$ 375.00

80% coinsurance clause complied with. Entire excess loss assessed contents policy.

◊ ◊ ◊ ◊

General Principle 1-D

This applies to insurance written to cover a specifically described group or class of related articles or objects, whether or not for an express amount, **without designation of location** such as:

> Stamp Collection
> Tractors
> Cattle or Animals

Illustrative Problem (1) — Loss to a stamp collection.

Coverage

Inland marine — scheduled floater policy covering stamp collection	$ 2,500.00
Fire policy — household contents form	10,000.00

Property

	Value	Loss
Stamp collection	$ 2,500.00	$2,500.00
Other contents	12,500.00	None
	$15,000.00	$2,500.00

Solution

Entire loss to stamp collection assessed the inland marine policy.

General Principle 1-D

Illustrative Problem (2) — Loss to builder's tools and equipment at the construction location.

Coverage

Inland marine — contractor's equipment floater	$ 5,000.00
Fire policy—builder's risk insuring at construction site (including builder's tools and equipment)	50,000.00

Property

	Value	Loss
Builder's tools and equipment	$5,000.00	$500.00

Solution

Entire loss assessed the inland marine contractor's equipment floater policy.

◊　　◊　　◊　　◊

General Principle 1-E

This applies to insurance written to cover at a designated location and not specific as to an "article" or "object" or as to a "group or class of related articles or objects" and shall be excess as to "1-A," "1-B," 1-C" and "1-D," but primary as to any other insurance.

Illustrative Problem (1)

Coverage

Household contents policy	$5,000.00
Personal property floater	7,500.00
No credit or pickup endorsement	
Fire loss — on-premises	$ 500.00

Solution

Entire loss assessed to the household contents policy.

◊　　◊　　◊　　◊

See General Principle 1-B — Illustrative Problem (2)

◊　　◊　　◊　　◊

General Principle 1-F

This applies to insurance without designation of location and not specific as to an "article" or "object" or as to "group or class of related articles or objects" and shall be excess to "1-A," "1-B," "1-C," "1-D" and "1-E," such as:

Floater Policies
Trip Transit
Tourist Baggage
Trip Travel
Sportman's
Certificate (covering contents of rental trailers or other similar type of coverages)
Armored Car

Illustrative Problem (1) — A fire loss to personal effects contained within a vehicle.

Coverage

Automobile policy — covering wearing apparel or personal effects	$ 100.00
Personal property floater — unscheduled personal property	5,000.00

Property

	Value	Loss
Personal effects	$ 90.00	$ 90.00

Solution

Entire loss assessed to the automobile policy.

(The coverage under the automobile policy is confined to personal effects while they are in or upon the automobile.)

For the purpose of this Principle a vehicle is considered as a specified location even though mobile.

General Principle 1-F

Illustrative Problem (2) — Fire loss to contents of a rental trailer.

Coverage

Inland marine — certificate covering contents of a rental trailer (subject to a $100.00 deductible clause)	$ 800.00
Fire policy — household contents	4,500.00
Off-premises	450.00

Property	Value	Loss
Contents of rental trailer	$2,500.00	$750.00

Solution

Inland marine certificate is primary insurance. However, same is subject to a $100.00 deductible clause and claim under each type of insurance is:

Primary insurance (inland marine)

Amount of loss	$750.00	
Less deductible	100.00	
Claim		$650.00

Excess insurance (fire)

Amount of loss	$750.00	
Less amount paid under primary insurance	650.00	
Claim		100.00
Total Claim		. $750.00

General Principle 1-G

Two or more insurances which are not concurrent but providing coverage as set forth in "1-A" through "1-F" shall contribute.

Illustrative Problem (1)

Coverage

Household contents or (homeowners 1, 2 or 4) —
$5,000.00 on household and personal property
Personal property floater —
$7,500.00 on unscheduled personal property
No credit or pickup endorsement

Property

Fire loss to unscheduled personal property (off-premises) $100.00

Solution

The loss is covered under both policies. As loss is off-premises household contents coverage is limited to 10% of the insurance. The loss is distributed in accordance with Principle 1-G.

Household contents policy

		Limit of Liability	Pays
Amount of policy	$5,000.00		
Off-premises coverage 10% or	500.00		
Loss	100.00		
Limit of liability		$100.00	$ 50.00

Personal property floater

Coverage	$7,500.00		
Loss	100.00		
Limit of liability		100.00	50.00
		$200.00	$100.00

General Principle 1-G

Illustrative Problem (2)

Coverage

Homeowners MIC-5
    $15,000.00 on unscheduled personal property
    No credit or pickup endorsement
Personal property floater —
    $5,000.00 on unscheduled personal property
    No credit or pickup endorsement

Property

Fire loss to unscheduled personal property (on-premises) $500.00

Solution
Apportionment based on Principle 1-G.

Homeowners MIC-5		Limit of Liability	Pays
Coverage	$15,000.00		
Loss	500.00		
Limit of liability		$ 500.00	$250.00
Personal property floater			
Coverage	$ 5,000.00		
Loss	500.00		
Limit of liability		500.00	250.00
		$1,000.00	$500.00

◊   ◊   ◊   ◊

Illustrative Problem (3)

Coverage

Homeowners MIC-1, 2 or 4 —
    $7,500.00 on unscheduled personal property
    No credit or pickup endorsement
Household contents policy
    $5,000.00 on household and personal property

Fire loss — to unscheduled personal property (on-premises) $1,000.00

Solution
Apportionment based on Principle 1-G.

Homeowners MIC-1, 2 or 4		Limit of Liability	Pays
Coverage	$7,500.00		
Loss	1,000.00		
Limit of liability		$1,000.00	$ 500.00
Household contents			
Coverage	$5,000.00		
Loss	1,000.00		
Limit of liability		1,000.00	500.00
		$2,000.00	$1,000.00

General Principle 1-G

Illustrative Problem (4)

Coverage

Homeowners MIC-5
  $12,000.00 on unscheduled personal property
  $ 100.00 diminishing deductible
  No credit or pickup endorsement

Personal property floater
  $5,000.00 on unscheduled personal property
  No credit or pickup endorsement

Property

Loss to unscheduled personal property (on-premises) $450.00

Solution

Apportionment based on Principle 1-G.

Step 1 — Establish limits of liability for each of the separate coverages.

	Limit of Liability
Homeowners	
Coverage $12,000.00	
Loss 450.00	
Claim — 125% of ($450.00 less [1]deductible of $100.00) $350.00 or 437.50	
([1]application of diminishing deductible establishes the deduction as $12.50 rather than $100.00)	
Limit of liability	$437.50
Personal property floater	
Coverage $10,000.00	
Loss 450.00	
Limit of liability	450.00
	$887.50

Step 2 — Assess loss separately covered to insurance which alone affords coverage.

The [1]$12.50 deductible of the homeowners policy is assessed to the personal property floater.

Step 3 — Contribution to area of common coverage.

Loss to area of common coverage is $450.00 less $12.50 or $437.50.

The amount paid under the personal property floater to the area it alone covers is deducted from its limit of liability. The remaining limit of liability then contributes with the limit of liability of the homeowners policy to pay loss to area of common coverage.

	Limit of Liability	Pays
Homeowners	$437.50	$218.75
Personal property floater (remaining limit of liability $450.00 less $12.50)	437.50	218.75
	$875.00	$437.50

Total claim under each policy is:

Homeowners —		
Share of area of common coverage loss		$218.75
Personal property floater —		
Deductible	$ 12.50	
Share of area of common coverage loss	218.75	231.25
		$450.00

[1] See Definitions.

General Principle 1-G

Illustrative Problem (5)

Coverage

Homeowners MIC-5

$12,000.00 on unscheduled personal property
$ 100.00 diminishing deductible
No credit or pickup endorsement

Personal property floater

$10,000.00 on unscheduled personal property
$ 25.00 deductible
No credit or pickup endorsement

Property

Loss to unscheduled personal property (on-premises) $450.00

Solution

Apportionment based on Principle 1-G.

Step 1 — Establish limits of liability for each of the separate coverages.

		Limit of Liability
Homeowners		
Coverage	$12,000.00	
Loss	450.00	
Claim — 125% of ($450.00 less deductible of $100.00) $350.00 or	437.50	
(application of diminishing deductible establishes the deduction as $12.50 rather than $100.00)		
Limit of liability		$ 437.50
Personal property floater		
Coverage	$10,000.00	
Loss	450.00	
Claim — $450.00 less $25.00 or	425.00	
Limit of liability		425.00
		$ 862.50

The amount of the lowest deductible ($12.50) represents a sum not insured under either policy.

Step 2 — Assess loss separately covered to insurance which alone affords coverage.

The difference between the highest and lowest deductible ($25.00 less $12.50) or $12.50 is assessed to the policy having the lowest deductible.

Step 3 — Contribution to area of common coverage.

The amount of $12.50 paid under the homeowners policy to area it alone covers is deducted from its limit of liability. The remaining limit of liability then contributes with the limit of liability of the personal property floater to pay loss to area of common coverage.

Loss in excess of the highest deductible or ($450.00 less $25.00) $425.00 is the loss to area of common coverage.

	Limit of Liability	Pays
Homeowners (remaining limit of liability $437.50 less $12.50)	$425.00	$212.50
Personal property floater	425.00	212.50
	$850.00	$425.00

Total claim under each policy is:

Homeowners —		
Deductible	$ 12.50	
Share of area of common coverage loss	212.50	
		$225.00
Personal property floater —		
Share of area of common coverage loss		212.50
		$437.50

General Principle 1-G

Illustrative Problem (6)

Coverage

Homeowners MIC-5

> $20,000.00 on unscheduled personal property
> $ 250.00 limit on jewelry
> $ 100.00 diminishing deductible
> No credit or pickup endorsement

Personal property floater

> $17,750.00 on unscheduled personal property
> $ 250.00 limit on jewelry
> $ 50.00 deductible
> No credit or pickup endorsement

Property

> Loss to jewelry $415.00

Solution

Apportionment based on Principle 1-G.

	Limit of Liability	Pays
Homeowners		
Coverage	$20,000.00	
Loss	415.00	
Claim—125% of ($415.00 less $100.00) $315.00 or	393.75	
Policy limit on jewelry	250.00	
Limit of liability		$ 250.00 $ 230.56
Personal property floater		
Coverage	$17,750.00	
Loss	415.00	
Policy limit on jewelry	250.00	
Application of deductible $250.00 less $50.00 or	200.00	
Limit of liability		200.00 184.44
		$ 450.00 $ 415.00

◊   ◊   ◊   ◊

Illustrative Problem (7)

Coverage

Homeowners

> $25,000.00 on dwelling
> No credit or pickup endorsement

Standard fire dwelling form

> $10,000.00 on dwelling

Property

Loss to dwelling — $1,000.00

Solution

Apportionment based on Principle 1-G.

	Limit of Liability	Pays
Homeowners		
Coverage	$25,000.00	
Loss	1,000.00	
Limit of liability	$ 1,000.00 $ 500.00	
Standard dwelling form		
Coverage	10,000.00	
Loss	1,000.00	
Limit of liability		$ 1,000.00 $ 500.00
		$ 2,000.00 $ 1,000.00

General Principle 1-G

Illustrative Problem (8) — Burglary loss involving premise damage to owner-occupied risk.

Coverage

Casualty
Mercantile open stock policy .... $ 15,000.00

Fire policy subject to extended coverage and vandalism
and malicious mischief endorsements
Building and contents $100,000.00

Property	Value	Loss
Stock	$ 37,500.00	$1,000.00
Premise damage	87,500.00	500.00
	$125,000.00	$1,500.00

Step 1 — Establish limit of liability.

Mercantile open stock policy			Limit of Liability
Insurance		$ 15,000.00	
Loss —			
Stock	$ 1,000.00		
Premise damage	500.00	1,500.00	
Limit of liability			$1,500.00

Fire policy (E.C.E. and V. and M.M.)		
Insurance	$100,000.00	
Loss — premise damage	500.00	
(fire policy does not cover loss to stock)		
Limit of liability		$ 500.00
		$2,000.00

Step 2 — Loss separately covered assessed to policy which alone affords coverage.
Stock loss assessed the mercantile open stock policy which alone affords coverage and the remaining limit of liability participates with the fire policy (E.C.E. and V. and M.M.) to pay loss to area of common coverage.

Stock loss assessed mercantile open stock policy $1,000.00

Step 3 — Contribution to area of common coverage on basis of available limits of liability.
Loss to area of common coverage is $500.00.

	Limit of Liability	Pays
Mercantile open stock policy (remaining limit of liability)	$ 500.00	$ 250.00
Fire policy (E.C.E. and V. and M.M.)	500.00	250.00
	$ 1,000.00	$ 500.00

Claim under each policy is:
Mercantile open stock policy

Stock	$ 1,000.00
Area of common coverage pays	250.00
	$1,250.00

Fire policy (E.C.E. and V. and M.M.)

Area of common coverage pays	250.00
	$1,500.00

General Principle 1-G

Illustrative Problem (9) — One policy subject to a deductible clause.

Coverage

"Fire Group" $75,000.00
"Boiler Group" .... 50,000.00 — $1,000.00 deductible clause

Property

Loss $15,000.00

Solution

Step 1 — Establish limit of liability.

		Limit of Liability
"Fire Group"		
Insurance	$75,000.00	
Loss	15,000.00	
Limit of liability		$15,000.00
"Boiler Group"		
Insurance	50,000.00	
Loss	15,000.00	
Claim $15,000.00 less $1,000.00 or	14,000.00	14,000.00
Limit of liability		$29,000.00

Step 2 — Assess loss separately covered to policy which alone affords coverage.

The $1,000.00 uninsured under the "Boiler Group" is first assessed to the "Fire Group" which alone affords coverage and the remaining limit of liability participates with the "Fire Group" to pay loss to area of common coverage.

Step 3 — Contribution to area of common coverage on basis of available limits of liability.

Loss to area of common coverage is $14,000.00.

	Limit of Liability	Pays
"Fire Group" (remaining limit of liability)	$14,000.00	$ 7,000.00
"Boiler Group"	14,000.00	7,000.00
	$28,000.00	$14,000.00

Claim under each policy is:

"Fire Group"

Deductible	$ 1,000.00	
Area of common coverage pays	7,000.00	
		$ 8,000.00

"Boiler Group"

Area of common coverage pays	7,000.00
	$15,000.00

General Principle 1-G

Illustrative Problem (10) — One policy subject to a deductible clause.

Coverage

"Fire Group"	$500,000.00
"Boiler Group"	50,000.00 — $5,000.00 deductible clause

Property

Loss $525,000.00

Solution

Step 1 — Establish limits of liability for each group.

"Fire Group"

		Limit of Liability
Insurance	$500,000.00	
Loss	525,000.00	
Payable under policy limitations	500,000.00	
Limit of liability		$500,000.00

"Boiler Group"

Insurance	50,000.00	
Loss	525,000.00	
Payable under policy limitations	50,000.00	
Limit of liability		$ 50,000.00

Step 2 — Assess loss separately covered to group which alone affords coverage.

The $5,000.00 deductible of the "Boiler Group" is assessed to the "Fire Group" which alone affords coverage. Its remaining limit of liability contributes with the "Boiler Group" to pay loss to area of common coverage.

Step 3 — Contribution to area of common coverage on basis of available limits of liability.

Loss to area of common coverage is $520,000.00 ($525,000.00 — $5,000.00)

	Limit of Liability	Pays
"Fire Group" (remaining limit of liability)	$495,000.00	$472,293.58
"Boiler Group"	50,000.00	47,706.42
	$545,000.00	$520,000.00

Summary of claim to each group is:

"Fire Group"

Deductible	$ 5,000.00	
Share of loss to area of common coverage	472,293.58	$477,293.58

"Boiler Group"

Share of loss to area of common coverage	47,706.42
	$525,000.00

General Principle 1-G

Illustrative Problem (11) — Each group subject to a deductible clause.

Coverage

"Fire Group" .... $75,000.00 — $ 200.00 deductible clause
"Boiler Group" .... 50,000.00 — $1,000.00 deductible clause

Property

Loss $15,000.00

Solution

Step 1 — Establish limit of liability.

		Limit of Liability

"Fire Group"

Insurance	$75,000.00	
Loss	15,000.00	
Claim $15,000.00 less $200.00 or	14,800.00	
Limit of liability		$14,800.00

"Boiler Group"

Insurance	$50,000.00	
Loss	15,000.00	
Claim $15,000.00 less $1,000.00 or	14,000.00	
Limit of liability		14,000.00
		$28,800.00

Step 2 — Assess loss separately covered to policy which alone affords coverage.

The difference between the highest and lowest deductibles is assessed to the "Fire Group" which alone affords coverage and the remaining limit of liability participates with the "Boiler Group" to pay loss to area of common coverage.

Step 3 — Contribution to area of common coverage on basis of available limits of liability.

Loss to area of common coverage is $14,000.00

	Limit of Liability	Pays
"Fire Group" (remaining limit of liability)	$14,000.00	$ 7,000.00
"Boiler Group"	14,000.00	7,000.00
	$28,000.00	$14,000.00

Claim under each policy is:

"Fire Group"

Differential between the highest and lowest deductible — $1,000.00 less $200.00 or	$ 800.00	
Area of common coverage pays	7,000.00	
		$ 7,800.00

"Boiler Group"

Area of common coverage pays	7,000.00
	$14,800.00

Note: Lowest deductible assumed by insured.

General Principle 1-G

Illustrative Problem (12) — Time element loss.

Coverage

"Fire Group"	$761,000.00 — 80% coinsurance clause
"Boiler Group"	(Valued Form) $3,000.00 daily indemnity
	Commencement of liability — 1st Midnight
	Limit of loss $100,000.00

Other considerations — Time of occurrence 12:01 A.M.; plant operates twenty-four hours per day; occurrence causes 100% shutdown of operations.

Business Interruption

	Value	Loss
Value	$1,128,055.00	

Period of suspension

80 hours or 3⅓ days

1st 24-hour period	$5,198.00	
2nd 24-hour period	5,198.00	
3rd 24-hour period	5,198.00	
4th 8-hour period	1,732.66	$17,326.66

Step No. 1 — Establish respective limits of liability.

"Fire Group"

		Limit of Liability
Insurance	$761,000.00	
Loss	17,326.66	
Application of 80% coinsurance clause —		
$761,000.00/$902,444.00 of $17,326.66	14,610.97	$14,610.97

"Boiler Group"

	Limit of Liability
Insurance — $3,000.00/day from 1st Midnight	
1st 24-hour period — 12:01 A.M. — 12:00 Mdnt —	no coverage
2nd 24-hour period — 12:00 Mdnt — 12:00 Mdnt —	$3,000.00
3rd 24-hour period — 12:00 Mdnt — 12:00 Mdnt —	3,000.00
4th 8-hour period — 12:00 Mdnt — 8:00 A.M. —	1,000.00
	$ 7,000.00
Total	$21,610.97

Step 2 — Assess part of loss separately covered to policy which alone affords coverage.

Loss for first 24-hour period assessed to "Fire Group" — $5,198.00

"Fire Group" remaining limit $9,412.97 ($14,610.97 — $5,198.00) available for contribution in area of common coverage.

Step 3 — Contribution to area of common coverage on basis of available limits of liability.

Loss to area of common coverage is ($17,326.66 — $5,198.00) $12,128.66

	Limit of Liability	Loss
"Fire Group" (remaining limit)	$ 9,412.97	$ 6,955.88
"Boiler Group" limit	7,000.00	5,172.78
	$16,412.97	$12,128.66

Claim under each policy is:

"Fire Group"

1st 24-hour period	$ 5,198.00
Contribution to area of common coverage	6,955.88
	$12,153.88

"Boiler Group"

Contribution to area of common coverage	5,172.78
Insured recovers	$17,326.66

Note: Example not intended to imply that loss under "Valued Form" of boiler-machinery policy must necessarily be adjusted on an "hourly" basis.

General Principle 1-G

Illustrative Problem (13) — Time element loss.

Coverage

"Fire Group" $761,000.00 — 80% coinsurance clause
"Boiler Group"   Valued U and O — daily indemnity $5,500.00
                      Liability commences 1st Mdnt; limit loss $550,000.00

Other considerations — Time of occurrence 12:01 A.M.; plant operates twenty-four hours per day; occurrence causes 100% shutdown of operations.

Property

Business interruption	Value	Loss
Value	$1,128,055.00	

Period of suspension

80 hours or 3⅓ days

1st 24-hour period	$5,198.00	
2nd 24-hour period	5,198.00	
3rd 24-hour period	5,198.00	
4th 8-hour period	1,732.66	
		$17,326.66

Step 1 — Establish respective limits of liability.

		Limit of Liability
"Fire Group"		
Insurance	$761,000.00	
Loss	17,326.66	
Application 80% coinsurance clause $761,000.00/$902,444.00 of $17,326.66		$14,610.97

"Boiler Group"

Insurance — $5,500.00/day from 1st Midnight

1st 24-hour period — 12:01 A.M. — 12:00 Mdnt —	no coverage	
2nd 24-hour period — 12:00 Mdnt — 12:00 Mdnt —	$5,500.00	
3rd 24-hour period — 12:00 Mdnt — 12:00 Mdnt —	5,500.00	
4th 8-hour period — 12:00 Mdnt — 8:00 A.M. —	1,833.33	
	$12,833.33	
Total	$27,444.30	

Step 2 — Assess loss separately covered to policy which alone affords coverage.

Loss for first 24-hour period assessed "Fire Group" — $5,198.00

"Fire Group" remaining limit $9,412.97 ($14,610.97 — $5,198.00) available for contribution in area of common coverage.

Step 3 — Contribution to area of common coverage basis of available limits of liability.

Loss to area of common coverage is ($17,326.66 — $5,198.00) $12,128.66

	Limit of Liability	Pays
"Fire Group" (remaining limit)	$ 9,412.97	$ 5,131.94
"Boiler Group" limit	12,833.33	6,996.72
	$22,246.30	$12,128.66

Claim under each policy is:

"Fire Group"

1st 24-hour period	$5,198.00
Contribution to area of common coverage	5,131.94
	$10,329.94

"Boiler Group"

Contribution to area of common coverage	6,996.72
Insured recovers	$17,326.66

Note: Example not intended to imply that loss under "Valued Form" of boiler-machinery policy must necessarily be adjusted on an "hourly" basis.

General Principle 1-G

Illustrative Problem (14) — Boiler-machinery — fire overlap
Fire policies coverage is non-concurrent

Coverage

"Fire Group"

Building	$ 50,000.00
Building and contents	75,000.00
	$125,000.00

"Boiler Group"

Amount of Insurance	$100,000.00

Property	Value	Loss
Building	$ 90,000.00	$15,000.00
Contents	75,000.00	5,000.00
	$165,000.00	$20,000.00

Solution

Step 1 — Establish limits of liability of each group for contribution purposes.
The liability of the "Fire Group" policies is determined by order of precedence as established by General Principles 1-A through 1-G.

"Fire Group"

Building policy — primary insurance in accordance with Principle 1-A and Specific Principles — Fire-Fire.

	Limit of Liability
Entire building loss would be assessed to specific insurance	$15,000.00

Building and contents policy — excess insurance in accordance with General Condition 1.

Building and contents value and loss	$165,000.00	$20,000.00	
Less value covered by primary insurance (building)	50,000.00		
Less amount assessed to primary insurance		$15,000.00	
Excess value and loss	$115,000.00	$ 5,000.00	
Limit of liability			$ 5,000.00
"Fire Group" limit of liability			$20,000.00

"Boiler Group"

Amount of insurance	$100,000.00	
Loss	20,000.00	
Limit of liability		$20,000.00
		$40,000.00

Step 2 — Distribution of loss to each group.

	Limit of Liability	Pays
"Fire Group"	$20,000.00	$10,000.00
"Boiler Group"	20,000.00	10,000.00
	$40,000.00	$20,000.00

Distribution of the Fire Group's share of loss to their policy or group of concurrent policies —

	Limit of Liability	Pays
Building policy	$15,000.00	$ 7,500.00
Building and contents policy	5,000.00	2,500.00
	$20,000.00	$10,000.00

General Principle 1-G

Illustrative Problem (15) — Boiler-machinery overlap
Fire policies coverage is non-concurrent

Coverage

"Fire Group"

Building	$ 50,000.00
Building and contents	75,000.00
	$125,000.00

"Boiler Group"

Amount of insurance —	$100,000.00
(subject to $1,000.00 deductible clause)	

Property	Value	Loss
Building	$ 90,000.00	$15,000.00
Contents	75,000.00	5,000.00
	$165,000.00	$20,000.00

Solution

Step 1 — Establish limits of liability of each group for contribution purposes.

The liability of the "Fire Group" policies is determined by order of precedence as established by General Principles 1-A through 1-G.

	Limit of Liability

"Fire Group"

Building policy — primary insurance in accordance with Principle 1-A and Specific Principles — Fire-Fire

Entire loss would be assessed to specific insurance $15,000.00

Building and contents policy — excess insurance in accordance with General Condition 1.

Building and contents value and loss	$165,000.00	$20,000.00	
Less value covered by primary insurance (building)	50,000.00		
Less amount assessed to primary insurance		15,000.00	
Excess value and loss	$115,000.00	$ 5,000.00	
Limit of liability			$ 5,000.00

"Fire Group" limit of liability $20,000.00

"Boiler Group"

Amount of insurance	$100,000.00	
Loss	20,000.00	
Claim $20,000.00 less $1,000.00 or $19,000.00		$19,000.00
Limit of liability		$39,000.00

Step 2 — Assess loss separately covered to group which alone affords coverage.

The $1,000.00 not insured under the "Boiler-Machinery Group" is first paid by the "Fire Group" which alone affords coverage. The remaining limit of liability of the "Fire Group" contributes with the "Boiler Group" to pay loss to area of common coverage.

The amount of $1,000.00 is assessed to the "Fire Group."

General Principle 1-G Illustrative Problem (15) — continued

Step 3 — Contribution to area of common coverage on basis of available limits of liability.
Loss to area of common coverage is $20,000.00 less $1,000.00 or $19,000.00

	Limit of Liability	Pays
"Fire Group" (remaining limit of liability)	$19,000.00	$ 9,500.00
"Boiler Group"	19,000.00	9,500.00
	$38,000.00	$19,000.00

Claim under each group is:
"Fire Group"

Amount of deductible	$ 1,000.00	
Area of common coverage	9,500.00	
	$10,500.00	$10,500.00

Distribution of the Fire Group's share of loss to their policy or group of concurrent policies —

	Limit of Liability	Pays
Building policy	$15,000.00	$ 7,875.00
Building and contents	5,000.00	2,625.00
	$20,000.00	$10,500.00

"Boiler Group"

Area of common coverage	$ 9,500.00
	$20,000.00

◊   ◊   ◊   ◊

Illustrative Problem (16) — Boiler-machinery — fire overlap
Fire policies coverage is non-concurrent

Coverage

"Fire Group"

Building	$ 50,000.00 — 80% coinsurance
Building and contents	75,000.00 — 80% coinsurance
	$125,000.00

"Boiler Group"

Amount of insurance	$100,000.00

Property	Value	Loss
Building	$ 90,000.00	$15,000.00
Contents	75,000.00	5,000.00
	$165,000.00	$20,000.00

Solution
Step 1 — Establish limits of liability of each group for contribution purposes.
The liability of the "Fire Group" policies is determined by order of precedence as established by General Principles 1-A through 1-G.

General Principle 1-G Illustrative Problem (16) — continued

Limit of
Liability

"Fire Group"

Building policy — primary insurance in accordance with Principle 1-**A** and Specific Principles — Fire-Fire.

Under application of 80% coinsurance clause, limit of liability would be: $50,000.00/$72,000.00 of $15,000.00 or $10,416.67

Building and contents — excess insurance in accordance with **General Condition 1.**

Building and contents value and loss	$165,000.00	$20,000.00
Less value covered by primary insurance (building)	50,000.00	
Less amount assessed to primary insurance		10,416.67
Excess value and loss	$115,000.00	$ 9,583.33

Under application of 80% coinsurance clause, limit of liability would be: $75,000.00/$92,000.00 of $9,583.33 or .... $ 7,812.50

"Fire Group" limit of liability $18,229.17

"Boiler Group"

Amount of insurance	$100,000.00
Loss	20,000.00
Limit of liability	$20,000.00

$38,229.17

Step 2 — Distribution of loss to each group.

	Limit of Liability	Pays
"Fire Group"	$18,229.17	$ 9,536.78
"Boiler Group"	20,000.00	10,463.22
	$38,229.17	$20,000.00

Distribution of the Fire Group's share of loss to their policy or group of concurrent policies —

	Limit of Liability	Pays
Building policy	$10,416.67	$ 5,449.59
Building and contents policy	7,812.50	4,087.19
	$18,229.17	$ 9,536.78

General Principle 1-G

Illustrative Problem (17) — Boiler-machinery — fire overlap
Boiler-machinery policy subject to a deductible
Fire policies coverage is non-concurrent

Coverage
"Fire Group"

Building	$ 50,000.00—80% coinsurance
Building and contents	75,000.00—80% coinsurance
	$125,000.00

"Boiler Group"

Amount of insurance	$100,000.00—$1,000.00 deductible

Property	Value	Loss
Building	$ 90,000.00	$15,000.00
Contents	75,000.00	5,000.00
	$165,000.00	$20,000.00

Solution

Step 1 — Establish limits of liability of each group for contribution purposes.
The liability of the "Fire Group" policies is determined in order of precedence as established by
General Principles 1-A through 1-G.

Limit of
Liability

"Fire Group"
Building policy — primary insurance in accordance with Principle 1-A
and Specific Principles — Fire-Fire.
Under application of 80% coinsurance clause, limit of liability would be:
$50,000.00/$72,000.00 of $15,000.00 .... $10,416.67

Building and contents — excess insurance in accordance with General Condition 1.

Building and contents value and loss	$165,000.00	$20,000.00
Less value covered by primary insurance (building)	50,000.00	
Less amount assessed to primary insurance		10,416.67
Excess value and loss	$115,000.00	$ 9,583.33

Under application of 80% coinsurance clause, limit of liability would be:
$75,000.00/$92,000.00 of $9,583.33 or .... $ 7,812.50

"Fire Group" limit of liability $18,229.17

"Boiler Group"

Amount of insurance	$100,000.00	
Loss	20,000.00	
Claim $20,000.00 less $1,000.00 or	19,000.00	
Limit of liability		$19,000.00
		$37,229.17

Step 2 — Assess loss separately covered to group which alone affords coverage.
The $1,000.00 not insured under the "Boiler-Machinery Group" is first paid by the "Fire Group"
which alone affords coverage. The remaining limit of liability of the "Fire Group" contributes with
the "Boiler Group" to pay loss to area of common coverage.

The amount of $1,000.00 is assessed to the "Fire Group."

General Principle 1-G Illustrative Problem (17) — continued

Step 3 — **Contribution to area of common coverage basis on available limits of liability.**
Loss to area of common coverage is:
$20,000.00 less $1,000.00 or $19,000.00

	Limit of Liability	Pays
"Fire Group" (remaining limit of liability)	$17,229.17	$ 9,035.65
"Boiler Group"	19,000.00	9,964.35
	$36,229.17	$19,000.00

Claim under each group is:
"Fire Group"

Amount of deductible	$ 1,000.00	
Area of common coverage	9,035.65	
	$10,035.65	$10,035.65

Distribution of the Fire Group's share of the loss to their policy or group of concurrent policies —

	Limit of Liability	Pays
Building policy	$10,416.67	$ 5,734.66
Building and contents policy	7,812.50	4,300.99
	$18,229.17	$10,035.65

"Boiler Group"

Area of common coverage		$ 9,964.35
		$20,000.00

◊   ◊   ◊   ◊

Illustrative Problem (18)   Fire-Fire coverage.

Coverage

A. Stock	$30,000.00
B. Contents, including improvements and betterments	20,000.00
C. Contents, exclusive of improvements and betterments	10,000.00
	$60,000.00

No coinsurance clause under any policy.

Property	Value	Loss
Stock	$60,000.00	$ 5,000.00
Furniture and fixtures	10,000.00	1,000.00
Improvements and betterments	2,500.00	500.00
	$72,500.00	$ 6,500.00

Solution
Primary insurance — Policy A
Stock loss is assessed to specific insurance in accordance with Principle 1-C.

Excess insurance — Policies B and C
Loss to property other than stock is distributed according to Principle 1-G-(1).

General Principle 1-G Illustrative Problem (18) — continued

Step 1 — Establish limit of liability.

		Limit of Liability
Policy B, including improvements and betterments		
Insurance	$20,000.00	
Loss	1,500.00	
Limit of liability		$ 1,500.00
Policy C, excluding improvements and betterments		
Insurance	10,000.00	
Loss	1,000.00	
Limit of liability		1,000.00
		$ 2,500.00

Step 2 — Assess loss separately covered to policy which alone affords coverage.

Improvements and betterments loss is first assessed to Policy B which alone affords coverage and the remaining limit of liability participates with Policy C to pay loss to area of common coverage.

Improvements and betterments loss assessed Policy B.

Step 3 — Contribution to area of common coverage on basis of available limits of liability.

Loss to area of common coverage — $1,000.00

	Limit of Liability	Pays
Policy B (remaining limit of liability)	$1,000.00	$ 500.00
Policy C	1,000.00	500.00
	$2,000.00	$1,000.00

Total claim to each policy is:

Policy A

Stock	$5,000.00

Policy B

Improvements and betterments	$ 500.00	
Contents, other than stock and improvements and betterments	$ 500.00	$1,000.00

Policy C

Contents, other than stock and improvements and betterments	500.00
	$6,500.00

General Principle 2-E

Installment-Sales or Deferred-Payment
Merchandise Insurance:

Illustrative Problem (1)

Coverage
Inland marine
Policy issued to vendor.

Installment-sales floater (dual-interest.)
$30,000.00 on the interest of the insured and of purchasers in merchandise sold by the insured under a deferred-payment or conditional-sales agreement.

Evidence of insurance issued by vendor to vendee.

Fire insurance
Policy issued to purchaser —
$5,000.00 on household furniture.

Property, location and cause.

Property damaged — Refrigerator which had been purchased under a conditional-sales agreement
    or destroyed
Amount of loss   — $250.00
Location of loss   — Purchaser's residence
Cause of loss   — Fire

Solution

Distribution of loss is based on subdivision (1)-(a) of General Principle 2-E.
The loss is assessed to the installment-sales floater policy as primary coverage.

Note: With coverages outlined above the result would be the same in an "on-premises" or "off-premises" situation.

General Principle 2-E

Illustrative Problem (2)

Coverage
Inland marine
Policy issued to vendor.

Installment-sales floater (dual-interest.)

$30,000.00 on the interest of the insured and of purchasers in merchandise sold by the insured under a deferred-payment or conditional-sales agreement.

Certificate of insurance issued by vendor to vendee.

Fire insurance
Policy issued to purchaser —
$1,500.00 on tractor (Farm Form)

Property, location and cause.

    Property damaged — Tractor which had been purchased under a conditional-sales agreement
      or destroyed
    Amount of loss   — $2,500.00
    Location of loss — Purchaser's farm
    Cause of loss   — Fire

Solution

Distribution of loss is based on subdivision (1)-(b) of General Principle 2-E which provides loss be divided in accordance with the Limit of Liability Rule (General Condition 2).

	Limit of Liability	Pays
Inland marine		
Coverage	$30,000.00	
Loss	2,500.00	
Limit of liability	$2,500.00	$1,562.50
Fire insurance		
Coverage	1,500.00	
Loss	2,500.00	
Limit of liability	1,500.00	937.50
	$4,000.00	$2,500.00

Note: With coverages outlined above the result would be the same in an "on-premises" or "off-premises" situation.

General Principle 2-E

Illustrative Problem (3)

Coverage
Inland marine
Policy issued to vendor.

Installment-sales floater (dual-interest).

$30,000.00 on the interest of the insured and of purchasers in merchandise sold by the insured under a deferred-payment or conditional-sales agreement.

No evidence of insurance issued by vendor to vendee.

Fire insurance — homeowners MIC 1 or 2
Policy issued to purchaser —
$8,000.00 on unscheduled personal property.

Property, location and cause.

Property damaged or destroyed	— Television set which had been purchased under conditional-sales agreement.
Amount of loss	— $500.00
Location of loss	— Purchaser's residence
Cause of loss	— Fire

Solution

Distribution of loss is based on subdivision (2)-(a) of General Principle 2-E.

Loss is assessed to the homeowners policy as primary coverage.

General Principle 2-E

Illustrative Problem (4)

Coverage
Inland marine
Policy issued to vendor.

Installment-sales floater (dual-interest).

$30,000.00 on the interest of the insured and of purchasers in merchandise sold by the insured under a deferred-payment or conditional-sales agreement.

No evidence of insurance issued by vendor to vendee.

Fire insurance — homeowners MIC 5
Policy issued to purchaser —
$15,000.00 on unscheduled personal property xxx while in all situations anywhere in the world.
(10% of the limit of liability for coverage C for unscheduled personal property ordinarily situated throughout the year at residences other than the described dwelling.)

Property, location and cause.

Property damaged or destroyed	— Riding power lawn mower which had been purchased under a conditional-sales agreement.
Amount of loss	— $500.00
Location of loss	— Purchaser's secondary residence
Cause of loss	— Fire

Solution

Distribution of loss is based on subdivision (2)-(b) of General Principle 2-E, which provides loss be divided in accordance with the Limit of Liability Rule (General Conditon 2).

		Limit of Liability	Pays
Inland marine			
Coverage	$30,000.00		
Loss	500.00		
Limit of liability		$ 500.00	$250.00
Fire insurance — homeowners MIC 5			
Coverage — secondary residence	1,500.00		
Loss	500.00		
Limit of liability		500.00	250.00
		$1,000.00	$500.00

General Condition 1
See General Principle 1-B — Illustrative Problem (2).

PART II

SPECIFIC PRINCIPLES
CASUALTY - CASUALTY

Overlap of first-party property coverage situations occurring between or among casualty coverages only are to be resolved in accordance with General Principles 1-A through 1-G; 2-A through 2-E; General Conditions and Definitions.

PART II

SPECIFIC PRINCIPLES
FIRE - FIRE

Overlap of first-party coverage situations occurring between or among fire coverages only are to be resolved in accordance with General Principles 1-A through 1-G; 2-A through 2-E; General Conditions; Specific Principles and Definitions.

Explanatory Notes and Examples

Under overlapping situations between fire-fire coverages:

1. A building is construed to be an object.

2. The following are construed to be a group of related articles or objects and come within the provisions of General Principle 1-C or 1-D:
    (a) stock (merchandise),
    (b) machinery,
    (c) furniture and fixtures,
    (d) improvements and betterments.

3. Coverage on any combination of the above in 1 or 2 and coverage on CONTENTS or on personal property are not construed to be coverage on a group of related articles or objects, but come within the provisions of General Principle 1-E or 1-F.

PART II

SPECIFIC PRINCIPLES
INLAND - INLAND

Overlap of first-party coverage situations occurring between or among inland coverages only are to be resolved in accordance with General Principles 1-A through 1-G; 2-A through 2-E; General Conditions; Specific Principles and Definitions, subject to the following specific exceptions:

1. Policies issued to common or contract carriers covering their legal liability for cargo shall be deemed to insure independently of any policy issued to a shipper, consignee, owner or agent to the same extent as if no other insurance existed, subject, nevertheless, to pro rata contributions from and with other similar policies issued to the carrier.

2. Overlapping insurance shall be deemed to exist in the case of termination, by expiration or cancellation, of a motor truck cargo liability policy with Interstate Commerce Commission and State Endorsement(s) expiring subsequent thereto, and a succeeding motor truck cargo liability policy whose ICC and State Endorsement(s) attach upon the termination dates of the endorsement(s) attached to the succeeded policy. In the case of such overlapping insurance between a succeeded insurer's unexpired ICC and State Endorsement(s) and a succeeding insurer's ICC and State Endorsement(s) whether issued or not: It is agreed that the succeeding insurer shall assume any liability under ICC or State Endorsement(s) from the date of attachment of the succeeding policy but not in excess of the limits stated in the ICC or State Endorsement(s).

3. Overlapping insurance shall be deemed to exist whenever insured loss or damage may have occurred during continuous coverage under successive policies of two or more companies and the date of loss cannot be determined but may be presumed to have been during the existence of such policies, the loss shall be prorated between the companies on the basis of time each company was at risk prior to discovery of loss, the total of such time in no case to exceed thirty-six months nor to extend in the case of missing property beyond the time the property was last seen nor in the case of damage beyond the time the property was last known to be in sound condition.

4. When a furriers customers policy has been extended to cover excess legal liability and the amount charged the bailor for storage or services and insurance was predicated on the declared valuation stated in the receipt issued by the furrier for the article lost or damaged, the bailor's insurer shall accept in final settlement the amount of the loss or damage not exceeding such declared valuation, unless such loss or damage was due to unauthorized use or disposition of the article by the bailee.

   When one bailee sends property to another bailee, insurance covering the bailee in possession of the property at the time of the loss is to be considered primary in relation to the first bailee's insurance. The measure of liability under the insurance declared to be primary shall be determined as follows notwithstanding any limitation of subsequently determined excess liability stated in the original bailee's contract of bailment with the owner or agent:

   A. If a receipt shall have been issued by the bailee in custody, with a declared valuation, or stated limitation of liability, the measure of liability shall be such declared valuation, or stated limitation, but in no event exceeding the actual cash value of the property.

   B. If a receipt shall have been issued by the bailee in custody with no declared valuation, or no stated limitation of liability, or if no receipt shall have been issued, the measure of liability shall be the actual cash value of the property, unless there is in effect a signed contract or other agreement in writing between the parties specifically providing for a lesser liability between the parties.[5]

---

[5]See Examples.

EXAMPLES — Specific Principle 4

(Inland-Inland)

Example 1. A coat worth $3,000 is stored by "A" with the furrier who issues a fur storage receipt with a declared value of $500. "B" asks the furrier to manufacture a coat like "A's". The furrier agrees, and without "A's" knowledge or consent removes her coat from the storage vault to his workroom where it is used as a model, and while there it is stolen. This is an unauthorized use of the coat, and the furrier should be liable for the full value.

Example 2. The same coat is stored under a $500 receipt, and without "A's" knowledge or consent, the furrier removes the coat from the storage vault for display or exhibition and, while on a form in the store or window, it is stolen. This is an unauthorized use of the coat and the furrier should be liable for full value.

Example 3. The same coat is stored under a $500 receipt, and repairs are ordered and agreed upon. The receipt bears a statement: "All work done on our premises." The coat, without the knowledge of "A," is sent to another and independent contractor where the work is to be done. It is damaged by fire on these premises and is a total loss. This is an unauthorized use of the coat and the furrier should be liable for the full value for such a breach of contract.

Example 4. Assuming the same bailment, the furrier, being in financial difficulties, takes the coat to a pawnbroker, where it is pledged for a loan. "A" should recover damages (i.e., cost of replevin, et cetera) up to the full value from the furrier for such unauthorized use or disposition of the property.

Note: Where the personal property insurer does not control the right of recovery against the furrier, due to insufficient insurance, and a recovery is made by the owner in excess of the receipt valuation, the property insurer should refund to the excess liability insurer such amount as it has received in excess of the receipt valuation.

DEFINITIONS

of

Insurance Terms for the

Purpose of these Guiding Principles

AFFIXED — A television aerial or antenna is affixed to the building or outbuilding when substantially attached with the weight of the antenna borne principally by the building.

BLANKET — (Casualty) — When a policy covers at a stated location and any number of other unstated or non-scheduled locations as well, it is said to be "blanket."

(Fire and Inland Marine) — When a single amount of insurance covers several unrelated items, the policy is said to be written "blanket."

Example

One amount of insurance covering two or more buildings or a building and its contents.

CONCURRENT POLICIES — Concurrent policies are those insuring the same interest and the identical property involved in the loss or claim, which divide the risk of a specific major hazard between or among policies or companies, even though policy dates and amounts vary and certain policies contain reduced rate contribution, average, coinsurance, or deductible clauses, while others do not.

Examples

Two or more standard fire policies.
Two or more contractors installment floaters.
Two or more furriers customers policies.
Two or more mercantile theft policies.

A policy(ies) providing coverage under more than one underwriting classification; i.e., casualty--fidelity--fire--inland marine or multiple-line, shall **not** be considered concurrent to policy(ies) limited to one classification.

Examples

A standard fire policy and a homeowners or MIC.
A boiler-machinery and a fire policy.
A special multi-peril motel policy and a mercantile theft policy.

EXCESS PROVISION — A provision in a policy which stipulates that the policy is liable only after other insurance, covering the risk, has been exhausted — not to be confused with "pure excess" insurance. However, depositors forgery insurance which by its terms is primary to employee dishonesty coverage shall remain so.

FLOATER POLICY (FLOATING) — A policy under the terms of which protection follows movable property, covering it wherever it may be.

Example

A policy on tourist's baggage.

LIMIT OF LIABILITY RULE — As described in **General Condition 2.**

LIMITED PURPOSE — A policy(ies) is said to be for a more limited purpose when it is designed to provide coverage for a specific exposure as contrary to one which includes that exposure and other exposures as well.

Example

A trip transit policy is a more limited purpose policy than a household furniture policy with off-premises coverage.

LOCATION — A site specifically defined in the policy.

OVERLAPPING — When two or more types of insurance cover the same risk, the insurance is said to be "overlapping."

RETROSPECTIVE RATING — A plan under which the final premium for a risk is adjusted on basis of its own loss experience during the policy period.

QUESTIONS AND PROBLEMS

1. A disappearing deductible reads as follows: "This company shall be liable only when such loss in each occurrence exceeds $50. When loss is between $50 and $500 this Company shall be liable for 111% of the loss in excess of $50 and when loss is $500 or more, this loss deductible clause shall not apply."

   a. Calculate the Company's liability when the loss is $50.

   b. Calculate the Company's liability when the loss is $400.

   c. Calculate the Company's liability when the loss is $501.

   d. What is a *straight* deductible?

   e. What is a *percentage* deductible?

2. The waiver of inventory and appraisement clause, usually made a part of the coinsurance, contribution, or average clauses, provides: "In event that the claim for any loss is both less than $10,000 or less than 5% of the total amount of insurance upon the property described ... no special inventory or appraisement of the undamaged property shall be required. . . . however, nothing herein shall be construed to waive application of the (coinsurance, contribution or average clause) first paragraph of this clause."

   a. Explain in your own words the purpose and significance of this clause.

   b. Assume you are adjusting a loss estimated at $5,000, with $500,000 insurance, and the insured is obviously a coinsurer. The insured tells you he is not required to furnish a statement of values according to the waiver of inventory and appraisement clause. What action, if any, can you take? Explain.

3. **a.** What is the purpose of the Guiding Principles?

   b. How are differences of opinion resolved when the parties disagree on the precise application of the Guiding Principles?

Reports to Insurers

Reports are sometimes made orally, but generally they are written. An oral report may be no more formal than a telephone call to the field representative or a statement by the loss official that the claim representative has inspected the scene of the loss and estimates the amount as so many dollars. On the other hand, a serious situation involving a large loss or one with complications involving coverage or liability may be reported orally to the representatives of the insurers in a formal meeting, with a chairman to put motions and a secretary to record the proceedings and write up minutes. A written report may be nothing more than the claim representative's signature, approving a proof of loss for a small amount, or a form letter stating the amount of the adjustment and saying that nothing worth commenting upon was found. It may, however, be lengthy and highly detailed.

KINDS AND PURPOSE

Reports are of three general kinds: (1) *preliminary* and *interim reports* made for the purpose of keeping the insurer up to date on what is happening, (2) *interim reports* on unadjusted losses in which the claim representative presents situations that raise questions of expediency or liability and asks for the insurer's instructions, and (3) *closing* or *final reports* on losses which have been adjusted.

On any loss, the report should be factual and concise. On a loss that is large or complicated or that has unusual or doubtful situations, the report should be comprehensive.

A report should put the person who reads it in possession of information and comment that will justify taking some definite action. In preparing a report, the claim representative should consider the circumstances attending the loss or the claim and present those that are pertinent to an understanding of what has happened and what should be done. The material of a report should be arranged in orderly fashion and should be presented so as to emphasize what is important.

Reports should be made in the language ordinarily used by underwriters and loss personnel. If accurate description of unusual properties, processes, or other subjects requires the use of uncommon names, terms, or expressions, it is well to explain their meaning. Any conclusion or opinion stated should be supported by the reason for it.

In many instances, reports should be accompanied by exhibits, estimates, statements, diagrams, sketches, or photographs. These should be identified by name, letter, or number.

The great majority of written reports are made by the claim representative. In some offices, however, a competent secretary writes reports from memorandums and figures in the claim representative's file.

In emergencies, as when preliminary reports are expected by the underwriters within 24 hours, the newspaper-reporting method can be followed to advantage. The claim representative, after going over the property and picking up all available information, telephones the report to headquarters, where it is written up and mailed or otherwise delivered.

While the primary purpose of a report made on an adjusted loss is to present information and the claim representative's opinion about the loss and its adjustment, most underwriters desire comment in their reports on "risk characteristics" that can be used by the underwriters to their advantage in future underwriting.

Preliminary Reports

A preliminary report may be no more than an acknowledgment of the assignment and a statement of insurance involved and the cause and extent of damage or loss, and an estimate of the loss to the insurer. On losses involving large amounts of money, complicated questions of coverage, salvage, subrogation, or troublesome circumstances, the preliminary report should be sufficiently comprehensive to communicate factually to the insurer all relevant information.

It is generally considered good practice to make a preliminary report on any loss over a few hundred dollars that cannot be closed within 10 days from the date of the assignment. However, on routine losses under a few hundred dollars, with no complications or unusual circumstances, a preliminary report is ordinarily acceptable if the loss remains open for more than 30 days. Individual insurers have different rules and procedures to be followed. The claim representative should be guided accordingly. The report should always include an estimate of the amount of loss.

Where agents are given authority to assign losses, there may be a tendency for them to overlook sending written loss notices to insurers after reporting losses to the claim representative. Early preliminary reports are, therefore, desired and expected by the insurer on such losses. Notices of loss are likewise sent to insurers by agents or brokers without any estimate of amount. Consequently, the claim representative is expected to report promptly an estimate of the amount of each loss assigned.

Insurers are required by law to set up a reserve against every reported loss. In order to do so they need an estimate of the amount. Excessive overestimating is as detrimental as underestimating. In either case the insurer's financial and operating statements will be distorted.

Because the great majority of losses involve small sums of money in which there is no question of coverage and the adjustment is made on first contact with the insured, the first report received by the insurer often includes closing papers and is the only report made.

Interim Reports

Interim reports are made to inform the insurer of any change of circumstances in the occurrence of the loss and of the progress being made in the investigation, in determination of loss, or in adjustment negotiations. An interim report may be no more than a status report stating that there has been no change since the last report and telling the insurer to move the file ahead in the diary 30 days, 60 days, or whatever number of days is indicated by the particular circumstances.

Insurers frequently require periodic *status* reports, not only to be kept advised but, more importantly, to be certain the claim representative has not been neglectful in servicing the insured or in following up on essential or urgent elements of the investigation. Keeping the insurer up to date on all important developments can greatly reduce the need of the insurer to request routine status reports.

Interim reports should also confirm that the present reserve carried is adequate or should clearly specify any change upward or downward.

Reports Asking for Instructions

Insurers rarely delegate to other than their own salaried employees authority to decide questions of coverage or liability. Consequently, such questions must generally be submitted to the insurers for their decision. Questions of expediency also arise from time to time. In either case, the claim representative should make a report on the situation and ask for instructions. In submitting such questions the report should set forth all circumstances that the insurer must have in mind in order to make a wise decision.

Whenever feasible, a clear statement of the question asked should be made in the beginning of the report under a caption such as Question Submitted or similar wording. No question should be submitted to an insurer if a more thorough investigation or a reading of the policy will provide the answer. Likewise, it is not good practice to ask a question of an insurer without providing all the available facts upon which an opinion or answer can be based.

The kinds of question submitted to insurers for advice or instructions vary considerably but are generally of the following nature:

1. Matters of the individual insurer's interpretation of policy wording, particularly where there is no general concurrence in the industry.
2. Cases where the insurer's relationship with important producers or insureds may be affected by any decision.
3. Whether any policy provisions or conditions are to be waived.
4. Whether payment is to be made in excess of an amount the claim representative feels is adequate.
5. Whether specific Requirements in Case of Loss will be enforced.
6. Whether to defend or compromise cases of doubtful liability.
7. Whether to prosecute or compromise subrogation against third parties.
8. The exercise of company options.
9. The advisability of going to appraisal or examining the insured under oath.
10. Questions of extent of insurable interest.
11. Whether a valid contract existed at the time of loss.
12. Questions of contribution or apportionment.
13. Whether a peril insured against caused the loss.
14. Questions concerning whether the property involved is covered by the policy.

Closing or Final Reports

On small losses the closing, or final, report is very often the only report submitted. It summarizes the result of the investigation and agreement upon amount and states the recommendation for payment. Claim representatives should shorten their reports to the minimum that will present relevant facts concerning the loss. The insurer should not be burdened with a page of reading matter that can be condensed into a paragraph, or a paragraph that can be condensed into a sentence.

Status Reports on Salvage or Subrogation

Frequently, after a closing or final report, activity continues on a loss by reason of salvage operations or subrogation proceedings. The latter could extend into several years where litigation is involved. The salvor who handles the salvage and the attorney who handles the subrogation usually report periodically to the claim representative representing the insurer. He or she in turn forwards status reports to the insurer. In situations where the claim representative is providing a service for the subrogation attorney or acting as a witness in court he or she should report periodically to the insurer to keep the insurer up to date.

STRUCTURE OF REPORTS

Captions

The caption of a report should identify the loss to the insurer. It should show:

Company claim number—if known.
Adjuster's claim number.
Insured—name as it appears on the policy.
Location—street and number, city or town, and state.
Kind of loss—fire, windstorm, water damage, etc.
Date of loss—month, day, year, and hour of day.
Policy number—also form numbers involved in claim.
Agent—name and location.

When policies issued by more than one insurer are involved and a single report is prepared, addressed to the "Insurers Interested" or "Companies at Interest," the policy number of each insurer should be inserted in the caption, unless a list of insurers (giving policy numbers and amounts) is incorporated into the report.

Topical Headings

The topical headings under which material can be presented are: Summary; Insured; Insurance; Risk (building or other property covered); Interest, Title, Encumbrance, or Possession (one or more according to what is to be reported); Origin—or Fire, Windstorm, Explosion (or other peril that caused loss); Loss or Damage; Liability: Survey or Inspection; Protection From Further Damage; Preparation for Adjustment; Claim and Adjustment; Salvage; Subrogation; Payment; Recommendations; Comment.

Occasionally, a special circumstance will justify a heading not mentioned. Very few reports require more than six or seven sections. Material pertinent under one heading should not appear under another.

A topical heading need not be used in a report if the subject is not important or relevant to the claim and adjustment. An exception may be the use of such topical headings as Salvage or Subrogation; unless, in the appropriate situations, these headings are marked "None," the type of loss may lead the insurer to question whether salvage or subrogation has been overlooked.

Generally no heading should be used if the subject has been adequately covered in a previous report.

The Committee on Procedures and Standards of the Property Loss Research Bureau (PLRB), together with a Consulting Committee of independent adjusters, specifies the following topical headings for closing reports in *Procedures and Standards on Property Loss Adjustments:*

Closing Reports
(a) On routine small losses involving no unusual circumstances, short-form closing reports will be sufficient.

(b) On all other losses the information obtained should be furnished under the following captions: (It is not necessary to repeat any information furnished in previous reports.)
1. Source of assignment
2. Coverage—including: Source of policy information:
   Type of coverage
3. Policy violations
4. Insured—including: Description; Insurable interest; Previous and present address; Previous losses
5. Risk: Description of risk and recommendations
6. Title, mortgage and/or encumbrances
7. Origin
8. Adjustment and general remarks—including: General description of damage; Explanation of adjustments or any unusual problems in connection therewith
9. Subrogation: Yes or No. If "Yes," complete report on subrogation investigation with statements, photographs, or other pertinent data
10. Salvage: Yes or No. If "Yes," state disposition
11. Recommendations—including: Further insurance; Restoration of loss, if known; Payment
12. Enclosures

Statement of loss attached to proof should clearly indicate the name of the adjuster who actually handled claim.

OUTLINE GUIDE FOR REPORTING
Summary

A summary is given only in a final report, as until the loss is closed, no summary can be made. It generally is set up as the first section of the report with these column heads: Item, Sound Value, Loss, Insurance, Claim.

Items are stated as building, contents, business interruption, rents, or other subject matter. If more than one item is involved, each should be detailed. If, under any item, the claim is less than the insurance and also less than the loss, there should be added a statement, substantially as follows:

The amount claimed is the limit of liability under the ...% coinsurance (or other) clause.

Insured

In reports on ordinary losses, most insurers expect only short and simple statements relative to the insured. As examples:

1. The insured is employed as a bookkeeper in the local hardware store of Smith & Jones. He states that he has suffered no previous losses.
2. The insured is a nationally known producer of copper products. It has suffered a number of losses, none of which has been criticized.

In reports on losses of doubtful origin, or difficult of adjustment, or presenting unusual situations, any of the following items of information may be pertinent and should be covered.

1. For an individual.
   a. Approximate age, status, whether single, married, widow, or widower; if married, name of wife or husband.
   b. In dwelling losses, occupation and business address.
   c. In mercantile or manufacturing losses, home address.
   d. Citizen of what country.
   e. State and country of residence, and how long continuously a resident.
   f. Previous places of residence.
2. For a group, partnership, association, or corporation.
   a. Names of the individuals making up the group; partners, officers, and important employees.
   b. State in which incorporated.
   c. Authorized and paid-in capital.
3. For all classes of insureds.
   a. Financial stability.
   b. In contents losses, whether premises occupied is owned or not owned.
   c. Present business, previous business, and where located.
   d. Previous fires or other losses, if any; location, amount of insurance collected, names under which losses occurred.
   e. Moved since loss, and to what location.
   f. Attitude in adjustment negotiations: fairminded, cooperative, mercenary, difficult; support with reasons for the characterization.
   g. Recommendations on whether to continue to insure the insured.

Insurance

The insurance is frequently reported on in considerable detail in preliminary reports, particularly those that present situations in which the claim representative submits the facts and asks the insurer to advise how to proceed. The insurance is only occasionally discussed in final reports.

Preliminary reports include:

1. List of policies by numbers; binders or other contracts of insurance, alphabetically by names of insurers, commencement and expiration dates, amounts of insurance, total amount; if policies are not all concurrent, group any two or more that are, and show group total.
2. Name of agent issuing each contract and location of agency.
3. Form numbers; subject matter covered, location if there is doubt or dispute about the location at which the insurance covers; limitation clauses, loss-payable or mortgagee clauses, warranties, or other provisions that have any bearing on loss.
4. Examination of policies, when and where made; if not examined, why not; source of information.

In final or closing reports, no list of insurance is necessary, because the proof of loss shows details and lists all policies in an apportionment.

Risk

In ordinary losses, brief descriptions are in order; for example:

1. One-story frame, ranch-type, one-family dwelling.
2. Two-story ordinary brick, two-family residence.

3. Stock and equipment usual to a drug-store.
4. One-story brick building and contents usual to men's clothing store.

In unusual losses, any of the following may be pertinent to an understanding of the loss, a check of an application or representations, and a consideration by the underwriter of the desirability of the risk for future insurance and of the amount to be carried on or in it, if it is acceptable:

I. Building—construction.
   A. Fire-resistive, ordinary brick, frame, cement block, or other accepted description.
   B. Number of stories.
   C. Size and age, actual or estimated.
   D. Improvements and betterments—description.
   E. Defects and possibility of correction.
   F. Physical condition: sound, in need of repairs, deteriorated, or obsolescent.
   G. Contribution to cause or magnitude of loss.
II. Personal property—description.
   A. Property in hands of a manufacturer—class.
      1. Raw stock—kind of materials.
      2. Stock in process.
      3. Finished stock—kind, location, and storage method.
      4. Property of others—kind.
      5. Concentration of values.
      6. Contribution to cause or magnitude of loss.
   B. Property held for sale—class.
      1. Merchandise—kind, location, and storage method.
      2. Property of others—on consignment.
      3. Concentration of values.
      4. Contribution to cause or magnitude of loss.
   C. Property in use.
      1. Usual or incidental to the occupancy as a dwelling.
         a. Scheduled or unscheduled.

      b. On or off premises.
      c. Property of insured or others.
      d. Physical condition.
      2. Machinery, equipment, furniture, and fixtures—types and use.
         a. On or off premises.
         b. Property of others—leased—title.
         c. Physical condition.
         d. Location on premises.
III. Occupancy.
   A. Mercantile, manufacturing, office, warehouse, hotel, dwelling, school, or other.
   B. Any part, or all, unoccupied or vacant.
   C. Other occupancies and names of occupants if pertinent, particularly when loss originated in or because of another occupancy.
   D. Contribution to origin, spread, or magnitude or loss.
   E. Contribution to amount of the insured's loss.
IV. Protection against.
   A. Fire: within or beyond protection of public fire station; within or beyond 500 feet of public hydrant; private protection; sprinklered.
   B. Theft: police protection; private protection; special devices, safes, alarms.
   C. Lightning: lightning rods, arrestors, proper grounds.
   D. Explosion: controls in processing; approved electrical wiring, devices, and fixtures.
   E. Water damage: proper maintenance of heating, plumbing, and air-conditioning systems; control of wet manufacturing processes.
   F. Sprinkler leakage: proper maintenance; use of guards on heads; use of heads suitable for withstanding normal temperatures.
   G. Flood: dikes; window and door covers; pumps.
   H. Hurricanes: shutters; approved roofing; wind-resistive construction.

V. Exposures.
  A. Fire: building, lumber pile, brush or forests, grass field, rubbish burners, railroads, hazardous manufacturing processes.
  B. Theft: exhibiting of jewelry and furs publicly, jewelry samples carried by salesmen, furs and jewels in retail stores, valuables on exhibit.
  C. Lightning: greatest exposures in Southeast.
  D. Explosion: gas holder, tanks, plants using explosives or operating with nuclear devices, places where explosives are handled, blasting,—distance in feet from risk.
  E. Water damage: improper construction or maintenance of heating and plumbing systems and fixtures; deteriorated underground water mains, sewer systems, or steam pipes; defective or deteriorated building construction such as skylights, windows, doors, and roofs; careless tenants; wet manufacturing process.
  F. Sprinkler leakage: deteriorated systems, inadequate heat in premises, careless tenants.
  G. Flood: rivers or bodies of water; distance in feet from risk; normal elevation; record of floods; drain facilities in area in event of cloudburst.
  H. Hurricane: location—Southeast, Eastern Seaboard, Gulf States.
  I. Tornado, hail: location—Midwest States.
  J. Vandalism, malicious mischief: schools, churches, vacant or unoccupied buildings, buildings under construction.
  K. Earthquake, mudslide, other earth movement.
VI. Neighborhood loss record.
  A. Good or bad.
  B. Deteriorating; increase in arson, burglary, malicious mischief, rioting.

  C. Accepted reason.
VII. Value of risk.
  A. Replacement cost.
  B. Replacement cost less physical depreciation.
  C. Market value—actual cash value.
  D. Secondhand value.
  E. Probability of replacement if destroyed.
VIII. Recommendation.
  A. Continue insurance: after correction of any unsafe condition, or after inspection.
  B. Discontinue insurance; reason.

Interest, Title, Possession, Encumbrance

In the majority of losses, the claim representative can report: "Sole ownership, no encumbrance." In some losses, however, he or she must report on one or more of the following:

1. Insured's interest.
  a. Nature and extent.
  b. When and how acquired.
  c. If by contract of purchase, date, execution date, principal sum, payments stipulated, default, proviso as to bearing of any loss or maintenance of insurance.
2. Interests of others.
  a. Names of others holding or claiming interests.
  b. Nature and extent of the interest of each.
  c. Insured, by stipulation in the insured's policy or separately.
  d. Not insured.
3. Title.
  a. Name of title holder.
4. Possession: real property.
  a. Owner.
  b. Tenant at will.
  c. Lessee: terms of lease, duration, rental, fire clause, option to buy, insurance requirements; any independent insurance carried.
5. Possession: personal property.
  a. Owner.

b. Lessee: terms of lease, duration, rental, fire clause, option to buy, insurance requirements; any independent insurance carried.

c. Bailee: contract of bailment, written, oral, trade custom; charges; insurance carried on liability, on the property.

6. Encumbrance.

    a. Name of person holding.

    b. Nature, amount, date due; debt at date of loss; record or default; foreclosure threatened or begun.

    c. Covered by loss payable clause or mortgagee clause in insured's policies, or by independent insurance.

    d. Not covered; requirements of encumbrance as to insurance.

Origin or Occurrence of Loss

The time, place, and cause of loss are the essentials to be covered. In ordinary losses, little needs to be said. In unusual losses, there may be a considerable story to tell. Any special investigation should be concisely reported. The general requirements are:

1. Time.

    a. Date, hour, and minute.

    b. If indefinite, the best approximation.

2. Place.

    a. On the premises described, in a policy covering at specific location.

    b. On other premises or elsewhere, under extension of coverage or floating insurance.

3. Cause.

    a. Definite or uncertain.

    b. If uncertain, the insured's theory, the claim representative's theory.

    c. Direct loss.

    d. Named peril.

    e. All-risks.

    f. Witnesses.

    g. Statements.

4. Discovery—when and by whom.

5. Alarm or report—when given or made, and by whom.

Additional points to be covered in reporting on specific causes of loss include:

1. Fire.

    a. In what part of whose premises did it originate?

    b. How was it fought, by public or private protection; apparatus used—hose streams, barrels, and buckets?

    c. If property was sprinklered, number of heads that opened, their kind and location. Has system been restored?

    d. If fire was spread due to combustible materials, openings in floors or walls, or concealed spaces—comment.

    e. If fire was confined, what were the features of construction, occupancy, or protection that confined it?

    f. Limits of burning, smoking, and wetting?

    g. If fire originated in another building or from any external exposure, what is the distance?

    h. Persons interviewed and their statements: fire chief, police, fire marshal, watchman; clock records.

    i. Results of examination of debris.

    j. Are American Insurance Association, Property Loss Research Bureau, or other agencies investigating?

2. Lightning.

    a. Direct hit, near miss, or ground surge?

    b. Other damage in neighborhood, witnesses, weather bureau. Have other possible causes (power surge, short circuits, deteriorated apparatus) been eliminated?

    c. Was property rodded, lightning arrestors grounded?

3. Windstorm and hail.

    a. Exclusion of certain kinds of loss or property.

    b. Did the wind claimed to have caused the damage qualify as a windstorm?

    c. Weather bureau records of time and velocity, airport or other sources, other wind or hail damage in neighborhood.

4. Explosion.

    a. Kind of explosion: dust, blasting, pressure vessel, nitrate or other material, furnace, boiler, manufacturing process, leaking gas, etc.

    b. Was the damage the result of a happening which is specifically excluded in the policy as an explosion (i.e., electrical arcing, water hammer, etc.)?

c. Reports of authorities or experts on cause.

5. Riot and civil commotion.
   a. Does the occurrence meet the definition of riot or civil commotion used in the particular jurisdiction?
   b. Is the city, county, or state liable?
   c. Did any loss occur due to change of temperature, humidity, etc.?
   d. Was a burglary insurance carrier involved?

6. Vehicle—aircraft.
   a. Does the policy require actual physical contact?
   b. Does the policy exclude damage by a vehicle owned or operated by the occupant or tenant of the premises?
   c. Was the police report checked for identification of vehicle and driver?
   d. Identification of aircraft made? Private, commercial, or military?
   e. Property excluded by policy; driveways, walks, lawns, shrubs, etc.?

7. Sonic boom—full explanation for any claim for structural damage.

8. Smoke.
   a. Description of unit from which smoke emanated. Location.
   b. Conditions pertaining to sudden and accidental damage as opposed to accumulative.

9. Vandalism and malicious mischief.
   a. Who committed the act?
   b. Was the act done willfully with malicious intent?
   c. Was any person or persons apprehended? Charged?
   d. Exclusion: theft, glass breakage, etc.
   e. Is there any question of vacancy beyond the period permitted?
   f. Include police reports if any.

10. Theft, burglary, mysterious disappearance.
    a. Who last saw the missing article?
    b. Where was it?
    c. Was opportunity for theft present?
    d. Did it disappear under circumstances that were mysterious?
    e. If burglary, was there evidence of forcible entry? Did alarm operate?
    f. If there was a locked-car provision, is evidence of forcible entry visible?
    g. Was the occurrence reported to police? Were pawn shops notified? Was a reward offered? Have police taken action? Include police reports.
    h. Was the thief apprehended? Was the property recovered? Has a search been made?
    i. Was a complete statement taken from the insured or others to obtain the history and value of the item, and to obtain clues leading to persons having knowledge of the value and location of the item, such as delivery people and servants?
    j. Are there exclusions and limits applicable on the premises? Away from the premises?

11. Falling objects—Is the definition of "falling object" met?

12. Weight of ice, snow, or sleet.
    a. Was the loss actually caused by weight?
    b. Was there physical injury to the building covered or containing property covered?
    c. Did the claim include property specifically excluded?

13. Collapse.
    a. Was the damage the result of an actual collapse of part or all of a building?
    b. Describe the exact circumstances of the collapse. Was an expert used in determining the circumstances?
    c. Did the claim include specifically excluded property?

14. Accidental discharge or leakage of water.
    a. Was the discharge, leakage, or overflow actually accidental?
    b. Was the damaged property described in the policy?
    c. Is the substance discharged water from *within* the plumbing, heating, or air-conditioning system, or domestic appliance?

15. Sprinkler leakage.
    a. From what pipe, connection, valve, tank, or other part of the sprinkler system did the water escape?

b. What specific peril caused the leakage?
c. Did the alarms operate?
d. Has the system been restored or reactivated?

16. Breakage of glass.
    a. Description of glass involved (i.e., window, door, mirror constituting part of building, etc.).
    b. How was it broken?
    c. Damage by flying fragments.

17. Freezing of plumbing, heating, and air-conditioning systems.
    a. Description of exact cause of freezing.
    b. Circumstances relating to any vacancy or unoccupancy provision of the policy.

18. Electrical injury.
    a. Give a complete description of the peril that was the direct cause of the loss, and give your reason for classifying it as a "risk of loss" (direct? fortuitous?).
    b. If the peril is also a "named peril," refer to the specific peril in this outline.

Extent of Loss

The condition of the property immediately after the loss should be described so that the underwriter or loss supervisor will be informed how and to what extent the property was affected, as follows:

1. Buildings.
   a. Total losses: consumed, collapsed, blown to pieces, washed away.
   b. Partial losses: character and degree of damages; sections destroyed, scorched, smoked, or wet; debris; weather damage.

2. Personal property.
   a. Total losses: consumed, exploded, stolen, melted, buried, or contaminated beyond recovery.
   b. Partial losses: articles or lots involved, their location and arrangement; character and degree of damage, loss, or destruction: scorched, smoked, wet, buried under debris, mangled, stained, contaminated, damaged by weather.

Circumstances Affecting Liability

The circumstances creating any question of liability should be presented, together with the insured's statement and a summary of the evidence in hand. The position or attitude of any agent should be given.

The statement should include:
1. The question raised: forfeiture, coverage.
2. Facts.
3. Evidence in hand.
4. Insured's statement or explanation.
5. Agent's knowledge and attitude.

Survey or Inspection

In many reports it is unnecessary to discuss survey or inspection. In reports on unusual losses a full account of surveys or inspections is advisable.

Date.
Place.
By whom.
Others present.
Property surveyed.
Conditions noted.

Protection Against Further Damage

Steps taken to prevent further damage should be detailed.

1. Buildings.
   a. Temporary or permanent repairs to roofs or openings.
   b. Emergency shoring.
   c. Evacuating water.
   d. Draining plumbing.
   e. Restoring heat.

2. Personal property.
   a. Assembling scattered articles.
   b. Separating damaged and undamaged.
   c. Drying, wiping, greasing.
   d. Removing for better protection.
   e. Putting into work or reconditioning process.

Preparation for Adjustment

Preparation for adjustment is only occasionally reported on.

1. Examination of property.
   a. By claim representative.

b. By expert.
2. Estimates or inventories.
    a. By claim representative.
    b. By expert.
    c. Jointly with insured's representatives.
3. Examination of records.
    a. By claim representative.
    b. By expert.
4. Photographs.
5. Diagrams.
6. Chemical tests.
7. Impressions.
8. Rubbings.

Claim and Adjustment

A detailed account of how the claim was presented and what was done to bring about an adjustment is in order when reporting on a large loss or one requiring more than ordinary time, effort, or expense to adjust.

1. Claim.
    a. Amount; if more than one item of insurance, amount under each item.
    b. Evidence offered in support: estimate, inventory, statement, original records, repair bills; name of any estimator, inventory maker, accountant, or repairer.
2. Claim representative's figures.
    a. Amount.
    b. By whom made up.
3. Joint figures—if no formal claim was made, but figures were made up jointly, so state.
4. Experts—reason for use.

Subrogation

A section on subrogation is in order when circumstances indicate that the insured has a right to recover from a third party.

1. Circumstances creating right of recovery.
    a. Cause of loss.
    b. Negligent act or ommission.
    c. Person or party at fault.
2. If right has been waived—give details of any release or other agreement.
3. Investigation.
    a. Evidence gathered: statements of witnesses, diagrams, photographs, physical evidence.

b. Financial responsibility of wrongdoer.
    c. Insurance carried by wrongdoer that may be available.
4. Attorney recommended.
    a. Name.
    b. Opinion if consulted.
    c. Fee basis.
5. Subrogation or loan receipt.
    a. Taken by claim representative.
    b. To be sent with draft.
    c. Attorney will draft special form.
6. Uninsured interest.
    a. Name of attorney who will represent insured.
    b. Basis for apportioning any recovery if one has been agreed upon.

Salvage

If salvage was taken over or sold, details should be reported.

1. Reason for selling or taking.
2. Property.
    a. Description, quantity, sound value.
    b. Name of purchaser or salvor.
    c. Terms of sale or contract for handling.
3. When taken over for later sale.
    a. Probable net returns.
    b. Probable date of payment.

Payment

In many reports a routine statement recommending payment appears immediately after the summary. In some reports, one or more of the following points may require attention:

1. Date recommended.
    a. Prompt.
    b. At expiration of contract period, generally 60 days.
    c. Subject to later report.
2. How draft should be drawn.
    a. Insured only.
    b. Insured and payee or payees named in policy; if payees are not designated by name, guarantee given.
    c. Payee only.
    d. Insured and other persons.
    e. Assignee only.
    f. Legal representatives.

3. Special receipts or releases.
    a. Subrogation or loan receipt.
    b. Special release.
4. Circumstances delaying payment.
    a. Attachments, garnishments, notices of interest.
    b. Contested assignments.
5. Attorney.
    a. Attorney to whom question of payment has been, or should be, referred.
    b. Have garnishments, attachments, or assignments been given to him or her?

Comment

It is advisable to direct the insurer's attention to such circumstances as a series of fires in a single class of risks or a given territory, to local conditions affecting losses, and to forms or clauses that produce controversy.

Enclosures

Enclosures should be listed in detail. If there are many, it is well to number them so that identification will be easy. When the bill of an expert, attorney, or other person is enclosed for payment, it is well to show the amount when listing it.

STATEMENT OF LOSS

In closing reports, a statement of loss either is included as a separate exhibit or, on minor claims and those involving only a few items, may be shown directly on the back of the Proof of Loss. In some areas it is typed separately and affixed to the back of the Proof of Loss.

A statement of loss is actually an accurate presentation of how the amount of the agreed or adjusted loss was determined.

There is no standard form which can be used in all situations, as much will depend upon the size and kind of loss and also how complicated or involved the adjustment is. The essential consideration is to make certain that a person examining the statement will have no difficulty in following the figures and can readily pick out information relating to the insurance, the property involved, the insurable value of that property,

the amount claimed if relevant, amounts agreed to, application of any contribution or limiting clauses, and apportionment with other applicable insurance.

The section of the report covering claim and adjustment should be written so that it will follow the order of the statement of loss and can be checked against it. It is unnecessary to copy schedules of personal property which are submitted with the report, or to copy details of the contractor's estimates or those of other experts used in measuring the loss. These may be marked for identification and such identification referred to in the statement of loss. On the other hand, it is not satisfactory to include figures in the statement without any explanation of their source or how they came to be there. Where the working papers and such things as inventories are voluminous, they are often retained in the file with a notation to the insurer that they are available if desired. If the claim representative retains pertinent papers in the office he or she should retain them long enough to conform with the record-destruction program of the insurer—usually five to seven years.

REPORTS AS PRIVILEGED COMMUNICATIONS

The report to the insurer is a privileged communication but, like all other communications, may by accident or misjudgment fall into the hands of some third party. It is, therefore, advisable to refrain from making statements or using language in a report that might be used to charge the claim representative with libel or slander or that might be embarrassing in business or socially.[1]

It is unwise, in a written report, to charge a person with arson or any other willful destruction or damage to property, or with hiding it or disposing of it and reporting it as stolen.[2] When commenting on doubtful or suspicious circumstances, it is well to use such expressions as "I have been informed,"

[1]See also Chap. 2, "Unfair Claim-Handling Practices."
[2]See also Chap. 10, "Arson Investigation and Detection."

"I understand," and "It is reported." In reporting on arrests, it is better to say "He or she was arrested and charged with theft" than to say "The police arrested the thief."

A detailed statement of the condition of undesirable property will not arouse resentment, but a general derogatory statement may do so. A factual statement—that there are water stains on ceilings, indicating that the roof has leaked; that the paint has peeled or faded; that the right end of the front porch has sunk where the supports have decayed; and that the glass has been broken out of the five windows—will not anger the owner of the building. On the other hand, if the claim representative reported that the same building was a rundown dilapidated piece of property, the owner and producer might take offense at the statement if the report came into their possession.

Criticism of producers or underwriters should be avoided. If they have been at fault, an exact statement of what they have done will speak for itself.

Appendix

A. ADJUSTER'S LICENSING STATUTES*

State	License	Written Exam	Staff Adjuster	Independent Adjuster	Public Adjuster	License Required for Catastrophe
Alabama	Yes	None	No	Yes	No	No
Alaska	Yes	Yes	No	Yes	No	No
Arizona	Yes	None	No	Yes	Yes	No
Arkansas	Yes	None	No	Yes	No	No
California	Yes	None	No	Yes	Yes	No
Colorado	Yes	Yes	Yes	Yes	Yes	No
Connecticut	Yes	Yes	Yes (Casualty only)	Yes (Casualty only)	Yes	No
Delaware	Yes	Yes	Yes	Yes	No	No
District of Columbia	None	—	—	—	—	—
Florida	Yes	Yes	Yes	Yes	Yes	Permit issued
Georgia	Yes	Yes	No	Yes	Yes	No
Hawaii	Yes	Yes	No	Yes	Yes	No
Idaho	Yes	Yes	No	Yes	No	No
Illinois	None	—	—	—	—	—
Indiana	Yes	Yes	No	No	Yes	No
Iowa	None	—	—	—	—	—
Kansas	None	—	—	—	—	—
Kentucky	Yes	None	No	Yes	Yes	No
Louisiana	None	—	—	—	—	—
Maine	Yes	Yes	No	Yes	No	No
Maryland	Yes	Yes	No	No	Yes	No comment
Massachusetts	Yes	None	No	No	Yes	No comment
Michigan	Yes	Yes	No	Yes	Yes	No comment
Minnesota	Yes	Yes	No	Yes	Yes	Registration
Mississippi	No (fee)	None	No	Yes	No	No comment
Missouri	None	—	—	—	—	—
Montana	Yes	None	No	Yes	No	No
Nebraska	None	—	—	—	—	—
Nevada	Yes	Yes	No	Yes	Yes	No

*Used with permission of the Property Loss Research Bureau.

State	License	Written Exam	Staff Adjuster	Independent Adjuster	Public Adjuster	License Required for Catastrophe
New Hampshire	Yes	Yes	Yes	Yes	No	Temporary license
New Jersey	None	—	—	—	—	—
New Mexico	Yes	None	Yes	Yes	Yes	Temporary license
New York	Yes	Yes	No	Yes	Yes	Temporary permit
North Carolina	Yes	Yes	Yes	Yes	Yes	Registration only
North Dakota	None	—	—	—	—	—
Ohio	Yes	Yes	No	No	Yes	No
Oklahoma	Yes	Yes	Yes	Yes	Yes	Registration only
Oregon	Yes	Yes	No	Yes	Yes	Temporary permit
Pennsylvania	Yes	None	No	No	Yes (Solicitors also)	No
Puerto Rico	Yes	Yes	Yes	Yes	Yes	Special authority
Rhode Island	Yes	Yes	No	Yes	No	Temporary license
South Carolina	Yes	None	Yes	Yes	No	No (See brief for qualifications) †
South Dakota	None	—	—	—	—	—
Tennessee	Fee	None	Nothing in insurance code (appears to be an occupational tax)			
Texas	Yes	Yes	Yes	Yes	No	Temporary permit
Utah	Yes	Yes	No	Yes	Yes	No comment
Vermont	Yes	None	Yes	Yes	Yes	No comment
Virginia	None	—	—	—	—	—
Washington	Yes	Yes	No	Yes	Yes	No
West Virginia	None	—	—	—	—	—
Wisconsin	Yes	None	No	Yes	Yes	No comment
Wyoming	Yes	None	No	Yes	No	No

†Not shown.

B. CERTIFICATE OF SATISFACTION

CERTIFICATE OF SATISFACTION

DL 25374-1
FILE NUMBER

NH-12145-C
POLICY No.   CERT. No.

Boston, MA
AGENCY AT

DATE Dec. 3   19 76

P. T. Smyth
AGENT

To   A.B.C. Multiple-Line Insurance Company

of   Boston, Massachusetts

THIS IS TO CERTIFY, that the loss and damage by   Fire

of   11th   day of   November   , 19 76 , to   my upholstered sora

has been repaired/~~replaced~~ to   my   entire satisfaction by   Quality Repair Shoppe, 125 Third Avenue,

Boston, MA 02100   the cost of such repairs/replacements to be paid
to them whose receipt shall be sufficient acquittance for all claims under the above policy for loss and damage by reason of said

Fire

WITNESS: *Barbara L. Conte*
                              Insured

Mabel Stucker

UNIFORM STANDARD Form No. 3917 Approved by
PRINTED IN U.S.A.

C. STATEMENT IN PROOF OF LOSS, INCLUDING SUBROGATION AND SATISFACTION AGREEMENTS; AND AUTOMOBILE PROOF OF LOSS, INCLUDING SUBROGATION AGREEMENT

SWORN STATEMENT IN PROOF OF LOSS
AND SUBROGATION AGREEMENT

$20,000.00
AMOUNT OF POLICY AT TIME OF LOSS

HO-38465
POLICY NUMBER

June 5, 1976
DATE ISSUED

Chicago, Illinois
AGENCY AT

June 5, 1977
DATE EXPIRES

Universal
AGENT

To the Noco Insurance Company, Chicago, Illinois _____ (Insurer)
By the above policy you insured John and Marie Detweiler _____
against loss by Fire and Other Perils _____to the property described under Schedule "A."

1. **Time and Origin:** A Wind and Hail _____ loss occurred about the hour of 3 o'clock P.M.,
   STATE KIND
   on the 3d day of May 1977. The cause and origin of the said loss were: Hail
   _____

2. **Occupancy:** The building described, or containing the property described, was occupied at the time of the loss as follows, and for no other purpose whatever: Dwelling _____

3. **Title and Interest:** At the time of the loss the interest of your insured in the property described therein was Owner _____No other person or persons had any interest therein or incumbrance thereon, except: None _____

4. **Changes:** Since the said policy was issued there has been no assignment thereof, or change of interest, use, occupancy, possession, location or exposure of the property described, except: None _____

5. **Total Insurance:** The total amount of insurance upon the property described by this policy was, at the time of the loss, $20,000.00 _____, as more particularly specified in the apportionment attached under Schedule "C," besides which there was no policy or other contract of insurance, written or oral, valid or invalid.

(FULL REPLACEMENT COST FIGURES TO BE INSERTED ONLY WHEN CONSIDERED IN THE ADJUSTMENT)	FULL REPLACEMENT COST	ACTUAL CASH VALUE
6. The value of said property at the time of loss was......	$ 24,000.00	$ 20,000.00
7. The whole loss and damage was...........................	$ 500.00	$ 400.00

8. The amount (less Ded. of $100.00 _____) claimed under this policy is $400.00

9. The said loss did not originate by any act, design or procurement on the part of your insured, or this affiant; nothing has been done by or with the privity or consent of your insured or this affiant, to violate the conditions of the policy, or render it void; no articles are mentioned herein or in annexed schedules but such as were destroyed or damaged at the time of said loss; no property saved has in any manner been concealed, and no attempt to deceive the said company, as to the extent of said loss, has in any manner been made. Any other information that may be required will be furnished and considered a part of this proof.

10. The insured hereby assigns, transfers, and sets over to the Insurer any and all claims or causes of action of whatsoever kind and nature which the Insured now has, or may hereafter have, to recover against any person or persons as the result of said occurrence and loss above described, ro the extent of the payment above made; the Insured agrees that the Insurer may enforce the same in such manner as shall be necessary or appropriate for the use and benefit of the Insurer, either in its own name or in the name of the Insured; that the Insured will furnish such papers, information, or evidence as shall be within the Insured's possession or control for the purpose of enforcing such claim, demand, or cause of action. The Insured covenants that no release or settlement of any such claim, demand, or cause of action has been made.

11. The statements and agreements on the reverse side hereof or attached hereto are made a part of this instrument.

12. The furnishing of this blank or the preparation of proofs by a representative of the above insurance company is not a waiver of any of its rights.

State of Illinois _____

John Detweiler

County of Cook _____

John and Marie Detweiler _____ Insured

Subscribed and sworn to before me this _____day of _____19_____

_____Notary Public

(OVER)

SCHEDULE "A"—POLICY FORM

Policy Form No. HO-2 _____ Dated Ed. 2-75 _____
Item 1. $20,000.00 ___ on Dwelling (Replacement Cost Coverage) _____
Item 2. $_____ on _____
Item 3. $_____ on _____
Item 4. $_____ on _____
Situated 243 Thorne Street, Chicago, IL 60600 _____
Coinsurance, Average, Distribution, or Deductible Clauses, if any $100 Deductible _____
Loss, if any, payable to Insured _____

SCHEDULE "B"
STATEMENT OF ACTUAL CASH VALUE AND LOSS AND DAMAGE

		ACTUAL CASH VALUE		LOSS AND DAMAGE	
	Remove and replace 1,000 s.f. 235-1b asphalt shingles.				
	Removal and cartage	$100.00			
	15-1b saturated felt paper	40.00			
	10 squares shingles @ 27¢	270.00			
	Nails	6.67			
		$416.67			
	20% overhead, profit	83.33			
Totals:		$500.00			

SCHEDULE "C" — APPORTIONMENT

POLICY NO.	EXPIRES	NAME OF COMPANY	ITEM NO._____		ITEM NO._____	
			INSURES	PAYS	INSURES	PAYS
Totals:						

Jack Smith _____ Adjuster

SATISFACTION AGREEMENT

The insured hereby acknowledges repair or replacement of loss and damage to the Insured's entire satisfaction and agrees that the payment of the sum of_____Dollars, ($_____), by the Insurer to_____, the person or firm making the repair or replacement, shall constitute a full performance of the obligation of the Insurer under its said policy.

Dated_____19____   _____

THE INSURED

EK 115 6-73 15M   PRINTED IN U.S.A.

SWORN STATEMENT IN PROOF OF LOSS (AUTOMOBILE)

$ __ACV__ ___ CTF $ _____
AMOUNT OF POLICY

__February 1, 1976__
DATE ISSUED

__February 1, 1977__
EXPIRATION DATE

TO __A.B.C. Insurance__ _____ COMPANY

of __New York__ _____

Name of
Insured __Thomas D. Jones__

_____1234_____
OUR FILE No.

__60 23 45__
POLICY NO.   CERT. NO.

__Wichita, Kansas__
AGENCY AT

__National Agency__
AGENT

By your Policy of Insurance above described, you insured

COMPANY CLAIM No.

(HEREINAFTER CALLED INSURED) ACCORDING TO THE TERMS AND CONDITIONS CONTAINED THEREIN, INCLUDING THE WRITTEN PORTION THEREOF AND ALL ENDORSEMENTS, TRANSFERS AND ASSIGNMENTS ATTACHED THERETO, ON AUTOMOBILE DESCRIBED AS FOLLOWS:

MAKE	TYPE OF BODY	YEAR MODEL	TONNAGE	SERIAL NUMBER	MOTOR NUMBER
Ford	4-Dr S	1974		345678	

COVERAGE   AGAINST THE PERILS of __Comprehensive and $100.00 Deductible Collision__

DATE OF LOSS   A Loss occurred on the __2d__ day of __March__ _____ 19__76__ about the hour of __8__ o'clock __A.__ M.,
which loss upon the best knowledge and belief of Insured was caused by __collision with another vehicle__

CAUSE

LOCATION   __Wichita, Kansas__

WARRANTIES   Insured's occupation or business is __Salesperson__

Employer's name and address __Kerry Jewelry Shop, 49 Carteret Street, Wichita, KS 67200__

Said automobile is usually kept in __private__ located __1123 Spring Street, Wichita, KS 67200__
(PUBLIC OR PRIVATE GARAGE)

PURCHASE   SAID AUTOMOBILE WAS purchased __new__ from __Frankel Ford__ _____ by Insured
(NEW OR USED)

on __March 12,__ 19__74__ Cash $ _____ Trade Allowance $ _____ and ___ notes of $ _____
a total cost of $ _____ and at the time of said loss the unpaid balance of purchase price was $ _____
When your policy was issued to the Insured, Insured was the sole and unconditional owner of the automobile described. No incumbrance of said property existed nor has since been made nor has there been any change in the title, use, location or possession of said automobile.

OWNERSHIP   __Friendly Finance Company__

VALUE   THE ACTUAL CASH VALUE of above described automobile at the time of said loss was . . . . . . $__3,500.00__

WHOLE LOSS   THE ACTUAL LOSS AND DAMAGE to above described automobile as a result of said loss was . . . . . . $ __371.93__
(AS SHOWN BY ANNEXED SCHEDULE)

WHOLE INSURANCE   THE TOTAL INSURANCE covering peril above stated, including this policy and all other policies (whether valid or not), binders or agreements to insure, was at the time of said loss __less deductible__ $ __100.00__

AMOUNT CLAIMED   INSURED HEREBY CLAIMS OF THIS COMPANY and will accept from this Company in full release and satisfaction in compromise settlement of all claims under this policy the sum of . . . . $ __271.93__

ASSIGNMENT OF INTEREST   Upon payment of claim for total loss by theft of automobile above described, the Insured does undertake to execute all instruments necessary to transfer, assign and set over unto the Insurer all rights, title, and interest in said automobile, and will help the said Insurer, or proper authorities, to identify said automobile, if found, and will render all assistance possible to recover the said automobile or to apprehend the thieves.

SUBROGATION   The Insured hereby covenants that no release has been or will be given to or settlement or compromise made with any third party who may be liable in damages to the Insured and the Insured in consideration of the payment made under this policy hereby subrogates the said Company to all rights and causes of action the said Insured has against any person, persons or corporation whomsoever for damage arising out of or incident to said loss or damage to said property and authorizes said Company to sue in the name of the Insured but at the cost of the Company any such third party, pledging full cooperation in such action.

STATEMENTS OF INSURED   The said automobile has not been used for carrying passengers for compensation, or rented, or leased, or operated in any race or speed contest, nor for any illegal purpose, during the term of this policy.

The said loss did not originate by any act, design or procurement on the part of the Insured or this affiant; nothing has been done by or with the privity or consent of Insured or this affiant, to violate the conditions of this policy, or render it void; all articles mentioned herein or in the schedule annexed hereto belong to said automobile and were in possession of the Insured at the time of said loss; no property saved has been in any manner concealed; no attempt to deceive the said Insurer, as to the extent of said loss, has in any manner been made, and no material fact is withheld that the said Insurer should be advised of. Any other information that may be required will be furnished on demand and considered a part of this proof.

The furnishing of this blank or the preparation of proofs by a representative of the above insurance company is not a waiver of any of its rights.

State of __Kansas__ _____   _Thomas D. Jones_ _____

County of __Sedgwick__ _____

Subscribed and sworn to before me this _____ day of _____ , 19 _____
Insured.

Form G/T 101-R-7-70 U.S.A.   _____
Notary Public.

STATEMENT OF LOSS			
Item--1974 Ford Sedan			
Cash value as agreed	$3,500.00		
Loss as determined:			
Repair per Glen's Garage invoice $371.93		$371.93	
Less deductible 100.00			$271.93
Value, Loss, and Claim	$3,500.00	$371.93	$271.93

CERTIFICATE OF SATISFACTION AND AUTHORIZATION TO PAY OTHER THAN INSURED

(THIS MAY ALSO BE USED WHEN LOSS IS PAID TO INSURED AND LOSS PAYEE BY AGENT)

The loss or damage for which this claim is made has been made good to my/our entire satisfaction and I/we hereby release and discharge the __A.B.C. Insurance Company__ from all claims and demands for loss or damage which occurred on or about the __2d__ day of __March__, 19__76__, and authorize payment to

__Glen's Garage__

the sum of __Two Hundred Seventy-One and 93/100__ Dollars ($271.93------), whose receipt for same shall be a complete acquittance.

Date __March 9, 1976__

S. Weiss
(Witness)

Thomas D. Jones
(Insured)

_____
(Mortgagee)

Ann Romney
Adjuster

Form G/T 101-R-7-70 U.S.A.

D. PROPERTY ARBITRATION RULES AND REGULATIONS

The Guiding Principles General Condition 9, November 1, 1963, provides as follows:

> Differences of opinion respecting the application or effect of these Principles shall be submitted for arbitration in the manner determined by the participating Associations. . . .

To implement this directive, and

For the purpose of arbitration of differences of opinion in first-party property losses and claims arising outside the scope of the Guiding Principles,

The American Insurance Association and the Property Loss Research Bureau hereby promulgate the following rules and regulations:

1. An agreement to arbitrate becomes effective when it is filed with either the American Insurance Association or the Property Loss Research Bureau.

2. The companies shall furnish a signed, agreed statement of fact within thirty (30) days after the filing of an arbitration agreement. In case of disagreement, each company shall submit its own statement. Companies may, if they so desire, submit briefs. Statements of fact, briefs and all other material shall be submitted. Five legible copies are required.

3. Parties to the arbitration will promptly furnish any additional factual information desired by the arbitrators.

4. Arbitrators for cases involving fire and/or casualty insurance shall be designated jointly by the American Insurance Association and the Property Loss Research Bureau.

5. Arbitrators shall be appointed from the membership of the Loss Arbitration Committee, members of the American Insurance Association, Subscribers to the Property Claim Services, the Property Loss Research Bureau, or any combination thereof. Three arbitrators shall constitute an arbitration panel.

6. Each arbitrator shall submit a written opinion. The decision of the majority of the arbitrators shall be final and binding and shall be reported to the companies, party to the arbitration. Upon request, the staff is authorized to furnish the company or companies a resume of the opinion and conclusion reached by the majority.

7. If there is no majority decision, the arbitrators shall be discharged and a new panel of arbitrators shall be appointed to consider the case de novo but on the statements and/or briefs already submitted.

8. No member of either the Loss Arbitration Committee, the Claims Committee, Subscriber to the Property Claim Services, or the Property Loss Research Bureau shall serve on an arbitration panel considering any matter in which his company is directly, or indirectly interested.

9. Companies involved in differences of opinion in first-party property losses are not required to be a member of the American Insurance Association, or Subscribers to the Property Claim Services of the American Insurance Association, or the Property Loss Research Bureau, provided the companies at interest are agreeable to execute the Property Arbitration Agreement form.

10. These Rules and Regulations are not applicable to arbitration of automobile physical damage losses.

11. It is urged that the interested insurers promptly agree among themselves upon a method of payment to the insured pending arbitration.

PROPERTY ARBITRATION AGREEMENT

Whereas, differences of opinion have arisen between the undersigned companies (hereafter referred to as the companies) pertaining to their liabilities for loss incurred at

_____, and

Whereas, the companies are desirous of effecting settlement of these differences of opinion without resorting to litigation,

Now Therefore, the companies agree to submit the said differences of opinion to arbitration in accordance with the Property Arbitration Rules and Regulations provided therefor by the American Insurance Association and the Property Loss Research Bureau.

The companies further agree that the decision of a majority of the arbitrators shall be final and binding.

Dated at _____ this _____ day of _____ 19_____.

_____ Ins. Co.   _____ Ins. Co.

By _____   By _____

_____ Ins. Co.   _____ Ins. Co.

By _____   By _____

_____ Ins. Co.   _____ Ins. Co.

By _____   By _____

_____ Ins. Co.   _____ Ins. Co.

By _____   By _____

AMERICAN INSURANCE ASSOCIATION   PROPERTY LOSS RESEARCH BUREAU
CLAIMS COMMITTEE—PROPERTY   20 North Wacker Drive
  CLAIM SERVICES   Chicago, Illinois 60606
85 John Street
New York, New York 10038

E. NEW YORK STANDARD FIRE POLICY

NO. _____
REPLACES POLICY NO.

**COVERAGE AFFORDED BY THIS POLICY IS
PROVIDED BY THE COMPANY INDICATED BELOW**

☐ STATE FARM FIRE AND CASUALTY COMPANY

☐ STATE FARM GENERAL INSURANCE COMPANY

A STOCK COMPANY/BLOOMINGTON, ILLINOIS

STATE FARM INSURANCE

DECLARATIONS
INSURED'S NAME AND MAILING ADDRESS

Jane Bonkosky
27 Arbor Lane
Evansville, IN 47700

INCEPTION DATE 5/1/77	POLICY PERIOD one year	EXPIRATION OF POLICY PERIOD 5/1/78	

☐ THIS POLICY WILL BE RENEWED AUTOMATICALLY, SUBJECT TO PROVISIONS OF THE FORMS THEN CURRENT, FOR EACH SUCCEEDING POLICY PERIOD THEREAFTER AND IS SUBJECT TO TERMINATION BY THIS COMPANY ONLY AFTER WRITTEN NOTICE TO INSURED AND MORTGAGEE IN COMPLIANCE WITH POLICY PROVISIONS. THE PREMIUM FOR SUCCEEDING POLICY PERIODS WILL BE COMPUTED AT THIS COMPANY'S RATES THEN CURRENT.

DESCRIPTION OF DWELLING
THE DWELLING IS OF FRAME CONSTRUCTION WITH APPROVED ROOF, OCCUPIED BY NOT MORE THAN TWO FAMILIES. EXCEPTIONS IF ANY ARE:

LOCATION OF PREMISES (IF DIFFERENT THAN SHOWN ABOVE)	CONSTRUCTION	TYPE OF ROOF	NUMBER OF FAMILIES
	Fr.	Slate	1

HOMEOWNERS POLICY

☐ FORM 1   ☐ FORM 2   ☐ FORM 3   ☐ FORM 4

INSURANCE IS PROVIDED ONLY WITH RESPECT TO THOSE OF THE FOLLOWING COVERAGES WHICH ARE INDICATED BY A SPECIFIC LIMIT OF LIABILITY APPLICABLE THERETO.

STANDARD FIRE POLICY

INSURANCE IS PROVIDED AGAINST THOSE PERILS AND FOR ONLY THOSE COVERAGES INDICATED BELOW BY A PREMIUM CHARGE AND AGAINST OTHER PERILS AND FOR OTHER COVERAGES ONLY WHEN ENDORSED HEREON OR ADDED HERETO.

PREMIUM	PROPERTY AND COVERAGES	POLICY LIMITS OF LIABILITY	POLICY LIMITS OF LIABILITY	PROPERTY	PERILS AND COVERAGES	RATE	PREMIUM
BASIC POLICY PREMIUM $	A. DWELLING	$40,000	$	DWELLING	FIRE		$
ADDITIONAL PREMIUM $	B. UNSCHEDULED PERSONAL PROPERTY	$20,000	$	CONTENTS	AND		$
PREPAID PREMIUM (Automatic Renewal or 3 Year Term Policies)	C. ADDITIONAL LIVING EXPENSE	$ 8,000	$		LIGHTNING		$
$			$				$
TOTAL POLICY PREMIUM (If Paid In Installments)	E. PERSONAL LIABILITY (EACH OCCURRENCE)	$ Nil		OTHER PERILS AND COVERAGES			
$	F. MEDICAL PAYMENTS (EACH PERSON)	$ Nil	$ XXXX	EXTENDED COVERAGE			$
INSTALLMENT PREMIUM $	(EACH ACCIDENT)	$25000	$				$

SECTION I / SECTION II

LOSS DEDUCTIBLE CLAUSE(S) APPLICABLE IF INDICATED BY AN ☒ :

☐ NO. 1   ☒ NO. 1 & NO. 2

☐ NO. 1, NO. 2 & NO. 3   ☐ NO. 4 .... $_____

☐ OTHER:

	$
PREPAID PREMIUM (Automatic Renewal or 3 Yr. Term Policies)	$
TOTAL POLICY PREMIUM (If Paid In Installments)	$
INSTALLMENT PREMIUM	$

SUBJECT TO THE FOLLOWING FORMS AND ENDORSEMENTS:

MORTGAGEE	COUNTERSIGNATURE
None	DATE: May 21, 1977
	AGENT: Thomas Kester

In Consideration of the Provisions and Stipulations Herein or Added Hereto and of the Premium Above Specified (or specified in endorsement(s) made a part hereof), this Company, for the **term shown above** from **inception date shown above** at noon (Standard Time) to **expiration date shown above** at noon (Standard Time) at location of property involved, to an amount not exceeding the limit of liability above specified, does insure **the Insured named in the Declarations above** and legal representatives, to the extent of the actual cash value of the property at the time of loss, but not exceeding the amount which it would cost to repair or replace the property with material of like kind and quality within a reasonable time after such loss, without allowance for any increased cost of repair or reconstruction by reason of any ordinance or law regulating construction or repair, and without compensation for loss resulting from interruption of business or manufacture, nor in any event for more than the interest of the Insured, against all DIRECT LOSS BY FIRE, LIGHTNING AND OTHER PERILS INSURED AGAINST IN THIS POLICY INCLUDING REMOVAL FROM PREMISES ENDANGERED BY THE PERILS INSURED AGAINST IN THIS POLICY, EXCEPT AS HEREINAFTER PROVIDED, to the property described herein while located or contained as described in this policy, or pro rata for **five days** at each proper place to which any of the property shall necessarily be removed for preservation from the perils insured against in this policy, but not elsewhere.

Assignment of this policy shall not be valid except with the written consent of this Company.

This policy is made and accepted subject to the foregoing provisions and stipulations and those hereinafter stated, which are hereby made a part of this policy, together with such other provisions, stipulations and agreements as may be added hereto, as provided in this policy.

FP-3001.1

Line		
1	Concealment,	This entire policy shall be void if, whether
2	fraud.	before or after a loss, the insured has wil-
3		fully concealed or misrepresented any ma-
4	terial fact or circumstance concerning this insurance or the
5	subject thereof, or the interest of the insured therein, or in case
6	of any fraud or false swearing by the insured relating thereto.
7	Uninsurable	This policy shall not cover accounts, bills,
8	and	currency, deeds, evidences of debt, money or
9	excepted property.	securities; nor, unless specifically named
10		hereon in writing, bullion or manuscripts.
11	Perils not	This Company shall not be liable for loss by
12	included.	fire or other perils insured against in this
13		policy caused, directly or indirectly, by: (a)
14	enemy attack by armed forces, including action taken by mili-
15	tary, naval or air forces in resisting an actual or an immediately
16	impending enemy attack; (b) invasion; (c) insurrection; (d)
17	rebellion; (e) revolution; (f) civil war; (g) usurped power; (h)
18	order of any civil authority except acts of destruction at the time
19	of and for the purpose of preventing the spread of fire, provided
20	that such fire did not originate from any of the perils excluded
21	by this policy; (i) neglect of the insured to use all reasonable
22	means to save and preserve the property at and after a loss, or
23	when the property is endangered by fire in neighboring prem-
24	ises; (j) nor shall this Company be liable for loss by theft.
25	Other insurance.	Other insurance may be prohibited or the
26		amount of insurance may be limited by en-
27	dorsement attached hereto.
28	Conditions suspending or restricting insurance. Unless other-
29	wise provided in writing added hereto this Company shall not
30	be liable for loss occurring
31	(a) while the hazard is increased by any means within the con-
32	trol or knowledge of the insured; or
33	(b) while a described building, whether intended for occupancy
34	by owner or tenant, is vacant or unoccupied beyond a period of
35	sixty consecutive days; or
36	(c) as a result of explosion or riot, unless fire ensue, and in
37	that event for loss by fire only.
38	Other perils	Any other peril to be insured against or sub-
39	or subjects.	ject of insurance to be covered in this policy
40		shall be by endorsement in writing hereon or
41	added hereto.
42	Added provisions.	The extent of the application of insurance
43		under this policy and of the contribution to
44	be made by this Company in case of loss, and any other pro-
45	vision or agreement not inconsistent with the provisions of this
46	policy, may be provided for in writing added hereto, but no pro-
47	vision may be waived except such as by the terms of this policy
48	is subject to change.
49	Waiver	No permission affecting this insurance shall
50	provisions.	exist, or waiver of any provision be valid,
51		unless granted herein or expressed in writing
52	added hereto. No provision, stipulation or forfeiture shall be
53	held to be waived by any requirement or proceeding on the part
54	of this Company relating to appraisal or to any examination
55	provided for herein.
56	Cancellation	This policy shall be cancelled at any time
57	of policy.	at the request of the insured, in which case
58		this Company shall, upon demand and sur-
59	render of this policy, refund the excess of paid premium above
60	the customary short rates for the expired term. This pol-
61	icy may be cancelled at any time by this Company by giving
62	to the insured a five days' written notice of cancellation with
63	or without tender of the excess of paid premium above the pro
64	rata premium for the expired time, which excess, if not ten-
65	dered, shall be refunded on demand. Notice of cancellation shall
66	state that said excess premium (if not tendered) will be re-
67	funded on demand.
68	Mortgage	If loss hereunder is made payable, in whole
69	interests and	or in part, to a designated mortgagee not
70	obligations.	named herein as the insured, such interest in
71		this policy may be cancelled by giving to such
72		mortgagee a ten days' written notice of can-
73	cellation.
74	If the insured fails to render proof of loss such mortgagee, upon
75	notice, shall render proof of loss in the form herein specified
76	within sixty (60) days thereafter and shall be subject to the pro-
77	visions hereof relating to appraisal and time of payment and of
78	bringing suit. If this Company shall claim that no liability ex-
79	isted as to the mortgagor or owner, it shall, to the extent of pay-
80	ment of loss to the mortgagee, be subrogated to all the mort-
81	gagee's rights of recovery, but without impairing mortgagee's
82	right to sue; or it may pay off the mortgage debt and require
83	an assignment thereof and of the mortgage. Other provisions
84	relating to the interests and obligations of such mortgagee may
85	be added hereto by agreement in writing.
86	Pro rata liability.	This Company shall not be liable for a greater
87		proportion of any loss than the amount
88	hereby insured shall bear to the whole insurance covering the
89	property against the peril involved, whether collectible or not.
90	Requirements in	The insured shall give immediate written
91	case loss occurs.	notice to this Company of any loss, protect
92		the property from further damage, forthwith
93	separate the damaged and undamaged personal property, put
94	it in the best possible order, furnish a complete inventory of
95	the destroyed, damaged and undamaged property, showing in
96	detail quantities, costs, actual cash value and amount of loss
97	claimed; and within sixty days after the loss, unless such time
98	is extended in writing by this Company, the insured shall render
99	to this Company a proof of loss, signed and sworn to by the
100	insured, stating the knowledge and belief of the insured as to
101	the following: the time and origin of the loss, the interest of the
102	insured and of all others in the property, the actual cash value of
103	each item thereof and the amount of loss thereto, all encum-
104	brances thereon, all other contracts of insurance, whether valid
105	or not, covering any of said property, any changes in the title,
106	use, occupation, location, possession or exposures of said prop-
107	erty since the issuing of this policy, by whom and for what
108	purpose any building herein described and the several parts
109	thereof were occupied at the time of loss and whether or not it
110	then stood on leased ground, and shall furnish a copy of all the
111	descriptions and schedules in all policies and, if required, verified
112	plans and specifications of any building, fixtures or machinery
113	destroyed or damaged. The insured, as often as may be reason-
114	ably required, shall exhibit to any person designated by this
115	Company all that remains of any property herein described, and
116	submit to examinations under oath by any person named by this
117	Company, and subscribe the same; and, as often as may be
118	reasonably required, shall produce for examination all books of
119	account, bills, invoices and other vouchers, or certified copies
120	thereof if originals be lost, at such reasonable time and place as
121	may be designated by this Company or its representative, and
122	shall permit extracts and copies thereof to be made.
123	Appraisal.	In case the insured and this Company shall
124		fail to agree as to the actual cash value or
125	the amount of loss, then, on the written demand of either, each
126	shall select a competent and disinterested appraiser and notify
127	the other of the appraiser selected within twenty days of such
128	demand. The appraisers shall first select a competent and dis-
129	interested umpire; and failing for fifteen days to agree upon
130	such umpire, then, on request of the insured or this Company,
131	such umpire shall be selected by a judge of a court of record in
132	the state in which the property covered is located. The ap-
133	praisers shall then appraise the loss, stating separately actual
134	cash value and loss to each item; and, failing to agree, shall
135	submit their differences, only, to the umpire. An award in writ-
136	ing, so itemized, of any two when filed with this Company shall
137	determine the amount of actual cash value and loss. Each
138	appraiser shall be paid by the party selecting him and the ex-
139	penses of appraisal and umpire shall be paid by the parties
140	equally.
141	Company's	It shall be optional with this Company to
142	options.	take all, or any part, of the property at the
143		agreed or appraised value, and also to re-
144	pair, rebuild or replace the property destroyed or damaged with
145	other of like kind and quality within a reasonable time, on giv-
146	ing notice of its intention so to do within thirty days after the
147	receipt of the proof of loss herein required.
148	Abandonment.	There can be no abandonment to this Com-
149		pany of any property.
150	When loss	The amount of loss for which this Company
151	payable.	may be liable shall be payable sixty days
152		after proof of loss, as herein provided, is
153	received by this Company and ascertainment of the loss is made
154	either by agreement between the insured and this Company ex-
155	pressed in writing or by the filing with this Company of an
156	award as herein provided.
157	Suit.	No suit or action on this policy for the recov-
158		ery of any claim shall be sustainable in any
159	court of law or equity unless all the requirements of this policy
160	shall have been complied with, and unless commenced within
161	twelve months next after inception of the loss.
162	Subrogation.	This Company may require from the insured
163		an assignment of all right of recovery against
164	any party for loss to the extent that payment therefor is made
165	by this Company.

IN WITNESS WHEREOF, this Company has executed and attested these presents; but this policy shall not be valid unless countersigned by the duly authorized Agent of this Company at the agency hereinbefore mentioned.

Walter F. Vermier   Secretary   *Edward B. Frost*   President

The Board of Directors, in accordance with Article VI(c), of this Company's Articles of Incorporation, may from time to time distribute equitably to the holders of the participating policies issued by said Company such sums out of its earnings as in its judgment is proper.

F. ODOMETER (MILEAGE) STATEMENT; AFFIDAVIT OF VEHICLE THEFT

ODOMETER (MILEAGE) STATEMENT (FORM)

ODOMETER (MILEAGE) STATEMENT

580.9 R(2-73)

(FEDERAL REGULATIONS REQUIRE YOU TO STATE THE ODOMETER MILEAGE UPON TRANSFER OF OWNERSHIP. AN INACCURATE STATEMENT MAY MAKE YOU LIABLE FOR DAMAGES TO YOUR TRANSFEREE, PURSUANT TO § 409 (a) OF THE MOTOR VEHICLE INFORMATION AND COST SAVINGS ACT OF 1972, PUBLIC LAW 92-513.)

MAKE	COLOR(S)	BODY TYPE	YEAR	MODEL
AMC	Blue	2-Dr S	1974	Hornet

VEHICLE IDENTIFICATION NUMBER	LAST PLATE NUMBER	STATE	YR.
R34 003119	WYZ 123	NC	76

I, Marion T. Foley , STATE THAT THE ODOMETER
  TRANSFEROR

MILEAGE INDICATED ON THE VEHICLE DESCRIBED ABOVE IS 48,650
  ODOMETER READING

MILES AND IS AS INDICATED BELOW   (CHECK ONE)

[X] ACTUAL MILEAGE   [ ] TOTAL CUMULATIVE MILES (IF OVER 100,000)

[ ] TRUE MILEAGE UNKNOWN

TRANSFEROR'S (SELLER'S) CURRENT ADDRESS:

21 Reservoir Road

Greensboro, NC 27400

February 1, 1976   x _Marion T. Foley_
DATE OF THIS STATEMENT   TRANSFEROR'S (SELLER'S) SIGNATURE

I, _Jack Yates_ .
  (BUYER'S SIGNATURE)

HEREBY CERTIFY THAT I HAVE RECEIVED A COPY OF THE ABOVE ODOMETER (MILEAGE) STATEMENT.

AFFIDAVIT OF VEHICLE THEFT

All Questions Must Be Answered

Kemper INSURANCE COMPANIES

Claim No. QXR-23456

Name of Insured **Paula Branksma** Home Phone **555-3715** Bus. Phone **555-0370**

Address **37 River Road** **Flint** **MI** **48500**
Street and No. City State Zip Code

Date of theft **February 3, 1977** Time **8 to 10** ☐ AM ☒ PM Was vehicle locked? ☒ Yes ☐ No

Specific location from where vehicle was taken **Corner of Third and Saginaw Streets**

Name of person who left vehicle at this location **Insured**

When was theft discovered? Date **February 3, 1977** **10** Time ☐ AM ☒ PM

Were keys left in car? ☐ Yes ☒ No Who reported theft to police? **Insured**

Location of police station **First Precinct** Investigating Officer **Peter Vanzant** **158**
Name Badge No.

Make of Vehicle **Ford** Year **1970** Model **Galaxy**

Body Type **2-Dr S** Color **Tan** Motor No. **PT 45678-1** Complete Serial No. **CqL-293847**

License Plate No. **LP-123** No. of Cylinders **8** H.P. **350** Mileage **50,000**

EQUIPMENT MOUNTED ON VEHICLE AT TIME OF THEFT — CHECK ALL ITEMS APPLICABLE

		Factory		Dealer Installed					
Radio ☒	Heater ☒	Air Cond ☐		Air Cond ☐		Power Steering ☐		Power Brakes ☐	
Vinyl Roof ☐	Power Windows ☐	Power Seats ☐		Tinted Glass ☐		Stereo ☐		W/W Tires ☐	
Magnesium Wheels ☐	Auto Trans ☒	Standard Trans ☐		Floor Shift ☐		Console ☐			

☐ All others (specify) **CB radio and antenna**

Date car purchased **June 4, 1974** New ☐ Used ☒ Purchase cost $ **1,000**

Dealer **Green & Company** **960 Main Avenue** **Flint, MI**
Name Address City - State

Finance Co. **None**
Name Address City - State

Account No. ____ Bal. due on loan $ ____

Are keys in your possession? ☒ Yes ☐ No Ig. Key No. **1203** Trk. Key No. **1204**

Do you have other auto theft insurance? ☒ Yes ☐ No

If "Yes" **A.B.C. Insurance Co., 15 Everly Pl., Detroit, MI 48200 G.D.-41**
Name of Ins. Co. Address Policy No.

Describe any distinguishing features, such as dents, special paint, etc. **Not a dent in the car.**

The above statement is true to the best of my knowledge and belief.

Policy Holder **Paula Branksma**
Signature

This affidavit completed this **12th** day of **February**, 197**7**

EK 279-1 11-74 10M PRINTED IN U.S.A

G. HOLD HARMLESS AGREEMENT

HOLD HARMLESS AGREEMENT

WE, __Brian and Harriet Finnegan_____

_____in consideration of the payment

of __Four Hundred Seventy-One and 43/100_____DOLLARS ($__471.43____)

by the __A.B.C. Insurance Company_____

do hereby agree to hold the said __A.B.C. Insurance Company_____

_____

harmless from any further claim in respect to Policy No. __12345_____Cert. No._____and it is further understood

and agreed that in consideration of the payment of the above mentioned sum, we hereby release and relinquish all rights to

collect from the said __A.B.C. Insurance Company_____

under the above mentioned policy and certificate, and in the event of any further claim, we agree to defend any suit or go to any

trouble or expense to protect the __A.B.C. Insurance Company_____

_____

from any further claim under the above referred to policy, and to assume full responsibility for any necessary further payment

or compromise of such claims.

    IN WITNESS WHEREOF the parties hereto have hereunto set their hands and seals this __9th_____day of

__May 1977_____ At__San Antonio, Texas_____

WITNESS

_Gabriel Cobb_____

_Brian Finnegan_____

_Harriet Finnegan_____

STATE OF_____ ⎫
                ⎬ SS:
COUNTY OF_____ ⎭

On this_____ day of _____, 19___, before me appeared_____

to me personally known, and who acknowledged the execution of the foregoing instrument as_____free act and deed,

or the consideration set forth therein.

My Commission Expires_____   _____

                                                                  Notary Public.

UNIFORM STANDARD Form No. 3911
UNIFORM PRINTING & SUPPLY BY CHICAGO BROOKLYN LOWELL
PRINTED IN U.S.A.

H. PROPERTY LOSS NOTICE; AUTO—OTHER LIABILITY ACCIDENT NOTICE

ACCORD — **Property Loss Notice**

1 PRODUCER (FOR COMPANY USE)	**CLAIM NO** PL-36274KG
A. B. Dann	**COMPANY**
2 PRODUCER CODE 12345-u	Paramount Insurance Company
	PREVIOUSLY REPORTED ☐ YES ☒ NO

3 POLICY NUMBER	**POLICY DATES**	**MISCELLANEOUS INFORMATION**
PL3647	1/2/77-1/2/78	

4 LAST NAME	**FIRST**	**INITIAL**	**SPECIAL I.D. OR SOCIAL SECURITY NO**
Feldheim	Harry	R.	

5 PROPERTY ADDRESS	ZIP	**RESIDENCE PHONE**	**BUSINESS PHONE**
123 First Street, Columbus, OH 43200		555-9876	None

MAIL ADDRESS, IF DIFFERENT ZIP

6 WHERE CAN INSURED BE CONTACTED?	**WHEN?**
At home	All day

7 DATE AND TIME OF LOSS	**LOSS LOCATION IF DIFFERENT THAN PROPERTY ADDRESS**	**POLICE TO WHOM REPORTED (THEFT)**
4/24/77 6 PM		

8 KIND OF LOSS (fire, wind, explosion, etc.)	**PROBABLE AMT., ENTIRE LOSS**	**PROBABLE AMT., THIS POLICY**	**CAT. #**
Fire	$1,000	$1,000	

9 DESCRIPTION OF LOSS & DAMAGE (Use Reverse, if Necessary.)

Fat caught fire on stove. Burned floor, cabinets, and ceiling tile. Insured's builder has estimate.

10 MORTGAGEE • If none, so indicate

None

FIRE, ALLIED LINES & MULTI-PERIL POLICIES • Complete below only items involved in loss.

ITEM	AMOUNT	BLDG.	CTS.	OTHER	% COINS	Coverage and/or Description of Property Insured.
11 1	$25,000	x	x	x	None	Two-story approved-roof brick veneer dwelling-- three bedrooms and two-car attached garage. Small apartment in basement.
12	$					
13	$					

HOMEOWNERS POLICIES • Complete below Coverages A,B,C,D & additional coverages. EXCEPT LIABILITY.

	COVERAGE A	COVERAGE B	COVERAGE C	COVERAGE D	DESCRIBE ADDITIONAL COVERAGES PROVIDED.	
14 S	DWELLING	APPURTENANT PRIVATE STRUCTURES	UNSCHEDULED PERSONAL PROPERTY	ADDITIONAL LIVING EXPENSES	$	ON
15 C	$	$	$	$	$	ON
16 I	PERCENT OF COINSURANCE APPLICABLE				$	ON

17 SUBJECT TO FORM NOS. • Insert form nos. & edition dates.

DF-2 (Ed. 7-75)

18 DEDUCTIBLE WINDSTORM & HAIL	**DEDUCTIBLE OTHER PERILS**	**DEDUCTIBLE MISCELLANEOUS** • Explain.
$100	$50	$

19 OTHER INSURANCE • List names of companies, policy numbers & amounts.

None

20 REMARKS • If emergency handling required or if subrogation possibilities, explain:

Needs prompt attention as kitchen is useless.

ADJUSTER ASSIGNED

4/24/75	A. B. Dann, Agent	Branch Claim Office	*A. B. Dann*
DATE	REPORTED BY	REPORTED TO	SIGNATURE OF PRODUCER OR INSURED

ACORD 1   AGENCY-COMPANY OPERATIONS RESEARCH AND DEVELOPMENT

528

acord	■ Auto ■ Other Liability Accident Notice	(Inc. Section II Package Policies)

PRODUCER — 1

PRODUCER

J. R. Metz

2 PRODUCER CODE

LTD-4520

3 POLICY NUMBER

Pls-10894-p

(FOR COMPANY USE)	POLICY DATES	MISCELLANEOUS INFORMATION
	1/2/76-1/2/77	

CLAIM NO.

CL-12834-bz

COMPANY

A.B.C. Insurance Company

PREVIOUSLY REPORTED ☐ YES ☐ NO

INSURED

4 LAST NAME Arvilla   **FIRST NAME** Robert   **INITIAL** T.

SPECIAL I.D. OR SOCIAL SECURITY NO. 345-45-9870

5 ADDRESS 2 Hastings Street, Tulsa, OK 74100   **ZIP**

RESIDENCE PHONE 555-2344   **BUSINESS PHONE** 555-2244

6 WHERE CAN INSURED BE CONTACTED? At home

WHEN? After 6 p.m.

ACCIDENT

7 DATE & TIME OF ACCIDENT OR LOSS, ~~A.M.~~ 6/4/76   3 **P.M.**

LOCATION OF ACCIDENT (Including City & State) Corner of 5th Street and Lewis Avenue, Tulsa

POLICE TO WHOM REPORTED Local

8 DESCRIPTION OF ACCIDENT OR LOSS (Use Reverse, if Necessary.)

Insured, driving alone under the influence of pain pills, struck a tree. Damage

confined to front end of vehicle. No personal injuries.

CAT. #

POLICY

9 BODILY INJURY	PROPERTY DAMAGE	SINGLE LIMIT	MEDICAL PAYMENTS	COMPREHENSIVE/DED.	COLLISION/DED.	OTHER DED.
	Yes					

10 LOSS PAYEE (If none, so indicate.) None

OTHER COVERAGES (No-Fault, Towing, U.M., Product Liability, etc.)

INSURED VEHICLE — AUTO ONLY

11 VEH. NO.	YEAR	MAKE	MODEL	VIN (Vehicle Identification No.)	PLATE NO.	OTHER INSURANCE
1	74	Chrysler	2-Dr	9H34P459C	ES123 OK	☐ YES ☒ NO

12 NAME OF OWNER (X) SAME AS POLICYHOLDER   **ADDRESS (X) SAME AS POLICYHOLDER**   **PHONE**

13 NAME OF DRIVER (X) SAME AS OWNER   **AGE** 60   **ADDRESS (X) SAME AS OWNER**   **PHONE**

14 RELATION TO INSURED (Employee, Family, etc.)   **PURPOSE OF USE** Pleasure   **USED WITH PERMISSION** ☐ YES ☐ NO

15 DESCRIBE DAMAGE Front bumper, radiator, and grill   **REPAIR ESTIMATE** $345.00   **WHERE CAN CAR BE SEEN?** Art's Garage, Tulsa, OK   **WHEN?** Anytime

PROPERTY DAMAGE

16 OWNER   **ADDRESS**   **PHONE**

17 OTHER DRIVER (   ) SAME AS OWNER   **ADDRESS**   **PHONE**

18 DESCRIBE PROPERTY (If Auto: Make, Year, Plate No.)   **OTHER CAR OR PROPERTY INSURED** ☐ YES ☐ NO   **COMPANY OR AGENCY NAME & POLICY NO.**

19 DESCRIBE DAMAGE   **REPAIR ESTIMATE** $ **WHERE CAN CAR BE SEEN?**   **AGE** **INS. VEH.** **OTHER VEH.** **PED.**

INJURED

20 NAME   **ADDRESS**   **PHONE**   **EXTENT OF INJURY**

CLAIMANT — NON AUTO

21 OCCUPATION   **EMPLOYED BY**   **RELATION TO INSURED (Employee, Family, Etc.)**

22 PROBABLE DISABILITY **WEEKS**   **RETURNED TO WORK** ☐ YES ☐ NO   **WHY ON PREMISES**   **INS. VEH.** **OTHER VEH.** **OTHER**

WITNESS

23 NAME Rose Sheehan   **ADDRESS** 10 Uptown Street, Tulsa, OK 74100   **PHONE** None

24 Pedestrian

25 REMARKS

Would like prompt attention.

6/5/76	Agent	Claim Office	J. R. Metz
DATE	REPORTED BY	REPORTED TO	SIGNATURE (PRODUCER, INSURED OR, DRIVER)

ACORD 2   AGENCY-COMPANY OPERATIONS RESEARCH AND DEVELOPMENT

I. LETTER DEMANDING EXAMINATION UNDER OATH*

CLEMENS, TREE, AND CHIAPETTA
Counselors at Law
21 Roper Avenue
Albuquerque, New Mexico 87100

January 18, 1976

Re: Insured: Mark and Nancy Shator
Date of Loss: January 2, 1976
Policy 457
Company: A.B.C. Insurance Company

Mr. and Mrs. Mark Shator
416 Ray Street
Albuquerque, NM 87100

Dear Sir or Madam:

You will please take notice that under the terms and conditions of the policy of insurance issued by the undersigned insurance company, you are hereby required to submit to an examination under oath at my office on or about January 24, 1976, concerning your alleged loss by a casualty which occurred on January 2, 1976, and to subscribe the same and to produce at the same time and place aforesaid for examination all books of account, bills, invoices, and other vouchers, or certified copies thereof if the originals be lost, in any way relating to the alleged loss and to permit extracts and copies thereof to be made.

You will please take further notice that in the policy of insurance listed above, it is provided as a condition thereof that the company shall not be held to waive any provision or stipulation of the policy, or any forfeiture thereof, by any requirement or proceeding on its part relating to the examinations called hereby, and the undersigned company hereby expressly notifies you that in calling the said examinations and in requiring the production of books, etc., thereon, the undersigned company will not waive any provision or stipulation of said policy, or any forfeiture thereof, nor does the undersigned company waive any of its rights.

Very truly yours,

Arthur Jones

Arthur Jones
Attorney
For A.B.C. Insurance Company

AJ/am
Registered mail, return receipt requested

*Sample letter recommended by Max J. Gwertzman, attorney, Gwertzman, Nagelberg & Pfeffer, Counselors at Law, New York.

J. MEMORANDUM OF APPRAISAL

GENERAL ADJUSTMENT BUREAU, INC.

MEMORANDUM OF APPRAISAL

This memorandum by and between ___Sarah D. Berkowitz___

of the first part and the ___A.B.C. Insurance___

_____ Company of the second part:

WITNESSETH: that whereas the party of the first part claims to have sustained a loss by ___Fire___

occurring on the ___15th___ day of ___March___ 19_77_ to and upon the following described property to wit: one-family, frame, composition-roof dwelling situated at 347 Lavern Street, Richmond, California 94800 and

WHEREAS policy # ___6789___ issued by the party of the second part to the party of the first part provides as follows:

"2. Appraisal

If the insured and the company fail to agree as to the amount of loss, each shall, on the written demand of either, made within sixty days after receipt of proof of loss by the company, select a competent and disinterested appraiser, and the appraisal shall be made at a reasonable time and place. The appraisers shall first select a competent and disinterested umpire, and failing for fifteen days to agree upon such umpire, then, on the request of the insured or the company, such umpire shall be selected by a judge of a court of record in the county and state in which such appraisal is pending. The appraisers shall then appraise the loss, stating separately the actual cash value at the time of loss and the amount of loss, and failing to agree shall submit their differences to the umpire. An award in writing of any two shall determine the amount of loss. The insured and the company shall each pay his or its chosen appraiser and shall bear equally the other expenses of the appraisal and umpire."

and,

WHEREAS, a disagreement has arisen between the parties hereto as to the amount of such loss.

THEREFORE THIS MEMORANDUM WITNESSETH: that in conformity to the terms and conditions of the policy of the party of the second part, ___Ernest R. Orillas___

_____ and ___James MacDonald___

have been selected and are hereby appointed appraisers, to appraise, in accordance with the terms and conditions of said policy, the actual cash value of said property and the amount of loss directly caused by said ___Fire___ to and upon the same.

It is further mutually agreed that the ___A.B.C. Insurance___

_____ Company shall not be held to have waived any of its rights by any act relating to appraisal.

WITNESS our hands (in duplicate) at ___Richmond, California___ this ___20th___ day of ___March___ 19_77_

A.B.C. Insurance Company

P. Corona, Claim Representative

Sarah D. Berkowitz
Insured

328

DECLARATION OF APPRAISERS

STATE OF _____ }
COUNTY OF _____ } ss.

    We, the undersigned, do solemnly swear that we will act with strict impartiality in making an appraisement of the actual cash value and the amount of loss upon the property hereinbefore mentioned, in accordance with the foregoing appointment, and that we will make a true, just and conscientious award of the same, according to the best of our knowledge, skill and judgment. We are not related to the insured, either as creditors or otherwise, and are not interested in said property or the insurance thereon.

_____ } APPRAISERS
_____ }

Subscribed and sworn to before me this_____day of _____ 19____

_____
NOTARY PUBLIC

SELECTION OF UMPIRE

    We, the undersigned, hereby select and appoint _____
to act as umpire to settle matters of difference that shall exist between us, if any, by reason of and in compliance with the foregoing agreement and appointment.

    Witness our hands this _____ day of _____ 19____

_____

_____

QUALIFICATION OF UMPIRE

STATE OF _____ }
COUNTY OF_____ } ss.

    I, the undersigned, hereby accept the appointment of umpire, as provided in the foregoing agreement, and solemnly swear that I will act with strict impartiality in all matters of difference that shall be submitted to me in connection with this appointment, and I will make a true, just and conscientious award according to the best of my knowledge, skill and judgment. I am not related to any of the parties to this memorandum, nor interested as a creditor or otherwise in said property or the insurance thereon.

Subscribed and sworn to before me this _____day of _____ 19____

_____
NOTARY PUBLIC

AWARD

    We, the undersigned, pursuant to the within appointment, DO HEREBY CERTIFY that we have truly and conscientiously performed the duties assigned us, agreeably to the foregoing stipulations, and have appraised and determined and do hereby award as the actual cash value of said property on the _____ day of

_____ 19____and the amount of loss thereto by the _____
on that day, the following sums, to wit:

    ACTUAL CASH VALUE $_____

    AMOUNT OF LOSS $_____

    Witness our hands this_____day of _____ 19____

_____ } APPRAISERS
_____ }

_____ UMPIRE

K. LETTER DEMANDING APPRAISAL

DART ADJUSTING COMPANY
1 Canal Street
Tampa, Florida 33600

January 10, 1977

Re: Policy 2345
     Fire Loss: January 1, 1977

Mr. J. B. Intilli
10 Arch Street
Tampa, FL 33600

Dear Sir:

This is to inform you that, on behalf of A.B.C. Insurance Company
covering your property under the captioned policy and situated at 10
Arch Street, we do not agree with you on the actual cash value of the
property involved or on the amount of loss and damage you have claimed
as a result of the fire of January 1, 1977.

We direct your attention to the following provision for Appraisal in
your policy, lines 123 to 140 inclusive:

```
123   APPRAISAL.  In case the insured and this company shall
124   fail to agree as to the actual cash value of
125   the amount of loss, then, on the written demand of either, each
126   shall select a competent and disinterested appraiser and notify
127   the other of the appraiser selected within twenty days of such
128   demand.  The appraisers shall first select a competent and dis-
129   interested umpire; and failing for fifteen days to agree upon
130   such umpire, then, on request of the insured or this Company
131   such umpire shall be selected by a judge of a court of record in
132   the state in which the property covered is located.  The ap-
133   praisers shall then appraise the loss, stating separately actual
134   cash value and loss to each item; and, failing to agree, shall
135   submit their differences, only, to the umpire.  An award in writ-
136   ing, so itemized, of any two when filed with this Company shall
```

Mr. J. B. Intilli
Page 2
January 10, 1977

137   determine the amount of actual cash value and loss. Each
138   appraiser shall be paid by the party selecting him and the ex-
139   penses of appraisal and umpire shall be paid by the parties
140   equally.

By this letter, and in accord with the foregoing, we hereby demand an
appraisal and name Gerhard Goetzman, 7 Borden Avenue, Tampa, as appraiser
for A.B.C. Insurance Company. Please notify us of the name of your appraisers within 20 days from the date of this letter in order that the
appraisers may select an umpire and proceed to appraise the actual cash
value and loss to each item.

This demand shall not be construed as a waiver or an estoppel to assert
all the rights of the Company relating to or arising out of said fire
and loss.

Yours truly,

A.B.C. INSURANCE COMPANY
By Dart Adjusting Company

Jerry Todman

Jerry Todman
Adjuster

JT/da
Registered mail, return receipt requested

L. NON-WAIVER AGREEMENT

NON-WAIVER AGREEMENT

IT IS AGREED that any action taken by the insurance company, or companies, signing this agreement in ascertaining the amount of the actual cash value; and the amount of the loss and damage which occurred

_____ June 25 _____ 19 76 __ to ___ the two-story brick dwelling _____
                                                    Property

located at ___ 124 Paddock Street _____ Jacksonville _____ Illinois ____
                  Street Address   City   State

and in investigating the cause thereof, shall not waive or invalidate any of the conditions of the policies of insurance, and shall not waive or invalidate any rights whatever of any party to this agreement.

NOTICE, is hereby given and accepted, and it is hereby mutually understood and agreed, that no representative of any insurance company signing this agreement has power or authority to waive any of the conditions of their respective policies, unless such waiver be specifically made in writing.

THE SOLE OBJECT AND INTENT of this agreement is to provide for the determination of the amount of the actual cash value and the amount of the loss and damage, and an investigation of the cause thereof, without regard to the liability of said insurance companies, and to preserve all the rights of the insurance company, or companies, and the insured.

WITNESS our hands in duplicate, this _____ 4th _____ day of ___ August ___ 19 76 ___

INSURED	INSURANCE COMPANY, OR COMPANIES
George Adams, Sr.	A.B.C. Insurance Company
George Adams, Sr.	_Pat Burke_
	Claim Representative

WITNESSES

Ralph Ader

Ralph Ader

312

AGREEMENT AS TO ACTUAL CASH VALUE AND AMOUNT OF LOSS

(SUBJECT TO NON-WAIVER AGREEMENT, IF ANY, AND TO TERMS AND CONDITIONS OF APPLICABLE INSURANCE POLICIES AND AGREEMENTS)

IN ACCORDANCE WITH THE TERMS OF THIS AGREEMENT, it is agreed and determined that the actual cash value of the property, herein described, immediately preceding_____ June 25 _____ 19 76 and the loss and damage which occurred on that date is as follows:

ITEM	PROPERTY	ACTUAL CASH VALUE	LOSS AND DAMAGE
A	Dwelling	$50,000	$ 4,257.50
C	Unscheduled Personal Property	$28,500	$12,500.00

IT IS FURTHER AGREED that the above stipulation as to the actual cash value and the loss and damage is not a promise to pay any sum whatsoever, and that it creates no liability on the part of any insurance company signing this agreement, nor does it waive nor invalidate any rights whatever of the insurance company, or companies, or the insured.

WITNESS our hands in duplicate, this _____ 20th _____ day of _____ October _____ 19 76

INSURED	INSURANCE COMPANY, OR COMPANIES
George Adams, Sr.	A.B.C. Insurance Company
George Adams, Sr.	*Pat Burke*
	Claim Representative

WITNESSES

Arthur Jones

Arthur Jones

312 BACK

M. SUBROGATION AND LOAN RECEIPTS; TRUST AGREEMENT

SUBROGATION RECEIPT AND ASSIGNMENT

RECEIVED of the A.B.C. Insurance Company of New York, the sum of One Thousand Dollars ($1,000) being in full of all claims and demands for loss and damage by fire which occurred on the 2d day of June to property insured under their Policy numbered PU-2 issued at the X.Y.Z. Agency of said Company.

Now therefore, in consideration of said payment, we hereby assign, set over, transfer, subrogate and substitute the said A.B.C. Insurance Company of New York, its successors and assigns, to any and all rights, claims, interests or action which we have or ought to have against the Ace Welders, Inc., who may be liable or hereafter adjudged liable for the burning or destruction of said property, or against any person, persons or corporation, to the extent of the said sum of $1,000 and we hereby assign, transfer and set over the same to the said A.B.C. Insurance Company of New York or its successors or assigns as aforesaid: in accordance with the terms of said Policy of Insurance.

We hereby expressly authorize and empower the said A.B.C. Insurance Company to sue, compromise or settle in our name or otherwise to the extent of the money paid as aforesaid. It being understood that any action taken by said A.B.C. Insurance Company shall be without charge or cost to us or to our legal representative.

Dated this 30th day of June, 1976, at New York City

WITNESS

A. Foster, Claim Representative   X.Y.Z. Company, Inc.

John Broodman

LOAN RECEIPT

Loss Number LL-25   Dated August 2 1976
$1,000

    RECEIVED FROM The A.B.C. INSURANCE COMPANY the sum of One thousand Dollars
as a loan, without interest, under Policy No. T-234, repayable only in the
event and to the extent that any net recovery is made by me from any person or
persons, corporation or corporations, or other parties, on account of loss by
any casualty for which this Company may be liable, occasioned to my property
on or about July 3d day of 1976.
    As security for such repayment, I hereby pledge to said A.B.C. Insurance
Company whatever recovery I may make, and deliver to it herewith all documents
necessary to show our interest in said property and we hereby agree to promptly
present claim and, if necessary, to commence, enter into and prosecute suit
against such person or persons, corporation or corporations, through whose
negligence the aforesaid loss was caused, or who may otherwise be responsible
therefor, with all due diligence, in our own name, but at the expense of/and
under the exclusive direction and control of the said A.B.C. Insurance Company.

                       In presence of

B. Garson, Claim Representative   Jony Christides, Insured

P. Garson   *Jony Christides*

TRUST AGREEMENT

TO THE A.B.C. INSURANCE COMPANY:

    In connection with the loss and damage sustained by us under date of
July 4, 1976 and for which claim has been made under your Policy Number 3D, by
us, we hereby agree in accordance with our understanding, that we will make
claim and if necessary bring action in our name against all persons or parties
who may be responsible for the loss and damage sustained under date of July 4,
1976.
    Accordingly, we agree to bring action through any attorney whom you may
appoint in our name against the party or parties responsible for the loss sustained by us.
    We further agree that any monies that may be recovered by us in this
prospective claim or as a result of the action that may be brought by us, will
be held in trust for the benefit of the A.B.C. INSURANCE COMPANY and will be
repaid to the A.B.C. INSURANCE COMPANY.
    It is also agreed that all fees, expenses and costs in connection with
any actions that may be brought, will be borne by the A.B.C. INSURANCE COMPANY.

                       B.B. Manufacturers

                       B. Black
                       President

N. LETTERS REJECTING PROOF OF LOSS*

REJECTION OF VALUE AND LOSS STATED IN PROOF OF LOSS TO INDICATE NO ADJUSTMENT OF LOSS

BLANK ADJUSTMENT COMPANY
7 Berger Road
Duluth, Minnesota 55800

February 15, 1977

Re: Assured: Karl Olesen
Date of Loss: January 20, 1977
Policy 92804
Mutual Fire Insurance Company

Mr. Karl Olesen
100 Broadway
Duluth, MN 55800

Dear Sir:

We are this day in receipt of a Proof of Loss which was filed with us on the 15th day of February, 1977.

We are accepting this proof in compliance with the policy conditions concerning the filing of a Proof of Loss.

However, we expressly reject any and all statements contained in the said Proof of Loss with reference to the amount of sound value and the amount of loss, and we expressly reserve all of our rights and defenses in connection with the ascertainment as to the value and loss, if any, and we do not in any way in acknowledging the receipt of this Proof of Loss waive any of the rights and defenses which the Mutual Fire Insurance Company possesses under its Policy 92804.

Very truly yours,

MUTUAL FIRE INSURANCE COMPANY
By Blank Adjustment Company

(Mrs.) Ann P. Hollis

Ann P. Hollis
Adjuster

* Sample letters recommended by Max J. Gwertzman, attorney, and presented at the Mutual Loss Managers' Conference, Hotel Roosevelt, New York, March 8–11, 1965.

REJECTION OF PROOF OF LOSS BECAUSE OF DEFECTS IN PROOF

BLANK ADJUSTMENT COMPANY
7 Berger Road
Duluth, Minnesota 55800

February 15, 1977

Re: Assured: Karl Olesen
     Date of Loss: January 20, 1977

Mr. Karl Olesen
100 Broadway
Duluth, MN 55800

Dear Sir:

We have received from you a paper which purports to be a Proof of Loss
under Policy Number 92804 in connection with an alleged loss of
January 20, 1977, at 1100 North Street, Duluth, Minnesota.

We are hereby returning this document to you and expressly rejecting it
as a proper Proof of Loss since it does not comply with the provisions
of your policy of insurance with the Mutual Fire Insurance Company.

Your attention is directed to the following defects in the purported
Proof of Loss:

1. The statement was not filed within the time fixed for filing Proof
   of Loss under the terms of the policy.
2. The statement was not sworn to by you.
3. The statement does not set out:
   a. The time of the fire.
   b. The origin of the fire.
   c. The actual cash value of each item of property on which loss
      has been claimed.

Any other Proof of Loss that may be filed by you will be considered an
entirely new document and will be accepted or rejected solely in connection with the matters and items contained therein.

The Mutual Fire Insurance Company, in rejecting this purported Proof of
Loss, expressly reserves all of its rights and defenses under the policy
of insurance and does not in any way waive compliance with all the terms
and conditions of the policy of insurance.

Very truly yours,

MUTUAL FIRE INSURANCE COMPANY
By Blank Adjustment Company

(Ms.) Ann P. Hollis

Ann P. Hollis
Adjuster

O. AGREEMENTS FOR THE REMOVAL OF STOCK

AGREEMENT FOR THE REMOVAL OF STOCK
FOR BETTER PROTECTION AND/OR DISPOSITION

THIS MEMORANDUM WITNESSETH: That whereas, the stock described as insured by policies

issued to __Taylor Wholesale Company__

has been damaged by fire, water or other casualty occurring on or about the __6th__ day of __April__ ,

19 __77__ .

WHEREAS, It is to the benefit of all who may have an interest in the stock contained in building

located at __29 Grace Street, Amarillo, TX 79100__

_____that same be handled with as little delay as
possible without waiting to determine the respective ownership or interests or liabilities under policies
purporting to insure same.

IT IS HEREBY MUTUALLY UNDERSTOOD AND AGREED that all the remains of said
stock shall be turned over to the M. F. Bank & Company, Inc., to be by them put in best possible
order and sold in the interest of whom it may concern. The proceeds of such sale, less the Salvage
Company's expenses (which shall include necessary traveling expense and maintenance of the officers
or agents of the Company) of handling the same, plus __0__ % commission on gross sales shall be held
by them as Trustee until loss is adjusted and then turned over by them to the parties to whom said proceeds
belong.

IN WITNESS WHEREOF, we have hereunto attached our hands and seals on __three__ copies and

one original at: __Insured's office in Amarillo__ this day

of __April 8__ , 19 __77__ .

WITNESS BY,

_____   _____
Peter Rocha   _Martin Barkoff_
Pamela Gleason   A.B.C. Insurance Company
                                  For the Insurance Company

_____   _Art Guilet_

_____   Taylor Wholesale Company
                                  For the Insured

                                  R. P. Jones, President
                                  M. F. Bank & Company, Inc.

AGREEMENT FOR THE REMOVAL OF STOCK
FOR BETTER PROTECTION

No. 1 — PROTECTION

THIS MEMORANDUM WITNESSETH: That whereas, the stock described as insured by

policies issued to ___Kiddie Toy Manufacturing Company_____

has been damaged by fire, water or other casualty occurring on or about the___10th___day

of_____December_____, 19_76_

WHEREAS, it is to the benefit of all who may have an interest in___damaged_____

stock contained in building located at___21 Bloom Street, Gadsden, AL 35900_____

_____

that same be handled with as little delay as possible without waiting to determine the respective
ownership or interests or liabilities under policies purporting to insure this property;

IT IS HEREBY MUTUALLY UNDERSTOOD AND AGREED: that all the remains of said
stock as specified shall be turned over to M. F. Bank & Company, Inc., to be by them put in
best possible order; and all costs and expenses of such operations shall be charged against the
property, but there can be no abandonment to the insurers of the property described.

IN WITNESS WHEREOF, we have hereunto attached our hands and seals on___two___

copies and one original at___Insured's office in Gadsden_____, this___12th___day

of_____December_____, 19_76_.

WITNESS BY:

_____   _____

_____   _____

Marcie Tobin   _Alexandra Thomasin_

Sam Englehardt   A.B.C. Insurance Company
                                   For the Insurance Company

                                   V. K. Horne, Treasurer
                                   For the Insured

                                   B. Gunn
                                   M. F. Bank & Company, Inc.

P. NFIA: NOTICE OF LOSS;
WORKSHEET—CONTENTS—PERSONAL PROPERTY;
WORKSHEET—BUILDING; ADJUSTER'S REPORT

NOTICE OF LOSS
NATIONAL FLOOD INSURERS ASSOCIATION
(SEE REVERSE SIDE FOR INSTRUCTIONS)

**INSURANCE COMPANIES MEMBERS OF
NATIONAL FLOOD INSURERS ASSOCIATION**

1. NAME OF SERVICING COMPANY A.B.C. Insurance Company	7. POLICY NUMBER FL 001
	8. POLICY PERIOD (FROM, TO) 1/1/77 to 1/1/78

2. AGENCY NAME AND MAILING ADDRESS (RUBBER STAMP OR TYPE) X.Y.Z. Agency, Inc. 12 West Street Biloxi, MS 39500	9. DATE OF LOSS 4/20/77
	10. KIND OF LOSS [X] Flood [ ] Mudslide

11. PROBABLE AMOUNT OF LOSS—ALL PERILS **$6,000**   12. ESTIMATE OF LOSS—THIS POLICY **$3,000**

13. OTHER INSURANCE (SEE ITEM 18)   [X] Yes   [ ] No   [X] Buildings   [X] Contents

3. INSURED Louis Beaumont	14. REMARKS: BRIEF DESCRIPTION OF DAMAGE (if emergency handling required, explain why.)
4. PROPERTY ADDRESS 150 Hobart Drive Biloxi, Mississippi 39500 PHONE NO. 555-3456	High water from the Gulf and hurricane winds. Concrete block foundation on slab. Two feet of water on first floor. Oak on sleepers ruined, some doors peeling veneer. Finishings wet. Wind damaged roof, and attic contents wet from rain.
5. MAIL ADDRESS (IF DIFFERENT) PHONE NO.	
6. LOCATION OF PROPERTY IF REMOVED FOR PROTECTION Still on premises	

15. DESCRIPTION OF PROPERTY COVERED

ITEM NO.	AMOUNT INSURANCE	DESCRIPTION	
1 BLDG.	$40,000	On the __1__ Family __1__ Story Building of __Brick__ Veneer _____ Construction. Bsmt. Yes [ ] No [X]	16. MORTGAGEE (BUILDING) None
2 CONTS.	$20,000	On Contents in the Building described above [X] or in the ____ Family ____ Story Building of _____ _____ Construction. Bsmt. Yes [ ] No [ ]	17. LOSS PAYEE (CONTENTS) None

18. LIST ANY **OTHER** INSURANCE APPLICABLE TO THE PROPERTY DESCRIBED IN ITEM 15 ABOVE; INCLUDING COVERAGE ON SPECIFICALLY DESCRIBED ARTICLES, I.E., FURS, JEWELRY, ETC.

Limited Insurance Company   Homeowners Policy LC-143-T
Atlanta, Georgia   Covers: $40,000 Dw, $20,000 Cts

19. COPIES SENT TO ▶	NFIA	Servicing Company	X.Y.Z. Agency	CATASTROPHE SERIAL NO. Hur-21	CAT. ZONE NO. X	DATED 4/21/77

20. NAME OF ADJUSTER TO WHOM THIS NOTICE HAS BEEN FORWARDED Wright Adjusters, Inc.	21. NAME OF ADJUSTER HANDLING E/C OR OTHER INSURANCE LOSS Fire and Allied Adjusters

THIS SPACE FOR USE ONLY BY SERVICING OFFICE OR ASSOCIATION

NFIA-11 (Ed. 5-71)

INSTRUCTIONS FOR AGENTS OR BROKERS:

1. Complete this Notice of Loss in its entirety. **DO NOT OMIT ANY INFORMATION.**
2. Forward the completed notice to the Servicing Office shown on the Declarations Sheet of the Policy.
3. All losses under Flood Policies will be assigned to adjusters by the Servicing Office.
4. Agents and Brokers are not permitted to adjust losses under Flood Policies.
5. Additional Flood Notices of Loss may be obtained from the Servicing Office.

INSTRUCTIONS FOR ADJUSTERS:

1. Obtain necessary forms for the adjustment of Flood Losses from the Servicing Office assigning the loss.
2. Preliminary reports and estimates must be submitted to Servicing Office not later than ten working days from date of assignment.
3. Preliminary reports must indicate the height of the water, to the nearest foot, above or below the first floor level of the risk involved.

NATIONAL FLOOD INSURERS ASSOCIATION
WORKSHEET - CONTENTS - PERSONAL PROPERTY

Insured — Louis Beaumont   **Policy #:**   FL-001

150 Hobart Drive   **Co. Claim #:**   TF-4000

Location — Biloxi, MS 39500   **Date:**   April 20, 1977

1 ITEM	2 DESCRIPTION	3 QUANTITY	4 AGE	5 REPLACEMENT COST	6 LOSS OR DAMAGE	7 DEPRECIATION	8 A.C.V. FLOOD LOSS	9 A.C.V. WIND LOSS
1	3-pc living-room suite		5	$1,200	$1,200	$400	$800	--
2	Rugs, 9' x 12'	3	10	600	90	--	90	--
3	Food in pantry			100	100	--	--	$100
4	Master bedroom							
	Rugs, 6' x 8'	2	4	200	20	--	--	20
	Drapes--cleaning				50	--	--	50
	Bedding--cleaning				30	--	--	30
	Contents--dresser				100	--	--	100
5	Contents of attic ruined by							
	water (estimated)				150	--	--	150
	Total				$1,740	$400	$890	$450
	Deductibles						200	100
							$690	$350

NFIA-12 (Ed. 9-74)

NATIONAL FLOOD INSURERS ASSOCIATION

WORKSHEET - BUILDING

<u>5/10/77</u>
Date of Report

Insured and Location	Louis Beaumont 150 Hobart Drive Biloxi, MS 39500	Policy No. FL-001	Co. Claim Number TF-4000

Adjusting Firm and Location	Wright Adjusters, Inc. 10 Delaporte Street New Orleans, LA 70100	File No. 6FL-125	Date of Loss 4/20/77

Measure Dimensions and Draw Diagram of Ground Floor Area. Attach Snapshot.

Previous Flood Loss Record		
Prev. Loss	Date of Loss	Amount Paid
Yes ☐ No ☒		

Type of Bldg.
One story, brick veneer

Building Age
10 yr

Building Dimensions	Total Sq. Ft.	No. Rms.
30' x 50'	1,500 s.f.	6

No. Baths	Interior Wall Construction	Exterior Wall Construction
2	Drywall on furring	Brick veneer

Estimated Repl. Cost $45,000

Less Depreciation   5,000

Actual Cash Value $40,000

Quantity	Detailed Description	Full Cost Repair	Wind Loss	NFIA Loss	Grey Area		
					Total Grey	Total E.C.	Total NFIA
2,000 b.f.	1" x 3" red oak flooring	$1,000	--	$1,000	--	--	--
700 yd	Interior decorating	1,000	$800	200			
6	H.C. veneer doors	200	--	200			
22 s.f.	235 lb asphalt shingles	880	880	--			
	Demolition and debris	500	320	180			
	Total	$3,580	$2,000	$1,580			
	Deductibles		100	200			
			$1,900	$1,380			

NFIA-13 (Ed. 8-74)

NATIONAL FLOOD INSURERS ASSOCIATION

ADJUSTER'S REPORT

(THIS FORM MAY BE USED AS A FINAL REPORT EXCEPT IN THOSE CASES WHERE, IN THE OPINION OF THE ADJUSTER, A NARRATIVE REPORT IS NEEDED.)

INSURED ____Louis Beaumont____ POL. NO. __FL-001__ DATE OF LOSS __4/20/76__

PROPERTY ADDRESS __150 Hobart Drive, Biloxi, Jackson, MS 39500__ CAT. NO. __Hur-21__
(STREET OR LEGAL)   (CITY)   (COUNTY)   (STATE)

ENCLOSURES: ☒ ADJUSTER'S DETAILED ESTIMATE   ☒ INSURED'S ESTIMATE
☒ STATEMENT OF LOSS   ☒ PROOF OF LOSS   ☒ NEWS RELEASES   ☒ PHOTOGRAPHS __6__ (IF ENCLOSED)
(NUMBER)
☐ OTHER (Describe) __Bills and statements from dealers__

INSURANCE:
SERVICING
NFIA POLICY: SOURCE OF ASSIGNMENT   ☒ COMPANY   ☐ AGENT

NFIA COVERAGE FORM NO. __NFIA-1__ ED. DATE __Ed. 7-74__ VERIFIED FROM ☒ INS. POLICY
☒ AGENT'S DAILY   ☐ LOSS NOTICE
INSURANCE ON BUILDING $__40,000__ ON CONTENTS $__20,000__
DEDUCTIBLES ON BUILDING $ __200__ ON CONTENTS $ __200__

OTHER INSURANCE APPLICABLE:

COMPANY	POLICY NUMBER	BUILDING	CONTENTS
Limited Insurance Company, Atlanta, Georgia	LC-143-T	$40,000	$20,000
		$	$

NOTE: IF OTHER INSURANCE INVOLVED ATTACH A SCHEDULE OF INSURANCE AND APPORTIONMENT OF CLAIM.

MORTGAGEE (REAL PROPERTY) __None__
(NAME)   (ADDRESS)

LOSS PAYABLE (CONTENTS) __None__
(NAME)   (ADDRESS)

INSURED: AGE __35__ MARITAL STATUS __Married__   OCCUPATION __Plumber__
EMPLOYER: __Self__   ADDRESS __Has office in home__
PREVIOUS FLOOD LOSSES __None__
(DATE AND AMOUNT)

RISK:
BASEMENT: ☐ YES   ☒ NO   FOUNDATION: ☒ CONCRETE SLAB   ☐ OTHER ____
NEW CONSTRUCTION OR ADDITION SINCE AREA APPROVED FOR FLOOD __No__
(DATE AND DESCRIPTION)

DISTANCE FROM NEAREST BODY OF WATER __2 blocks__ NAME OF BODY OF WATER __Gulf of Mexico__
OCCUPANCY: ☒ OWNER - SINGLE   ☐ TENANT - SINGLE   ☐ MULTIPLE OCCUPANCY
CONTENTS: AGE __Various__ CONDITION __Good__ NO. ROOMS __6__
SALVAGE: ☐ YES   ☒ NO   VALUE ____ DISPOSITION ____

ORIGIN: DATE AND HOUR FLOODING BEGAN __8 a.m. 4/20__ DATE AND HOUR WATER ENTERED DWG. __Same__
DATE AND HOUR WATER RECEDED FROM FIRST FLOOR __11 p.m. 4/20/77__ FROM BASEMENT ____
MAXIMUM DEPTH OF FLOOD WATERS ABOVE OR BELOW FIRST FLOOR FLOORING __2 feet__
(TO NEAREST FOOT)

DATE AND HOUR OF ORIGIN OF OTHER DAMAGE __3 a.m. 4/20/77__
Hurricane winds, 90 mph at airport 2 miles east, preceded flooding.
(DESCRIBE ORIGIN OF OTHER DAMAGE I.E. "WINDS OF HURRICANE FORCE, FIRE, ETC.")

Q. BUSINESS INTERRUPTION WORKSHEET

COMBINATION BUSINESS INTERRUPTION WORK SHEET

N.C. FIRE INSURANCE RATING BUREAU

(For Use with Gross Earnings Form Nos. 3 and 4

for Mercantile, Non-Manufacturing or Manufacturing Risks)

Form No. 91-W-3

North Carolina

(3-69)

Name of Insured .. Reddy Manufacturing Company, Inc. ....

Location of Risk ... 20 Fess Avenue, Charlotte, NC 28200 ....

Date January 15, 1977

ALL ENTRIES TO BE ON AN ANNUAL BASIS	COLUMN 1 Actual Values for Year Ended 12/31, 1976	COLUMN 2 *Estimated Values for Year Ending 12/31/77
A. Total annual net sales value of production from Manufacturing Operations; and total annual net sales from Merchandising or Non-Manufacturing Operations, (Gross sales less discounts, returns, bad accounts and prepaid freight, if included in sales)	$650,000	$800,000
B. Add other earnings (if any) derived from operation of the business:		
1. Cash Discounts Received (not reflected in am'ts deducted under D)		
2. Commission or Rents from Leased Departments		
3.		
C. Total ("A" plus "B")	$650,000	$800,000
D. Deduct only cost of:		
1. Raw stock from which such production is derived	$139,000	$160,000
2. Supplies consisting of materials consumed directly in the conversion of such raw stock into finished stock or in supplying the service(s) sold by the Insured	11,000	20,000
3. Merchandise sold, including packaging materials therefor		
4. Service(s) purchased from outsiders (not employees of the insured) for resale which do not continue under contract		
5. Total Deductions	$150,000	$180,000
E. GROSS EARNINGS ("C" Minus "D")	$500,000	$620,000
F. Take 50, 60, 70 or 80% of "E", Column 2, as amount of insurance required, depending upon percentage Coinsurance Clause to be used (...... %)		$310,000
IF INSURANCE IS TO BE WRITTEN WITH ORDINARY PAYROLL EXCLUSION ENDORSEMENT, Deduct From "E" Above:		
G. All Ordinary Payroll Expense	$	$
H. Business Interruption Basis for Coinsurance ("E" minus "G")	$	$
I. Amount of Insurance—Take 80, 90 or 100% of H, Column 2, depending upon percentage Coinsurance Clause to be used (... %)		$
IF INSURANCE IS TO BE WRITTEN WITH ORDINARY PAYROLL-LIMITED COVERAGE ENDORSEMENT, Complete the Following:		
J. Select the largest Ordinary Payroll Expense for 90† consecutive calendar days	$	$
K. Business Interruption Basis for Coinsurance ("H" plus "J")	$	$
L. Amount of Insurance—Take 80, 90 or 100% of K, Column 2, depending upon percentage Coinsurance Clause to be used (... %)		$

*INSTRUCTIONS: THE COINSURANCE CLAUSE ALWAYS APPLIES TO THE **FUTURE** (never the PAST). Column 2 is merely a projection of known past values (shown in Column 1) to the next 12 months from the date the computation is prepared.

Do not inadvertently enter Cost of Sales as Cost of Raw Stock under "D" above. This item should not include any labor. "Freight in" may be considered as a part of the cost of raw stock.

Business Interruption values should be checked at regular intervals and the agent or broker notified at once of any actual or impending change that would affect values during the next 12 months from the date such change becomes known.

†**NOTE:** 120, 150 or 180 days may be selected as provided in the rules.

(over)

EXPLANATORY NOTES:

1. To obtain annual net sales value from Manufacturing Operations, the following procedure is recommended:

Net sales of Insured's product during the year (i.e. gross sales less discounts granted, returns, allowances, bad debts, and prepaid freight, if included in sales figures) .... $...............

DEDUCT — Inventory of FINISHED STOCK at beginning of year priced at sales value .... $...............

                                  Balance....... $...............

ADD — Inventory of FINISHED STOCK on hand at end of year priced at sales value .... $...............

TOTAL — Annual Net Sales Value of production during the year .. $...............

2. To obtain cost of raw stock, merchandise sold, or supplies consisting of materials consumed, the following procedure is recommended:

Inventory (incl. stock in process) at beginning of year .... $...............

ADD — Cost of raw stock, merchandise and such supplies purchased during the year (including cartage and transportation charges on said incoming purchases) .... $...............

                           TOTAL............ $...............

DEDUCT — Inventory (incl. stock in process) at end of year .... $...............

Amount for deductions 1, 2, and 3 of Item D .... $...............

Note: Adjust for any inventory increase or decrease caused by price fluctuations.

Note: Under deduction 2 of "D" the words "supplies consisting of materials" are intended to refer only to tangible or physical supplies (i.e. materials), and the deduction of intangible supplies (such as heat and power) is not permitted nor shall intangible supplies which are not "materials" be deemed to be raw stock.

(91-W-3—3-69)

R. SPECIAL WAVEWASH STATEMENT

General Adjustment Bureau, Inc.

SPECIAL WAVEWASH STATEMENT

TYPE OF LOSS	Wind and wavewash	GAB FILE NO.	
DATE OF LOSS	September 10, 1976	ADJUSTER	

INSURED _____ Edward and Anne McDonough

LOCATION _____ 110 Lester Street, Long Beach, NY 11561

ITEM NO. _____ Dwelling _____ TYPE OF CONSTRUCTION _____ 2-story, frame

ADDITIONS _____ X _____ DIMENSIONS _____ 36' x 50' _____ SQ. FT. AREA _____ 1,800

NO. ROOMS _____ 6 _____ NO. BATHS _____ 2 _____ AGE _____ 5 yr _____ GENERAL CONDITION _____ Good

EST. REPLACEMENT COST $ 36,000 _____ DEPRECIATION $ 4,000 _____ A.C.V. $ 32,000

	DETAILS OF LOSS	TOTAL REPAIR OR REPL.COST	WATER	DEBATABLE	WIND
FOUNDATION	C.B. undermined, west side	$ 1,200	$1,200	$ --	$ --
DIMENSION LUMBER	First floor studs, front	200	200	--	--
EXTERIOR SIDING	Entire front and west side	1,000	400	200	400
SHEATHING	Same	150	100	50	--
ROOFING	Replace asphalt shingles	800	--	--	800
INT. WALLS & CEILINGS	Drywall	600	100	100	400
FLOORING	1" x 3" oak	1,200	1,000	200	--
MILLWORK	Baseboard and doors	700	700	--	--
HARDWARE	Included				
INTERIOR PAINT	Preparation, two coats	1,500	300	200	1,000
EXTERIOR PAINT	One and two coats	800	100	--	700
ELECTRICAL	Rewire entire house	750	400	200	150
PLUMBING - AIR COND.	Drain and clean	800	100	300	400
DEMOLITION - DEBRIS		1,800	900	500	400
OTHER					
TOTALS		$ 11,500	$ 5,500	$ 1,750	$ 4,250

COMPROMISE OF DEBATABLE TOTAL ADDED — $ 750

TOTAL COST OF WIND REPAIRS OR REPLACEMENTS — $ 5,000

LESS DEPRECIATION $ R.C. , DEDUCTIBLE $ 200 , COINSURANCE $ -- — $ 200

INSURANCE $ 32,000 AND INSURED CLAIMS $4,800 — $ 4,800

APPLICATION OF DEDUCTIBLE OR COINSURANCE CLAUSE:

610 - (1-67)

550

S. INSURED'S STATEMENT FOR BURGLARY, THEFT, AND MYSTERIOUS DISAPPEARANCE LOSSES

Kemper INSURANCE

INSURED'S STATEMENT

Claim No. B6245-C

Name: Josephine Stuckert
Address: 412 Fay Street, Portland, OR 97200

Home Telephone: (503) 555-4251
Business Telephone: None

Occupation: Retired
Place of Employment:

Location of Loss: Same

Date of Loss: June 5, 1976
Time of Loss: Between 2 and 6 p.m.

Please Describe Occurrence: Entree to house by way of forced garage window. Rooms and dresser drawers ransacked, property stolen.

When And How Discovered? By insured when she came home.

Was Loss Reported To Police? Yes
Where (Station or Precinct)? 4th Avenue Precinct

Did Police Investigate? Yes
Any Suspects? None yet

Was there any evidence of burglary or theft other than the disappearance of the property? (Please Describe Evidence and/or Damage) Garage window sash broken and pry marks on sill.

Where Was Property Last Seen? In the home

When? Just prior to burglary

Were you away from the premises when the loss occurred? Yes

For what purpose? Shopping

Was there anyone on premises who could have taken the property? (Such as workman or maid) No

Were the involved premises or vehicle locked? Yes
How was entry gained?

If loss from vehicle, where was it parked?

If loss from parking lot, were keys given to attendant?

(Over please)

EK 399 6-72 30M

PRINTED IN U.S.A.

551

The following articles were taken:

Description of Item	Model and Serial No.	Name of Owner	Where Purchased	Date of Purchase	Purchase Price
See list attached					

(If more space is required, please furnish above information on a separate sheet of paper.)

Please attach any cancelled checks, bills or receipts to substantiate the missing and/or damaged property. Also, if damaged by forcible entry, attach estimate or bill for repair of premises.

Have there been any other similar occurrences in the neighborhood? __Yes__ If yes, please describe __Several homes__ broken into in recent months. Police believe local teenage group responsible.

Have you had any previous losses? __No__ If so, please describe

Do you have any other Insurance which might cover this loss? __No__ Please give details

The foregoing statement and that on the reverse side is true and correct to the best of my knowledge.

Date __June 15, 1976__ Signed _(Mrs.) Josephine Stuckert_

T. BOILER AND MACHINERY POLICY JACKET

INSURING AGREEMENT

In consideration of the Premium, the Company agrees with the Insured respecting loss from an Accident, as defined herein, occurring during the Policy Period, to an Object, as defined herein, while the Object is in use or connected ready for use at the Location specified for it in the Schedule, subject to the Declarations, to the Exclusions, to the Conditions, to other terms of this policy and to the Schedules and Endorsements issued to form a part thereof, as follows:

Coverage A—Loss on Property of Insured

1. Actual Cash Value—

To pay for loss on the property of the Insured directly damaged by such Accident or, if the Company so elects, to repair or replace such damaged property;

2. Repair or Replacement—

(Applies unless Coverage A2 is shown as "EXCLUDED" in Item 5 of the Declarations of the policy.) The Company agrees that loss on property of the Insured as specified in Coverage A1 of the Insuring Agreement of the policy shall mean the amount actually expended by the Insured to repair or replace such property of the Insured and condition 5 of the policy is deleted, all subject to the following provisions:

(a) The damaged property shall be repaired or replaced within twelve months from the date of the Accident unless such period is extended with written consent of the Company.

(b) If a coinsurance clause is applicable to the payment of loss under Coverage A1 of the Insuring Agreement of the policy, the words "replacement cost" are substituted for the words "actual cash value" wherever they appear in said coinsurance clause.

(c) The Company's liability for any repair or replacement shall be limited to the smaller of the following: (1) the cost at the time of the Accident to repair the said property, or (2) the cost at the time of the Accident to replace the said property on the same site with property of like kind, capacity, size and quality; provided that in the event the replacement is by property of a better kind or quality or of larger capacity or size, the liability of the Company shall not exceed the amount that would be paid if the replacement had been made by property of like kind, capacity, size and quality.

(d) The Company shall not be liable for: (1) any increase in the cost of repair or replacement necessitated by any ordinance or law regulating or restricting repair, alteration, construction or installation, (2) loss or damage to property useless to the Insured or obsolete to the Insured, or (3) the cost of repairing or replacing any part or parts of an Object which is in excess of the cost of repairing or replacing the entire Object.

(e) If any damaged property is not repaired or replaced, the Company's liability as respects such property shall be limited to the amount that would have been paid had Coverage A2 been shown as "EXCLUDED" in the Declarations of the policy.

Coverage B—Expediting Expenses

To pay, to the extent of any indemnity remaining after payment of all loss as may be required under Coverage A, for the reasonable extra cost of temporary repair and of expediting the repair of such damaged property of the Insured, including overtime and the extra cost of express or other rapid means of transportation, provided the Company's liability under Coverage B shall not exceed $1,000;

Coverage C—Property Damage Liability

To pay, to the extent of any indemnity remaining after payment of all loss as may be required under Coverages A and B, such amounts as the Insured shall become obligated to pay by reason of the liability of the Insured for loss on property of others directly damaged by such Accident, including liability for loss of use of such damaged property of others;

Coverage D—Bodily Injury Liability

To pay, to the extent of any indemnity remaining after payment of all loss as may be required under Coverages A, B and C, such amounts as the Insured shall become obligated to pay by reason of the liability of the Insured, including liability for care and loss of services, because of bodily injury, sickness or disease, including death at any time resulting therefrom, sustained by any person and caused by such Accident, except that the indemnity hereunder shall not apply to any obligation for which the Insured or any Company as insurer of the Insured may be liable under any workmen's compensation, unemployment compensation or disability benefits law, or under any similar law; or to such bodily injury, sickness, disease or death of any employee of the Insured arising out of and in the course of his employment by the Insured; to pay, irrespective of the Limit per Accident, for such immediate medical and surgical relief to others as shall be rendered at the time of the Accident;

Coverage E—Defense, Settlement, Supplementary Payments

To defend the Insured against claim or suit alleging liability under Coverage C, and under Coverage D if insurance under Coverage D is included, unless or until the Company shall elect to effect settlement thereof, and to pay all costs taxed against the Insured in any legal proceeding defended by the Company in accordance with such Coverages, all interest accruing after entry of judgment rendered in connection therewith up to the date of payment by the Company of its share of such judgment, all premiums on appeal bonds required in such legal proceedings, all premiums on bonds to release attachments for an amount not in excess of the applicable limits of liability for Coverages C and D, and all expenses incurred by the Company for such defense; the amounts incurred under Coverage E are payable by the Company irrespective of the Limit per Accident, except settlements of claims and suits;

Coverage F—Automatic Coverage

With respect to any property hereafter acquired by the Insured, any Object in use or connected ready for use at the time said property is acquired and which would be included by any Blanket Group Description designated and described in any Schedule forming a part of the policy shall be considered as added to the policy as of the time said property is acquired by the Insured, all subject to the following conditions:

(1) The Insured shall notify the Company in writing within 90 days after the date said property is acquired.

(2) The Insured agrees to pay an additional premium for insurance in accordance with the Company's Manual of Rules and Rates in force on the date said property is acquired.

(3) Loss from an Accident to any Object shall be subject to the highest Limit per Accident applicable to any Object which would be included by any Blanket Group Description designated and described in any Schedule forming a part of the policy.

(4) The Company shall not be liable under this Coverage for Use and Occupancy, Outage, Consequential Damage or any other indirect loss resulting from an Accident to any Object.

(5) This Coverage shall only apply to any Object within the Continental United States, Alaska, Hawaii, Puerto Rico, American Virgin Islands or Canada.

EXCLUSIONS

This policy does not apply:

1. To loss from an Accident caused directly or indirectly by

(a) hostile or warlike action, including action in hindering, combating or defending against an actual, impending or expected attack, by

    (i) any government or sovereign power (de jure or de facto) or any authority maintaining or using military, naval or air forces,

    (ii) military, naval or air forces, or

    (iii) an agent of any such government, power, authority or forces;

(b) insurrection, rebellion, revolution, civil war or usurped power, including any action in hindering, combating or defending against such an occurrence, or by confiscation by order of any government or public authority;

2. To loss, whether it be direct or indirect, proximate or remote,

(a) from an Accident caused directly or indirectly by nuclear reaction, nuclear radiation or radioactive contamination, all whether controlled or uncontrolled; or

(b) from nuclear reaction, nuclear radiation or radioactive contamination, all whether controlled or uncontrolled, caused directly or indirectly by, contributed to or aggravated by an Accident;

nor shall the Company be liable for any loss covered in whole or in part by any contract of insurance, carried by the Insured, which also covers any hazard or peril of nuclear reaction, or nuclear radiation;

3. To any increase in the loss necessitated by any ordinance or law regulating or restricting repair, alteration, construction or installation;

4. Under Coverages A and B to loss

(a) from fire concomitant with or following an Accident or from the use of water or other means to extinguish fire,

(b) from an Accident caused directly or indirectly by fire or from the use of water or other means to extinguish fire,

(c) from a combustion explosion outside the Object concomitant with or following an Accident,

(d) from an Accident caused directly or indirectly by a combustion explosion outside the Object,

(e) from flood unless an Accident ensues and the Company shall then be liable only for loss from such ensuing Accident,

(f) from delay or interruption of business or manufacturing process,

(g) from lack of power, light, heat, steam or refrigeration, and

(h) from any other indirect result of an Accident.

ATTACH DECLARATIONS PAGE, SCHEDULES AND ENDORSEMENTS
This is not a complete and valid contract without an accompanying Declarations Page, properly countersigned, together with one or more Schedules.

SHORT RATE CANCELLATION TABLE
Showing percentage of premium to be taken as earned premium

Less than one month shall count as a whole month and the percentage to be used shall be that specified for the next succeeding number of whole months.

MONTHS POLICY IN FORCE	ONE YEAR POLICY	TWO YEAR POLICY	THREE YEAR POLICY	MONTHS POLICY IN FORCE	TWO YEAR POLICY	THREE YEAR POLICY	MONTHS POLICY IN FORCE	THREE YEAR POLICY
1	31.3%	17.9%	12.5%	13	60.7%	42.5%	25	72.5%
2	37.5	21.4	15.0	14	64.3	45.0	26	75.0
3	43.8	25.0	17.5	15	67.9	47.5	27	77.5
4	50.0	28.6	20.0	16	71.4	50.0	28	80.0
5	56.3	32.1	22.5	17	75.0	52.5	29	82.5
6	62.5	35.7	25.0	18	78.6	55.0	30	85.0
7	68.8	39.3	27.5	19	82.1	57.5	31	87.5
8	75.0	42.9	30.0	20	85.7	60.0	32	90.0
9	81.3	46.4	32.5	21	89.3	62.5	33	92.5
10	87.5	50.0	35.0	22	92.9	65.0	34	95.0
11	93.8	53.6	37.5	23	96.4	67.5	35	97.5
12	100.0	57.1	40.0	24	100.0	70.0	36	100.0

(The use of this Table is subject to the Minimum Premium Requirements Rules and the Premium Gradation Rules as referred to in the Cancellation Condition of the Policy.)

CONDITIONS

1. Notice of Accident and Adjustment. When an Accident occurs, written notice shall be given by or on behalf of the Insured to the Company or any of its authorized agents as soon as practicable. The Insured shall give like notice of any claim made on account of such Accident. The Company shall have reasonable time and opportunity to examine the property and the premises of the Insured before repairs are undertaken or physical evidence of the Accident is removed, except for protection or salvage. Proof of loss shall be made by the Insured in such form as the Company may require. If suit is brought against the Insured for loss to which this insurance is applicable, the Insured shall immediately forward to the Company any summons or other process served upon the Insured. The Insured upon request of the Company shall render every assistance in facilitating the investigation and adjustment of any claim, submitting to examination and interrogation by any representative of the Company.

In the event of disagreement between the Company and the Insured as to the amount of loss on the property of the Insured for which the Company is liable under this policy, each shall, on the written demand of either, select a competent and disinterested appraiser. The appraisers shall first select a competent and disinterested umpire, and failing for fifteen days to agree upon such umpire, then on the request of the Insured or the Company, such umpire shall be selected by a judge of a court of record in the State or Province in which such appraisal is pending. The appraisers shall then appraise the loss, stating separately the actual cash value at the time of loss and the amount of loss and upon failure to agree shall submit their difference to the umpire. An award in writing of any two of said three persons shall determine the amount of said loss. The Insured and the Company shall pay the appraisers respectively chosen by each and shall share and pay equally for the umpire and for other expenses of appraisal. The Company shall not be held to have waived any of its rights by any act relating to appraisal.

The Insured shall not voluntarily assume any liability or incur any expense, other than at the Insured's own cost, except as otherwise expressly permitted in this policy, or interfere in any negotiation for settlement or any legal proceeding, without the consent of the Company previously given in writing.

2. Inspection. The Company shall be permitted but not obligated to inspect, at all reasonable times, each Object designated and described in a Schedule forming a part of the policy. Neither the Company's right to make inspections nor the making thereof nor any report thereon shall constitute an undertaking, on behalf of or for the benefit of the named Insured or others, to determine or warrant that such Object is safe or healthful.

3. Suspension. Upon the discovery of a dangerous condition with respect to any Object, any representative of the Company may immediately suspend the insurance with respect to an Accident to said Object by written notice mailed or delivered to the Insured at the Address of the Insured, as specified in the Declarations, or at the location of the Object as specified for it in the Schedule. Insurance so suspended may be reinstated by the Company but only by an Endorsement issued to form a part of this policy. The Insured shall be allowed the unearned portion of the premium paid for such suspended insurance, pro rata, for the period of suspension.

4. Limit Per Accident. The Company's total liability for loss from any One Accident shall not exceed the amount specified as Limit per Accident. The term "One Accident" shall be taken as including all resultant or concomitant Accidents whether to one Object or to more than one Object or to part of an Object. The inclusion herein of more than one Insured shall not operate to increase the limits of the Company's liability.

5. Property Valuation—Coverage A1. The limit of the Company's liability under Coverage A1 for loss on the property of the Insured shall not exceed the actual cash value thereof at the time of the Accident. If, as respects the damaged property of the Insured, the repair or replacement of any part or parts of an Object is involved, the Company shall not be liable for the cost of such repair or replacement in excess of the actual cash value of said part or parts or in excess of the actual cash value of the Object, whichever value is less. Actual cash value in all cases shall be ascertained with proper deductions for depreciation, however caused.

6. Other Insurance—Property. The words "joint loss," as used herein, means loss to which both this insurance and other insurance carried by the Insured apply. In the event of such "joint loss,"

(a) The Company shall be liable under this policy only for the proportion of the said joint loss that the amount which would have been payable under this policy on account of said joint loss, had no other insurance existed, bears to the combined total of the said amount and the amount which would have been payable under all other insurance on account of said joint loss, had there been no insurance under this policy, but

(b) In case the policy or policies affording such other insurance do not contain a clause similar to Clause (a), the Company shall be liable under this policy only for the proportion of said joint loss that the amount insured under this policy, applicable to said joint loss, bears to the whole amount of insurance, applicable to said joint loss.

7. Other Insurance—Liability. The insurance, if any, afforded by this policy with respect to loss under Coverages C and D shall be excess insurance over any other valid and collectible insurance available to the Insured. As used herein, the words "other valid and collectible insurance" include any deductible or self-insured retention provisions to which such insurance may be subject.

8. Cancellation. This policy may be cancelled by the Insured by mailing to the Company written notice stating when thereafter such cancellation shall be effective. This policy may be cancelled by the Company by mailing to the Insured at the Address of the Insured, as specified in the Declarations, written notice stating when not less than ten days thereafter such cancellation shall be effective. The mailing of notice as aforesaid shall be sufficient proof of notice and the effective date and hour of cancellation stated in the notice shall become the end of the Policy Period. Delivery of such written notice either by the Insured or by the Company shall be equivalent to mailing.

If the Insured cancels, the earned premium shall be computed in accordance with the Short Rate Cancellation Table printed hereon. If the Company cancels, the earned premium shall be computed pro rata. Premium adjustment may be made at the time cancellation is effected and, if not then made, shall be made as soon as practicable after cancellation becomes effective. The Company's check or the check of its representative mailed or delivered as aforesaid shall be a sufficient tender of any refund of premium due the Insured.

JACKET PAGE 2

CONDITIONS (Continued)

The determination of the return premium for any cancellation shall be subject to the Minimum Premium Requirements Rules set forth in the Company's Manual of Rules and Rates applicable. If the premium for this policy has been determined by applying any discount in accordance with a Premium Gradation Plan, the determination of the return premium for any cancellation shall also be subject to the Premium Gradation Rules set forth in the Company's Manual of Rules and Rates applicable.

9. Subrogation. In the event of any payment under this policy, the Company shall be subrogated to the Insured's rights of recovery therefor against any person or organization and the Insured shall execute and deliver instruments and papers and do whatever else is necessary to secure such rights. The Insured shall do nothing after the Accident to prejudice such rights.

10. Action Against Company—Except Coverages C and D. No action shall lie against the Company unless, as a condition precedent thereto, the Insured shall have fully complied with all the terms of this policy, nor unless commenced within fourteen months from the date of the Accident.

11. Action Against Company—Coverages C and D. No action shall lie against the Company unless, as a condition precedent thereto, the Insured shall have fully complied with all the terms of this policy, nor until the amount of the Insured's obligation to pay has been finally determined either by judgment against the Insured after trial or by written agreement of the Insured, the claimant and the Company. The Insured upon request of the Company shall aid in effecting settlements, in securing evidence and the attendance of witnesses and in prosecuting appeals.

Any person or organization or the legal representative thereof who has secured such judgment or written agreement shall thereafter be entitled to recover under this policy to the extent of the insurance afforded by this policy. Nothing contained in this policy shall give any person or organization any right to join the Company as a codefendant in any action against the Insured to determine the Insured's liability.

Bankruptcy or insolvency of the Insured or of the Insured's estate shall not relieve the Company of any of its obligations hereunder.

12. Assignment. Assignment of interest under this policy shall not bind the Company until its consent is endorsed hereon; if, however, the Insured shall die or be adjudged bankrupt or insolvent during the Policy Period, this policy, unless cancelled, shall, if written notice be given to the Company within sixty days after the date of such death or adjudication, cover the Insured's legal representative as the Insured.

13. Changes. By accepting this policy, the Insured agrees that this policy embodies all agreements existing between the Insured and the Company or any of its agents relating to this insurance. Notice to any agent or knowledge possessed by any agent or by any other person shall not effect a waiver or a change in any part of this policy or estop the Company from asserting any rights under this policy; nor shall the terms of this policy be waived or changed, except by Endorsement issued to form a part of this policy, signed by a duly authorized officer or representative of the Company. The additional or return premium for any such Endorsement shall be computed in accordance with the Company's Manual of Rules and Rates applicable to such change.

14. Premium Gradation. If the premium for this policy has been determined by applying any discount in accordance with a Premium Gradation Plan, the determination of the additional or return premium for any subsequent change in the policy shall be subject to the Premium Gradation Rules set forth in the Company's Manual of Rules and Rates applicable.

15. Schedules. The insurance afforded hereunder shall apply only to loss from an Accident to an Object designated and described in a Schedule forming a part hereof, bearing the signature of the duly authorized officer or representative of the Company and containing the description of such Object, the definition thereof, the definition of Accident and other provisions as applicable to the said Object.

16. Malicious Mischief. Subject to Exclusion (1) of this policy, any Accident, as defined in any Schedule forming a part hereof, arising out of strike, riot, civil commotion, acts of sabotage, vandalism or malicious mischief, shall be considered "accidental" within the terms of said definition.

17. Blanket Group Plan. With respect to a described group of Objects opposite which the word "Blanket" is entered in the column captioned "Description of Object" of any Schedule forming a part of this policy, each Object, of such group of Objects, shall be considered as being designated and described in such Schedule. The premiums for all kinds of insurance afforded by this policy as applicable thereto shall be adjusted as follows:

(a) Any premium applicable to such group or groups of Objects shall be adjusted, as of the effective date such insurance applies, on the basis of the information obtained at the time of the Company's survey of such Objects that are in use or connected ready for use as of such effective date;

(b) The premium, including revisions of premium due to changes in the rating of Objects under the Blanket Group Plan, shall be adjusted pro rata at the end of each policy year on the basis of the information obtained by the Company, either as respects such Objects added to such Group Plan that are in use or connected ready for use prior to the end of such policy year or as respects such Objects withdrawn, during such policy year, from such Group Plan using the rates in effect at the time the applicable insurance was made effective as though such changes and such insurance had been specifically effected or terminated at the end of the first six months of the policy year, except that if, as respects a described group of Objects, insurance under the Blanket Group Plan is in effect for only a part of a policy year, such adjustments shall be computed as of the mid-date of such part of the policy year. The term "Policy Year" shall be understood to mean a period of one year from the effective date of this policy or any anniversary thereof.

As respects the Company previously designated, the following correlative provision forms a part of this policy:

Mutual Policy Conditions.   LUMBERMENS MUTUAL CASUALTY COMPANY   AMERICAN MANUFACTURERS MUTUAL INSURANCE COMPANY

This is a perpetual mutual corporation owned by and operated for the benefit of its members. This is a non-assessable, participating policy under which the Board of Directors in its discretion may determine and pay unabsorbed premium deposit refunds (dividends) to the Insured.

As respects the State of Texas, such provision is amended as follows:

Mutuals—Membership and Voting Notice. The Insured is notified that by virtue of this policy he is a member of the Company so designated, and is entitled to vote either in person or by proxy at any and all meetings of said Company. The Annual Meetings are held in its Home Office at the place and time stated on the front cover.

Mutuals—Participation Clause Without Contingent Liability. No Contingent Liability: This policy is non-assessable. The policyholder is a member of such Company and shall participate, to the extent and upon the conditions fixed and determined by the Board of Directors in accordance with the provisions of law, in the distribution of dividends so fixed and determined.

Dividends.   AMERICAN MOTORISTS INSURANCE COMPANY   FEDERAL KEMPER INSURANCE COMPANY

This policy is participating and shall be entitled to receive unabsorbed premium deposit refunds as apportioned by the directors.

As respects the State of Texas, such provision is amended to read as follows:

Dividend Provision—Participating Companies. The named Insured shall be entitled to participate in a distribution of the surplus of the Company, as determined by its Board of Directors from time to time, after approval in accordance with the provisions of the Texas Insurance Code, of 1951, as amended.

IN WITNESS WHEREOF, the Company designated on the Declarations Page has caused this policy to be signed by its President and Secretary, but this policy shall not be valid unless countersigned on the Declarations Page by a duly authorized representative of the Company.

LUMBERMENS MUTUAL CASUALTY COMPANY
AMERICAN MOTORISTS INSURANCE COMPANY
AMERICAN MANUFACTURERS MUTUAL INSURANCE COMPANY

FEDERAL KEMPER INSURANCE COMPANY

Secretary   *President*   *Secretary*   *President*

RK 400-9   JACKET PAGE 3   (ED. 4-73) 1-75 10M   PRINTED IN U.S.A.

U. MORTGAGEE, ARTICLES OF SUBROGATION AND ASSIGNMENT

ARTICLES OF SUBROGATION AND ASSIGNMENT

BE IT KNOWN, That the————————————————————————Insurance Company, of
————————did insure————————————————————under its Policy No.————
issued at its Agency at————————————as follows:————
————————————————————for the period of————years, commencing
on the————day of————————19—and continuing until the————day of————19——, to
which said Policy there was attached a Mortgage Clause, making loss or damage under said Policy payable for
assured's account unto————————trustee or mortgagee, or——successors in trust, as——interest
may appear, and providing that whenever said Company should pay any sum for loss under said Policy No.
————and should claim that, as to the grantors in the mortgage or trust deed, or to the owners of the property
so insured, no liability therefor existed, then said Company should at once be subrogated to all the rights of the
said trustee or mortgagee under all the securities held for the debt by him or them.
    Said mortgage or trust deed having been given by————————————————to————————
and dated the————day of————————A.D. 19—, and recorded on the————day of————————A.D.
19—, in the Recorder's Office of————————County, in the State of————————in book————
of————————————, at page————AND IT APPEARING that on the————day of————19—, a fire
occurred by which the property originally insured was damaged or destroyed to the amount of————
————————————————Dollars, and the said————————Insurance Company hereby
claiming that, as to the said assured under the said Policy and the present owner of the property so insured
under said Policy above mentioned, no legal claim exists against said Company, and that said Company is in
no manner liable to them or either of them under the terms and conditions of said Policy. Now, THEREFORE, in
consideration of————————Dollars, this day paid to————————the trustee or mortgagee under
said mortgage clause by said————————Insurance Company, the receipt whereof is hereby acknowledged, said sum being in full settlement of said Company's liability to said trustee or mortgagee by reason of
said loss and damage under said Policy, the said————mortgagee or trustee does hereby assign, set over,
transfer and subrogate to the said————————Insurance Company, all the right, title, claim and
interest to the amount of————————Dollars, which——, the said————————
trustee or mortgagee has in said trust deed or mortgage above described, and in and to the note or notes therein
described. And it is agreed that all interest which hereafter accrues upon said sum of————————
Dollars aforesaid, shall inure and be paid to said Insurance Company, and that no release of any kind or for
any amount of said notes or mortgage, or any part thereof, shall be made by said trustee or mortgagee until
said Company shall have received therefrom said sum of————Dollars, paid said trustee or mortgagee as
aforesaid, with interest thereon at the same rate as provided in and by said notes from the date thereof until paid.
    Said————————trustee or mortgagee, hereby authorizes and empowers said————
Insurance Company to sue, foreclose, compromise or settle, in——name or otherwise, for said amount, and
it is hereby fully substituted in——place and subrogated to all——rights in the premises to the amount so
paid, it being agreed, however, that any action taken by said Company shall be without cost to said——
trustee or mortgagee, as aforesaid.

————————————————————[SEAL]
                                                            Trustee
————————————————————[SEAL]
                                            Legal Owner of Said Note

STATE OF————————————⎫ss.
COUNTY OF————————————⎭   I,————————————————
a————————————in and for said County, in the State aforesaid, do hereby certify that————————
personally known to me to be the same person whose name is subscribed to the foregoing instrument, appeared
before me this day in person and acknowledged that he signed, sealed and delivered the said instrument as his
free and voluntary act, for the uses and purposes therein set forth.
    Given under my hand and seal this————day of————————————A.D. 19——

————————————————
————————————————

Bibliography

BOOKS AND ARTICLES

Adjuster's Explanatory Review, National Flood Insurance Association (NFIA), 1975.

Adjuster's Licensing Statutes, Property Loss Research Bureau (PLRB), 1975.

Analysis of Proof Requirements in Arson Cases in Selected States, Defense Research Institute, Milwaukee, Wis., 1975.

Annotation of the 1943 New York Standard Fire Insurance Policy, Section of Insurance Law, American Bar Association, Chicago, 1967.

Arnold, Ralph W., "Living With Unfair Claim Practices Acts," *Best's Review*, 1975.

Bickelhaupt, David L., *General Insurance*, Richard D. Irwin, Inc., Homewood, Ill., 1974.

Black, Henry Campbell, *Black's Law Dictionary*, West Publishing Company, St. Paul, Minn.

Blasting Damage: A Guide for Adjusters and Engineers, American Insurance Association, 1972.

Brainard, Calvin H., *Automobile Insurance*, Richard D. Irwin, Inc., Homewood, Ill., 1961.

Condominium Insurance, Property Loss Research Bureau, 1974.

Cotton, Bert, "Metered Fire Insurance," *New York Insurance Law Journal*, April 1958.

Daynard, Harold S., *Paths and By-Paths in Inland Marine Insurance*, The Insurance Advocate, Roberts Publishing Company, New York, 1949.

———, *Trends in Adjusting*, Daynard & Van Thunen Company, New York, 1967.

Donaldson, James H., *Casualty Claim Practice*, Richard D. Irwin, Inc., Homewood, Ill., 1969.

Econ, Dan, *Role of the Adjuster in Arson Losses*, Massachusetts Property Insur-ance Underwriting Association, Arson Seminar, November 1974, Boston.

Esposito, Karen, Editorial Assistant, "Policy Readability: How the Industry Has Reacted," *Best's Review*, 1975.

The Fire Fighter's Responsibility in Arson Detection, National Fire Protection Association (NFPA), 1971.

Flood Adjuster's Handbook, Property Loss Research Bureau, 1971.

Guinane, George E., CPCU, *Homeowners Guide: An Interpretation of Policy Coverages*, The Rough Notes Company, Inc., Indianapolis, 1975.

Gwertzman, Max J., A *Legal Analysis of Examination Under Oath*, The Insurance Advocate, Roberts Publishing Company, New York, 1960.

———, A *Legal Analysis of the Standard Fire Insurance Policy*, The Insurance Advocate, Roberts Publishing Company, New York, 1963.

Huff, William H., *Unfair Claim Settlement Practices*, Loss Managers' Conference, Property Loss Research Bureau, Arlington Heights, Ill., 1973.

Klein, Henry C., *Business Interruption Insurance*, The Rough Notes Company, Inc., Indianapolis, 1964.

Lecomte, John E., *The Role of the Attorney in the Investigation and Defense of an Arson Loss*, Massachusetts Property Insurance Underwriting Association, Arson Seminar, November 1974, Boston.

Magarick, Pat, *Successful Handling of Casualty Claims*, Boardman, Clark Company, Ltd., 1974.

Mehr, Robert I., and Emerson Cammack, *Principles of Insurance*, Richard D. Irwin, Inc., Homewood, Ill., 1972.

Morrison, John W., *Judicial Approaches: Trend Setting Decisions*, Loss Managers' Conference, Property Loss Research Bureau, Denver, 1975.

Nierenberg, Gerard I., *Fundamentals of Negotiating*, Hawthorn Books, New York, 1973.

Proceedings of numerous loss managers' conferences, Property Loss Research Bureau.

Property Claim Services Bulletins, American Insurance Association.

Provencher, R. G., National Director, Investigations, Division of General Adjustment Bureau, Inc., *Was It Arson?* General Adjustment Bureau, Inc., 1975.

Question and Answer Service for Members, Property Loss Research Bureau.

Raymond, John, "Punitive Damage in Property Insurance Claims," *Best's Review*, June 1975.

Riegel, Robert, and J. S. Miller, *Insurance Principles and Practices, Property and Liability*, Prentice-Hall, Inc., Englewood Cliffs, N.J., 1968.

Riot and Civil Disorder Losses Under Standard Reinsurance Contract, U.S. Department of Housing and Urban Development, 1974.

Thomas, Paul I., *How to Estimate Building Losses and Construction Costs*, Prentice-Hall, Inc., Englewood Cliffs, N.J., 1976.

Withers, K. W., *Business Interruption Insurance Coverage and Adjustment*, San Francisco, 1957.

Young, E. Neil, John R. Lewis, and J. Finley Lee, "Insurance Contract Interpretations: Issues and Trends," *Insurance Law Journal*, No. 625, February 1975.

MANUALS

Auto Damage Manual, Kemper Insurance Companies, 1975.

Automobile Physical Damage Coverage and Investigation, Employers-Commercial Union Companies, 1976.

Boiler and Machinery Technical Claim Manual, Kemper Insurance Companies, 1976.

Operator's Manual, National Automobile Theft Bureau, 1975.

Index